MW00779113

IDENTITY AND SOCIAL CHANGE

IDENTITY AND SOCIAL CHANGE

Edited by

Joseph E. Davis

Transaction Publishers
New Brunswick (U.S.A.) and London (U.K.)

First paperback printing 2015
Copyright © 2000 by Transaction Publishers, New Brunswick, New Jersey.

All rights reserved under International and Pan-American Copyright Conventions. No part of this book may be reproduced or transmitted in any form or by any means, electronic or mechanical, including photocopy, recording, or any information storage and retrieval system, without prior permission in writing from the publisher. All inquiries should be addressed to Transaction Publishers, 10 Corporate Place South, Piscataway, New Jersey 08854. www.transactionpub.com

This book is printed on acid-free paper that meets the American National Standard for Permanence of Paper for Printed Library Materials.

Library of Congress Catalog Number: 00-037390
ISBN: 978-0-7658-0034-3 (cloth); 978-1-4128-5710-9 (paper)
eBook: 978-1-4128-2580-1
Printed in the United States of America

Library of Congress Cataloging-in-Publication Data

Identity and social change / edited by Joseph E. Davis
        p.   cm.
    Includes bibliographical references and index.
    ISBN 0-7658-0034-9 (alk. paper)
    1. Group identity.   2. Identity (Psychology)   3. Social change.
  I. Davis, Joseph E.

HM753 .I34 2000
303.4—dc21

                                                        00-037390

Contents

Introduction: Social Change and the Problem of Identity

Joseph E. Davis

Identity is a problem. The concept emerged as a problem, and, if Zygmunt Bauman is correct, can only exist as a problem (1996: 19). On one level, identity is a problem because of the philosophical and moral weight it has been made to carry. Modern understandings of the self—identity, the person—have been shaped by the emphasis on the cognitive and self-sustaining subject in Enlightenment philosophy, as well as by the stress on moral introspection and subjectivity arising from a number of crucial post-Reformation movements (Taylor 1989; Ferguson, this volume). These sources defined a conception of inwardness that assigned the self an inner depth, a power of disengaged reason, and a capacity and need for self-exploration. They freighted the self with a unity, consciousness, and moral charge it has been hard-pressed to bear. At least since Marx's theory of alienation, the integral and self-sufficient subject has been a recurrent topic of criticism and critique.

On another level, personal and social identities are a problem because of the destabilizing and uprooting social forces of modern life. Historic social changes, including the pluralization of authorities, the de-institutionalization of private life, the multiplication of role expectations and identity schemes, the disembedding from geographical place, the diversification of contexts of interaction, and the decline of overarching systems of meaning, together with accompanying changes in social practices—religious, economic, familial, technological—created a new uncertainty and a new task. The uncertainty and the task was how to place oneself amidst a pluralism of incommensurable beliefs and behaviors, maintain that placement, and have it recognized by others. While by no

1

means distributed evenly in time or space, structural, institutional, and cultural transformations created, and continue to create, a distinctively new environment. In this environment identities must be constructed and situated amid competing cultural discourses and social practices, each of which tends to assert claims to priority. This pluralism creates not only challenges for individuals and identity-forming institutions, but, as Cascardi has argued, can also appear as contradictions within the "subject-self" (1992; cited in Calhoun 1994: 12).

These two ways in which identity is problematic are interrelated. The cognitive and moral weight attached to selves arose because social transformations and changes in social practices worked to produce a new problemization of subjectivity. At the same time, attributing a deep inwardness to the self made an increasingly pluralistic and free-floating environment the source of new forms and new levels of uncertainty about self-placement and self-definition and their recognition by others. Conceptions of the self and the task of placement/distinction, then, are related to each other and both are in turn related to changes in the broader environment.

Given this interrelationship, it should be unsurprising that during a time of rapid and profound change, as has been characteristic of postwar Western society, questions of identity have reappeared with a new force and a new urgency. No less than a "veritable discursive explosion" (Hall 1996: 1) has occurred in recent years around questions of self, subjectivity, agency, and multiple identities. These issues have been taken up by scholars of a wide variety, as well as by self-help writers, psychiatrists, business consultants, social movement activists, and many others. They are central to a host of current discussions dealing with such topics as the body, gender, ethnicity, therapy, citizenship, nationalism, education, postmodernism, multiculturalism, and ethics.

Amidst this outpouring of writing around the concept of identity, the most influential has emerged from the movements of identity politics and academic postmodernism. In these movements, attention is focused on the construction of difference, the solidarity of marginalized groups, and the epistemological status of the subject. While of far-reaching significance, both theoretically and socially, the circumscribed concerns of identity politics and postmodernism have led to a general neglect of the structural and institutional forces behind a wider problematization of identity. Moreover, particularly in postmodernist formulations, a disjunction has opened between discursive and social practices, with identity instability and fragmentation read not through structural or institutional changes but through the instabilities and fragmented nature of language and interpretation.

There is a need to expand the study of identity beyond issues of group-based identifications and epistemology. *Identity and Social Change* is a contribution to such an enlarged effort. Working from several vantage points and disciplines yet within a theoretical framework of identity as socially constituted, the contributors explore key social changes and social practices and the issues they raise for questions of subjectivity, identity, and identity formation. In the process, they also challenge key aspects of existing theoretical formulations and explore opportunities and prospects for the future.

To set the volume in context, I begin by briefly considering the currently dominant approaches to the study of identity and their limitations.

Identity and Difference

A concern to put identity into a context of social change is certainly not new; it has a long history in the social sciences. In addition to a persisting concern with the rise of the individual, for the postwar generation of scholars the conflict between individual needs and social demands, and the effects of this conflict and rapid social change for the adapting person, were central issues. Attention focused on the self-society nexus, along with concerns over the disruptions in self-concept and personality brought about by the significant social dislocations and transformations of "mass society"—urbanization, bureaucratization, the rise of a consumption ethic, technological advances, the decline of community, and so on. Further, many writers sought to trace the emergence of a new personality type or character, shaped by or adapted to changing social, cultural, and economic conditions. "Other-directed" (Riesman et al. 1950), an "antinomian personality" (Adler 1972), an "untrammeled self" (Bell 1976), and a "narcissistic personality" (Lasch 1979) are but a few of the influential ways in which the new character type was portrayed. Some writers in this tradition saw social changes leading to painful uneasiness and destructive alienation and instability. For others, however, the effects of change were believed to be more salutary, leading to experimentation with new and adaptive ways to meet social demands and efforts to break free from narrow and restrictive social roles.

A concern with the impact of larger social forces on consciousness and identity and with changes in the way that people structure their sense of self has not disappeared. But over at least the past two decades, the study of identity has shifted to issues of collective identity and political action. One stream of the new scholarship, the social constructionist, has concentrated on identities of race, ethnicity/nation, gender, and sexuality. In this now large literature, collective identities are treated not as some natural or primordial property of a group's members, but as subjective, symbolic entities that are negotiated and renegotiated in social interaction. No unique features are seen to distinguish group members from all other people. Rather, basic distinctions and boundaries, including biological distinctions, such as the inscription of gender on the body, are called into question and reformulated as the outcome of specific social practices and sociopolitical processes.

Following the politicization of identity by the social movements of the 1960s and 1970s, another and enormously influential stream of research emerged concerning the constitution of collective identities and the political implications that result from group struggles to self-characterize and claim social franchise. This is the literature on identity politics, which has also been concerned with identities of race, ethnicity, nationality, gender, and sexuality, but goes beyond these identities to include collective definitions in such "new social movements" as animal rights and environmentalism. The analytical focus in identity politics has centered on the issue of difference, and the interrelated problems of social recognition and self-recognition. In their incisive critique of social hierarchies, writers in this tradition deconstruct a discourse of natural boundaries as a politics of domination by which one group categorizes and regulates the identities of marginalized and devalued others (Fuss 1995). Sampson, for instance, argues,

> African-Americans become the image the white majority has of them. They become the image because the power of the image-constructors lies also in their ability to construct a world that conforms to their images of it. (1993: 26)

Subaltern identities (e.g., African-American), in other words, are shaped in part by the definition of "otherness" projected onto them in the construction and ongoing maintenance of the dominant identity. To counter such oppressive and exclusionary practices, proponents of a politics of identity frame identity in terms of group or category membership—woman, gay/lesbian, African-American, and so on. This discrete and demarcated social identity serves in turn as a common basis for making moral and political claims of the state and for seeking recognition and legitimacy in the wider culture.

While identity politics stresses difference, its emphasis on category membership has often led to a reassertion of fixed notions of identity and even natural boundaries between those in and outside the category. Yet another influential stream of writing about issues of identity, the academic postmodernist, also begins with a deconstruction of established identity categories and their accompanying power-discourse formations. But it pushes the issue of difference and "otherness" further. From a searching epistemological critique of the rationally centered and unified subject of Enlightenment philosophy, academic postmodernists, influenced by French poststructuralism, call for the abandonment of all such "essentialist" or unitary notions of the self. These notions, they argue, imply stable categories, first principles, unvarying standards, and mutually exclusive oppositions (Young 1990: 98-9). They deny or repress difference, and thus the full range of "being," by denying or repressing the ambiguity, plurality, and particularity of experience and signification. Emphasizing and even valorizing difference, postmodernist writers such as Derrida, Foucault, and Rorty argue that the subject is "decentered" because it is constituted in the precarious relations of difference. They frame identity as constructed in and through discourse and, therefore, "by nature as heterogeneous, shifting, and tenuous as signification itself" (Dunn 1998: 28). In effect, as texts are unstable and fluid, so also is the self. If the modern self, as suggested at the outset, was made to carry a heavy philosophical and moral weight, in the stronger postmodernist formulations the self seems to shoulder no burden at all. As something unified and consistent, it effectively ceases to exist, dissolved into a more or less random assemblage of experiences.

Broadening the Inquiry

In their different but also overlapping ways, constructionism, identity politics, and postmodernism have contributed to a new problemization and destabilization of identity categories. Emphasizing the role and functions of power, each movement has advanced a deconstructive critique of established categories. In much of the writing on identity politics, this critique has also been accompanied by a new recognition and legitimacy for marginalized identities. The postmodernist/poststructuralist writing, on the other hand, has gone the furthest in deconstructing all essentialist conceptions of identity and putting them "under erasure." At the same time, all these movements can also be seen as themselves symptomatic of a far more general problemization of identity, personal and collective, in our time. As Kenneth Gergen (this volume) notes, for instance, the very intelligibility of poststructuralist theoretical ideas about the dissolution of the self suggests a base in common experiences in the wider culture. The relatively limited concerns of constructionism and identity politics, and the epistemological preoccupations of postmodernism, however, have tended to obscure broader structural and institutional changes. These broader changes are significant for the emergence of these movements and the identity issues they address, as well as for questions of identity and identity formation which they typically occlude.

Further, both identity politics and postmodernism tend to detach identity from the social processes in which it is rooted. Identity politics, with its prioritizing of categorical identities, "allows a kind of abstraction," according to Craig Calhoun, "from the concrete interactions and social relationships within which identities are constantly renegotiated" (1994: 26). As a result, "complex notions of persons or networks of concrete social relations" are downplayed and the "capacity for an internal dialogicality" (1994: 26, 27) is effectively denied. In postmodernist writings, observation and deduction are de-emphasized in favor of an elevated concern with discourse (Cerulo 1997: 391). Discourse is prioritized over the dynamics of social relations; text and culture are prioritized over lived cultural conditions and sociohistorical context. One of the ironic consequences of this theoretical stance is a framing of the subject as externally determined, constituted in discursive structures and practices beyond human consciousness (Dunn 1998: 177-79). Here too, though in a manner different from identity politics, the account of human subjectivity is both limited and limiting.

While by no means exhaustive, these reflections on deficiencies in the dominant approaches are perhaps sufficient to suggest a need to broaden the scope and terms of inquiry. Treating the problemization of identity within a larger context of structural and institutional change would focus attention beyond currently more circumscribed concerns. Framing identity and difference theoretically as always constructed within webs of complex social interaction would resist reductionisms and offer enhanced possibilities for understanding both determinisms and human agency. Further, an enlarged and more social-relational approach to the study of identity and identity formation would provide analytic purchase on *both* the challenges and the opportunities—individually, culturally, and politically—that characterize our historical moment.

Identity and Social Change

With an aim to make a contribution toward just such a wider and socially regrounded project, a colloquium series on identity was organized at the University of Virginia under the auspices of the Institute for Advanced Studies in Culture. Earlier versions of the chapters by Bauman, Davis, Ferguson, Gergen, Harvey, and Nagel were first delivered in that series. Mike Featherstone and Robert Dunn were unable to participate but subsequently prepared papers for this volume. Half European scholars and half American, our collective effort was directed to exploring, within a framework of identity as socially constituted, the concrete impacts of economic, technological, and cultural change—broadly "social change"—as well as shifts in social practices for understanding problemizations of identity and subjectivity and their representations in contemporary society. Moving beyond the frequent abstractions of "theory" to lived experience, we also sought to examine the progressive as well as regressive possibilities of social change for individuals, social actors, and communities.

Recent analyses of social and cultural change stress a number of significant and interrelated transformations (e.g., Bauman 1992; Castells 1996; Dunn 1998; Giddens 1991; Harvey 1990; Lash 1990; Featherstone 1995). One cluster of changes involves structural transformations in the capitalist system and the global expansion of consumerism with its relentless momentum toward change, product differentiation, and immediate gratification. Another cluster centers in the growth of new information and communication technologies with an accompanying intensification and mobility of images and the freeing of interaction from physical co-presence. Yet a third cluster involves changes at the cultural level, variously characterized as shifts toward simulation, aestheticization, the dissolution of symbolic hierarchies, the valuation of novelty, the decline of grand narratives, and the rejection of tradition. Each of these transformations, in turn, shape institutional practices—production and consumption regimes, family life, the allocation of public resources, etc.—and strain not only collective and cultural identities but the routine social roles and personal identities of everyday life.

These broad transformations are "the changing landscape" on which the contributors in part 1 of this volume locate key questions of identity and subjectivity. This part opens with Zygmunt Bauman's reflections on the ceaseless drive toward change inherent in consumerism and the differential effects it produces on our experiences of time, distance, and place. He suggests that the much-vaunted liberations of postmodern life, both economically and psychologically, require a class of disadvantaged persons whose subjective experience of social change is not one of opportunities but of constraints. Drawing on theoretical insights from Marx, David Harvey links the micro-level discourse of the body with the macro-level discourse of economic globalization. Bringing these hitherto separate discourses together, he argues, illuminates consequences for worker subjectivity of the explosive growth of the wage labor system worldwide and the possibilities of a "body politics" for those similarly situated in the labor process. Analyzing the challenges to citizenship and national identity posed by globalization and new information technologies, Mike Featherstone outlines a rethinking of citizenship and identity-formation in light of the new realities of the public sphere(s) and new opportunities for connectedness in a global culture. Finally, focusing on ethnic identities, Joane Nagel identifies key economic, social, and cultural changes that have redefined the meaning and "worth" of ethnicity, and help to explain the paradoxical contemporary controversies over the authenticity of ethnic self-designations.

Recent analyses of social and cultural change have also tended to stress the differentiation, discontinuity, and fragmentation of meaning and experience, both personal and collective. For some, the consequence of this condition is a breakdown in individuals' sense of identity and self-coherence (e.g., Baudrillard 1981, 1983; Deleuze and Guattari 1987; Jameson 1991; Melucci 1996). A commodified, technologically mediated, and depthless culture, these observers argue, produces an unstable and fluid self characterized by a preoccupation with surface and performance, a blurring of boundaries between inner and outer worlds, a generalized ironic outlook, contingent commitments, and an endless negotiation and experimentation with alternative identities. In the more pessimistic readings of this postmodern self, an analogy is drawn with the schizophrenic, who cannot unify past, present, and future and so experiences the world as a series of intense and disconnected immediacies.

The question of "identity and dissolution" forms the general backdrop for the chapters in part 2. Robert G. Dunn begins by examining the relationship between new processes of cultural commodification and consequent attenuations of self and social relations. He argues that the commodification effects of media, marketplace, and new simulational orders of experience point not to a dissolution of the subject but to a general destabilization of identity formation processes with outcomes for individuals and communities both liberating and problematizing. The techno-cultural revolution spawned by the proliferation of low-cost communications technologies, Kenneth J. Gergen argues, undermines the traditional conceptions of a private self as the locus of moral agency and of community as the generative matrix for moral action. He sees new potential for sustaining moral meaning in the contemporary social context, however, in an as-yet nascent movement to push beyond the self/society binary toward a broader moral-cultural rationale of "relatedness." In an analysis of the moral transformation process in psychotherapies that address self-fragmentation, Joseph E. Davis argues that identity and moral subjectivity are inseparably linked. This linkage, he suggests, casts doubt on general readings of identity dissolution and the liberating potential of fragmented subjectivity. In the final chapter, Harvie Ferguson traces the history of the modern use of irony to communicate what could only be communicated indirectly: the inner depth of the self. In contemporary society, he argues, which prioritizes surface over depth and outer over inner, models of "deep" selfhood have disappeared and so irony has now become a technique for losing rather than gaining the self.

As noted earlier, most of the papers collected here were first delivered in earlier versions at the University of Virginia as part of a colloquium series on identity I organized for the Institute for Advanced Studies in Culture. My thanks to the Institute, and especially its executive director, Professor James Davison Hunter, for sponsoring the colloquium and my work in preparing this book for publication. My thanks also to Kristine Kay Harmon of the Institute for her expert editorial assistance.

References

Adler, N. 1972. *The Underground Stream: New Life Styles and the Antinomian Personality*. New York: Harper and Row.

Baudrillard, J. 1981. *For a Critique of the Political Economy of the Sign*. St. Louis, MO: Telos.

———. 1983. *Simulations*. New York: Semiotext(e).

Bauman, Z. 1992. *Intimations of Postmodernity*. London: Routledge.
————. 1996. "From Pilgrim to Tourist—or a Short History of Identity." Pp. 18-35 in *Questions of Cultural Identity*, edited by S. Hall and P. DuGay. Thousand Oaks, CA: Sage.
Bell, D. 1976. *The Cultural Contradictions of Capitalism*. New York: Basic Books.
Calhoun, C. 1994. "Social Theory and the Politics of Identity." Pp. 9-36 in *Social Theory and the Politics of Identity*, edited by C. Calhoun. Oxford: Blackwell.
Cascardi, A.J. 1992. *The Subject of Modernity*. New York: Cambridge University Press.
Castells, M. 1996. *The Information Age, Volume 1: The Rise of the Network Society*. Malden, MA: Blackwell.
Cerulo, K.A. 1997. Identity Construction: New Issues, New Directions." *Annual Review of Sociology* 23: 385-409.
Deleuze, G., and F. Guattari. 1987. *A Thousand Plateaus: Capitalism and Schizophrenia*. Minneapolis: University of Minnesota Press.
Dunn, R.G. 1998. *Identity Crises: A Social Critique of Postmodernity*. Minneapolis: University of Minnesota Press.
Featherstone, M. 1995. *Undoing Culture: Globalization, Postmodernism and Identity*. London: Sage.
Fuss, D. 1995. *Identification Papers*. New York: Routledge.
Giddens, A. 1991. *Modernity and Self-Identity*. Stanford, CA: Stanford University Press.
Hall, S. 1996. "Introduction: Who Needs 'Identity'?" Pp. 1-17 in *Questions of Cultural Identity*, S. Hall and P. DuGay. Thousand Oaks, CA: Sage.
Harvey, D. 1990. *The Condition of Postmodernity*. Cambridge, MA: Blackwell.
Jameson, F. 1991. *Postmodernism, or, The Cultural Logic of Late Capitalism*. Durham, NC: Duke University Press.
Lasch, C. 1979. *The Culture of Narcissism: American Life in an Age of Diminishing Expectation*. New York: W.W. Norton.
Lash, S. 1990. *The Sociology of Postmodernism*. London: Routledge.
Melucci, A. 1996. *The Playing Self: Person and Meaning in the Planetary Society*. Cambridge: Cambridge University Press.
Riesman, D., with N. Glazer and R. Denny. 1950. *The Lonely Crowd: A Study of the Changing American Character*. New Haven, CT: Yale University Press.
Sampson, E.E. 1993. *Celebrating the Other: A Dialogic Account of Human Nature*. Boulder, CO: Westview Press.
Taylor, C. 1989. *Sources of the Self: The Making of the Modern Identity*. Cambridge, MA: Harvard University Press.
Young, I.M. 1990. *Justice and the Politics of Difference*. Princeton, NJ: Princeton University Press.

Part 1

The Changing Landscape

1

Tourists and Vagabonds:
Or, Living in Postmodern Times

Zygmunt Bauman

Nowadays, we are all on the move. We change places—moving homes or traveling to and from places that are not our homes. We are all on the move even when we stay physically put. While glued to a chair, we zip between cable or satellite channels with a speed much beyond the capacity of supersonic jets and cosmic rockets, staying nowhere long. We flit through the Web, netting and mixing on one computer screen messages born in opposite corners of the globe. In the world we inhabit, distance does not matter much; it exists as if solely to be canceled—it offers a constant invitation to traverse. It has stopped being an obstacle; one needs but a split second to conquer it. There are no "natural borders" anymore. Wherever we happen to be at the moment, we cannot help knowing that we could be elsewhere, so there is less and less reason to be anywhere in particular. Spiritually at least, we are all travelers.

But we are also on the move in another, deeper sense, whether or not we take to the roads or leap through the channels and whether or not we like doing it. One cannot stay put in this postmodern world of ours—a world with reference points set on wheels, known for their vexing habit of vanishing from view before the instruction they offer has been pondered and acted upon. Professor Ricardo Petrella of the Catholic University of Louvain sums it up very well: "Globalization drags economies toward the production of the ephemeral, the volatile (through a massive and universal reduction of the life-span of products and services) and the precarious (temporary, flexible, and part-time jobs)" (Petrella 1997: 17). In order to elbow their way through the dense, deregulated thicket of global competitiveness and into the limelight of public attention, goods and services must seduce their prospective consumers and out-seduce their competitors. But then they must make room, and quickly, for other objects of desire, lest the global chase of profit and ever-greater profit (re-baptized as "economic growth") should ground to a halt. Today's industry is geared increasingly to the production of attractions and temptations. And attractions tempt and seduce only as long as they beckon from that faraway place that we call the future.

Being a Consumer in a Consumer Society

Our postmodern society is a consumer society. When we call it a consumer society, we have in mind something more than the trivial and sedate circumstance that all members of that society are consumers—all human beings, and not just *human* beings, have been consumers since time immemorial. What we do have in mind is that ours is a "consumer society" in the similarly profound and fundamental sense in which the society of our predecessors, modern society in its industrial phase, used to be a "producer society." That older type of modern society once engaged its members primarily as producers and soldiers; society shaped its members by dictating the need to play those two roles, and the norm that society held up to its members was the ability and the willingness to play them. In its present late-modern (Giddens), second-modern (Beck), or postmodern stage, modern society has little need for mass industrial labor and conscript armies, but it needs—and engages—its members in their capacity as consumers.

The role that our present-day society holds up to its members is the role of the consumer, and the members of our society are likewise judged by their ability and willingness to play that role. The difference between our present-day society and its immediate predecessor is not as radical as abandoning one role and picking up another instead. In neither of its two stages could modern society do without its members producing things to be consumed, and members of both do, of course, consume. The consumer of a consumer society, however, is a sharply different creature from the consumer of any other society thus far. The difference is one of emphasis and priorities—a shift of emphasis that makes an enormous difference to virtually every aspect of society, culture, and individual life. The differences are so deep and multiform that they fully justify speaking of our society as a society of a separate and distinct kind—a *consumer society*.

Ideally, all acquired habits should "lie on the shoulders" of that new type of consumer just like the ethically inspired vocational and acquisitive passions used to lie, as Max Weber repeated after Richard Baxter, "on the shoulders of the 'saint like a light cloak, which can be thrown aside at any moment'" (Weber 1976: 181). And the habits are indeed continually, daily, and at first opportunity thrown aside, and never given the chance to firm up into the iron bars of a cage (except one meta-habit: the "habit of changing habits"). Ideally, nothing should be embraced by a consumer firmly, nothing should command a commitment forever, and no needs should be seen as fully satisfied, no desires considered ultimate. There ought to be a proviso "until further notice" attached to any oath of loyalty and any commitment. It is the volatility, the in-built temporality of all engagements that counts, and counts more than the commitment itself, which is not allowed to outlast the time necessary for consuming the object of desire (or the desirability of that object) anyway.

That all consumption takes time is in fact the bane of the consumer society and a major worry for the merchandisers of consumer goods. The consumer's satisfaction ought to be *instant* and this in a double sense. Consumed goods should bring satisfaction immediately, requiring no learning of skills and no lengthy groundwork, but the satisfaction should end the moment the time needed for consumption is up, and that time ought to be reduced to a bare minimum. The needed reduction is best achieved if consumers cannot hold their attention nor focus their desire on any object for long; if they are impatient, impetuous, and restive; and above all if they are easily excitable and predisposed to quickly lose interest. Indeed, when the waiting is taken out of wanting and the wanting out of waiting, the consumptive capacity of consumers may be stretched far beyond the limits set by any natural or acquired needs or designed by the physical endurability of the objects of desire. The traditional relationship between needs and their satisfaction is then reversed: the promise and hope of satisfaction precedes the need promised to be satisfied and will be always greater than the extant need—yet not too great to preclude the desire for the goods that carry that promise.

As a matter of fact, the promise is all the more attractive the less the need in question is familiar; there is a lot of fun in living through an experience one did not know existed. The excitement of a new and unprecedented sensation—not the greed of acquiring and possessing, nor wealth in its material, tangible sense—is the name of the consumer game. Consumers are first and foremost gatherers of sensations; they are collectors of things only in a secondary and derivative sense. As Mark C. Taylor and Esa Saarinen put it, "Desire does not desire satisfaction. To the contrary, desire desires desire" (1994: 11). Such is the case with the ideal consumer. The prospect of the desire fading off, dissipating, and having nothing in sight to resurrect it, or the prospect of a world with nothing left in it to be desired, must be the most sinister of the ideal consumer's horrors (and, of course, of the consumer-goods merchandiser's horrors).

To increase their capacity for consumption, consumers must never be left to rest. They need to be constantly exposed to new temptations to keep them in the state of perpetual suspicion and steady disaffection. The bait commanding them to shift attention needs to confirm the suspicion while offering a way out of disaffection: "You reckoned you'd seen it all? You ain't seen nothing yet!" It is often said that the consumer market seduces its customers. But in order to do so, it needs customers who *want* to be seduced (just as to command his laborers, the factory boss needed a crew with the habits of discipline and command-following firmly entrenched). In a properly working consumer society, consumers seek actively to be seduced. They live from attraction to attraction, from temptation to temptation—each attraction and each temptation being somewhat different and perhaps stronger than its predecessor. In many ways they are just like their fathers, the producers, who lived from one turn of the conveyer belt to an identical next.

This cycle of desire is a compulsion, a must, for the fully fledged, mature consumer; yet that must, that internalized pressure, that impossibility of living one's life in any other way, is seen as the free exercise of one's will. The market might have already selected them as consumers and so taken away their freedom to ignore its blandishments, but in every successive visit to the marketplace, consumers have every reason to feel that they are the ones in command. They are the judges, the critics, and the choosers. They can, after all, refuse their allegiance to any one of the infinite choices on display—except the choice of choosing among them.

It is the combination of the consumer, constantly greedy for new attractions and fast bored with attractions already had, and of the world in all its dimensions—economic, political, personal—transformed after the pattern of the consumer market and, like that market, ready to oblige and change its attractions with ever-accelerating speed, that wipes out all fixed signposts from an individual map of the world or from the plans for a life itinerary. Indeed, traveling hopefully is in this situation much better than to arrive. Arrival has that musty smell of the end of the road, that bitter taste of monotony and stagnation that signals the end to everything for which the ideal consumer lives and considers the sense of living. To enjoy the best this world has to offer, you may do all sorts of things except one: to declare, after Goethe's Faust: "O moment, you are beautiful, last forever!"

Divided We Move

And so we are all traveling, whether we like it or not. We have not been asked about our feelings anyway. Thrown into a vast and open sea with no tracks and milestones fast sinking, we may rejoice in the breathtaking vistas of new discoveries or tremble out of fear of drowning. How does one voyage on these stormy seas—seas that certainly call for strong ships and skillful navigation? This becomes the question. Even more so when one understands that the greater the expanse of free sailing, the more the sailor's fate tends to be polarized and the deeper the chasm between poles.

But there is a catch. Everybody may be cast into the mode of consumer; everybody may wish to be a consumer and indulge in the opportunities which that mode of life holds. But not everybody *can* be a consumer. Desire is not enough; to squeeze the pleasure out of desire, one must have a reasonable hope of obtaining the desired object, and while that hope is reasonable for some, it is futile for others. All of us are doomed to the life of choices, but not all of us have the means to be choosers.

You can tell one kind of society from another by the dimensions along which it stratifies its members, and, like all other societies, the postmodern consumer society is a stratified one. Those "high up" and "low down" are plotted in a society of consumers along the lines of mobility—the freedom to choose where to be. Those "high up" travel through life to their hearts' content and pick and choose their destinations by the joys they offer. Those "low down" are thrown out from the site they would rather stay in, and if they do not move, it is the site that is pulled from under their feet. When they travel, their destination, more often than not, is of somebody else's choosing and seldom enjoyable; and when they arrive, they occupy a highly unprepossessing site that they would gladly leave behind if they had anywhere else to go. But they don't. They have nowhere else to go; there is nowhere else where they are likely to be welcomed.

As it happens, the degree of global polarization has broken all registered and remembered records in the last three decades. According to the United Nations' *Program for Development* (1994 edition), the top fifth of the world population in 1960 was thirty times richer than the bottom fifth; in 1991 it was already sixty-one times richer. Nothing in the foreseeable future indicates a slowing down of the widening of this gap, much less a reversal. In 1991, the top fifth of the world population enjoyed 84.7 percent of the world's gross product, 84.2 percent of its global trade, and 85 percent of its internal investment, against, respectively, the bottom fifth's 1.4 percent, 0.9 percent, and 0.9 percent share. The top fifth consumed 70 percent of the world's energy, 75 percent of its metals, and 85 percent of its timber. On the other hand, the debt of the economically weak countries of the "Third World," which was more or less stable at around $200 billion in 1970, has since grown tenfold and is today fast approaching the mind-boggling figure of $2 trillion.

Commenting on the findings of the 1996 U.N. *Human Development Report* that the total wealth of the top 358 "global billionaires" equaled the combined incomes of the 2.3 billion poorest people (45 percent of the world's population), Victor Keegan of the *Guardian* (1996) called the present reshuffling of the world's resources "a new form of highway robbery." Indeed, only 22 percent of the global wealth belongs to the so-called "developing countries," which account for about 80 percent of the world population. This is by no means the end of the story, as the share of current income received by the poor is smaller still: in 1991, 85 percent of the world's population received only 15 percent of the world's income. No wonder that in the last thirty years the abysmally meager 2.3 percent of global wealth owned by 20 percent of the poorest countries fell further still, to 1.4 percent. The global network of communication, acclaimed as the gateway to a new and unheard of freedom, is clearly very selectively used; a narrow cleft in a thick wall, rather than a gate. "All computers do for the Third World these days is to chronicle their decline more efficiently," says Keegan. And he concludes: "If (as one American critic observed) the 358 [billionaires] decided to keep $5 million or so each, to tide themselves over, and give the rest away, they could virtually double the annual incomes of nearly half the people on Earth. And pigs would fly" (1996: T2). In the words of John Kavanagh of the *Institute of Policy Research* in Washington,

> Globalization has given more opportunities for the extremely wealthy to make money more quickly. These individuals have utilized the latest technology to move large sums of money around the globe extremely quickly and speculate ever more efficiently. Unfortunately, the technology makes no impact on the lives of the world poor. In fact, globalization is a paradox: while it is very beneficial to a very few, it leaves out or marginalizes two-thirds of the world's population. (Quoted in Balls and Jenkins 1996)

Global polarization is replicated on only a slightly reduced scale in the inner-societal polarization in most affluent countries. Throughout the affluent part of the globe, we hear of the unprecedented phenomenon of the permanent, perhaps even hereditary, "underclass," and of the equally unprecedented phenomenon of "structural unemployment." The long-forgotten category of "working poor" (people who are employed and earn money yet whose wages fail to lift them above the threshold of poverty) has made an unexpected comeback. Whether measured globally or nationally, the gap between the affluent and the poor grows steadily.

Two Spaces, Two Times

Although this trend may be measured economically, the phenomenon itself is more than just an issue of economic divisions. The two worlds at the top and bottom of the emergent hierarchy differ sharply and have become increasingly *incommunicado* to each other. If for the first world—the world of the rich and the affluent—space has lost its constraining quality and is easily traversed in both its "real" and "virtual" renditions, for the other world—that of the useless and unwanted poor, the "structurally redundant"—real space is fast closing up. And the deprivation is made yet more painful by the obtrusive media display of space conquest and the "virtual accessibility" of distances that stay stubbornly unreachable in the nonvirtual reality. The shrinking of space abolishes the flow of time. The inhabitants of the first world live in a perpetual present, going through a succession of episodes hygienically insulated from both their past and their future. These people are constantly busy and perpetually "short of time," since each moment of time is nonextensive. People marooned in the opposite world are crushed under the burden of abundant, redundant, and useless time that they have nothing with which to fill. They do not "control" time, but neither are they controlled by it, unlike their clocking-in, clocking-out ancestors who were subject to the faceless rhythm of factory time. They can only kill time, as they are slowly killed by it.

Residents of the first world live in *time*; space does not matter for them, since every distance can be spanned instantaneously. It is this experience which Jean Baudrillard (1983) encapsulated in his image of "hyperreality," where the virtual and the real are no longer separable, since both share and miss in the same measure that "objectivity," "externality," and "punishing power" which Emile Durkheim listed as the symptoms of reality. Residents of the second world live in *space*—heavy, resilient, untouchable—which ties down time and keeps it beyond the residents' control. Their time is void; in their time, "nothing ever happens." Only virtual television time has a structure, a "timetable." Other time is monotonously ticking away. It comes and goes, making no demands and leaving no apparent trace. Immaterial, time has no power over that all-too-real space to which the residents of the second world are confined.

For the increasingly cosmopolitan, extraterritorial, first world global businessmen, global culture managers, and global academics, state borders are leveled, just as they are dismantled for commodities, capital, and finances. For the inhabitants of the second world, the walls built of immigration controls, residence laws, and of "clean streets" and "zero tolerance" statutes grow taller, and the moats separating them from the sites of their desire and dreamed-of redemption grow deeper. The first travel at will. The second travel surreptitiously, often illegally, sometimes paying more for the crowded storage of a stinking un-seaworthy boat than others pay for business-class luxuries, and are frowned upon, and perhaps deported, once they arrive.

It would be advisable, therefore, to follow Roland Robertson's (1995) suggestion and instead of "globalization" speak of *glocalization*—a bizarre blend of globalizing/emancipating and localizing/ascriptive tendencies. This more complex term concentrates our attention on the fact that what is now going on in the world polarizes mobility—that ability to use time to annul the limitations of space. Ability or disability to move divides the world into the globalized and the localized. "Globalization" and "localization" may be inseparable sides of the same coin, but the two parts of the world population seem to be living on different sides, facing one side only—much like the people of the Earth see and scan only one hemisphere of the moon. Some inhabit the globe; others are chained to their place.

Moving Through the World Versus the World Moving By

The cultural consequences of polarization are enormous. Agnes Heller recalls meeting on one of her long-distance flights a middle-aged woman, who was an employee of an international trade firm. The woman spoke five languages and owned apartments in three different places:

> She constantly migrates, and among many places, and always to and fro. She does it alone, not as a member of a community, although many people act like her.... The kind of culture she participates in is not a culture of a certain place; it is the culture of a time. It is a culture of the *absolute present*.

> Let us accompany her on her constant trips from Singapore to Hong Kong, London, Stockholm, New Hampshire, Tokyo, Prague, and so on. She stays in the same Hilton hotel, eats the same tuna sandwich for lunch, or, if she wishes, eats Chinese food in Paris and French food in Hong Kong. She uses the same type of fax, and telephones, and computers, watches the same films, and discusses the same kind of problems with the same kind of people. (Heller 1995): 41

Agnes Heller herself, like many of us an academic globetrotter, finds it easy to empathize with her anonymous companion's experience. She adds, *pro domo sua*, "Even foreign universities are not foreign. After one delivers a lecture, one can expect the same questions in Singapore, Tokyo, Paris, or Manchester. They are not foreign places, nor are they homes" (Heller 1995).

Jeremy Seabrook remembers another woman, Michelle, from a neighboring council estate:

> At fifteen her hair was one day red, the next blonde, then jet-black, then teased into Afro kinks and after that rat-tails, then plaited, and then cropped so that it glistened close to the skull....Her lips were scarlet, then purple, then black. Her face was ghost-white and then peach-colored, then bronze as if it were cast in metal. Pursued by dreams of flight, she left home at sixteen to be with her boyfriend, who was twenty-six....At eighteen she returned to her mother, with two children....She sat in the bedroom which she had fled three years earlier; the faded photos of yesterday's pop stars still stared down from the walls. She said she felt a hundred years old. She was weary. She'd tried all that life could offer her. Nothing else was left. (Seabrook 1985: 59)

Heller's fellow-passenger lives in an imaginary home she does not need and thus does not mind being imaginary. Seabrook's acquaintance performs imaginary flights from the home she resents for being stultifyingly real. Virtuality of space serves both, but to each offers different services with sharply different results. To Heller's travel companion, the virtuality of space helps to dissolve whatever constraints a real home may impose—to dematerialize space. To Seabrook's neighbor, the virtuality brings into relief the awesome and abhorring power of a home turned into a prison—it decomposes time. The first experience is lived through as postmodern freedom. The second as the postmodern version of slavery.

The first experience is, paradigmatically, that of the *tourist* (and it does not matter whether the purpose of the trip is business or pleasure). The tourists become wanderers and put the dreams of homesickness above the realities of home. They do so because they want to, because they consider it the most reasonable life-strategy "under the circumstances," or because they have been seduced by the true or imaginary pleasures of a sensation-gatherer's life. But not all wanderers are on the move because they prefer being on the move to staying put or because they want to go where they are going. Many would perhaps go elsewhere or refuse to embark on a life of wandering altogether were they asked. Only they were never asked. If they are on the move, it is because "staying at home" in a world made to the measure of the tourist is a humiliation and a drudgery. They are on the move because they have been pushed from behind, having been first spiritually uprooted from the place that holds no promise by a force of seduction or propulsion too powerful, and often too mysterious, to resist. They see their plight as anything but a manifestation of freedom. These are the *vagabonds*, or dark vagrant moons reflecting the bright light of tourist suns and following their orbit, the mutants of postmodern evolution, the freaks of the brave new species. The vagabonds are the waste of the world that has dedicated itself to tourist services.

The tourists stay or move at their heart's desire. They abandon a site when a new untried opportunity beckons elsewhere. The vagabonds, however, know that they won't stay in one place for long, however strongly they wish to, since nowhere they stop are they welcome. The tourists move because they find the world within their reach irresistibly *attractive*. The vagabonds move because they find the world within their reach unbearably inhospitable. The tourists travel because they want to, the vagabonds because they have no other bearable choice. The vagabonds are, one may say, involuntary tourists, but the notion of "involuntary tourist" is a contradiction in terms. However much the tourist strategy may be a necessity in a world marked by shifting walls and mobile roads, freedom of choice is the tourist's flesh and blood. Take it away, and the attraction, the poetry and, indeed, the livability of the tourist's life are all but gone.

What is acclaimed today as "globalization" is geared to the tourists' dreams and desires. Its second effect, its side effect, is the transformation of many others into vagabonds. Vagabonds are the travelers who are refused the right to turn into tourists. They are allowed neither to stay put (there is no site-guaranteed permanence) nor to search for a better place to be. Once emancipated from space, capital needs no more itinerant labor (while its most emancipated, most high-tech avant-garde needs hardly any labor, mobile or immobile). And so the pressure to pull down the last remaining barriers to the free movement of money, commodities, and information goes hand-in-hand with the pressure to dig new moats and erect new walls (variously called "immigration" or "nationality" laws), barring the movement of those who are uprooted, spiritually or bodily, as a result. Enforced localization guards the natural selectivity of the globalizing effects. The widely noted, increasingly worrying polarization of the world and its population is not an alien, disturbing influence in the process of globalization. It is its effect.

For Better or Worse United

The vagabond is the alter ego of the tourist, and the tourist's most ardent admirer. Ask the vagabonds what sort of life they would wish to live given the chance and you will get a pretty accurate description of the tourist's bliss. Vagabonds have no other images of a good life. They have no alternative utopia, no political agenda of their own. The sole thing they want is to be allowed to be tourists—like the rest of us. In the restless world, tourism is the only acceptable, human form of restlessness.

The tourist and the vagabond are both consumers, and the postmodern consumers are sensation-seekers and collectors of experience; their relationship to the world is primarily *aesthetic*. They perceive the world as a matrix of possible experiences (in the sense of *Erlebnisse*, a state one lives through, not *Erfahrungen*, occurrences that happen to one—the seminal distinction made in German but sorely missing in English), and map the world according to the experiences occasioned. Both vagabonds and tourists are moved—attracted or repelled—by the promised quality of sensations. They both "savor" the world, as seasoned museumgoers savor their *tête-à-tête* with a work of art. This attitude to the world unites them, makes them similar to each other. This similarity enables the vagabonds to empathize with tourists and to desire to share in their lifestyle. The tourists try hard to forget the similarity; though much to their dismay, they cannot quite suppress it.

Both the tourist and the vagabond have been made into consumers, but the vagabond is a *flawed* consumer. Vagabonds are not really able to afford the kind of sophisticated choice in which consumers are expected to excel. Their limited resources severely limit their potential for consumption. This fault makes their position in society precarious. They breach the norm and sap the order. They spoil the fun, they do not lubricate the wheels of the consumer society, and they add little to the prosperity of the tourist economy. They are "useless," in the sole sense of "use" one can think of in a society of consumers and in a society of tourists. And because they are useless, they are also unwanted, and hence the natural targets for stigmatizing and scapegoating. Their crime, however, consists in wanting to be like tourists yet lacking the means to act on their wishes.

If the tourists view the vagabonds as unsavory, disreputable, and offensive, and resent their unsolicited company, it is for deeper reasons than the much-publicized "public costs" of keeping them alive. The tourists have the horror of the vagabonds for much the same reason for which the vagabonds look up to the tourists as their gurus and idols; in the society of travelers, in the traveling society, tourism and vagrancy are two sides of the same coin. The vagabond, let me repeat, is the alter ego of the tourist. The line that divides them is tenuous and not always clearly drawn. One can easily step over it without noticing. There is this abominable likeness.

Among the tourists, some are always on the go and always confident that they go in the right direction and that the going is the right thing to do. These happy and self-assured tourists seldom entertain a thought that their adventures might end, that their tourism might descend into vagabondage. Similarly, there are some convinced vagabonds who long ago threw in the towel and abandoned all hope of ever rising to the rank of tourists. But between these two extremes there is a large part, perhaps the majority, of the society of consumers/travelers who cannot be sure where they stand at the moment and are even less sure if their standing can be maintained. There are so many banana skins on the road, and so many high curbs on which one can stumble: most jobs, after all, are temporary; shares may go up as well as down; skills are continuously devalued and superseded by new and improved proficiencies; partnerships are shifting and temporary; one's prized assets become obsolete in no time; exquisite neighborhoods grow shoddy and run-down; values worth pursuit and ends worth investment come and go. Just as no life insurance policy can protect the policy owner from death, so none of the seeming assurances of the tourist's lifestyle can protect against a decline into vagabondage.

The vagabond, then, is the tourist's nightmare, the tourist's "inner demon," which needs to be exorcised, and daily. The sight of the vagabond makes the tourist tremble, not because of what the vagabond is but because of what the tourist may become. In forcing the vagabond off the street, confining him to a far-away and "no-go" ghetto, demanding his exile or incarceration, the tourist desperately seeks deportation of his own fears. A world without vagabonds will be a world in which the tourist need never wake up a vagabond. A world without vagabonds is the utopia of the tourist society.

The irony is, though, that the life of the tourist would not be half as enjoyable as it is if there were no vagabonds around to demonstrate what the alternative to that life—the sole alternative that consumer society renders realistic—is like. Tourist life is not a bed of roses, and the roses most likely to be found there have thorns. There are many hardships one needs to suffer for the sake of tourist freedoms: the impossibility of slowing down, the uncertainty surrounding every choice, and the risks attached to every decision most prominent among them. The joy of choosing loses much of its allure when choosing you must, and adventure is stripped of a good deal of its attraction when one's whole life becomes a ceaseless string of adventures. There is a lot, in fact, the tourist could complain about. The temptation to seek another way to happiness is never far away. It can never be extinguished, only pushed aside, and not for long. What makes the tourist life endurable, what turns its hardships into minor irritants and permits the temptation to change to be resisted, is the self-same sight of the vagabond that makes the tourist shudder.

And so, paradoxically, the tourist's life is all the more bearable, even enjoyable, for being haunted by the nightmarish alternative of the vagabond's existence. In an equally paradoxical sense, tourists have a vested interest in rendering the vagabond alternative as dreadful and execrable as possible. The worse the plight of the vagabond, the better it feels to be a tourist. Were there no vagabonds, the tourists would need to invent them. The consumer society needs both. They are bound together by a Gordian knot no one seems to know how to untie and no one seems to have a sword to cut.

So we go on moving, the tourists and the vagabonds, the half-tourists and the half-vagabonds that we have become in the postmodern society of relentless consumption.

References

Balls, G., and M. Jenkins. 1996. "Too Much for Them, Not Enough for Us." *Independent on Sunday* (21 July): 18.

Baudrillard, J. 1983. *Simulations*. New York: Semiotext(e), Inc.

Heller, A. 1995. "Where Are We at Home?" *Thesis Eleven* N, 41.

Keegan, V. 1996. "Highway Robbery by the Super-Rich." *Guardian* (22 July): T2.

Petrella, R. 1997. "Une Machine Infernale." *Le Monde Diplomatique* (June).

Robertson, R. 1995. "Glocalization: Time-Space and Homogeneity-Heterogeneity." Pp. 25-44 in *Global Modernities*, edited by M. Featherstone, S. Lash, and R. Robertson. London: Sage.

Seabrook, J. 1985. *Landscapes of Poverty*. Oxford: Blackwell.

Taylor, M.C., and E. Saarinen. 1994. "Telerotics." In *Imagologies: Media Philosophy*. London: Routledge.

United Nations Development Program. 1994. *Program for Development, 1994*. New York: Oxford University Press.

Weber, M. 1976. *The Protestant Ethic and the Spirit of Capitalism*. Trans. T. Parsons. London: Allen and Unwin.

2

The Work of Postmodernity: The Laboring Body in Global Space

David Harvey

The rise of the term "postmodernity" to considerable currency not only in academic circles but also in the mass media betokens a discursive shift in how we collectively represent, understand, and interpret the world. This shift depended upon a reconfiguration of all manner of conceptual apparatuses in many different spheres. It is doubtful, for example, if postmodernism could have acquired the currency and purchase it undoubtedly has without the rise of concepts to do with chaos, complexity, fractals, and the like within mathematics and the sciences, for no matter how badly misunderstood these ideas might be in the humanities or in the media, they still add their authority to the destabilization of traditional concepts that is such a hallmark of postmodern sensibility.

But to destabilize concepts in perpetuity is one thing. To have at hand a stable enough language to communicate anything at all is quite another. And so beneath all of the shifting, fragmentation, and disruption of concepts, it is not hard to detect a subterranean set of concerns and ideas that have become epicenters of our thinking and which constitute relatively stable arenas of discursive activity.

In this essay I will consider two concepts—"globalization" and "the body"—that have risen to prominence in contemporary discussions and which define separate but major arenas of discursive activity. While there is, of course, considerable dispute over the significance and meaning of these terms, the convergence of attention upon them hardly suggests a chaotic, or even random motion in our conceptual universe. Cursory analysis of them yields, furthermore, detectable traces of deep continuities which, once excavated, suggest that *displacement* rather than *disruption* has characterized the shift from modern to postmodern perspectives. Systematic displacements are somewhat easier to analyze than chaotic disruptions and I propose to look more closely at them with the aid of one of the discourses—that of Marx—which postmodernism was supposed to have so decisively displaced. Globalization and the body take on specific meanings and significances, it will be seen, when set against the material conditions defined by the capitalist system of wage labor. That system, organized through market processes which are orchestrated by specific configurations of corporate and state powers, has produced not only the phenomenon of globalization but a very distinctive sort of body politics. Bringing the two discourses together reveals, furthermore, some interesting unities between them. But why invoke the outdated and supposedly discredited Marx?

Marx Redux

For the last twenty-eight years (with the exception of one) I have run either a reading group or a course on Marx's *Capital,* Volume One. While this may seem the mark of a peculiarly stodgy academic mind, it yields me a rare time-series of data points on reactions to and interest in this particular text.

In the early years there was great political enthusiasm for it on the part of self-styled radical academics. The group formed (in parallel with many others across American campuses at the time) to try to find a theoretical basis, a way of understanding all of the chaos and political disruption evident in the world (the civil rights movement in the United States; the urban uprisings that followed the assassination of Martin Luther King; the growing opposition to the imperialist war in Vietnam; the massive student movements that shook the world from Paris to Mexico City, Berkeley, and Bangkok; the Prague "Spring" and its subsequent repression by the Soviets—just to name a few of the signal events that made it seem as if the world as we knew it was falling apart). In the midst of all this confusing turmoil there was a crying need for solid intellectual guidance. Many of us turned to Marx for help.

Several young faculty members and graduate students (some of whom have since gone on to be famous) participated from all manner of disciplines (math sciences to English). We all puzzled our way through *Capital* and I soon found myself teaching it well beyond the confines of the university. Teaching undergraduates was somewhat fraught, for their radicalism was anti-intellectual; many thought it rather unradical to demand that they read let alone understand and write about such a long and tortuous book.

The situation is different now. I teach *Capital* as a conventional course. I rarely if ever see any faculty members and the graduate student audience has largely disappeared (except for those few who plan to work with me and who take the course as some kind of "ritual of passage" before they go on to more important things). Of course many academics refer to Marx, but mainly as an outmoded "structuralist" and "modernist" or denigrate him as insufficiently concerned with more important questions of gender, race, sexuality, human desires, or whatever. Undergraduates still take the course but for them this is no longer a political act. The Berlin Wall fell down and the fear of communism dissipated. The course has a good reputation. Depending on their timetable and their requirements, some of them end up in Marx's *Capital* rather than in Aristotle's *Ethics* or Plato's *Republic*.

This contrast between then and now is hardly surprising. But there is another tale to be told that makes matters more confusing. In the 1970s it was hard to find the direct relevance of *Capital* to the political issues that dominated the day. We needed Lenin to get us from Marx to an understanding of the imperialist war that so unnerved us in Vietnam. We needed a theory of civil society (Gramsci at least) to get us from Marx to civil rights, and a theory of the state (such as Miliband or Poulantzas) to get us to a critique of state repressions and welfare state expenditures manipulated to requirements of capital accumulation. We needed the Frankfurt School to understand questions of legitimacy, technological rationality, and the environment. In short, we needed a whole host of mediations to get from *Capital* to most of the political issues that concerned us. The text did not have that much immediate relevance to daily life.

The situation is different today. The text teems with ideas as to how to explain our current state. There is the fetish of the market that caught Kathy Lee Gifford when she was told that the line of clothing she was selling through Wal-Mart was made either by thirteen-year-olds in Honduras paid a mere pittance, or by sweated women workers in New York who had not been paid for weeks. There is also the whole savage history of downsizing (prominently reported in the *New York Times*), the scandals over child labor in South Asia, and Michael Jordan's $30 million retainer for Nike set against media accounts of the appalling conditions of Nike workers in Indonesia and Vietnam. The press is full of complaints as to how technological change is destroying employment opportunities, weakening the institutions of organized labor, and increasing rather than lessening the intensity and hours of labor (all central themes of Marx's chapter on "Machinery and Modern Industry"). And then there is the whole question of how an "industrial reserve army" of labor has been produced, sustained, and manipulated in the interests of capital accumulation these last decades—illuminated by the public admission of Alan Budd, an erstwhile advisor to Margaret Thatcher, that the fight against inflation in the early 1980s was a cover for raising unemployment and reducing the strength of the working class. He said, "What was engineered—in Marxist terms—was a crisis in capitalism which re-created a reserve army of labour, and has allowed the capitalists to make high profits ever since" (Brooks 1992).

Students who stray into the course soon feel the heat of a devastating critique of a free market neo-liberalism run riot. For their final paper I give them bundles of cuttings from the *New York Times* (a respectable source, after all) and suggest they use them to answer an imaginary letter from a parent/relative/friend from home that says:

> I hear you are taking a course on Marx's *Das Kapital*. I have never read it myself though I hear it is both interesting and difficult. But thank heavens we have put that nineteenth-century nonsense behind us now. Life was hard and terrible in those days, but we have come to our collective senses and made a world that Marx would surely never recognize....

The students write illuminating letters. Though they dare not send them, few finish the course without having their views disrupted by the sheer power of a text that connects so trenchantly with conditions around us.

This text of Marx's was much sought after and studied in radical circles at a time when it had little direct relationship to daily life. Scarcely anyone cares to consider it now even though the material conditions are so ripe for its application. So it is worth examining what happens when this all-too-pertinent text is used to frame contemporary understandings of globalization and the body.

A Tale of Two Eras

There are, of course, all kinds of aspects to the massive discursive shift that has paralleled the demise of Marxian thinking these last two decades. But it is worth starting by noting the dominance of an almost fairytale belief, held on all sides alike, that once upon a time there was structuralism, modernism, industrialism, Marxism, or what have you, and now there is poststructuralism, postmodernism, postindustrialism, post-Marxism, postcolonialism, and so forth. Like all hegemonic tales, this one is rarely spoken of in such a simplistic way. To do so would be particularly embarrassing to those who deny in principle the significance of this type of "metanarrative." Yet the prevalence of "the post" (and the associated inability to say what it is that we might be "pre") is a dominant in the discursive shift that has occurred. It then becomes impossible to discuss Marx or Marxism outside of these dominant terms of debate. For example, a strong theme of reaction to my own recent work, particularly *Justice, Nature and the Geography of Difference,* is to express surprise and disbelief at how I seem to merge modernist and postmodernist, structuralist and poststructuralist arguments (see, e.g., Eagleton 1997). But Marx had not read Saussure or Levi-Strauss and while there are some powerful structuralist readings of Marx (principally provided by Althusser) the evidence that Marx was a structuralist or even a modernist *avant la lettre*, as these terms came to be understood in the 1970s, is neither overwhelming nor conclusive. It is here that basing analyses on Marx directly (as opposed to accounts of Marx) collides with the beguiling power of this fairytale reading of our recent discursive history. Put bluntly, we do not read Marx these days (no matter whether he is relevant or not) because he is someone whose work lies in a category that we are supposed to be "post."

Now it is interesting to look at Marx's *oeuvre* through the lenses provided by contemporary concerns and fashions. He was, of course, an avid critic of classical bourgeois political economy and devoted much of his life to "deconstructing" its dominant principles. His technique, focusing on the absences (or "aporias" as we now often refer to them), was pioneering and rigorously textual. He was deeply concerned with language (discourse) and was acutely aware of how discursive shifts (of the sort he examined in depth in *The Eighteenth Brumaire*) carried their own distinctive political freight (how else was "the poetry of the future" to be construed?). He understood in a very deep sense the relationship between knowledge and "situatedness" ("positionality"), though it was, of course, the "standpoint" of the worker that was the focus of his attention. I could go on and on in this vein, but my point here is not to try to prove that much of what passes for innovative in our recent discursive history is already prefigured in Marx, but to point to the damage that the fairytale reading of the differences between the "then" and the "now" is doing to our abilities to confront the changes occurring around us.

Bearing this in mind, let us go back to "globalization" and "the body" as two important foci of thought and analysis in recent times. Both terms were little if at all in evidence as analytical tools in the early 1970s. Both are now powerfully present; they may even reasonably be regarded as conceptual dominants. "Globalization," for example, was entirely unknown before the mid-1970s. Innumerable conferences now study the idea and there is a vast literature on the subject, coming at it from all angles. It is a frequent topic of commentary in the media. It is now one of the most hegemonic concepts for understanding the political economy of international capitalism. And its uses extend far beyond the business world to embrace questions of politics, culture, national identity, and the like. It is, so to speak, an accepted fact of life. And while the shift into postmodern modes can hardly be credited with inventing it, it is surely one of those terms that postmodernism simply could not operate without. Does not the whole idea of the globe suggest a radical decentering of everything (there is no natural center to the surface of a globe)? Is it not globalization that has so hollowed out the nation state and so decentered political power that everything dissolves into multicultural identity politics? So where did this concept of globalization come from? Does it describe something essentially new?

"Globalization" seems first to have acquired its prominence as American Express advertised the global reach of its credit card in the mid-1970s. The term then spread like wildfire in the financial and business press, mainly as legitimation for the deregulation of financial markets. It then helped make the diminution of state powers to regulate capital flows seem inevitable and became an extraordinarily powerful political tool in the disempowerment of national and local working class movements and trade union power (labor discipline and fiscal austerity—often imposed by the International Monetary Fund and the World Bank—became essential to achieving internal stability and international competitiveness). By the mid-1980s "globalization" helped create a heady atmosphere of entrepreneurial optimism around the theme of the liberation of markets (and of the artifacts of culture) from state control. It became a central concept, in short, associated with the brave new world of globalizing neoliberalism. The term helped make it seem as if we were entering upon a new era (with a touch of teleological inevitability thrown in) and thereby became part of that package of concepts that distinguished between then and now in terms of political possibilities. The more the left accepted this discourse as a description of the state of the world (even if it was a state to be criticized and rebelled against), the more it circumscribed its own political possibilities. That so many of us took the concept on board so uncritically in the 1980s and 1990s, allowing it to displace the far more politically charged concepts of imperialism and neocolonialism, should give us pause. The passage from Marxian understandings to those based on notions of globalization was disempowering for the left.

What of the body? Here the tale, though analogous, is substantively different. The extraordinary efflorescence of interest in "the body" as a grounding for all sorts of theoretical inquiries over the last two decades has a dual origin. In the first place, the questions raised through what is known as "second-wave feminism" could not be answered without close attention being paid to the "nature-nurture" problem and it was inevitable that the status and understanding of "the body" became central to theoretical debate. Questions of gender, sexuality, the power of symbolic orders, and the significance of psychoanalysis also repositioned the body as both subject and object of discussion and debate. And to the degree that all of this opened up a terrain of inquiry that was well beyond traditional conceptual apparatuses (such as that contained in Marx), an extensive and original theorizing of the body became essential to progressive and emancipatory politics (this was particularly the case with respect to feminist and queer theory).

The second impulse to return to the body arose out of the movements of poststructuralism in general and deconstruction in particular. The effect of these movements was to generate a loss of confidence in all previously established categories (such as those proposed by Marx) for understanding the world. This in turn provoked a return to the body as the irreducible basis for understanding. Lowe argues that

> there still remains one referent apart from all the other destabilized referents, whose presence cannot be denied, and that is the body referent, our very own lived body. This body referent is in fact the referent of all referents, in the sense that ultimately all signifieds, values, or meanings refer to the delineation and satisfaction of the needs of the body. Precisely because all other referents are now destabilized, the body referent, our own body, has emerged as a problem. (1995: 14)

The convergence of these two broad movements has refocused attention upon the body as the basis for understanding and, in certain circles at least, as the privileged site of political resistance and emancipatory politics.

Consider, now, the positioning of these two discursive regimes in our contemporary constructions. "Globalization" is the most macro of all discourses that we have available to us while that of "the body" is surely the most micro (unless, of course, we go to the levels of molecular biology and propose that everything is to be understood in terms of DNA). These two discursive regimes operate at opposite ends of the spectrum in the scalars we might use to understand social and political life. Yet little or no systematic attempt has been made to integrate "body talk" with "globalization talk." The only strong connection to have emerged in recent years concerns individual and human rights (e.g., the work of Amnesty International), and, more specifically, the right of women to control their own bodies and reproductive strategies as a means to approach global population problems (dominant themes in the Cairo Conference on Population in 1994 and the Beijing Women's Conference of 1996). Environmental movements often try to forge similar connections, linking personal health and consumption practices with global problems of toxic waste generation, ozone depletion, global warming, and the like. These instances illustrate the potency of linking the two seemingly disparate discursive regimes of the personal and the global. In what follows, therefore, I shall sketch a way in which "globalization" and "the body" might be more closely integrated with each other. But first I need to give a fuller description of what these different discursive regimes might be about.

Globalization

One of the most compelling and concise descriptions of globalization is given by Marx and Engels in *The Communist Manifesto*. Modern industry, they wrote, not only creates the world market, but the need for a constant expansion of that market "chases the bourgeoisie over the whole surface of the globe" so that it "must nestle everywhere, settle everywhere, establish connections everywhere." Through its exploitation of the world market, the bourgeoisie has

> given a cosmopolitan character to production and consumption in every country....
> All old established national industries have been destroyed or are daily being

destroyed. They are dislodged by new industries, whose introduction becomes a life and death question for all civilized nations, by industries that no longer work up indigenous raw material, but raw material drawn from the remotest zones; industries whose products are consumed, not only at home, but in every quarter of the globe. In place of the old wants, satisfied by the production of the country, we find new wants, requiring for their satisfaction the products of distant lands and climes. In place of the old local and national seclusion and self-sufficiency, we have intercourse in every direction, universal interdependence of nations. And as in material, so also in (cultural) production. The (cultural) creations of individual nations become common property. National one-sidedness and narrow-mindedness become more and more impossible, and from the numerous national and local (cultures), there arises a world (culture). (Marx and Engels 1952: 46-7)

The fact that such a remarkable statement could be made more than 150 years ago suggests that globalization is a long-standing process rather than something that recently arose. I have argued elsewhere that the pursuit of a "spatial fix" to the contradictions of capitalism has been a permanently revolutionary feature in the history of global capital accumulation since at least 1492, if not before (Harvey 1982, 1996b). Wallerstein (1974), for example, traces the origins of the modern world system back to at least the long sixteenth century. The Pax Britannica at the close of the nineteenth century, like the Pax Americana post-World War II (operated under the Bretton Woods Agreement), were certainly global systems of power and capital accumulation (Arrighi 1994).

But to argue that globalization has long been with us is not to claim that nothing has changed. Three main forces have shifted the balance of that process since around 1970 or so (Harvey 1996b; forthcoming). A ratcheting downwards in the cost of transporting people and commodities removed locational restraints on production and consumption activities at the same time that the deregulation of financial markets permitted, with the aid of the information revolution, the creation of more fluid conditions of movement of finance and money capitals on the world stage (Chesnais 1996). The effect was to create conditions for a radical dispersal of manufacturing, resource extraction, and agricultural commodity production activities across the face of the globe. This meant massive proletarianization worldwide (a doubling of the number of wage workers in the world in twenty years) accompanied by deindustrialization in the traditional heartlands of advanced capitalism. Such processes gained added significance with the political collapse of the Soviet bloc, its opening as a field of accumulation, and the insertion of the remaining principle communist power (China) into the capitalist world market as a major competitor.

There were all kinds of cognate features to globalization, including strong migratory currents of populations throughout the world—powerful processes of rapid urbanization that spawned cities of 20 million or so (mostly in the so-called developing world). Perhaps even more important was political reterritorialization through the emergence of sub- and supranational powers and the patent diminution of nation state powers to control capital flow across state borders. This did not mean a general diminution in the role of the state, but political reterritorialization did change the state's orientation away from any kind of populist or socialist agenda, towards what is euphemistically called "creating a good business climate" (i.e., controlling the aspirations and powers of organized labor).

"Globalization," as we came to know it from the 1970s on, focused broadly on these innovative aspects of a globalization process that had been long-standing within the historical-geographical dynamic of capital accumulation. A variety of challenges to this dominant account can be constructed, particularly with respect to the supposed diminution of nation-state power (see Chesnais 1996; Hirst and Thompson 1996; Harvey 1996b; ILO 1996). But, plainly, this globalization process has been characterized by massive transformations in the conditions of wage labor throughout the world, which in turn have serious implications for the laboring body as the bearer of that key commodity called "labor power." So how, then, are these implications understood in contemporary theorizations of the body?

The Body

Viewing the body as the irreducible locus for the determination of all values, meanings, and significations is not new. It was fundamental to many strains of pre-Socratic philosophy, and the idea that "man" or "the body" is "the measure of all things" has had an extraordinarily long and interesting history. The contemporary return to "the body" as "the measure of all things" provides, therefore, an opportunity to reassert the bases (epistemological and ontological) of all forms of inquiry. The *manner* of this return is crucial to determining how values and meanings are to be constructed and understood and how politics can be imagined. Foucault, for one, strove to shift our political horizons away from monolithic categories such as class, and hence away from class politics, to embrace the micro-politics of the body as an alternative site for radical politics. Foucault writes,

This work done at the limits of ourselves must, on the one hand, open up a realm of historical enquiry, and, on the other, put itself to the test of reality, of contemporary reality, both to grasp the points where change is possible and desirable, and to determine the precise form this change should take. This means that the historical ontology of ourselves must turn away from all projects that claim to be global or radical. In fact we know from experience that the claim to escape from the system of contemporary reality so as to produce the overall programs of another society, of another way of thinking, another culture, another vision of the world, has led only to the return of the most dangerous traditions. (1984: 46)

The warning is salutary and deserves to be taken seriously. But the turning away from all projects that claim to be global leads Foucault to prefer projects that are "always partial and local." It drives a wedge between the discourses of "globalization" and "the body" so as to conform to Foucault's other view on the inherent heterogeneity, radical pluralism, and incompatibility of multiple discourses.

While not everyone has followed Foucault into such a political position, it is undeniable that much of the recent discourse about the body has been constructed as an antidote to discourses about class and has played an important role in generating that massive discursive shift away from interest in Marx that I began by outlining. And the recent discourse has, *pari passu*, made it not only undesirable but seemingly impossible to try to link discourses about globalization and the body in any systematic way. Yet there is something odd about how this construction has occurred, for there is much in the contemporary literature on the body that is perfectly consistent with the fundamentals of Marx's argument.

Consider, for example, the two fundamental themes that dominate the recent literature. Writers as diverse as Elias (1978), Bourdieu (1984), Stafford (1991), Haraway (1991), Butler (1993), Diprose (1994), Grosz (1994), and Martin (1994) agree that the body is an unfinished project, historically and geographically malleable in certain ways. The body may not be infinitely or even easily malleable, and certain of its inherent ("natural") qualities cannot be erased. But the body is evolving and changing in ways that reflect both an internal transformative dynamics (often the focus of psychoanalytic work) and external processes (most often invoked in social constructionist approaches). The malleability of the body is an idea that is powerfully present in Gramsci's analysis of Fordism and can be traced back, as I have shown elsewhere (Harvey 1998), to the very core of Marx's work from *The Economic and Philosophic Manuscripts of 1844* to *Capital*. The second theme, broadly consistent with (if not implicitly contained in) the first, is that the body is not a closed and sealed entity, but a relational "thing" that is created, bounded, sustained, and ultimately dissolved in a spatio-temporal flow of multiple processes. This entails a relational-dialectical view (most clearly articulated in queer theory) in which the body (construed as a thing-like entity endowed with transformative powers) internalizes the effects of the processes that create, support, sustain, and dissolve it. Here, too, an argument can be made that a relational dialectical reading of Marx's work (see Harvey 1996a) is entirely compatible with such a view. The body which we inhabit and which is supposedly the irreducible measure of all things is not itself irreducible. There is far more agreement between, say, Marx and Foucault on this point than there is fundamental difference. Much of what Foucault has to say, particularly in his early works such as *Discipline and Punish*, is prefigured in Marx's chapters in *Capital* on "The Working Day" and "Primitive Accumulation." Conversely, there is much in Foucault that can be read as a friendly and thoughtful extension of Marx's concerns rather than as a rejection and rebuttal.

But we here encounter a conundrum. On the one hand, to return to the human body as the fount of all experience is presently regarded as a means (now increasingly privileged) to challenge the whole network of abstractions (scientific, social, political-economic) through which social relations, power relations, institutions, and material practices get defined, represented, and regulated. But on the other hand, no human body is outside the social processes of determination. To return to the body is, therefore, to instantiate the very social processes being purportedly rebelled against. If, for example, workers are transformed (as Marx suggests in *Capital*) into appendages of capital in both the workplace and the consumption sphere (or, as Foucault prefers it, bodies are made over into "docile bodies" by the rise of a powerful disciplinary apparatus from the eighteenth century onwards), then how can their bodies be a measure, sign, or receiver of anything outside of the circulation of capital or of the various mechanisms that discipline workers? Or, to take a more contemporary version of the same argument, if we are all now "cyborgs," as Haraway (1991) in her celebrated manifesto on the topic suggests, then how can we measure anything outside of that deadly embrace of the machine as extension of our own body and of the body as extension of the machine?

So while return to the body as the site of a more authentic (epistemological and ontological) grounding of the theoretical abstractions that have for too long ruled purely as abstractions may be justified (and provide a proper grounding, as in the cases of feminism and queer theory, for an emancipatory and progressive politics), that return cannot in and of itself guarantee anything except either the production of a narcissistic self-referentiality or the sacrifice of any sense of collective political possibilities. So whose body is it that is to be the measure of all things? Exactly how and what is it in a position to measure? And what politics might flow there from? Such questions cannot be answered without a prior understanding of exactly how bodies are socially produced. And on that matter Marx does have something illuminating and important to say.

The Bodily Subject as Variable Capital

Marx has a coherent theory of the bodily subject under capitalism. His account, though limited, is nevertheless powerful as a tool for understanding the social production and reproduction of bodies and of subjectivities within the dynamics of capital accumulation. His analysis also indicates how and why the two discursive regimes of the body and globalization might be reconciled.

The fundamental process that Marx looks at is that of the circulation of capital. This is understood as the use of *money* to buy a bundle of *commodities* (plant, equipment, raw materials, energy—all means of production—and labor power) in order to engage in the *production* of *commodities* for sale so as to acquire more *money* (*profit*, understood by Marx as *surplus value* and measured as the difference between what labor power creates and what the laborer gets as a money wage). This process is viewed in its continuity: as more money is invested, capital accumulates. Marx is interested in the relations and qualities of the different "moments" that exist within this overall process, the different forms it can take (as landed capital, commercial capital, finance capital, as well as industrial capital) and, above all, in its internal contradictions and crisis tendencies (see Harvey 1982). The process is fundamentally powered by the quest for exchange values. To the degree that money, the primary form of exchange value, is fungible and fluid across space and time, money assumes a globality and universality that commands and subsumes the other exchange processes necessary to support capital accumulation. In short, the monetary drive underlies the process of globalization and, hardly surprisingly, the revolution in international financial arrangements since the 1970s has been at the heart of what we now term "globalization."

But there are other circulation processes necessary to the proper functioning of the general circulation and accumulation of capital. I concentrate on just one—the circulation of what Marx calls "variable capital." In this circulation process the laborer as person takes his/her abilities to dispense labor power to market. He/she exchanges labor power's use value to the capitalist for a money wage which permits him/her to buy use values (commodities) in order to live and thus be able to return to the labor market again and again. The circulation of variable capital is about the reproduction of the laborer and therefore about the continuous reproduction of labor power as a commodity. Plainly, the reproduction of that labor power is a necessary condition for the continuous circulation and accumulation of capital.

By using the term "variable capital," Marx makes it seem as if capital circulates "through the body of the laborer" and thereby "turns the laborer into a mere appendage of the circulation of capital itself" (Harvey 1982: 157). It then becomes clear why Haraway (see Harvey and Haraway 1995: 510) considers it so "crystal clear" that "the body is an accumulation strategy in the deepest sense" and why Foucault (1995: 221) agrees that "the two processes—the accumulation of men and the accumulation of capital—cannot be separated." The circulation of variable capital describes the conditions under which laboring bodies and subjectivities get produced and reproduced within the circulation and accumulation of capital. Note, however, that variable capital circulates with *use value* (the concrete capacities of the laboring person and the food, shelter, etc. that sustains that person) rather than *exchange value* (money) as its beginning and end point. Variable capital is thereby constrained in ways that the circulation of exchange values (capital) is not. Variable capital circulation is always about the particular and the concrete, whereas money is the general representative of value (abstract labor) on the world stage. Laboring is always localized and contingent as opposed to universal and global. Consequently, the point of intersection between the circulation of variable capital and the circulation of (money) capital is the point at which the concrete, particular, and contingent aspects of the laboring body intersects with the abstract, universal, and rule-bound certitudes of capitalist laws of accumulation on the world stage. This is, in short, the point where body politics and globalization processes intersect.

The Laboring Body in Global Space

So how are we to understand the laboring body under conditions of contemporary globalization? I sketch in a few obvious points.

Consider, first, the sheer size of the global proletariat. The World Bank (1995) estimates that the global labor force doubled in size between 1966 and 1995. By the latter date, an estimated 2.5 billion men and women were active participants in labor markets and thereby captive to the conditions of wage labor. Most of this wage labor force was living under the most appalling conditions:

> The more than a billion individuals living on a dollar or less a day depend....on pitifully low returns to hard work. In many countries workers lack representation and work in unhealthy, dangerous, or demeaning conditions. Meanwhile 120 million or so are unemployed worldwide, and millions more have given up hope of finding work. (World Bank 1995: 1-2)

This condition exists at a time of rapid growth in average levels of productivity per worker (reported also to have doubled since 1965 worldwide) and in world trade, fueled in part by reductions in costs of movement and in part by a wave of trade liberalization and sharp increases in the international flow of direct investments. The latter helped construct transnationally integrated production systems largely organized through intra-firm trade. As a result, says a report of the International Labor Office:

> the number of workers employed in export- and import-competing industries has grown significantly. In this sense, therefore, it could be said that labour markets across the world are becoming more interlinked....Some observers see in these developments the emergence of a global labour market wherein "the world has become a huge bazaar with nations peddling their workforces in competition against one another, offering the lowest prices for doing business"....The core apprehension is that intensifying global competition will generate pressures to lower wages and labour standards across the world. (ILO 1996: 12)

This process of ever-stronger interlinkage has been intensified by "the increasing participation in the world economy of populous developing countries such as China, India and Indonesia." With respect to China, for example, the United Nations Development Program reports,

> The share of labour-intensive manufactures in total exports rose from 36% in 1975 to 74% in 1990....Between 1985 and 1993 employment in textiles increased by 20%, in clothing and fibre products by 43%, in plastic products by 51%. China is now a major exporter of labour-intensive products to many industrial countries....For all its dynamic job creation, China still faces a formidable employment

challenge. Economic reforms have released a "floating population" of around 80 million most of whom are seeking work. The State Planning Commission estimates that some 20 million workers will be shed from state enterprises over the next five years and that 120 million more will leave rural areas hoping for work in the cities. Labour intensive economic growth will need to continue at a rapid pace if all these people are to find work. (UNDP 1996: 94)

I quote this instance to illustrate the massive movements into the global labor force that have been and are underway. And China is not alone in this. The export-oriented garment industry of Bangladesh hardly existed twenty years ago, but it now employs more than a million workers (80 per cent of them women and half of them crowded into Dhaka). Cities like Jakarta, Bangkok, and Bombay, as Seabrook (1996) reports, have become meccas for the formation of a transnational working class—heavily dependent upon women—living in conditions of poverty, violence, chronic environmental degradation, and fierce repression.

It is hardly surprising that the insertion of this proletarianized mass into global trading networks has been associated with wide-ranging social convulsions and upheavals (see Moody 1997) as well as changing structural conditions, such as the spiraling inequalities between regions (that left sub-Saharan Africa far behind as East and Southeast Asia surged ahead) and between classes.On this last point, the most recent report of the U.N. Development Program notes:

> Nearly 30 years ago the Pearson Commission began its report with the recognition that "the widening gap between the developed and the developing countries has become the central problem of our times." But over the past three decades the income gap between the world's richest fifth and its poorest fifth more than doubled, to 74 to 1. And with that gap comes migration, environmental pressure, conflict, instability and other problems rooted in poverty and inequality. (UNDP 1999: 10)

The U.N. had earlier estimated that "between 1960 and 1991 the share of the richest 20% rose from 70% of global income to 85%—while that of the poorest declined from 2.3% to 1.4%." By 1991, "more than 85% of the world's population received only 15% of its income" and "the net worth of the 358 richest people, the dollar billionaires, is equal to the combined income of the poorest 45% of the world population—2.3 billion people" (UNDP 1996). In 1995 in the United States, the net wealth of Bill Gates alone was greater than the combined net worth of the poorest 40 percent of Americans (106 million people). These trends toward spiraling inequalities show no sign of abating:

The world's 200 richest people more than doubled their net worth in the four years to 1998, to more than $1 trillion. The assets of the top three billionaires are more than the combined GNP of all least developed countries and their 600 million people. (UNDP 1999: 3)

This polarization is simply astounding, rendering hollow the World Bank's extraordinary claim that international integration coupled with free market liberalism and low levels of government interference is the best way to deliver growth and rising living standards for workers. It also renders hollow a wide-ranging set of ideological claims that the free market will create a "stakeholder" society within a rapidly democ-ratizing capitalism. Within the era of the "so-called people's market" in the United States, for example, "Federal Reserve statistics show that 60 percent of Americans own no stock at all" (not even through pension funds). Furthermore, "the wealthiest 1 percent of Americans own nearly 50 percent of all stock; the bottom 80 percent own only 3 percent" (Smith 1998). It is then not hard to see who has benefited most from the run-up in the stock market over the last decade.

Marx, of course, had shown conclusively in *Capital* that the effect of unrestricted freedoms of the market (of the sort pursued relentlessly under neoliberalism these last thirty years) would be increasing "accu-mulation of wealth at one pole" and further "accumulation of misery, the ferment of labour, slavery, ignorance, brutalization and moral degra-dation at the opposite pole, i.e. on the side of the class that produces its own product as capital." Polanyi (1957) later followed Marx in a thor-ough critique of a free market utopianism that could only result in the destruction of the natural world and the social order, a critical tradition that John Gray (1998) has recently resurrected albeit from a conservative perspective.

It is against this background that it becomes easier to assess the power of the tales assembled by Seabrook:

Indonesia, in the name of the free market system, promotes the grossest violations of human rights, and undermines the right to subsist of those on whose labour its competitive advantage rests. The small and medium-sized units which subcontract to the multinationals are the precise localities where the sound of the hammering, tapping, beating of metal comes from the forges where the chains are made for industrial bondage.... (1996: 101)

Many transnationals are subcontracting here: Levi Strauss, Nike, Reebok. A lot of the subcontractors are Korean-owned. They all tend to low wages and brutal man-

> agement. Nike and Levis issue a code of conduct as to criteria for investment; but in reality, under the tender system they always go for the lowest cost of production....Some subcontractors move out of Jakarta to smaller towns, where workers are even less capable of combining to improve their conditions. (1996: 105)

Or, at a more personal level there is the account given by two sisters, Hira and Mira, who until recently worked for a Singaporean-owned subcontractor for Levi Strauss:

> We are regularly insulted, as a matter of course. When the boss gets angry he calls the women dogs, pigs, sluts, all of which we have to endure patiently without reacting....We work officially from seven in the morning until three (salary less than $2 per day), but there is often compulsory overtime, sometimes—especially if there is an urgent order to be delivered—until nine. However tired we are, we are not allowed to go home. We may get an extra 200 rupiah (10 US cents)....We go on foot to the factory from where we live. Inside it is very hot. The building has a metal roof, and there is not much space for all the workers. It is very cramped. There are over 200 people working there, mostly women, but there is only one toilet for the whole factory....when we come home from work, we have no energy left to do anything but eat and sleep. (Seabrook 1996: 90-1)

Home is a single room, two meters by three, costing $16 a month; it costs nearly ten cents to get two cans of water and at least $1.50 a day to eat.

In *Capital* Marx recounts the story of the milliner, Mary Anne Walkely, twenty years of age, who often worked thirty hours without a break (though revived by occasional supplies of sherry, port, and coffee) until, after a particularly hard spell necessitated by preparing "magnificent dresses for the noble ladies invited to the ball in honour of the newly imported Princess of Wales," died, according to the doctor's testimony, "from long hours of work in an over-crowded work-room, and a too small and badly ventilated bedroom" (Marx 1976: 364). Compare that with a contemporary account of conditions of labor in Nike plants in Vietnam:

> [Mr. Nguyen] found that the treatment of workers by the factory managers in Vietnam (usually Korean or Taiwanese nationals) is a "constant source of humiliation," that verbal abuse and sexual harassment occur frequently, and that "corporal punishment" is often used. He found that extreme amounts of forced overtime are imposed on Vietnamese workers. "It is a common occurrence," Mr. Nguyen wrote in his report, "to have several workers faint from exhaustion, heat and poor nutrition during their shifts." We were told that several workers even coughed up blood before fainting. Rather than crack down on the abusive conditions in the factories, Nike has resorted to an elaborate international public relations campaign

to give the appearance that it cares about its workers. But no amount of public relations will change the fact that a full-time worker who makes $1.60 a day is likely to spend a fair amount of time hungry if three very simple meals cost $2.10. (Herbert 1997: A29)

The material conditions that sparked the moral outrage expressed in Marx's *Capital* have not gone away. They are embodied in everything from Nike shoes, Disney products, and GAP clothing to Liz Claiborne products. As in the nineteenth century, part of the response has been reformist middle-class outrage backed by the power of working-class movements to regulate conditions of labor worldwide (Moody 1997). Campaigns against "sweatshop labor" worldwide and for a code of "fair labor practices," perhaps certified by a "fair labor label" on the products we buy, as well as the specific campaigns against Nike and other major corporations are a case in point (Ross 1997; Goodman 1996; Greenhouse 1997a; 1997b).

Can Workers of the World Unite?

The obvious conclusion which Marx and Engels drew from this sort of thing was that workers of the world should unite in political struggle. But if the material setting for the *Manifesto* or for *Capital* has not radically changed, our political willingness to embrace such a simple political slogan as a response certainly has. The work of postmodernism is to deny the possibility of such a politics. Under postmodern rules of engagement, all universals are suspect if not proscribed and what could be more universalistic than to make the claim that workers everywhere have common interests that can be brought together into a common political project? To even suggest that labor struggles are a fundamental form of body politics offends postmodern (particularly Foucauldian) sensibilities.

To be sure, postmodern objections are not without substance. Even if the global proletariat is far larger and even if the superficial imperative for workers of the world to unite is greater than ever, the barriers to that unity are formidable. The workforce is geographically dispersed, culturally heterogeneous, ethnically and religiously diverse, stratified by gender, race and habits, linguistically fragmented, and differentiated by beliefs and understandings. Modes of resistance to capitalism and aspirations for alternatives are radically differentiated. The political and economic gap between, for example, the most affluent workers in Germany and the United States and the poorest wage workers in Indonesia and Mali is huge. A certain segment of the working class (mostly but not exclusively in the advanced capitalist countries and often possessing by far the most powerful political voice) has a great deal to lose besides its chains. Consider another point: while women have always been an important component of the workforce, their participation has now become much more general and this poses acute questions of gender (and alternative dimensions to body politics and cultural habits) in working class politics. A strongly feminized proletarian movement (not an impossibility in our times) might turn out to be a very different agent of political transformation than a movement led almost exclusively by men. Organizing labor in the face of all these differences poses particular problems and makes it reasonable to question whether workers of the world will ever be in a position to unite in struggle.

The Universality of Rights

It would be an egregious error to conflate the "global" of globalization with more general claims to universality (of truths, moral precepts, ethics, or of rights). Yet it would also be wrong to miss the rather powerful connection between them. The recent phase of globalization has posed a whole series of open questions concerning universality. It has forced us to consider, in political rhetoric and to some degree in terms of political-economic fact, the rules and customs through which we might relate to each other in a world of mutual interdependency. This commonality is willy-nilly imposed upon the whole world of difference and otherness that is the normal grist for political theorizing in postmodern circles. In fact, the whole postmodern movement might well be construed as a movement that celebrates or mourns that which is on the brink of disappearing. "Otherness" and "difference" (and even the idea of "culture" itself as a regulatory ideal, as Readings 1996 so trenchantly points out) become important to us precisely because they are of less and less practical relevance within the contemporary political economy of globalization.

The globalization of capital accumulation and market exchange implies widespread (though often informal, grudging, corrupted, and even superficial) acceptance of certain bourgeois notions of law, rights, freedoms, and even moral claims about goodness and virtue. This is the albeit often weak but nevertheless omnipresent political corollary of maintaining an open field for capital investment, accumulation, and labor and resource exploitation across the surface of the earth. But if the rights of capital are operative as universals, then why not the global and universal rights of labor?

Consider, in this regard, Articles 22 to 25 of the 1948 U.N. Declaration on Human Rights:

Article 22:

Everyone, as a member of society, has the right to social security and is entitled to realization, through national effort and international cooperation and in accordance with the organization and resources of each State, of the economic, social and cultural rights indispensable for his dignity and the free development of his personality.

Article 23:

1. Everyone has the right to work, to free choice of employment, to just and favourable conditions of work and to protection against unemployment.

2. Everyone, without any discrimination, has the right to equal pay for equal work.

3. Everyone who works has the right to just and favourable remuneration ensuring himself and his family an existence worthy of human dignity, and supplemented, if necessary, by other means of social protection.

4. Everyone has the right to form and to join trade unions for the protection of his interests.

Article 24:

Everyone has the right to rest and leisure, including reasonable limitation of working hours and periodic holidays with pay.

Article 25:

1. Everyone has the right to a standard of living adequate for the health and well-being of himself and of his family, including food, clothing, housing and medical care and necessary social services, and the right to security in the event of unemployment, sickness, disability, widowhood, old age or other lack of livelihood in circumstances beyond his control.

2. Motherhood and childhood are entitled to special care and assistance. All children, whether born in or out of wedlock, shall enjoy the same social protection.

What is striking about these articles (particularly when stripped of their strong gender bias and their fixation on a bourgeois notion of the family—itself an easy indicator as to how fraught all universal declarations are) is the degree to which hardly any attention has been paid over the last fifty years to their implementation or application and how almost all countries that were signatories to the Universal Declaration are in gross violation of them. Strict enforcement of such rights would entail massive and in some senses quite revolutionary transformations in the political economy of capitalism.

The contradictions and paradoxes of globalization offer, it seems, opportunities for an alternative progressive politics in which universal rights of this sort might take on specific meaning. These are rights, furthermore, that attach to individual bodies. Globalization opens up a terrain of both conceptual and theoretical debate, as well as a terrain of political struggles (shadowy forms of which can already be discerned).

Consider, for example, the general idea that laborers everywhere should be treated with dignity, that they should be accorded a "living wage" that guarantees them the minimum of economic security and adequate access to life chances. That universal conception, thoroughly consistent with the Universal Declaration of 1948, plainly runs up against the conditions of uneven geographical development that capital has both fed upon and, in many instances, actively produced. Such rights challenge neoliberalism because they interfere with the functioning of labor markets. Yet we also know that a "living wage" means something different depending upon historical-geographical conditions. A living wage in Dhaka or Bombay is not the same as that which might be required in Johannesburg, Duluth, Lulea, or New York City. Does this imply that the struggle for a global right to a living wage is impossible or unreasonable?

On July 17-19, 1998, some forty representatives from worker rights organizations in the United States, the Caribbean, Central America, Mexico, Canada, and Europe met to consider exactly that question (see Benjamin 1998). They concluded that a campaign for setting a living wage as a global standard (initially in the shoe and apparel industries) was both feasible and worthwhile even though any formula to calculate that wage, no matter how carefully crafted to take account of cultural, social, and economic differences between countries and regions, would doubtless be the focus of intense controversy. It would, moreover, be unlikely to enjoy universal acceptance. But, they concluded, "the more controversy over this formula and the more alternative formulas proposed the better." Simply drawing the industry and the public into a debate over which formula to adopt forces the issue of a living wage, defined as "a wage with dignity," to the forefront of the political agenda in exactly the same way that the adoption of the Universal Declaration of Human Rights in 1948 placed certain issues about universal human rights (however controversial or fuzzy) irrevocably upon the global agenda.

The Rights of Labor and of Species Being

Marx, of course, was not very impressed with talk about rights. He often saw it as an attempt to impose one distinctive set of rights—those defined by the bourgeoisie—as a universal standard to which everyone should aspire. But if workers of the world are to unite then surely it has to be around some conception of their rights. And on questions of rights the bourgeoisie has created such a maelstrom of contradictions on the world stage that it has opened several paths toward a progressive and universalizing politics at the global scale. To turn our backs on such universals at this stage in our history, however fraught or even tainted, is to turn our backs on all manner of prospects for progressive political action. Perhaps the central contradiction of globalization at this point in our history is the way in which it brings to the fore its own nemesis in terms of a fundamental reconception of the universal right for everyone to be treated with dignity and respect as a fully endowed member of our species. In short, globalization poses the question of our "species being" on planet earth all over again. The connection between globalization and body politics yields clear political messages. Whether or not we will have the courage to listen to and act upon them is another matter.

References

Arrighi, G. 1994. *The Long Twentieth Century*. London: Verso.
Bourdieu, P. 1984. *Distinction: A Social Critique of the Judgement of Taste*. London: Routledge.
Brooks, R. 1992. "Maggie's Man: We Were Wrong." *Observer* (June 21).
Butler, J. 1993. *Bodies that Matter: On the Discursive Limits of "Sex."* New York: Routledge.
Chesnais, F. 1996. *La Mondialisation Financiere: Genese, Cout et Enjeux*. Paris: Syros.
Diprose, R. 1994. *The Bodies of Women: Ethics, Embodiment and Sexual Difference*. London: Routledge.
Eagleton, T. 1997. "Spaced Out." *London Review of Books* (April 24): 22-23.
Elias, N. 1978. *The Civilizing Process: The History of Manners*. Oxford: Blackwell.
Foucault, M. 1984. *The Foucault Reader*. Harmondsworth: Penguin Books.
———. 1995. *Discipline and Punish: The Birth of the Prison*. New York: Vintage Books.
Goodman, E. 1996. "Why Not a Labor Label?" *Baltimore Sun* (July 19): 25A.

Gramsci, A. 1971. *Selections from the Prison Notebooks*. London: Lawrence and Wishart.

Gray, J. 1998. *False Dawn: The Illusions of Global Capitalism*. London: Grantat Books.

Greenhouse, S. 1997a. "Voluntary Rules on Apparel Labor Proving Elusive." *New York Times* (February 1): 1.

———. 1997b. "Accord to Combat Sweatshop Labor Faces Obstacles." *New York Times* (April 13): 1.

Grosz, E. 1994. "Bodies-cities." Pp. 241-253 in *Sexuality and Space*, edited by B. Colomina. Princeton, NJ: Princeton University School of Architecture.

Haraway, D. 1991. *Simians, Cyborgs, and Women: The Reinvention of Nature*. London: Routledge.

Harvey, D. 1982. *The Limits to Capital*. Oxford: Blackwell.

———. 1996a. *Justice, Nature and the Geography of Difference*. Oxford: Blackwell.

———. 1996b. "Globalization in Question." *Rethinking Marxism* 8: 1-17.

———. 1998. "The Body as an Accumulation Strategy." *Society and Space* 16: 401-421.

———. Forthcoming. *Spaces of Hope*. Edinburgh: Edinburgh University Press.

Harvey, D., and D. Haraway. 1995. "Nature, Politics and Possibilities: A Debate and Discussion with David Harvey and Donna Haraway." *Society and Space* 13: 507-528.

Herbert, B. 1997. "Brutality in Vietnam." *New York Times* (March 28): A29.

Hirst, P., and G. Thompson. 1996. *Globalization in Question: The International Economy and the Possibilities of Governance*. Oxford: Blackwell.

International Labour Office. 1996. *World Employment 1996/97: National Policies in a Global Context*. Geneva: International Labour Office.

Lowe, D. 1995. *The Body in Late-Capitalist USA*. Durham, NC: Duke University Press.

Martin, E. 1994. *Flexible Bodies*. Boston: Beacon Press.

Marx, K. 1976. *Capital*. Vol.1. New York: Vintage Books.

Marx, K., and F. Engels. 1952 (1848). *Manifesto of the Communist Party*. Moscow: Progress Publishers.

Merrifield, A. Forthcoming. "The Urbanization of Labor: Living Wage Activism in the American City." *Social Text*.

Moody, K. 1997. *Workers in a Lean World*. London: Verso.

Polanyi, K. 1957. *The Great Transformation*. New York: Beacon Press.

Readings, B. 1998. *The University in Ruins*. Cambridge, MA: Harvard University Press.

Ross, A., ed. 1997. *No Sweat*. London: Verso.

Seabrook, J. 1996. *In the Cities of the South: Scenes from a Developing World*. London: Verso.

Smith, H. 1998. "How the Middle Class Can Share in the Wealth." *New York Times* (April 19): B18.

Stafford, B. 1991. *Body Criticism: Imaging the Unseen in Enlightenment Art and Medicine*. Cambridge, MA: The MIT Press.

United Nations Development Program. 1996. *Human Development Report, 1996*. New York: Oxford University Press.

———. 1999. *Human Development Report, 1999*. New York: Oxford University Press.

Wallerstein, I. 1974. *The Modern World System*. New York: Academic Press.

World Bank. 1995. *World Development Report: Workers in an Integrating World*. New York: Oxford University Press.

3

Public Life, Information Technology, and the Global City: New Possibilities for Citizenship and Identity Formation

Mike Featherstone

It is often argued that globalization processes are profoundly changing the nature of social and cultural life by threatening the boundaries of the nation-state. Yet, if we are entering what some seek to designate as the "global age" (Albrow 1996), we need to undertake theoretical and substantive investigations of the practices and spaces in which the new forms of social life and identity formation are enacted. This chapter examines the possibilities for the generation of new public spaces and forms of citizenship within global cities. It does so by inquiring into the potential for new forms of public association and identity formation in the public sphere: both the actual public life of global cities as well as the virtual public life which is beginning to develop through electronic networks.

There has been a good deal of interest in identity in recent years, yet relatively little analysis of the relationship between identity formation and citizenship. The term "identity" is used in a bewildering range of ways in the contemporary social sciences and humanities. It can be applied to a person, a place, a nation, and even the world. It can be applied to inanimate objects, as is the case with the bar-code which gives a consumer object or credit card an identity mark. In some usages "identity" is the inheritor of the terms "personality" and "selfhood"; in others it is seen as a quality of a culture, a nation, and even a society (Habermas having asked the question, "Can modern societies have an identity?"). A central aspect of identity, according to the *Oxford English Dictionary* (second edition), is defined as "the sameness of a person or thing at all times or in all circumstances; the condition or fact that a person or thing is itself and not something else; individuality, personality." It is this consistency of sameness which has been challenged under the banner of postmodernism. Instead of unity and sameness we have references to "multiple identities" and "fragmented identities." Those associated with postmodernism have mounted a strong critique of the notion of a unified identity through their emphasis on otherness, difference, and cultural complexity (Featherstone 1991, 1995). From this perspective, identities are always unstable and processual, subject to slippage, blurring, and entanglement with others (Hall 1996). This postmodern, anti-essentialist critique of identity thinking is something which emphasizes that instability and lack of fixity should not necessarily be seen as pathological and signs of an identity crisis. This contrasts with some of the theories of identity in the past, as, for example, in the 1950s, when the maintenance of a stable centered self was seen by psychologists as important for mental health. In the wake of the new social movements and identity politics which have developed since the 1960s, today we find advocates of the positive effects of developing multiple identities and composing a discontinuous life course (see Turkle 1995; Shotter 1993; Featherstone and Hepworth 1998: 170-72).

There are, of course, still those who emphasize the need to see identity formation as a life project, such as Anthony Giddens (1991). Here the emphasis is upon reflexive self-formation through the active construction of lifestyles, to cope with the identity problems and ontological insecurity which are seen as having accompanied the erosion of tradition through the unprecedented rapid pace of social change. In contrast to the need to cope with ontological insecurity and the unfolding of identity over time, there are others who view the process of identity construction through the metaphor of movement in space. Rather than a modernist concern with unfolding temporality, the quest for unity, and accurate representation, there is a postmodern emphasis upon space, fluidity, and discontinuity. Rosi Braidotti, for example, explores the metaphor of the nomad as a transgressive identity:

> As a figuration of contemporary subjectivity, therefore, the nomad is a postmeta-physical intensive, multiple entity, functioning in a net of interconnections. S/he

cannot be reduced to a linear, teleological form of subjectivity but is rather the site of multiple connections. (1994: 36)

She goes on to advocate the importance of suspending the belief in fixed identities in favor of identity seen as a game of masks, something which is partial and fragmentary (Braidotti 1994: 224-5; see also the critique of Braidotti by Pels 1999 and Braidotti's 1999 response).[1] Towards the end of her book, Braidotti (1994: 257) remarks that the crucial question confronting feminists who acknowledge the importance of multiple locations, mobility, and cultural diversity, is how to combine this recognition of differences with alliances across class, age, and ethnicity. Recognizing that this directs the analysis towards questions of citizenship, she asks how far can women hope to escape the limitations of national citizenship to become citizens of the world.

Generally, discussions of identity have not taken place on the same ground as those of citizenship. This is because the concern with identity has sought to work with constructing and deconstructing structures of selfhood, which entails the filling out of a particular content. From this perspective the notion of citizenship seems empty and formal. It is something which, in its commitment to the principle of universality, seems to be identityless (Donald 1996: 175). Citizenship is seen as occupying a much higher level of abstraction, as something fabricated and guaranteed by the state. Yet there is a potential connection between identity and citizenship when we consider the relationship in terms of national identity. The sense of belonging to a common culture, in which the nation becomes actualized as an "imagined community," as Benedict Anderson (1991) argues, can be seen as a product of print capitalism, something which only becomes clearly formulated within modernity. The sense of belonging points to a strong level of identification and solidarity in which the nation takes on the mantle of religion. Patriotism and national community have a cultural exclusivism; they mark the boundaries of a particular culture with its own conception of the sacred, something from which others are necessarily barred. This process tends to blur civic and ethnic identity to the extent that it becomes very difficult to conceptualize national identity as separate from that of the state. Hence the politics of citizenship are conceived as inseparable from the politics of identity, something ordered and guaranteed by the nation-state (Donald 1996: 173).

This provokes a number of questions. If this is the only tradition of citizenship, are there not notions of citizen rights which can be separated from ethnicity and the national community? Is it possible to consider notions of citizenship and rights which extend beyond the boundaries of the nation-state: to think of global citizenship and transnational human rights (Santos 1999)? Can we think of flexible notions of citizenship which could parallel the more flexible notions of identity formation, the "doubles" or multiple identifications which are generated in a world in which globalization and information technology encourage greater mobility and migration? In what kinds of spaces are these new forms of identity and citizenship being developed? How do these new public spaces relate to the concept of the public sphere developed by Habermas (1989) and others? To what extent, in the wake of global migration and electronic communication technologies, should we now speak of trans-national public spheres (Appadurai 1996)?

The Western notion of citizenship is derived from the Ancient Greek city-state, along with the independent city that emerged in the late Middle Ages (see Weber 1958). The notion of the active assembly of citizens, or their chosen representatives, coming together in public spaces to debate the common good, has become central to our conception of the democratic process. This conception all too easily made the transition from city to nation, and images of the revolutionary fighter for civil rights and citizenship—the right to representation, fair trial and due process—became interwoven with images of the nation. The citizen became the national citizen with the republic transformed into the nation, where members not only had rights and liberties, but duties, including the duty to fight, to sacrifice and die for one's country (Habermas 1994: 23). Images of citizen and nation became woven into various mythologies and traditions and were made sacred through regular ritual practices and enactments. In these practices and enactments, the excitement, emotional bonding, and solidarity of the heroic times of citizens' actions to create or save the nation could be regenerated (see Hunt 1988 on the sacred and the French revolutionary tradition).

At the same time, there were always those who saw the potential of citizenship as transcending the nation-state. Dahrendorf argues that "citizenship is never complete until it is world citizenship. Exclusion is the enemy of citizenship" (1994: 17). This tradition gained much of its impetus from Kant with his vision of world civil society and cosmopolitanism. Habermas actively draws upon this tradition with the Kantian notion of *mundigkeit*, or coming of age, a term which has the connotation of a maturation of the capacity to think for oneself and respect the rights of others. For Habermas (1971), only in a world in which the last human being is free and responsible can we, too, be free. Therefore, we have a self-interest in the freedom of the other. For only if our interactant and associate provides the mirror for our own aspirations can we ultimately recognize and realize them.

Citizenship, then, suggests the notion of full participation in public life, a wider sphere than political life (van Steenbergen 1994: 2). According to T. H. Marshall (1977), whose ideas have been very influential, the ideal of citizenship suggests full participation in the community, which extends beyond the notion of civil and political rights. It suggests social and economic rights, the right to welfare, health, education, and employment. Yet the dismantling of welfare states in the wake of the return to neoliberal policies in the 1980s, which was buttressed by the deregulation of financial markets and the integration of the global economy, would now seem to make this broader conception of citizenship a remote possibility. We see a new focus on the excluded amidst calls to extend and rethink the notion of citizenship to take into account the globalization process. We hear calls for global citizenship (Falk 1994), cultural citizenship (Turner 1994), technological citizenship (Beck 1996), sexual citizenship (Weeks 1998), and "deep citizenship" (Clarke 1996). Yet what are the means of association which can bind together the people designated by these categories? What is the basis of these peoples' common ground and interests? What public spaces will they inhabit and how will they interact and exchange information? What authorities and agencies can they appeal to for redress and implementation of their rights?

More specifically, how will the process of globalization effect our sense of public space, a space in which these notions can be anchored? What types of public spaces will develop in global cities? Can the traditional forms be revised, or will new forms emerge which can sustain a more differentiated range of citizenship positions, with cultural citizenship and technological citizenship being added to the more often cited political, civic, social, and economic forms? Will these new forms require new spaces, such as the virtual public spaces of the Internet, which are based upon the new information technology? Or will there be a progressive privatization of public space, with the replacement of the active citizen by the passive consumer? Will the new forms of citizenship be merely attenuated forms, not won in struggles, but granted by consumer culture industries and corporations? Here one thinks of being a passport holder of Walt Disney World, or a McCitizen (Probyn 1998; Barber 1996). Will we see an increasing impoverishment of public life, with a retreat from public participation into the intimacy of the private sphere as Habermas (1989) and Sennett (1976) have argued in their different ways?

The Global City and Information Technology

According to Virilio (1993: 72), we now live in the world city. Today we live in synchronized world time made possible by the development of information technology. The distinction between the city and the countryside has been obliterated—we can participate or work in the world city from any planetary location. While there are implications in this notion which I will take up in the next section, it is worth noting that the logical extension of the world city is to end the significance of the real, or geographically located, city. Virilio writes with a typically French provocative style, yet he articulates something which has been strong in the public imagination ever since Toffler (1980) in *The Third Wave* conjured up the vision of the electronic cottage as our future. Toffler argued that the information revolution would bring a return to the putting-out system common in the eighteenth century, except that the materials to be worked on in the home are not now dropped off at the cottage doorstep, but rather come in the form of electronic data transfers down the telephone lines. Computerization means that information industries, and increasingly other forms of business organizations, can be located anywhere. Hence, they will flee expensive city rentals for low-cost areas on the periphery or in the countryside. The city is dying; the end of the city is in sight (Sassen 1994: 1, 124).

Yet the abandonment of the city for the electronic virtual world city has not happened, nor does it seem likely to happen in the near future. If the predictions of the United Nations are to be believed, we will see a massive expansion in cities over the next fifteen years. Tokyo will increase from 25 to 29 million, São Paulo will increase from 19 to 25 million, Bombay will increase from 13 to 26 million. In addition to the growing list of megacities, we can add Guangzhou, itself a city of 6.5 million people, which will merge with Hong Kong and other cities around the Pearl River Delta to make a further megacity of 40-50 million people (Castells 1996: 403-5). These megacities articulate the global economy, acting as key nodes in the information networks which play a crucial role in the world economy (Castells 1996: 404). They are premised upon the massive expansion in direct foreign investment in the 1980s, which accelerated with the deregulation of financial markets after the "big bang" of 1986 (Dezalay 1990). International financial flows have grown more rapidly and today the monetary value of these flows is larger than the value of international trade or direct foreign investment (Sassen 1994: 9).

Deregulation and capital flows have been accompanied by a rise in the number and financial power of transnational corporations. Global cities have grown in power and influence as key nodes, the command points, for the coordination and integration of an increasingly complex and differentiated global economy. Information technology, with its advanced telecommunications and networked computers, makes possible both geographical dispersal—hence neutralizing distance—and integration, as the information necessarily flows towards and through specific centers. With the post-Fordist type of "just-in-time" production systems, industrial plants can be spatially dislocated and shifted to the optimum and currently most profitable global locations—a move made possible by the increasing capacity of corporate management headquarters to coordinate and integrate the process in a flexible way through information technology. Yet global cities are not just centers of corporate management; the management itself depends upon the close availability of financial and other specialized services, which in turn participate in their own global networks, as well as networks across sectors.

In addition to specialized corporate and financial services, global cities also generally contain culture industries and services (design, fashion, information, publishing, television, film, recording, leisure, tourism, and consumption). Culture has assumed an increased economic importance, not only with the expansion of consumer culture, but also with the demand, given the need to deal with an expanded and diversified "glocal" market (global-local, where goods are tailored to local needs, see Robertson 1995), for practical information drawing from diverse cultures around the world. An increasingly competitive global market, where there is a strong impetus to innovate and devise new customized products, drives a new concern to manipulate cultural differences.

The image we have of international financial flows is often one of virtual flows of data, disembedded from time and place, with constantly shifting sets of figures on computer screens. Yet the screens have to be located somewhere, and the data is only useful if it is interpreted. The sheer volume of data increases the problem of judgment, of what to attend to and what to ignore, of how to present coherent synopsis which formulate trends. It can be argued therefore that with the increase in the volume of data, much of it about unknown third parties with whom one must deal, trust becomes a problem. Abstract data systems themselves do not provide the answers, rather we rely on interpretive schemata and conventions performed by trusted others. To minimize risk we need not only to look up credit ratings, but also to consult trusted specialists, or meet people face-to-face. As trust depends upon our judgment about a person, we prefer to talk to them face-to-face in order to "weigh their words," listen to their tone of voice, and observe their body language, in order to decode their habitus and place them within our hierarchy of contacts (something which Goffman 1971 captured in his concept of "face-work").

In short, intensified flows of information create, not just solve problems. Information flows introduce new levels of complexity and uncertainty which need to be managed. The growth of specialized financial media—books, magazines, newspapers, television, and radio—cater not just to the demand for data updates (trade figures, interest rate changes) but also to the perspective of experts who can contextualize the information and theorize likely trends (Thrift 1996: 222). As financial markets have increased in size, complexity, and volatility, so the need for interpretive accounts has grown. Various experts and market gurus put forward a range of theories, some based upon vast data-sets or charts of market trends, others on psychology, chaos theory, and even astrology. Rational modeling and reflexive criteria are by no means in the ascendancy (Thrift 1996: 224-5).

Hence, global cities are not just nodes in informational networks, but places where people meet and associate. Electronic communication does not reduce the need for face-to-face contact, it increases it. Consequently, cosmopolitan business and financial elites, along with professionals, specialists, and cultural intermediaries, need restaurants, bars, hotels, clubs, exhibitions, and galleries where they can meet and make contacts and work their networks, both at local and global levels. This leads to the gentrification of specific areas of cities and the expansion of cultural and entertainment industries.

What is the status of these new quasi-public spaces of meeting and mixing? In one sense they represent a continuity with the marketplace or forum which was not only a place to trade goods, but a place to trade information. These places had some of the characteristics of a fair, with its aesthetic sign play and mixing of exotica, strange goods, animals, and bodies cultivating excitement and sensory stimuli (Featherstone 1991: ch. 5). They are places of rumor and intelligence gathering, where there is also a daily informal stock exchange rating of the viability and reputation of the main individual and corporate players in the field, based upon the gossip of their associates. The same functions may well go on today in global cities across a range of sites. Yet unlike the forum in the ancient city, the market in the early modern period with its regulation through corporations and burghers, or indeed the court society at Versailles, the contemporary world of face-to-face contacts in global cities is much more fluid and open-ended.[2]

How do these new sites for association of the growing strata of businessmen, professionals, and intermediaries within global cities compare to the coffee houses and salons of eighteenth-century London and other European cities discussed by Habermas (1989) in his account of the rise of the bourgeois public sphere? Is there any possibility of a similar public sphere function in prospect? The short answer would be not too much, since, one assumes, questions of citizenship, rights, and serious intellectual discourse are very limited at the new sites. Yet is this the whole story? If there is to be a set of people who become concerned with issues of global citizenship, transnational human rights and the fate of the planet as a whole, it has been argued that it will be drawn from this strata that makes up sectors of the new middle class (Isin 1996). Those who work in transnational organizations or who are professionals and specialists in global cities are people who have become familiar with other cultures through their work (the Internet, media, travel) and are most likely to develop cosmopolitan affiliations. Their habitus is likely to be more flexible through their need to interact with people from a range of different cultures, and their identifications may well become more multiple and less rooted in their national culture of origin. From this group, especially the various sets of cultural intermediaries, we would expect to find those who are more likely to develop the dispositions of the respectful interpreter of cultural differences, rather than that of the confident legislator who assumes he/she knows what others really need (Bauman 1987, 1988). While this group has the potential to generate modes of public association and become carriers of global citizenship, it is hard to see them becoming the new class (Gouldner 1979; Isin 1996). Despite the enhanced role of culture and information in the global economy, they seem destined to become at best, in Bourdieu's phrase, "the dominated fraction of the dominant class." In terms of economic power and wealth creation, they have a long way to go to challenge the traditional financial and business community either in terms of individual wealth or influence, unless the current wave of global marketization is reversed and we see a move towards global political institution building, which would include increased democratization through an invigorated global public sphere.

At the same time, it is clear that global cities, despite drawing in members of the new middle classes, also draw in a range of other groups. Alongside the high-waged professional occupations there is a whole infrastructure of low-waged, nonprofessional jobs (Sassen 1994: 123). There is a strong gender dimension to this labor force, with women forming the bulk of the low-paid clerical workers, cleaners, restaurant, bar, and hotel workers. Many in this intrastructure are also migrant workers: people, not just capital, flow around the world as part of the globalization process, and inhabit city areas which are the low-cost equivalent of gentrification (Tagg 1996). The low-wage economy, with deregulation and the casualization of labor, also leads to the generation of new urban poor. Alongside the images of the gentrifying city and its yuppies, which were particularly strong in the late 1980s, we now have images of degentrification and deproletarianization, with the unemployed, homeless, immigrants, and minorities engaging in struggles to defend particular spaces (e.g., the struggle over Tomkins Square Park in New York's Lower East Side, see Smith 1996). Global cities are sites for a range of struggles in which the identities of various urban spaces and the image of the city as a whole are contested (Sassen 1996).

The unevenness within global cities is noticeable, not least with regard to access to the new information technology. While New York City contains the highest concentration of fiber-optic cable in the world, Harlem contains only one building which is cabled up (Sassen 1999: 60). The global elites and middle-class professional groups are netted up, and can exchange information and travel, whereas the lower class and poor are often separated and confined to particular places. This is the familiar "dual or divided city" with its polarized class structure (Fainstein et al. 1992), and typified as much by walls as by flows. For some (Davis 1990, 1992; Dear and Flusty 1999) Los Angeles is the future prototype for the global city. It is a city characterized by fortress enclaves, private policing of middle-and upper-class neighborhoods and apartment complexes, panopticon shopping malls, carceral inner city surveillance areas (typified in films such as *Blade Runner* and *Escape from LA*), along with downgraded or disappearing public spaces.

Yet is there one particular future for all global cities? It may well be the case that this image of the fortress city is but one representation of the global city, something which does an injustice to the levels of cultural complexity which we are now discovering beneath the quest for universal models.

It may well be that the prior cultural orthodoxy of older urban representations has been undermined by the new sense of multiplicity, complexity, and heterodoxy generated as cities discover they are multicultural (King 1996: 2). Or perhaps we should say that there are more voices speaking back and contesting the dominant images of the city which previously circulated in academic and public arenas with relatively little contestation. There are now more types of cultural productions which inscribe meaning and signs onto the urban fabric, and a greater reflexivity and rapidity of feedback of "the voices from the streets" into design, fashion, and advertising than ever before. It may well be the case that Jane Jacobs is right when she remarks "it is arguable whether this sudden interest in what might generally be defined as the cultural dimension of the city is responding to a material shift in cities, or it is simply the city being seen anew" (1993, quoted in King 1996: 3). One of the effects of the development of cultural modernism and consumer culture since the mid-nineteenth century has been the massive accumulation of texts and images of the city, which are now increasingly ransacked by cultural intermediaries working in culture industries and public sphere activists engaged in various struggles over the aestheticization of the urban landscape and the general cultural identity of the city.

We have therefore become more conscious that the city is a process, that places are processes which do not have a singular or essential identity; rather they are actively constructed through the interactions, experiences, narratives, images, and accounts of various groups (Massey 1993; Arantes 1996). This is given greater impetus through globalization, which is pulling cities into tighter competing reference groups and forcing them to reflect on their capacity to market themselves to attract investment (Featherstone 1995a). Constructing a successful city image becomes an important strategy for urban growth. Hence the heritage, tourist, and marketing industries seek to stimulate the arts, city tourism, culture industries, preservation, and gentrification processes as part of a general reinvention of place (Zukin 1996: 45). This reinvention is particularly evident in the alliances of local businesses, cultural organizations (such as libraries and museums), universities, and city governments, which are quickly put together to promote the city in competitions for international prestige events such as the Olympic Games.

In global cities, then, new spaces come into being, places become redesignated and there is a general aestheticization of the cityscape and investment in culture which create a more vibrant public life. Yet it is difficult to see where new spaces, which could favor the public sphere interactions sought by Habermas (1989), could develop. The redevelopment of financial and corporate districts themselves offers little prospect. The bars, restaurants, clubs, and hotels are quasi-public, quasi-private areas of interaction, areas for deals, news, and gossip; they are mixed areas for sociability and public life, which lack the overt public sphere function that coffee houses and salons fulfilled in the eighteenth century. The salons were spaces of formal discourse and argumentation, with strict rules and conventions in terms of body language, volume of speech, listening, turn-taking, and the absence of alcohol. The participants were allegedly committed to the public use of reason and had an Enlightenment faith in the powers of rational discourse—something which, in our current phase of informality, the mixing of styles, and syncretism, is hard to imagine could be resurrected. Habermas (1989) is clear that the eighteenth-century public sphere was a bourgeois one, yet it was also a gender-specific dialogue among middle-class property-owning men, and racially specific in its exclusion of blacks and other ethnicities.

The many critics of Habermas have pointed out that his assumption of a single, universal public sphere is flawed. They argue that it makes more sense to imagine a range of competing public spheres, or counter publics, based upon social movements (Calhoun 1992), the working class (Negt and Kluge 1997), women (Fraser 1996), and blacks (Baker 1994). Some of these spheres, such as the feminist public sphere, remain attached to the lifeworld and define themselves against the universalizing and homogenizing logic of the global megaculture (Hartley 1996: 71). In general the notion of the public sphere would seem to value linear reason over the wandering arguments of everyday life, consensus over sociability, communicative ethics over aesthetics, and the mind over the body. Indeed, with regard to the latter it has been suggested that

Habermas tends to reduce language to its cognitive dimension and thus to miss "the communication before communication," the energies, moments of warmth, and possibilities of violence which open bodies to communication and represent a substratum of life which can never be entirely eradicated (Noys 1997; Crossley 1997).

Mediated Bodies

"How could we apply the ideal speech situation to a visit to the cinema?" one skeptical critic asks; the short answer is: with difficulty (Stevenson 1995, quoted in McGuigan 1996: 178). Many people's experience of public space may well have been one in which aesthetics was mixed with ethics. Myriam Hanson (1991), for example, argues that the cinema should be regarded as one of the central public sphere institutions which developed in the twentieth century. The cinema provided visual collective representations once only confined to architecture. In many ways the cinema provided a virtual space within an actual public space, which could mobilize strangers into common experiences, emotional responses, and feelings of solidarity. It can be argued that it offers a form of the virtual mobile gaze (Featherstone 1998).

Yet one feels that for Habermas, the cinema and the mass media are still tainted with an overall propaganda function, and he remains to some extent under the influence of Adorno, who assumed that Hollywood and the culture industries were merely a form of mass deception (Horkheimer and Adorno 1971). In his view, popular aesthetics were to be viewed with suspicion, as offering commercially constructed simple pleasures, amusements, and diversions which stood in the way of the quest for communicative reason. Given this influence, it is not surprising that Habermas regards the twentieth century so negatively and speaks of the refeudalization of the public sphere. But his model of the public sphere may be too firmly based upon face-to-face communication. Although Habermas gave print a significant role, he sees newspapers as being read aloud and discussed in coffee houses, hence the positive potential of newspaper reading in private tends to be neglected. Habermas' conception of the public sphere is essentially a dialogical one, with individuals interacting in a shared locale as equal participants (Thompson 1993: 186). The new despatialized, nondialogical kinds of publicness, which we find in the contemporary media and in the new forms of electronic communication, are prejudged negatively. Indeed, in the volume from the conference which was held to celebrate the English translation of *The Structural Transformation of the Public Sphere* (Calhoun 1992), Habermas's lengthy reply to all his critics conspicuously neglects to address the question of the contemporary media.

But need the fact that the twentieth-century media—radio, television, and film—are monological, not dialogical, be so negative for the development of the public sphere and citizenship? John Thompson (1995: 82-4), in an attempt to theorize the role of media in modern life, has argued that it makes sense to distinguish between three forms of interaction: face-to-face interaction, mediated interaction, and mediated quasi-interaction. Face-to-face interaction takes place in a context of co-presence and is essentially dialogical, with a multiplicity of supplementary symbolic cues (body language, tone of voice, etc.). Mediated interaction, such as letter-writing or a telephone conversation, involves the use of a technical medium for transmission across time and space. Participants are not co-present, so there is a narrowing of the range of symbolic cues available and hence a need for a more open-ended quality to the interaction with more interpretive and contextual work required. Mediated quasi-interaction refers to the type of social relations provided by the media of mass communication (books, newspapers, radio, television, cinema, etc.). Like mediated interaction, there is a separation of the parties in time and space. Unlike face-to-face and mediated interaction, however, in which the orientation is towards specific others, mediated quasi-interaction produces symbolic forms made available for an indefinite range of possible recipients. The interaction is also based on a one-way flow of information, information which was constructed at a particular place and time (in unseen "back regions") separate from the receiver, with the inability of the receiver to respond to the sender.

One of the main dangers which Habermas was concerned about was the use of the media for propaganda and the aestheticization of politics with carefully staged performances by celebrity politicians which dupe the masses. Yet despite the dangers of the concentration of ownership and a narrowing of choice through the monopoly control of media conglomerates, the possibility of restricting the output of the electronic media to a few channels with carefully controlled program output may well be difficult to achieve. In addition, there is a good deal of literature which argues that the question of reception is more differentiated, active, and complex than has been previously assumed.

A further crucial point is that the face-to-face dialogical model of the public sphere may not itself be any more conducive for democracy and citizenship than a deliberative model of democracy.[3] It may well be that reading newspapers and books and watching television programs can provide individuals with knowledge they would otherwise never have access to, and enable them to reflect and deliberate, to form their opinions free from the rhetorical gestures, committed gazes, and all the embodied modes of persuasion we find in face-to-face interactions (Thompson 1995: 256). The distance and "coolness" of the television program may well facilitate careful deliberation and rational judgment. It may also be the case that, rather than assume that ethics needs to be anchored in face-to-face commitments, with the possibility of moral responsibility seen as generated through those human beings who we are in close contact with, the media extends our frame of reference by encouraging identifications and empathy with others in distant parts of the world (Thompson 1995: 262).

These distant others need not necessarily be human beings, for the capacity of the television camera to take us close into other worlds, be they of different cultures, animals, or even insects or plants, may well generate new forms of emotional bonding, solidarity, and respect. An extended sense of collective membership which refuses to stop at the boundary of my own locality or nation-state creates a sense of sympathy and fellow-feeling for a potentially wide range of phenomena. There may well be forms of object-centered sociality in which organisms and machines are experienced with feelings of solidarity and even described as "my friends" (Knorr Cetina 1997). This could generate not only a sense of respect for the object, but a sense of its integrity and identity, its right to exist; an ethical stance toward the object which gives it rights and membership. In effect, we share an interest in its "objectualization," something which could well lead to the formulation of citizen rights for things and a rejection of the big gulf between humans as subjects and nature and technology as objects, with the former capable of communicative interaction and the latter implicated in the generation of our instrumental rational way of approaching life in order to increase our control and domination. This dangerous merging of the human and the object increasingly interpenetrates the lifeworld and drives out the potential for genuine critical communication. Hence, we need to move beyond this type of strong dualism between humans and nature, and humans and technology. Posthumanism need not be a frightening prospect.

The process of the "objectualization" of living things and machines may well be akin to the processes of individualization which are central to many accounts of the development of human beings towards responsibility and maturity (Knorr Cetina 1997). While one may well want to reject parallels to stage developmental models of personality or moral responsibility (e.g., Habermas 1978, who follows Kohlberg), it is salutary to dwell on the basis of our sense of the other's fitness for autonomy and responsibility. One dimension of this may well be a sense of care, that the other is worth caring for and should be allowed to exist in its own terms.

A further dimension of the sense of sympathy is our awareness that bodies are vulnerable, they bruise, cut, bleed, and get sick. Richard Sennett (1996) has discussed the work of Elaine Scarry (1985) on the body in pain in the context of the generation of civic bodies. Scarry argues that we are only aware we have a body when things go wrong, such as when it is in pain. Yet we have all experienced the body in pain; human suffering binds us together. In the context of the city, the plan and the abstract grid brings forth the idea of the empty city, free of the litter and memories of the past. As Sennett remarks, "Pain could be erased by erasing place" (1996: 376). On the other hand, in the contemporary multicultural global city, the moral difficulty of generating a sense of sympathy for the other can be furthered by our sense of bodily pain. For Sennett, the body which acknowledges pain, which accepts pain, is ready to become a civic body, sensible to the pain of others on the street. This connection of pain and the body suggests two further points.

Firstly, citizenship and public sphere participation are not helped by conceptualizing them only in terms of communicative discourse, in which the participants focus solely on the words and try to eliminate the bodies of the speakers and audience as if they are so much "static" or "interference" we seek to "tune out" in order to hear better. Maybe we can hear better when we look at bodies. Maybe citizenship and our sense of membership and identification with others will be furthered by our respect for the vulnerability of their bodies.

Secondly, human beings are not the only ones who feel pain and suffer. Animals, insects, plants, and nature at large can be assumed in various ways to experience pain and consequently should be allowed to have rights. Television documentaries about the natural world are very popular and, given the success of environmental movements such as Greenpeace, Friends of the Earth, the World Wildlife Fund, and so on, we find a greater sense of sympathy with nature and sense that it has the right to exist on its own terms. Television pictures of the infliction of pain and suffering by humans on animals, such as the hunting of whales or culling of seals, or the suffering inflicted on seabirds by oil pollution, or forests with trees stripped of leaves (what the Germans call *Waldsterben*, or forest-murder, see Heimer 1997) can invoke a sense of global citizenship and ecological responsibility (Falk 1994; Beck 1996). If humans are to be regarded as embodied persons, and nature too can be seen as our outer body, then questions of health, pain, and suffering in some ways unite us with all living things.

Virtual Publics and Cities of Bits

John Thompson's book *The Media and Modernity* was published in 1995, yet it fails to discuss the Internet and the development of cyberspace. These are important developments in terms of his typology of face-to-face, mediated, and mediated quasi-interaction. The Internet is clearly a form of mediated interaction, sharing some of the characteristics of the letter and telephone. Like the letter it is a scriptural form, yet it is almost like the telephone in that the exchanges between parties can be almost instantaneous and relatively simple to initiate. It is like a conversation, except that it uses the written word; it is also possible for multiple users to participate in the same "conversation."

Yet the next stage of the Internet, which we are just beginning to see, really deserves a classificatory category of its own; for simplicity we can call it virtual interactivity, although this only captures limited dimensions of its characteristics. In the first place, it is beginning to take a multimedia form, combining text, speech, music, and images. Apart from the integration of previously dispersed forms, the massive potential difference from the conventional media is the extent of on-line programming and archive material available for access through increased "bandwidth" (Negroponte 1994). Also important is the capacity to configure material in databases, which can be accessed and searched rapidly. The data is hypertexted or hyperlinked, which can be contrasted to the linear mode we are used to in reading books and other texts, in the way it permits jumps within and across texts. New discontinuous, parallel-accessing modes of reading and viewing akin to television channel-hopping are in the process of being developed, as the formal integrity of a separate document, file, or book gives way. The following implications should be mentioned.

In the first place, these developments promise the fulfillment of a long-held dream of humanity, that of completeness, with every piece of written or recorded knowledge (image/music/text) potentially immediately available. Yet one corollary of the availability of a digital database of human culture is the problem of navigation and selectivity: now that everything is available, where do we go and why do we go there?

But along with completeness, there is a second notable feature to this next stage of the Internet: interactivity. This does not mean that the Internet can be used like a telephone, but that the material downloaded, or used in conversational mode, can be edited and reformed. With text it is possible to write in the middle of other people's text—to effectively become a co-author—which threatens to make available a whole mass of co-written hybrid versions of texts, as well as to undermine the authority of book writers and intellectuals. In addition, similar possibilities of co-production are possible with the digitalization of images—it will be easy to alter, morph, and reconstruct existing film and television output, or construct new output which is no longer based on montage (Cubitt 1998).

A third and potentially radical feature of the new medium is the possibility of three-dimensional representation and fuller sensory replication. There are already three-dimensional programs available on the Internet that have the potential to reconfigure the existing flat page format to enable the user to move through data-architecturally constructed space (VRML is predicted to replace HTML). Yet the potential of cyberspace, by incorporating virtual reality into the process, is to simulate an intensely realistic space, which offers a high degree of instantiation or immersion—a space which one can rapidly move or "fly" through.

The potential of the Internet, if it takes the form of cyberspace, is not to remain a tool or technique, but to become a parallel world with its own spatial economy and architecture. While the global cities have financial and business districts full of people working through screens, there are power stakes in the architecture, speed, and accessibility of the virtual data city. The potential world city referred to by Virilio is in effect a data city in which people will work, associate, and play. The Internet, then, offers the potential for the construction of *Cities of Bits,* to use the title of Mitchell's (1995) book. The inspiration for cities of data comes from William Gibson's famous definition of cyberspace as

a graphic representation of data abstracted from the bank of every computer in the human system. Unthinkable complexity. Lines of light receding on the non-

space of the mind. Clusters and constellations of data. Like city lights receding.
(1986: 51)

In order to provide ease of access to the data constellations we can fly
into, they become coded in readily identifiable iconic forms. One could
imagine a complex city of different types of data, which also contained
virtual streets and effective public spaces. This immediately makes one
think back to the real global informational city and questions of access
and the growth of private space at the expense of public space. The public spaces would be juxtaposed to private intranets whose closed access
building form would make up much of the datacity. William Gibson's
vision draws a good deal on Mike Davis's depiction of 1980s Los Angeles. Hence within Gibsonian cyberspace we have extreme deregulation
and privatization, a virtual world in which corporations can play out
their power games.[4]

What is the potential for the development of public space in this new
world? In the first place, the prospects of a Habermasian public sphere
emerging from the Internet and cyberspace do not look very good. How
can one have public interaction when one will never meet the other in-
teractants? How can trust be generated without embodied face-to-face
interaction?

Yet there are those like Rheingold (1994) who argue that virtual
communities can revitalize citizenship democracy. People will form
personal relationships in cyberspace; indeed it is interesting to read the
accounts of BBS (bulletin board), MOO, and MUD (multi-user domain)
friendships, where people develop intimate, emotionally rewarding
attachments with complete strangers, reversing some of our long-held
sociological assumptions about primary and secondary relationships. For
Rheingold the loss of community which many bemoan in contemporary
societies will now be regenerated through BBSs and MOOs, which have
relatively democratic access and modes of address in which users leave
behind their everyday status and power resources. One can rediscover
one's citizenship rights and involvement in a whole range of issues. One
can escape from those significant others and superiors who "know what
you think" and feel entitled to "speak on your behalf." Violence—both
actual and symbolic—which silences the voices of the less powerful
becomes more difficult to effect. New forms of trust with distant others
may emerge. In a society where many of the major risks are cumulative
and invisible—for example, ecological threats, pollution, radiation,
AIDS, and so on—we rely more and more on indirect information

about them. A technology which is in part a "super-telephone" can aid verification of information by the ease with which information can be exchanged and checked (Leeson 1996a: 51).

These are the conditions for the development of what some would call the postmodern public sphere (Hartley 1996; Poster 1995)—a notion that contests the myth of the extendibility of the Enlightenment public sphere and asks us to see the democratic potential of the mass media and cyberspace forms. Hartley (1996: 156) asks us to reflect on and reconsider an intellectual tradition which has favored production over consumption, urban over suburban, masculine over feminine, authority over the popular, truth over desire, word over image, and the printed archive over the popular screen. The Internet and cyberspace, then, may well force us to rethink our notions of citizenship and public space.

Yet there are also clear problems with this pioneering and subversive vision. In conventional terms, as we have just mentioned, trust is generated over time as we get to know people, as we digest their actions and words and observe their gestures and body language in co-present interactions. Liminal moments are usually well circumscribed, at least if one lives in Anglo-Saxon, North European, or North American cultures, although consumer culture and advertising generate a wider range of liminoid repertoires and a sense of the constructability of persona and performing selves, which invade everyday life. In the Habermasian discourse on the public sphere, masks and disguises are misinformation to be filtered out; they are resonant with the lack of seriousness of the carnival, or with the artfulness and deception of the courtier in the court society, to be contrasted with the solid, serious, purposeful bourgeois gentleman—the clarifier of truth.

The Internet and cyberspace will make masking and disguise both easy and routine. Already we see that in MOOs and BBSs there is the phenomenon of computer cross-dressing: age, gender, ethnicity are all seen as reconstructable. Indeed there are also accounts of people interacting on the Internet with "bots" (computer programs which masquerade as persons, being coded up to give a sophisticated and flexible range of responses, see Leeson 1996b). If one develops regular interactions with a person who is in disguise, or with a machine, how does this affect trust? There are clearly gains as well as losses to be considered here, for example, the loss of the ideal of pure communication, of compete truthfulness and trust: a romantic ideal of complete and self-sufficient identity which draws on Rousseau and others. Instead of the masculine and bourgeois ideal, there may well be more realistic possibilities for communication and participation by accepting masking and performance as part of everyday life and not seeking to eradicate it. Many academics and intellectuals often inhabit the tradition of Rousseau and have a long-standing prejudice in favor of sincerity over acting.[5]

Likewise, the Internet may well encourage us to accept the notion of multiple identities (Turkle 1995). The Windows format many of us operate with when using personal computers already encourages parallel processing, carrying out many tasks at once. The lack of a strong identity, the possibility of fragmentation and splitting into multiple selves, formerly regarded as pathological, is now increasingly normalized and brought into psychological orthodoxy, and surfaces in the popular psychology how-to-do-it literature (Shotter 1993).

There exists a further problem in terms of the generation of the "civic bodies" Sennett (1996) speaks of. The simulated puppet bodies we use to represent ourselves in virtual reality seem a long way from the body in pain, the aging body which reminds us of our common human fate and vulnerability. One can know little about the body in pain from the representation the person chooses to employ: it could well be a sick and invalid person who chooses a youthful, active body to represent him- or herself. One can seemingly escape the lived body and interact only with the virtual body, something which, it has been argued, reveals a continuity between the cyberspace aficionados and the idealistic tendencies of Western thought, with its long-held preference for the mind over the body. Cyberspace offers the seductive possibilities of pure, unencumbered mind, able to travel and transform itself, to float free of the messiness and disgust of decaying bodies, of what is contemptuously referred to as "the meat" (see Featherstone 1995b; Featherstone and Burrows 1995). It offers a technological dream of mastery, of the elimination of death and suffering bodies, which Sennett is critical of in respect to the urban plan: the city swept clean of the refuse of human misery. Yet it may well be that the new forms of association have potential to go beyond the type of opposition Sennett speaks of, and that technological mastery of the planned kind ceases to have a coherent worldview in a time of greater pragmatism and syncretism. Indeed, as I mentioned in the previous section, some of the dichotomies between human beings and nature, and humans and machines, are being actively deconstructed by social developments and theoretical formulations.

At the same time we have to step back from the virtual city and ask questions about its relation to the actual cities we live in. There are many utopian strands in the writing on cyberspace, coupled with a sense of inevitability of the triumph of the new modes. For those influenced by Deleuze and Guattari (1983, 1987) the net is the archetypal rhizomic structure, a nonsystematic, labyrinthine form which is impossible to control or destroy. There is a strong "cyberrevolutionary" strand in the writings about the Internet which uses the language of the unstoppable cybernetic machine (Terranova 1996). The evolution of information bits is likened to that of those other bits of information, genes. Parallels are made between DNA codes with their genes and electronic information codes with their memes (Terranova 1996: 75), both seen as independent systems of life.

The danger is that the group of people who develop such systems and operate the Internet will become increasingly detached from other people who inhabit the global informational cities. In short there will be large groups of informationally poor and excluded people who cannot participate. With the existing global economic order, with increasing marketization, deregulation, and downsizing, it is difficult to see social structure or agencies who will be interested in incorporating the unemployed underclass and the excluded. Rather, we can assume the option will be confinement and policing. Yet it is not the technology which is creating this problem. Indeed it can be argued that the new information technology with its post-scriptural modes of communication favors everyday life, the world of discordant voices, and speech over the linear mode of written language. The fate of the excluded raises important questions about membership in the public sphere, about the limits of our existing notions of citizenship. It points to the need to rethink citizenship and cultural rights, to work towards notions of global cultural citizenship which will go a little further than the McCitizen.

Notes

An earlier version of Featherstone's chapter was first delivered in December 1997 at the Conference on Cityscapes, UNICAMP, São Paulo, Brazil. —Ed.

1.   Braidotti's position is echoed by many others in contemporary cultural studies who follow postmodern and postcolonial theories. Trinh T. Minh-ha, for example, writes, "The differences made *between* entities comprehended as absolute presences—hence the notions of *pure origin* and *true self*—are an out-growth of a dualistic system of thought peculiar to the Occident (the 'onto-theology' which characterizes Western

metaphysics). They should be distinguished from the differences grasped *both between* and *within* entities, each of these being understood as multiple presence. Not One, not two either. 'I' is, therefore not a unified subject, a fixed identity, or that solid mass covered with layers of superficialities one has gradually to peel off before one can see its true face. 'I' is, itself, *infinite layers*" (1989, quoted in Lemert 1993: 605).

2. In this context it is interesting to note that the early forms of newspapers which developed in the seventeenth and eighteenth centuries had a dual function of news about trade and finance along with other cultural and political matters. It has been argued that the early broadsheets contained trade and financial information and that other news was introduced as a "filler" (see Thompson 1995: 66-8 on early newspapers). These ancillary matters to trade, then, were also perceived as important contextual information which could themselves have useful business payoffs. This points to the hybrid nature of the genesis of the public sphere.

3. For a number of arguments which challenge the notion of the corruption of the public sphere by the media in the past and which question whether there was ever a more open and public city in the past, see Robbins (1993).

4. For a discussion of the architecture of cyberspace, in which "liquid architecture" becomes possible, see Novak (1992).

5. Elias's 1983 work on court society is an important correction to this tradition; see also the discussion in Sennett (1976) and Vowinckel (1987).

References

Albrow, M. 1996. *The Global Age*. Cambridge: Polity.

Anderson, B. 1991. *Imagined Communities*. rev. ed. London: Verso.

Appadurai, A. 1996. *Modernity at Large*. Minneapolis: University of Minnesota Press.

Arantes, A. 1996. "The War of Places: Symbolic Boundaries and Liminality in Urban Space." *Theory, Culture & Society* 13(4): 81-91.

Baker, H. 1994. "Critical Memory and the Black Public Sphere." *Public Culture* 7(1): 3-34.

Barber, B.R. 1996. *Jihad vs. McWorld*. New York: Balantine Books.

Bauman, Z. 1987. *Legislators and Interpreters*. Oxford: Polity.

———. 1988. "Is There a Postmodern Sociology?" *Theory, Culture & Society* 5(2-3): 217-238.

Beck, U. 1996. "World Risk Society." *Theory, Culture & Society* 13(4): 1-32.

Braidotti, R. 1994. *Nomadic Subjects*. New York: Columbia University Press

———. 1999. "Response to Pels." *Theory, Culture & Society* 16(1): 87-94.

Calhoun, C., ed. 1992. *Habermas and the Public Sphere*. Cambridge, MA: The MIT Press.

Castells, M. 1996. *The Information Age, Volume 1: The Rise of the Network Society*. Oxford: Blackwell.

Clarke, B. 1996. *Deep Citizenship*. London: Pluto.

Crossley, N. 1997. "Corporeality and Communicative Action." *Body & Society* 3(1): 17-46.

Cubitt, S. 1998. *Digital Aesthetics*. London: Sage.

Dahrendorf, R. 1994. "The Changing Quality of Citizenship." Pp. 10-19 in *The Condition of Citizenship*, edited by B. van Steenbergen. London: Sage.

Davis, M. 1990. *City of Quartz: Excavating the Future in Los Angeles*. London: Verso.

———. 1992. "Beyond *Blade Runner*: Urban Control and the Ecology of Fear." Westfield, NJ.: Open Magazine Pamphlet Series.

Dear, M., and S. Flusty. 1999. "Postmodern Urbanism and the Spatial Logic of Global Capitalism." Pp. 64-85 in *Spaces of Culture*, edited by M. Featherstone and S. Lash. London: Sage.

Deleuze, G., and F. Guattari. 1983. *Anti-Oedipus: Capitalism and Schizophrenia*. Minneapolis: University of Minnesota Press.

———. 1987. *A Thousand Plateaus: Capitalism and Schizophrenia*. Minneapolis: University of Minnesota Press.

Dezalay, Y. 1990. "The *Big Bang* and the Law." In *Global Culture: Nationalism, Globalization, and Modernity*, edited by M. Featherstone. London: Sage.

Donald, J. 1996. "The Citizen and the Man About Town." Pp. 170-190 in *Questions of Cultural Identity*, edited by S. Hall and P. Du Gay. London: Sage.

Elias, N. 1983. *The Court Society*. Oxford: Basil Blackwell.

Falk, R. 1994. "The Making of Global Citizenship." Pp. 127-140 in *The Condition of Citizenship*, edited by B. van Steenbergen. London: Sage.

Fainstein, S.S., I. Gordon, and M. Harloe, eds. 1992. *Divided Cities: New York & London in the Contemporary World*. Oxford: Blackwell.

Featherstone, M. 1991. *Consumer Culture and Postmodernism*. London: Sage.

———. 1995a. *Undoing Culture: Globalization, Postmodernism and Identity*. London: Sage.

———. 1995b. "Post-Bodies, Ageing and Virtual Reality." Pp. 227-244 in *Images of Aging: Cultural Representations of Later Life*, edited by M. Featherstone and A. Wernick. London: Routledge.

———. 1998. "The *Flâneur*, the City and Virtual Public Life." *Urban Studies* 35(5-6): 909-917.

Featherstone, M., and R. Burrows. 1995. "Introduction." Pp. 1-20 in *Cyberspace/Cyberbodies/Cyberpunk: Cultures of Technological Embodiment*, edited by M. Featherstone and R. Burrows. London: Sage.

Featherstone, M. and M. Hepworth. 1998. "The Male Menopause: Lay Accounts and the Reconstruction of Everyday Life." Pp. 276-301 in *The Body in Everyday Life*, edited by S. Nettleton and J. Watson. London: Routledge.

Fraser, N. 1996. "Rethinking the Public Sphere: A Contribution to the Critique of Actually Existing Democracy." Pp. 109-142 in *Habermas and the Public Sphere*, edited by C. Calhoun. Cambridge, MA: The MIT Press.

Gibson, W. 1986. *Neuromancer*. New York: Fantasia Press.

Giddens, A. 1991. *Modernity and Self Identity*. Cambridge: Polity Press.

Goffman, E. 1971. *The Presentation of Self in Everyday Life*. Harmondsworth: Penguin.

Gouldner, A. 1979. *The Future of the Intellectuals and the Rise of the New Class*. London: Macmillan.

Habermas, J. 1971. *Theory and Practice*. London: Heinemann.

———. 1978. "Ego Development and Moral Identity." In *Towards a Reconstruction of Historical Materialism*. Boston: Continuum.

———. 1981. *The Theory of Communicative Action: Volume 1*. London: Heinemann.

———. 1989. *The Structural Transformation of the Public Sphere*. Cambridge: Polity Press.

———. 1994. "Citizenship and National Identity." Pp. 20-35 in *The Condition of Citizenship*, edited by B. van Steenbergen. London: Sage.

Hall, S. 1996. "Introduction: Who Needs Identity?" Pp. 1-17 in *Questions of Cultural Identity*, edited by S. Hall and P. Du Gay. London: Sage.

Hanson, M. 1991. *Babel and Babylon: Spectatorship in American Silent Films*. Cambridge, MA: Harvard University Press.

Hartley, J. 1996. *Popular Reality: Journalism, Modernity, Popular Culture*. London: Arnold.

Heimer, J. 1997. *A Comparison between the English and German Green Movements.* Unpublished doctoral dissertation, University of Teesside.

Horkheimer, M., and T.W. Adorno. 1971. *Dialectic of Enlightenment.* New York: Herder and Herder.

Hunt, L. 1988. "The Sacred and the French Revolution." Pp. 25-43 in *Durkheimian Sociology: Cultural Studies,* edited by J. Alexander. Cambridge: Cambridge University Press.

Isin, E.F. 1996. "Global Citizenship." York University, Ontario. Mimeographed.

Jacobs, J. 1993. "The City Unbounded; Qualitative Approaches to the City." *Urban Studies* 4(5): 827-848.

King, A.D. 1996. "Introduction." Pp. 1-19 in *Re-Presenting the City: Ethnicity, Capital and Culture in the 21st-Century Metropolis,* edited by A.D. King. London: Macmillan.

Knorr Cetina, K. 1997. "Postsocial (Knowledge) Societies: Objectualization, Individualization and the Idea of an Object Centered Sociality." *Theory, Culture & Society* 14(4): 1-30.

Lemert, C., ed. 1993. *Social Theory: The Multicultural and Classic Readings.* Boulder, CO: Westview Press.

Leeson, L.H. 1996a. "Jaron Larnier Interview." Pp. 43-53 in *Clicking In: Hot Links to a Digital Culture,* edited by L.H. Leeson. Seattle, WA: Bay Press.

———. 1996b. "Sandy Stone Interview." Pp. 105-115 in *Clicking In: Hot Links to a Digital Culture,* edited by L.H. Leeson. Seattle, WA: Bay Press.

Marshall, T.H. 1977. *Class, Citizenship and Social Development.* Chicago: University of Chicago Press.

McGuigan, J. 1996. *Culture and the Public Sphere.* London: Routledge.

Massey, D. 1993. "Power Geometry and a Progressive Sense of Place." Pp. 59-69 in *Mapping the Futures: Local Cultures, Global Change,* edited by J. Bird, et al. London: Routledge.

Minh-ha, T.T. 1989. *Woman, Native, Other: Writing, Postcoloniality and Feminism.* Bloomington: Indiana University Press.

Mitchell, W.J. 1995. *City of Bits.* Cambridge, MA: The MIT Press.

Negroponte, N. 1994. *Being Digital.* New York: Alfred A. Knopf.

Negt, O. and Kluge, A. 1997. *The Public Sphere and Experience.* Minneapolis: University of Minnesota Press.

Novak, M. 1992. "Liquid Architectures in Cyberspace." Pp. 225-254 in *Cyberspace: First Steps,* edited by M. Benedikt. Cambridge, MA: The MIT Press.

Noys, B. 1997. "Communicative Unreason: Bataille and Habermas." *Theory, Culture & Society* 14(1): 59-76.

Pels, D. 1999. "Privileged Nomads: On the Strangeness of Intellectuals and the Intellectuality of Strangeness." *Theory, Culture & Society* 16(1): 63-86.

Poster, M. 1995. "Postmodern Virtualities." Pp. 79-96 in *Cyberspace/Cyberbodies/Cyberpunk: Cultures of Technological Embodiment,* edited by M. Featherstone and R. Burrows. London: Sage.

Probyn, E. 1998. "*Mc*-Identites. Food and the Familial Citizen." *Theory, Culture & Society* 15(2): 155-174.

Rheingold, H. 1994. *The Virtual Community: Finding Connection in a Computerized World.* London: Secker and Warburg.

Robertson, R. 1995. "Glocalization: Time-Space and Homogeneity-Heterogeneity." Pp. 25-44 in *Global Modernities,* edited by M. Featherstone, S. Lash, and R. Robertson. London: Sage.

Robbins, B., ed. 1993. *The Phantom Public Sphere.* Minneapolis: University of Minnesota Press.

Santos, B.S. 1999. "Towards a Multicultural Conception of Human Rights." Pp. 214-229 in *Spaces of Culture: City, Nation, World*, edited by M. Featherstone and S. Lash. London: Sage.

Sassen, S. 1994. *Cities in a World Economy*. Thousand Oaks, CA: Sage.

————. 1996. "Identity in the Global City." Pp. 131-152 in *The Geography of Identity*, edited by P. Yaeger. Ann Arbor: University of Michigan Press.

————. 1999. "Electronic Space and Power." Pp. 49-63 in *Spaces of Culture: City, Nation, World*, edited by M. Featherstone and S. Lash. London: Sage.

Sennett, R. 1976. *The Fall of Public Man*. Cambridge: Cambridge University Press.

————. 1996. *Flesh and Stone: The Body and the City in Western Civilization*. London: Faber.

Scarry, E. 1985. *The Body In Pain*. New York: Oxford University Press.

Shotter, J. 1993. *Cultural Politics of Everyday Life*. Milton Keynes: Open University Press.

Smith, N. 1996. "After Tompkins Square Park: Degentrification and the Revanchist City." Pp. 93-107 in *Re-Presenting the City: Ethnicity, Capital and Culture in the 21st-Century Metropolis*, edited by A.D. King. London: Macmillan.

van Steenbergen, B., ed. 1994. *The Condition of Citizenship*. London: Sage.

Stevenson, N. 1995. *Understanding Media Cultures: Social Theory and Mass Communication*. London: Sage.

Tagg, J. 1996. "This City Which is Not One." Pp. 179-182 in *Re-Presenting the City: Ethnicity, Capital and Culture in the 21st-Century Metropolis*, edited by A.D. King. London: Macmillan.

Terranova, T. 1996. "Digital Darwin: Nature, Evolution and Control in the Rhetoric of Electronic Communication." *New Formations* 29: 69-83.

Thompson, J.B. 1993. "The Theory of the Public Sphere." *Theory, Culture & Society* 10(3): 173-190.

————. 1995. *The Media and Modernity*. Cambridge: Polity.

Thrift, N. 1996. *Spatial Formations*. London: Sage.

Turkle, S. 1995. *Life on the Screen*. New York: Simon and Schuster.

Toffler, A. 1980. *The Third Wave*. London: Collins.

Turner, B.S. 1994. "Postmodern Culture/Modern Citizens." Pp. 153-168 in *The Condition of Citizenship*, edited by B. van Steenbergen. London: Sage.

Virilio, P. 1993. "Marginal Groups." *Daidalos* 50(Dec.): 72-81.

Vowinckel, G. 1987. "Command or Refine." *Theory, Culture & Society* 4(2-3): 489-514.

Weber, M. 1958. *The City*. Glencoe, IL: The Free Press.

Weeks, J. 1998. "The Sexual Citizen." *Theory, Culture & Society* 15(3-4): 35-52.

Zukin, S. 1996. "Space and Symbols in an Age of Decline." Pp. 43-59 in *Re-Presenting the City: Ethnicity, Capital and Culture in the 21st-Century Metropolis*, edited by A.D. King. London: Macmillan.

4

False Faces: Ethnic Identity, Authenticity, and Fraud in Native American Discourse and Politics

Joane Nagel

The Paradox of Declining and Rising Ethnicity

Racial and ethnic identities remain important individual and collective characteristics in contemporary societies. The expectations of early post-World War II social theorists that race and ethnicity would recede in favor of national identities in Western countries have not been met. The belief was that as immigrant and indigenous groups participated in civic institutions (churches, schools, voluntary associations) and the national economy, they would assimilate and adopt the dominant culture. Interestingly, there *is* indeed clear evidence of assimilation among second, third, and subsequent generations of immigrants in many Western countries like the U.S., Canada, Australia, the United Kingdom, and France, to mention a few. As measured by such indicators as native language loss and national language acquisition, intermarriage, and decline in traditional religious practices, the children and grandchildren of immigrants do seem to be integrating. However, during the past few decades, despite these signs of assimilation, we have also seen resurgences in racial, ethnic, and national identifications, and the formation of new organizations and ethnic movements in most states around the world.

What can account for this apparent paradox of simultaneous declining and increasing ethnic identification and community? There have been several social, political, economic, and cultural processes at work during the postwar period, which have combined with the assimilation processes and pressures not only to maintain ethnic differences, but actually to increase ethnic diversity in many countries.

One factor has been global migration. Migration is the engine that produces new ethnic groups; migration can be internal, from rural to urban centers, or international, spanning national borders. In both cases—internal and international—ethnic communities and enclaves are formed, often in cities, that serve to build ethnic networks and self-awareness, that infuse established communities with new traditional ethnic membership, and that can create a backlash among dominant groups in response to a perceived ethnic "invasion."

Another factor encouraging ethnic emergence of new groups and resurgence of established groups has been political policies that reinforce and recognize ethnicity as a basis for political claimsmaking. This politicization of ethnicity can occur for many reasons. The political rights movement of one ethnic group can spread to other ethnic groups seeking similar rights or recognition (e.g., the U.S. African American civil rights movement served as a model for ethnic movements among many other groups: Latinos, Native Americans, Asian Americans). Official political policies, recognizing particular ethnic problems or extending ethnic rights, can generate similar demands among other groups (e.g., the Canadian recognition of the rights of French speakers led members of other language communities to seek language rights protections).

Another political factor can be ethnic representation in the political system. Electoral politics can lead to strategies of ethnic bloc voting. Ethnic electoral competition can encourage ethnic mobilization as well as a shifting of ethnic boundaries from smaller groups (e.g., Mexican Americans, Cuban Americans, Puerto Ricans) to larger identities and groups (Latinos, Hispanics). In some cases this takes the form of ethnic mobilization or alliances to get out the vote for a particular candidate. In other cases, it can result in ethnic political parties (e.g., Canada's *Parti Quebecqois*).

Ethnicity and economics are also linked in ways that can generate ethnic renewal. Affirmative action policies are under attack in many countries, in such places as different as the U.S. and India, in part because of controversies about the authenticity of ethnic candidates for affirmative action. Controversies can center on the class position of the individual (is s/he really in *need* of affirmative action recognition?) or on the ethnic background of the individual (is s/he really a bonafide member of the group in which membership is claimed?). Despite such queries, the moral right to restitution and the potential advantage of affirmative action can encourage individuals to identify themselves ethnically and can lead ethnic communities to defend affirmative action policies.

Finally, there is a cultural value to ethnicity in many national settings. Despite the costs borne by members of racial and ethnic communities (racism, discrimination, even genocide), there is also a symbolic importance to having an ethnic identity in many contemporary societies. Sometimes this takes the form of recreational ethnicity where members of ethnic communities participate in festivals and fairs to celebrate a common ancestry and reenact shared traditions. Sometimes this takes a more serious or ceremonial form involving religious or traditional practices, membership rituals, or self or collective rededications to ethnic community and lifeways. Just as it is a disadvantage in the modern world to be without a country, in many countries, one is adrift if one is without an ethnicity.

False Faces: Tensions between Self and Other Ethnic Claims

An important factor in understanding these paradoxical patterns of declining and rising ethnicity in contemporary states is the way in which ethnicity is determined. Ethnicity is best understood as a dynamic, constantly evolving property of both individual identity and group organization. The construction of ethnic identity and culture is the result of both structure and agency—a dialectic played out by ethnic groups and the larger society. Ethnicity is the product of actions undertaken by ethnic groups as they shape and reshape their self-definition and culture; however, ethnicity is also constructed by external social, economic, and political processes and actors as they shape and reshape ethnic categories and definitions. Ethnic identity is the result of a dialectical process involving internal and external opinions and processes, as well as the individual's self-identification and outsiders' ethnic designations—that is, what *you* think is your ethnicity, versus what *they* think is your ethnicity. Since ethnicity changes situationally, the individual carries a portfolio of ethnic identities which are more or less salient in various situations and vis-à-vis various audiences. As the audiences change, the socially defined array of ethnic choices open to the individual changes. This produces a "layering" of ethnic identities which combines with the ascriptive character of ethnicity to reveal the negotiated, problematic nature of ethnic identity. Sometimes one or more of the identities an individual claims are questioned by others who assert that the individual is putting forth an ethnic false face.

When debates about ethnic authenticity arise, they are often because of a lack of fit between individual self-identification and outsiders' beliefs about the individual's ethnicity. This tension is particularly ironic when it occurs in U.S. society because of the long-standing American tradition of and respect for self-invention. A central component of individual identity cosmology in American culture is the individual's right to self-reinvention and upward mobility: "Go west, young man" and seek your fortune and a new life (identity). This presumed reinvention flies in the face of both informal and formal criteria for authentic ethnicity, such as the requirement that an individual have particular ancestry or other qualifications in order to claim membership in an ethnic group. For instance, many Americans claim to have some degree of American Indian ancestry. These self-identifications are often challenged by the U.S. federal government and by individual American Indian tribal governments, each of which has formal rules defining who is an Indian or a tribal member (e.g., particular degrees of "blood quantum," Indian ancestry or tribal membership of one or both parents, residency on the reservation). These rules are often designed to protect severely limited tribal resources from claims by individuals making casual assertions of Indian identity. Recent demographic trends in Native America have brought issues of American Indian ethnic authenticity to the foreground in many Indian communities.

The Decline and Resurgence of American Indian Self-Identification

At the time of European contact with North America, scholars estimate there were several million inhabitants living in several thousand communities, speaking several hundred languages, practicing hundreds of distinct cultural and religious traditions (Swanton 1952; Driver 1961; Thornton 1987a; Snipp 1989).[1] During the next four hundred years, as a result of disease, warfare, forced relocations, and the destruction of economic, political, and social institutions, the number of Native American individuals and communities was decimated, and the survival of many indigenous languages and cultures was threatened. The number of American Indians counted by census takers in the 1900 census was fewer than one-quarter million, and Indian communities on reservation and federal land numbered fewer than 500. The conditions confronting American Indians were so grave that many researchers and policymakers feared for the cultural and demographic survival of Indian societies (see Meriam 1928).

Despite this devastating history, something remarkable occurred in the second half of the twentieth century. The demographic decline of the Indian population was reversed, and many Indian communities embarked on programs of cultural, linguistic, and religious preservation and renewal and programs of economic and political development. This paper briefly outlines the reasons scholars have given for the recent increase in the American Indian population and the accompanying renewal of native culture and community. The main purpose of the paper, however, is to examine the consequences for American Indian ethnicity—an increased complexity and diversity—that resulted from the resurgence of American Indian ethnic identification and the renascence of tribal cultures during the 1970s and 1980s.[2] I argue that the American Indian demographic resurgence and cultural renewal of the 1970s, 1980s, and 1990s generated complications and controversies about the nature and boundaries of American Indian ethnicity. The events in recent American history that contributed to the rise in American Indian ethnic identification included the rights movements of the 1960s and 1970s, shifts in federal Indian policy, and most important, the rise of American Indian activism, namely, the Red Power movement of the 1970s. American civil rights history, federal Indian policy, and Indian activism all combined to energize and transform American Indian ethnicity and community during the postwar period. The result has been a Native American renaissance, but that rebirth has raised questions about American Indian genealogical and cultural authenticity and the extent to which native ancestry can be used to claim membership in official Indian communities and access to tribally controlled material and symbolic resources.[3]

In order to understand the destabilizing effects of recent increases in the Native American population, it is important to review recent Indian demographic history. In 1990, nearly 1.9 million Americans reported their race to be "American Indian." This figure reflects the dramatic growth in the American Indian population during the twentieth century—more than an eightfold increase from approximately one-quarter million in 1900 to nearly 2 million at the end of the century. Table 4.1 shows the increases in the American Indian population from 1900-1990.

TABLE 4.1
American Indian Population - 1890-1990

Year	Number	% Change
1890	248,253	
1900	237,196	-5
1910	276,927	17
1920	244,437	-13
1930	343,352	40
1940	345,252	1
1950	357,499	4
1960	523,591	46
1970	792,730	51
1980	1,364,033	72
1990	1,878,285	38

Sources: 1890-1970: Thornton (1987a: 160)
1980 and 1990: U.S. Bureau of the Census (1991b: Table 1).

The figures in table 4.1 show a slow, but steady increase in the Indian population from 1900 to 1950, that demographers attribute mainly to a rise in birthrates and a decline in infant and general mortality rates among the American Indian population resulting from improved health and social services available to rural and reservation Indians. The spurt of growth from 1950-1960 (46 percent) reflects a change in 1960 racial classification procedures, when the Census Bureau began relying on self-reports (rather than enumerator designations) of race and ancestry. Increases in the American Indian population from 1960 to 1990 outpaced rising birthrates and declining deathrates, growing 51 percent from 1960-1970, 72 percent from 1970-1980, and 38 percent from 1980-1990. While some of this change can be attributed to improvements in census enumeration techniques, particularly for rural Indian populations, researchers note that the large increases in the Indian population after 1960 cannot be accounted for by changes in enumeration techniques or definitions, or by more traditional demographic explanations such as increased immigration or improved life expectancy (Passel and Berman 1986: 164; see also Snipp 1989; Stiffarm and Lane 1992; Thornton 1987a).

Scholars have concluded that something more *social* than demographic must have produced the particularly high increases in the number of American Indians that occurred after 1960, especially the large rise from 1970 to 1980 (Harris 1994; Eschbach 1995). Given the Census Bureau's self-reporting approach to racial identification, researchers have posited that the increase in the American Indian population in recent decades is the result of changes in individuals' ethnic identification. That is, for some reason, an increased number of individuals were motivated, for the first time, to declare their race "Indian" in each decade after 1960, but particularly in 1980. For instance, census researchers Passel and Berman argue that the unexplained percentage of Indian population growth from 1970-1980 (about half of the increase) is the result of "changes in self-definition" by individuals who reported a non-Indian race (or who were not included) in the 1970 census, but who reported their race to be Indian in the 1980 census (1986: 164).

I propose three related explanations for this increased propensity of Americans to identify their race as American Indian after 1960: (1) federal Indian policies which laid the groundwork and provided a rationale for increased Indian ethnic self-identification; (2) changes in American ethnic politics brought about by the civil rights movement which enhanced the social worth and meaning of ethnicity generally, and which provided a model and expanded political opportunity structure for Indian activism (i.e., the Red Power movement) during the 1960s and 1970s; and (3) the self-renewing, self-reinventing capacity of the Red Power movement itself, which started a tidal wave of Indian ethnic renewal that surged across reservation and urban Indian communities, revitalizing cultures, restoring Indian ethnic pride, and ultimately sweeping away an entire era of federal Indian policy.[4]

The argument that American Indian activism led to a renewal of Indian ethnic pride and motivated a cultural renascence is the reverse of traditional models of activism in which identity is thought simply to *precede* rather than grow out of protest activity. However, in *Cultures of Solidarity*, Fantasia (1988) shows that through direct involvement in protest as well as through association with protest movements, individual and collective identity often emerge for the first time or are strengthened and redefined. Following this view of identity and activism, Red Power can be seen as both affirming and intensifying American Indian ethnicity. Thus, the Red Power movement was arguably the single most powerful force in the emergence and resurgence of Indian self-identification and in the construction and reconstruction of tribal communities and cultures during the 1970s and 1980s.

Many changes in American Indian policy were brought about by the pressures placed on policymakers by Red Power activists. The 1970s, 1980s, and 1990s brought about a major reversal in federal Indian policy, away from "termination" in which tribal rights were minimized with the ultimate goal of ending tribal federal treaty rights, toward "self-determination" in which tribal sovereignty was reaffirmed and where tribes regained many old rights and obtained a number of new powers. One of these powers was to gain control over sacred materials, funerary objects, and burial remains historically in the hands of non-Indian institutions like natural history museums. These new rights and their enforcement both empowered Indian communities, but also generated debates about Indian ethnic authenticity, as the next sections illustrate.

The Problematics of American Indian Ethnic Renewal

In January, 1994, I visited the Field Museum of Natural History in Chicago as part of a group of scholars working at the Newberry Library's D'Arcy McNickle Center for American Indian History. The Field Museum's extensive collection of Native American art and artifacts has come under attack in recent years following the passage of the 1990 Native American Graves Protection and Repatriation Act (NAGPRA), which required U.S. museums to catalog their Indian holdings in order to identify the tribal affiliation of all human remains and sacred objects and to contact Indian communities in order to return these remains and artifacts should the tribes wish them returned. Nor surprisingly, NAGPRA has created quite a stir among U.S. museum curators since museums are generally busy collecting and displaying art and artifacts, not returning their holdings to originators or their descendants.

During this visit, as I walked through the Field museum's extensive display of Indian artifacts, I came upon a large display case that was empty except for the labels of the objects that were missing from its shelves and a letter from Peterson Zah, then president of the Navajo Nation. On Navajo Nation letterhead, President Zah informed the Field Museum that representatives from the Nation had visited the museum, had examined the "nightway" masks that were displayed in the case, and had determined that the masks "should not be seen by uninitiated eyes." The museum was instructed to remove the masks from public display, and to await a decision from the tribe about their final disposition. Several months later, a Navajo Nation delegation went to the museum and conducted a private ceremony, removing the nightway masks from the case. Also in the case were some Iroquois "false face" masks. All of the masks were removed and stored in the museum's back areas.

While visiting the Field, I queried one of the museum's staff members about the case, the masks, and their likely return to the Navajo Nation. One staff member commented that many of the masks had never been "danced" or used in any sacred setting, and some of the masks had indeed been made by Navajo artisans specifically for collectors. The question of which mask was an "authentic" sacred object and which mask was simply a work of art was difficult for museum staff to determine, as were the conditions and terms of the masks' purchase. These ambiguities, as well as the precedent that would be set if the museum returned the masks without documentation of ownership, resulted in delays in returning the masks to the Navajo Nation. Negotiations for return of the nightway masks to the Navajo Nation were still underway in 1997. These kinds of negotiations and disputes have been underway in museums around the country for the past several years and will, no doubt, extend well into the next century (see Tallman 1993; Klein 1995; Josephy et al. 1998) as museums and Indian nations struggle to come to terms with the provisions of NAGPRA.

The question of the "real" nature, origins, and ownership of the nightway and false face masks held in the Field Museum of Natural History is only one of several debates about authenticity that involve ethnic or national communities, their membership, and their property in the U.S. and around the world. The Greek government has, for years, attempted to get back the Elgin marbles from Britain, and the government of Egypt has made numerous claims on extensive Egyptian art, sculpture, artifacts, funerary remains (mummies), and precious jewels held by museums outside of Egypt. In these cases the issue is not whether or not the objects in question are authentically sacred, but rather debate centers on who has a right to possess them. Art and artifacts are not the only targets of authenticity and rights debates. Challenges to authenticity can be leveled against individuals and their claims to ethnic group membership, as the next case illustrates.

In 1982 I visited an American Indian community center in an eastern city.[5] I was greeted by the director, a man wearing jeans and a plaid shirt, whose dark hair was woven into braids bound by beaded ties. He told me about the Indian center's history and about its current activities which were designed to provide a sense of community for the city's several thousand American Indian residents. The most successful undertaking, he reported, was a summer camp program. The program involved local Indian children from diverse tribal backgrounds—most of whom had been born and lived their lives in the city—who were sent to spend two weeks on the director's home reservation more than a thousand miles away, to learn about reservation life and their native heritage. I found the conversation interesting and informative. Several months later, while I was visiting a Bureau of Indian Affairs office in Washington, D.C., the Indian center director's name came up in conversation. To my surprise, I was told matter-of-factly by a person working at the BIA (who identified himself as a member of a recognized Indian tribe) that the director, Sam Smith (not his name), was "not really an Indian." When I inquired into this statement, the official went on to say that, "well, maybe his grandmother had some Indian blood," but, he reiterated, "Sam Smith is not really an Indian."

As one reads through the Indian affairs literature, the question of who is really an Indian comes up again and again. The query is often made in an atmosphere of skepticism and sometimes bitter contention.[6] The question is posed to tribes as well as to individuals. For instance, in an "open letter" to the governor of Georgia, Cherokee Nation of Oklahoma principal chief, Wilma Mankiller, denounced the state's decision to officially recognize two groups claiming Cherokee ancestry, expressing concern that these groups were "using the Cherokee Nation's name, history, culture, and reputation...and posing as Indian tribes" (1993: A-4). Such concerns often arise because of the potential loss of scarce tribal resources to an ever-increasing pool of collective and individual recipients. For example, in the Pacific Northwest, the efforts of the Samish and Snohomish tribes to obtain federal recognition, and thus rights to treaty-protected salmon fishing and a share of federal Indian resources, were opposed by other recognized tribes in the region, most notably the Tulalips, whose attorney summarized the dispute as a matter of resources and authenticity: "It boils down to trying to protect tribal fisheries from groups which the Tulalips view as not genuine Indians" (Egan 1992: 8).

Contemporary American Indian individuals and communities, like other minorities in American society, are often called upon to prove their ethnic authenticity. This is an irony in a country with a long tradition of racial segregation and a near-obsession with ethnic classification and identification. We all know the historical facts surrounding what Harris (1964) referred to as "hypodescent," or the "one drop rule," in the classification and treatment of Americans of African descent in the United States. Beginning with slavery, passing through official segregation to the present, to have any discernible African ancestry is to be black (see Feagin 1991; Hacker 1992). Despite the clear reality of the black/white racial boundary in U.S. society, there remain disputes inside and outside the African American community about who is "really" black. In March, 1997, *Newsweek* magazine ran a cover story asking this question, and focused on differences of class and region that create divisions in the black community and which make unified action difficult. Collas (1994) reports that questions can also arise about the racial credentials of individuals with dark skin, particularly those whose friendships and marriages cross the color line. Such policing is referred to by Williams (personal communication) as the "soul patrol."

The demands for ethnic proof facing many African Americans or Native Americans reflect the contemporary debate about race and ethnicity in America. Racial controversies today are not so much centered on those differences that divide us. Rather the claims and counterclaims of American ethnic groups (white and nonwhite) have to do more with the economics and politics of ethnicity—who has access to what resources based on what ethnic designations. With an emphasis on rights and resources, very quickly ethnic arguments settle down to issues of proof and authenticity. Who is *really* Indian or Latino or black? Which ethnic groups are *really* disadvantaged (all racial groups or just some: blacks, but not Asians, or only some Asians—Japanese, no, Hmong, yes; what about Asian Indians?)?

Who is *Really* an Indian?

Individual American Indian ethnicity is at least as problematic as that of other American ethnic groups, in part because of wide variability in the criteria and standards of proof of Indian ancestry and Indian-ness. Again, the doubts and suspicions seem greatest when ethnically tied resources are at stake, and when benefits are seen to accrue to individuals who claim Indian ancestry or special Indian knowledge. An example is the author Jamake Highwater, in particular his book, *The Primal Mind* (1981), which has served as a kind of lightning rod for ethnic inauthenticity charges from both ends of the political spectrum, and from Indians and non-Indians alike. For example, the following statements about Highwater are striking in their similarity despite the rather opposite standpoints of their authors. They come from two scholars—one Indian, one non-Indian, writing in two recently published books—one dedicated to outlining the history of American exploitation and repression of American Indians, the other intent on challenging the legitimacy of many American Indian economic, political, and cultural claims and programs.

The first author is Wendy Rose (1992), writing in *The State of Native America: Genocide, Colonization, and Resistance.* Disturbed by the popularity of *The Primal Mind* and its zealous readership, Rose recounts an incident where

> I was confronted by a non-native man who took it upon himself to "explain" to me how Jamake Highwater's transparently bogus ramblings had "done more for Indians than the work of any other writer." When I and several Indian colleagues sharply disagreed, the man informed us we were "hopelessly deluded." (1992: 414)

Representing quite another perspective, one less sympathetic to many contemporary Indian claims, Alice Kehoe (1990), writing in *The Invented Indian,* makes oddly similar comments.

> Exactly who Jamake Highwater is has been subject to controversy. He claims to be Blackfoot and also Cherokee; he admits to having been a choreographer in San Francisco under the name J. Marks; he denies being a Greek-American filmmaker from Toledo, Ohio, named Gregory J. Markopoulos. Whatever he once was, Highwater is a talented popular writer whose assertion of American Indian identity has lent credibility to his representation of Indian religion as 'primal vision.' (1990: 196)[7]

Though the apparent agendas of these two authors are vastly different,[8] their critique is essentially the same—a challenge to authenticity, one that is extended to a wide variety of authors, artists, scholars, activists, and individuals claiming Indian identity or interests. The authenticity debate often, though not exclusively, centers on ancestry, namely, just how much and what kind of Indian background qualifies individuals or groups to have the rights of American Indians.

Another source of controversy concerns how an individual acquires authentic Indian ethnicity—through self-definition or by the acknowledgment of others. Again, resources seem to be a key issue. For instance, at its annual meeting in Phoenix in 1993, the Association of American

Indian and Alaskan Native Professors (AAIANP) issued a statement on "ethnic fraud" stressing the importance of official tribal recognition of individuals' Indianness in classifying university students and faculty. The statement was intended to register the organization's concern about "ethnic fraud and offer recommendations to ensure the accuracy of American Indian/Alaska Native identification in American colleges and universities....and to affirm and ensure American Indian/Alaska Native identity in the hiring process. We are asking that colleges and universities 'Require documentation of enrollment in a state or federally recognized nation/tribe with preference given to those who meet this criterion.'"[9] David Cornsilk, assistant director of admissions at Bacone College in Muskogee, Oklahoma, provided this rationale for such a policy:

> I believe in membership as the foundation of sovereignty...I believe the authority of the tribe, the right of the tribe, stems from the group, the community...I don't believe in the right of self-identification. I believe that's an assault on the right of the group. (Quoted in Reynolds 1993: A3)

Tim Giago, editor of *Indian Country Today* and the *Lakota Times*, affirmed the tribal membership approach to establishing Indian authenticity, and underlined the issue of resources in making distinctions between "real" Indians and others who claim Indian ancestry:

> It was in the 1970s that people claiming to be Indian began to take jobs intended for Indians and to write books claiming to be authorities on Indians. These instant "wannabees" did us far more harm than good. Not only did they often give out misleading information about Indians, they also took jobs that left many qualified genuine Native Americans out in the cold....before you can truly be considered an Indian you must become an enrolled member of a tribe. I think most Indians would agree that this is the only way you can truly be accepted as Indian. (1991: 3)

Alphonse Ortiz echoed these concerns about scarce resources allocated to self-identified recipients:

> These are people who have no business soaking up jobs and grants, people who have made no claim to being Indian up to their early adulthood, and then when there's something to be gained they're opportunists of the rankest stripe, of the worst order....we resent these people who just come in and when the going's good skim the riches off the surface. (Quoted in Reynolds 1993: A1)

This emphasis on official enrollment (membership) in recognized tribes in determining Indian ethnicity is at odds with the way in which most Americans (and perhaps most American Indians) acquire their ethnicity. Though estimates vary, somewhere between two-thirds and one-half of American Indians counted in the 1980 and 1990 censuses were enrolled members of recognized tribes.[10] Thus, the official enrollment rule would throw into question the ethnicity of a significant proportion of Americans who designed their "race" as Indian in the U.S. Census, not to mention the millions more who identified an Indian ethnic ancestry on census forms.[11] As we have seen, in contemporary America, ethnicity is a negotiated status, determined by the interplay between external ascription and individual self-identification. The AA-IANP's reliance on external (tribal) ascription represents a challenge to the notion that ethnicity is, at least in part, an individual choice (a notion which, as we shall see below, is shared by the U.S. Census Bureau).[12]

The discrepancy between the narrow, ascriptive tribal enrollment criteria for Indian ethnicity and the broader, self-designation approach to determining Indianness is not merely the eccentric policy of a single organization (the AAIANP). The personal accounts of individuals who have come to identify themselves as Native Americans in their adult years, and outside the boundaries of a recognized tribe, report skepticism and antagonism about their ethnicity from Indians and non-Indians alike. For instance, Jim (Hoppy) Hopkins, a thirty-five-year-old firefighter in Orange County, California, became Jim Red Eagle (Wamni Watak'pe) in 1992. He made the decision to change his name "to one that has significance and meaning...reclaiming another part of my heritage" (Red Eagle 1992: 15-16). He reported his decision was delayed by family resistance: "I know that a negative reaction from my relations is the overwhelming reason why I did not make the change years ago." Describing his return to his native roots at age forty, Z.G. Standing Bear reported a similar reaction from relatives when he decided to change his name: "'What are you trying to prove?' one said, 'all that stuff is over and done with'" (Standing Bear 1988: 366). Both men felt they had to account for their ethnicity. Red Eagle was motivated to write an article in an Orange County Fire Department newsletter, and Standing Bear developed strategies to anticipate the questions of non-Indian colleagues and students:

> I went on a journey back in 1984. I'd finished a particular phase of my spiritual training where you're not supposed to cut your hair. So I let my hair grow and have braids. Now when I go to give a talk, like to criminal justice groups, I have to explain my appearance, otherwise they can't get past the braids.[13]

Given the constructed nature of ethnicity and reality generally, there is no paucity of answers to questions about who is really an Indian, and there is a dearth of consensus about which answers are sound. The debates can be trying to the targets of authenticity inquiries, as critical author and activist Ward Churchill's comments reveal:

> I'm forever being asked not only my "tribe," but my "percentage of Indian blood." I've given the matter a lot of thought, and find that I prefer to make the computation based on all of me rather than just the fluid coursing through my veins. Calculated this way, I can report that I am precisely 52.5 pounds Indian—about 35 pounds Creek and the remainder Cherokee—88 pounds Teutonic, 43.5 pounds some sort of English, and all the rest "undetermined." Maybe that last part should just be described as "human." It all seems rather silly as a means of assessing who I am, don't you think? (Quoted by Jaimes 1992a: 123)

While many methods of calculating individual Indian or tribal authenticity are, unfortunately, ludicrous and sometimes offensive (analyses of urine and earwax, chemical tasting abilities) (Snipp 1989: 30-1), the enterprise is by no means capricious. Calculating authenticity turns out to be deadly serious in the many cases where individual and community resources hang in the balance. These cases routinely involve such important matters as child custody rights, health benefits, scholarships, legitimate means of livelihood, land claims, mineral and resource rights and royalty payments, political and criminal jurisdiction, taxation, and a myriad of other personal and financial matters. The truth is embedded in the common sociological fact: while ethnicity is socially and politically constructed, and is thus arbitrary, variable, and constantly negotiated, it is no less real in its consequences.

Official Measures of "Indianness"

Debates over legitimate Native American ethnic boundaries reflect the interplay between micro and macro politics. The interests and political processes in native communities are played out in the larger federal Indian policy arena. Both Native American and federal politics occur in a context of economic interests and resource competition, both of which are often crucial to native community survival. It is important to keep this in mind when listening to various voices speaking on behalf of one set of criteria or another. Also important to acknowledge is the legitimating and legal power of "official" federal criteria of Indianness.

There are many official and unofficial yardsticks for measuring the Indianness of individuals and groups—all reflect a definition of and concern about Indian ethnic authenticity. There are federal definitions of Indians and tribes, state definitions, tribal definitions, and individual definitions. The literature surveying and critiquing various definitions and practices for determining Indian legality and authenticity is immense (e.g., Hagan 1985; Cohen 1982; Snipp 1989). A broad survey of definitions is less useful here than some examples followed by observations about what is common and controversial about them. Underlying both the debates about and the solutions to the Indian question is a set of simultaneously accepted and challenged assumptions about primordiality and authenticity.

One example of an official definition of Indianness is a currently very powerful and equally controversial list of criteria applied to groups petitioning the federal government for formal recognition as Indian tribes. As noted above, in 1978, the federal government issued a set of seven criteria for tribal recognition to be administered by the Office of Federal Acknowledgment in the Bureau of Indian Affairs in the Interior Department.[14] These regulations were formalized at the close of three decades of work by the Indian Claims Commission (ICC), hearing and disposing of mainly historical land claims of various Indian communities. In preparing cases for the ICC a number of groups reorganized themselves, conducted historical research, and sought official tribal status.[15] Other Indian communities also joined the petitioning process. By 1997 there were 185 petitions, of which thirty-seven were resolved and 148 still pending (U.S. Bureau of Indian Affairs 1997).

According to Acknowledgment Office criteria, in order to qualify for official recognition, petitioning groups must provide evidence to show that "a single Indian group has existed since its first sustained contact with European cultures on a continuous basis to the present; that its members live in a distinct, autonomous community perceived by others as Indian; that it has maintained some sort of authority with a governing system by which its members abide; that all its members can be traced genealogically to an historic tribe" (Quinn 1990: 152). This detailed list stresses historical, social, and political continuity and a clearly identified continuous membership, and reflects the anthropological roots of the Acknowledgment Office's criteria. For instance, Fried's (1975) widely cited definition of a tribe also emphasizes boundaries and networks of kinship, economic production and consumption, defense, language, and culture.

In sharp contrast to these definitions stressing historical continuity and cultural content are the more limited, self-defining criteria of the Indian Reorganization Act of 1934, which encouraged Indian communities to form tribal corporations for purposes of economic development and cultural revitalization. Briefly stated, the IRA defined a tribe simply as "any Indian tribe, organized band, pueblo, or the Indians residing on one reservation" (Cohen 1982: 13). A comparison of this inclusive IRA approach, which basically requires only a reservation location for any group of Indians to be a tribe, with the Acknowledgment Office's extensive set of criteria, illustrates the widely varied rules of recognition that have been applied by only one federal agency—the Indian Service.

Further variation occurs when comparisons are made across federal government agencies. For instance, the current Census Bureau's official definition of who is an Indian depends entirely on self-identification, while the Indian Health Service requires enrollment in a recognized tribe or possession of a particular blood quantum. Even the most restrictive of these federal rules may seem lax when compared to the specific enrollment rules of particular recognized tribes, which can specify amount or type of ancestry or particular residency requirements for membership.

Unofficial definitions of group or individual Indianness are similarly diverse and varying in stringency. But no matter the stringency of the rules, questions of authenticity persist, sometimes even when official criteria are met. Ironically, in some instances the burdens of proof can become more and more onerous as one moves closer inside Indian communities. Divisions among tribal populations on reservations along age, kinship, religion, or degree of ancestry (e.g., "mixed blood," "full blood") lines, are often reported as the bases for claims and counterclaims about individual ethnic legitimacy and/or rights to represent tribal interests (e.g., Forbes 1981; Thompson and Peterson 1975; Churchill 1991). Commenting on the disunity such internal distinctions can cause, Tim Giago, who on many occasions has criticized lax definitions of Indianness, nevertheless asks: "Don't we have enough problems trying to unite without....additional headaches? Why must people be categorized as full-bloods, mixed-bloods, etc.?" (cited in Jaimes 1992a: 129).

Who *Should* be Indian?

Imbedded in many discussions of formal and informal definitions of Indian authenticity and membership regulations, there resides a question about whether the rules defining Indianness and tribal membership should be relaxed or tightened, that is, made more inclusionary or more exclusionary. For instance, Trosper describes the adoption of tighter, more exclusionary enrollment rules by the Flathead Tribe of Montana in response to pressures to "terminate" (i.e., dissolve the federal trust relationship) the tribe in the 1950s. Federal officials charged that Flathead's Salish and Kootenai tribal members were acculturated and no longer needed federal services or protection. This prompted a move by tribal leaders to pursue a kind of ethnic purification strategy by adopting a stricter set of blood quantum rules to designate membership. Thornton (1987b) reports an opposite, loosening or inclusionary strategy on the part of some nonreservation-based groups, mainly in Oklahoma, where such groups as the Cherokees or Choctaws face less competition among members for shares of tribally held or land-based resources. In these instances, inclusion can have positive political consequences in an electoral system, since a relatively large percentage of the Oklahoma population (12.9 percent in the 1990 Census) is American Indian.

In recent years, there has been introduced an increasingly exclusionary approach to the issue of what constitutes "Indian" art. The ensuing controversy points once again to the resource competition which underlies much of the debate about ethnic authenticity, and not just in the case of American Indians, though that is the subject at hand. The Indian Arts and Crafts Act of 1990 (IACA) requires the certification of Indian artists, in part, in response to complaints (by art buyers and artists) about foreign and non-Indian competition in the lucrative trade in American Indian art.[16] The U.S. federal government attempted to set standards of ethnic artistic authenticity by legislatively defining genuine Indian art and ethnicity. According to the IACA, in order for art to be "Indian art," the artist must prove Indian ancestry and must be "certified as an Indian artisan by a [federally recognized] Indian tribe" (*United States Statutes at Large* 1990: 4663). By this legal definition, nonenrolled or noncertified artists of Indian ancestry cannot produce Indian art, nor can artists who are members of non-recognized tribes. The Act has led a number of Indian artists to seek official tribal status (some have refused), and has excluded some recognized American Indian artists from galleries, museums, and exhibits (*Kansas City Star* 1991: J-5; Jaimes 1992a: 131). Similar local restrictions on who can sell Indian art and where it can be sold have caused bitter divisions among American Indians and other minority communities in the Southwest (Evans-Pritchard 1987).

Jaimes (1992a: 131) is highly critical of blood quantum rules for determining Indian authenticity, labeling the 1990 American Indian Arts and Crafts Act as a "contemporary reassertion of eugenics principles," which requires proof of Indian ancestry issued by federally recognized tribes in order to sell Indian art. And Forbes (1990: 48) finds the intrusion of authorities into the ethnic designation process a violation of "the human right of [ethnic] self-identification....Self-identification ought, it seems to me, to be a basic right upon which legislators, clerks, officials, and teachers cannot infringe."

Some critics call for the entire abolishment of ancestry or blood quantum regulation of tribal membership, arguing that such rules, particularly when applied by the federal government, tend to heighten tension among Native Americans, creating disunity and suspicion. For instance, activist Russell Means raises questions about the meaning and legitimacy of ancestry tests of Indianness:

> Our treaties say nothing about your having to be such-and-such a degree of blood in order to be covered....when the federal government made its guarantees to our nations in exchange for our land, it committed to provide certain services to us as we defined ourselves. As nations, and as a *people*. This seems to have been forgotten. Now we have Indian people who spend most of their time trying to prevent other Indian people from being recognized as such, just so that a few more crumbs—crumbs from the federal table—may be available to them, personally. I don't have to tell you that this isn't the Indian way of doing things. The Indian way would be to get together and demand what is coming to each and every one of us, instead of trying to cancel each other out. We are acting like colonized peoples, like subject peoples. (In Jaimes 1992a: 139)

Like Means, Stiffarm and Lane challenge the assumptions underlying ancestry and blood quantum tests of Indianness and tribal membership, asking whether American Indians

> will continue to allow themselves to be defined mainly by their colonizers, in exclusively racial/familial terms (as "tribes"), or whether they will (re)assume responsibility for advancing the more general and coherently political definition of themselves they once held, as *nations* defining membership/citizenship in terms of culture, socialization, and commitment to the good of the group. (1992: 45)

Stiffarm and Lane wonder whether American Indian tribes cannot take seriously their semi-sovereign status with regard to citizenship, bringing "'outsiders'...into their membership by way of marriage, birth, adoption, and naturalization" (1992: 45).

Such a strategy would certainly open the door to an expansion of Indian ethnic membership, as well as tribal citizenship, which might be resisted by Indian communities faced with distributing already scarce resources and by a federal bureaucracy attempting to keep the lid on or reduce Indian expenditures.[17] However, many tribes may be forced to come to terms with their own blood quantum rules in the very near future. The rate of racial intermarriage for American Indians is the highest of all American racial categories, with fewer than half of American Indians marrying other Indians, compared with racial endogamy rates of 95 percent and higher for whites, blacks, and Asians (Snipp 1989: 157; Sandefur and McKinnell 1986). The consequence of this intermarriage is an increase in the number of Indian/non-Indian offspring with ever-diminishing degrees of Indian ancestry. One result of tribal blood quantum restrictions, even as low as one-quarter, is that an increasing proportion of these children will not qualify for tribal membership even though one or both of their parents are tribal members, and despite their having lived on the reservation since birth.

Conclusion

Disputes about ethnic authenticity appear to be part of the ethnic boundary formation, maintenance, and change process. Authenticity controversies can arise over individual claims to ethnic ancestry or membership, over group claims to ethnic distinctiveness or rights reserved for particular ancestry or cultural communities, over the purity of particular ethnic products or objects and who has the right to control their disposition or marketing, and over the rules for designating official ethnic groups and their rights. In the contemporary world, these debates are often politically regulated and often become official disputes that require adjudication in legal arenas.

It is important to note that questions of authenticity are not limited to the realm of ethnicity. We see authenticity of identity, behavior, or group membership challenged in other social realms as well: "Who is really poor?" "Who is really a Christian?" "Who is really a man?" Some of these challenges to poverty, religiosity, or manliness are posed in official settings (e.g., in a welfare office), sometimes in unofficial settings (in church or on the sports field), but they all reflect the construction, reconstruction, and deconstruction of identity and community, and the search for "false faces" that seems to preoccupy postmodern society.

Notes

1. Estimates of the exact number of indigenous North Americans range from a low of 1 million (Kroeber 1939) to as many as 18 million (Dobyns 1983).
2. Some scholars and activists argue that American Indians should not be described as an "ethnic" group, and that to do so relegates indigenous peoples to the status of immigrant minority populations with no rights to sovereignty or nationhood (see Trask 1990, 1991; Morris 1989); others argue that in the arena of American politics, American Indians can make claims *both* as aboriginal nations with treaty rights *and* as an ethnic minority group with rights similar to other minority populations (see Deloria and Lytle 1984; Stiffarm and Lane 1992). Following Weber (1978) and Barth (1969), I define an ethnic group as a community of people who see themselves as descended from a common ancestor and whom others consider part of a distinct community; thus both Indian tribes and the larger supratribal "Indian" category can be considered ethnic groups.
3. While this paper will focus on the specific case of Native Americans, I believe that the issues of ethnic membership boundaries, community rebuilding and renewal, and individual and cultural authenticity are characteristic of debates underway in many ethnic, racial, and nationalist movements and communities around the world. The interplay among political policy, individual ethnic identification, and ethnic activism tends to raise questions of rights, duties, and membership in many communities and countries. Thus the case of American Indian ethnic renewal has implications for a wide variety of indigenous and non-indigenous communities, ranging from native rights movements throughout the Americas, in Hawaii and the Pacific, Asia, Africa, and Europe, to the definition of and rights of newly resurgent nationalist groups in the states and territories of the former Soviet bloc, to the fictive national boundaries of postcolonial Africa and Asia, and across both the North and the South globally.
4. The policy that was swept away was widely known as "termination" (or assimilation) policy. In its place was instituted a "self-determination" policy which affirmed Indian treaty rights and self-government, and renounced assimilation as a goal of federal Indian policy (see Fixico 1986).
5. I will use the terms "American Indian," "Native American," "Indian," and "native" interchangeably in this paper. This varying usage is consistent with formal and informal designations of Americans of indigenous ancestry by themselves and others, and these terms are used widely and interchangeably by both native and non-native researchers and writers (e.g., see Snipp 1992, footnote 1).
6. See the introduction and first chapter of James Clifton's (1990) edited work, *The Invented Indian*, as well as the chapters by some of his contributors (especially David Henige and Stephen Feraca), for a particularly virulent challenge to the ethnic authenticity of a variety of American Indian individuals and groups.
7. William T. Hagan also raises the question of personal benefit from Indian self-representation: "According to Highwater, the 'grand climax' of his 'professional and personal life' came when he was adopted by Blackfeet in Canada....Highwater used the term 'professional and personal life' advisedly, because he had used his Indian ancestry to advance himself professionally as an author and TV producer" (1985: 320). For additional discussions of Highwater's ancestry, see *Akwesasne Notes* issues 16(4): 10-12 (1984) and 17(6): 5 (1985).
8. The article by Wendy Rose (who is identified as a Hopi in the biographical sketch section) appears in a volume in South End Press's Race and Resistance Series, *The State of Native America: Genocide, Colonization, and Resistance*, edited by M. Annette Jaimes. The tone of the volume is set by Evelyn Hu-DeHart in the concluding

paragraph of the Preface: "For those who wish to understand the anguish of native peoples as the country and the world prepare to celebrate the arrival of Columbus and the Europeans, and for those who wish to know the merits of expanding our basically Eurocentric curriculum to a more pluralistic, inclusive one, this book is a good place to start" (Jaimes 1992: x). In contrast, Alice Kehoe's article appears in *The Invented Indian*, edited by James Clifton, who sets the tone for this volume with introductory comments about the Menominee Indian tribe's restoration efforts in the 1970s, led in part by a group of activists known as the Menominee Warriors Society, whom Clifton characterizes as "mainly young, urban, lower-class males and the women who adored them....[who] were covertly coached in their deftly played confrontational tactics by a political splinter-group—Wisconsin's tiny band of zealous Trotskyites....joined by a perfectly weird medley of the other protest groupies who invariably show up when storms brew in Indian Country" (1990: 8).

9. Press release, Association of American Indian and Alaskan Native Professors, June 28, 1993. The concerns of AAIANP parallel a wider skepticism about ethnic claims in general (not just those of Native Americans) when rights, jobs, and resources are at stake. In discussing the minority status of a particular individual, a fellow academic once told me, "I don't know if s/he's really a _____, or has just found a horse to ride to tenure."

10. The Indian Health Service conducted a survey of federally recognized tribes to obtain tribal enrollment figures in 1986, and counted 746,175 enrolled members in 213 tribes in the lower 48 states (see Lister 1987). This is a significant undercount, since there are more than 350 recognized tribes. However, most of the more sizable tribes (e.g., the Navajos and Cherokees of Oklahoma) were included in the survey. The 1980 and 1990 census figures for American Indians were 1,364,033 and 1,873,536 respectively (see U.S. Bureau of the Census 1991a, Table 1).

11. In his analysis of the 1980 census, Karl Eschbach (1992: 42) found that an even smaller percentage of individuals reporting an Indian race were reservation residents (about one-quarter), further removing the majority of self-identified Indians from their reservation roots.

12. Sometimes the nuances and differences in perspective concerning what constitutes authentic Indianness are difficult to negotiate. Two cases come to mind. The first case involved the reaction of a Mohawk woman's tribe to her marriage to a Pottawatomie man: "When we got married, I received a letter from the tribe. It said they were very happy that I'd gotten married. They wished that I'd married an Indian. My husband hit the overhead...what they had meant was in the tribe...[husband speaking: "The letter stated 'married a non-Indian'"]....I guess they never heard of a Pottawatomie" (Chicago American Indian Oral History Project, Interview 001, Leroy and Pat Wesaw, January 5, 1983). The second case involved the following discussion of tribal politics: "Our tribe is split. There's two factions. Then another guy was put in as tribal chairman who wasn't really even a native person. His mother was a Pawnee who was counted as a Wichita during a census.... Well, if he's anything, he's a Pawnee, but he looks white, he doesn't even look Indian" (anonymous interview, summer, 1993).

13. Telephone interview with Z.G. Standing Bear, June 25, 1993, Valdosta, Georgia.

14. Part 83 of Title 25 of the *Code of Federal Regulations*.

15. Hagan (1985) argues that Indian Claims Commission litigation contributed to the rejuvenation of many tribes, by way of financial settlements which increased the value of tribal membership and left tribes more firmly entrenched as government wards.

16. My thanks to Matt Snipp for pointing out the advantages to art collectors and buyers of having legally guaranteed "genuine" Indian art, and for noting the racism inherent in an assertion that the ability to produce certain kinds of art ("primitive?") is somehow racially or biologically linked. On the other side of the issue is the encroachment of non-Indian-produced and imported art into the Indian art market and the implications for the livelihoods of Indian artists of these often cheap imports. For instance, while visiting a craft shop near the Northern Cheyenne reservation in Montana, a tribe whose members have long been known for their skill at beadwork, I picked up a small beaded necklace and pouch only to find a "Made in China" label inside. The shop was run by a native person whose livelihood obviously depended on the sale of both imported and native crafts. However, the low price of this imported beaded item clearly undercut the work of native craftspersons. The dilemma posed by this situation was, in part, what the 1990 Arts and Crafts Act attempted to resolve.

17. For instance, in 1986, the Reagan administration put forth a proposal to adopt an official 1/4 blood quantum definition of "Indian" for the purposes of receiving services from the Indian Health Service. Tribal organizations, led by the National Congress of American Indians, protested and lobbied effectively to stop the effort. There is no reason to believe that this will be the last such attempt (see Jaimes 1992: 133-35).

References

Barth, F. 1969. *Ethnic Groups and Boundaries*. Boston: Little, Brown.

Churchill, W. 1991. "Genocide in Arizona? The 'Navajo-Hopi Land Dispute' in Perspective." Pp. 104-146 in *Critical Issues in Native North America*, Vol. 2, edited by W. Churchill. Copenhagen: International Work Group for Indigenous Affairs, Document No. 68.

Clifton, J., ed. 1990. *The Invented Indian: Cultural Fictions and Government Policies*. New Brunswick, NJ: Transaction Publishers.

Cohen, F.S. 1982. *Felix S. Cohen's Handbook of Federal Indian Law*. Charlottesville, VA: Michie Bobbs-Merrill.

Collas, S. 1994. "Transgressing Racial Boundaries: The Maintenance of the Racial Order." Paper presented at the annual meeting of the American Sociological Association, Los Angeles, August. Mimeographed.

Deloria, V., Jr., and C. Lytle. 1984. *The Nations Within: The Past and Future of American Indian Sovereignty*. New York: Pantheon Books.

Dobyns, H. 1983. *Their Number Become Thinned*. Knoxville: University of Tennessee Press.

Driver, H.E. 1961. *Indians of North America*. Chicago: University of Chicago Press.

Egan, T. 1992. "Indians Become Foes in Bid for Tribal Rights." *New York Times* (September 9): 26.

Eschbach, K. 1992. "Shifting Boundaries: Regional Variation in Patterns of Identification as American Indians." Unpublished doctoral dissertation, Harvard University.

———. 1995. "The Enduring and Vanishing American Indian: American Indian Population Growth and Intermarriage in 1990." *Ethnic and Racial Studies* 18: 89-108.

Evans-Pritchard, D. 1987. "The Portal Case: Authenticity, Tourism, Traditions, and the Law." *Journal of American Folklore* 100: 287-296.

Fantasia, R. 1988. *Cultures of Solidarity*. Berkeley: University of California Press.

Feagin, J.R. 1991. "The Continuing Significance of Race: Antiblack Discrimination in Public Places." *American Sociological Review* 56: 101-116.

Fixico, D. 1986. *Termination and Relocation: Federal Indian Policy, 1945-1960.* Albuquerque: University of New Mexico Press.

Forbes, J. 1981. *Native Americans and Nixon: Presidential Politics and Minority Self-Determination, 1969-1972.* Native American Politics Series, No. 2. Los Angeles: American Indian Studies Center.

———. 1990. "The Manipulation of Race, Cast and Identity: Classifying Afroamericans, Native-Americans and Red-Black People." *Journal of Ethnic Studies* 17: 1-51.

Fried, M.H. 1975. *The Notion of Tribe.* Menlo Park, CA: Cummings Publishing.

Giago, T. 1991. "Big Increases in 1990 Census not Necessarily Good for Tribes." *Lakota Times* (March 12).

Hacker, A. 1992. *Two Nations: Black and White, Separate, Hostile, and Unequal.* New York: Charles Scribner's Sons.

Hagan, W.T. 1985. "Full Blood, Mixed Blood, Generic, and Ersatz: The Problem of Indian Identity." *Arizona and the West* 27(4): 309-326.

Harris, D. 1994. "The 1990 Census Count of American Indians: What Do the Numbers Really Mean?" *Social Science Quarterly* 75: 580-593.

Harris, M. 1964. *Patterns of Race in the Americas.* New York: W.W. Norton.

Highwater, J. 1980. "Second-Class Indians." *American Indian Journal* 6(July): 7-9.

———. 1981. *The Primal Mind: Vision and Reality in Indian America.* New York: Harper and Row.

Jaimes, M.A., ed. 1992. *The State of Native America: Genocide, Colonization, and Resistance.* Boston: South End Press.

———. 1992a. "Federal Indian Identification Policy: An Usurpation of Indigenous Sovereignty in North America." Pp. 123-128 in *The State of Native America: Genocide, Colonization, and Resistance*, edited by M.A. Jaimes. Boston: South End Press.

Josephy, A.P., Jr., J. Nagel, and T. Johnson. 1998. *Red Power: The American Indians' Fight for Freedom.* rev. ed. Lincoln: University of Nebraska Press.

Kansas City Star. 1991. "Indian Art Protection Law may end up Hurting the Artists." (August 4): J-5.

Kehoe, A.B. 1990. "Primal Gaia: Primitivists and Plastic Medicine Men." Pp. 193-209 in *The Invented Indian: Cultural Fictions and Government Policies*, edited by J. Clifton. New Brunswick, NJ: Transaction Publishers.

Klein, J. 1995. "NAGPRA, Consultation and the Field Museum." *Registrars' Quarterly* (Fall): 7-8, 16.

Kroeber, A.L. 1939. *Cultural and Natural Areas of Native North America.* Vol. 38 of *American Archaeology and Ethnology.* Berkeley: University of California Press.

Lister, E. 1987. "Tribal Membership Rates and Requirements." Unpublished table. Washington, DC: U.S. Indian Health Service.

Mankiller, W. 1993. "An Open Letter to Governor of Georgia." *Indian Country Today* (May 26): A4.

Meriam, L., ed. 1928. *The Problem of Indian Administration.* Baltimore, MD: Johns Hopkins University Press.

Morris, G.T. 1989. "The International Status of Indigenous Nations within the United States." Pp. 1-14 in *Critical Issues in Native North America*, edited by W. Churchill. Copenhagen: International Work Group for Indigenous Affairs, Document No. 62.

Passel, J.S., and P.A. Berman. 1986. "Quality of 1980 Census Data for American Indians." *Social Biology* 33(3-4): 163-182.

Quinn, W.W., Jr. 1990. "The Southeast Syndrome: Notes on Indian Descendant Recruitment Organizations and their Perceptions of Native American Culture." *American Indian Quarterly* 14(2): 147-154.

Red Eagle, J. 1992. "The Importance of a Name." *Fire Line* 6: 15-16.

Reynolds, J. 1993. "Indian Writers: Real or Imagined." *Indian Country Today* (September 8): A1, A3.

Rose, W. 1992. "The Great Pretenders: Further Reflections on Whiteshamanism." Pp. 403-421 in *The State of Native America: Genocide, Colonization, and Resistance*, edited by M.A. Jaimes. Boston: South End Press.

Sandefur, G.D., and T. McKinnell. 1986. "American Indian Intermarriage." *Social Science Research* 15: 347-371.

Snipp, C.M. 1989. *American Indians: The First of This Land*. New York: Russell Sage Foundation.

————. 1992. "Sociological Perspectives on American Indians." *Annual Review of Sociology* 18: 351-371.

Standing Bear, Z.G. 1988. "Questions of Assertion, Diversity, and Spirituality: Simultaneously Becoming a Minority and a Sociologist." *American Sociologist* 19(4): 363-371.

Stiffarm, L.A., and P. Lane, Jr. 1992. "The Demography of Native North America: A Question of American Indian Survival." Pp. 23-53 in *The State of Native America: Genocide, Colonization, and Resistance*, edited by M.A. Jaimes. Boston: South End Press.

Swanton, J. 1952. *The Indian Tribes of North America*. Washington, DC: The Smithsonian Institution Press.

Tallman, V. 1993. "Repatriation Demanded Across the Country." *Indian Country Today* (September 22): A7.

Thompson, B., and J.H. Peterson, Jr. 1975. "Mississippi Choctaw Identity: Genesis and Change." Pp. 179-196 in *The New Ethnicity: Perspectives from Ethnology*, edited by J.W. Bennett. St. Paul, MN: West Publishing Company.

Thornton, R. 1987a. *American Indian Holocaust and Survival*. Norman: University of Oklahoma Press.

————. 1987b. "Tribal History, Tribal Population, and Tribal Membership Requirements." Newberry Library Research Conference Report No. 8. Chicago: Newberry Library.

Trask, H-K. 1990. "Politics in the Pacific Islands: Imperialism and Native Self-Determination." *Amerasia* 16: 1-19.

————. 1991. "Natives and Anthropologists: The Colonial Struggle." *The Contemporary Pacific* 3: 159-167.

United States Statutes at Large. 1990. 101st Congress, 2nd Session, "Vol. 104," Part 6: 4662-4665. Washington, DC: Government Printing Office.

U.S. Bureau of Indian Affairs. 1997. "Summary Status of Acknowledgment Cases (as of May 7, 1992)." Unpublished table. Washington, DC: Office of Federal Acknowledgment.

U.S. Bureau of the Census. 1991a. "Census Bureau Completes Distribution of 1990 Redistricting Tabulations to States." Census Bureau Press Release CB91-100, Monday, March 11.

————. 1991b. "Census Bureau Releases 1990 Census Counts on Specific Racial Groups." Census Bureau Press Release CB91-215, Wednesday, June 12.

Weber, M. 1978. *Economy and Society: An Outline of Interpretative Sociology. Vol.1. G. Roth and C. Wittich, eds. Berkeley: University of California Press.*

Part 2

Identity and Dissolution

5

Identity, Commodification, and Consumer Culture

Robert G. Dunn

The rise of identity politics over the last thirty years or so has inspired a large body of scholarly discourse—theoretical, political, and historical—on questions of identity and difference. These writings have both driven and been fueled by a growing theoretical interest in the problems of subjectivity and agency, particularly in the areas of epistemology and culture. Much of this work reflects a loosely postmodern outlook and has often drawn on the theoretical insights of poststructuralism.

The social movements and global changes driving the politicization of identity have led most writers and theoreticians to frame issues of group and category-based identity more or less directly and immediately in the terms given by these developments themselves, including how they are experienced and constructed by group-identified subjects. The marginalization and subsequent resurgence of collective identities of race, ethnicity, gender, and sexual preference have raised issues of group identifications, power, and recognition within a "postcolonial" context of expanding opportunities and new inequalities linked to domestic and global capitalism. A less distinct but more complex postmodern politics of difference growing out of identity politics has likewise shared a

The editor gratefully acknowledges the University of Minnesota Press for permission to use previously published material from Robert G. Dunn, *Identity Crises: A Social Critique of Postmodernity*, published by the University of Minnesota Press, and copyright 1998 by the Regents of the University of Minnesota.

concern for group-based affiliations and the need for collective political and cultural struggle but in a context of "multiculturalism" and the
transformative possibilities of multiple and fluid identities.

Although the importance and impact of identity and difference/multi-
cultural politics can hardly be overestimated, the problem of identity in
the contemporary world extends ultimately beyond the significance of
these particular movements and their cultural and political practices and
representations. Identity issues are at the very core of postmodernism as
a theoretical and epistemological movement as well as of postmodernity
as a sociohistorical condition. I argue that the politics of identity and
difference are only one manifestation of a generalized and structurally
induced *destabilization* of identity occurring in the West and perhaps
throughout the world. This destabilization is an effect of the convergence
of structural and cultural changes linked to recent transformations in
advanced capitalism as concentrated most visibly in the United States.

It is necessary, therefore, to address contemporary problems of
identity outside of the limited frameworks of identity politics and multiculturalism. My own treatment of identity adopts a sociohistorical perspective, examining structural and cultural changes effecting (however
unevenly) whole populations. The analysis I present shifts attention from
group-centered identifications and alliances to salient changes in general processes and structures of identity formation in highly developed
commodity society. In this respect, I wish to examine major features of
the impact of a consumption-oriented culture on historical changes in
identity and identity formation, looking specifically at the relationship
between cultural commodification and the attenuation of self and social
relations. By introducing historical and structural perspectives into current debates, I hope to delineate a more comprehensive and systematic
approach to the problems of identity in our time.

The Commodification of Culture: Modern and Postmodern Trends

The makings of a commercialized culture organized around the visual
senses and the possession and use of "symbolic goods" first emerged in
the modernizing urban environment of nineteenth-century Europe, most
notably in France. The Haussmannization of Paris, with its broad boule-
vards and other expansive public spaces, symbolized not only the growing influence of the bourgeoisie but a new visual awareness concentrated
in the worlds of fashion, leisure, recreation, consumerism, the art market,
and other elements of an ascendant middle class society (Clark 1984).

The visual pleasures of bourgeois Paris would soon be transformed by the powers of the camera into full-blown capitalist modernity in the form of what Guy Debord (1977) called "the spectacle." The spectacle was comprised of visual images "fuse(d) in a common stream," constituting a "pseudo-world apart" from lived social relations. Debord understood the visual mode of perception as a descendant of the commodity form, whereby the "degradation of *being* into *having*" was followed by "a generalized sliding of *having* into *appearing*" (paragraphs 2, 3, and 17; emphasis in the original). In this view, a link is established between the economic and social processes of commodification and the emergence of a culture constituted in visual images. Following the camera, in more recent times an historical succession of technologies (film, television, video, CD-rom) have appropriated the visual experiences and pleasures accompanying an expanding world of commodities.

The increasing containment of cultural expression and meaning within the commodity form has extended "the spectacle" into the deepest recesses of individual experience. The logic of visual technology intensifies the culture of consumption by tying the privatizing tendencies already inherent in commodities to the consumption of visual images. The dramatic spread of commodity culture in the twentieth century is attributable to the capacity of such media to colonize cultural experience within the realm of privatized consumption.

While the exchange of goods and services within the cultural framework of modernity served to engender a landscape of visual stimulation, the triumph of television and video have entirely transformed the relationship between visual experience and material objects. In the argument of Jean Baudrillard (1981), relations of economic exchange have now thoroughly penetrated culture, producing what he calls the "commodity/sign form." This is a structure of *semiotic* exchange involving both a commodification of culture, in which cultural constructions are reduced to the status of commodities, and what might be called a "culturalization" of the commodity, in which commodities are constructed semiotically within a cultural language of consumption, as perhaps best exemplified by television advertising.

The point at which commodities function as signs while signs circulate as commodities marks a reversal of a significant moment in modernity in which aesthetic expression, productively but only momentarily autonomized in its own realm, is reintegrated into the spheres of production and consumption through the technological reproduction of images.

This "aestheticization" of society has been theorized as a principal consequence of commodity culture and has been widely characterized as a watershed of postmodernity (Featherstone 1991; Huyssen 1986; Jameson 1984, 1991). It is worth noting a troubling paradox of this whole movement: just as the aesthetic dimension is reintegrated into everyday social life, the world of images seems to acquire its own autonomy within an expanding universe of media entertainment and advertising. Thus, while the aesthetic dimension loses its formerly privileged position in the world of modern art, the new *vehicle* of aesthetic value—the commercialized image—is elevated by technologies of reproduction and commodities to a plane of purely functional, instrumental logic, re-autonomizing the aesthetic dimension within the framework of consumer capitalism.

In a society suffused with exchange value the very logic of culture undergoes dramatic change. This is most notably evident in the blurring of boundaries between "high" and "popular" culture, seen as a collapse of evaluative norms which enforce the separation of "serious" artistic production governed by specialized elites from popular expression and corporate-based products mass-marketed as "entertainment." These are conditions under which the modernist conception of culture as a specialized, class-based realm of aesthetic and intellectual practice gives way, oddly enough, to the traditional anthropological conception: culture as coterminous with the realm of everyday life and social practices. Paralleling the disintegration of the boundaries between high and popular culture is the gradual dissolution of representation as a distinctly *separate realm* of signification. However, whereas for preliterate groups cultural and aesthetic meaning was symbolically attached to natural and hand-crafted objects, today these same values have been transmuted into the semiotic attributes of media images and other commodities, thereby losing their symbolic character. Relatedly, we can now speak of a distinct "cultural economy" (Lash 1990), an institutional merging of cultural productions and commercial interests. Thus, the commodity/ sign form for all practical purposes obliterates distinctions between the commercial functions of the economy and the production and appropriation of cultural experiences and meanings. This can be illustrated on the one hand by mass advertising, which appropriates popular forms of experience and expression, and on the other hand by the recontextualization of high culture within a framework of consumption—whether in media, concert, museum, or other format—along with high culture's increasing dependence on corporate sponsorship and marketing strategies.

The long path of cultural commodification through modernity to postmodernity thereby leads to a highly commercialized field of new kinds of objects and experiences, constituted in the circulation and consumption of commodities, specifically the commodities' visual characteristics. It is the consequences of this development for identity and identity formation that I wish to explore in the remainder of this paper.

The Imperatives of Consumption:
Promises and Threats of a Postmodern Subjectivity

Identities in modern society—while embattled, alienated, and proliferating—have tended nonetheless to remain connected to the social roles and relationships of family, religion, and other traditional groupings while at the same time becoming more firmly anchored in the occupational and class statuses of an expanding industrial economy. The structures of modern life typically have provided for an identity premised on relatively fixed boundaries of the self, which in turn are based upon distinctions between "interior" and "exterior," "self" and "other," "individual" and "society."

In the more recent discourses of postmodernism and postmodernity, however, we find an image of a "fluid" self characterized by fragmentation, discontinuity, and a dissolution of boundaries between inner and outer worlds. This tendency toward fragmentation and dissolution has been linked to the vast and rapidly changing landscape of consumer capitalism and the evolving means of signification constituting mass culture and informational society. In these theories, technologically mediated forms of culture tend either (1) to occlude or obliterate social relations, and by implication the self (Baudrillard 1981, 1983a, 1983b), or (2) to "decenter" social identities towards an unstable, fragile, and fluid self dispersed by the representational processes of media and other technologies (Harvey 1990; Jameson 1983, 1984; Lash 1990; Poster 1990).

A contrast might be suggested, therefore, between a modern form of identity—secured by the internal mental and emotional states of individuals but produced in multiple structures of social interaction and institutions—and a postmodern form arising directly from the effects of externally mediated forms of signification and technologically based modes of cultural experience. Such forms would include consumer goods, telecommunications, and informational technologies. In this view, sources of identity have shifted historically from the internalization and integration of social roles to the appropriation of disposable commodities, images, and techniques, selected and discarded at will from the extensive repertoire of consumer culture. In this argument, to the *extent* that communication and information technologies supplant older forms of sociation, roles and identities lose their interactional quality as they become a mere extension of the instrumental and performative functions of various cultural media.

This instrumentalization of roles and identities would seem to foreshadow a demise of the modern individual, understood as constituted by reason, emotion, and other elements of an interiorized subjectivity or "inner life." Moreover, to the degree that social roles become mere objects of performance and commodity exchange, they would seem to threaten foundational ethical precepts of Western society, which presuppose a grounding of social attachments and commitments. In some writings about postmodernism, and in line with Fredric Jameson's (1984) argument about a decline in "depth models" of subjectivity, these ethics are seen as inconsistent with a culture that playfully celebrates "surface" and "multiplicity" (Dunn 1991; Jameson 1984; Newman 1985; Russell 1985). In this view, a commodified and technologized culture is seen as separating the construction of subjectivity from the social process, reconstituting it in a realm of images or "signifiers." A related argument sees the collapse of older processes of identification as creating a detached and mobile "nomadic" subject endlessly negotiating different identities in an open field of possibilities (Melucci 1996; Deleuze and Guattari 1983).

Within this cluster of postmodern notions, however, it is possible to delineate two different theoretical positions. First, in its "stronger" version the subject of the postmodernists is no longer "an individual" but a fluid set of "effects" produced by processes of signification or discourse. As the theoretical voice of postmodernism, poststructuralism has adopted a notion of discursively determined "subject-positions," which it has deployed against Enlightenment conceptions of a substantial self or ego. Repudiating notions of "the individual," poststructuralists have proclaimed the "death of the subject," appealing to the various deconstructions of the subject in Freud, Nietzsche, and Heidegger, and the fields of semiotics and structuralism, the latter of which are the original sources specifically of Jean Baudrillard's apocalyptic claims about the disappearance of the subject in commodity society. This conception displaces essentialist and unified notions of "the individual" by repositioning the latter in unstable structures of language, discourse, and power, thereby rendering the subject a shifting set of "textual effects." Such a view verges on denying subjectivity and identity altogether, claiming their complete disintegration in processes of signification.

However, a "weaker" and, I argue, more compelling version of the postmodernist subject speaks less of dissolution than of changes in the subject's formation. In this argument, postmodern society *destabilizes* the subject through the commodification of culture. This implies a disintegration of integrated, productivist roles as the subject becomes fragmented through new regimes of consumption and leisure. In this version of postmodern subjectivity, I suggest, identity formation is transformed by the commodification process in at least four basic respects. First, the individual is turned into a *consumer*, and increasingly a consumer of signs and images. While social identities persist (e.g., employee, parent, student), these identities are now subsumed by the role of consumption, which now shapes and conditions the individual's social orientations and relationships. Second, the *sources* of identity formation change as tangible, role-based relationships are subordinated to the disembodied visual images of mass culture. Third, identity formation is *exteriorized* in the sense that its locus shifts from the inner self to the outer world of objects and images valorized by commodity culture. Identity formation in postmodernity (as in premodernity) thus deeply roots itself in culture, but this now occurs primarily through the appropriation of commodities and commodified images rather than by means of communal participation in a traditional group (Lash and Friedman 1992). Fourth, and as a consequence, the self tends to lose its sense of autonomy from the outside world; as a result, identity becomes susceptible of chronic instability, inconsistency, and/or incoherence. The fragmenting effects of the commodity form thus *problematize* the integrative and continuous features of self-identity as the self becomes increasingly absorbed by the disjunctive features of mass culture.

In this weaker version of postmodern identity, the self is transformed by a culture of consumerism, and identity and self are destabilized by technological processes of signification, reconstituted and reshaped by the commodity form. Images, fashions, and lifestyles manufactured by the media industries become sources of self-image and vehicles by which the self perceives others. The "other-directed" orientation of developed modernity (Riesman et al. 1950) is thus overwhelmed by consumerism, mass media, and advertising. To the extent that we define ourselves through acts of consumption, our relationship to others and self is mediated by commodities and the form they take as images. In this view, mass culture tends to substitute ready-made images for identifications with "real" social objects. Social identifications are displaced by collections of image attributes consumed through television, movies, mass periodicals, advertising, and other cultural commodities.

In this argument, the displacement of social relations by commodities (however incomplete) has two consequences. First, consumer culture becomes a primary means for the construction of self. Style and fashion offer themselves as a source of incessantly changing and highly personalized identities. People "fashion" themselves through clothing, food, music, automobiles, television shows, and other commodities, in what Axel Honneth refers to as a "*process of fictionalization* of reality.... through which the atomized individual becomes an imitator of styles of existence prefabricated by media" (1992: 165; emphasis in the original). Second, the collective identities of class, gender, sexuality, race, and ethnicity, along with conventionalized institutional social roles, are weakened or replaced by more "individualized" and fluid "lifestyle" identities constructed in relation both to consumer goods (Featherstone 1991; Shields 1992) and media images such as film stars, advertising persona, television personalities, and fictional media characters (Kellner 1992). To the extent this occurs, the moorings of the self in socially delineated statuses, roles, and relationships are weakened, and processes of self-definition come to depend increasingly on an appropriation of the attributes of commodities. An integrated social conception of self is thereby replaced by a loose aggregate of personality traits assembled through the consumption of goods and images.

In an older discourse of social criticism, the shift of identity formation from social roles to a packaged world of mass culture was seen as a breakdown of the socialization process and associational life. In this earlier rendition of perceived threat to social values, the influence of family, church, neighborhood, and school weakens in the face of mass media, particularly television. In this view, centralized media systems undermine the authority of traditional socializing agencies responsible for the formation of stable identities and group memberships. Here, a market in cultural goods works to erode the social contexts and loyalties in which meaning and identity traditionally took shape, leaving the individual adrift in a world of commercialized distractions. Thus, identities are no longer influenced by the validations and controls of social groupings but are prefabricated and mass-marketed to consumers who appropriate them according to their own personal needs and desires.

Subsequent changes in the production and consumption of culture, however, have significantly changed this earlier critique of mass culture. Whereas previously, mass culture was condemned for its standardizing features—the dominant tendency in the early postwar years of economic expansion—recent decades have seen increased cultural fragmentation and dispersal, inviting a postmodern rereading of old criticisms (Collins 1989: 7). The increasing fragmentations of mass culture have provoked a more ambivalent and often celebratory attitude, in which a new sense of heterogeneity in cultural consumption is approached somewhat optimistically. The postmodernist construction of mass culture, then, attempts to preempt the formerly one-sided and negative view propounded by elitist critics. As a result, when measured against modern ideologies of identity, the actual impact of consumer culture now seems more ambiguous.

The more optimistic postmodernist view, on the one hand, sees in a continually changing marketplace of goods and images a realm of personal freedom, an alternative to established cultural and social norms. Honneth (1992) sees an underlying feature of the postmodern as the replacement of "self-realization," which presupposed "some life goal," by the Nietzschean idea of "experimental self-creation." In Honneth's words, "here, human subjects are presented whose possibilities for freedom are best realized when, independent of all normative expectations and bonds, they are able to creatively produce new self-images all the time" (167). Such self-creation is offered through the freedom to select from a wide range of goods and experiences, such as clothing, hairstyles, music, or television shows, without constraints of tradition or convention. Consumerism in this sense provides a potentially liberating experience, facilitating an expressive self by providing an arena of conscious experimentation and choice in the construction and elaboration of identity (Lash and Friedman 1992: 7).

The posing of such possibilities by consumerism and the media, along with the commercial co-optation of new cultural attitudes and values spawned by the sixties counterculture, have led many observers to proclaim ours an era variously of "self-fulfillment," "hedonism," or "narcissism" (Bell 1977; Bellah et al. 1985; Lasch 1979; Schur 1976; Turner 1976; Yankelovich 1981). While such concepts are of only limited value in characterizing present-day culture as "postmodern," they clearly reflect the shift from the productivist values of modernity to the consumptionist ethos of postmodernity. At the same time, however, although such tendencies are obviously compatible with notions of self-creation, they also reflect the extremely individualistic and frequently self-seeking and pathological forms this has often assumed in the U.S. (Lasch 1979, 1984). Nevertheless, some postmodernist readings see in the very nature of consumer culture expanded possibilities for the development of new kinds of identification. On one level, this can be seen in the various ways that consumer culture has *pluralized* style, differentiating and articulating new social and cultural identities around gender, race, ethnicity, age, and sexuality (e.g., the independent woman, the youthful and fit senior citizen). On another level, and within these new vocabularies, this culture introduces multiple possibilities for the articulation of *personal* style, whether in the form of individually constructed lifestyle identities (e.g., new looks in women's and men's clothing fashions) or as part of lifestyle identifications with collective groups and categories (e.g., upwardly mobile, professional African Americans). On both levels, consumer culture provides a range of models to choose from in the construction of novel identities, be they commercially marketed styles or individualized constructions. This has been accomplished through increasingly segmented markets and sales strategies that target consumers with specialized tastes. Post-Fordist economic regimes of product differentiation, target marketing, and rapid goods turnover has thus overcome many of the leveling effects of standardization widely criticized in earlier mass society theory (Harvey 1990). Contrary to the critics of mass culture and consumerism, then, contemporary consumer culture has thus in a sense made it possible to contemplate the commodity as a vehicle for a more fully and creatively developed self.

On the other hand, the original (modernist) critics of mass culture have attacked consumerist ideologies of choice for masking the basic powerlessness of individuals in a corporate-dominated society. Choice in consumer goods and media images, this argument runs, represents a spurious compensation for a real decline in power and influence in politics and the workplace. Consumer individualism, additionally, serves as a pale imitation of "authentic" individualism based upon the values of achievement and individual self-worth. Consumer choice, in this view, has replaced real social and political recognition, trivializing freedom through its reduction to the category of "taste." Consumerism, to the extent that it privatizes choice by enforcing loyalty to the values of leisure and lifestyle, has a depoliticizing effect, turning workers—who might otherwise be militant and in solidarity—into consumers, and citizens-who might otherwise engage in collective action—into spectators (Alt 1975, 1976; Brenkman 1979; Debord 1977). Moreover, tendencies towards conformity remain inherent in a cultural system in which social success depends upon criteria of style and fashion sanctioned by the media and other corporate institutions. While consumer culture often seems packed with novelty, in fact rapid stylistic turnover simply disguises the underlying structures of predictability and control characteristic of commercialism and corporate marketing practices. Personal choice is short-circuited by market-based and market-controlled norms of popularity and conformity, as illustrated especially in the strategies of mass advertising.

From this perspective the incursions of mass culture thus pose troubling questions about the impact of ready-made cultural products on the self. Cultural commodification makes the formation of personal and social identities increasingly dependent on the prerogatives of the corporate economy. In this view, new cultural articulations of gender, race, and so on, while recognizing difference and contributing to collective forms of identification, are nevertheless *marketed* identities. In a society shaped by the marketing of goods and images, the criteria of self-definition become instrumental, impersonal, and distant, and self-construction comes to depend increasingly on the agendas and strategies of large-scale corporate enterprises.

To summarize, the externalization of identity-forming processes in mass culture can be seen as both liberating and problematizing. On the one hand, the proliferation of commodities and the play of images promise seemingly limitless possibilities for creative self-expansion and experience. Despite their predetermined, market character, the self in this view retains a capacity for making of commodified images and products what it will, reading and using the meanings and pleasures inherent in these products in ways that cannot be either anticipated or fixed in advance. On the other hand, the tendency toward the absorption of self-identity into a world of images/commodities can be seen as threatening the boundary between the self and the outer world, problematizing both (Lasch 1984: 153). If and to the extent that a distinction between inner self and outer world is no longer sustainable (Lasch 1984: 32), the self is reduced to a function of the operation of sign systems, and identity becomes as scattered and fleeting as market-based manufactured culture. In this scenario, the multiplicity of discourses, sensations, and messages flooding commercial culture overwhelm and fragment the subject, fore-shadowing the demise of meaning and selfhood and the loss of personal freedom.

Television as a Commodity Form:
Consumption and the Displacement of Social Relations

As forms of mass broadcasting and systems of formulas for market-ing manufactured entertainment, television and other mass media raise important questions about changes in the material sources of identity formation, such as the rise of celebrity in the form of packaged identity models. But given the relational nature of identity formation, it seems even more important to explore the technologically based effects of televisual flow and fragmentation on the viewing experience, and how these in turn dramatically change the conditions of identity formation. As a result of its very form, television broadcasting works against the unity and cohesion assumed by modern modes of representation and conventional sociological conceptions of identity. As a commercially driven commodity form, television exemplifies the transformation to consumption relations and the inherently fragmenting effects of a cor-porate-based consumer culture. Furthermore, television is a major form of mass privatization. Television presupposes an isolated viewer/con-sumer; viewing presupposes a certain withdrawal from the contexts of social interaction. Television spectatorship, then, can be thought of as a socially disengaged experience of a simulated, ongoing, and highly frag-mented world of visual images. While television viewers often watch with others, the *act* of viewing necessitates disengagement from social interaction for an immersion in a fabricated world of visual stimuli. Furthermore, even though viewers might hold to an inner sense of self against which they measure or judge what they see on television, the decision to watch often comes from a desire for pleasurable distractions involving an "escape" from self and other.

The "escapist" character of television viewing is inseparable from the simulational and constructed nature of the televisual world itself. While in various ways making claims to "reality," television in fact constitutes only ready-made representations, substituting for real social relations their artificial construction as images. To the extent that identification processes might still be at work in television viewing, they shift from social contexts of interaction to artificially created visual experiences.

Whereas in social interaction identity is shaped and sustained by the on-going and mutually reinforcing responses of self and others, in television viewing the self enters into a fundamentally different process of reacting to and appropriating prefabricated messages. As such, identity is both opened to innovative possibilities and limited by the preformed mean-ings upon which television as a mass medium depends. Television can unsettle identity, offering a fantasy world of action and desire that opens to the play of mind and the imagination. Needless to say, television also promotes a powerful form of social "realism," however artificial, by formulaically condensing and privatizing familiar aspects of social experience and by rhetorically prescribing ways of thinking and acting in the social world. But as commodity form, television binds the self back into structures of consumption inherent in its programming, for-mulas, and visual codes. While creating a realm of image play (Lembo forthcoming), television simultaneously conditions and adapts the self to participation in consumption relations by substituting for socially based identity formation a fragmentary and disorganized collection of *image-based* identities.

Social interaction connects the self to others' actions and responses by means of an internally shared set of common and negotiated meanings. These continually emerging ties, as Hewitt (1984) argues, contribute to an individual's sense of continuity, providing a framework for self-iden-tification and differentiation. The consumption relationship, in contrast, weakens and ruptures these ties. As a functional object, television elicits responses without itself responding (Baudrillard 1981; Debord 1977). Instead, television works to absorb the symbolic and social processes of lived interaction into industrially finished products, harnessing these processes for predetermined and instrumental purposes. It is in this sense that television as a consumption relationship "externalizes" processes of identity formation, shifting the locus of self-construction from the inter-nal relations of interaction to the consumption of packaged images.

The "nonsocial relational" character of the television viewing expe-rience is emblematic of the transformation of the problem of identity formation from the modern alienation of self-other relations to a post-modern isolation and fragmentation of the self in consumption relations. Although the implications of this situation for questions of identity are profound, its real effects are unclear. Two hypothetical possibilities sug-gest themselves. On the one hand, television viewing can be seen as an activity relatively free of direct social and cultural constraints and thus offering experiential openings to new forms of identity that viewers construct in self-determining ways. Identifications are in one sense viewer directed and controlled, implying a kind of free floating identity-making process which is buoyed by an endless supply of images and sensations. In this respect, television viewing as an act of consumption provides a potentially inventive and imaginative means of self-construction free of conventional social influences.

On the other hand, if the capacity for self-definition is by its nature socially relational, dependent on the concrete encounters of group life, we might expect the experience of television viewing as privatized entertainment to impede or undermine identity forming processes. Involved in privatized entertainment, the self forgoes social engagement for the visual and dramatic pleasures of the screen. Although some viewers actively construct their own private meanings while they watch, thereby enhancing their inner lives, television as simulation displaces viewers from socially formative processes of interaction.

While critical theorists of television's ideological effects have been preoccupied with its hegemonic influences on viewers, the fragmenting effects of television as a visual medium dramatically change the kinds of questions that need to be raised about the mass media. Not only is the experience of television largely inconsistent with the formation of stable and unified identities, a condition *presupposed* by the ideological effects model, but television's lack of cohesiveness would seem to be incompatible with the development of a coherent sense of self. As a consumption relationship, television tends to undermine the unifying and differentiating capacities that have come to be associated with self-development. The fragmentation of experience, the temporary and disposable character of self identifications, and the externalization of the self in signs and images thus deeply problematize modern conceptions of the means and possibilities of self-definition.

Commodification, the Market, and the Waning of Class Identity

Historical claims that the United States is a "classless" society certainly have no basis in fact. Yet, the many *appearances* of classlessness in this country are inescapable, and these appearances are in complex ways closely linked to the level of commodification characterizing advanced capitalist society.

Historically, the leveling effects of commodification have operated on multiple but interrelated levels. First, from its inception, the modern commodity contained within itself an inherently democratizing logic. Despite its role as marker of distinction there has always been a powerful countertendency within the commodity to *diminish* social class differences, insofar as the act of consumption reduces (*and* elevates) various segments of the population to the common level of *consumer.* Second, the commodity form has evolved within a Fordist strategy of accumulation, based on standardized mass production and creating at least the *appearance* of a commonly shared culture of consumer goods. Third, the historical transition from production to consumption has resulted in a major ideological shift from occupational to consumer roles, followed by the conversion of the latter into vehicles of "lifestyle" affiliation rather than class standing, which turns privatized consumption into the primary source of identity and shared culture. As a consequence of these changes, commodification has weakened class consciousness by creating a common denominator (or what Baudrillard 1981 calls a "democracy") of consumption.

The democratizing tendencies inherent in consumption have been rapidly accelerated in the postwar period by a post-Fordist regime of flexible accumulation (Harvey 1990), characterized by a rapidly shifting marketplace in which status distinctions are continually blurred and redrawn. The blurring of status, furthermore, has been intensified by a massive extension of consumer credit. Through increased consumption rates and an expansion of taste levels made possible by a widespread rise in purchasing power, the relationship between objective class position and "lifestyle" position has been weakened, as members of lower income brackets buy into the lifestyle of the middle class, just as the middle class now increasingly avails itself of an upper-class lifestyle. Finally, the commodity system in and of itself provides a semblance of growing equality by stimulating a "democratization of style" whereby higher lifestyles are "marketed down" to the lower class levels, superficially spreading the signs of affluence through cheaper versions of expensive commodities.

At the same time, flexible economic accumulation rests on a strategy of "difference." Whereas mass production and consumption democratize by emphasizing the characteristics of *sameness*, flexible accumulation democratizes by elaborating *differences*. Importantly, the differences marketed under this new system are not those of class as traditionally conceived, but of *lifestyle* as differentiated by a complex array of both economic and non-economic factors, including income, gender, family status, ethnicity, race, age, and sexuality. Thus, the market forces accompanying post-Fordist economics work to destabilize the identities of class and occupation by introducing new kinds of lifestyle-based distinctions that operate at an increasing distance from class position.

The excess, rapid turnover, and ceaseless differentiation of commodities characteristic of the post-Fordist mode of accumulation produce an eclectic and continually shifting mixture of cultural goods and significations, all competing for consumer attention. The resulting erosion of class hierarchy intensifies the search for status distinctions through the appropriation of goods and services from an ever-expanding marketplace of lifestyle identities. Consumers thus face a heterogeneous, capricious, and often ambiguous landscape of symbolic goods. Despite the persistence of real inequalities in income and education, flexible accumulation strategies tend to decouple consumption from social structure (Pakulski and Waters 1996), segregating the production of "status symbols" from the class structure. This entails a major shift in *perception* from class to lifestyle criteria and more generally from patterns of differentiation within the *social* sphere to the production of differences in the realm of *culture*.

The diminution of class identities, however, is accompanied by three further market-driven developments. First, we can plausibly assume that a certain fragmentation of self is inevitable in the growing cultural heterogeneity, and especially the incessant changeability, of status symbols in the marketplace. Second, the "core" identities of class, gender, race, ethnicity, age, and sexuality undergo cultural deconstruction as part of the dissolution of older modernist hierarchies of cultural authority stemming from consumerism and the symbolic inflation of cultural goods in a high-demand, excessively differentiated society. While the market breaks down older identities, however, it also introduces new fluidities in identity, facilitating its redefinition along more inclusionary and democratizing lines. Third, a tendency is set in motion for identification processes to shift generally away from core identities to consumer roles. However, while individuals increasingly see themselves and act as consumers, far from replacing core identities consumerism *reshapes* or *inflects* these identities in new ways, providing new contexts for their construction and reconstruction.

Simulation and the Postmodern "Crisis of the Real"

The technological intensification of signification processes through consumerism, entertainment, and information systems has raised the specter of a drastically transformed order of experience, whereby the problematizing effects of visual culture are surpassed by a state of affairs in which the foundations of meaning formation have been completely abolished. This marks a transition from Debord's problem of the spectacle—the abstracting and reifying powers of capital that convert everything into an image—to Baudrillard's theory of the simulacra (1983a), in which signification acquires a life and operational logic all its own, a mutation of the visual and informational world of signs and images into a transcendent order of simulation (Best 1994; Wakefield 1990).

Appropriating a concept from Marshall McLuhan (Kellner 1989), Baudrillard, the celebrated theorist of the "crisis of the real," has characterized the reversal of the modernizing process of cultural differentiation at the level of the mode of representation as a case of "implosion." The "sign" of semiotic theory was clearly delineated under modernity into signifier (image, word), signified (meaning, concept), and referent (reality), corresponding to the three autonomous spheres of culture (aesthetic, theoretical, and moral-practical). With the collapse of these spheres, the structure of the sign itself collapsed, reducing the mode of signification to the signifier, abolishing both signified and referent in a world of freely circulating and self-referential signs and images. Thus, not only has meaning been thrown into question, but representation and reality themselves have been increasingly problematized (Lash 1990). Visual imagery, which bears a close resemblance to the reality it "represents," begins to replace that reality. Thus, signifier and referent begin to merge. Indeed, images can be so literal and immediate as to make them more real than "the real" itself, what Baudrillard (1983a, 1983b) refers to as "hyperreality." But just as the hyperreal substitutes for the real, the social environment becomes so pervaded by the means of representation that reality in the sense of daily existence simultaneously comes to be comprised of images (Lash 1990). Thus, signifier and referent invade each other's realms, threatening the distinction between the real and its representation.

The contemporary cultural scene is replete with examples of the technological transformation of cultural experience into a simulated, artificial reality, and the displacement of direct, unmediated experience by simulated versions. There are a number of dimensions to this process. First is the extent to which reality becomes so thoroughly mediated as to threaten its displacement by technologically based images. This is evident in the deployment of video technology at sporting events, concerts, and other events where spectators present at the event are provided with video replays and various entertainments and commercials on a huge screen *while* they are watching the event itself, as if video reproduction and amplification made the event more real, more material, and even more legitimate. This replicates an earlier transition in media culture when television viewers were sometimes heard to comment that an event did not seem "real" until they had seen it on television. In another example, huge video screens often dominate the stages of rock concerts, such that the monitors are grabbing almost as much attention as the actual performances. Here, rock fans experience the pleasures of enormous video images of musical celebrities *while* the latter are performing in their physical presence. While in such examples the media do not literally replace reality, the media are endowed by spectators with a power to verify and sanction reality and a visual pleasure that makes reality subservient to its representation.

A second dimension of technological simulation bears on questions concerning the distinction between reality and illusion, truth and falsehood. For example, computerized electronic imaging of photography is a Baudrillardian development threatening to completely undermine the veracity of the still picture. Computerized alterations of visual images in the media, especially in photojournalism, is an increasingly accepted practice (Ritchin 1990), and even has emerged as a new form of entertainment.

Visual media in general have the capacity to invent, construct, or modify reality in accordance with the goals of mass consumption. A pragmatics of effect occupy the very core of these media, and so by nature they operate to produce a desired result on their recipients. The technologies of photography, film, and video are used in the context of mass entertainment and consumption to produce preferred outcomes in the audience. This further implies that, regarding notions of truth and falsehood, the simulational powers of technology need to be read within the context of their social uses and economic motivations (a point overlooked by Baudrillard and other technological determinists).

A third dimension of simulation is the most complex and perhaps most unsettling of all. How does the emergence of a simulated order of visual technology effect the distinction between the "real" and the "imaginary," our very sense or understanding of reality? Perhaps the purest manifestation yet of the simulacrum is the arrival of what is variously called "virtual" or "artificial" reality, a total sensory environment that is electronically simulated. Consider also the familiar example of MTV. As imaginary visualizations of music, this genre employs the most sophisticated techniques of visual production to construct a completely "other" world of play, eroticism, magic, the bizarre, and the phantasmagoric. Constructed from elements of social reality, MTV represents a high-tech version of romantic fantasy at its extreme, resulting in a complete obliteration of space and time. At the same time, MTV exploits many of the possibilities of video as an art form by transforming music into highly creative visual productions, adapting them to the structures of commercial television. Similarly, computerization has led to the evolution of vast informational networks and electronic communication systems that threaten to collapse everything into digitized information appearing on a screen. But at the same time, a whole new cult-like culture comprised of computer hackers, musicians and artists, science fiction freaks, futurists, and others have formed around computer technology. Dubbed "cyberpunk" and hailed as a "counterculture of the computer age," this miscellany of rebellious visionaries and experimentalists are attempting to explore the virtues and artistic possibilities of artificially created environments. Turning high tech to their own purposes, the cyberpunks celebrate the fusion of humans and machines in a surrealistic world of computer technology.

The emergence of a simulated environment raises difficult questions for a theory of identity formation. While the case for the abolition of "reality" by "simulation" is obviously overstated by Baudrillard, simulational technology nonetheless constitutes a pervasive set of forces undermining a unified and stable sense of identity. New sites and spaces of technologically mediated experience compete with and threaten social experiences of self and other by subverting or replacing the relationships upon which they depend. Such forces undermine the conditions of continuity, integration, identification, and differentiation posited by Hewitt (1984) as the major constituents of identity.

Cultural Change and the Problematics of Postmodern Identity

My sketch of the consequences of commodification, television, the marketplace, and new simulational orders of experience point to some general conclusions regarding the impact of cultural change on identity formation. First, privatized modes of consumption tend to disrupt and weaken identity through rapid change in goods and styles. The transitory and temporary sense of the world of objects experienced in a rapid-turnover consumer culture disrupts feelings of self-continuity and wholeness. Second, the multiplication of sites and spaces where identity and selfhood might form produces numerous discontinuities in the self's experience of itself and others. Third, the fragmentation of experience inherent in various forms of media and related technologies problematizes unified conceptions of self and other. Not only is a sense of temporality disrupted by new kinds of visual spatialization and disjunction but identification processes come to be shaped by the consumption of fabricated or virtual images. Such discontinuities undermine feelings of wholeness and a sense of boundary. Fourth, and closely related, consumerism and the media produce a present-oriented culture in which a sense of the passage of time, and more generally history itself, is often obliterated by the immediacy of objects and images and their claims to reality.

Lastly, a general withdrawal of the self from public or associational life into private spaces of consumption deprives the self of opportunities for identifications with and differentiations from others in the context of socially or spatially based community. This withdrawal needs to be understood as involving the destruction of an older "public sphere" and its replacement by a new *kind* of public sphere(s) constituted by communications technologies and consumer culture. What is left of the historical public sphere penetrates the private domestic realm via the direct intrusions of mass media (e.g., television talk shows). More precisely, the spatial reorganization of society and culture around communications technologies effectively *abolishes* the conventional distinction between "public" and "private." The overriding tendency toward "privatization" is in this sense a more complicated matter of destroying the very concept of the "private" by eliminating the boundary between private and public in an unbounded, expanded space of potentially endless signification and consumption.

Thinking about the destabilization of identity thus depends upon a consideration of the consequences of cultural transformation and the particular direction and forms this transformation has taken as a result of the economic and technological dynamics of an expanding capitalist society. However, while identity has been problematized, in the sense of a questioning of the nature and boundaries of self, other, and outside world, the dominance of signification processes in the production and consumption of culture raises issues not only about the loss of self but of new possibilities of regeneration within a consumerist orientation. In short, consumerism, paradoxically, extends a certain initiative to the consuming individual. While the experience of technology might problematize identity, the workings of the market, as we have seen, simultaneously create the conditions of possibility for a wider and deeper democratization of culture and society in which new and more complex identities might get constructed.

Conclusion: Consumption, Community, and the Fate of Identity

Addressing the fate of the individual in modern society, many thinkers turned to the emerging social potentialities of an expanding and newly institutionalized market society in search of the horizons and limits of individuality and identity. Encountering the limits of the market economy, this search eventually led to the concept of "community." In classical social theory and other discourses on the crises of modernity, it was ultimately the problem of community, and specifically its alleged decline following the passing of traditional society, that provided the framework for a critique of the structural forces threatening to engulf the individual.

While critiques of modernity have often exaggerated the decline of community and its negative consequences, the forms and nature of community have nevertheless changed dramatically as a consequence of modernization and specifically the processes of commodification. Aside from industrialization and urbanization, perhaps the most powerfully disruptive change has been the rise of mass communications. Presupposing a detached, isolated, and anonymous individual, mass communications have both reflected and hastened a decline in communal ties. However, whether with regard to remnants of "organic" community left over from traditional society, or modern forms of community structured by work, neighborhood, education, or similar settings, and despite earlier fears, modern society has managed to sustain a semblance of communal life, however weakened or changed in nature, creating new symbolic and social possibilities for the individual within a market framework.

But in an era of technologically mediated culture and privatized consumption, notions of community acquire even greater urgency, insofar as this concept gives us a strategy for thinking normatively and critically about identity formation in postmodern society. Consumerism, mass media, and information systems represent a major departure from both traditional and modern forms of community, creating "artificial" or "virtual" communities based on consumption and technology. Television viewing, computer networks, and video entertainment are forms of collective behavior constituted and mediated by technologies whose uses and contents destabilize our sense of place and time. These modes of participation represent a break from natural interactional settings, engendering practices and forms of consciousness inconsistent with the kinds of expectations associated with conventional social relationships. The more abstract and ephemeral kinds of community created by modernity and mass society—movements, fads, lifestyles, and so on—have now been transformed into technologically mediated forms of consumption, if not replaced altogether by "virtual" forms of communication, interaction, and experience (Poster 1995).

On the positive side, theorists have attempted to characterize the changed nature and dimensions of community formation in contemporary mass culture with concepts such as "interpretive communities" (Lindlof 1988), "thin culture" (Lichterman 1992), and "lifestyle enclaves" (Bellah et al. 1985), all of which designate to varying degrees the replacement of "real" community by aggregate and anonymous collectivities. Thus, mass culture tends to generate the elements of both virtual and surrogate communities, both of which afford their participants new experiences of membership and belonging, however vague their temporal and spatial boundaries.

On the negative side, however, these and related efforts to assess the condition of community remain conceptually and empirically problematic, given the diversity and complexity of various substitute forms and their relationship to the values of traditional community life. Certainly notions of mediated, situated, and virtual community generally capture the present state of affairs. Yet, to the extent that such formations are incapable of functioning as authentic and enduring communities, the fate of identity might seem to depend largely on the extent to which commodified and technologized forms of culture weaken earlier kinds of social groupings and contexts of interaction, or allow them to survive. In addition, despite identifying new forms of community, real or potential, these and other writings about the search for associational life generally tend to understate the consumerist nature of these communities, their origins in mass culture, and therefore the extent to which they are shaped by the marketplace. In spite of some observable continuities with earlier forms of community, the collectivities formed by these media often offer only limited opportunities for genuine social participation.

The commodification of society and culture has relocated the search for identity in the act of consumption and the fragmentary and fleeting experiences of mass culture and telecommunications. Through a proliferation of cultural and symbolic possibilities, mass culture provides new means and sources for the formation of social and personal identity. However, the temporary and situated nature of consumption relations denies to self the grounding, definition, and validation afforded by social forms of community and the enduring ties enjoyed by members of traditional groupings. While some excitement and creativity might accompany the novelties of mass culture and the concomitant emergence of fluid, mobile, and unpredictable identities, the boundaries and capacities of the self depend to a large extent upon forms of sociation precluded by the structures of mass consumption, at least in its present forms.

The fate of identity, thus, would seem closely linked to distinctions between activities of "consuming" on the one hand and those of "relating, interacting, sharing" on the other, opposing tendencies which intermingle, combine, antagonize, reconcile, and merge in ever-changing combinations. Thinking through the problem of identity in a postmodern society therefore would require analysis of the ongoing interrelations and tensions between the powers and pleasures of consumption and the search for social connectedness. In a commodified society, consumption and social relationality persistently contend as sources of selfhood and personal meaning, alternately reinforcing and undermining each other.

At the same time, it seems undeniable that the transition from modernity to postmodernity involves an important shift in the mode of identity formation from social relations to the commodity form. To the extent that technologically mediated forms of experience position individuals as consumers of commodified culture, traditional and modern social structures gradually lose their effectiveness as reliable and stable sources of identification and meaning. Moreover, the inherently fragmenting effects of the commodity tend to *problematize* identity by situating consumers in spaces and sites of consumption that work against the construction of unified and consistent definitions of self.

While modernity places great strains on self-conception by expanding and differentiating the field of social relations, the technological and semiotic environment of consumerism invades, absorbs, fractures, and reconstitutes this field in ways that throw self-conception more deeply into question. Thus, theorizing and investigating differences between modernity and postmodernity as sociohistorical and cultural conditions is an urgent task with consequences for our very comprehension of the future possibilities of self and identity.

References

Alt, J. 1975. "Work, Culture, and Crisis." *Telos* 23: 168-182.

———. 1976. "Beyond Class: The Decline of Industrial Labor and Leisure." *Telos* 28: 55-80.

Baudrillard, J. 1981. *For A Critique of the Political Economy of the Sign.* St. Louis, MO: Telos Press.

———. 1983a. *Simulations.* New York: Semiotext(e), Inc.

———. 1983b. "The Ecstasy of Communication." Pp. 126-134 in *The Anti-Aesthetic: Essays on Postmodern Culture,* edited by H. Foster. Port Townsend, WA: Bay Press.

Bell, D. 1977. *The Cultural Contradictions of Capitalism.* New York: Basic Books.

Bellah, R.N., R. Madsen, W.M. Sullivan, A. Swidler, and S. Tipton. 1985. *Habits of the Heart: Individualism and Commitment in American Life.* Berkeley: University of California Press.

Best, S. 1994. "The Commodification of Reality and the Reality of Commodification: Baudrillard, Debord, and Postmodern Theory." Pp. 41-67 in *Baudrillard: A Critical Reader,* edited by D. Kellner. Oxford: Blackwell.

Brenkman, J. 1979. "Mass Media: From Collective Experience to the Culture of Privatization." *Social Text* 1: 94-109.

Clark, T.J. 1984. *The Painting of Modern Life: Paris in the Art of Manet and His Followers.* Princeton, NJ: Princeton University Press.

Collins, J. 1989. *Uncommon Cultures: Popular Culture and Post-Modernism.* New York: Routledge.

Debord, G. 1977. *Society of the Spectacle.* Detroit, MI: Black and Red.

Deleuze, G., and F. Guattari. 1983. *Anti-Oedipus: Capitalism and Schizophrenia.* Minneapolis: University of Minnesota Press.

Dunn, R. 1991. "Postmodernism: Populism, Mass Culture, and Avant-Garde." *Theory, Culture and Society* 8(1): 111-135.

Featherstone, M. 1991. *Consumer Culture and Postmodernism.* London: Sage.

Harvey, D. 1990. *The Condition of Postmodernity.* Oxford: Basil Blackwell.

Hewitt, J.P. 1984. *Self and Society: A Symbolic Interactionist Social Psychology.* 3 ed. Boston: Allyn and Bacon.

Honneth, A. 1992. "Pluralization and Recognition: On the Self-Misunderstanding of Postmodern Social Theorists." Pp. 163-172 in *Between Totalitarianism and Postmodernity,* edited by P. Beilharz, G. Robinson, and J. Rundell. Cambridge, MA: The MIT Press.

Huyssen, A. 1986. *After the Great Divide: Modernism, Mass Culture, Postmodernism.* Bloomington: Indiana University Press.

Jameson, F. 1983. "Postmodernism and Consumer Society." Pp. 11-125 in *The Anti-Aesthetic: Essays on Postmodern Culture*, edited by H. Foster. Port Townsend, WA: Bay Press.

———. 1984. "Postmodernism, or the Cultural Logic of Late Capitalism." *New Left Review* 146: 53-92.

———. 1991. *Postmodernism, or The Cultural Logic of Late Capitalism*. Durham, NC: Duke University Press.

Kellner, D. 1989. *Jean Baudrillard: From Marxism to Postmodernism and Beyond*. Stanford, CA: Stanford University Press.

———. 1992. "Popular Culture and the Construction of Postmodern Identities." Pp. 141-177 in *Modernity and Identity*, edited by S. Lash and J. Friedman. Oxford: Blackwell.

Lasch, C. 1979. *The Culture of Narcissism: American Life in an Age of Diminishing Expectations*. New York: W.W. Norton.

———. 1984. *The Minimal Self: Psychic Survival in Troubled Times*. New York: W.W. Norton.

Lash, S. 1990. *The Sociology of Postmodernism*. London: Routledge.

Lash, S., and J. Friedman, eds. 1992. *Modernity and Identity*. Oxford: Basil Blackwell.

Lembo, R. Forthcoming. *Thinking Through Television*. New York: Cambridge University Press.

Lichterman, P. 1992. "Self-Help Reading as a Thin Culture." *Media, Culture and Society* 14: 421-447.

Lindlof, T.R. 1988. "Media Audiences as Interpretive Communities." *Communication Yearbook* 11: 81-107.

Melucci, A. 1996. *The Playing Self: Person and Meaning in the Planetary Society*. Cambridge: Cambridge University Press.

Newman, C. 1985. *The Post-Modern Aura: The Act of Fiction in an Age of Inflation*. Evanston, IL: Northwestern University Press.

Pakulski, J., and M. Waters. 1996. *The Death of Class*. London: Sage.

Poster, M. 1990. *The Mode of Information: Poststructuralism and Social Context*. Chicago: University of Chicago Press.

———. 1995. *The Second Media Age*. Cambridge, MA: Polity Press.

Riesman, D., with N. Glazer and R. Denney. 1950. *The Lonely Crowd: A Study of the Changing American Character*. New Haven: Yale University Press.

Ritchin, F. 1990. *In Our Own Image: The Coming Revolution in Photography*. New York: Aperture.

Russell, C. 1985. *Poets, Prophets, and Revolutionaries: The Literary Avant-Garde From Rimbaud Through Postmodernism*. New York: Oxford University Press.

Schur, E. 1976. *The Awareness Trap: Self-Absorption Instead of Social Change*. New York: Quadrangle.

Shields, R., ed. 1992. *Lifestyle Shopping: The Subject of Consumption*. London: Routledge.

Turner, R. 1976. "The Real Self: From Institution to Impulse." *American Journal of Sociology* 81: 989-1016.

Yankelovich, D. 1981. *New Rules*. New York: Random House.

Wakefield, N. 1990. *Postmodernism: The Twilight of the Real*. London: Pluto.

6

Technology, Self, and the Moral Project

Kenneth J. Gergen

Largely owing to the closely coupled beliefs in knowledge as a cumulative commodity of universal application, scholarly inquiry too seldom confronts the immediately pressing issues of the day. Textual traditions—with their fixed objects of study and their aspirations to speak beyond history and culture—tend to engulf the new and the immediate. And because contemporary issues seldom fall neatly into the established categories of knowledge (e.g., psychology, sociology, political science, history) they are often shoved to the periphery of interest. The scholarly traditions grapple but tenuously, for example, with immediately pressing problems of the environment, the globalization process, sustainable economics, genocidal politics, or international terrorism. The consequences of this configuration have been particularly unfortunate in the case of what may be viewed as a techno-cultural revolution. Although technological artifacts have come to play a pivotal role in contemporary cultural life, critical appraisal has been slow to develop. As many believe, Western cultural life has already been radically and irreversibly transformed by technology. If we may speak of a "postmodern culture" it is essentially one in which technology is a quintessential ingredient. Yet, scholarly study has moved but slowly.

There are significant exceptions to these resistant tendencies, and a slowly arousing consciousness of the ways in which, for example, individual mentalities, family life, communal relations, power, and ideology are implicated in the technological transformation (Alkalimat,

Gills, and Williams 1995; Kelley 1994; Meyrowitz 1985; Poster 1995; Rheingold 1993; Sproull and Kiesler 1991; Stone 1995; Turkle 1995). The present effort extends this domain of concern to consider the issue of moral order. One of the central challenges for any culture is that of securing an acceptable, if not virtuous mode of collective life. In effect, every culture is challenged by what we may loosely term a *moral project*, an attempt to achieve a sustainable and agreeable (as opposed to an agonistic and ultimately self-destroying) mode of cultural life. At least since the Enlightenment, we in Western culture have wished to answer this challenge by some means other than force of arms. Rather, in place of this crude form of control, we have generally wished to link institutional order to a rational scaffold. That is, we have sought to generate an intelligibility that can be shared by all, and the implications of which are realized through various institutional traditions. For over three centuries, hopes for the moral society have rested on two major and conflicting rationales, the one centered on individual moral deliberation, and the other on community commitment. These two fulcra of moral action serve as the chief focus of the present offering.

We must suppose that forms of moral intelligibility and their accompanying institutions are neither developed nor sustained in a vacuum. Their genesis and possible demise depend importantly on existing conditions—both material and cultural. Whether a system of religion flourishes, for example, will depend on existing conditions of communication, education, government policy, and so on. As proposed, technological artifacts have become an increasingly significant feature of the contemporary ethos. Thus, the central question posed by the present analysis: can the traditional conceptions of self and community (and their associated institutions) be sustained as the techno-cultural revolution bursts into the twenty-first century? In both cases there is substantial reason for doubt.

To be more specific, my particular concern is with the accumulating *technologies of sociation*, from the telephone, automobile, mass transportation systems, and radio early in the century, to the jet plane, television, Internet, satellite transmission, fax, and cellular phone in the latter. These relatively low-cost technologies dramatically expand and intensify the domain of social connection. Whether we speak in terms of the "information age," the "globalization process," or a "new world order," we find that daily life is marked by a steady expansion in the range of opinions, values, perspectives, attitudes, images, personalities, and information to which we are exposed (for an extended treatment of this process, see Gergen 1991a). It is my view that the technologically based transformation of this century—and surely deepening within the next—significantly undermines the potentials of both individualism and communalism to secure a morally viable society. Required in the emerging technological conditions are new forms of intelligibility and associated institutions. After considering the erosion of our twin traditions, I shall outline a possible successor project in the form of what I shall call *relational being*.

The Self: Death by Technology

Drawing from early Greek, Judaic, and Christian traditions, but most fully articulated within the course of the Enlightenment, we have traditionally viewed the single individual as the atom of the moral society. Whether we speak in terms of psyche, soul, agency, rational deliberation, or conscious choice, we generally hold that moral action is derived from particular conditions of individual mind. Thus philosophers seek to establish essential criteria for moral decision making, religious institutions are concerned with states of individual conscience, courts of law inquire into the individual's capacity to know right from wrong, and parents are concerned with the moral education of their young. The general presumption is that the virtuous mind propels meritorious conduct, and that with sufficient numbers of individuals performing worthy acts, we achieve the good society.

Yet, as Walter Ong's (1982) exploration of oral as opposed to literate or print societies suggests, our conception of individual minds is vitally dependent on the technological ethos. The shift from an oral to a print culture, Ong proposes, significantly altered the common forms of thought. Thus, for example, in oral societies people were more likely to depend on recall, concrete as opposed to abstract categories, and redundancy as opposed to precision. Yet, there is an important sense in which this fascinating thesis is insufficiently realized. While Ong wished to locate forms of mental life within a cultural context, he had no access into mental conditions themselves. That is, the analysis may be viewed as a treatise not on mental conditions but on cultural constructions of the mind. It is not thought in itself that changed but our way of defining what it is to think.[1]

To extend the implications of Ong's analysis, we may ask whether the conception of mind as a critical focus of study—something we must know about—was not solidified by the expansion of printed media. In an oral society, where the determination of the real and the good grows from face-to-face negotiation, there is little reason to launch inquiry into the speaker's private meaning. Through words, facial expressions, gestures, physical context, and the constant adjustments to audience expression, meanings are made transparent. However, when print allows words to spring from the face-to-face relationship—when the discourse is insinuated into myriad contexts separated in time and space from its origins—then the hermeneutic problem becomes focal. To wonder and speculate about "the mind behind the words" is to create the reality of this mind. To grant this mental condition the status of originary source of action is to solidify its importance. Both hermeneutic study and psychological science have since assured the reality of a meaningful mind with moral intent.

Given the potential dependency of conceptions of self on technological conditions, let us consider our contemporary ethos. In particular, what is to be said about the increasing insinuation of the technologies of sociation into our lives and its effects on our beliefs in individual minds? In my view the transformation of the technological ethos slowly undermines the intelligibility of the individual self as an originary source of moral action. The reasons are many and cumulative; I limit discussion here to several concatenating tendencies (for a more extended analysis of the "loss of self" in the media age, see Turkle 1995 and Gergen 1996).

Polyvocality

By dramatically expanding the range of information to which we are exposed, the range of persons with whom we have significant interchange, and the range of opinion available within multiple media sites, so do we become privy to multiple realities. Or more simply, the comfort of parochial univocality is disturbed. From the spheres of national politics and economics to local concerns with education, environment, or mental health we are confronted with a plethora of conflicting information and opinion. And so it is with matters of moral consequence. Whether it is a matter of Supreme Court nominees, abortion policies, or affirmative action, for example, one is deluged with conflicting moral standpoints. To the extent that these standpoints are intelligible, they also enter the compendium of resources available for the individual's own deliberations. In a Bakhtinian vein, the individual approaches a state of radical polyvocality.

If one does acquire an increasingly diverse vocabulary of deliberation, how is a satisfactory decision to be reached? The inward examination of consciousness yields not coherence but cacophony; there is not a "still small voice of conscience" but a chorus of competing contenders. It is one's moral duty to pay taxes, for example, but also to provide for one's dependents, to keep for oneself the rewards of one's labor, and to withhold monies from unjust governmental policies; it is one's moral duty to give aid to starving Africans, but also to help the poor of one's own country, to prevent population growth, and to avoid meddling in the politics of otherwise sovereign nations. Where in the mix of myriad moralities is the signal of certitude?

If immersion in a panoply of intelligibilities leaves one's moral resources in a state of complex fragmentation, then in what degree are these resources guiding or directing? Or more cogently for the present analysis, if "inward looking" becomes increasingly less useful for matters of moral action, does the concern with "my state of mind" not lose its urgency? The more compelling option is for the individual to turn outward to social context—to detect the ambient opinion, to negotiate, compromise, and improvise. And in this move from the private interior to the social sphere, the presumption of a private self as a source of moral direction is subverted. If negotiating the complexities of multiplicity becomes normalized, so does the conception of mind as moral touchstone grow stale.

Plasticity

As the technologies of sociation increase our immersion in information and evaluation, so do they expand the scope and complexity of our activities. We engage in a greater range of relationships distributed over numerous and variegated sites, from the face-to-face encounters in the neighborhood and workplace, to professional and recreational relationships that often span continents. Further, because of the rapid movement of information and opinion, the half life of various products and policies is shortened, and the opportunities for novel departures expanded. The composition of the workplace is thus in continuous flux. The working person shifts jobs more frequently, often with an accompanying move to another location. In the early 1990s one of three American workers had been with their employer for less than a year, and almost two out of three for less than five years.

As a result of these developments, the individual is challenged with an increasingly variegated array of behavioral demands. With each new performance site, new patterns of action may be required; dispositions, appetites, personae—all may be acquired and abandoned and reappropriated as conditions invite or demand. With movements through time and space, oppositional accents may often be fashioned: firm here and soft there, commanding and then obedient, sophisticated and then crude, righteous and immoral, conventional and rebellious. For many people such chameleon-like shifts are now unremarkable; they constitute the normal hurly-burly of daily life. At times the challenges may be enjoyed, even sought. It was only four decades ago when David Riesman's (1950) celebrated book, *The Lonely Crowd*, championed the virtues of the inner-directed man, and condemned the other-directed individual for lack of character—a man without a gyroscopic center of being. In the new techno-based ethos there is little need for the inner-directed, one-style-for-all individual. Such a person is narrow, parochial, inflexible. In the fast pace of the technological society, concern with the inner life is a luxury—if not a waste of time. We now celebrate protean being. In either case, the interior self recedes in significance (see, e.g., Lifton 1993).

Repetition

Let us consider a more subtle mode of self-erosion, owing in this instance to the increasing inundation of images, stories, and information. Consider here those confirmatory moments of individual authorship, moments in which the sense of authentic action becomes palpably transparent. Given the Western tradition of individualism, these are typically moments in which we apprehend our actions as unique, in which we are not merely duplicating models, obeying orders, or following conventions. Rather, in the innovative act we locate a guarantee of self as originary source, a creative agent, an author of one's own morality. Yet, in a world in which the technologies facilitate an enormous sophistication in "how it goes," such moments become increasingly rare. How is it, for example, that a young couple, who for twenty years have been inundated by romance narratives—on television and radio, in film, in magazines and books—can utter a sweet word of endearment without a haunting sense of cliche? Or in Umberto Eco's terms, how can a man who loves a cultivated woman say to her, "'I love you madly," when "he knows that she knows (and that she knows that he knows) that these words have already been written by Barbara Cartland?" (Eco 1983: 67).

In what sense can one stand out from the crowd in a singular display of moral fortitude, and not hear the voices of John Wayne, Gary Cooper, or Harrison Ford just over the shoulder?

Should one attempt to secure confirmation of agency from a public action—political remonstrance, religious expression, musical performance, and the like—the problems of authenticity are even more acute. First, the existing technologies do not allow us to escape the past. Rather, images of the past are stored, resurrected, and recreated as never before. In this sense, the leap from oral to print memory was only the beginning of a dramatic technological infusion of cultural memory. Thus, it becomes increasingly difficult to avoid observations of how any notable action is historically prepared. To perform publicly is to incite incessant commentaries about how one is, for example, "just like the 60s," "has his roots in Billy Sunday revivalism," or "draws his inspiration from Jimmy Hendrix." Should the public demonstration gain media interest there is also a slow conversion from the authentic to the instrumental. That is, what may have once seemed spontaneous is now converted to a performance "for the media" and its public. Indulgence in political passion, for example, becomes muted by the attentions one must give to wardrobe, voice projection, and facial expression. One cannot simply "play the music," but must be concerned with hairstyling, posture, and girth. In a world in which the local is rapidly transported to the global, the half-life of moral authenticity rapidly diminishes.

Transience

To the extent that one is surrounded by a cast of others, all of whom respond to each other in a similar way, a sense of unified self may result. One may come to understand, for example, that he is the first son of an esteemed high school teacher and a devoted mother, a star of the baseball team, and a devout Catholic. This sense of perdurable character also furnishes a standard against which the morality of one's acts can be judged. One can know that "this just isn't me," that "If I did that I would feel insufferable guilt." However, with the accumulating effects of the technologies of sociation, one now becomes transient, a nomad, or a "homeless mind" (Berger, Berger, and Kellner 1973). The continuous reminders of one's identity—of who one is and always has been—no longer prevail. The internal standard grows pallid, and in the end, one must imagine that it counts for little in the generation of moral action.

There is a more subtle effect of such techno-induced transience. It is not only a coherent community that lends itself to the sense of personal depth. It is also the availability of others who provide the time and attention necessary for a sense of an unfolding interior to emerge. The process of psychoanalysis is illustrative. As the analyst listens with hovering interest to the words of the analysand, and these words prompt questions of deeper meaning, there is created for the analysand the sense of palpable interiority, the reality of a realm beyond the superficially given, or in effect, a sense of individual depth. The process requires time and attention. And so it is in daily life; one acquires the sense of depth primarily when there is ample time for exploration, time for moving beyond instrumental calculations to matters of "deeper desire" and forgotten fantasies, to "what really counts." Yet, it is precisely this kind of "time off the merry-go-round" that is increasingly difficult to locate. In the techno-dominated world, one must keep moving, the network is vast, commitments are many, expectations are endless, opportunities abound, and time is a scarce commodity.

Each of these tendencies—toward polyvocality, plasticity, repetition, and transience—function so as to undermine the longstanding presumptions of a palpable self, personal consciousness as an agentive source, or interior character as a touchstone of the moral life.[2] Yet, while lamentable in certain respects, the waning intelligibility of moral selves is much welcomed in other quarters. Both intellectually and ideologically the concept of the self as moral atom is flawed. On the conceptual level, it is not simply that the conception of moral agency recapitulates the thorny problems of epistemological dualism—subject vs. object, mind vs. body, minds knowing other minds—but that the very idea of an *independent* decision-maker is uncompelling. How, it is asked, could moral thought take place except within the categories supplied by the culture? If we subtracted the entire vocabulary of the culture from individual subjectivity, how could the individual form questions about justice, duty, rights, or moral goods? In Michael Sandel's terms, "To imagine a person incapable of constitutive attachments...is not to conceive an ideally free and rational agent, but to imagine a person wholly without character, without moral depth" (1982: 179).

These conceptual problems are conjoined to widespread ideological critique. Alexis de Tocqueville's observations of nineteenth-century American life set the stage: "Individualism is a calm and considered feeling which disposes each citizen to isolate himself from the mass of his fellows...he gladly leaves the greater society to look after itself" (1969: 506). Within recent decades these views have been echoed and amplified by many. Christopher Lasch (1979) has traced linkages between individualist presumptions and cultural tendencies toward narcissism; Bellah and his colleagues (1985) argue that certain forms of individualism work against the possibility for committed relationships and dedication to community; for Edward Sampson (1993) the presumption of a self-contained individual leads to an insensitivity to minority voices, suppression of the other, and social division. Ultimately, the conception of an interior origin of action defines the society in terms of unbreachable isolation. If what is most central to our existence is hidden from the other, and vice versa, we are forever left with a sense of profound isolation, an inability to ever know what lies behind the other's visage. By constituting an interior self we inevitably create the Other from whom we shall forever remain alien.

Techno/Community: All Against All Redux

As we find, there are many reasons for welcoming a decline in attempts to lodge moral action in independent minds. It is not simply the conceptual and political limits inherent in individualism that are at stake here. Rather, for many analysts there is a far superior candidate available for achieving the moral project, namely the community. As Alasdair MacIntyre has proposed, to be an individual self—that is, one who is identified within a narrative of past, present, and future—requires a community. To be a moral self, then, is "to be accountable for the actions and experiences which compose a narratible life within a community" (1984: 202). In this sense, the moral project is achieved by sustaining the best of a community's traditions. In effect: "The virtues find their point and purpose not only in sustaining those relationships necessary if the variety of goods internal to practices are to be achieved...but also in sustaining those traditions which provide both practices and individual lives with their necessary historical context" (207). On the more political level, this view resonates with the shift from a rights-based to a duty-based orientation toward societal life, as advocated by the communitarian movement.

Let us again, however, consider the community as moral resource in the age of technology. Again the way is paved for such reflection by an earlier classic, in this case Benedict Anderson's *Imagined Communities*

(1991). As Anderson proposes, the emergence of nation states was importantly facilitated by the development of print technology—which not only succeeded in unifying and codifying particular languages, but could be used to generate a sense of common interest and common future. In effect, we cannot separate issues of social organization from the technological context. In light of the contemporary context, then, what are the potentials of community-based morality?

If by community we mean a group of people relating face-to-face across time in a geographically circumscribed habitat, there would appear little hope for success in the moral project. As I attempted to outline in *The Saturated Self* (1991a), twentieth-century technologies of sociation are everywhere eroding the traditional face-to-face community as a generative matrix for moral action. Mass transportation systems have separated home from workplace, and neighborhoods from commercial and entertainment centers; families are frequently scattered across continents, and largely owing to career demands the average American now moves households over eleven times during his or her life. Even when neighbors or families are within physical proximity, face-to-face interaction has dramatically diminished. Technologically mediated exchange—through telephone, television, radio, CD players, computers, and the like—is steadily reducing dependency on those in the immediate surrounds. In these and many other ways, both the geographically circumscribed neighborhood and the traditional family unit are losing their capacity to generate and sustain moral commitment.[3] Thus, while theoretically more appealing than individualism, the emerging technological ethos poses substantial and ever intensifying limits to lodging morality in geographically based communities.

Yet, while technological developments are reducing the significance of face-to-face communities within the culture, we are also witnessing a striking increase in the number and importance of *technologically mediated communities*. These are communities whose participants rely largely on communication technologies for sustaining their realities, values, and agendas. Television evangelism is an obvious case in point. Several million Americans are linked primarily through mediated communication to a set of beliefs that affect decisions from local school systems across the country to the posture of national political parties (see, e.g., Hoover 1988). Less obvious is the organization of over 20,000 non-governmental organizations (NGOs) operating internationally—to combat starvation, overpopulation, AIDS, environmental erosion, and other threats to human well-being—and over a million such private organizations advancing human welfare within the United States. Such organizations are vitally dependent on existing communication technology for continuing sustenance.

Less public in their moral agenda are the countless computer-mediated or *virtual* communities emerging over the past decade. The sense of community often created within such groups is illustrated in Howard Rheingold's *The Virtual Community*:

> Finding the WELL (a computer mediated community) was like discovering a cozy little world...hidden within the walls of my house; an entire cast of characters welcomed me to the troupe with great merriment as soon as I found the secret door.... A full-scale subculture was growing on the other side of my telephone jack, and they invited me to help create something new. The virtual village of a few hundred people I stumbled upon in 1985 grew to eight thousand by 1993. (1993: 7)

The emergence of these communities is now facilitated by the World Wide Web, on which virtually any organization can mount a colorful invitation to participate. At present there are, for example, highly active web sites inviting membership in the Druid religion and in pantheism. The potential power of these forms of mediated engagement in people's lives is perhaps most dramatically evidenced in the ability of the techno-generated cult, Heaven's Gate, to precipitate mass suicide.

If moral dispositions are solidified through relationships, one might see great promise in twentieth-century communication technologies. Here we find a mushrooming of new communities, many of them specifically constructed around visions of the good. Yet the very advantages of technologically based organization may simultaneously pose the greatest danger. Rapidly, inexpensively, and with little regard to geographic distance, self-organizing enclaves are created and sustained. At the same time, however, the ease and efficacy of organization is accompanied by strong centripetal or inner-directed tendencies. With the flick of a switch the individual enters the totalizing reality of the group. In many cases, the techno-mediated relationships are complemented by printed media (newsletters, newspapers, magazines) and face-to-face meetings (religious services, conferences, demonstrations, picnics). The social and political agenda invites a lifestyle of full engagement. Healy comments on the tendencies toward cyber-segmentation:

> At my university...the IRC addicts are just as segregated as the occupants of my son's high school lunch room. In our computer lab the Vietnamese students hang out on Vietnamese channels, just as at Ben's school they all sit at their own tables at lunch....On the net...talk tends not to get "overheard;" the boundaries

separating virtual conversants are less substantial, but their effect is more dramatic. Two virtual places may be "separated" by only a keystroke, but their inhabitants will never meet. (1997: 62)

Accompanying such segmentation is a tendency for moral/political positions to become polarized and rigidified. The in-group reality becomes more convincing, the out-group is seen as more malevolent. When the moral/political agendas become manifest in public action, jarring conflict is almost inevitable. And it is thus that our technologies have hastened what James Davison Hunter (1991) has called "the culture wars"—with blacks vs. whites, women vs. men, gays vs. straights, pro life vs. pro choice, right vs. left, young vs. old, minorities vs. the majority, and so on. It is when a commitment to justice, dignity, freedom, and moral integrity lead to the bombing of the Federal Building in Oklahoma that we began to confront the impasse of community-based morality.

Toward Relational Being

As the preceding analysis suggests, our legacy for pursuing the moral project is severely delimited. In light of the emerging technological context, neither individualism nor communalism holds substantial promise for securing an acceptable mode of cultural life. Both traditions are deeply flawed—conceptually, ideologically, or practically. Indeed, with the emerging clash of global cultures one might view these traditions as potential hazards to our future well-being. On what conceptual grounds are we thus to proceed? Are there significant alternatives to individualism and communalism offering promise for theorizing the moral project in the twenty-first century? In my view, there is a subtle but significant movement taking place, one that will demand nurturant and creative attention in order to bear fruit. It is a movement that works to subvert the self/society binary and to bring about an apotheosis of relationship. It is the attempt to subsume both self and community within a broader reality of relatedness.

In certain respects the emerging technologies again create the space for a relational conception of being. Of particular relevance is the development of chat rooms, bulletin boards, list serves, and other Internet facilities that enable relationships to take place without specific lodgement in individual bodies (see especially Turkle 1995 and Stone 1995). That is, identities can be put forward that may or may not be linked in any specific way to the concrete existence of the participants, and these cyber-identities may carry on active and engaging relationships. Most significant for our purposes, we have here relationships that proceed not on the basis of "real selves" (originary minds within a body), but on the basis of self-positionings or discursive formations. (One "real self" may indeed generate multiple self-positions, and in some cases even set these into animated public interchange.) Further, it is only the coordinated functioning of these discursive formations that enable "community" to be achieved. In effect, community has no geographic locus outside the web of discourse by which it is constituted. We approach here pure relatedness, without self or community in the traditional sense.

The image of relationship without self or community does have other sources in the techno-sphere. For several decades the computer has served as one of the chief metaphors for human functioning. The cognitive revolution in psychology, along with the artificial intelligence movement and cognitive science, have derived much of their intelligibility from various equations of person and computer. However, with the dramatic expansion of the internet and World Wide Web, the computer gradually loses its rhetorical fascination. The internet is a domain that brings instantaneous relationship to an exponentially increasing population throughout the globe. It is a domain so vast and so powerful that it can scarcely be controlled by the nation state. It is legislated by no institution; it functions virtually outside the law. In this context the computer is merely a gateway into a domain without obvious end. The metaphor of the computer, limited and parochial, is gradually replaced by the *network*: a world that stretches toward infinity.

In the same way that the cultural ethos has stimulated the scholarship of self and of community, so does it now function as an impetus to scholarly concern with relationship. Such attempts not only create a reality of relationship, but move slowly toward linking this reality to new conceptions and practices of moral significance. Such writings now emerge in many corners of the academy. For example, guided by such works as Jean Baker Miller's *Toward a New Psychology of Women* (1983), feminist scholars and practitioners have elaborated a relational view of self with broad therapeutic and moral implications. The work of the Stone Center, in particular, views the individual mind as inseparable from the relations of which one is a part.[4] One's "self-esteem," for example, is not a private possession, but a derivative of a relational matrix. This work bears a certain affinity to the broad-ranging discussion of Levinas's conception of moral responsibility. For Levinas (1969), ethics begins with the putting into question of the ego or knowing subject; morality begins with recognizing the face of the other as Other, and responding with selfless dedication. Both the feminist and Levinasian movements celebrate relationship over self or community. However, in my view, neither is entirely sufficient in crossing the self/other divide. We find here—and as well in the work of their predecessors, George Herbert Mead and Martin Buber—that the concept of relationship presupposes something in the way of an essential self. For Levinas, and Buber in particular, the *other* (or the *thou*) is the object of a contemplative or integral consciousness. For the relational feminists as well as Mead, we find an implicit presumption of an essentialized self that is a necessary prerequisite for comprehending the other's mental states. There is no empathy or symbolic interaction until there are selves to comprehend the other's interior. In all these cases, ethical actions ultimately derive from a particular condition of individual mind.

On another front, psychologists have joined with cultural anthropologists to generate an image of individual mental functioning as inseparable from cultural milieu. For example, Bruner's highly influential work draws sustenance from Lev Vygotsky in proposing that "it is culture, not biology, that shapes...the human mind, that gives meaning to action by situating its underlying intentional states in an interpretive system" (1990: 34). In a similar vein, anthropologist Richard Shweder proposes that the mind is "content-driven, domain-specific, and constructively stimulus-bound; and it cannot be extricated from the historically variable and culturally diverse intentional worlds in which it plays a constitutive part" (1990: 13). A similar view is echoed in Michael Cole's volume, *Cultural Psychology* (1996), in which a substantial account is generated of the way in which mental functioning is shaped through the use of cultural tools. Yet, in my view, these accounts also remain substantially wedded to the traditional self/society binary. In contrast to the preceding lines of argument, it is not the private self that is privileged but the culture as origin of the self. There is little in the way of mind until there is culture; culture (community) functions as an ontological prior. As Michael Cole quotes Theodore Adorno, "Culture might be precisely that condition that excludes a mentality capable of measuring it" (1996: 7).

More successful in escaping the thrall of the traditional binary has been a movement bringing together scholars from across the humanities and social sciences in a resuscitation of Mikhail Bakhtin's (1981) writings on dialogism. Focal attention shifts in this case from expositions of psychological process sui generis to characterizing self *within* ongoing relationships, replacing the concern over internal residues of cultural experience with an examination of ongoing social (self-other) process from which individual functioning cannot be extricated. In such accounts, the self-other (individual/culture) binary is virtually destroyed. For example, drawing from Bakhtin's work, Edward Sampson proposes that

> all meaning, including the meaning of one's self, is rooted in the social process and must be seen as an ongoing accomplishment of that process. Neither meaning nor self is a precondition for social interaction; rather, these emerge from and are sustained by conversations occurring between people. (1993: 99)

Similarly, in his development of a "rhetorically responsive" view of human action, John Shotter is concerned with the way "responsive meanings are always first 'sensed' or 'felt' from within a conversation....and amenable to yet further responsive (sensible) development" (1993: 180).

Meaning and Morality

These are interesting and important excursions into a new image of relationship. At the same time, it is too early to determine the full moral import of dialogic accounts. Among the major problems to be solved is how to reconcile a description of all intelligible action as dialogical with an ethical prescription of dialogue over monologue. If all intelligible human action is dialogic, what actions can be identified as immoral, and on what grounds are we to argue their moral inferiority? If an intelligible view of monologue (something other than dialogue) can successfully be generated, then proponents also run the risk of violating the ethic in the very articulation of dialogicality—which itself seems propelled by a unified ontology, rationality, and ethics.

There is yet another movement that, while overlapping in significant degree with the preceding one, offers a significant alternative. Here we find a certain species of social constructionist scholarship with particularly deep roots in Wittgenstein's later works (1953). Perhaps the key argument derived from Wittgenstein in this case is one which traces meaning to action. Rather than meaning deriving from individual minds (the self) or from the community (from whence interjected into selves), meaning is a byproduct of language use within relationship. Meaning is thus removed from hidden recesses of the mind and from the community, and placed in the coordination of actions—visible, present, and continuous. When extended in this way, we find that both self and community are derivatives of relationship. To speak of self (our intentions, thoughts, emotions, etc.) or community (our religion, ethnicity, nation, etc.) is already to participate in discursive traditions, and these traditions are developed and sustained within relationship. In this sense, relationship becomes a logical prior to all that we take to be real, objective, true, or moral.

Resonating with this line of argument is a body of scholarship that attempts first to deconstruct the dualist presumption of self (within bodies), and then reconstruct the language of self in relational terms. The attempt, then, is to eliminate psychological states and conditions as explanations for action, and to reconstitute psychological predicates within the sphere of social process. The flavor of the critique is already captured in the preceding discussion of limits to individualist explanation. However, in the relational reconstitution of self, Potter and Wetherell's work provides an early entry. Here the term "attitude" is shorn of mental referents and is used to index positional claims within social intercourse. To possess an attitude (or an opinion), on this account, is to take a position in an ongoing conversation. The "attitude," then, cannot be extricated from the discursive relationship (Potter and Wetherell 1987). In the same way, we can understand "reason" as a form of discourse—not an effective form of mentation but of effective rhetoric (Myerson 1994). Memory from this standpoint is not something that occurs in mind or brain, but a particular kind of social action indexed by such phrases as "I remember" (Middleton and Edwards 1990). Or, as Shotter proposes, memory is a "social institution" (1990: 129). Terms of emotion are reconstituted as constituents of culturally specific performances, and these performances are embedded within reiterative patterns of interchange. In effect, one cannot extricate the dancer from the dance.

Unlike much of the preceding work, such theorizing is not typically devoted to illuminating the truth about human action. Rather, social constructionism generally eschews the warrants of "truth" and "objectivity" in favor of a use-based conception of language. Thus, the attempt in such theorizing is primarily to furnish a range of discursive resources that might enlarge the potentials for human interchange. This aversion to truth warrants also brings us face-to-face with the challenge of the moral project. In what sense can relational accounts, born of a constructionist sensibility, serve as moral resources for the future? At the outset it would seem that the constructionist aversion to fundamental or foundational claims carries over into moral stipulations. If so, then constructionism is placed under attack for its lack of moral standpoint—its "moral relativism." In effect, there is no moral standpoint here but a vacuum.

Yet, it is precisely within its groundlessness that we locate the moral potential of constructionism for the postmodern world. There is no attempt here to suppress an ethic or ideology, nor is there any attempt to ground such positions in a foundation or first philosophy. Rather, from the constructionist perspective, what we do have available in our discourses are resources either for creating or subverting the process of meaning making—which is to say, resources that are essential for creating any sense of the good (worth, value, ideals)—or destroying it. There is no foundational warrant for championing creation over destruction. However, if we value any form of action whatsoever, then we may have a stake in fostering processes of relationship from which values emerge and are sustained. Social construction does invite, then, inquiry into sustaining relationships from which meaning is generated. Without meaning there is no morality.

If the invitation is accepted, one might initially be drawn toward the promulgation of discourse ethics, as in the case of Habermas's (1993) significant efforts. However, in light of the antifoundationalist thrust of constructionist reasoning there is little interest in such transcendental warrants for particular kinds of conversation. And, given arguments for the use-based character of meaning, there is little desire to generate abstract, context-free "rules for good conversations." Rather, for many constructionists there is more to be gained by turning from scholarship to societal practices. The practices of particular concern to morality are those relevant to sustaining conditions of meaning. Let us consider more closely.

In most sectors of life discursive relations proceed without severe obstruction. As we converse with family, friends, neighbors, and so on there will emerge implicit (and sometimes explicit) moral codes—agreements on what is proper, appropriate, or desirable. In effect, normal human interchange will yield up standards of the good. In this sense, the moral project is always already in motion. No foundational rationality is required for the sense of the good to emerge. However, the major problem from a constructionist perspective is not the generation of morality, but the existence of multiple moralities. It is when enclaves of the good come to see their local standards as universal and alternative commitments as inferior or threatening, that the stage is set for the dissolution of meaning. It is in the process of mutual annihilation that we confront the destruction of relationship—thus the end of moral meaning. Thus, the chief focus for the architect of relational practice is the domain of conflicting realities.

It is thus that the present offering ends with yet another beginning. There are many practitioners and theorists now engaged in crafting processes for restoring the meaning-making process. Such efforts issue from the disparate domains of family therapy, organizational study, communication, counseling, education, and community work. These explorations are scarcely the private preserve of constructionists; the efforts themselves are communal.[5] Within such explorations, however, lie potentials for what may become significant societal resources for sustaining moral meaning.

Notes

1. Such a conclusion would also be congenial with a rapidly growing body of literature on the historical and cultural construction of the mind. See, for example, Foucault (1978), Lutz (1988), and Graumann and Gergen (1996).
2. These conclusions are surely resonant with other accounts of "the loss," "decentering," or "deconstruction" of the self in recent scholarship. However, where key writings by Foucault, Lacan, and Derrida derive their conclusions from theoretical premises, the present analysis attempts to trace the sense of dissolution to particular circumstances of cultural technology. In effect, one might suppose that the very intelligibility of the theoretical analyses may be derived from common experiences in contemporary culture.
3. For further discussion of technology and the erosion of the traditional family, see Meyrowitz (1985) and Gergen (1991b).
4. On the work of the Stone Center, see, http://www.wellesley.edu/counseling/wip.html#rd.
5. The work of the Taos Institute represents a concerted effort of constructionist scholars and practitioners to develop means of transforming relationships. See http://www.serve.com/taos.

References

Alkalimat, A., D. Gills, and K. Williams, eds. 1995. *Job-tech: The Technological Revolution and Its Impact on Society*. Chicago: Twenty-First Century Books.
Anderson, B. 1991. *Imagined Communities*. 2 ed. New York: Verso.
Bakhtin, M.M. 1981. *The Dialogic Imagination*. Austin: University of Texas Press.
Bellah, R.N., R. Madsen, W.M. Sullivan, A. Swidler, and S. Tipton. 1985. *Habits of the Heart: Individualism and Commitment in American Life*. Berkeley: University of California Press.

Berger, P.L., B. Berger, and H. Kellner. 1973. *The Homeless Mind*. New York: Vintage.

Bruner, J.S. 1990. *Acts of Meaning*. Cambridge, MA: Harvard University Press.

Cole, M. 1996. *Cultural Psychology*. Cambridge, MA: Harvard University Press.

Eco, U. 1983. *Postscript to The Name of the Rose*. San Diego, CA: Harcourt Brace Jovanovich.

Foucault, M. 1978. *The History of Sexuality*." Vol.1. New York: Pantheon.

Gergen, K.J. 1991a. *The Saturated Self*. New York: Basic Books.

————. 1991b. "The Saturated Family." *Family Therapy Networker* 15(Sept./Oct.): 26-35.

————. 1996. "Technology and the Self: From the Essential to the Sublime." Pp. 127-140 in *Constructing the Self in a Mediated Age*, edited by D. Grodin and T. Lindlof. Beverly Hills, CA: Sage.

Graumann, C.F. and K.J. Gergen, eds. 1996. *Historical Dimensions of Psychological Discourse*. New York: Cambridge University Press.

Habermas, J. 1993. *Justification and Application: Remarks on Discourse Ethics*. Cambridge, MA: The MIT Press.

Healy, D. 1997. "Cyberspace and Place." In *Internet Culture*, edited by D. Porter. New York: Routledge.

Hoover, S.M. 1988. *Mass Media Religion*. Beverly Hills, CA: Sage.

Hunter, J.D. 1991. *Culture Wars: The Struggle to Define America*. New York: Basic Books.

Kelley, K. 1994. *Out of Control: The New Biology of Machines, Socials Systems and the Economic World*. Reading, MA: Addison-Wesley.

Lasch, C. 1979. *The Culture of Narcissism*. New York: Norton.

Levinas, E. 1969. *Totality and Infinity*. Pittsburgh, PA: Duquesne University Press.

Lifton, R. 1993. *The Protean Self*. New York: Basic Books.

Lutz, C.A. 1988. *Unnatural Emotions*. Chicago: University of Chicago Press.

MacIntyre, A. 1984. *After Virtue*. 2 ed. Notre Dame, IN: University of Notre Dame Press.

Meyrowitz, J. 1985. *No Sense of Place: The Impact of Electronic Media on Social Behavior*. New York: Oxford University Press.

Middleton, D., and D. Edwards. 1990. *Collective Remembering*. London: Sage.

Miller, J.B. 1983. *Toward a New Psychology of Women*. New York: Penguin.

Myerson, G. 1994. *Rhetoric, Reason and Society*. London: Sage.

Ong, W.J. 1982. *Orality and Literacy*. London: Methuen.

Poster, M. 1995. *The Second Media Age*. Cambridge, MA: Polity Press.

Potter, J., and M. Wetherell. 1987. *Discourse and Social Psychology: Beyond Attitudes and Behavior*. London: Sage.

Rheingold, H. 1993. *The Virtual Community: Homesteading on the Electronic Frontier*. Reading, MA: Addison-Wesley.

Riesman, D., with N. Glazer and R. Denney. 1950. *The Lonely Crowd: A Study of the Changing American Character*. New Haven, CT: Yale University Press.

Sampson, E.E. 1993. *Celebrating the Other*. Boulder, CO: Westview Press.

Sandel, M.J. 1982. *Liberalism and the Limits of Justice*. Cambridge: Cambridge University Press.

Shotter, J. 1990. "The Social Construction of Remembering and Forgetting." Pp. 120-138 in *Collective Remembering*, edited by D. Middleton and D. Edwards. London: Sage.

————. 1993. *Cultural Politics of Everyday Life*. Toronto: University of Toronto Press.

Shweder, R.A. 1990. "Cultural Psychology: What Is It?" Pp. 1-43 in *Cultural Psychology: Essays on Comparative Human Development*, edited by J.W. Stigler, R.A. Shweder, and G. Herdt. New York: Cambridge University Press.

Sproull, L., and S. Kiesler. 1991. *Connections: New Ways of Working in the Networked Organization.* Cambridge, MA: The MIT Press.

Stone, A.R. 1995. *The War of Desire and Technology at the Close of the Mechanical Age.* Cambridge, MA: The MIT Press.

Tocqueville, A. de. 1969. *Democracy in America.* New York: Doubleday.

Turkle, S. 1995. *Life on the Screen: Identity in the Age of the Internet.* New York: Simon and Schuster.

Wittgenstein, L. 1953. *Philosophical Investigations*, trans. G. Anscombe. New York: Macmillan.

7

Not Dead Yet:
Psychotherapy, Morality, and the
Question of Identity Dissolution

Joseph E. Davis

Although originating from diverse vantage points, recent social theory about the concept of identity has been typically concerned with an erosion of the belief in an essence or foundational identity defining the person. Writers on postmodernism, for instance, argue that the individual's sense of identity and biographical continuity has been superseded by fragmentation and superficial play with the endless flow of images and sensations encountered in consumer culture. Philosophers of various stripes have advanced a comprehensive epistemological critique of the idea of the rational and unified subject at the heart of post-Cartesian philosophy. Many psychologists, whose discipline has been concerned to proffer models of the self's inner structure, now question the very notion of the self. And even in the literature on identity politics, with its typical emphasis on individuals identifying themselves in or with groups and categories, some writers challenge essentialist accounts of collective identities (the notion that all members of the collectivity uniquely share core features), and reject definitions of self in terms of birth or inner life experience (e.g., O'Hara 1989). In each of these discourses and others, the deconstructive critique of identity has attacked the idea of an underlying, coherent self. Identity fragmentation and multiplicity have been central themes.

In deconstructive critiques, fragmentation and malleable identities are sometimes championed as a form of personal liberation. Some post-modernists celebrate a self characterized by variation, by change, by flux, by an irony toward life and a free-floating approach to work, ideas, attitudes, and feelings. This self is not stable and centered but multiple and "nomadic," experimenting with and resymbolizing itself, linking disparate identity elements in a constant stream of new combinations (see Anderson 1998; Lifton 1993; Deleuze and Guattari 1983; Melucci 1996). In these celebratory versions of postmodernism, the performative ability to transcend and reconstitute one's self is the very definition of freedom. Similarly, in some of the popular psychological literature, the older notion of life stages has been replaced by a view of life as "an improvisatory art" (Bateson 1989: 3), and the possibility of multiple selves is regarded as healthy and adaptive. A healthy multiplicity has also been suggested by social psychologists (Gergen 1991; Markus and Nurius 1986; Sampson 1993), and even within the multiple personality literature, one can find plaudits for the ability of some multiples to dissociate creatively, and thus, in part, acclaim for multiplicity itself (see Brown 1999).

Deconstructive and emancipatory views, however, by no means cover the field. The experience of identity as multiple, discontinuous, and shifting has long been seen to represent a disability, and in more extreme cases a mental disorder, and in many quarters it still is. Over the past few decades whole movements with high rates of participation, including the New Age and recovery movements, have arisen that seek to aid participants in the face of a wide range of identity tribulations to achieve unity, biographical coherence, and a teleological sense of life as a meaningful project (Bellah et al. 1985; Brown 1997; Irvine 1999; Rice 1996). Popular and professional seminars, programs, and books, along with teachers, counselors, and guides have proliferated, each offering advice on how to consolidate and hold the right identity. Further, new or reconstituted categories of disorder and therapy have spread that explicitly attend to fragmented selves. Multiple personality disorder (now called dissociative identity disorder) and post-traumatic stress disorder are but two of the more outstanding examples. With the exceptions noted above, there is no celebration of fragmentation or multiplicity in these psychological discourses and treatment practices. Health involves wholeness and self-integration.

In this chapter, I explore a site, adult survivor therapy, at which identity instability and experiences of fragmentation are addressed as a disability, and where the attitudinal goal for clients is to embrace a view of themselves and their lives as meaningful, coherent, and centered. To achieve an identity transformation, two languages of the self are employed. The first is used throughout therapy to characterize the self-understandings and orientations that the client is encouraged to reject. This is the "false self," and it is pictured as determined and fixed through unconscious processes arising directly from traumatic formative experiences. The second language is used to characterize the self-understandings and orientations that the client is encouraged to adopt. This is the "true self," and it is pictured as determining itself, drawing its purposes and life-plans from within yet able to improvise and change as the need or desire arises.

I want to suggest here that the practice of using these two seemingly incompatible languages, while paradoxical, is not contradictory. The tension between social determination and individual agency in survivor therapy, I argue, can be resolved by focusing on the moral transformations that are constitutive of the identity-change process. Survivor therapy, and other practices like it, I hope to show, are designed to alter clients' identities by altering their suppositions toward what it is good to do and good to be. Rather than contradict, the two languages of the self serve this common goal. The determinative view of the self, defined on the basis of scientific and universalistic moral claims, pathologizes client orientations to the self and others linked to it. At the same time, it provides the epistemological "other" against which the self-determining view and its moral orientations are constructed and their adoption warranted. Constructing the false self, in other words, dictates an identity change, a change in moral orientations, and in precisely the terms in which the true self is depicted.

Addressing identity crises and experiences of fragmentation in this way, and leading clients to develop a more reflexive and coherent view of themselves, I argue, casts doubt on the general reading of identity dissolution, emancipatory or otherwise, that has been advanced by prominent social theorists. The practice of survivor therapy implies that identity cannot be decoupled from moral subjectivity, however much the second language of the self, the language of reflexive self-definition, obscures the connection. Therapists proffer a moral evaluation of victimization and its consequences and new normative orientations to the client to help create biographical continuity and a sense of meaning and direction to the life project. Implicitly, moral frameworks are treated as foundational to the self. If this view is correct, if a moral disposition to the world and a prior assent to certain moral criteria is inescapable for psychological order and self-consistency, a point that has been argued by the philosopher Charles Taylor (1989), then the self cannot be radically fragmented or "protean" without at the same time being in crises. Accounts of identity dissolution, and thereby accounts of the effects of social and cultural change on the self, inadequately account for identity itself and the integrative possibilities by which identities can be reconstituted or transformed.

In developing the argument, I begin with an analysis of the therapy process and the key stages through which the therapist leads the client. I then consider in more detail the paradoxical disjunction between the end of the therapeutic process, the model of a self-determining self toward which the therapy aims, and the strongly determinative self language by which the therapist leads the client to realize it. I conclude by considering how the disjunction between these two languages might be resolved and what it implies for questions of identity dissolution.

Adult Survivor Therapy

Adult survivor therapies, or as they are sometimes called, incest survivor therapies, are relatively new. They emerged over the past two decades amidst considerable social activism on child sexual abuse and in tandem with new theories of the long-term effects of sexual maltreatment. In the new theories, which broke quite sharply from older approaches, mental health researchers and therapists argued that sexual abuse (which could be very broadly defined and include experiences that involved no touch) not only profoundly harmed children, but when inadequately resolved, typically resulted in debilitating distresses, dysfunctional behavior patterns, or mental illnesses in victims' adult lives. An experience of abuse, these theorists argued, is psychologically traumatic, and so in order to survive, victims must build an internal defense structure to protect themselves. In some cases, victims block or split off, by mental mechanisms of repression or dissociation, all memory of the abuse from consciousness. More commonly, victims block out only some memories and emotions, deny their experience was abusive, or fail to recognize the extent to which it has determined their life.

Although victims' trauma defenses are functional for psychic survival, the theory goes, they do not prevent abuse from being harmful and become disorders in themselves over time. The personally hidden nature of the trauma, and the social secrecy and nonrecognition that surround it, also contributes to the false and distorted mode of being that victims take on.

As the new trauma theories arose, therapists designed a variety of treatment models for addressing the adult problems believed to represent the enduring effects of abuse. Most of these models are theoretically eclectic. Consistent with their eclectic orientation, they present techniques from a variety of therapeutic schools to address specific problems. Psychodynamic techniques, for example, are often recommended for unearthing memories and working through them; cognitive techniques are recommended for handling "faulty thinking"; and behavioral techniques are recommended for desensitizing client emotional responses to traumatic memories. While there is a great deal of overlap, these models do not share all the same assumptions, and do not recommend all the same approaches or the same stages. For purposes of analysis, however, I have created a composite picture of the process based on a grounded theory (Strauss 1987) analysis of the professional and self-help therapeutic literatures (see Davis 1999 for methodological details). Obviously, with a composite, some specificity, nuance, and variability in clinical practice is lost. Yet the structure that I briefly present here, with varying modifications, is common to the different models.

One further prefatory point. I describe survivor therapy in terms of a narrative reconstruction of a client's life story, yet, as I will consider further below, none of the treatment models is organized on a "narrativist" or "constructivist" basis. Narrativists conceive psychotherapy as an exercise in reconceptualizing life stories and identities that are believed to be constraining or incoherent. In this modality, therapists assist clients to construct a new life story, one that builds on an understanding of what their old stories have done for them but at the same time offers new potential for positive feelings and accomplishments (e.g., Gergen 1994; Howard 1990; Neimeyer 1995).[1] Although the survivor therapeutic process is not theoretically narrativist, I frame it in a narrative metaphor because in coding the treatment literature, story editing, building, and replacing emerged as the decisive features. Survivor therapy is an iterative process, emphasizing the development of narrative facility as the client tells and retells (and perhaps also writes out, even experimenting with different voices and literary styles) a developing account of her life and its significance. As one guidebook for therapists notes,

> the words chosen must be the patient's own—carefully selected, always subject to change and reformulation. The therapeutic process, like a piece of sculpture, brings the patient ever closer to a final construction with which she can feel satisfied; but the work remains 'in progress' for some time. (Davies and Frawley 1994: 212)

Not every element of therapy involves storytelling as such. In many of the therapist's techniques, the client performs rather than narrates new understandings, such as in expressing emotion, role-playing with assertiveness, engaging in "body work," and confronting the alleged abuser. Yet each non-storytelling element serves as a precondition of constructing a narrative or makes its conveyance in a narrative possible. The client can tell a story about self-assertiveness once assertiveness is expressed, for instance, or anger, once discharged, can then be added to the story that brought it about. Survivor therapy, then, is a fundamentally narrative process. By way of this process, survivor therapists bring clients to terms with their tarnished past self and to a recognition of certain beliefs about the self and others that constitutes the basis for a new and emergent identity.

Discovering the True Self

The construction of a new life story in survivor therapy is a negotiated accomplishment. To foster abuse resolution and personal healing, the therapist employs what I will call a "mediating narrative" to authorize and structure the client's rejection of old self-understandings and the appropriation of new. The mediating narrative is the symbolic vehicle, the sequence of words, acts, and rituals that are used by therapists to convey a message of personal transformation through a reordered self, and that mediates the transformation by providing a template for achieving it. This narrative structure unfolds in three stages—about the past, present, and future—which, taken together, represent a developing plot directed toward the new understandings of the self and relationships that constitute the endpoint attitudinal ideals of health and wholeness. To reach the endpoint, the therapist organizes each element of therapy, including, importantly, the therapeutic relationship, to foster a "narrative fit" (Goodman 1978), helping the client to reflect upon and evaluate her experience and repeatedly renarrate it until it is internally consistent with the narrative model.[2]

When they come to therapy, clients do not typically link their adult problems with sexual abuse as a child, and may not report abuse even when asked. Survivor therapists therefore work to discover if clients were abused. Since a client's own understandings of her past may be partially or completely unreliable, therapists cannot always rely on her disclosures to determine if she was a victim. They use lists of presenting symptoms and in-therapy comments and behavior to identify and diagnose possible victims. Because abuse is believed to cause a very wide range of behavioral, cognitive, and emotional disorders, these symptom lists are typically quite long, including depression, sexual problems, over- or undereating, anxiety, marital conflicts, and the problems typically associated with post-traumatic stress disorder—for example, flashbacks, sleep disturbances, dissociation and identity splits, and amnesia.

After diagnosing a client as an adult survivor, the therapist works to create a relationship with her that is the foundation and an important vehicle for his efforts. He works not only to build a cordial, relaxed, and freely interactive ethos, but he structures the relationship to embody and promote each of the key changes he believes the client needs to make. In order to promote change, the therapist may also recommend participation in a therapy or survivor group. The right group supports therapy by providing peer affirmation and support for every step of the process, as well as ready models for emulation and identification. In a group, momentum for change is mobilized, the rightness of the change is authorized, and an incentive—continuing membership, others' expectations—is created to stay the course.

As the relationship with the therapist takes shape, the client is prepared to begin the journey to self discovery.

The Victim Story. In the initial stage of therapy, the therapist helps the client, whatever her current understanding, to construct a victim story about her experience. To construct the story, the therapist takes the client through a series of steps in which she slowly detaches herself from and deconstructs her previous identity.

In the first step, the therapist helps the client to remember childhood sexual episodes and to discuss them in detail. While clients are believed to block memories to varying degrees, all clients, whatever their level of recall, are expected to recover some new memories. Therapists authorize and promote memory work by giving the client "permission to remember," actively encouraging her to seek out memories and bring them to mind, and validating memories as they surface by believing them. Some use memory-enhancement techniques, such as hypnosis and age regression to help with the recovery process. Therapists also promote new memories by interpreting otherwise unexplained bodily pain or discomfort and nightmares as abuse memories. By talking through the past, and, perhaps for the first time, having memories of abuse or interpreting an experience as abuse, the client is beginning to construct a personal victim account.

In constructing a victim story, and to promote further memory recovery, the therapist also directs the client to reenact and describe abuse emotions. Therapists believe that abuse emotions are bottled up within or split off from the direct consciousness of the client but remain present and active. In order to overcome emotional inhibition and to encourage a mood state in which memories can more easily be remembered, therapists encourage clients to release appropriate emotion and may use relaxation techniques, cues, and selective validation for this purpose. Many emotions, some positive and many negative, are expected to flood over the client during this phase. Therapists may help the client sort out and explore her emotions by providing a language to describe them. To move the process along, therapists sometimes suggest emotions, help the client to label her emotions, and validate acceptable emotions (not, for instance, guilt) as real and genuine. By taking the client through the emotions of sexual abuse, the therapist solidifies her sense of past victimization. New memories are brought forth, and doubts about her memories are further eroded by a kind of experiencing of abuse through emotional reenactment. Victim "feeling states" are added to and can be conveyed and triggered by the emerging victim account.

By themselves, the memories and feelings of abuse tell only part of the victim story. The other part of the story concerns the consequences. In order to tell this part, the client needs to recognize that what happened to her, whatever its specific details, was serious victimization. She also needs to recognize that her victimization has had serious long-term consequences and caused many, though not necessarily all, her adult problems. Despite the memory and emotion work up to this point in therapy, the client may still resist this recognition. Therapists, therefore, work to promote it. Among other methods, they explain the connection between past trauma and current problems, sometimes using the theory of post-traumatic stress disorder to do so, and by encouraging clients to read the autobiographical accounts of other adult victims or to attend survivor group meetings.

The client's recognition of victimization and its causal relationship to her adult problems represents a milestone in treatment. Victimization and its aftereffects are the interpretative key offered to clients to make sense of their painful and otherwise disconnected experiences, to help them to see a general pattern to their life, and to locate responsibility for negative outcomes. In survivor therapy, victimization and its aftereffects account for how her life has come to be what it is.

At this point in therapy, the essential elements of the victim story—memories, emotions, connection between past and present—are coming into place. Through a slow, halting process of being told and retold, the client's self-narrative is taking the shape of the mediating narrative. The client has narrated conditioning and disempowerment through victimization into her self-history. She is now ready, if she was not earlier, to "break silence" and disclose to carefully selected others her victim story. Therapists advise clients to use disclosure as a basis for "realigning" (Meiselman 1990: 102) their significant relationships, including some and excluding others depending on how they respond. Those socially included are the prosurvivors. These are the people who will patiently listen to and "honor" her victim story as she tells and retells it, working it out. After disclosure, and for at least the time she is in therapy, the therapist recommends that the client's primary relationships be with her prosurvivors. Those excluded after disclosure are the family members and friends of the client who do not accept her story or who defend the alleged abuser.

Being able to give an account of victimization, including to others, is the sign that the client is ready for stage two, the survivor story. The transition to the survivor story involves a ritual of grieving and symbolically letting go of the past. The victim story is not the last word. It is only the beginning. To encourage the client to make the transition to a new story, the therapist focuses her on what she has lost and on what she stands to gain by moving beyond the victim story. The victim story defines the past, while letting go prepares the client to tell a different story about her present and future.

The Survivor Story. The victim story, rightly told, is the essential beginning for the whole mediating narrative of survivor therapy. It is the foundation for the larger lesson of *who the client can become* that the whole narrative anticipates and is designed to communicate. It teaches the client that the abuse theory has explanatory power for her life situation; it is the key to decoding her experience. It teaches her that her life and how she copes with it is, perhaps in large measure, abuse-determined rather than self-determined. It teaches her that she is disempowered. The victim story also teaches her that identifying and overcoming the effects of abuse in her life and relationships is the key to future happiness and life satisfaction. It mandates and authorizes a new beginning.

In the second stage of therapy, the therapist again leads the client in a narrative process, but now the time frame shifts. Therapy is moving away from a concern with the past to a concern with changing the way the client presently views herself and lives her life. To build a sense of agency and spur the client's motivation for the next steps, the therapist emphasizes her strength, not her past powerlessness. She suffered trauma, he tells her, and lived to tell about it. She is, therefore, a "survivor," possessor of the inner resources that enable victims to persevere. To persevere, therapists argue, is to resist the complete obliteration of the "true self," the originary self that is strong and healthy. In contrasting two selves or two parts of the self, the therapist communicates to the client a central therapeutic idea: the story of her life is really two stories. One story, victimization, signifies the part of herself conditioned by abuse and expressed in her symptoms and other problems identified during therapy. The other story, survival, signifies the part of herself that has remained true and that is expressed in her inner strength, resilience, and willingness to struggle. In the second stage of therapy, the therapist contrasts these two stories, and the two parts of the client signified by each, crediting the client's true self with any progress. In this way, he encourages her to feel that the change is arising from within, that she is gaining mastery and learning to trust her own true perceptions, and that he is simply drawing out and recognizing a reality that is already present. The telling of the survivor story begins with the therapist leading the client to affirm that she possesses the survivor qualities, and because she has them, has the power to heal.

In the survivor story stage, the therapist takes the client through a process of reframing her view of herself and others in light of the new trauma psychology. Already in stage one, the therapist led the client to link her adult problems with childhood abuse and to commit herself to reject all that being an abuse victim entails. Now he uses the trauma theory to identify a broader pattern of deviations from therapeutic norms in matters of the client's sense of self-worth, the way she manages her personal boundaries, the coherence of her identity, and her social skills and relationships. In the process of decoding her life according to the trauma theory, the therapist persuades her to see problems with the way she is living that go well beyond the issues that brought her to therapy. He creates for her a fuller picture of the "false self" that, he argues, has informed and divided her identity, and uses this picture as a benchmark against which to contrast the self that she can become.

The survivor story is a story of personal change, a story about overcoming the conditioned responses of the false self. Building on the idea of her "survivor strength," the therapist emphasizes risk-taking, experimentation, efficacious action, personal development, and new possibilities for relationships. As in the victim story, where the therapist has the client act out key elements of the drama—for example, remembering, expressing anger, disclosing, grieving—so in the survivor story, he will lead the client to act out a new way of knowing and possessing the self. These actions are the preconditions for telling the story and create experiences which can then be conveyed in it.

Throughout the survivor stage, the therapist uses the therapy sessions as a workshop for addressing problems linked to childhood abuse, most particularly low self-esteem, uncertain personal boundaries, identity fragmentation, and social dysfunction. In this lengthy process, he teaches and models for the client new assumptions about the self and its basic goodness, new understandings of her rights and how to assert them, new images of the body, new norms of emotional expression, and new standards of relating to others and choosing relationships. To this end, he provides practical instruction and experiential learning opportunities so that the client can experience for herself the rightness of new interpretations. Contrasting a victim self with a survivor self, he suggests the inadequacy of her previous ways of thinking and acting, and defines them in terms of a stunted self-development.

As the therapist leads the client through the reorientations of the survivor story, he readies her to confront the alleged abuser, and perhaps others as well. The therapist advocates confrontation because, when handled properly, it expresses the survivor story themes of innocence and empowerment and reinforces them. The confrontation of the alleged abuser is a kind of personal (witnesses may or may not be present) degradation ceremony (Garfinkel 1956), in which the client expresses her moral indignation by denouncing the alleged abuser and degrading his total identity. She forcefully asserts her victimization, the harm it has caused her, and his complete responsibility for moral injustice. She asserts her innocence, her moral status as aggrieved party, and her right

to shame and degrade him. For therapists, whatever its public consequences, the confrontation reinforces the survivor story by providing
the client with an emotionally charged context in which to demonstrate
to herself that she is no longer a victim and no longer silent, and to
"showcase" her new "emotional strength, power, and control" (Bolton
et al. 1989: 117). It may also force a further and desired realigning of
relationships, both with the alleged abuser, no matter what his response
to the confrontation, and with others who take sides.

Although principally framed as a story about growth and healing,
the survivor story is nonetheless built directly on the victim story about
abuse. Survivor strength is defined in terms of resistance to abuse, and
personal change in terms of overcoming a self conditioned by abuse.
As therapy moves toward its denouement, therapists encourage clients
to move beyond and "let go" of the view of themselves as a survivor.
Abuse remains a part of their story, but at this advanced point in therapy,
the transitional stories of victim and survivor have accomplished their
purpose. The therapist now readies the client to end therapy and reincor-
porate into normal life with a positive story, the thriver story, that moves
abuse and overcoming abuse to the background. He will not ask the client to let go of the thriver story but rather to embrace it as the ongoing
story of her life. When therapy ends, the thriver story is just beginning.

The Thriver Story. The thriver story is the end of the mediating narrative and its climax. It is the conclusion that is anticipated throughout
the process of constructing the narrative, guiding the building of the
therapeutic relationship, the selective recruitment of past events (whether
real or imagined), and the interpretation of present life circumstances.
It is the goal, the lesson toward which the whole narrative builds and
takes its meaning. It is the promise used to motivate the client and justify
the effort undertaken to deconstruct a previous identity and construct a
new one.

The thriver story is a story of liberation. According to the plot of the
mediating narrative as it has unfolded in the victim and survivor stories,
the pathological secret has been identified and its effects progressively
overcome. The hold of the past on the client has been broken, she has
been freed from who she was, freed from the wrong story, freed from
encumbering relationships, and is in possession of the power to become
someone new. In the thriver story, she is free to let her true self flourish fully for the first time. She can live with new vitality and satisfaction, express her creativity, enjoy intimacy, define her goals and strive

to reach them. She can become who she wants to be and do what she wants to do. In the thriver story, the future is unscripted, open and full of possibilities.

In leading the client to tell the thriver story, the therapist emphasizes themes aimed to confirm her transformation and motivate her to continue to act according to the new norms and relationship strategies she has learned. By linking her old ideas and behavior with abuse, and by framing his teaching in terms of health and normal development in the survivor stage, he has already made a forceful case for not returning to old or other patterns. Moreover, because the thriver story represents a commitment to a continued course of action, ordering her self and renegotiating her relationships through that story constrains the client to continue to act in a manner consistent with the commitment. In the thriver story, the therapist connects future growth and vitality with a consistent living of the new story and emphasizes themes of self-determination and responsibility to reinforce it.

In leading the client to tell the thriver story, the therapist contrasts two journeys, one now nearly complete and another about to begin. In the first journey, to healing, the client has moved, via the mediating narrative, from a life that was abuse-determined to a life capable of being self-determined, from a life shaped by domination to a life empowered with agency. In the second journey, she will move into the future choosing her own path. For the second journey, as thriver, she no longer requires the dependence on and guidance of the therapist. She is ready, he argues, for "healthy separation" (Courtois 1988: 10); she is now able to reflexively direct her own journey.

Therapy ends when the therapist is satisfied that the thriver story and the endpoints of the mediating narrative, the attitudinal signs of health, are increasingly defining the client's self-understanding. If all has gone well, the client's symptoms, especially signs of distress but also impaired functioning, are also expected to have decreased or disappeared.

The Disjunction of Self Languages

Throughout the stages of survivor therapy two different and seemingly irreconcilable languages of the self are in operation. One language, used for the new self-narrative, is based on understandings of the self as self-defining. According to survivor therapists, the "thriver" client is ready to terminate therapy because she is finally realizing her true self as she appropriates and acts from new assumptions about the self and others. In these new assumptions the self is multidimensional and has the potential to grow in many possible and simultaneous directions.[3] The self is also properly unencumbered. There are no binding obligations or social roles that take precedence over the self's autonomy. The appropriate conditions of nonrestraint and choice, however, cannot be taken for granted. The freedom to choose who one wants to be or become must be vigilantly protected from the encroachments of other people, social conventions, and old habits of mind. At the same time, life choices must also remain flexible and open to renegotiation and new circumstances. Growth in the ethic of survivor therapy is incompatible with the closing off of personal options and an unwillingness to make revisions as the need or desire arises.

While a self-language of invention, agency, and reflexivity characterizes the endpoint of therapy, the discourse used in the antecedent narrative reconstruction process is based on very different premises. To reach the thriver stage, the client has first had to narrate her experience in the precise terms of the victim and the survivor. This narration, as noted above, is not conceived as a "narrativist" or "constructivist" exercise. Narrativist and constructivist therapists describe their goal as an imaginative reconstruction of personal experience. When old identities have become problematic, often due to painful interpersonal experience, or are simply felt to be unsatisfactory in some way, the constructivist method is to help individuals to build new self-narratives that reorient them, that open new courses of action, that are felt to be more meaningful and suited to their needs. No argument, however, is made for the truth of new self-narratives, only for their utility. For these therapists, old self-narratives are altered or discarded not because they are wrong in some overarching sense, but because they are undesirable under present circumstances (Gergen 1994: 245).

In the identity reconstruction in survivor therapy, by contrast, the interpretations offered to the client for understanding her experience, and that warrant intervention strategies, are cast in terms of empirical truth claims. These claims arise from scientifically argued theories about the nature of sexual abuse and the determinative effects of psychological trauma. Sharp distinctions are drawn between proper and improper development, and the effort to reconstruct childhood is in part an effort to correct development that has departed from predefined and fixed standards. Further, survivor therapy is deep in oppositions between health/normalcy on the one hand and disorder/deviancy on the other. While the treatment manuals describe therapy as an alliance in which the client is in charge of her healing, in which she is "the expert of her own experience" (Courtois 1988: 169), they also instruct therapists to direct every element of the process according to normative, and presumably universalistic, rules about what does and does not constitute healthy attitudes, beliefs, emotions, and behaviors. In each stage of the treatment process, therapists are working to overcome the client's resistance, arouse appropriate emotions, reassign moral responsibility, teach and model correct ideas about the self, and consolidate the changes made. This is not a coercive process, as the critics of recovered abuse memories have charged, but neither is it, as therapists claim, the mere emancipating and recognizing of a hitherto silenced voice. Distinctly normative and nonnegotiable orientations to the old self-narrative mandate and specify the identity change.

A language of reflexive self-definition for the endpoint ideal, a language of determination by external forces for the change process: how can we understand this discursive disjunction and the seemingly contradictory orientations it entails? One possibility might be a kind of cultural lag between the goal of identity change and the means used to achieve it. Survivor therapy, from this angle, goes halfway toward a nonfoundationalist ethic. It leads clients toward the thriver view of the self, yet still relies on the outmoded and incompatible warrants of science and the tendency to universalizing presumptions. Over time, if this view has merit, we should expect the language of the change process to "catch up" and conform more closely with the language of the endpoint perspective. The future direction of such therapy would be toward some form of constructivism, which prescinds from strong evaluations and a belief in the moral foundations of action. A vocabulary of negotiation and imaginative narrative reconstruction would replace normative language and a scripted change process.

Rather than an inconsistency in the therapeutic means, a second way to look at the disjunction of self languages, and I believe the more persuasive, is to see them as working in tandem. Despite the talk of clients liberating their true self, all the stages of the mediating narrative, as I've tried to show, are fitted together to bring about a fundamental moral reorientation. This process involves the deconstruction of an old identity, for which the language of external determination is used, and the embracing of a new identity, for which the language of self-definition is employed. In the victim and survivor stages, memories and emotions are emplotted according to a moral evaluation of victimization and a sweeping theory of its enduring personal consequences. Telling a story of how their identity was externally determined prevents clients from taking a contingent or morally uncertain view of their past, and it links particular views of the self and of other people with pathology (as outcomes of abuse).[4] In identifying the unhealthy views, the views to be rejected, this picture of the false self and its origins in turn points indirectly toward the type of self it is good to be. Thus, the first language, of external determination, is internally related to and sets up the use of the second. In the thriver stage, the language of self determination gives more direct expression to the already outlined ideal self and its orientations toward what is good, what is worthwhile, and what has meaning. If clients come away with a more unified and stable sense of self, it would appear to be because they now possess a narrative, socially recognized by significant others, that "redeems" the past by emplotting formative early experiences with adult dysfunctions and distresses and a vision of life yet to live. The consistency of perspective embodied in this self-narrative provides meaning, coherence, and direction to their life.

A similar coordinated use of contrasting languages of determination and agency can be observed in other cases as well. Changing identities through the use of different languages of the self is not unique to survivor therapy. A significant part of the vast network of "anonymous" self-help groups, for instance, seeks to lead members to much the same therapeutic ethic. In this case, the means of bringing the member to new assumptions about personal autonomy and self-direction is by employing a medical model of addiction applied to excessive behaviors ranging from gambling to shopping to caring for pets (Rice 1996). Pathologizing past experience and its conditioning of the self is the medium through which members are prepared to understand that they can be self-defining. So too in the discourse of identity politics. Using a social constructionist methodology, activists and academics challenge the suppression of difference and otherness by arguing for the social origins of knowledge and its service of political ideologies and structures of power that impose distinct feelings and experiences of subordination on the marginalized. The objectivity, and thus authority, of one version of reality is deconstructed as inherently biased and originary of a false self so as to replace it with the marginalized alternative, which is defined as permitting full agency and self-determination. As in survivor therapy, the different languages of the self work together. Moral and/or scientific premises are drawn upon to show that a past self-narrative, a false self, was internalized via experiences and interaction external to the self. The false self, in turn, serves as the mirror opposite for the moral ideals of the endpoint or true self, which is presented as determining itself.

If the paradox involved in these identity changing processes can be resolved by understanding the two languages of the self as working together, then, at a minimum, the account of the endpoint self is deeply inadequate. The identity-framing work of survivor therapists and others suggests that moral orientations are foundational to the self. The description of the endpoint ideal, however, provides at most a very truncated account of this constitutive role. The true self, conceptually set up by the stark contrast with the image of the false self, is depicted as without social interactional foundation and directed according to its own internal criteria. Besides being discordant with the actual identity change process, this view is also not sustainable as an account of identity. A brief look at the work of Charles Taylor (1989) on how identity and moral subjectivity are joined will help to explain why.[5]

In Taylor's view, individual identity is constituted in and through the taking of moral positions. We all act, he argues, within moral frameworks of "constitutive goods" that enable us to make qualitative distinctions of "right or wrong, better or worse, higher or lower." These evaluative distinctions "are not rendered valid by our desires, inclinations, or choices, but rather stand independent of these and offer standards by which they can be judged" (1989: 4). Constitutive goods, then, orient our other views and choices and supply the moral criteria that establish why our particular preferences and values are good or valuable or ought to be done. Only through a commitment to constitutive goods can we know where we stand, establish an identity, and render life events and choices meaningful. Who we are, in this view, is defined by what matters to us, by where we stand with regard to "higher" or more fundamental questions of the good. Not everyone, of course, has the same constitutive goods, but having such orienting principles, Taylor argues, is inescapable.

Further, moral frameworks, in Taylor's view, are fundamentally social. Identity is not simply a matter of defining where I stand, where I am speaking from, but also whom I am speaking to (1989: 36). Our basic moral positions and sense of personal identity, then, depend on some reference to a defining moral community. We are selves only in relation to certain interlocutors, both those who were essential to our achieving self-definition, and to those who are now crucial to our "continuing grasp of languages of self-understanding" (1989: 36). We cannot be a "self" outside these "webs of interlocution," for the language through which we articulate our moral frameworks and self-understandings is always relating us to others. He notes,

> We may sharply shift the balance in our definition of identity, dethrone the given historic community as a pole of identity, and relate only to the community defined by adherence to the good (of the saved, or the true believers, or the wise). But this doesn't sever our dependence on webs of interlocution. It only changes the webs, and the nature of our dependence. (1989: 39)

Any conception of the human person, therefore, as finding his or her bearings within, as drawing his or her "purposes, goals, and life-plans" out of themselves, is based on ignoring or denying the webs of interlocution within which identity is maintained.

If Taylor's argument has merit, then the account of the self in survivor therapy and in other practices like it is inadequate because it denies moral and social sources. The individual's initial orientations to certain questions of the good are described as determined from the outside while new orientations to those questions are presented as arising from within. The change in moral frameworks and the social sources of this change, including identification with the therapist, are thus concealed. And neither determination nor agency nor their interrelationship is elucidated by establishing a one-dimensional and oppositional hierarchy between them. Self-knowledge is not a discovery, it is a construction. The practice in survivor therapy and the other cases makes this plain, while the languages of the self that are used deny it.

The Question of Identity Dissolution

The practice of survivor therapy and other programs like it, along with the conceptual linkage of identity and moral subjectivity advanced by Taylor, have implications for how we think about the nature of identity, fragmentation, and the impact of social change. Conceiving identity within a theory of moral and social relations challenges key ideas advanced by social theorists in each of these areas. First, philosophical understandings of the self tend to focus on self-awareness, and thus personal identity is principally a matter of self-consciousness. While an awareness of oneself as an agent is certainly fundamental, identity is more than self-consciousness. "We are not simply *aware* of ourselves," to quote Craig Calhoun on this point, "we *matter* to ourselves in very basic ways" (1991: 237, italics in original). Making sense of our lives in relation to the good, having an orientation in moral space, as Taylor puts it, and thus some sense of direction, is not an option, a project that can be dispensed with. Rather, and contrary to the rejection of a belief in the moral foundations of action in postmodern thought, it is a structural requirement of human agency.

Further, because human experience is temporal, the never-complete and not always fully conscious project of self-understanding invariably has an historical dimension. Indeed, as a number of scholars have argued, it is in and through narrative emplotment, an interpretive process which looks both back in time and projects into the future, that our lives and our selves attain meaning (e.g., Kerby 1991; MacIntyre 1984; Somers 1994). Selecting and plotting our experience within a narrative, determined by our moral frameworks and always in a context of complex relationships, establishes a meaningful unity, or at least continuity, to our development and future direction, to where we have been and where we are going. Life events and episodes are ordered in relationship to the entire story, *our whole life*, which emerges in and through them. The effort to overcome fragmentation in survivor therapy, particularly in its emphasis on the narrative form and the interpretation and emplotment of action and emotion, illustrates the salience of this temporal dimension and the role it plays in creating a sense of biographical coherence and direction.

Second, as noted at the outset, a number of contemporary formulations view fragmentation of the self as adaptive and/or liberating. But if personal identity requires that we determine our place in relation to the good and orient ourselves by it, then these formulations miss something essential. We cannot be continuously indifferent about whether what we do and how we do it are good or worthwhile or to a purpose. Without some orientation, however achieved, the self is adrift and the meaning of personal experience remains undetermined. On the account I am offering here, such a state of inner confusion cannot be judged adaptive or liberating. Coherence, in this view, is essential to a functioning personality, to all that we mean by agency and full personhood. This is not to say that the self cannot be fragmented or become fragmented. The experience of adult survivor therapy clients suggests that identity instability and incoherence are clearly possible. But it also suggests that such fragmentation is a "tribulation of the self," to use Giddens's (1991) phrase, that drives a search for resolution and personal moorings, and not only by those with the extreme experiences labeled "dissociative identity disorder." In seeking to strengthen client and member identities, therapies, self-help groups, and identity movements respond to a felt need for purpose and value, for wholeness and unity. Judging from their high rates of participation, it is a widely felt need.

Finally, these reflections have important implications for how we think about the impact of social and cultural change. An influential stream of accounts have analyzed the proliferation and fragmentation of discourses, that allegedly result from the bombardment of fragmented signs and images in a simulational consumer culture, as leading to a fragmentation of the subject (see Featherstone 1995; Harvey 1990; Jameson 1984). That a deep problemization and destabilization (Dunn, this volume) of identity and identity-forming processes is at work in contemporary society is not in question. But, from the point of view argued here, these formulations fail to take account of another important feature of contemporary society, namely, the drive toward identity restabilization and reconstruction. Survivor therapy, and the other movements I have briefly touched upon, are examples of this powerful tendency. This drive, and the cultural options and moral communities (however tenuous or enduring) it produces, challenge theoretical correspondences between textual instability and identity instability and the assumption that as the social world becomes "aestheticized" and dispersed so too does the self. These movements draw attention, rather, to the multiple and dynamic ways in which identity challenges can be engaged and even promote an integration of the self. And they draw attention to the tensions both within and between contending cultural discourses. In contemporary society, tendencies toward dispersal *and* toward integration are operative, constraining *and* empowering projects of identity.

Further, changing forms of identity or subjectivity should not be read as simply the reflection of broader social and cultural transformations. Changes in technology, production and consumption regimes, demography, culture, and so on, have important implications for the ways that we understand our world and place ourselves in relation to it. Giddens, for example, has argued that broad institutional changes have led to a sequestering of key types of experience--sickness, death, sexuality, and so on—from day-to-day life. This sequestration represses basic moral and existential components of human life and so creates a social context of "substantial moral deprivation" (Giddens 1991: 169). Taylor notes that the social forces of modernity have eroded and pluralized traditional moral frameworks. There are now a plurality of moral frameworks, none of which is shared by everyone, and hence none of which can simply be articulated in universal terms or "sink to the phenomenological status of unquestioned fact" (1989: 17). Clearly, under conditions of moral deprivation and pluralism, and in a social environment that frequently emphasizes immediacy, sensation, simultaneity, and surface, finding a stable and socially recognized place in relation to the good can be profoundly challenging. Even for those with a clear and self-conscious grasp of their moral frameworks, a loss of meaning is always a potential threat. But social conditions do not in themselves determine how we understand ourselves, much less destroy our capacity to render our experience meaningful and coherent. We are also agents, negotiating the meaning of our experience within a social horizon on which social and cultural forces place limitations as well as open up formative possibilities.

Against the view that identity fragmentation or decentering is liberating, and against the view that identity coherence and a teleological belief that life is a meaningful project are simply no longer possible, I have argued that moral orientations and a sense of direction and life order are both necessary to full personhood and attainable, even if in a tentative form and without ultimate confidence. Depthlessness and loss of meaning are not the whole story about our time or our selves. Disconnected from lived experience, recent theory has obscured the creative and generative possibilities by which identities might be narratively reconstituted or transformed. The search for believable frameworks, temporal continuity, depth, and substance also characterize our historical moment. Reports of their death, of the dissolution of identity and moral coherence, have been greatly exaggerated.

Notes

1. Narrative approaches to psychotherapy are generally identified with the new constructivist (Neimeyer and Mahoney 1995) or constructionist (Gergen 1985) movements in psychotherapy. In these movements, therapy involves the articulation, elaboration, and revising of those constructions that the client uses to organize his or her experiences and sense of identity.
2. To simplify the prose, I use the masculine pronoun for therapists and the feminine for clients. Most survivor clients are women, with estimates running over 90 percent. While there is no data on the sex of survivor therapists, it would appear that they are predominantly women as well.

3. This brief exposition necessarily relies on inferences, as assumptions about the self tend to remain latent, taken for granted rather than delineated. I make no claim that all therapists who do survivor therapy necessarily share them.
4. Berger and Luckmann (1966: 157-63) argue that significant identity transformations ("alterations") involve a biographical rupture in which the earlier identity is subsumed under a negative category. In this process, old identities are not merely discounted, they are "annihilated." Linking pre-therapy orientations with externally induced pathology certainly accomplishes such an annihilation.
5. This discussion of Taylor has benefited from the important overview of his work by Calhoun (1991).

References

Anderson, W.T. 1998. *The Future of the Self: Inventing the Postmodern Person*. New York: Putnam.

Bateson, M.C. 1989. *Composing a Life*. New York: The Atlantic Monthly Press.

Bellah, R.N., R. Madsen, W.M. Sullivan, A. Swidler, and S.M. Tipton. 1985. *Habits of the Heart: Individualism and Commitment in American Life*. New York: Harper & Row.

Berger, P.L., and T. Luckmann. 1966. *The Social Construction of Reality*. New York: Doubleday Anchor.

Bolton Jr., F.G., L.A. Morris, and A.E. MacEachron. 1989. *Males at Risk*. Newbury Park, CA: Sage.

Brown, M.F. 1997. *The Channeling Zone: American Spirituality in an Anxious Age*. Cambridge, MA: Harvard University Press.

———. 1999. "The New Alienists: Healing the Shattered Self at Century's End." Pp. 137-156 in *Paranoia within Reason: A Casebook on Conspiracy as Explanation*, edited by G.E. Marcus. Chicago: University of Chicago Press.

Calhoun, C. 1991. "Morality, Identity, and Historical Explanation: Charles Taylor on the Sources of the Self." *Sociological Theory* 9: 232-263.

Courtois, C.A. 1988. *Healing the Incest Wound: Adult Survivors in Therapy*. New York: W. W. Norton.

Davis, J.E. 1999. *Accounts of Innocence: Sexual Abuse, Psychotherapy, and the Construction of Moral Meanings*. Unpublished manuscript, University of Virginia.

Davies, J.M., and M.G. Frawley. 1994. *Treating the Adult Survivor of Childhood Sexual Abuse: A Psychoanalytic Perspective*. New York: Basic Books.

Deleuze, G., and F. Guattari. 1987. *A Thousand Plateaus: Capitalism and Schizophrenia*. Minneapolis: University of Minnesota Press.

Featherstone, M. 1995. *Undoing Culture: Globalization, Postmodernism and Identity*. London: Sage.

Garfinkel, H. 1956. "Conditions of Successful Degradation Ceremonies." *American Journal of Sociology* 61: 420-424.

Gergen, K.J. 1985. "The Social Constructionist Movement in Modern Psychology." *American Psychologist* 40: 266-275.

———. 1991. *The Saturated Self*. New York: Basic Books.

———. 1994. *Realities and Relationships: Soundings in Social Construction*. Cambridge, MA: Harvard University Press.

Giddens, A. 1991. *Modernity and Self-Identity*. Stanford, CA: Stanford University Press.

Goodman, N. 1978. *Ways of Worldmaking*. Indianapolis, IN: Hackett.

Harvey, D. 1990. *The Condition of Postmodernity*. Cambridge, MA: Blackwell.

Howard, G.S. 1990. "Narrative Psychotherapy." Pp. 199-201 in *What is Psychotherapy?*, edited by J.K. Zeig and W.M. Munion. San Francisco, CA: Jossey-Bass.

Irvine, L. 1999. *Codependent Forevermore: The Invention of Self in a Twelve Step Group*. Chicago: University of Chicago Press.

Jameson, F. 1984. "Postmodernism, or The Cultural Logic of Late Capitalism." *New Left Review* 146: 53-92.

Kerby, P.A. 1991. *Narrative and the Self*. Bloomington: Indiana University Press.

Lifton, R.J. 1993. *The Protean Self*. New York: Basic Books.

MacIntyre, A. 1984. *After Virtue: A Study in Moral Theory*. 2 ed. Notre Dame, IN: University of Notre Dame Press.

Markus, H., and P. Nurius. 1986. "Possible Selves." *American Psychologist* 41: 954-969.

Meiselman, K.C. 1990. *Resolving the Trauma of Incest: Reintegration Therapy with Survivors*. San Francisco, CA: Jossey-Bass.

Melucci, A. 1996. *The Playing Self: Person and Meaning in the Planetary Society*. Cambridge: Cambridge University Press.

Neimeyer, R.A. 1995. "Client-Generated Narratives in Psychotherapy." Pp. 231-246 in *Constructivism in Psychotherapy*, edited by R.A. Neimeyer and M.J. Mahoney. Washington, DC: American Psychological Association.

Neimeyer, R.A., and M.J. Mahoney, eds. 1995. *Constructivism in Psychotherapy*. Washington, DC: American Psychological Association.

O'Hara, M. 1989. "Constructing Emancipatory Realities." *AHP Perspective* (August/September).

Rice, J.S. 1996. *A Disease of One's Own: Psychotherapy, Addiction, and the Emergence of Co-Dependency*. New Brunswick, NJ: Transaction Publishers.

Sampson, E.E. 1993. *Celebrating the Other: A Dialogic Account of Human Nature*. Boulder, CO: Westview Press.

Somers, M.R. 1994. "The Narrative Constitution of Identity: A Relational and Network Approach." *Theory and Society* 23: 605-649.

Strauss, A.L. 1987. *Qualitative Analysis for Social Scientists*. New York: Cambridge University Press.

Taylor, C. 1989. *Sources of the Self: The Making of the Modern Identity*. Cambridge, MA: Harvard University Press.

8

Deception and Despair:
Ironic Self-Identity in Modern Society

Harvie Ferguson

"The ironist is always only making himself seem to be other than he really is."

—Søren Kierkegaard

In contemporary society nothing is quite what it seems. Every appearance is deceptive; is *mere* appearance. Reality hides from us so that both the scientist and the artist, having learned to mistrust their senses, look to some other and more stable world as the source and explanation of the ceaseless and incomprehensible flux in which they find themselves. Confined to the surface of life, descriptions of ourselves, as well as of everyday objects and events, are tainted with the arbitrary and contingent. In such a world any statement, to be truthful, must, it seems, refer beyond immediate experience to another, and more substantial, reality.

In terms of identity this has often been taken to mean that, at an individual level "authentic" selfhood, or at a collective level "humanity," is a secret and inward presence. But the expression of this inner truth requires either a distortion of its superficial appearance or a superficial declaration of its opposite. Self-expression, thus, is forced into an ironic mold. More generally, as both modernity and irony expose the "contrast of an appearance and reality" (Muecke 1969: 5), modernity is preeminently a culture of irony.

Yet sociologists, interested to the point of obsession with issues of identity, have been slow to acknowledge and explore its subversive twin, irony. Skeptical of philosophical discourse, intent on revealing the "structure" of society (in terms of either a positivistic explanation of external "facts" of social life, or their meaningful interpretation as direct expressions of cultural values), and, no doubt, insufficiently secure within academic institutions to take themselves less seriously, sociologists have generally ignored the rich discourse on irony which developed as an essential aspect of modern self-understanding (Eagleton 1996 represents a welcome shift of focus).

Where a systematic foundation for a social theory of irony might have become evident—most notably in the specifically American practice of symbolic interactionism with its roots in the social philosophy of George Herbert Mead—it has been little developed in relation to a "standard model" of normatively binding, "authentic," and direct communication. The writings of Erving Goffman, not only explicitly in his notion of "role distance," but implicitly and more generally in terms of his dramaturgical conception of social interaction, might well be proposed as a major exception to such a generalization. The understanding of social action as a process of "self-presentation," with its explicit recognition that role-playing always involves a more or less grudging surrender to, and concealment within, a socially provided persona, might be viewed as both a social theory of irony and an ironic social theory. However, Goffman's conception of role-playing remains nonironic; there is no contrast here (as there is, for example, in Rousseau), between a "superficial" performance and an "authentic" and frustrated inwardness; rather, the partial disengagement from every social action is predicated on the multiplicity of such wholly conventional roles. There is nothing "left over" from such performances and, therefore, no "depth" of selfhood in which irony might take root (Burns 1995: 130-35).

Clearly, identity, irony, and modernity are linked directly and indirectly in a number of complicated ways. These interconnections and the distinctions in which they are rooted can only be clarified by following the advice of Henri-Frédéric Amiel—the nineteenth-century writer whose *Journal Intime* in part exemplifies one such interrelation—who urges us "to look at ourselves socially and historically" (1906: 126). The following essay suggests one possible historical reconstruction of ourselves; and argues that modern philosophical and aesthetic traditions which reflect on irony offer rich insights into both the enigmas of personal and social identity and the character of modern experience.

Identity and Irony

Yet there is something decidedly odd, even paradoxical, in coupling irony and identity. It is not simply that ironic statements appear to be negative, inward, and secretive, whereas signs of identity seem to be affirmative, outward, and open. More importantly, irony seems continually to undo (grammatically if not in other ways) every effort to establish an identity; it corrodes the very inwardness it appears designed to preserve. Worse, neither the notion of irony nor identity separately enjoy a settled position within their own domain of meaning. The concept of identity is notoriously troublesome; one need only consider the continuing debate over the interpretation and current relevance of such widely divergent philosophical positions as those represented by Hume and Leibniz to be made wary of the plethora of contemporary positions which claim originality on the matter.

The emergence and development of modern society, in fact, has been marked by continuous and inconclusive discussion of the "problem" of identity. Indeed, no period since the Renaissance can be claimed to be free from a veritable "crisis of identity," which has penetrated every aspect of life and provided the raw material for many of the distinctive cultural products of modern societies. It is not only that the conditions of modernity pose uniquely difficult problems for individuals; more significantly, it is in these conditions that the very possibility of individuality has taken root. Problems of identity are endemic to modern society because modern society, in terms of the explicit conceptions of its forms of organization and underlying order which have emerged and developed along with and as part of that social organization, is viewed in terms of "sovereign individuals" who, whatever their position and role in that society, remain "internally" free (Abercrombie, Hill, and Turner 1986).

These ideological commitments suggest two opposed but linked notions of identity. Firstly, identity means simply that each individual is the same as every other individual; that they are identical. In terms of the distribution of public social roles, the division of labor and the large-scale organizations in which individuals are organized as anonymous units, no *essential* differences distinguish those in authority from those in subordinate position: those who are highly rewarded from those who are not. That is to say, personal qualities are irrelevant to modern forms of social differentiation. Secondly, however, identity in everyday usage refers to the unique individuality of the person, to the absolute difference upon which the experience of the self and its world is founded. In this perspective, it is not the distinctiveness, but the *arbitrariness* of the individual which is problematic. This is the central difficulty which emerged in the Romantic tradition of modernity, exemplified by Rousseau. The absolute inner freedom of the individual provided each person, so to speak, with impregnable grounds of difference, but left each individual with the task of creating his or her own uniqueness. The difficulty posed by the principle of inner freedom was to realize uniqueness in a satisfying manner, so that the emerging personality was not continually plagued by doubt with the sense that it had not become "truly" itself.

Not quite matching these two meanings of identity, it is also important to note the distinct levels at which the concept was applied. Social identity conceives the individual in relation to a specific group or community, while personal identity refers to this same relation, as it were, from the "inside," in terms of an individual perspective on social relations. In this context two specifically modern themes emerge. Firstly, a fateful disjunction (or series of disjunctions) between a personal and a social identity (or series of such identities) has become visible. And, secondly, an equally momentous rupture can now be felt between the experience of the private self as an "ego" and the self-evidential "I" of discourse.

The argument here is that both these meanings and both these perspectives can be understood historically in terms of the distinctive character of modern social relations as a process of individuation. Thus, rather than apply well-known sociological criticisms of such schema—to insist once again on their misleading and even illusory nature—it is useful to ask how such a view becomes not only possible but mandatory. It is not the error of utilitarian social theory which must be exorcised, but a clearer insight into the sense in which it was (and may yet still be) valid.

Typically, expressions of identity link the individual to a social group: "I am Scottish, I am middle-aged, I am white, I am a sociologist, I am... etc." Some of these designations are of given characteristics, some refer to variable and contingent matters of social relations. All, however, are conceived as voluntary in the sense that "identification" is an accomplished act. I need not identify myself as "Scottish"; clearly I cannot, without lying, say "I am English" or "I am French," though I might, in some contexts, prefer to say "I am British" or "I am European." Such social identities slide effortlessly from the personal to the collective pronoun: " we are Scottish," "we are white," "we are middle-aged," and so on. Not infrequently a negative form is adopted: —"we are *not* English, *not* black, *not* old..."— with obvious evaluative implications. Such statements are frequently rhetorical, involving exaggeration of one sort or another, but they are rarely expressed ironically. Generically these forms of social identification might be rendered as "I am us."

Personal identity, on the other hand, is usually expressed in terms of universal characteristics of inwardness: "I am happy, I am ambitious, I am truthful..." and apparently express the fixed characteristics of the "personality" of the individual. A person might typically say "I am modest" or "I am sympathetic" and, frequently with emphasis, "*Of course* I am..." Such expressions are often given the complication of a negative form, "I am not unsympathetic, untruthful..." These expressions are frequently ironic, and express just the opposite of what they claim; that, in fact, "I am immodest, unsympathetic, untruthful..." Indeed, many of the most gifted of modern psychologists and philosophers have claimed that expressions of personal identity can *only* be made in an ironic form. In its generic form these expressions might be rendered as "I am not myself."

The relation of irony and identity, then, is concerned primarily with the construction of *personal* identities. The concept of irony, however, has itself been subject to the most varied judgments. Hegel, for example, condemned irony as the purest abstraction and uncontrolled subjectivism, while Kierkegaard, criticizing Hegel for *his* abstraction, claimed irony was a means of returning modern thought to concreteness, a view more recently endorsed by Thomas Mann—widely regarded as the master of the twentieth-century ironic novel—who claims bluntly that "objectivity is irony." In the Socratic tradition, espoused in its modern form by Kierkegaard, irony is an essential mark of individuation, a sign of an impregnable and ultimately incommunicable inwardness; while for Pushkin, according to Belinsky, the more his artistic and ironic self-representation was perfected "the more his own identity crumbled" (Greenleaf 1994: 4), and the more deeply he became ensnared in the "endlessly self-negating subject" (Handwerk 1985: 30). And, from quite another perspective, Wayne Booth views irony as predicated on "amiable communities of interpretation" which neither hypostasize nor annihilate a sense of individuality" (1974).

When irony becomes a general standpoint or perspective on the world it seems to imply both intellectual detachment and emotional coldness. Thomas Mann, thus, has also claimed that "the ironist is conservative and essentially unpolitical" (1987: 419). And Joseph Conrad remarks that "revolutionaries hate irony which is the negation of all saving instincts, of all faith, of all devotion, of all actions" (Enright 1986: 21). Richard Rorty, however, finds in the ironist's unfinished redescription of modern experience the most significant intellectual and moral weaponry aimed against the conservatism of "common sense" (1989: 74), a view which echoes Vladimir Jankélévitch's celebration of irony as an "eternal introduction" to life (1964: 36).

And while Thomas Mann, again, claims that "irony is eroticism" (1987: 419), he also talks of its "cool and fastidious attitude toward humanity." This seeming inconsistency is noted as well by Haakon Chevalier, who claims, in analyzing the writings of Anatole France as exemplary of the type, that the ironist's "relation to life is at once intimate and impersonal" (1932: 173). Irony, indeed, is a strange and protean relation; perhaps it is even self-contradictory. Søren Kierkegaard, who wrote one of the most challenging books on the concept, argues that "It is a position that continually cancels itself; a nothing that devours everything and a something one can never grab hold of, something that is and is not at the same time, but something that at rock bottom is comic" (1989: 131). All might agree with Friedrich Schlegel's brief characterization: "irony is the form of paradox" (1971: 149).

But before succumbing to the vertigo implicit in every attempt to analyze irony or identity, far less their interrelation, it may be helpful to distinguish two quite different senses in which "not being myself" might, in a loose way at least, appropriately describe a particular form of personal identity. I might not be myself because I am another self, or appear to be another self; and I might not be myself because I am other than a self: a distinction roughly between deception, including self-deception, and despair.

Both deception and despair are specific forms of *social* relation, the possibility and meaning of which depends upon the conditions of modern life. Deception is an ever-present possibility where social encounters are frequently, even predominantly, among strangers; it is the counterpoint to the generalized and distinctive form of trust, which as Durkheim demonstrated, is one of the enabling assumptions of modern society (Durkheim 1933; Luhmann 1979). And despair is the inevitable outcome of the equally modern demand not only to experience the world in terms of a private, interior, and individuated selfhood, but to realize and validate that selfhood in terms of a meaningful pattern of social action (Ferguson 1995).

Modernity and Identity

The "problem" of identity is central to the emergence and development of modern society; personal identity is, in effect, a phenomenon of modernity. This is simply because, from the time of the Renaissance and particularly through the emergence of capitalism, the world was experienced for the first time from the perspective of the "ego"; it became (however mistakenly), first and foremost "my" world and for some, indeed, the world in a sense becomes nothing but an objectification of the ego (Elias 1991).

Modernity, in the sense of a new view of the world, begins with the breakdown of a feudalized hierarchical cosmos in which there is no categorical separation of objects from other objects, or objects from subjects; and the development of a new order of things founded upon the universal empty dimensionality of a characterless space and time, the separation within these dimensions of objects one from another, and the differentiation of subject and object. All objects within this new cosmos are fundamentally identical in terms of the universal laws of nature to which they are subjected; they are indifferent, in other words, to place as an essential qualification of their nature. Matter is then conceptualized in terms simply of differing quantities of a common substance uniquely characterized by location and motion. Objects are distinguished unambiguously in terms of their position in space and time, rather than in terms of a differing "essence" linked to their unchanging place within the Chain of Being. Presence, which had previously been distributed throughout the world and was shared as a given order of the world, in which could be directly sensed a fundamental but unseen reality, was transformed into an inward and personal sense of self-certainty (Koyré 1957; Ferguson 1990).

In contrast to the new cosmos of dead matter, human subjects were uniquely defined in terms of internal qualities which could be known directly only by themselves: in terms, that is to say, of their immediate experience. This is not to claim that human subjectivity has somehow escaped the universalizing tendencies of modernity and preserved itself, so to speak, in a premodern time bubble. Although many modern commentators prefer to describe human identity in terms of a premodern language, and would like the "soul" to represent an untransformed and changeless essence of the human individual, it is, in fact, only because human reality was transformed that this new way of describing and understanding the world of nature as a self-sufficient domain of objects became meaningful. And, indeed, the very possibility of human self-understanding as a uniquely individuated innerworld was predicated on this same transformation.

"Objectively" speaking, persons, rather like objects in the natural world, became identical and could be differentiated only by reference to relational and functional characteristics. They were "essentially" the same creature. Humanity was everywhere the same. For modern society it became increasingly obvious that objective and "natural" differences among people were insignificant in comparison with what were socially more significant but ultimately arbitrary distinctions of rank and position. Descartes, whose philosophical work can conveniently be taken as a starting point for reflections on the nature of modernity, clearly understood this and, indeed, went significantly further in recognizing that the distinguishing inner quality of humanness, which he took to be the possession of Reason, was also universal. "Good sense," he says in the opening paragraph of his *Discourse on Method*, "is the best distributed thing in the world....the power of judging well and of distinguishing the true from the false—which is what we properly call "good sense," or "reason"—is naturally equal in all men" (1984: 111).

The implication of this insight, which over a protracted period became (ideally at least!) institutionalized in the demand for, and granting of, individual citizenship rights, universal and impersonal standards of justice, the gradual democratization of politics, the extension of free access to markets for all commodities, and so on, was that individuals were not simply conceived as equal in legal or political terms, but were, again theoretically, viewed as interchangeable units within the social division of labor. There was, of course, reluctance to accept the full force of the logic of "sovereign individualism" among those who were the beneficiaries of irrational privileges of all sorts, albeit that it was, for the most part, members of those very privileged groups who had done the most to unleash the forces of modernism in whose name all such demands were made and all such institutionalization accomplished (Unger 1975; Abercrombie, Hill, and Turner 1986).

Reflection on the nature of modernity concentrated primarily on issues of rights, justice, and the difficulties of creating a new social order given universal criteria of humanity. But, as is frequently the case, events overtook the arguments. A more or less unjust, but more or less self-regulating, bourgeois order embodying at least some of these principles was established through the mechanism of the market, which, in due course, became a singular fact of life that was impossible to ignore and against which it was very difficult to rebel.

From the perspective of the present it might seem that the more intractable problem was, in fact, not the establishment of social order in which all should be treated as equivalent elements or atoms of a social cosmos, but, rather, given this hypothetical condition, how value could be attached separately to each individual as a unique subject. If all were ultimately the same, how could each be distinguished one from another?

Two approaches to this difficulty, which were in principle related but which in practice remained somewhat separate, may be distinguished. Firstly, a unique identity could be specified for any individual in terms of the specific ensemble of social relations in which he or she was implicated. This might be designated the "social identity" of the individual. Thus, while for modern society each individual constitutes a theoretically equivalent atom of society, each is distinguished in terms of a complex relational field and a pattern of interaction unique to their experience. This, as in different ways both Durkheim and Simmel pointed out, is quite characteristic of modern society and by no means signifies the immanent collapse of the social order. Indeed, modern society has become more stable than any previous large-scale social order precisely because of its high level of social differentiation, which not only distinguishes, and in principle values, each individual, but draws each into necessary relationships of interdependence with others. Social identity, however, which was simply the extreme point of a process of social differentiation predicated on the liberation of individuals into the empty space of the market, seemed to be quite distinct from and did not seem to account for the continuous presence of an inner "self." The second approach, therefore, viewed "personal identity" as characterized, rather, by the extent to which it was experienced as something anterior to, and detachable from, the performance of any specific social obligation. Above all, personal identity was a process of self-creation and the realization of universal human freedom in the form of a unique individuality.

The fundamental reconstruction of the cosmos as matter in motion, and the universalization of space and time, meant that all *qualities* (and thus all experienced immediacy in which personal identity might take root) became personal, inward, individuated, and secretive. The withdrawal of human subjectivity into itself, its self-enclosure as the individual self or "ego," is as characteristic of the birth of modernity as is the capitalist market, bureaucratic organization, or the centralized state. And from its inception this inwardness raised difficulties. The paradox of self-fashioning was explored by Renaissance writers, particularly by Cervantes and Montaigne, who dwelt on the logical and psychological problems that attended any effort to construct from the flux of experience, and sustain in the face of the world, an image of selfhood as the animating soul of the individual (Greenblatt 1980; Garber 1982). It seemed more likely than not that every such effort would collapse under the weight of its own improbability, and the whole project end in madness or melancholy.

Indeed, the solipsistic character of modern selfhood as the process of self-creation turned out to have serious implications, not only for any conception of subjectivity but, equally, for any notion of objectivity. The problem with objectivity is just that, in the end, it is another form of subjectivity. The world, including the world of objects, can only be known in terms of an inner experience which remains irreducibly subjective. But what is the subject? The difficulty here—ignoring a host of related problems—is that while the subject could be defined only in terms of its freedom from objects—its voluntaristic self-generation of itself—the world which ought now to be included as an aspect of this freedom stood out against it as an intractable and given reality. The subject, thus, was divided against itself in a conflict between its finite and infinite aspects, between its ideal and actual reality.

However, even ignoring these paralyzing difficulties, more benign views of the emerging problem of personal identity ran into problems of their own. The interior self-certainty and self-presence, celebrated by Descartes as the only reality beyond doubt, cannot express itself as such; in expressing itself it either loses itself in the transparent and abstract universality of the *cogito,* or enters into the objectified and therefore doubtful world of objects. The self-evidential "I" is forced to *represent* itself as a sign, and is thus drained of its immediate presence in relation to, and difference from, the world of similarly represented objects. And the very character of a sign is to be other than itself; every utterance thus draws attention to itself as ironic (Sperber and Wilson 1981). How then can the self express its inner truth in a direct fashion? How can the self become real for others? How can quality be conveyed?

The peculiarity of bourgeois society was that it made obligatory the realization of this paradoxical inner-freedom. This is the fundamental theme of Max Weber's (1930) famous essay on *The Protestant Ethic and the Spirit of Capitalism*. In his view, the Lutheran Reformation internalized and stripped traditional conceptions of religious faith of all their remaining elements of magic. Where in premodern society Christianity could easily be identified with the observance of specific practices and, in particular, with the confession of specific creedal statements, such practices and beliefs now had to be held inwardly as a spontaneous faith; as a groundless trust in God. Faith was the depth of inwardness which, unlike the *cogito*, preserved all the unique characteristics of inward experience within itself. It thus remained incommunicable. This, of course, became the central problem, doctrinal and practical, for the reformed churches. If faith is wholly inward and ineffable can it be the basis for a community; can it, in fact, support or respond to a church? The religious and ecclesiastical difficulties need not detain us; what is significant here is the model of soulful interiority which it provided for later generations of secular writers. Thus, just as Weber argues that for later generations of capitalist entrepreneurs the religious foundation of modern asceticism has become irrelevant, so we can also see in the development of bourgeois individualism a secular adaptation of Luther's profound religious psychology. The bourgeois is obliged to express his (and latterly her) individuality as a personal identity. It is not sufficient to realize the universal and, becoming like everyone else, display through a network of activities and relations a unique social pattern, each must strive to become that unique individual of which they alone contain the potential. Each must express, in other words, an authentic selfhood.

In this demand, of course, the bourgeois culture of modernity betrayed the subtle insights of Montaigne and of Cervantes as much as it trivialized the intellectual rigor of Luther. If selfhood was uniquely self-enclosed then it could not be expressed, and if it could be expressed then it was not wholly inward.

The demand for self-realization, nonetheless, came to prominence in the culture of the Enlightenment, and particularly in the writings of Rousseau for whom, as "the inventor of the psychological interior," it remained a key problem (Ginzburg 1991; Greenleaf 1994: 228). He is among the first, and remains the most eloquent, of what might be termed the bourgeois critics of modernity. He takes seriously the modern secular duty of self-actualization; indeed, he takes it more seriously than, in fact, it had ever been intended. He makes absolute the demand for self-realization and, consequently, agonizes over his repeated failure to authenticate his sense of inward uniqueness in transparently expressive acts. From his First Discourse, the prize-winning essay on the progress of the arts and sciences, he berates bourgeois society for its hypocrisy and playacting; "We no longer dare seem what we really are," he complains. We cannot make ourselves understood, our goodness and warmth is somehow translated into their opposites. Everyone appears in society as if performing on a stage and, thus, "we never know with whom we are to deal." Soon we begin to suspect that "jealousy, suspicion, fear, coldness, reserve, hatred, and fraud lie constantly concealed under the uniform and deceitful veil of politeness" (Rousseau 1973: 6-7). A century later Amiel complains of the same obscuring gentility:

> In society people are expected to behave as if they lived on ambrosia and concerned themselves with nothing but the loftiest interests. Anxiety, need, passion, have no existence. All realism is suppressed as brutal....All vehemence, all natural expression, all real suffering, all careless familiarity, or any frank sign of passion, are startling and distasteful in this delicate *milieu*. (1906: 183)

Bourgeois individualism, in practice, was always half-hearted; it valued only the appearance of authenticity and required nothing more taxing than carefully staged hypocrisy. Briefly, Goethe's edifying greatness could be invoked as an example of *Bildung*, of the realization of authentic inwardness in terms of action in the external world, of a reciprocal and mutually supportive relation of inner freedom and the givenness of the world, of a self-sustaining interaction of cultivation and culture. But of the generation which sought to follow this example, few succeeded. By and large those who, from Pascal to Dostoevsky's degenerate "underground man," took life seriously, and demanded of themselves a more rigorous discipline than the conventions of everyday life required, were abandoned to melancholy and the abysmal depths of solipsistic selfhood.

In modern society, the depth of the soul was accorded a special reality and value—provided only that it remain invisible. The inner self, we might say, was to the social actor what the process of production was to the commodity; a reality upon which all ultimately turned, but which, in order to operate effectively, concealed itself beneath a world of appearances. Rousseau (1953), with a sure intuition, thus turned away from utopian literary and social experimentation to a continuous practice of memory: to self-recollection as a constructive process of self-creation. His unique autobiographical project had an immense effect on his contemporaries, and with Freud's and Proust's equally heroic confessions, it continues to provide an influential framework for the conceptualization of modern selfhood. It still seems plausible to many that "there is one method of making oneself unique, if only in one's own eyes: one has simply to recall one's youth" (Metter 1995: 10).

Breaking out of the self-enclosing character of subjectivity could not be tackled head-on. In some ways, Cervantes (1950) and Montaigne (1991) had already grasped this important insight. The self of the text was an unreliable narrator. But the author of the text, and the characters in the text—fictional beings in support of which an entire world had to be created—carried the *weight* of authentic selfhood more convincingly than could any living person, caught up, as they inevitably were, in the self-undermining paradoxes of direct communication; thus Montaigne's insistence that "I am myself the subject of my book" and the fictionalized autobiography of Rousseau's *Confessions*. So the fictionalized self became an essential and authentic mask, not just to the writer (though the novelist borrowed this device, which provided the foundations of a new realism), but to every otherwise hermetically enclosed self.

Modernity and Irony

Authentic selfhood, it seems, resists direct exposure and can only be expressed fictionally—that is, inauthentically. This contradiction is one form of modern irony and might be viewed as a version of Amiel's so-called "Law of Irony": "the refutation of the self by itself, the concrete realisation of the absurd" (1906: 235).

Premodern Irony
But to grasp this specifically modern notion of irony we need to retreat a little. Irony, after all, is not in itself a modern phenomenon. It has

ancient roots and a continuous history in the development of Western society. The Greek *Eiron* was a minor stock character in tragic drama, a sly and cunning individual usually paired with *Alazon,* a proud and boastful bully, whom he regularly got the better of through cleverness and deception. Irony thus came to mean "sly, mocking pretence and deception" (N. Knox 1961: 3). In Plato's earlier dialogues, however, and in Aristophanes's *Clouds*, irony became identified as a particular questioning attitude to the world. Socratic questioning, on the other hand, with its insistent refrain claiming ignorance, which threw the interrogated back on his or her own intellectual resources, was generally understood in the ancient world as nothing more than modesty. In Aristotle, this form of irony was thus dignified as self-deprecating modesty.

In ancient examples, as well as throughout the late classical and medieval period, irony was a frequently used trope or figure which typically took the form of condemning or blaming while apparently praising. Irony might distinguish a specific statement or, as in Cicero, might characterize an entire passage of speech or prose. Though its usage in the Latin Medieval West was restricted almost exclusively to its rhetorical sense, the term continued to be discussed by grammarians and used by authors and speakers. But, where classical authors had favored irony as a distinguished and polished discourse, some medieval writers, following Augustine, became suspicious of its rhetorical force. Augustine linked irony with mendacity and dissimulation and criticized its borrowed authority, its assumption of superiority, and its distraction from reasoned argument (D. Knox 1989).

But what remained central to the whole notion of irony was that it was not intended to take in the reader or listener; its deception is transparent. Irony is a pretence but it is "recognized that this pretence was unmasked by gestures, intonation, context, and so on," and in this way it could remain a polemical device, "a vehicle for expressing mockery, reproach, indignation and the like, particularly when ostensibly praising what was in fact being condemned" (D. Knox 1989: 149). Mark Anthony's celebrated speech, for example, denounces Brutus as "an honorable man." Indeed, elaborate and precise lexicons of appropriate gestures through which to convey irony were produced as part of the standard curriculum in rhetoric.

More generally, as has already been suggested, the emergence of the novel as a literary form, and the modernity it reflected, established irony on a new and more comprehensive foundation. Irony, we might say, had to await the emergence of modern society, to find its true point of

reference. The rupture between appearance and reality, all along hinted
at by the use of irony to unmask pretensions, became, in Cervantes,
Montaigne, Shakespeare, and Calderón the point of departure for a new
representation of the world of human experience. Irony then ceased to
be one figure of speech among others, more or less useful for rhetorical
purposes as the circumstances dictated, and became, rather, the only
possible form through which the truth of modern experience could be
expressed (Muecke 1970; D. Knox 1989).

Romantic Irony

The centrality of irony to the mode of presentation of major literary works of the Renaissance went largely unremarked prior to the
establishment of a more or less self-regulating bourgeois economy and
society within which the values of personal identity and uniqueness
were theoretically recognized but practically suppressed. As part of what
has already been referred to as the bourgeois critique of modernity, the
Romantic movement not only espoused these values of personal identity
and uniqueness, but celebrated Shakespeare and Cervantes in particular
as the sources of their modern embodiment.

It was Friedrich Schlegel who, more than any other, elevated irony
into a metaphysics of modernity. Inspired by Renaissance examples
of irony, the writings of Goethe, German idealist philosophy, and the
French Revolution, Schlegel redefined the tasks of poetry and criticism
as nothing less than the realization of the promise of human freedom
implicit in modernity. During the last few years of the eighteenth century
he was "carried away....with the ego's wonderful creative powers, its divine independence, and the royal rulership it gave man over the domain
of things and thoughts" (Wernaer 1966: 138).

Favoring an aphoristic style, Schlegel championed the notion that
irony was pre-adapted, as it were, to express the real character of modernity as infinite subjectivity. Irony, he claims, "is the form of paradox"
and paradox is essential to every representation of human reality whose
depths remain inexpressible by direct means. The unlimited potentiality
of human subjectivity to assume any form, to empty itself into an infinite
variety of particularities and realize itself in as yet unknown ways, is a
limit to positive representation. But there is, after all, something infinite
and radical in irony so that its ceaseless negations might be regarded
as a superior form to, rather than a barely adequate substitute for, such

a mode of representation. Schlegel claims, indeed, that his conception of irony "contains and arouses a feeling of indissoluble antagonism between the absolute and the relative, between the impossibility and the necessity of complete communication....by its means one transcends oneself" (1971: 155). And self-transcendence is the very essence of modern selfhood.

Irony makes us smile, yet it is no joke; there is no release of tension or aggression, no telling of secrets which undoes conventional repressions and disorders the body in laughter. The smile of irony is essentially one of self-congratulation and superiority. Irony is a form of self-flattery in which the "I" becomes superior to everything other than itself; it establishes its own authority and expresses its autonomy in every self-motivated and self-willed expressive action. Heinrich Böll, for example, talks of "keeping your superiority feelings fresh in a refrigerator of irony" (Enright 1986: 25). This kind of pleasure, the smile of self-indulgence, is important for modernity because it makes the hard task of self-fashioning appear as if it were already accomplished. In irony, the "I" wins through and triumphantly surveys the infinity of its own realm. It places us, as Goethe claimed, "above happiness or unhappiness, good or evil, death or life" (Muecke 1970: 37).

The conception of Romantic irony which Schlegel formulated was given its philosophically most influential form by Karl Solger whose definition of irony as "infinite absolute negativity" was taken over both by Hegel and Kierkegaard. As Kierkegaard expresses it: "It is negative because it only negates; it is infinite because it does not negate this or that phenomenon; it is absolute because that by virtue of which it negates is a higher something that still is not" (1989: 261). In irony, in short, the subject realizes itself and holds itself "in negative independence of everything." Of course, this "infinitizing" of human subjectivity is symmetrical with the establishment of modern cosmology, with the infinitizing and absolutizing of space and time within which the commonality of bodies are located and differentiated. And it is, in that sense, a completion, rather than a rejection, of the real character of modernity.

Irony, because it refuses to align itself with any positive statement and "refuses to become involved any more with the world" (Kierkegaard 1989: 124), continually renews itself, endlessly detaching itself from immediacy to provide the subject, so to speak, with a temporary platform from which to look down upon events and activities which had previously been absorbing. Irony transforms the human subject into a spectator, again as Kierkegaard has it, the ironist "travels around, so to speak, in an exclusive incognito and looks down pityingly from this high position on ordinary prosaic talk." This provides the ironist with a specific "subjective pleasure as the subject frees himself by means of irony from the restraint in which the continuity of life's condition holds him" (1989: 248).

For the Romantics, as for their critics including Hegel and Kierkegaard, irony is not primarily a matter of literary taste or philosophical adequacy; it is a practical problem and a practical task. Irony is a way of life, a form of existence rather than a representation of existence. It involves a polemical attitude to everyday life, a continual stepping aside or stepping back from involvement in the world.

Critics of Romantic Irony

It is just this detachment—detachment in the name of nothing other than a theoretical possibility in which the entire world is annulled—that enraged Hegel and provided Kierkegaard with a point of departure for his own post-Romantic view of irony. They do not simply distrust, however much they are also attracted by, the dialectical brilliance of the ironic. They argued, rather, that irony in Schlegel's and Solger's sense misrepresents the real character of modern life.

Hegel's antipathy to Romanticism is focused on criticism of the notion of irony. Like Kierkegaard, he distinguishes between Socratic and Romantic irony, and, like Kierkegaard, he has the greatest admiration for the former. He claims that "Socrates expresses real existence as the universal 'I,' as the consciousness which rests in itself," but the Romantics distorted this notion of consciousness as the "inmost, deepest life" and interpreted it as "just the subjective and arbitrary will" (1892, vol. 3: 385, 401). He also criticizes Schlegel's conception of self-transcendence as vacuous. For him, Hegel claims, "Irony knows itself to be the master of every possible content; it is serious about nothing, but plays with all forms," and he nicely describes the Romantic notion of irony as "the ego's persistent tendency to break through the boundary of its own self-identity" (1892, vol. 3: 507).

Hegel extended his criticism of Romanticism in *The Philosophy of Right*, arguing that it was nothing more than contemporary subjectivism. Romanticism, in fact, was not so much a theory as an ironic (that is to say, empty) theory of human subjectivity, "the supreme form in which this subjectivism is completely comprehended and expressed is that to which the term 'irony,' borrowed from Plato, has been applied" (1991: 180). However,

> In this shape, subjectivity is not only empty of all ethical content in the way of rights, duties, and laws, and is accordingly evil...in addition, its form is that of *subjective* emptiness, in that it knows itself as this emptiness of all content and, in this knowledge, knows itself as the absolute. (1942: 182)

Here consciousness of self lacks all ethical seriousness and resolves itself into "mere play." Although the subject has developed knowledge of the "objective side of ethics," it is

> without that self-forgetfulness and self-renunciation which seriously immerses itself in this objectivity and makes it the basis of action. Although it has a relation to this objectivity, it at the same time distances itself from it and knows *itself* as that which *wills* and *resolves in a particular way* but may *equally well* will and resolve otherwise. (1942: 182)

For Hegel identity requires self-limitation. The lack of objectivity, of the dialectic, and of Spirit as a controlling element, particularly in the form of religion, "induced the noble soul to abandon itself to feeling," from which concrete selfhood could never emerge.

Kierkegaard is just as fierce in his criticism of the Romantics but, in criticizing their ironic detachment in which they "become alien to the actuality of the whole substantial world," he simultaneously attacks Hegel's return to a purely abstract conception of the Absolute conditioning element of reality as Reason. The strength of irony, in his view, lies in its concreteness. Socrates remains a personality through his questioning and refuses to be carried away by dialectical sophistication or ironic flights of fancy. He never escapes from his existential determinants and for him the "divine freedom of the mind" is continually placed alongside and supports, rather than annuls, immediacy. Socratic irony, for Kierkegaard, is the main instrument of what he terms the "maieutic art"—an obstetric procedure, to bring forth that which is hidden—so that Socratic dissimulation is justified because the confession of ignorance and repeated requests for clarification undermines all sophistical responses to the concrete issues posed by reality. The Socratic ironist only appears to be other than he or she is, and does so only to force the other to realize who he or she is or might become.

Romantic irony, however, which raises this form of negation "to a higher power" empties the world of every content. It is not a calculated use of dissimulation, but a new form, which Kierkegaard terms despair. The Romantic ironist lives, or would like to live, poetically. As a result he or she does not live at all—a being whose "life is nothing but words" (Kierkegaard 1989: 26). Rather than gaining authentic selfhood, the ironist has simply and literally lost touch with the world. Irony, in fact, is not positioned somewhere outside the world offering a vantage point from which the individual can confirm an eternal identity; it is an illusory independence and autonomy. "The ironist stands proudly inclosed within himself," writes Kierkegaard, and rejects everything else. But this is not a position from which anything can be rejected; "it is not because it is an antiquated actuality that must be replaced by a truer actuality, but because the ironist is the eternal *I* for which no actuality is adequate" (1989: 283) that the polemical stance comes to nothing. And, as a result, "he infinitizes his *I*, volatilizes it metaphysically and esthetically" (284).

But where Hegel had sought to counterpose the ironic dissolution of selfhood by a new positive element in philosophy, Kierkegaard rejects any metaphysical solution whatever to the problem. Hegel's system, in his view, ends in just the same "volatilization" of selfhood as does irony. The Absolute conceived philosophically converts the human subjectivity of self-identity and experience back into the universal *cogito,* an infinite abstraction in which all personal elements are swallowed up.

Paradoxically the ironist *and* the Hegelian, by so completely detaching themselves from actuality, in fact end by accepting it, as it were, by default: they soar so far above it that they completely ignore it. But this means that in terms of their actual existence, rather than in terms of their thought or their poetic effusions, they continue to live in the world as it is. And it is for this reason that irony can still be viewed as either subversive or as conservative. The ironist simultaneously escapes and is captured by actuality. He or she achieves a curious "negative unity" which is nothing but an arbitrary succession of words and images—the unity which Kierkegaard calls boredom.

Despair

Kierkegaard's thesis on irony ends at this important point of transition. He himself insisted that this work did not form part of his authorship proper and, until recently, it has been undervalued both as an analysis of irony and as a perspective from which his work as a whole might be read (Smyth 1986). In the present context, however, what is significant is that in this work he begins the transition from critical literary and philosophical terms to existential categories. Thus, rather as Marx moved from the critique of religion to the critique of political economy, Kierkegaard's understanding of modern identity moves from the critique of irony to the critique of boredom. He himself admits that the *Either* of *Either/Or* (1987) is conceived as "an ironical sequel to *Concept of Irony*" and provides an exemplary instance of modern irony, now conceptualized as boredom. Boredom is existential irony; irony is philosophical boredom. This is the irony of not having a self, of non-identity, rather than the irony of deception and dissimulation.

This is not only a shift from a metaphysical to an existential discourse, but a movement from the notion of the ironic self-confirming strategy of Socratic irony, to the self-undoing of modern or Romantic irony. Taken out of its literary and philosophical context, Romantic irony is a non-identity. On the one hand, it is a volatilization of the self into abstraction, and, on the other hand, the self is abandoned to the concrete arbitrariness of the moment.

Kierkegaard's method throughout the subsequent development of his writing is to attempt to use Socratic irony to confirm himself, while representing the emptiness of Romantic irony. By deception he hopes to discourse existentially on despair without himself falling into despair; without losing himself in his books. At the same time, this method is Socratic in challenging the reader, and in drawing from the reader a positive response rather than a passive intellectual understanding. To this end he writes under a series of pseudonyms and, as carefully as had Cervantes, hides his part in the construction of the books in which every possible existential possibility given in the modern world is carefully anatomized. A series of characters are introduced, some reappearing in subsequent works to continue to argue their case and to represent as fully as possible the potentialities inherent in modern existence.

What emerges is a complex and many-layered presentation of modernity and modern self-identity as despair. The ironic, understood as boredom, is only the simplest and as it were the most primitive form of the general melancholy of modern existence. The philosophically most sophisticated of the Romantics, Karl Solger, had already drawn attention to melancholy as an inescapable element in modern life; and descriptive accounts of its psychology had figured in literary works since Goethe's (1989) *The Sorrows of Young Werther*, whose hero in many ways remained its prototype. But in Solger the heaviness and lassitude of the melancholic state, the "sadness without a cause" of which Burton and Montaigne had already spoken at length, was connected with the human failure to realize the theoretical freedom which could be grasped abstractly. For him an "immeasurable sadness permeates every form of life, since the absolute can only appear in limited, finite, and transitory form" (Behler 1988: 45). Solger, indeed, expresses the hopelessness of a deeper insight into Romantic irony: "we cannot help being seized by an immeasurable grief when we see what is most glorious of all dispersed into nothing on account of its necessary earthly existence" (Wheeler 1984: 145).

Kierkegaard's "young men," however, are melancholic as much from an excess of infinitude, as they are over the constraints of existence; as Settembrini remarks to Hans Castorp in *The Magic Mountain*: "A soul without a body is as inhuman and horrible as a body without a soul" (Mann 1960: 100). Given the demands and possibilities of modernity— the conceptualization of reality as crystallized in an inner self which authenticates itself in expressive action—Kierkegaard's characters throw themselves into the world, fail to recognize themselves in their actions, and fall back in upon themselves in fits of gloomy self-doubt and depression. The oscillation between unbounded enthusiasm and melancholic withdrawal from life are characteristic of what Kierkegaard calls the "present age" (1978). Characteristic, that is, for those true moderns who are unwilling simply to accept the normality of bourgeois-philistinism with its stultifying conventions.

Irony implies boredom and boredom implies despair; it leads to melancholy and to the spiritual crisis of modern self-identity. Irony, after all, viewed existentially rather than metaphysically, is no flight from actuality, but is rather a prelude to a deepening consciousness of its paradoxical and contradictory character. It is the beginning of that inward transformation which results, if not in a positive self-identity, then certainly in the overthrowing of both the superficiality of the present and all philosophical and poetic fantasies which seek to replace the present with abstract abbreviations of real life. In the *Concept of Irony*, Kierkegaard writes that, "As philosophers claim that no true philosophy is possible without doubt, so by the same token no authentic human life is possible without irony." Friedrich Schlegel had been almost right. He had claimed that "there is a kind of person for whom an enthusiasm for boredom represents the beginning of philosophy" (1971: 167). But in

Kierkegaard's view, boredom for all its lassitude and disinterest in the world is nonetheless a real-life relation which binds the subject to actuality. And he is not alone—Heidegger concurs. "Boredom," Heidegger remarks, "is the first deep plunge into existence," the first experience which "reveals being as a whole" (Bigelow 1987: 120).

Self-identity does not come easily. It is not, as it were, handed out ready-made; nor can it be self-generated as a free and spontaneous expression of itself. Identity is developed, rather, through a series of decisive inner transformations and crises; through actually deepening despair rather than in theoretically infinitizing irony. In the *Or* of *Either/ Or* (1987), the melancholic young man is advised to "choose despair," to bind himself more completely to his boredom and thus plunge more deeply into existence.

The incommunicability of inwardness means that irony is an essential aspect of modern social life, and not merely a decorative excess. Inasmuch as the soul is defined by communication, despair is an inescapable and central feature of existence. The irony of deception is less important here than the irony of despair. The conditions of modern society, it is true, provide for deception, making secrecy and the lie an important aspect of personal existence. Indeed, as Simmel pointed out, the secret and the lie has become an adornment of the personality and a means of protecting and enhancing the self (1950: 312-18, 334-36). But, given the reality of modernity as inwardness, the incommunicability of this reality means that every life relation becomes tinged with the irony of despair.

Anonymity and the End of Irony

Irony is a moment in the development of modern identity, and of the identity of modernity: the fathomless depth of inwardness is symmetrical with the infinite extension of time and space. Neither can be directly represented so that irony is appealing as a kind of negative communication through which personal identity can be forged and made known. But irony is a dangerous game; it insists in playing with the infinite, and in the infinite all sense of personal identity is swallowed up and lost.

Irony, however, is only one moment in this development. Since the Romantics, who advertised the stunning insights of the first moderns, irony has waned. Everyone, of course, must remain on nodding terms, so to speak, with the ironic. It remains significant as a technique of affirming membership in a specific "in-group." But irony in the Romantics' sense is no longer in evidence; as an all-embracing literary and meta-physical position, it seems to have had its day, and now it must be content with playing its part, with other figures, in the repertoire of modern rhetorical devices. Of course, discourse has now become a matter of living and breathing, a style of life rather than a mode of speech alone. But, all the same, few would confess, far less boast, of living out an ironic style of life.

Irony as a social form of communication exists in the period of developing individualism, a period in which voluntary communities and exclusive social groupings can form. The period of high modernity is inimical to irony in that sense because, for the most advanced societies, all communities tend ideally to be dissolved in the continuous flux of civil society.

The interchangeability of persons, the anonymity of large-scale organization, the division of labor, the legal-rational forms of authority, the decay of personal relations as a form of political organization and public life—these conditions mean that, most of the time, social interaction takes place among strangers devoid of distinguishing inwardness. Identity thus becomes a purely "inward" and personal marker, rather than something to be displayed. "Communities" are conjured by special occasions, as in large sporting events, which are expressive only of a carefully staged show of emotion. Among the most fervent supporters, as among the most devout fashion worshippers, nothing, in fact, is being communicated about the "inner-person." Modes of identification are at the same time displays of "role-distance." The privacy of the modern self becomes a secret even from itself—an obscure inner region that, in spite of the interpretive efforts of Freud, ultimately resists clarification. The individual cannot, thus, even use irony on himself or herself as a maieutic device to bring forth the hidden personality, as no such being any longer clothes itself in the possibility of existence.

Ought we refer, indeed, to the end of irony like the end of ideology—and for much the same reason? If irony betrays the "depth," hiddenness, and inwardness of the soul, and always works "from below the surface" (Muecke 1969: 5), then the contemporary age is no longer an age of irony. Now the soul is exposed, open, spread flat like the page of a book; there is nothing interior, underneath, or hidden. There is no disjunction or rupture upon which irony can get to work and in which it might take root. The most advanced societies are notoriously insensitive to irony. Identity is no longer linked to irony, nor is it secreted in the "ego." Rather, it openly displays itself in a vortex of disconnected experiences.

Now there is no need to be ironic because no one would imagine that "depth," authentic or otherwise, is being expressed. The nonironic identity of contemporary society, unlike that of premodern society, is not based on trust, or on openness, but on superficiality—on the glamour of the modern personality and of modern identity.

Personality, that is to say, is no longer that "deep" selfhood which can only be expressed indirectly and ironically, but has become an aspect of the network of relations in which it is implicated. Social and personal identities are reconciled in the unity of fashion. Personality and self-image are no longer fixed from within but easily adapt themselves to the continually changing circumstances of time and place. The personality, shiny and mirror-like, is a glamorous soul. This is not because the contemporary world has in some way lost sight of reality, or cut itself off from every form of humanly meaningful relation, but rather that, for the contemporary world, the surface of things has been consecrated as the paramount "reality." The contemporary world is conceptualized as continuous with the self, an extended, energetic, and sensitive surface upon which is registered the continuous flux of experience. Identity, in such a world, cannot be a function of interior self-expression or the outcome of a process of actualization; there is no interior to express or to actualize.

The nonironic mood—melancholic still, but no longer detached and superior, no longer heavy with suppressed passion—is very well-expressed, for example, in the contemporary American writer Richard Ford. His celebration of the ordinariness of American life, or one section of it at any rate, seems, to a European reader still charmed by irony, to be so sincere that it *must* be ironic through and through. However, given that it might be read in two ways, Ford plausibly represents a nonironic and yet nonnaive central character who claims at one point, "I can't bear all the complications, and long for something that is façades-only..." (1996: 37).

He depicts the amorphous, and more or less anonymous, drifting soul and the contemporary world of appearances on which it floats: "And for a moment I find it is really quite easy and agreeable not to know what's next..." (147). Ford's character experiences the serenity of finding pleasure without identity: "All we really want is to get to the point where the past can explain nothing about us and we can get on with life" (30).

The abandonment of the personal past, more than any other aspect of the novel, makes it clear that the sportswriter is serious about rejecting the unequal struggle of self-actualization. Though, of course, he cannot really be serious about that either. This lightness, the floating quality of the sportswriter (an ideal postmodern occupation), is quite unlike the detachment of the ironist. And, in spite of the phenomenological similarity, he is not bored, not "seriously" bored in Heidegger's sense, not the "profound boredom, drifting here and there in the abysses of our existence like a muffling fog, [which] removes all things and men and oneself with it into a remarkable indifference" (Heidegger 1977: 101). Rather, the sportswriter's drifting is engagement. He is fully absorbed in and by reality; it is just that this reality remains ill-defined and fluid. He is borne effortlessly, in directionless and intermittent currents of life. This characterization of contemporary life as an ubiquitous sense of drifting, in contrast to the rectilinear motion of self-actualizing intentions, resonates with much of the literature of this century and is by no means confined to recent examples. Its most complete and (ironically) its most profound expression can be found in Robert Musil's (1995) masterpiece, *The Man Without Qualities*.

Identity for a person without qualities becomes a more or less arbitrary matter of social relations. Identity can be multiple, transformative, and variable without impinging on the obstructive notion of an inner soul. Social identity is expressed not in terms of ego-based utterances but in terms of superficial signs: clothing, style of life, advertising, and so on.

Glamour is a nonironic nonidentity—a surface gloss, which, in fact, neither conceals nor reveals the "person." Glamorous personal accessories are, in this sense, nonironic commodity consumables, taken up and put down as is convenient. Once the ego-self relation is split apart, it becomes possible to parade quasi-self-identities like any other aspect of fashion. Glamour is exciting; in it the self loses itself, abandoning itself to appearance. Where the classical ego recognized itself in melancholy, in a gloomy despair, the contemporary self (nonself) recognizes itself in the despair of glamour. Glamour is the exclusiveness of money alone, and it requires no effort, no refinement of taste, to consume. Glamour does not expose the private—it is not conspicuous consumption—so much as it transforms the private into the visible innocence of the "man without qualities." The lives of the rich and famous become glamorous not because they are unable to conceal how they live privately, or because they court publicity to become yet more rich and famous, but because glamour in itself de-individuates and disintegrates all boundaries; the glamorous is essentially public.

Has, then, the "age of irony" passed to be replaced by an "age of glamour" in which appearance is consecrated as the only reality, in which both personal and social identities are assimilated to a new culture of consumerism? (Slater 1997) Possibly. Where it does not matter what sort of person one is—even to that person himself or herself—then neither identity nor irony remains important, and there are only the continuously shifting boundaries of impersonal and transient life contents. In this context, identity is a transitory selfhood, momentarily distinguished from what might be termed the "background radiation" of self-presence. This hardly amounts to an alternative spectator ego, watching over the whole comedy. There remains not much more than a bare impersonal presence, a quality of hereness and nowness, which lends to the fleeting experience of conventionalized selfhoods their peculiar, but intermittent, primacy.

Modernity thus moves through a period of "authentic" selfhood to one of "ironic" selfhood to a contemporary culture which might be termed "associative" selfhood—a continuous "loosening" of the tie between an "inner" soul and an "outer" form of social relation. A certain contemporary infatuation with the notion of "irony" as the inauthentic is surely misplaced. The age of irony is primarily the age of high capitalism; the postmodern is, in contrast, the age of glamour.

Yet we remain aware of ourselves as individuals; personal identities are not wholly dissolved into immediate relations. Or, rather, of the modes of identity and non-identity available to us, "old-fashioned" individualism remains a possibility. It seems that modes of experience persist in us, or through us, which not only have their origin in the past but continue, as it were, to point to a vanished social and cultural context. We do not live only in the contemporary world, but also in every period of the development of Western society—premodern as well as modern. We thus "feel" ourselves to be in one moment souls enclosed in bodies, and then, in the next moment, we are spread out as extended surfaces, or become primitive cosmological schemas.

Identities, thus, are continuous oscillations, movements from one world to another. And irony, its protean form adapting to contemporary conditions, now expresses the freedom of this movement and the false limitations of accepting any position or perspective as genuine and authentic. Contemporary identity has the added advantage, as it were, of being a self-conscious form of historicism and perspectivism. Without irony we remain unaware of this and cannot commit ourselves even to the possibility of variety. Irony, thus, has become a technique of losing rather than gaining the soul. Indeed, contemporary irony has become self-consciously historical and social. It is a succession of forms, now "postmodern" superficiality, now the depth of the soul—a succession from which we do not detach ourselves, but adopt in relation to it, at appropriate moments, an "ironic" or a nonironic standpoint. This perspectivism might be regarded as itself a thoroughgoing irony. The idle playing with forms with which Hegel charged the Romantics has become, rather than an extreme measure of individuation, the general condition of contemporary life. At best it might be considered a version of Thomas Mann's practice of irony as "the intellect of conservatism," that, ever-conscious of the artificiality of pure reason, undermines all radicalism based on principles with a generous humanism, tolerant of formal contradictions (Mann 1987: 430).

In the postmodern world, all distinctions become fluid, boundaries dissolve, and everything can just as well appear to be its opposite; irony becomes the perpetual sense that things could be somewhat different, though never fundamentally or radically different. Modernity has become so well established (as postmodernity) that it can now allow individuals not simply the reconciling luxury of an inner and harmless freedom—a personal identity conceived as a soul—but also the freedom to express themselves, and, even more significantly, to act without expressing themselves and to abandon altogether the pursuit of personal identity. Modernity has become so effectively institutionalized that it no longer requires that its subjects be individuated, personalized, and identified in terms of the unique qualities of inwardness.

In this perspective the inexplicable succession of events and images exercises a fatal power over us. The world becomes so confident in its appearance (glamour) that it parades itself before us and humiliates our puny efforts to assert ourselves, ironically or actually, over its objectivity. Now, rather than the exalted subject rising ironically above the world of its own limiting objectivity, the irresistible force of this very objectivity transforms every subject into a plaything of its casual irony. Hugo von Hofmannsthal once remarked that "there is nothing like a lost war to teach us the significance of this irony that permeates our whole earthly existence." War "puts everything into relationship

with everything else—the seemingly great with the seemingly small....
it reduces the heroic to the mechanical." This culminates in "the most
devastating and irresistible irony" of the present,

> to wit, the contrast between the magnificent ideals....and the confused tangle of
> obstinate realities...the endless round of details which is the basis of reality, and
> which mocks at our rash efforts to synthesize life, our admittedly false attempts
> to escape from the mechanics of existence. (Hofmannsthal 1924: 175-77)

Schlegel also had seen irony in the character of modern life itself and
not in a peculiarly detached and superior attitude to it, or mood within it.
But Hofmannsthal strikes a more ancient note, a characteristic of irony
to pull down and reassert the trivial minutiae of everyday life, to debunk
and empty out the verbosity and rhetoric of leaders and teachers. Now
irony does not require wit or a writer; the complexity of everyday existence is capable of asserting itself over all such elevated conceptions of
life. Irony, where it exists at all, does not any longer provide an escape,
a soaring sense of freedom, but rather confirms the inescapable necessity of our mundane and transparently conventional existence. Irony
ends, then, by being absorbed into, rather than in standing apart from,
the conditions of contemporary life; it becomes glamour or "universal
cynicism" (Jankélévitch 1964).

References

Abercrombie, N., S. Hill, and B.S. Turner. 1986. *Sovereign Individuals of Capitalism*.
London: Allen and Unwin.

Amiel, H-F. 1906. *Amiel's Journal: The Journal Intime of Henri-Frédéric Amiel*. London: Macmillan.

Behler, E. 1988. "The Theory of Irony in German Romanticism." Pp. 43-81 in *Romantic
Irony*, edited by F. Garber. Budapest: Akadémiai Kiadó.

Bigelow, P. 1987. *Kierkegaard and the Problem of Writing*. Tallahassee: Florida State
University Press.

Booth, W.C. 1974. *A Rhetoric of Irony*. Chicago: University of Chicago Press.

Burns, T. 1995. *Erving Goffman*. London: Routledge.

de Cervantes, M. 1950. *Don Quixote*, trans. J.M. Cohen. Harmondsworth: Penguin.

Chevalier, H.M. 1932. *The Ironic Temper: Anatole France and His Time*. Oxford: Oxford
University Press.

Descartes, R. 1984. *The Philosophical Writings of Descartes*. Vol.1. Cambridge: Cambridge University Press.

Durkheim, E. 1933. *The Division of Labor in Society*, trans. G. Simpson. New York:
The Free Press.

Eagleton, T. 1996. *The Ideology of the Aesthetic*. Oxford: Blackwell.

Elias, N. 1991. *The Society of Individuals*, trans. E. Jephcott. Oxford: Blackwell.

Enright, D.J. 1986. *The Alluring Problem: An Essay on Irony.* Oxford: Oxford University Press.
Ferguson, H. 1990. *The Science of Pleasure: Cosmos and Psyche in the Bourgeois World View.* London: Routledge.
———. 1995. *Melancholy and the Critique of Modernity.* London: Routledge.
Ford, R. 1996. *The Sportswriter.* London: Harvill.
Garber, F. 1982. *The Autonomy of the Self from Richardson to Huysmans.* Princeton, NJ: Princeton University Press.
Ginzburg, L. 1991. *On Psychological Prose*, trans. J. Rosengrant. Princeton, NJ: Princeton University Press.
von Goethe, J.W. 1989. *The Sorrows of Young Werther*, trans. M. Hulse. Harmondsworth: Penguin.
Greenblatt, S. 1980. *Renaissance Self-Fashioning: From More to Shakespeare.* Chicago: University of Chicago Press.
Greenleaf, M. 1994. *Pushkin and Romantic Fashion: Fragment, Elegy, Orient, Irony.* Stanford, CA: Stanford University Press.
Handwerk, G.J. 1985. *Irony and Ethics in Narrative: From Schlegel to Lacan.* New Haven, CT: Yale University Press.
Heidegger, M. 1977. "What is Metaphysics?" Pp. 91-112 in *Basic Writings from Being and Time (1927) to The Task of Thinking (1964)*, edited by D.F. Krell. New York: Harper and Row.
Hegel, G.W.F. 1892. *Lectures on the History of Philosophy.* 3 vols., trans. E.S. Haldane. London: Kegan Paul, Trench and Trubner.
———. 1991. *Elements of a Philosophy of Right*, edited by A.W. Wood, trans. H.B. Nisbet. Oxford: Oxford University Press.
von Hofmannsthal, H. 1924. "Two Essays." *London Mercury* 9(50): 175-180.
Jankélévitch, V. 1964. *L'Ironie.* Paris: Flammarion.
Kierkegaard, S. 1978. *Two Ages*, trans. H.V. Hong and E.H. Hong. Princeton, NJ: Princeton University Press.
———. 1987. *Either/Or.* 2 vols., trans. H.V. Hong and E.H. Hong. Princeton, NJ: Princeton University Press.
———. 1989. *The Concept of Irony*, edited by H.V. Hong and E.H. Hong. Princeton, NJ: Princeton University Press.
Knox, D. 1989. *Ironia: Medieval and Renaissance Ideas of Irony.* Leiden: E.J. Brill.
Knox, N. 1961. *The Word Irony and its Context, 1500-1755.* Durham, NC: Duke University Press.
Koyré, A. 1957. *From the Closed World to the Infinite Universe.* Baltimore, MD: Johns Hopkins University Press.
Luhmann, N. 1979. *Trust and Power.* Chichester: Wiley.
de Montaigne, M. 1991. *The Complete Essays of Michel de Montaigne*, trans. M.A. Screech. London: Allen Lane, The Penguin Press.
Mann, T. 1960. *The Magic Mountain*, trans. H.T. Lowe-Porter. Harmondsworth: Penguin.
———. 1987. *Reflections of a Nonpolitical Man*, trans. W.D. Morris. New York: Ungar.
Metter, I. 1995. *The Fifth Corner of the Room*, trans. M. Duncan. London: Havrill.
Muecke, D.C. 1969. *The Compass of Irony.* London: Methuen.
———. 1970. *Irony.* London: Methuen.
Musil, R. 1995. *The Man Without Qualities*, trans. S. Wilkins and B. Pike. London: Picador.

Rorty, R. 1989. *Contingency, Irony, and Solidarity*. Cambridge: Cambridge University Press.

Rousseau, J-J. 1953. *The Confessions of Jean-Jacques Rousseau*, trans. J.M. Cohen. Harmondsworth: Penguin.

———. 1973. *The Social Contract and Discourses*, trans. G.D.H. Cole. London: Everyman.

Schlegel, F. 1971. *Lucinde and The Fragments*, trans. P. Firchow. Minneapolis: University of Minnesota Press.

Simmel, G. 1950. *The Sociology of Georg Simmel*, trans. K.H. Wolff. Glencoe, IL: The Free Press.

Slater, D. 1997. *Consumer Culture and Modernity*. Cambridge, MA: Polity Press.

Smyth, J.V. 1986. *A Question of Eros: Irony in Sterne, Kierkegaard, and Barthes*. Tallahassee: Florida State University Press.

Sperber, D., and D. Wilson. 1981. "Irony and the Use-Mention Distinction." Pp. 295-318 in *Radical Pragmatics*, edited by P. Cole. New York: Academic Press.

Unger, R.M. 1975. *Knowledge and Politics*. London: The Free Press.

Weber, M. 1930. *The Protestant Ethic and the Spirit of Capitalism*, trans. T. Parsons. London: Allen and Unwin.

Wernaer, R.M. 1966. *Romanticism and the Romantic School in Germany*. New York: Haskell House.

Wheeler, K.M., ed. 1984. *German Aesthetic and Literary Criticism: The Romantic Ironists and Goethe*. Cambridge: Cambridge University Press.

Contributors

Zygmunt Bauman is Emeritus Professor of Sociology at the Universities of Leeds and Warsaw. His many books include *Legislators and Interpreters; Postmodernity and Its Discontents; Globalization: The Human Consequences; In Search of Politics;* and *Liquid Modernity.*

Joseph E. Davis is Program Director of the Institute for Advanced Studies in Culture and Research Assistant Professor of Sociology at the University of Virginia. His articles have appeared in academic journals such as *Qualitative Sociology*, the *Journal of Policy History*, and *The Hedgehog Review*, as well as in more popular publications. He is author of a book on the theoretical foundations of anti-cultism and editor of a forthcoming volume on narrative and social movements.

Robert G. Dunn is Professor of Sociology at California State University, Hayward. He is the author of *Identity Crises: A Social Critique of Postmodernity*. His articles have appeared in journals such as *Media, Culture, and Society; Theory, Culture and Society;* and *Socialist Review*. He is currently at work on a book dealing with consumption, identity, and the self.

Mike Featherstone is Professor of Sociology at Nottingham Trent University. He is the editor of the journal, *Theory, Culture, and Society*, as well as a book series by that title at Sage Publishers. He is the editor of many books, as well as author, most recently, of *Undoing Culture: Globalization, Postmodernism and Identity* and *Consumer Culture and Postmodernism.*

Harvie Ferguson is Reader in Sociology at the University of Glasgow. His most recent books include *Melancholy and the Critique of Modernity: Søren Kierkegaard's Religious Psychology*; *The Lure of Dreams:*

205

Sigmund Freud and the Construction of Modernity; and *The Art of Detachment: Forms of Subjectivity in Modern Society.*

Kenneth J. Gergen is the Gil and Frank Mustin Professor of Psychology at Swarthmore College. He was awarded the Alexander von Humboldt Prize in the Humanities in 1989, and has been a Guggenheim Fellow and a Phi Beta Kappa Visiting Scholar. A prolific author, his most recent books include *The Saturated Self: Dilemmas of Identity in Contemporary Life* and *Realities and Relationships: Soundings in Social Construction.*

David Harvey is Professor of Geography at the Johns Hopkins University. From 1987-1993 he was Halford Mackinder Professor of Geography at Oxford University. He has been the recipient of many awards, including, most recently, the Patron's Medal of the Royal Geographical Society (1995) and the Vautrin Lud Prize in France (1995). His many books include *The Limits to Capital*; *The Condition of Postmodernity*; *Justice, Nature and the Geography of Difference*; and, forthcoming, *Spaces of Hope.*

Joane Nagel is University Distinguished Professor and Chair of the Department of Sociology at the University of Kansas. She has been the recipient of several teaching awards and guest lectureships, and is past president of the Midwest Sociological Society. She is the editor of several books, and author, most recently, of *American Indian Ethnic Renewal: Red Power and the Resurgence of Identity and Culture* and the forthcoming *Race, Ethnicity, and Sexuality: The Color of Sex.*

Index

212 Identity and Social Change

Reality, 19–20, 121–23, 175, 184, 189, 199
Reason, 146
Recovery movement, 152
Recreational ethnicity, 79
Red Eagle, Jim, 90–91
Red Power movement, 81, 83
relational being, 133
Relationship(s), 143–48, 159, 162
Relativism, 147
Renaissance, 177, 181, 184, 189
Repetition, 136–37, 138
Reproductive rights, 34
Rheingold, Howard, 69, 141
Riesman, David, 136
Rights, 34, 43, 46–49, 54–55, 59, 81, 139, 182–83
Robertson, Roland, 20
Role distance, 176, 197
Romantic irony, 189–192, 194–95
Rorty, Richard, 5, 180
Rose, Wendy, 88
Rousseau, J. J., 70–71, 176, 178, 186–87

Saarinen, Esa, 16
Sameness, 52
Sampson, Edward, 4, 139, 145
Sandel, Michael, 138
Satisfaction, 15
Scarry, Elaine, 66
Schlegel, Friedrich, 180, 189–91, 195, 202
Seabrook, Jeremy, 21–22, 42–44
Segregation, 87
Self, 52, 109–10, 115–16, 136, 146; actualization, 113, 167, 186; coherence, 151–52; creation, 60, 113–14, 184; deception, 180–81; dissolution of, 151, 193; inner, 184; languages of, 164, 167; and morality, 136–37, 140, 143-44, 151; privatization, 124–25, 181, 199; social sources, 168–69; unencumbered, 71, 164; unstable and fluid, 5. *See also* False self, Fictional self, True self
Self-esteem, 143, 161
Self-help, 2, 155, 166, 170
Self/society binary, 9, 142, 144
Semiotics, 107–08, 110, 121, 128
Sennett, Richard, 56, 66, 71–72
Sensations, 16
Sequestration, 170
Sexual abuse, 154, 157–58, 164
Sexuality, 4, 33, 55, 105, 114, 120–21
Shakespeare, W., 189
Shotter, John, 145–46

Shweder, Richard, 144
Sign, 185
Signification, 121–22
Simmel, G., 183, 196
Simulation, 7, 118, 121–23
Social dysfunction, 161
Social identity, 5, 167, 177–78, 183, 199
Social order, 183
Socratic irony, 192–93, 194–95
Solger, Karl, 190–91, 194–95
Solipsism, 184, 186
Soul, 182, 187, 197, 201–02
Space, 20–21; shrinking of, 19–20; virtuality of, 22
Spectacle, 107, 121
Spectator, 191
Spontaneity, 137
Stage development, 66
Standardization, 114
Standing Bear, Z. G., 90
Status symbols, 120–21
Stiffarm, L. A., 95
Stratification, 17
Structuralism, 31
Style, 112, 114
Subjectivity, 1, 2, 6, 110, 182, 184–85, 187, 190–93
Suffering, 66–67, 71
Superficiality, 195, 98, 201
Superiority, 188, 190
Surface, 110
Surplus value, 39
Survivor story, 159–162

Target marketing, 114
Taste, 114
Taylor, Charles, 154, 167–69, 171
Taylor, Mark C., 16
Technologically mediated exchange, 140–41
Technologies of sociation, 132, 134–35, 137, 140
Technology, 3, 109, 122–23, 131–32, 170
Teleology, 152, 171
Television, 65, 107, 112–13, 116–19, 122, 126, 140
Television evangelism, 140
Therapy, 2
Thin culture, 126
Thompson, John, 63–65, 67
Thriver story, 162–66
Time, 15, 20, 22, 126
Tocqueville, Alexis de, 138

West African Warfare in Bahia and Cuba

Soldier Slaves in the Atlantic World, 1807–1844

MANUEL BARCIA

OXFORD
UNIVERSITY PRESS

OXFORD
UNIVERSITY PRESS

Great Clarendon Street, Oxford, OX2 6DP,
United Kingdom

Oxford University Press is a department of the University of Oxford.
It furthers the University's objective of excellence in research, scholarship,
and education by publishing worldwide. Oxford is a registered trade mark of
Oxford University Press in the UK and in certain other countries

© Manuel Barcia 2014

The moral rights of the author have been asserted

First published 2014
First published in paperback 2016

All rights reserved. No part of this publication may be reproduced, stored in
a retrieval system, or transmitted, in any form or by any means, without the
prior permission in writing of Oxford University Press, or as expressly permitted
by law, by licence or under terms agreed with the appropriate reprographics
rights organization. Enquiries concerning reproduction outside the scope of the
above should be sent to the Rights Department, Oxford University Press, at the
address above

You must not circulate this work in any other form
and you must impose this same condition on any acquirer

Published in the United States of America by Oxford University Press
198 Madison Avenue, New York, NY 10016, United States of America

British Library Cataloguing in Publication Data
Data available

Library of Congress Cataloging in Publication Data
Data available

ISBN 978–0–19–871903–8 (Hbk.)
ISBN 978–0–19–875426–8 (Pbk.)

Links to third party websites are provided by Oxford in good faith and
for information only. Oxford disclaims any responsibility for the materials
contained in any third party website referenced in this work.

To little Kenny
Dee dee, da da

Acknowledgments

This book is the result of a long process that originated when I came to the realization that in order to understand the history of the African diaspora in the Americas, I had to learn West African history in an uncompromising manner. I began by writing a short paper that I presented in conferences and seminars that took place in Castellon, Leeds, Niamey, and Paris, and eventually ended up writing this volume.

In the course of my research I incurred debts to many people and institutions. First and foremost, I am greatly indebted to the Leverhulme Trust. It was thanks to a Leverhulme Research Fellowship that I was able to focus on this project and to finish it. Friends and colleagues who generously read parts of the manuscript broadened my understanding of the subject and gave precious advice on how to deal with a number of themes and issues. I am particularly thankful to Robin Law, Ann O'Hear, and Paul Lovejoy who took time to comment and advise on a number of aspects pertaining to the African side of the story I tell here. Numerous discussions with John Thornton improved my knowledge of African warfare on both sides of the Atlantic. Michelle Kelly and Ananya Kabir also read parts of the manuscript. Their opinions, and especially their encouragement, have been much appreciated. I consider myself very lucky to be able to count on such good friends and wonderful scholars.

The staff at the archives and libraries I visited in Havana, Matanzas, Salvador de Bahia, Rio de Janeiro, Aix-en-Provence, Seville, Madrid, Lisbon, London, Hull, York (Toronto), and Niamey proved helpful locating documents and allowing me to get hold of the information I needed. Special thanks are due to Gaelle Beaujean-Baltzer, Gabino La Rosa, Lisette Roura, and Jorge Garcell, for allowing me to use their photographs in this book, and to Philip Schwartzberg for the wonderful maps that adorn its pages. I would also like to thank my Ph.D. student Jennifer Nelson for going out of her way to secure the rights to reproduce some of the images used here.

Sandra Nickel and Mohammed Bashir Salau provided me with much needed translations of documents in Yoruba and Hausa, during the latter stages of the writing. I cannot thank them enough for their help.

I am equally indebted to a number of friends and colleagues who have been willing and ready to engage in discussions and to provide their academic and moral support whenever needed. Among them, Rosanne Adderley, Ana Lucia Araujo, Imilcy Balboa, Maria del Carmen Barcia, José Luis Belmonte, Robin Blackburn, Matt Childs, Lisa Earl Castillo, Emma Christopher, Mary Ellen Curtin, Rocío Davis, Jorge Felipe, Leida Fernández, Ada Ferrer, Aisha Finch, Dorothea Fischer-Hornung, Alejandro de la Fuente, Reinaldo Funes, Gloria García, Dick Geary, Alejandro Gómez, Dale Graden, Lillian Guerra, Gwendolyn Midlo Hall, Walter Hawthorne, Marial Iglesias, Sherry Johnson, Nurcan Kaya, David Lambert,

Jane Landers, Cara Levey, Milagros López-Peláez, Henry Lovejoy, Karen Mahe Lugo, Ghislaine Lydon, Jorge Macle, Beatriz Mamigonian, Rafael Marquese, Sonia Menéndez, Ismael Montana, Consuelo Naranjo, Olatunji Ojo, Ricardo Quiza, José Antonio Piqueras, João José Reis, Maria Dolores Ripoll, Anicia Rodríguez, Matthias Röhrig Assunção, Inés Roldán de Montaud, Benedetta Rossi, David Sartorius, Stuart Schwartz, Dale Tomich, William Van Norman, Claudia Varela, Sigfrido Vázquez, and Michael Zeuske.

Spending a semester at the Wilberforce Institute for the Study of Slavery and Emancipation (WISE) at the University of Hull allowed me to dedicate plenty of time to research on the topic at what was the start of the project. There I also benefited from the friendship and collegiality of David Richardson, Nick Evans, Doug Hamilton, Filipa Ribeiro da Silva, Carlos Silva Jr., Stacey Sommerdyck, and especially from the many discussions and schemes that I have had the pleasure to share ever since with Joel Quirk.

In and around the University of Leeds I have benefited from the friendship of really exceptional people who have made my days fun and productive. I am happy to count most of them as both colleagues and friends. My thanks go to Gregorio Alonso, Anyaa Anim-Addo, Nir Arielli, Warren Barner, Richard Cleminson, Stephanie Dennison, Alison Fell, Frank Finlay, David Frier, Paul Garner, Will Gould, Louise Gibbs, Stuart Green, Bettina Hermoso, Claire Honess, Graham Huggan, Annina Kaltenbrunner, Sofia Martinho, Jeremy Munday, Thea Pitman, Yasmin Reyes, Angel Smith, Duncan Wheeler, and any others that I might forget now. Particular thanks also to my Dynamite softball teammates for always cheering me up, even on those occasions when we are losing.

I would also like to acknowledge those with whom I've stayed in touch mostly thanks to the internet, but who have been a presence in my life over the past few years: Ileana Alvarez, Maria Eugenia Brito, Katia Enrique, Nurcan Kaya, Arturo López-Levy, Manuela Picq, and Erna Von der Walde, among many others that I may forget now.

Kristy Johnson did a wonderful job of copy-editing the manuscript. All four Oxford University Press anonymous readers gave priceless suggestions that have made this text more coherent and articulate. I would also like to thank Alexandra Walsham and especially Matthew Hilton for believing in this project and for encouraging me to submit the manuscript to the prestigious Past & Present book series. The editing team at Oxford University Press has been professional from day one. My thanks go to all of them, and especially to Stephanie Ireland and Cathryn Steele who were always in contact and ready to address my many queries and doubts.

To all my relatives in Canada, Greece, and Cuba I owe an immense debt of gratitude. My parents in particular have been always a constant presence, in spite of there being an ocean between us.

I am grateful to my wife Effie Kesidou for every moment and every conversation. I've been blessed to share my days with such a wonderful, intelligent woman and fellow scholar. This book is dedicated to our son, Kenneth, who joined us over a year ago, filling our life with an incalculable amount of nappies and love.

Contents

List of Maps

List of Figures

List of Tables

All water has a perfect memory, and is forever trying to get back to where it was.

Toni Morrison

Introduction

Esín rí ogun jó; Okó-ó rí ogun yó.
(The horse sees war and dances; the spear sees war and rejoices.)

Yoruba proverb

In 1804 a Fulani-led rebellion, commanded by Shehu [Sheik] Uthman dan Fodio against the Sarki of Gobir in West Africa, laid down the beginnings of one of the deepest and more transformative processes in the modern history of the Atlantic World. What in the beginning was meant to be a struggle against the repression exercised by Gobir upon the Islamic Fulani in the north soon became a full-blown *jihād* that engulfed most of the Sahel and led to the establishment of the Sokoto Caliphate in 1809.

Once Kebbi, Katsina, Daura, Kano, and Gobir were turned into parts of the Caliphate the *jihād* went south first towards Nupe, and then across the river Niger towards the formerly powerful Empire of Oyo. By the time it reached the Oyo territories around 1817, a series of historical events which occurred in and around Oyo had contributed to a qualitative change in the dynamics of the slave trade in this vast area of West Africa and, by extension, in the Atlantic World. The insubordination of Afonja, the supreme military commander or Are-Ona-Kakanfo of Oyo, under way since the mid-1790s and the consequent flight of the Muslim Hausa and other northern slaves from their Oyo owners to join Afonja and then the Fulani jihadists in Ilorin; the Owu wars in the southwest of the Yoruba-speaking territories that began *c.*1811 or 1812; the rise of Dahomey, especially after the ascension of King Ghezo to the throne in 1818; and the beginnings of the enforcement of the abolition of the transatlantic slave trade by the British—these among other events, would, in due course, have a deep impact upon the destinies of the peoples inhabiting vast regions of West Africa and the Americas.

The decline and eventual ending of the slave exports to a number of American territories, chiefly as a result of the British pressures to abolish this trade, meant that by the early 1820s only Brazil and Cuba continued to import large—indeed, ever larger—numbers of African slaves, challenging the efforts of the British government, its navy, and its Courts of Mixed Commissions and Vice-Admiralty. The combination of socio-political developments that occurred in and around Oyo, and the concentration of the transatlantic slave trade towards the aforementioned New World destinations, had dire and immediate consequences for the American societies to which these enslaved peoples were transplanted. Two near-simultaneous cycles of slave plots and insurrections organized and led by African-born men and women unfolded in the region of Bahia in the northeast of Brazil, and in the plantation area around the cities of Havana, Matanzas, and Cárdenas in the western part of the island of Cuba. Despite the conspicuously obvious similarities and the unambiguous connections existing between these two sets of events, no comparative study has been produced until today revealing and discussing the elements that were common to them, and how the background of their protagonists affected their developments. Additionally, until today, many of these conspiracies and insurgencies have not been the subject of individual studies, hindering our knowledge of the reasons that led these men and women to put their lives on the line to get their freedom back.[1]

One apparent distinctive feature of these events, however, has been mentioned by scholars before. The leaders of most of these movements had been enslaved in or around Oyo and had almost certainly been sent to Bahia and Cuba from one of the busy ports of the Slave Coast (i.e. Whydah, Porto Novo, Badagry, and Lagos) (see Maps 0.1a and 0.1b). The men, women, and children who were sent to Bahia and Cuba from these ports in the first half of the nineteenth century had the same or similar ethno-cultural backgrounds. They were, to put it in simple terms, victims of warfare and slave raiding in the region that stretches from the Gold Coast and the Slave Coast in the south to the limits of the Sahara desert in the north. They were Hausa-speakers and Bariba, Nupe, and Borno, and many of them were Yoruba-speakers who had been enslaved during the Fulani-led *jihād* or the Owu wars in the late 1810s and early 1820s, during the looting and pillaging of the new settlements in Egbado and Egbaland in the 1820s and early 1830s, and during the wars that led to the ultimate collapse of Old Oyo in the mid-1830s and the final defeat of the Fulani invaders at the battle of Osogbo in *c*.1838.

These men, women, and children, whether they were taken to Bahia or to Cuba, all had several things in common. Firstly, and most importantly, they were all well acquainted with war, regardless of whether they had been soldiers themselves or not. As a matter of fact, a large number of them had been enslaved precisely during the above-mentioned wars. Other cultural traits that identified them either totally or partially included their familiarity with Islam—some practiced it, some resisted it—and with local animist religions. For the Yoruba-speaking, most of whom considered themselves descendants of the mythical Oduduwa, the *orishas* or *orixás* had the power over all things on earth. The might of some of these orishas, like Ogun and Shango, extended to neighboring states like Dahomey. Another exceptionally

---

[1] Curiously for the Cuban case most of the existing studies have focused on the plots and revolts organized and led by Creole or free colored men and women. As a matter of fact until very recently only the conspiracies of Aponte of 1812 and La Escalera of 1843–4 had received individual monographs. In the Bahian case the situation is similar. Only the great revolt of 1835 has been the subject of a monograph. Other plots and revolts have been studied in individual articles, but much is still needed to understand the reasons and ideologies behind each of them. See Robert L. Paquette, *Sugar is Made with Blood: The Conspiracy of La Escalera and the Conflict between Empires over Slavery in Cuba* (Middleton, CT: Wesleyan University Press, 1987); Matt D. Childs, *The 1812 Aponte Rebellion and the Struggle against Atlantic Slavery* (Chapel Hill: The University of North Carolina Press, 2006); and João José Reis, *Slave Rebellion in Brazil: The Muslim Uprising of 1835 in Bahia* (Baltimore: The Johns Hopkins University Press, 1995), and also its more recent and revised version in Portuguese, *Rebelião escrava no Brasil: a história do levante dos Malês em 1835* (São Paulo: Companhia das Letras, 2003).

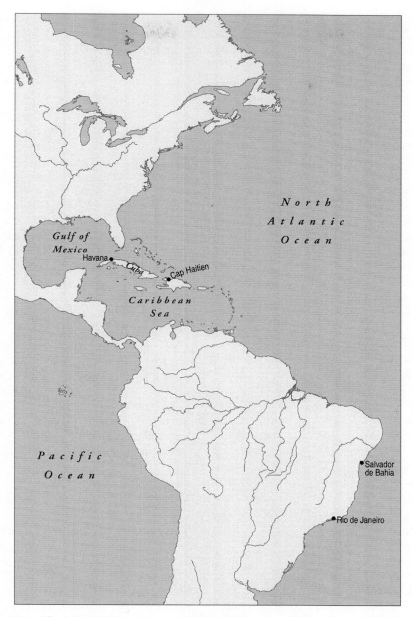

Map 0.1a The Atlantic Basin with some of the major ports involved in the transatlantic slave trade: North Atlantic Ocean

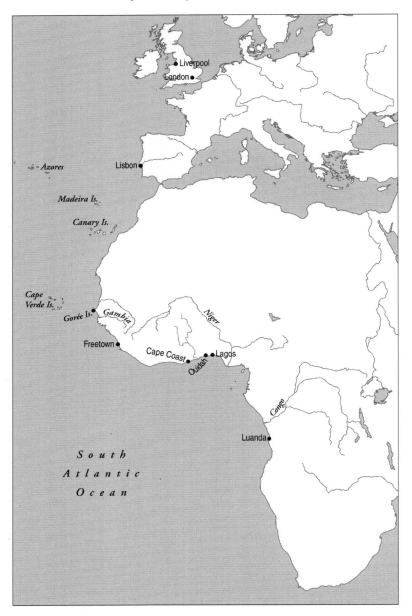

Map 0.1b The Atlantic Basin with some of the major ports involved in the transatlantic slave trade: South Atlantic Ocean

important cultural feature that they all shared was their knowledge of the Yoruba language, which allowed them to understand each other, despite the existence of a number of different linguistic subgroups in the region.[2]

These shared cultural features were taken across the Atlantic and reproduced and developed in the New World societies they were forced to move to and live in. The behavior they exhibited in West Africa was to a large extent also displayed in Bahia and western Cuba. Their presence meant that two chronologically near-simultaneous, remarkably similar processes of Africanization of the manifestations of slave resistance, and particularly of slave rebellion, were observed in both places. Bahia saw the Hausa slaves take arms in 1807—just three years after Uthman Dan Fodio had begun his rebellion against Gobir—and by 1835 when a combination of Nagô and Hausa slaves and freedmen took the streets of Salvador the repetition of African-led armed uprisings in the city and its hinterland was a regular occurrence.[3] Whilst Cuba had to wait until 1825 to see the first major African-led insurrection, what came after left no doubt of the role played by the Lucumí and their neighbors in almost all of the more than 40 movements that followed and that only came to a halt in 1844.[4]

Another important common characteristic of these two cycles of African-led insurgencies in Bahia and Cuba, was that many of them were organized and led by recently arrived African men and women, who were often identified as *bozales* or *negros novos* (new negroes). The fact that they were at the core of many of these armed movements either as initiators or as key participants, constitutes one of the clearest signs that their actions were often an uninterrupted perpetuation of similar actions they had carried out or witnessed in their homelands, since their time of assimilation to their new societies had been minimal. In other words, their West African experiences then, were key to their armed movements in the Americas.

This *bozal* character, however, is not the only signpost indicating a persistence of African warfare across the Atlantic. Another important aspect to add to this limited time of exposure to the day-to-day life in their New World societies was the places where they would be sent upon their arrival. For those who were sent to work as domestic slaves in cities, towns, and countryside states, the level of close contact with Brazilian and Cuban cultures and societies was ample. These men and women were likely to learn the new customs and languages faster, and they would also be exposed to news, rumors, and more importantly, to colonial- and imperial-accepted

<hr/>

[2] Reis and Mamigonian have noted this before while discussing the cultural similarities amongst the Nagôs in mid-nineteenth century Bahia. See João José Reis and Beatriz Gallotti Mamigonian, "Nagô and Mina: The Yoruba Diaspora in Brazil," in Toyin Falola and Matt D. Childs, eds., *The Yoruba Diaspora in the Atlantic World* (Bloomington and Indianapolis: Indiana University Press, 2004), 81. For an in-depth examination of the main cultural/linguistic areas in West and West Central Africa see John K. Thornton, *Africa and the Africans in the Making of the Atlantic World, 1400–1800* (Cambridge: Cambridge University Press, 1998), 184–92.
[3] The best two studies on the sequence of African-led plots and revolts occurred in Bahia are: Howard M. Prince, "Slave Rebellion in Bahia, 1807–1835," Ph.D dissertation, Columbia University, 1972; and Reis, *Rebelião escrava no Brasil*.
[4] See Manuel Barcia, "Revolts amongst Enslaved Africans in Nineteenth-Century Cuba: A New Look to an Old Problem," *The Journal of Caribbean History*, 39:2 (2005): 173–200.

brotherhoods, where their fellow countrymen and countrywomen were allowed to meet and celebrate old and new rituals. In addition to all this, they also had better chances of learning about the few legal provisions that allowed slaves to buy their freedom in both societies through manumission channels, and they also learned that there were ways of denouncing cruel masters if necessary.

The situation for those sent to remote plantations in the Recôncavo valley or to the vast fields south and east of Havana and Matanzas, was considerably different. There, they would be less exposed to the Portuguese and the Spanish languages, as well as to Brazilian and Cuban cultures. They would likely be destined to do hard labor on sugar cane fields where time and prospects for association and learning about their new environs were very limited. To these men and women, their only relief was that they would often find themselves surrounded by other fellow Africans, who often shared their own political, cultural, and religious backgrounds. There, African languages continued to thrive away from the white masters and overseers, and their beliefs and cosmologies were reproduced on a continual basis for years and decades. To them, colonial and imperial laws were not a viable option, at least not for the first few years, and thus, violent actions, often associated with their previous knowledge of warfare, were the more likely ways to resist. In other words, months and even years after arriving on these estates, they were still generally considered to be *bozal* Africans, instead of acculturated ones. As is shown in Appendices 1 and 2, *bozal* leadership and rural isolation often played crucial roles in the armed movements that are examined through a comparative lens in Chapters 4 and 5 of this book.

It is imperative, then, to address an essential question that arises from the proposition of a comparative approach of military actions whose protagonists were born and raised in Africa. How did a series of historical events that occurred in a specific geographical area of West Africa from the mid-1790s onwards (Afonja's rebellion, the Owu wars, the Fulani-led *jihād*, the migrations to Egbaland, etc.) affect life in cities and plantations of Bahia and western Cuba? This question could be also presented in an inverted form: To what extent were a series of conspiracies and insurrections that took place in Bahia and western Cuba in the first half of the nineteenth century the result—or the continuation—of events that occurred in and around Oyo in the same period? I will attempt to answer these questions by establishing the connections—often mentioned but so far not examined in any real depth—between warfare in West Africa and Bahia and Cuba in the first half of the nineteenth century, and by paying special attention to the Africans who were shipped in this period mostly from the Bight of Benin to cities and plantations on the other side of the Atlantic. I will look into their knowledge of warfare, their tactics and strategies, their armaments, their capabilities to overcome ethnic differences in order to form alliances with Africans who had arrived from other regions, and a number of factors that could be considered relevant for establishing and understanding these direct connections.

Thus, two essential arguments will be raised and discussed throughout this book. The first one relates to an issue that some scholars, including myself, have previously debated: the Africanization of slave rebellion in Bahia and Cuba from the early years of the nineteenth century.[5] This time, however, I intend to go one step further by stressing the central role played by the Yoruba-speakers (Nagô and Lucumí) and some of their closest neighbors in this process. I will do so from a comparative perspective and to a large extent by relying on a micro-historical approach that will allow me to read against the grain and interpret the court records that constitute the bulk of the sources used throughout. By stressing the role of the Nagô and the Lucumí, I intend to show that at least from the 1820s onwards this process of Africanization in Bahia and Cuba can be reasonably narrowed down to what we could call a *Nagoization* and *Lucumization* of slave rebellion, since the aims, tactics and strategies, weaponry, and knowledge of warfare exhibited by the leaders and most of the participants were either Nagô and Lucumí or closely related to their aims, tactics, and so on, having been learned during their time in West Africa. Even when not always Nagô or Lucumí in origin (i.e. the tactics and so on might be Dahomean, Hausa, or Fulani in origin) they were thoroughly filtered through Nagô and Lucumí traditions, practices, beliefs, and cosmologies.

Secondly, I will pay attention to the role that identity, memory, news, ideas, ideologies, ethics, and old and new allegiances played in these insurrectionary movements. I will attempt to uncover the direct links and continuities existing between the Yoruba- and Hausa-speaking peoples and other West African groups in Bahia and Cuba on one side, and the Bight of Benin and its interior on the other. After all, many of the ideas, the ideologies, the ways of waging war, including ethics, and the myriad of cultural manifestations that made their way from West Africa to the Americas in this period were, too, Atlantic and revolutionary, and had an impact of similar or bigger proportions upon slave resistance to that of those originating elsewhere in the Atlantic World.

The comparative transatlantic study of the two near-simultaneous cycles of slave movements that occurred in Bahia and western Cuba which lasted for most of the first half of the nineteenth century will be the natural way to bring forward these connections. This book is, thus, about war: about war in West Africa, and about war in two regions of the Americas.

THE NAGÔ IN BAHIA AND
THE LUCUMÍ IN CUBA

The terms used to refer to African people in Africa and the Americas did not always accurately define who they really were and which socio-cultural groups they belonged to. A number of recent studies on ethnicity on both sides of the Atlantic have brought up new ways of approaching the complicated issue of the diverse origins of those who were enslaved in Africa and sent to work in cities and plantations in the Americas. Douglas Chambers in particular has revived the

---

[5] Reis, *Slave Rebellion in Brazil*; Paul E. Lovejoy, "Jihad e escravidão: as origens dos escravos muçulmanos da Bahia," *Topoi: Revista de História*, 1:1 (2000): 11–44; Manuel Barcia, "A Not-so-Common Wind: Slave Revolts in the Age of Revolutions in Cuba and Brazil," *Review: The Journal of the Fernand Braudel Center*, 31:2 (2008): 169–94.

concept of neo-African diasporical "ethnies" to define those groups that shared ancestral mythical origins, historical memories and a sense of solidarity that dated back to their homelands.[6] To this list, I believe, the existence of a *lingua franca* could be added. Overall, although by no means a conclusive contribution, the idea of emerging ethnies in the diaspora goes a long way to explain what may have occurred among many groups of Africans in the diaspora over centuries. In the case of the Yoruba-speakers in nineteenth-century Bahia and Cuba, it might well be crucial to our understanding of the ways in which human relations developed in the diaspora and of their historical significance during acts of overt resistance.

There seems to be little doubt that those men and women who came to be known as Nagô in Bahia and Lucumí in Cuba came from closely related socio-cultural and geographical settings. That does not mean, however, that they could all be labeled "Yoruba." Historian Robin Law has rightly pointed out how in Cuba members of other ethnic groups such as Tapa (Nupe) and Arará (Ewe Fon) could be found under the generic term Lucumí.[7] Something similar probably happened to a certain extent in Bahia, where Hausa, Bariba, Nupe, and other West Africans were identified on occasion as Nagôs.[8] This assimilation of people belonging to other African ethnicities in the Americas constitutes a clear proof that emerging ethnies blossomed in Bahia and Cuba as they did elsewhere in the Americas.

Scholars have addressed the origin of both terms—Nagô and Lucumí—on several occasions. Although both served to create and solidify common cultural identities in the diaspora, there is evidence from African sources that Nagô and Lucumí were terms used in the Bight of Benin to define, if not peoples, at least geographical locations. Historians such as Robin Law, João José Reis, and Beatriz Gallotti Mamigonian agree that Nagô very likely referred to the territory called Anago by the Dahomeans, being their "immediate eastern neighbors in Yorubaland."[9] The origin of the term Lucumí seems somehow more complex. A number of variations of it— e.g. Ulkumi, Ulkama, Loucoumy, Lucamee—appeared in European sources from the seventeenth century.[10] Robin Law has lately addressed the problem again offering some fresh and challenging conclusions. Firstly, he has determined in a convincing manner that Lucumí did not refer to a group of people but to a geographical location; secondly, after a careful examination of the existing literature he has concluded that Lucumí or Ulkumi may have been in fact Ijebu, the southern Yoruba-speaking

---

[6] Douglas Chambers, "Ethnicity in the Diaspora: The Slave-Trade and the Creation of African 'Nations' in the Americas," *Slavery & Abolition*, 22:3 (2001): 25–39. See also Michael A. Gomez, *Exchanging our Country Marks: The Transformation of African Identities in the Colonial and Antebellum South* (Chapel Hill: The University of North Carolina Press, 1998) and Gwendolyn Midlo Hall, *Slavery and African Ethnicities in the Americas: Restoring the Links* (Chapel Hill: The University of North Carolina Press, 2007).

[7] Robin Law, "Ethnicity and the Slave Trade: 'Lucumi' and 'Nago' as Ethnonyms in West Africa," *History in Africa*, 24 (1997): 205–19; and "Ethnicities of Enslaved Africans in the Diaspora: On the Meanings of 'Mina' (Again)," *History in Africa*, 32 (2005): 266–8.

[8] Paul Lovejoy, "The Urban Background of Enslaved Muslims in the Americas," *Slavery & Abolition*, 26:3 (2005): 349–76 and "Jihad e escravidão." See also Reis and Mamigonian, "Nagô and Mina."

[9] Reis and Mamigonian, "Nagô and Mina," 81. See also Law, "Ethnicity and the Slave Trade," 212–15.

[10] Law, "Ethnicity and the Slave Trade," 210–12.

kingdom which had supplied the Europeans with slaves and cloth since the sixteenth century, or more likely "a state or a group of states inland from Ijebu."[11] Why this specific term became generic of the Yoruba-speaking people in a considerable area of the Atlantic World is still a matter for further discussion.

It is obvious that both Nagô and Lucumí were widely used on the American side of the Atlantic from an early time, despite never being "unambiguously documented in West Africa as a generic term for all Yoruba speakers before the mid nineteenth century."[12] The term Nagô, in particular, was not exclusive to Bahia or Brazil. There are references to Nagô slaves in Saint Domingue, Louisiana, and the West Indies in the eighteenth and early nineteenth centuries, a circumstance that suggests that the term was used almost everywhere in the Americas, bar the Spanish territories, to designate the Yoruba-speaking peoples.[13] Lucumí, on the other hand, was used from the sixteenth century in Spanish America and, at least in Cuba, continued to be used until the late nineteenth century.[14]

The existence of a common national or ethnic identity amongst the Nagô and Lucumí is a question that still has not been properly addressed and satisfactorily answered. In this work it will be discussed how, to a significant extent, Yoruba-speaking peoples used these terms to differentiate themselves from other Africans, within the parameters of an "us and them" dynamics. It will also become apparent that members of other ethnies saw them as a distinguishable group with certain characteristics and stereotypes inherently attached to them. More often than not I will use Nagô and Lucumí instead of Yoruba throughout the text, due to the simple fact that Yoruba was used in this period neither in Bahia nor in Cuba and its use would, therefore, be both anachronistic and inaccurate. The term Yoruba appeared in West African sources at least from the early seventeenth century onwards, when Ahmad Baba first mentioned it.[15] However, it was only by the mid-nineteenth century that it came to be widely used to identify the men and women that inhabited

---

[11] Law, "Ethnicity and the Slave Trade," 212.

[12] Law, "Ethnicity and the Slave Trade," 215.

[13] See David P. Geggus, "Sex, Ratio, Age and Ethnicity in the Atlantic Slave Trade: Data from French Shipping and Plantation Records," *Journal of African History*, 30 (1989): 23–44; Gwendolyn Midlo Hall, *African Slaves in Colonial Louisiana* (Baton Rouge: Louisiana State University Press, 1992), 291–2; Kevin Roberts, "The Influential Yoruba Past in Haiti," in Falola and Childs, eds., *The Yoruba Diaspora*, 177–8; Barry W. Higman, *Slave Populations of the British Caribbean, 1807–1834* (Baltimore and London: The Johns Hopkins University Press, 1984), 442–58.

[14] Alonso de Sandoval, *Treatise on Slavery: Selections from De Instauranda Aethiopum Salute* (Indianapolis and Cambridge: Hackett, 2008); Fernando Ortiz, *Los negros esclavos* (Havana: Ciencias Sociales, 1987), 41–56; Rafael L. López Valdés, "Notas para el estudio etnohistórico de los esclavos Lucumí de Cuba," in Lázara Menéndez, ed., *Estudios afro-cubanos: Selección de lecturas* (Havana: Universidad de la Habana, 1990), ii. 317–9; G. Aguirre Beltrán, "Tribal Origins of Slaves in Mexico," *Journal of Negro History*, 31 (1946): 322–4; David Pavy, "The Provenience of Colombia Negroes," *Journal of Negro History*, 52 (1967): 35–58; Frederick P. Bowser, *The African Slave in Colonial Peru, 1524–1650* (Stanford, CA: Stanford University Press, 1974), 40–3; Russell Lohse, "Africans in a Colony of Creoles: The Yoruba in Colonial Costa Rica," in Falola and Childs, eds., *The Yoruba Diaspora*, 130–56.

[15] Law, "Ethnicity and the Slave Trade," 206; Paul Lovejoy, "The Yoruba Factor in the Trans-Atlantic Slave Trade," in Falola and Childs, eds., *The Yoruba Diaspora*, 41.

the interior of the Bight of Benin and who spoke the same or very similar variations of the same language, and who saw Ile-Ife as their ancestral home.

According to Law, "consciousness of a Yoruba ethnicity first emerged in the diaspora, and more specifically in Sierra Leone"[16] where many Yoruba speakers—known there as Aku—had resettled after being liberated by the Courts of Mixed Commissions established there since 1819. Only after Yoruba-speaking Christian missionaries, such as Samuel Ajayi Crowther, liberated by the British squadron and landed in Sierra Leone, returned to their homes in the late 1830s and early 1840s, did the term come to represent them all as a cohesive "pan-ethnic and linguistic" group.[17]

The fact that the vast majority of the Yoruba-speaking peoples sent to the Americas made the journey together may have helped to preserve their identities within the most unfavorable of environments. Those exported from the Bight of Benin in the first half of the nineteenth century could hardly be labeled a "mutilated assemblage" of different peoples, to use Stephanie Smallwood's phrase.[18] In fact, if we are to rely on the existing records, they were very much the closest thing to a traveling community, an enforced and enslaved one certainly, but still a community that survived and developed in the diaspora.[19]

When discussing the peoples who have traditionally been referred to as Yoruba or Hausa, I will use the terms Yoruba-speaking and Hausa-speaking peoples instead, especially when I am discussing them within a West African context.[20] This classification is still far from resolving once and for all the problems associated with these broad categories and its use may make reading this book somehow more difficult. However, their use will hopefully allow us to move away from traditional, neocolonial monolithic ethnic categories that, to use David Northrup's words, use "language as a surrogate to culture and nation" and that "misrepresent African cultural diversity and reinforce stereotypes of African cultures as static."[21]

---

[16] Law, "Ethnicity and the Slave Trade," 206. See also Robin Law, "Local Amateur Scholarship in the Construction of the Yoruba Ethnicity, 1880–1914," in Louise de la Gorgondière, Kenneth King, and Sarah Vaughan, eds., *Ethnicity in Africa: Roots, Meanings and Interpretations* (Edinburgh: Centre of African Studies, 1996), 55–90.

[17] Lovejoy, "The Yoruba Factor," 41.

[18] Stephanie Smallwood, *Saltwater Slavery: A Middle Passage from Africa to American Diaspora* (Cambridge, MA: Harvard University Press, 2007), 121.

[19] Relying on pre-1800 sources Stephanie Smallwood has recently questioned the existence of "groups" or "crowds" of peoples in the Middle Passage. The experience of the Lucumí sent to the Americas in the first half of the nineteenth century strongly contradicts this assumption. The records of the Havana Court of Mixed Commission clearly show that most of those liberated Africans processed by the court were, in fact, from the same *naciones* or ethnies, a circumstance that points to close socio-cultural backgrounds and experiences. Documents from Cuban plantations also portray a similar situation, in some cases showing that kinship relations and military allegiances were kept almost intact across the Atlantic and despite the hardships of the journey.

[20] I will still use the term Hausa when discussing the slave movements that took place in Bahia between 1807 and 1835, because even if the problems associated with African cultural identities are still present, it would be an almost impossible task to define where exactly each of them had arrived from and, therefore, what sort of cultural heritage they had.

[21] David Northrup, "Igbo and Myth Igbo: Culture and Ethnicity in the Atlantic World, 1600–1850," *Slavery & Abolition*, 21:3 (2000): 18.

OYO, THE EARLY NINETEENTH-CENTURY YORUBA-SPEAKING DIASPORA, AND THE HISTORIANS

The history of the fall of Oyo and the enslavement of the Yoruba-speaking peoples in West Africa is of paramount importance for anyone interested in exploring the history of the Nagô and the Lucumí in Brazil and Cuba. Unfortunately, the historical sources about the events that started with the reign of Aláàfin Abiodun (*c*.1770–*c*.1789) and finished with the battle of Osogbo (*c*.1838) are incomplete, problematic, and contradictory.[22] To begin with, there is very little contemporary known material to work through, with the exception of the journals of Hugh Clapperton and the Lander brothers. For most of the time, even the dates of key historical events are unreliable to the point that dating itself has become a subject of academic work. Historians of the Yoruba, the Nupe, the Bariba, and the Fulani have been quick to recognize the problems inherent in their sources and have often been forced to rely heavily on the local and regional oral traditions.[23] However, despite these deficiencies, over the past half-century West African, European, and American scholars have opened their own exploration path and have produced a considerable number of books and articles that attempt, from different perspectives, to disentangle the many problems associated with the history of the region in the early nineteenth century.

Among the most significant issues they have dealt with are the chronological problems associated with the events that took place between the late eighteenth century and the mid-nineteenth century in the Yoruba-speaking territories, and ultimately the real impact of these events upon the demise of the formerly powerful West African state of Oyo. Since this book's main premise is precisely to provide a comparative study of how West African warfare was transplanted to the New World by those who were enslaved mainly through warfare in this part of West Africa, a brief discussion of how historians have addressed some of these issues is in order.

In 1988 Nigerian historian Toyin Falola published an article outlining the need for what he aptly called a "research agenda" that would address the history of the Yoruba in the nineteenth century. Although the article was mainly focused on the history of the Yoruba in West Africa, some of the issues raised by the author

---

[22] See Robin Law, ed., *Contemporary Source Material for the History of the Old Oyo Empire, 1627–1824* (Toronto: Harriet Tubman Resource Centre on the African Diaspora, 2002).

[23] See e.g. Robin Law, "The Chronology of the Yoruba Wars of the Early Nineteenth Century: A Reconsideration," *Journal of the Historical Society of Nigeria*, 5:2 (1970): 211–23; and "Making Sense of a Traditional Narrative: Political Disintegration in the Kingdom of Oyo," *Cahiers d'études africaines*, 22:87/88 (1982): 387–401; Michael Mason, "The Antecedents of Nineteenth-Century Islamic Government in Nupe," *The International Journal of African Historical Studies*, 10:1 (1977): 63–76; Finn Fuglestad, "A Reconsideration of Hausa History before the Jihad," *The Journal of African History*, 19:3 (1978): 319–39; Toyin Falola, "A Research Agenda on the Yoruba in the Nineteenth Century," *History in Africa*, 15 (1988): 211–27; Oyeronke Oyewumi, "Making History, Creating Gender: Some Methodological and Interpretive Questions in the Writing of Oyo Oral Traditions," *History in Africa*, 25 (1998): 263–305; Alaba Simpson, *Oral Tradition and Slave Trade in Nigeria, Ghana and Benin* (Paris: UNESCO, 2004).

transcended the geographical limits of the African continent. To begin with, Falola straightforwardly claimed that, even though the study of nineteenth-century wars had, until then, dominated the scholarship on the subject and period, historians were still far from knowing "everything" about them.[24] Falola's article was, predictably, only a departing point. In the following years other studies have enriched even further our knowledge of warfare practices in these territories. However, much still needs to be done, not least in the diaspora. The many plots and armed actions that feature prominently in this book are a testament to the relevance of the diaspora as an essential aspect to understand warfare in West Africa, and more specifically in Oyo and its neighboring states.

Back then Falola also called the attention of scholars to other issues that in his opinion had been neglected, among which he included "the ethics of war, the distinction (both in theory and practice) between wars, raids and brigandage, all of which are confused in the traditions as wars, the roles of youth and women, warfare on rivers and lagoons, the role of notable individuals (as opposed to that of state) in causing and ending wars," and many more.[25]

The roots of the lack of studies on some of these issues can be found in the previously mentioned fact that contemporary sources are not abundant and those that do exist are quite problematic. What Falola did not mention then, although he has since been one of the main advocates of the study of the Yoruba-speaking diaspora, is that light can be shed upon most of these issues by examining the history of the Nagô and the Lucumí in Brazil and Cuba, where the compulsive bureaucracy existing at the time translated into thousands of folios the various manifestations of resistance and to a certain extent also the daily life of these enforced African migrants and their descendants.

Inversely, anyone who attempts to explore the Yoruba-speaking diaspora in the Americas must look across the Atlantic and be ready to soak up West African history. Only by crossing that scholarly and geographical bridge and by acquiring a sound knowledge of the history of Oyo, Nupe, Borgu, Sokoto, Benin, and Dahomey, to mention but a few, can one make sense of the documents that may surface in the archives of Bahia, Rio de Janeiro, Havana, or Matanzas and that, contentious by nature, focus on issues such as ethnicity, religion, trade, migration and settlement, and warfare, among others.

Let us consider, for instance, the slave routes to the coast and their short- and long-term historical impact. From the time of Aláàfin Abiodun until the abandonment of Old Oyo in the mid-1830s these routes, as demonstrated by Robert S. Smith, Peter Morton-Williams, and others, moved eastwards.[26] Although these changes are discussed at length in Chapter 2, it must suffice to notice here that there is convincing evidence to demonstrate that enslaved Yoruba-speaking people made their way through the West African hinterland to places as far apart as the Gold Coast in the west and the ports of the Bight of Biafra in the east. These long and tortuous

---

[24] Falola, "A Research Agenda," 215.   [25] Falola, "A Research Agenda," 215–16.
[26] Robert S. Smith, *Kingdoms of the Yoruba* (London: Methuen & Co., 1969), 44–7; Peter Morton-Williams, "The Oyo Yoruba and the Atlantic Trade, 1670–1830," *Journal of the Historical Society of Nigeria*, 3:1 (1964): 25–45.

journeys across vast territories certainly contributed to the development of new and solid relations among those who were enslaved. These relations may have gone beyond previously existent ethnic associations and loyalties, and may have also led to friendships that could outlast the Middle Passage. The ways these men and women associated, plotted, and often rebelled in places like Bahia and western Cuba suggest that we still lack enough evidence to reveal accurately their possible ethnic origins, cultural—and on occasion multicultural—backgrounds, experiences, and behaviors. This comparative approach to the Yoruba-speaking diaspora, in turn, may help to shine a light on some of the darkest areas of knowledge mentioned by Falola in his 1988 article.

The study of Oyo's neighbors is as crucial to understanding the Yoruba-speaking diaspora as the study of Oyo itself. After all, we would know today much less about the events that led to the demise of Oyo, had it not been for the studies about Dahomey, Borgu, Nupe, Benin, the Sokoto Caliphate, and also about other Yoruba-speaking states that have been produced over the past decades which have illustrated the significance of the development of new polities in the region, the resurgence of others, and the interactions among them. Understanding the almost insurmountable rivalries existing between Dahomey and Oyo, or the circumstantial alliance between Borgu and the last Aláàfin of Old Oyo in the mid-1830s could be crucial if we are to determine why the Araràs (Dahomeans) could on occasion stay away from Lucumí-led movements in western Cuba and why the Bariba (Borgu) and the Nagô were happy to join forces in the 1835 revolt in Bahia. Equally important, are studies such as those provided by Joseph P. Smaldone and Paul Lovejoy about the emergence of the Sokoto Caliphate and, as a direct result, the spread of Islam across the former Hausa-speaking states, Nupe and part of Oyo, which constitute a vital input if we are to comprehend a myriad of aspects related to warfare in Bahia and Cuba, such as ethnic and group allegiances and alliances, tactics, weaponry, and religion.[27]

The study of the changes in the demographics of the slave trade in the region, carried out by an ever increasing number of scholars, especially since the publication, in 1999, of the first version of the Slave Trade Database co-edited by David Eltis, Stephen D. Behrendt, David Richardson, and Herbert S. Klein, have provided historians with a new functional and fairly reliable tool to assess the migration of the Yoruba-speaking populations not only inland but also across the Atlantic, and in some cases also in the Americas.[28] Some of the studies resulting from this Database have thrown light upon issues as diverse as the physical characteristics of the Yoruba speakers, even as compared to other West African groups, the stereotypes associated with some specific ethnicities and diasporical ethnies, and the actual rates of survival, suicides, and revolts before, during, and after the Middle

[27] Joseph P. Smaldone, *Warfare in the Sokoto Caliphate: Historical and Sociological Perspectives* (Cambridge: Cambridge University Press, 1977); Paul Lovejoy, *Slavery, Commerce and Production in the Sokoto Caliphate of West Africa* (Trenton and Asmara: Africa World Press, 2005).
[28] The Slave Trade Database was originally published by Cambridge University Press in a CD Rom format in 1999. The most recent and up-to-date version is hosted online by Emory University and can be consulted at: <http://www.slavevoyages.org>.

Passage. These new studies have also helped to answer some key questions about the enslavement of the Yoruba-speaking populations and their neighbors: who was enslaved, and when and how socio-political changes affected the trade, throughout the first half of the nineteenth century.[29]

Although scholarly works about the Yoruba-speaking peoples in the Middle Passage do not abound, a number of recently published books and articles have looked into what percentage of the slave trade they constituted, where were they sent to—both as slaves and as liberated men and women—, and in some more exceptional cases, their actual actions during the transatlantic crossing. Here, too, the role of the *Slavevoyages* database has been crucial by providing precious figures about the trade in the Bights. Taking advantage of this data, Paul E. Lovejoy and David Eltis have recently discussed a number of issues about the transatlantic slave trade and the role of the Yoruba speakers in it. Among them are the ports of destination in the Americas, the estimates of the actual numbers of people exported from the Bights after 1800, and the remarkable association between the rise of the exports of Yoruba-speaking individuals and the political problems that affected Oyo from the last decade of the eighteenth century.[30] Concurrently, Lovejoy has also called our attention to the changes that occurred over time in the numbers of people from particular ethnic groups who were exported from the ports of the Bights. Even more importantly, Lovejoy has been able to establish that the proportion of Yoruba-speaking women sent to the Americas was higher among those who were enslaved in the south, closer to the coast than those enslaved in the north, implying that almost certainly a higher number of Yoruba-speaking women from southern states, like Ijebu Ode, Ife, and Owu were sent to Bahia and Cuba.[31]

Another significant aspect in his approach to the Yoruba-speaking peoples and their neighbors has consistently been that of the role played by Islam before, during, and after the Middle Passage. As a matter of fact, Lovejoy has gone farther than any other scholar by crossing the Africanist–Americanist divide and attempting to make sense of the Islamic Yoruba-speaking—as well as the non-Yoruba-speaking—population in Bahia in the first half of the nineteenth century.[32] Although Lovejoy was quick to emphasize the possible problems that could arise from his interpretation, these did not stop him from attempting to establish the foundations for what I would dare to call a new methodological approach that relates events that took place in West Africa to those that took place in the Americas.[33]

In a recent study of shipboard insurrections in the Middle Passage, Eric Robert Taylor has also added new insights on the role of the Yoruba-speaking peoples and their neighbors in the Slave Trade. Although most of the sources used for his book refer to pre-nineteenth-century voyages, Taylor has been able to highlight that the

---

[29] David Eltis, "Welfare Trends among the Yoruba in the Early Nineteenth Century: The Anthropometric Evidence," *The Journal of Economic History*, 50:3 (1990): 521–40; Robin Law and Paul E. Lovejoy, "Borgu in the Atlantic Slave Trade," *African Economic History*, 27 (1999): 69–92; See also the various essays that are featured on <http://www.slavevoyages.org>.

[30] David Eltis, "The Diaspora of Yoruba Speakers, 1650–1865: Dimensions and Implications," in Falola and Childs, eds., *The Yoruba Diaspora*, 17–39; and Lovejoy, "The Yoruba Factor," 40–55.

[31] Lovejoy, "The Yoruba Factor," 47–9.   [32] Lovejoy, "Jihad e escravidão."

[33] A dialectic approach upon which this study is based. Lovejoy, "Jihad e escravidão," 153–7.

incidence of slave revolts in the Bight of Benin for this period was only second to that of the Senegambia region. If we added up the figures for the Bights of Benin and Biafra, they would constitute by far the largest percentage of slave insurrections anywhere along the African coast.[34] Figures for the post-1800 period are less forthcoming, but acts of resistance increased rather than diminished, as is apparent from Taylor's list of slave insurrections aboard slave trade ships that is included as an appendix at the end of his book.[35]

Whereas the sources for the history of the Yoruba-speaking people in West Africa and in the Middle Passage in the first half of the nineteenth century are not plentiful, the documents produced in the various territories of the Americas to which they and their neighbors were transplanted during these years are qualitatively and quantitatively much richer. Not surprisingly, over the past decades more and more studies have appeared discussing different aspects of their history on the American side of the Atlantic. Both in Brazil and Cuba the legacy of the Nagô and the Lucumí is undeniably rich and well entrenched in the cultures and idiosyncrasies of the Brazilian and Cuban people. Even today, anyone who visits Salvador de Bahia or Havana will almost certainly come across different manifestations of that legacy, notably Candomblé and Santería. Although the cult of the orixás or orishas remains as the most obvious and transcendental cultural inheritance passed to us by the enslaved Yoruba speakers who arrived in Cuban and Brazilian shores in the eighteenth and nineteenth centuries, many other expressions of this cultural legacy can still be found in fields as diverse as botany (through the use of medicinal herbs), music, dance, and even cinema and television.

Something similar could be stated for those British territories in the West Indies that received important numbers of liberated Yoruba-speaking people taken there as a result of the enforcement of British Abolitionism in the Atlantic World.[36] Recent studies about their heritage in the British West Indies, such as those by Rosanne M. Adderley, Maureen Warner-Lewis, and Rosalyn Howard have looked into the endurance of Yoruba cultural elements in places like Trinidad and Tobago and the Bahamas.[37] Both Adderley and Howard have revealed how their descendants in these British West Indies territories have preserved an identity that even today defines them as different from those who descend from other African ethnic groups who were also relocated there after the British abolition of the transatlantic slave trade.[38]

---

[34] Eric Robert Taylor, *If We Must Die: Shipboard Insurrections in the Era of the Atlantic Slave Trade* (Baton Rouge: Louisiana State University Press, 2006), 65.

[35] Taylor, *If We Must Die*, 209–13. The figures for the period post-1820 are likely to be heavily compromised, since the slave trade after this date was deemed illegal in the Atlantic. However, it is well known that, far from diminishing, the slave trade augmented in the following decades, making the chances of having African revolts on board slave vessels even more likely.

[36] See Rosanne M. Adderley, *New Negroes from Africa: Free African Immigrants in the Nineteenth-Century Caribbean* (Bloomington: Indiana University Press, 2007).

[37] Adderley, *New Negroes from Africa*; Maureen Warner-Lewis, "Ethnic and Religious Plurality among Yoruba Immigrants in the Nineteenth Century," in Paul E. Lovejoy, ed., *Identity in the Shadow of Slavery* (London: Continuum, 2000), 113–28; and Rosalyn Howard, "Yoruba in the British Caribbean: A Comparative Perspective on Trinidad and the Bahamas," in Falola and Childs, eds., *The Yoruba Diaspora*, 157–76.

[38] Adderley, *New Negroes from Africa*, chs. 4–6; Howard, "Yoruba in the British Caribbean," 167–8.

Although Yoruba speakers have left an indelible mark among the British West Indies cultures, it has been in Bahia and western Cuba that, due to the sheer size of their migration, their culture and outlook on the world have become more easily identifiable and indeed more interesting to both scholars and popular audiences. Not surprisingly, this popularity has led to the emergence of studies focusing on the cult of the orishas, which have been produced for and have monopolized academic and popular attention. In the cases of both Bahia and Cuba, scholarly rigor has been often neglected in order to satisfy a wider readership. This, of course, has also contributed to the spread of the cult of the orishas beyond the geographical borders of Brazil and Cuba. Today Ogun, Shango, and Obatala are venerated in places as far apart as Mexico City, Miami, New York, London, Madrid, Lisbon, and Moscow. As a matter of fact, Yoruba religious beliefs and rituals, though in very confusing fashions, have made it even to Hollywood. Blockbusters such as *The Believers* (1987) starring Martin Sheen and Helen Shaver and *Dance with the Devil* (1997) with Rosie Perez, Javier Bardem, and James Gandolfini have portrayed Yoruba religion as a shadowy satanic cult, in a way that resembles in an uncanny manner the way in which another African religion, Voodoo, has often been portrayed.[39]

This pre-eminence in contemporary cultural studies, however, has not been translated with the same enthusiasm into historical studies of the men, women, and children who were forced to make their way to the various ports of the Slave Coast from the late eighteenth century onwards, and who were then crammed into slave trade vessels and sent to Bahia and western Cuba as slaves.

Although some remarkable studies have indeed appeared over the past decades, much still needs to be done. Thanks to the works of scholars such as Howard Prince and João José Reis for Bahia, and José Luciano Franco, Pedro Deschamps Chapeaux, Matt D. Childs, and more recently Michelle Reid-Vazquez for Cuba, there has been a significant growth in our knowledge and understanding of the Nagô, the Lucumí, and those who were neither but who were in contact with them in West Africa, who made the Atlantic crossing with them below the decks of slave trade ships, and who, eventually, shared their same fate in cities, smallholdings, and plantations in both regions. Nonetheless, issues such as interethnic relations, the meaning of life and death, burial practices, the length of their periods of settlement, their chances of communicating with each other by using their African languages, their cosmologies, and even their religious practices, still call for more studies.

In the case of the relationship between warfare and the Nagô, the Lucumí, and their neighbors once transplanted to Bahia and Cuba, little has been written so far and, as I have already asserted, nothing exists from a comparative perspective. While Brazil, and more specifically Bahia, has been served by Prince and Reis with studies of nineteenth-century slave plots and insurrections, what happened in Cuba outside of the main conspiracies and revolts involving African slaves in the period

---

[39] The cult of the orishas has also often appeared in several well-known American sitcoms and series. Among those are *CSI Miami, Miami Vice, Third Watch, Law and Order, First 48, The Flash*, and more bizarrely in the 'Days of Wine and D'oh'ses' episode of *The Simpsons*.

(the 1812 and 1843–4 movements), has remained virtually unexamined. A couple of articles have addressed the Lucumí uprisings of August 1833 and March 1843, but the conclusions of both were limited in scope and to a certain extent repeated the tradition of Cuban scholarship that attributed grandeur to all acts of resistance against Spanish colonialism, in some cases going so far as to conclude that these movements had a proto-nationalist character.[40] My own study of the cycle of African-led slave movements that took place in Cuba between 1825 and 1844, though addressing the vital issue of the African character of these plots and rebellions, did not tackle the need for what I would now dare to call the most obvious case for comparing them with their counterparts in Bahia.[41] None of the scholars who produced outstanding studies on the conspiracies of Aponte and La Escalera in Cuba (Franco, Paquette, Childs) contemplated the possibility of engaging in a discussion that would encompass the two simultaneous processes of Africanization and, and from the 1820s, *Nagoization* and *Lucumization*, that took place in these regions from the first years of the nineteenth century until the mid-1840s.[42]

It is then apparent that despite the recent blossoming of academic scholarship on Brazilian and Cuban slavery in the Age of Revolution, some areas remain neglected. Due to reasons that go beyond the academic world, these areas are vaster in the Cuban case. West African historians have written precious little about Cuba and even less has been written by Cuban scholars about West Africa. The same cannot be said about the relationship between scholars who focus on Brazilian slavery and scholars who specialize in West Africa, which has undoubtedly grown larger over the past years. Africanists like Paul E. Lovejoy, Joseph Miller, and Elisée Soumonni have often resorted to the history of Brazil to better illustrate their arguments, while Brazilianists like Pierre Verger, João José Reis, James H. Sweet, and more recently Stefania Capone, Roquinaldo Ferreira, and Mariana Candido have highlighted the need for looking to West Africa if we are to make sense of the historical events that took place in Brazil.[43] Something similar is urgently needed in the Cuban case.

[40] Interestingly enough, while doing research for this book I have become convinced that there is far more information in Cuban and Spanish primary sources about Lucumí movements in Cuba than there is on the same subject in Brazilian and Portuguese sources. See Juan Iduarte, "Noticias sobre sublevaciones y conspiraciones de esclavos. Cafetal Salvador, 1833," *Revista de la Biblioteca Nacional José Martí*, 73:24, 1–2, 3ra época (1982): 117–52; Daniel Martínez García, "La sublevación de la Alcancía: su rehabilitación histórica en el proceso conspirativo que concluye en La Escalera (1844)" *Rábida*, 19 (2000): 41–8; Gloria García, *Conspiraciones y revueltas: la actividad política de los negros en Cuba, 1790–1845* (Santiago de Cuba: Oriente, 2003). Both Henry Lovejoy and William Van Norman have recently paid attention to the 1833 Salvador uprising again, offering new historical interpretations of the event. See Henry B. Lovejoy, "Old Oyo Influences on the Transformation of Lucumí Identity in Colonial Cuba" (Ph.D. diss. UCLA, 2012), 192–9; and William C. Van Norman Jr., *Shade-Grown Slavery: The Lives of Slaves on Coffee Plantations in Cuba* (Nashville: Vanderbilt University Press, 2013), 125–36.

[41] Barcia, "Revolts amongst Enslaved Africans in Nineteenth-Century Cuba," 173–200. I have since addressed this issue in an article published in 2008. See Barcia, "A Not-so-common Wind."

[42] José Luciano Franco, *La Conspiración de Aponte* (Havana: Archivo Nacional, 1963); Paquette, *Sugar is Made with Blood*; Childs, *The 1812 Aponte Rebellion*.

[43] See e.g.: Pierre Verger, *Trade Relations between the Bight of Benin and Bahia from the 17th to the 19th Century* (Ibadan: Ibadan University Press, 1976); Reis, *Slave Rebellion in Brazil*; James H. Sweet,

Much needs to be done in order to bring together the history of peoples, ideas, and ideologies that linked the three geographical regions at the core of this study. What social, political, economic, and natural environments did Yoruba speakers and their neighbors find in the New World upon their arrival? How can the study of this diaspora contribute to the historical body of knowledge associated with West Africa and in particular with the history of Oyo and its neighbors in the first half of the nineteenth century? Are the sources produced by the Portuguese, the Spanish, the Brazilians, and the Cubans relevant enough to offer new insights that may help to resolve some of the most crucial questions connected to the historical events that took place in the late eighteenth and early nineteenth century in Oyo, Owu, Dahomey, Nupe, Borgo, etc.? Were the many slave rebellions that took place in Bahia and Cuba in the first half of the nineteenth century a prolongation of wars that began in and around Oyo? If yes, to what extent?

As this book will hopefully reveal, Brazilian and Cuban sources can present scholars with valuable clues to expand our knowledge of early nineteenth-century West African history. They will certainly serve, using Paul Lovejoy's words, as "empirical evidence of historical change in Africa."[44] Unknown or unused documents related to the history of the Nagô and the Lucumí in Bahia and Cuba in this period are only starting to emerge and can potentially give us qualitative and quantitative brand new information about the Yoruba-speaking peoples and their neighbors in the diaspora and, more promisingly, in West Africa too.

Whilst perusing these historical sources I will pay attention to the processes of settlement, adaptation, and resistance that took place in Bahia and western Cuba in the first half of the nineteenth century. At their arrival in the Americas the Nagô, the Lucumí, and their enslaved neighbors were destined to work on plantations, smallholdings, and urban environments. In all these places they reproduced old forms of association and created new ones. Amongst the old ones, military loyalties played a significant role in their daily life and acquired an even greater relevance in the course of overt acts of resistance. Amongst the new ones were the *cabildos de nación* in Cuba and the various *irmandades* or brotherhoods that proliferated in Bahia, which were particularly useful for those who had access to an urban life. Although the *cabildos de nación* and *irmandades* had their historical roots in Africa, many of the ceremonies and practices associated with them were new, including the acceptance of members of other ethnies in their ranks. Both *cabildos de nación* and *irmandades* have been the subject of recent studies.[45] Due to their intrinsic

---

Recreating Africa: Culture, Kingship and Religion in the African-Portuguese World, 1441–1770 (Chapel Hill: The University of North Carolina Press, 2003); and Stefania Capone, *Searching for Africa in Brazil: Power and Tradition in Candomblé* (Durham, NC: Duke University Press, 2010); Roquinaldo Ferreira, *Cross-Cultural Exchange in the Atlantic World: Angola and Brazil during the Era of the Slave Trade* (Cambridge: Cambridge University Press, 2012); and Mariana Candido, *An African Slaving Port and the Atlantic World: Benguela and its Hinterland* (Cambridge: Cambridge University Press, 2013).

[44] Paul Lovejoy, "Identifying Enslaved Africans in the African Diaspora," in Lovejoy, *Identity in the Shadow of Slavery*, 9.

[45] See e.g. María del Carmen Barcia, *Los ilustres apellidos: negros en la Habana colonial* (Havana: Bologna, 2009); Lovejoy "Old Oyo Influences," 107–35; and Lucilene Reginaldo, "Irmandades e devoções de africanos e crioulos na Bahia setentista: histórias e experiências atlânticas," *Stockholm Review of Latin American Studies*, 4 (2009): 25–35.

urban environment and the limitations associated with their legal character I will visit them on occasions; however, I will attempt to reveal that their role, when it came to African-led armed movements, was often—though not always—limited. African loyalties, on the other hand, will be assessed throughout with the intention to show not only their survival in the diaspora, but also their blossoming under the harsh conditions of a slave life.

Critically and usually forgotten, upon their arrival in Bahia and Cuba the Nagô and the Lucumí found environments that resembled or reminded them of their homelands. They found similar tropical climates, which included temperatures, atmospheric pressure, and humidity levels to which they were accustomed. They also found animals, and more importantly, plants that were familiar to them and that they used for a variety of purposes, ranging from alimentation to medicine and religious ceremonies. To these men, women, and children, their new home-lands were not shockingly different from what they knew and thus one of their priorities, the reconstruction of their African lives, was at least from the environmental point of view a real possibility. They did so, sometimes on plantations and sometimes even in hideouts in mountains, forests, and swamps known as *quilombos* and *mocambos* in Brazil, and as *palenques* in Cuba, where the lack of authority of the white man may have created an even closer resemblance to conditions in their previous homes.

In spite of the overwhelming repression to which they were now subjected, the Nagô, the Lucumí, and their neighbors were also able to practice their African religions—Islam and Orisha cults. In the case of the former, its survival and what could be considered a revival in Bahia sharply contrast with the almost total lack of references about it in Cuba. Does that mean that Islam did not arrive in Cuba? Even though the evidence is sparse I will attempt to answer this question in this text basing my arguments on new and old sources and published works. In the case of the cult of the orishas, in contrast to the situation regarding Islam, there is very little doubt that a continuous and substantial process of transculturation allowed those who practiced it to merge their own deities with the awkwardly similar ones of the Catholic pantheon. From early on this process served as a decoy that permitted the survival of the millenarian Orisha cult within deeply religiously intolerant societies.

Another aspect that will be examined in depth here is that of the period of time spent in the New World societies by those slaves who rose in arms on different occasions. In my opinion, the length of this period was crucial. Recently arrived West Africans showed a determination to rise against their new social condition as soon as they landed in Bahia and Cuba. In some cases they even took arms before they were delivered to their final destinations and in some others, they did so as soon as the shackles came off their hands and feet. A number of revealing cases, many of which have never been studied in depth before, will help illustrate this point and will allow me to ask identity-related questions about whether at this stage these men and women saw themselves as prisoners of war rather than as slaves.

Halfway through this text I also question whether it is appropriate to use terms such as rebellion and revolt while studying these West African movements. I try to look at the way in which the leaders and participants saw and explained their own actions, with the intention to reveal how perhaps we, scholars, should be attempting to examine their struggles, if we want to understand the real meanings behind the actions we study.

Warfare in West Africa and warfare in those regions of the Americas where West African men, women, and children who had been enslaved as a result of war were taken show many common characteristics. From the way African soldiers dressed to the weapons and charms they carried, to the strategies of attack and retreat they were familiar with, West African warfare in Bahia and Cuba, rather than a survival, was more accurately a continuation of events that had begun on the African side of the Atlantic as a consequence of ideas and ideologies and political disputes associated with them. The expansion of Islam and the civil problems of Oyo are only two of the major factors associated with the transatlantic crossing of warfare ideas, ideologies, ethics, and technologies in the period.

In 1825, during his visit to Oyo, Clapperton found it was the norm and not the exception for confrontation to be "not a national war but a slaving one" in West Africa at the time.[46] Slavery and war were at the center of West African politics and economics in the first half of the nineteenth century, nowhere more so than in and around Oyo. Something similar can be said for Bahia and Cuba for the same period, although in all fairness full-blown wars never really affected either. The events that unfolded almost simultaneously in and around Salvador de Bahia and across the plantation region surrounding Havana, Matanzas, and Cárdenas in the first half of the nineteenth century can be traced back to Africa and more specifically to West Africa and often to Oyo, Sokoto, Dahomey, and other specific West African states. While highlighting the importance of starting the study of the African diaspora in Africa Paul Lovejoy stated some years ago that very often "the discussion of the African background has been too vague to establish many concrete links with the homeland."[47] Establishing those links is the main ambition behind this study.

In order to achieve this aim, the book has been divided into five chapters. Chapters 1, 2, and 3 examine the historical background and the life experiences of the men, women, and children who are at the center of this story. Where were they from? What sort of political, social, and cultural societies did they leave behind? How, when, and where were they likely enslaved? What were the characteristics of their enslavement journeys from their homes until they arrived in the Americas? In what way may the Middle Passage have affected them? It also explores the sort of world awaiting them on the other side of the Atlantic.

Chapters 4 and 5 focus on the transplantation of West African warfare to the Americas by scrutinizing the many military uprisings staged by West African men and women, often slaves, on Bahian and Cuban cities and plantations. After a discussion of the role of translation and the meanings of words for the interpretation

---

[46] Hugh Clapperton and Richard Lander, *Journal of a Second Expedition into the Interior of Africa from the Bight of Benin to Soccatoo* (London: John Murray, 1829), 47.

[47] Paul Lovejoy, "The African Diaspora: Revisionist Interpretations of Ethnicity, Culture and Religion under Slavery," *Studies in the World History of Slavery, Abolition and Emancipation*, 2:1 (1997): 3–4.

of what West Africans consistently referred to as actions of war, these two chapters move to assess and discuss West African warfare in Bahia and Cuba. Following the models used by scholars such as Robert S. Smith, Joseph P. Smaldone, and John K. Thornton to study warfare in West Africa, these chapters look into organization and strategies; leadership; military operations and tactics of war; gender, ethnicity, and the composition of the insurgent troops; and finally weapons and war paraphernalia. By following this methodology and centering on these aspects, these final chapters expose the concrete links existing between West African warfare on both sides of the Atlantic.

1

Between Glory and Decay
West African Atlantic States in the Age of Revolution

The best weapon against an enemy is another enemy.

Friedrich Nietzsche

On a clear morning, sometime between January and April 1821, the history of the quiet and peaceful village of Osogun was to change forever. Early in the morning, while many of its men were already out working on their farms, a force formed by Fulani and Yoruba-speaking marauders surrounded the small village and after a few hours of fighting took it by force. A teenage boy called Ajayi was one of the many residents who attempted to escape from the invaders. He, alongside his relatives and neighbors headed for the nearest prickly shrubs with the intention of evading capture. Unfortunately, Ajayi, his mother, grandmother, sisters, and several of his cousins were all captured by Muslim raiders, who threw noose ropes around the necks of their captives, tying them in the same way they might have done if seizing goats.

This event caused a long-lasting trauma to the boy; after that day Ajayi would never see his father again. A short time after being captured, he also witnessed a violent argument, between some of the invaders, over who would get to keep one of his cousins. At some point the Fulani man seemed to have even considered dismembering him if their wish to keep him was not to be accepted by his Yoruba-speaking counterpart. What followed next can only be imagined. Ajayi was separated from his loved ones and taken to Lagos via Iseyin, Dada, Ijaye, Itoko, Ikereku-Iwere, and Ikosi. By the time he reached his destination he was, as he put it himself, "a veteran in slavery."[1]

Ajayi's story of capture and enslavement was not by any means unique. What made him exceptional was the fact that he, unlike many thousands of fellow West Africans who went through similar experiences, was able to write down the events as he remembered them many years later. After the ship in which he was embarked, the *Esperanza Felix*, was seized by the British navy in April 1822, Ajayi was freed and taken to Freetown where he learned to read and write, and eventually went on to become the well-known Reverend Samuel Ajayi Crowther. Ajayi's story tells us

---

[1] J. F. Ade Ajayi, "Samuel Ajayi Crowther of Oyo," in Philip D. Curtin, ed., *Africa Remembered: Narratives by West Africans from the Era of the Slave Trade* (Madison: University of Wisconsin Press, 1967), 310.

about a place and time in which revolution, war, and slavery went hand in hand; a story that partially reflects the rise of a West African power, the Sokoto Caliphate, and the fall of another, the Empire of Oyo.

This chapter deals with the political and socio-economic changes that took place in and around Oyo from the early 1790s onwards. Zooming in from the general (creation and destruction of states, inter-state and internal wars, enslaving raids, etc.), to the particular (personal experiences of those who were enslaved and sent to the Atlantic World during this period), it will also address a number of issues and themes that were paramount to the functioning of these states such as the development or collapse of their civil institutions, laws, and rules. In other words, this chapter is about the world of war that the protagonists of this story left behind when they were sent towards the coast and embarked on vessels bound for the Americas.

THE BEGINNING OF THE END: THE STRENGTHENING OF OYO'S NEIGHBORS AND AFONJA'S INSUBORDINATION (*C.*1783–*C.*1817)

During the eighteenth century Oyo emerged as one of the strongest polities in West Africa (see Map 1.1). Its rulers, known as aláàfins, were continuously successful in waging war against most of their neighbors, in some cases by conquest and in others by imposing and extracting tribute. In that respect Oyo became a quintessential West African pre-colonial predatory state.[2] Its development was based on cyclical predatory wars that ensured the submission of its enemies and the procurement of slaves to supply its domestic market and the growing needs of the transatlantic and transaharan trades. These wars not only provided slaves and booty, but also contributed to the internal political and social stability of the kingdom. Nevertheless, powerful as they usually were, starting in 1754 Oyo's aláàfins went through a period in which their authority was little more than nominal, after the commander-in-chief of the army and leader of the Oyo Mesi, Basorun Gaha, took over the kingdom, going as far as disposing of three aláàfins and waging war whenever he saw fit.[3]

In 1770 a new Aláàfin, Abiodun, came to power and slowly but surely started to claim the lost alafinate authority back. Eventually, in 1774 an older and much debilitated Gaha was forced to deal with and crush an open insurrection in Ilorin led by the local chief Pasin, and not long after, Abiodun, supported by a number

---

[2] Some years ago Hubbell proposed what he aptly called the "predatory state model" to define and explain the character and reasons behind these wars in West Africa. According to him, "a primary purpose of warfare, oftentimes waged during the annual dry season, was to accumulate/capture those primarily human resources—slaves—vital to the perpetuation and reproduction of state institutions," Andrew Hubbell, "A View of the Slave Trade from the Margin: Souroudougou in the Late Nineteenth-Century Slave Trade of the Niger Bend," *Journal of African History*, 42:1 (2001): 27.

[3] Smith, *Kingdoms of the Yoruba*, 47–9, 137–41; Robin Law, "The Constitutional Troubles of Oyo in the Eighteenth Century," *Journal of African History*, 12:1 (1971): 25–44.

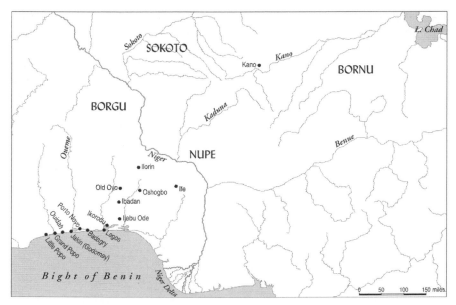

Map 1.1 The Bight of Benin and its interior

of unhappy chiefs organized a coup that ended with his de facto rule.[4] The following years saw the Aláàfin reclaim his supremacy and Oyo attain its greatest territorial extent,[5] but as various scholars have pointed out, the long-term damage to the mighty kingdom had been already done.[6] For example, J. A. Atanda claimed that underlying constitutional weaknesses within Oyo reduced the aláàfins "to impotence in practice," while none of the other high-ranking officers was at least in theory strong enough to assert power over the entire kingdom.[7] Robert S. Smith was even more specific by pinpointing the major internal problems that plagued the kingdom in the post-Gaha period. Among them were a decrease in the effectiveness of the army, the overdependence of Oyo upon the slave trade, the increase in the foreign and unfree population that helped lead to the fall of Ilorin to the jihadists in *c.*1823–*c.*1824, and, finally, a decline of impetus and morale at the center of government.[8]

---

[4] Gaha was captured and executed, as were many of his sons and relatives. See Samuel Johnson, *The History of the Yorubas: From the Earliest Times to the Beginning of the British Protectorate* (Cambridge: Cambridge University Press, 2010), 181–6; Smith, *Kingdoms of the Yoruba*, 47–8.

[5] Law, "The Constitutional Troubles of Oyo," 25.

[6] Smith has gone as far as suggesting that Gaha's ascendancy and his disposal of four different Aláàfins during those years could have been "symptoms of the approaching decline of Oyo." Smith, *Kingdoms of the Yoruba*, 47.

[7] J. A. Atanda, "The Fall of the Old Oyo Empire: A Re-consideration of its Cause," *Journal of the Historical Society of Nigeria*, 5:4 (1971): 478–9. See also Law, "The Constitutional Troubles of Oyo," 27–34.

[8] Smith, "Event and Portent: The Fall of Old Oyo, a Problem in Historical Explanation," *Africa: Journal of the International African Institute*, 41:3 (1971): 187–8.

Although domestically peace had been reestablished, Oyo's neighbors had begun to assess their odds of achieving independence. In the 1780s the sphere of influence of the kingdom expanded as never before, but also saw the first signs of external challenge to its traditional political and military supremacy. Although Aláàfin Abiodun still managed to reaffirm his control over Dahomey, as it is clear from the campaigns ordered by him and carried out by the Dahomean army in 1784 against Badagry and 1786 against Weme, others decided that the time had come to confront Oyo. The first indication of external weakening was the defeat suffered by an Oyo force at Kaiama in Borgu in 1783.[9] According to the report given by Lionel Abson, Governor of the English fort at Whydah, the Oyo army had received "a total overthrow from a country by name Barrabas (Bariba/Borgu) having lost in the battle 11 umbrellas and the generals under them."[10] Not much is known about this apparently disastrous campaign, and although Oyo recovered by establishing control over Mahi and the southern Egbado, things got much worse after the death of Abiodun in *c*.1789.

Barely two years later, around 1791, both external and internal problems began to accumulate. First, another hefty Oyo force was heavily defeated by a Nupe army. As a result, according to Archibald Dalzel, Oyo was "under the necessity of submitting to the victor's own terms, having lost thirteen umbrellas in the action."[11] Internally, Abiodun's successor, Awole, was soon at odds with both the Basorun Asamu, and more importantly, with the newly appointed Are-Ona-Kakanfo Afonja, who was soon to play a pivotal role in the events that led to the collapse of the kingdom. Afonja, alongside the Bale of Gbogun, Opele, defied the authority of the new Aláàfin, refused to pay him tribute, and conspired to bring him down. By the mid-1790s both Afonja and Opele had strengthened their own spheres of influence. When the Aláàfin finally decided to rid himself of Afonja, a mutiny jointly organized by Basorun Asamu, Opele, and Afonja culminated in what Robin Law has termed a *coup d'état* that forced the Aláàfin to take his own life.[12] According to Johnson, these events were followed by Opele's conquest of Dofian and Igbo-Owu, and by a failed attempt to take Igboho, where he was killed by an arrow.[13] In the meantime, Afonja asserted his authority in the north by limiting the power of the new aláàfins and by expanding his sphere of influence towards Igbomina.[14]

What until then had been a struggle for power within a unified state soon led to the secession of one of its provinces, for in around 1796 the Egba rebelled against Oyo during the regency of Basorun Asamu, and attained their independence, showing the way to other Oyo provinces and endangering the "important trade route to

---

[9] This Borgu force was very likely under the command of Sabi Agba (1775–85). See Julius O. Adekunle, *Politics and Society in Nigeria's Middle Belt: Borgu and the Emergence of a Political Identity* (Trenton, NJ, and Asmara: Africa World Press, 2004), 110–11.

[10] Lionel Abson to ?. Williams fort, Whydah, 26 September 1783. NA-UK: T 70/1545.

[11] And presumably 13 generals too. Archibald Dalzel, *The History of Dahomy, an Island Kingdom of Africa; Compiled from Authentic Memoirs; with an Introduction and Notes* (London: T. Spilsbury and Son, 1793), 229.

[12] Law, "The Constitutional Troubles of Oyo," 41.

[13] Johnson, *The History of the Yorubas*, 193.   [14] Johnson, *The History of the Yorubas*, 193–4.

the coast."[15] This combination of defeats at Borgu and Nupe, the insubordination of important provinces like Ilorin, Egba, and in due course Ekiti, and the now diminished authority of the aláàfins led to a period of instability characterized by the empowerment of Afonja in the north, by an increase of internal conflict, and by changes in the slave trade patterns observed until that time. By *c.*1812 the south of the kingdom saw the first skirmishes of the Owu wars, while north of Oyo an aggressive new state, the Sokoto Caliphate, began threatening the very existence of Oyo from the mid-1810s.

The relationship between Oyo and its northern neighbors had been traditionally complicated, and often determined by the size and strength of their armies. Nupe had always been a thorn in Oyo's side, and there is some evidence that points to a possible Nupe ascendancy over Oyo, at least from the second part of the eighteenth century. Relationships with Borgu were not better. Borgu and Oyo had been habitual rivals, and after Oyo's defeat at Kaiama in 1783, armed parties from Borgu increased their forays into Oyo territory. These attacks and acts of vandalism eventually became a serious problem to the point that by the time Hugh Clapperton visited the area they were considered to be one of the main dangers affecting Oyo's roads.[16] On the other hand, the relationship between Oyo and the various Hausa-speaking states, at least until the beginnings of the nineteenth century, had been mostly based on mutual trade benefits.[17] The slaves procured from the constant and consuming wars that plagued the Hausa-speaking states throughout the eighteenth century were, according to Lovejoy, "common in Oyo, both for domestic use and for employment in the military."[18]

In the late eighteenth century these Hausa-speaking states would experience a renaissance of Islamic militant discourses and practices associated with Mahdist beliefs and with the perceived need to reform, by arms if necessary, the corrupt form of Islam instituted by the rulers of each of these states.[19] Already in the 1770s an Islamic preacher and scholar, Jibrilu Dan Umaru, called for a *jihād* to reform this deviating Islamic rule. As Smaldone has rightly argued, although his call "went unheeded," three decades later one of his students' new calls would revolutionize the structure and balance of power in the entire Central Sudan.[20]

By the mid-1790s Uthman Dan Fodio had become a well-known scholar and the leader of the Qādiriyya Order across the Hausa-speaking territories.[21] As a

[15] Smith, *Kingdoms of the Yoruba*, 50. According to Gailey the Ekiti would soon follow the Egba in defying Oyo's authority and achieving their independence. Harry A. Gailey, *Lugard and the Abeokuta Uprising: The Demise of Egba Independence* (London: Frank Cass, 1982), 2.

[16] Clapperton noted in his journal, "it is enough to call a man a native of Borgoo, to designate him as a thief and a murderer." Clapperton and Lander, *Journal of a Second Expedition*, 107.

[17] For a discussion of the Hausa states before Dan Fodio's *jihād* see Finn Fuglestad, "A Reconsideration of Hausa History before the Jihad," 319–39.

[18] Lovejoy, *Slavery, Commerce and Production*, 57.

[19] Mervyn Hiskett, "The Nineteenth-Century Jihads in West Africa," in John E. Flint, ed., *The Cambridge History of Africa* (Cambridge: Cambridge University Press, 1976), v. 136.

[20] Smaldone, *Warfare in the Sokoto Caliphate*, 20.

[21] Hiskett, "The Nineteenth-Century Jihads in West Africa," 135–8; A. D. H. Bivar, "The Wathiqat ahl Al-Sudan: A Manifesto of the Fulani Jihad," *Journal of African History*, 2:2 (1961): 235–6. See also Uthman Dan Fodio, *For the Evangelization of the Nation.* DMAA-Niamey: CN, 262.

result of his Mahdist beliefs, his views of the socio-political status of these states, along with a number of mystic visions, Dan Fodio found himself more and more at odds with the rulers of Gobir, the kingdom where he had been born and where he had lived most of his life. These tensions increased during the government of Nafata (*c*.1795–*c*.1802) and reached a point of no return after the ascension of Yunfa in 1802. The new Sarki saw the Muslim reformists as a threat to the stability of Gobir and did everything in his power to undermine and restrain them. On his part, Dan Fodio considered all Hausa rulers as "unbelievers and nothing else,"[22] and went as far as to record a long list of ways in which they had, until then, oppressed and taken advantage of their people.[23] Yunfa's intolerance combined with Dan Fodio's confrontational position led to the outbreak of hostilities between the two sides in 1804.[24] A military campaign that initially seemed destined to be another minor episode in the history of Central Sudanic warfare, soon turned into a full-scale *jihād* that would affect in one way or another every state in the area. Within four years the Hausa-speaking states had been unified and brought under Fulani rule, and virtually every polity in the region was effectively under threat from the jihadist forces.[25]

The socio-political motives behind the Fulani-led *jihād* have been repeatedly discussed over the years. In addition to the perceived need for an Islamic reform, endemic warfare associated with social injustice and the enslavement of people—frequently Muslims—seemed to have also been fundamental reasons behind the call for the *jihād* of 1804.[26] The aforementioned factor apparently carried considerable weight in the minds of those who led the movement. In the decades that preceded the *jihād*, Hausa rulers and traders had profited from the enslavement of fellow Muslims on a continual basis. The slave trade towards the Bights, and also towards the Sahara, was a thriving business. Whilst discussing this issue Lovejoy noted that "Uthman dan Fodio complained about the enslavement of Muslims by the Hausa states," although he also pointed out that "the consolidation of the Sokoto Caliphate only increased the level of enslavement, including large numbers of Muslims."[27] Although the *jihād* appeared to have fallen short of limiting the enslavement of fellow Muslims, it did not fail to unify and

[22] Uthman Dan Fodio, *Tanbihu'l Ikhwan*. Translated in H. R. Palmer, "An Early Fulani Conception of Islam (Continued)," *Journal of the Royal African Society*, 14:53 (1914): 53.

[23] Uthman Dan Fodio, *Kitab al-farq*. Translated in M. Hiskett, "Kitab al-farq: A Work on the Habe Kingdoms Attributed to Uthman Dan Fodio," *Bulletin of the School of Oriental and African Studies*, 23:3 (1960): 567–9.

[24] Muhammed Bello, *Infaq Al-Maisur*, 1812, in C. E. J. Whitting, ed., *Infaku'l Maisuri* (London: Luzac & Company, 1957).

[25] Samuel N. Nwabara, "The Fulani Conquest and Rule of the Hausa Kingdom of Northern Nigeria (1804–1900)," *Journal de la Société des Africanistes*, 33:2 (1963): 233–5.

[26] Uthman Dan Fodio, *Important Issues about the People of Sudan*. DMAA-Niamey: CN, 280.

[27] Lovejoy, "Slavery, the Bilad al Sudan," *Slavery on the Frontiers of Islam*, 15. See also Olatunji Ojo, "Islam, Ethnicity and Slave Agitation: Hausa 'Mamlucks' in Nineteenth-Century Yorubaland," in Behnaz A. Mirzai, Ismael M. Montana, and Paul E. Lovejoy, *Slavery, Islam and Diaspora* (Trenton, NJ, and Asmara: Africa World Press, 2009), 104–5. The most recent study on the transaharan trade is Ismael M. Montana, *The Abolition of Slavery in Ottoman Tunisia* (Gainesville: University Press of Florida, 2013).

reform the formerly independent Hausa states into one single state: the Sokoto Caliphate.[28]

From 1804 onwards the jihadist forces swelled. Taking advantage of the long-standing rifts existing between the rulers of the various Hausa states, Dan Fodio and his commanders defeated each of them, eventually ushering in a new age of Islamic orthodox rule throughout the Hausa-speaking territories. The main leaders of the *jihād* seem to have been well versed in the art of war. In particular Dan Fodio's brother Abdullahi and son Muhammad Bello proved to be brilliant generals who inflicted defeat after defeat on their enemies.[29]

By September 1808, after three previous failed attempts, the jihadist forces finally took Alkalawa, the capital of Gobir.[30] As a direct result of the fall of Alkalawa, a "unified Islamic feudality," the Sokoto Caliphate was established in 1809, ushering in what is commonly considered as the second phase of the *jihād*.[31] Now, the jihadists moved towards the neighboring kingdoms of Kano and Zaria, and continued east as far as Borno, where an army led by Muhammad Al-Amin Al-Kanemi eventually stopped them. As a result of this advance the flag bearers of the Shehu founded new emirates. Hadejia, Katagum, Bauchi, and Gombe were all well established by 1811. In the following years the Caliphate was divided into a western section with its capital in Gwandu under Abdullahi's command, and an eastern section based in Sokoto under Bello's authority.[32]

The strengthening of the Caliphate's grip and authority throughout Hausaland allowed the jihadist forces to organize themselves and to support each other in the impending military campaigns. What at the beginning had been barely an Islamic guerrilla-like force resisting the armies sent from Gobir, by 1812 had become a respectable military force formed by a number of individual armies often linked to the new emirates who waged what Lovejoy has called "a continuous military campaign" with "enslavement as a basic aim."[33] Once the Hausa-speaking territories were finally secured the Islamic forces set their sights on their southern neighbors, Borgu, Nupe, and Oyo.

Over the following years the people of Borgu were attacked on numerous occasions by the jihadists. In spite of these unremitting attacks they were successful in repelling them to the point that Uthman Dan Fodio himself called all true Muslims to emigrate from those lands after giving up on them. According to Nehemiah Levtzion, the resistance presented against the *jihād* by many states, including Borgu, may have been the result of a conceptual opposition between the ruling

[28] For a more detailed assessment of slavery and the slave trade in the Caliphate of Sokoto see: David C. Tambo, "The Sokoto Caliphate Slave Trade in the Nineteenth Century," *International Journal of African Historical Studies*, 9:2 (1976): 187–217; Sean Stilwell, "Power, Honour and Shame: The Ideology of Royal Slavery in the Sokoto Caliphate," *Africa: Journal of the International African Institute*, 70:3 (2000): 394–421; Lovejoy, *Slavery, Commerce and Production in the Sokoto Caliphate of West Africa* (Trenton, NJ, and Asmara: Africa World Press, 2005).

[29] Hiskett has suggested that these skills may have been a result of them both being "literates fully familiar with the extensive Islamic military literature in classical Arabic." Hiskett, "The Nineteenth-Century Jihads in West Africa," 140.

[30] Bello, *Infaq Al-Maisur*, ch. 5.

[31] Hiskett, "The Nineteenth-Century Jihads in West Africa," 149.

[32] Smaldone, *Warfare in the Sokoto Caliphate*, 35–7.

[33] Lovejoy, *Slavery, Commerce and Production*, 20.

warrior elites, unwilling to relinquish or share the power they had traditionally held, with these new Islamic leaders.[34] Whilst Borgu remained mostly independent and for Dan Fodio and his followers considered to be within the realm of Dar-el-harb (the house of war), from the late 1810s Nupe was consumed by a civil war of which the jihadists took full advantage almost immediately. Upon the death of Mu'azu, the Etsu of Nupe, a succession conflict ensued between the two claimants to the throne, Majiya and Jimada. In order to secure power Majiya invited the jihadists, represented by Mallam Dendo, to back his claim, and eventually defeated and killed Jimada in *c.*1820. By the early 1830s and after a string of changes of alliances and military campaigns that included Majiya's unsuccessful attack against Ilorin, his escape, and his ultimate reinstatement to the throne as a puppet of Mallam Dendo, Nupe had, in practical terms, become another emirate of Sokoto.[35]

Further south, a not-so-dissimilar historical development took place well into Oyo's territory, specifically in and around Ilorin. There, Afonja, driven by his desire of strengthening his hold on northern Oyo, invited another Fulani Mallam called Alimi to be by his side, presumably as an advisor and spiritual leader. From the 1790s when he had played a pivotal role in the fall of Aláàfin Awole, Afonja had been in open insubordination against the rulers of Oyo. However, according to Falola and Heaton his rebellion had remained stagnant during all those years since "Oyo was not able to defeat him" and "neither was Afonja able to inflict any serious defeats on Oyo."[36]

This lack of progress apparently led Afonja to seek help, not only from military leaders such as the Onikoyi of Ikoyi, but also from defecting slaves and from Islamic spiritual leaders. The first of these to come and settle around Ilorin seems to have been Solagberu, a Yoruba-speaking Muslim from Kuwo who became an important ally of Afonja. Historical evidence suggests that throughout the 1810s ever increasing numbers of northern slaves, probably mostly Hausa speakers, began to run away from their Oyo masters and gather around Afonja and probably also around Solagberu, participating as soldiers in the military excursions sent from Ilorin against its neighbors, and in time launching their own raids into Oyo territory.[37]

When Mallam Alimi settled in Ilorin around 1817 or 1818 Afonja's independence from Oyo was a fact. Alimi, a Fulani cleric who had been preaching and selling charms throughout northern Oyo since around 1813, and who was well acquainted with Dan Fodio's *jihād*, soon became a key friend and advisor to Afonja, and an influential leader among the runaway Hausa-speaking slaves who were settling in and around Ilorin.[38]

Although Afonja never converted to Islam, for a few years he was successful in using these runaway slaves in his expeditions against the Igbolos, the Igbominas,

[34] Nehemiah Levtzion, *Muslims and Chiefs in West Africa: A Study of Islam in the Middle Volta Basin in the Pro-Colonial Period* (Oxford: Oxford University Press, 1968), 189.

[35] Mason, "The Antecedents of Nineteenth-Century Islamic Government in Nupe," 63–76.

[36] Toyin Falola and Matthew Heaton, *A History of Nigeria* (Cambridge: Cambridge University Press, 2008), 74–5.

[37] Reverend Samuel Ajayi Crowder was himself enslaved during one of these raids, as we have seen at the beginning of this chapter.

[38] Ann O'Hear, *Power Relations: Ilorin Slaves and their Successors* (Rochester, NY: Rochester University Press, 1997), 22, 47–8; Law, *The Oyo Empire, c.1600–c.1836* (Oxford: Oxford University Press, 1991), 256–7.

the Ekitis, and the Oyos.[39] When Clapperton visited Oyo's capital in the mid-1820s he noticed how afraid the Oyo were of these runaway slaves. He was told that the slaves had been in rebellion for two years and that they had taken control of "a large town" two days' journey from Oyo-Ile called "Lori" [Ilorin].[40] In spite of achieving a number of victories and of solidifying his ascendancy over Oyo, Afonja eventually paid a high price for relying too much on these Muslim troops. In the early 1820s he seemed to have fallen out with both Alimi and Solagberu, and was eventually a victim of what seems to have been in fact a "coup organized to establish Fulani control over Ilorin."[41] The loyalties of these runaway slaves now lay with Alimi and his sons, and when Afonja attempted to disband them they rose and surrounded and killed him before he could receive reinforcements from Ikoyi.[42] After his death in *c.*1823 Ilorin fell into Fulani hands for good. Since Alimi himself seems to have died soon before Afonja, probably also in 1823, and Solagberu was killed not long after, power fell to Alimi's son Abdusalami.[43] Upon Afonja's and Alimi's deaths, Ilorin became an emirate under Gwandu and Abdusalami its first emir, ruling between *c.*1823 and *c.*1834.

For the Oyo the news of the assassination of Afonja was as devastating as news can be. For all they had suffered while Afonja was alive, he was still one of them, an Oyo renegade, but still an Oyo. The continual incursions of Afonja's Muslim war-boys into Oyo territory, cruel and destructive as they were, could not compare to the new menace that a jihadist outpost well inside Oyo territory now posed to them. More importantly, as Law has argued, Afonja's death closed the period of internal strife between Oyo chiefs, giving way to a new period in which Ilorin, now an emirate under Gwandu, "represented an alien power whose object was the complete destruction of the Oyo kingdom."[44]

To have a new Gwandu emirate southeast of their capital Oyo-Ile was both frightening and unacceptable. This circumstance led the Aláàfin and his new Are-Ona-Kakanfo, Toyeje of Ogbomoso, to act in order to prevent any further gains into Oyo territory by the invaders. According to Robin Law, who has discussed the chronology of the period, a number of military campaigns ensued roughly between 1824 and 1830.[45] These campaigns, however, were doomed as far as Oyo was concerned even before they began. By this time Oyo was already experiencing a "severe commercial depression" that was a result of its lack of success in supplying the Europeans with enough slaves.[46]

---

[39] Johnson, *The History of the Yorubas*, 197–8; See also Report of the commission appointed to enquire into the fears of minorities and the means of allaying them, BPPO. 1857–58. Colonial Office. Nigeria, 74.

[40] Clapperton and Lander, *Journal of a Second Expedition*, 55.

[41] David D. Laitin, *Hegemony and Culture: Politics and Change among the Yoruba* (Chicago: University of Chicago Press, 1986), 115.

[42] Johnson, *The History of the Yorubas*, 198.

[43] Chief Samuel Ojo Bada, "The Frontier City of Ilorin," in Toyin Falola, ed., *Yoruba Gurus: Indigenous Production of Knowledge in Africa* (Trenton, NJ, and Asmara: Africa World Press, 2000), 161.

[44] Law, *The Oyo Empire*, 278.

[45] Law, "The Chronology of the Yoruba Wars of the Early Nineteenth Century," 215–19. Law even included a chronological table (219).

[46] Law, *The Oyo Empire*, 281.

The first of these campaigns occurred in *c*.1824, when the Oyo regular army fought an intense battle against the troops from Ilorin at Ogele. The Oyo army was eventually defeated and pursued by the jihadists. According to Johnson, the invaders then followed up their victory with the "destruction of many towns in the Ibolo province,"[47] causing much damage and even more distress among the Oyo. Sometime in 1824 or 1825, the Oyo gathered again, this time counting on the support of Majiya of Nupe, who was interested in destroying Ilorin where Mallam Dendo was hiding at the time, and attacked Ilorin for a second time. The combined Oyo and Nupe armies struggled from the onset to organize themselves in the wake of all the destruction left behind by the previous conflict. This campaign came to be known as the Mugba Mugba war (locust fruit war), due to the extraordinary situation in which the soldiers found themselves, being forced to live on the locust fruit in order to survive what by all accounts amounted almost to a famine. According to Johnson, once more the Oyo were unable to cope with the competent Fulani regular cavalry, and were heavily defeated for a second time.[48]

The Ogele and Mugba Mugba wars led to a breakdown of central authority in Oyo of unprecedented magnitude that coupled with the wars in the south limited considerably the power of Aláàfin Majotu. Not long after the Mugba Mugba war had ended, sometime between 1825 and 1830, two of the Aláàfin's most senior officers, Adegun, the Onikoyi of Ikoyi, and Toyeje, the new Are-Ona-Kakanfo, went to war against each other. Some petty quarrel between them led to an open armed conflict in which Toyeje, supported by Solagberu and an army from Ilorin, laid siege to Ikoyi, almost taking it before the tide turned against him when the Ilorin army was recalled by Abdusalami.[49] In what amounted to a realignment of the invading forces, almost immediately after these troops were sent again to Ikoyi, but this time in support of the Onikoyi, who had struck a deal with Abdusalami declaring his allegiance to the emirate.[50] The armies of Ikoyi and Ilorin then proceeded to inflict another heavy defeat upon the armies of Oyo at Pamo.

After this last routing the Oyo army was once again in retreat and disarray, and many of its remnants moved south in small guerrilla-like groups that contributed to the perpetuation of slave raids and wars that were already under way in places like Owu and Egba. Abdusalami's power in the northern territories of Oyo was almost total. After the Onikoyi declared his loyalty to Ilorin, the Emir's armies began to enter and raid the Oyo lands with an increased frequency, mostly in search of slaves to supply the transaharan and transatlantic slave trade markets.[51] Oyo was effectively torn into pieces and the authority of the Aláàfin shattered. At some point there were three claimants to the title of Are-Ona-Kakanfo, Edun of Gbogun, Ojo

---

[47] Johnson, *The History of the Yorubas*, 201.
[48] Johnson, *The History of the Yorubas*, 202. On the decline of the formerly mighty Oyo cavalry see: Robin Law, "A West African Cavalry State: The Kingdom of Oyo," *Journal of African History*, 16:1 (1975): 1–15.
[49] Johnson, *The History of the Yorubas*, 203; Smith, *Kingdoms of the Yoruba*, 142–3.
[50] Johnson, *The History of the Yorubas*, 203–4.
[51] See Jamie Bruce Lockhart and Paul E. Lovejoy, eds., *Hugh Clapperton into the Interior of Africa: Records of the Second Expedition, 1825–1827* (Leiden: Brill, 2005), 36.

Amepo of Akese, and Oluyedun, a son of Afonja who was at the time in Ibadan. As Law has pointed out, the dissolution of the Empire "could hardly be better illustrated than by this simultaneous existence of three claimants to its senior military title, none of whom had been appointed by the Aláàfin."[52]

These military campaigns had a profound effect on the ways in which the slave trade was conducted in the region and also on who was enslaved and exported, and where from and to. In the time of Afonja, small gangs of runaway slaves based in Ilorin were among those who conducted slave raids into Oyo terri-tory. The attack on Ajayi's village, with which this chapter begins, is only one among the many that took place then. After Afonja's death, to a considerable extent Ilorin "took over Oyo's role as slave supplier, both by capture and trade."[53] Incursions into Oyo were now more frequent and devastating than before, since the many disputes existing among the Oyo chiefs did not allow for an organized resistance against the Muslim invaders. Raids into Nupe and Borgu were also common at least from the time of Sokoto's consolidation as a Sudanese state in the mid-1810s.[54]

While Nupe and Ilorin fell to the Islamic forces in the 1820s, Oyo and the Yoruba-speaking states to the south had other problems to contend with. A war between Owu on one side and Ife and Ijebu on the other had broken out some-time midway through the 1810s and had developed into a full-fledged conflict by the mid-1820s. Additionally, after the ascension of King Ghezo to the Dahomean throne in 1818, the southwestern border of the Oyo Empire came under sustained attacks from its former vassals, who being discontented with shaking off Oyo's domination, also invaded and occupied several regions that had formerly belonged to Dahomey.

THE WARS IN THE SOUTH (*C.1812–C.1824*)

Disruptions in the supply of slaves to the port of Lagos were the main cause behind the conflict that began in *c.*1811 or 1812 in the Ife market town of Apomu. According to Law, the "shift of the main centre of the Atlantic slave trade from Porto Novo eastwards to Lagos"[55] led to an increased demand for slaves in the effervescent port of Lagos.[56] The response of Ijebu traders, who at the time were the port's main sup-pliers of slaves, was to acquire more and more slaves by any necessary means, even if that meant kidnapping fellow Yoruba-speaking traders. The consequences were almost immediate. Akijobi, the Olowu of Owu, following orders from Toyeje, then still Bale of Ogbomoso and Adegun, the Onikoyi of Ikoyi, proceeded to

---

[52] Law, *The Oyo Empire*, 286.
[53] Ann O'Hear, "The Enslavement of the Yoruba," in Toyin Falola and Matt D. Childs, eds., *The Yoruba Diaspora in the Atlantic World* (Indianapolis: Indiana University Press, 2004), 58.
[54] O'Hear, "The Enslavement of the Yoruba," 58; Law and Lovejoy, "Borgu in the Atlantic Slave Trade," 79–81.
[55] Law, *The Oyo Empire*, 274.
[56] A. L. Mabogunje and J. Omer-Cooper, *Owu in Yoruba History* (Ibadan: Ibadan University Press, 1971), 48–9.

attack several towns in Ife, including Apomu, with the intention of bringing the kidnappings to an end.[57]

Although the Olowu won this first war, during the following months and years the problems between Owu and Ife, far from being solved, increased to the point that by 1816–17 a second war broke out between them. This time, however, the Ife had secured the support of the Ijebu and their modernized army, against whom the Owu could only muster their traditional weapons, including their long and heavy cutlasses known as *agedengbe*, bows, and arrows.[58] The combined Ife–Ijebu army soon forced the Olowu and his soldiers into their capital city Owu, where a long siege followed. Owu resisted for a few years until the allied Ife–Ijebu army finally took and destroyed the town in *c.*1822, in part thanks to the reinforcements received from the "numerous refugee Oyos, who had fled southwards from the civil wars" in the north of the kingdom.[59] After the fall of Owu, the Ife–Ijebu army proceeded to ransack Ikija, and "the other towns of the Egba kingdom which fell one after the other."[60]

By then the situation in the south was nothing short of a civil war. The advancing Ife–Ijebu forces, swarming with Oyo refugees, mostly from the north, continued to push west killing and enslaving fellow Yoruba-speaking peoples, and leaving destruction in their wake. The now retreating Owu sought refuge in Egbaland, and also contributed to the destruction and sacking of a number of towns, notably Kesi. Once again following Law's chronology it is possible to speculate that by the mid-1820s some of the Egba and Owu refugees founded the new town of Abeokuta on the banks of the river Ogun, while a number of Ife and Ijebu joined by Oyo refugees settled in Ibadan, creating in this way two of the most important centers of power in the region for the years to come.[61]

While internal problems throughout Oyo continued to degenerate into wars and destruction and simultaneously with the secession and strengthening of Ilorin in the north, an old foe to the west, Dahomey, took advantage of the propitious situation to shake off Oyo's supremacy once and for all. In 1818 a coup led by Ghezo and supported by the notorious slave trader Francisco Felix de Souza, ousted king Adandozan and ushered in a new era in the relations between Dahomey and Oyo.[62] Although during the early years of Adandozan's reign Dahomey had challenged Oyo's domination with a series of attacks on Porto Novo, at the time of Ghezo's ascension in 1818 Dahomey was still an Oyo tributary.[63]

---

[57] Law, *The Oyo Empire*, 273–7; and "The Owu War in Yoruba History," *Journal of the Historical Society of Nigeria*, 2:1 (1973): 141–7.

[58] By this time the Ijebu had already managed to arm their soldiers with imported muskets. Law, *The Oyo Empire*, 275; Johnson, *The History of the Yorubas*, 206.

[59] Law, "The Owu War in Yoruba History," 146. See also Mabogunje and Omer-Cooper, *Owu in Yoruba History*, 76–7.

[60] Alfred Moloney to Sir Samuel Rowe. Government House, Lagos, 12 May 1881. BPPO. 1887 [C.4957] [C.5144] Lagos (West Africa). Correspondence respecting the war between native tribes in the interior and the negotiations for peace conducted by the government of Lagos, 4.

[61] Law, "The Chronology of the Yoruba Wars," 219–22.

[62] Elisée Soumonni, *Dahomey y el mundo Atlántico* (Amsterdam and Rio de Janeiro: SEPHIS, 2001), 8–9. See also Ana Lucia Araujo, "Dahomey, Portugal and Bahia: King Adandozan and the Atlantic Slave Trade," *Slavery & Abolition*, 33:1 (2012): 1–19.

[63] Archibald Dalzel reported that when in 1786 a Dahomean army attempted to take Porto Novo, then known as Ardrah, Aláàfin Abiodun forbade it from doing so, claiming that "Ardrah was Eyeo's

A few years after coming to power Ghezo, who was certainly aware of the problems that Oyo was facing, made an audacious move and after refusing to pay the periodic tribute, also assassinated two Oyo duty collectors that had been sent by the Aláàfin. Oyo then launched two attacks on Dahomey. The first one was rapidly met and repelled by a Dahomean army led by Ghezo himself at Paouignan. A second, much better organized force was also met and defeated by Ghezo at Kpaloko. The commander of the Oyo army, Ajanaku, "was taken prisoner and put to death and Kpaloko was taken by the Dahomeans."[64]

Ghezo followed up this victory by attacking some western Yoruba-speaking territories, especially the kingdoms of Ketu and Sabe and, according to a report dating from the late 1850s, also part of Egbaland. In all these territories he was said to have committed the same "atrocities" that he had committed earlier, burning their towns until they were lying in ruins and enslaving their people.[65] When Ghezo's offensive finally came to a halt the independence of Dahomey was all but a fact, and both Porto Novo and Mahi had become dependencies of the now flourishing kingdom. Ghezo would rule for the next 50 years, and together with Francisco Felix de Souza, his Bahian advisor and his slave trading colleagues would raise the slave trading profile of all the Atlantic ports under his rule, especially Whydah.

THE FALL OF OYO AND THE CONSOLIDATION OF THE SOKOTO CALIPHATE AND DAHOMEY (*C.*1824–*C.*1840)

By the late 1820s the territorial integrity of Oyo was heavily compromised. Dahomey's incursions on the west were significant and contributed to the civil unrest that pervaded the kingdom, but it was the renewed expansion of Ilorin's sphere of influence that really brought Oyo to a state of disorder and alarm. The kingdom's former main sources of income, slaves obtained through warfare, were now more difficult to procure. Soon the problem turned into a vicious circle. Since Oyo's armies were unable to provide the Atlantic ports with enough slaves, their ability to buy firearms was greatly reduced, which in turn led to a decline in their organization and prowess, and as a direct result to a commercial crisis that eventually contributed to their own demise. The formerly well-organized empire was now the stage for internal wars that were waged in an attempt to compensate for the lack of centralized command. Waves of refugees, often armed and violent, roamed across the region, in some cases joining armies that were already at war, and in others plundering

---

[Oyo's] calabash out of which nobody should be permitted to eat but himself." Dalzel, *The History of Dahomey*, 196. Smith, *Kingdoms of the Yoruba*, 49; and Yves Person, "Chronologie du royaume gun de Hogbonu (Porto Novo)," *Cahiers d'études africaines*, 15:58 (1975): 25–7.

[64] Law, *The Oyo Empire*, 272. See also Augustus A. Adeyinka, "King Gezo of Dahomey, 1818–1858: A Reassessment of a West African Monarch in the Nineteenth Century," *African Studies Review*, 17:3 (1974): 541–48.

[65] "Death of the Slave-Hunting King," *Friends Intelligencer*, 16 (Philadephia: William W. Moore, 1860): 143.

and kidnapping at their own will. Oyo's failure to keep hold of the slave trade routes also meant that in this period "most of the slaves coming from the north were by-passing Oyo altogether, being taken through Borgu and Dahomey for sale at Whydah."[66]

Although Oyo continued to exist as an independent polity, all its former splendor was now gone. When Richard Lander visited its capital Oyo-Ile in 1830 he found the place in a much neglected state. He commented:

> . . . one cannot help feeling rather melancholy in wandering through streets almost deserted, and over a vast extent of fertile land on which there is no human habitation, and scarcely a living thing to animate or cheer the prevailing solemnity. The walls of the town have been suffered to fall into decay; and are now no better than a heap of dust and ruins.[67]

This state of decay observed by Lander was a result of repeated failed military campaigns against Ilorin and Dahomey, of internal disorder and unrest, and the Aláàfin's loss of authority and power. After the Mugba Mugba war was over, Nupe fell into the hands of Mallam Dendo and the Sokoto Caliphate.[68] To the Aláàfin the loss of such an important ally as Majiya was a massive setback that contributed considerably to the further weakening of his tenure. The Muslim invaders sensed that their moment had finally arrived and undertook a series of campaigns against the formerly powerful kingdom.[69] Johnson's assessment of Oyo's situation in the late 1820s supports that given by Richard Lander during his 1830 visit to Oyo-Ile. The combination of an old Aláàfin who was virtually powerless, a crown prince corrupted and full of vices, an economy on the brink of collapse due to the loss of control of the slave trade, a drought and subsequent famine, and an epidemic of what was probably influenza, ultimately led to the depopulation of the north of the kingdom, to the death of Aláàfin Majotu, and to the overall weakening of the few regular troops that still remained loyal to the Aláàfin.[70]

Undermined as he was, Majotu still managed to preserve Oyo's independence until his death in *c.*1831. However, during the next two years and under his successor, Amodo, the Ilorin-based jihadists effectively made a vassal of Oyo. In spite of Amodo's renewed intentions to resist Ilorin advances, he was defeated and Oyo was taken and plundered by an Ilorin army sometime between 1831 and 1833. As a result, the new Aláàfin had to convert to Islam and his kingdom was forced to pay tribute to the newest of Gwandu's emirates.[71]

The fall of Oyo-Ile and Amodo's resolution eventually combined to bring about a new attack on Ilorin. Nevertheless, once more the Aláàfin's army was defeated, this time in the battle of Kanla. This defeat opened the Oyo country to the Ilorin

---

[66] Law, *The Oyo Empire*, 282.   [67] Lander, *Journal of a Second Expedition*, 169.
[68] Siegfried Frederick Nadel, *A Black Byzantium: the Kingdom of Nupe in Nigeria* (Oxford: Oxford University Press, 1951), 78–80; E. G. M. Dupigny, "Nupe Province," in Anthony Hamilton Millard Kirk-Greene, ed., *Gazetteers of the Northern Provinces of Nigeria: The Central Kingdoms: Kontagora, Nassarawa, Nupe, Ilorin* (London: Frank Cass, 1972), iii. 8–10.
[69] Smith, *Kingdoms of the Yoruba*, 144–5; Law, *The Oyo Empire*, 287–8.
[70] Johnson, *The History of the Yoruba*, 214–15.
[71] Smith, *Kingdoms of the Yoruba*, 145; Law, *The Oyo Empire*, 289.

troops. In the following months and years, Ilorin armies roamed across northern Oyo, taking the important towns of Ikoyi, Gbogun, and Epo and enslaving their people. They also invaded and reduced Saki and Ibarapa and were only stopped by the thick forest of Ijesa, where their cavalry was unable to exert any advantage over their enemies' infantry troops and was said to have suffered severe losses.[72] By 1833 only Ede, in the vicinity of the river Osun, and the new centers of power established away from the savanna in Ibadan and Ijaye had survived the offensive of the Ilorin troops. The Aláàfin, still entrenched in his capital Oyo-Ile, continued to be a tributary of Ilorin, though the territorial integrity of the empire was all but a thing of the past.

When Aláàfin Amodo died in *c.*1833 he was succeeded by Oluewu, a son of Aláàfin Awole. Unlike his father, Oluewu was a decisive leader who was capable of creating alliances and of posing a real threat to Ilorin. Soon after ascending to Oyo's throne Oluewu refused to travel to Ilorin, as his predecessor had done, to make a profession of Islam. In the face of a growing internal dissent from the Oyo Mesi, who perceived his behavior as dangerous, and of the external threat of an Ilorin-sponsored invasion, Oluewu resolved to form an allegiance with Borgu.[73] This unpredictable move teaming with an old foe showed that the new Aláàfin was ready to make concessions in order to reassert the lost authority of Oyo. A large military contingent including a considerable number of horsemen arrived in Oyo from Bussa, Nikki, Wawa, and Kaiama. Within a short space of time Oluewu had the Oyo Mesi under control and the army sent from Ogodo by the new emir of Ilorin, Shi'ta, was in full retreat.[74]

Seeing the assertive moves made by the new Aláàfin, some of the towns taken by Ilorin in previous years began to rebel against their occupation. Saki and Gbodo led the way, and the Aláàfin's army marched towards the latter in *c.*1834 and liberated it from the Ilorin.[75] The victory of Gbodo convinced some of the Oyo chiefs who had submitted to Ilorin, to defect and join the effort to reclaim Oyo's former glory. Among these chiefs were Atiba of Ago-Oja, Kurunmi of Ijaye, and Oluyole of Ibadan. During the next rainy season the Oyo army gathered at Ogbomoso and prepared for an all-out attack on Ilorin.[76] In the meantime Shi'ta also received reinforcements from Nupe and prepared for what would be a crucial encounter.[77]

Despite the swelling of its ranks the Oyo troops were, according to Johnson, plagued by internal rivalries and before the decisive battle against Ilorin took place,

---

[72] Johnson, *The History of the Yorubas*, 222; Smith, *Kingdoms of the Yoruba*, 145; Law, *The Oyo Empire*, 290–1; Robin Law has also noticed how the Ijesa forest had already stopped and defeated an Oyo army in the seventeenth century. See Law, "A West African Cavalry State," 9.

[73] Johnson, *The History of the Yorubas*, 258–9; Smith, *Kingdoms of the Yoruba*, 146; Law, *The Oyo Empire*, 294–5.

[74] Johnson, *The History of the Yorubas*, 260–1; Smith, *Kingdoms of the Yoruba*, 146–7; Law, *The Oyo Empire*, 294–5.

[75] Johnson, *The History of the Yorubas*, 260; Law, *The Oyo Empire*, 293.

[76] Johnson, *The History of the Yorubas*, 261–2; Smith, *Kingdoms of the Yoruba*, 147; Law, *The Oyo Empire*, 293–4.

[77] Who exactly sent reinforcements from Nupe is still not clear. For a discussion on this issue see Law, *The Oyo Empire*, 294.

some of the most important Oyo chiefs, including Atiba, stayed away and did not fight.[78] The day was won by Ilorin. Most of the Borgu commanders, with the exception of Gajere of Bussa, were killed in battle, while Aláàfin Oluewu was captured and later executed at Ilorin. The battle of Ilorin checked once and for all the Oyo illusions of regaining their former grandeur. Not only that, but also this defeat led to the eventual evacuation of the capital Oyo-Ile, now exposed more than ever to the possible attacks of Ilorin and Ogodo. The new Aláàfin, Atiba, decided to establish a new capital at Ago-Oja, a place that would ultimately come to be known as New Oyo. Oyo-Ile was abandoned and never populated again.[79]

Moving the kingdom's capital to the south was a strategically motivated decision that was soon to pay dividends. While Ilorin prepared a new invasion of the Oyo territories that had rebelled earlier, Atiba conferred the titles of Are-Ona-Kakanfo and Basorun to Kurunmi of Ijaye and Oluyole of Ibadan respectively.[80] Now the main Oyo armies were all stationed close together, able to support each other, better organized, and under the protection of the rainforest. When in *c*.1838 Ilorin troops marched on Osogbo, they were surprised and overwhelmingly defeated by an Ibadan force sent by Atiba. After this battle, the advance of Ilorin was stopped for good and a new order was born. The former might of Oyo had by then been already much diminished and after Shi'ta's death the conquering intentions of Ilorin receded. However, war continued to affect a vast area, from the emirates founded by the jihadist forces in the north to Dahomey, New Oyo, and Ijebu Ode, and not surprisingly the need for slaves to supply European merchants still constituted one of the main reasons behind the conflicts.

WAR, ENSLAVEMENT, AND HUMAN DISPLACEMENT

On a day in late September 1841 Reverend James Frederick Schön, visiting the town of Egga in Nupe, came across a shed "about twenty feet long and ten feet wide, full of people."[81] Upon entering and questioning the Hausa-speaking man who seemed to be in charge, he found out that 15 of those inside—12 women and three children—had been seized in war by the Fulani. The Hausa-speaking man in charge told Schön that he was not the owner of the slaves, but an agent charged with selling them. At that moment, he said, very few slaves remained. He then suggested that due to the lack of demand those in the shed would not be sold locally and that instead they would have to be sent to the slave market of Rabba, the largest in the region, where they would almost certainly be promptly purchased.[82]

---

[78] Johnson, *The History of the Yorubas*, 264–6.

[79] Johnson, *The History of the Yorubas*, 266–8; Augustus Mockler-Ferryman, *Up the Niger* (London: G. Phillip & Son, 1892), 172–3; Smith, *Kingdoms of the Yoruba*, 146–8; Law, *The Oyo Empire*, 294–6.

[80] Law, *The Oyo Empire*, 295.

[81] *Journals of the Rev. James Frederick Schön and Mr. Samuel Crowther who, with the Sanction of Her Majesty's Government accompanied the Expedition up the Niger, in 1841* (London: Hatchard and Son, 1842), 176.

[82] *Journals of the Rev. James Frederick Schön and Mr. Samuel Crowther*, 176–7.

The 12 women and three children found by Schön were by no means an unusual sight. The numerous military conflicts that plagued the interior of the Bight of Benin in the first half of the nineteenth century had an elevated human toll. Undoubtedly, along with the hegemonic ambitions of states such as Sokoto, Borno, and Dahomey, the need for slaves to supply the transatlantic and transaharan slave trades was at the very center of each of them. The repercussions of these wars were felt across Western and Central Sudan and throughout the Atlantic states. Fleeing groups of men, women, and children were forced to go from dwelling to dwelling in search for new homes and shelter, after theirs had been plundered, raided, and on occasion burned down to the ground. Often, displaced men and children as young as 13 or 14 years old joined regular armies or small gangs they found on their way, and started raiding and attacking more villages, contributing this way to the reproduction of the same cycle of death, displacement, and slavery that they had been victims of.[83]

Social and kinship networks were frequently broken down. Relatives and friends were torn apart, and sometimes sent in opposite directions to never see each other again. Some other luckier cases would be sent to distant places together, while others would be left behind to wonder about their fate. In some extraordinary cases a few would be able to reacquaint themselves with their relatives by returning to their homes after spending years in distant lands. In other even more exceptional cases, as happened to two Lucumí brothers in Havana in the 1830s, they would have the most improbable of encounters and would come face-to-face with their long-gone beloved relatives on the streets of a city on the other side of the ocean where they both had been sent as slaves.[84]

In many of these military conflicts women and children played central roles, which they would then repeat in their new homes after their Atlantic journeys. According to Bolanle Awe and Omatayo Olutoye in the Bight of Benin and its interior, "women had always featured in all phases of hostilities" and those who led men were often "women of distinction and noble birth."[85] This opinion is shared by other scholars, like T. M. Ilesanmi, who referred to an instance of warfare that occurred in the nineteenth century when a Fulani army attacked the Ijesa city of Ilesa at a time when only the women and children were in it. According to Ilesanmi, the Ijesa women laid a trap for the Fulani cavalry, and once they had fallen in it, they "pounced on the injured raiders and killed thousands of them with their waving rods."[86] Another story recounted by Fuso Afolayan refers to Tinubu of Abeokuta who, also in the nineteenth century, upon seeing her city under siege "dressed like a warrior . . . rallied the people, mobilized her numerous slaves and

[83] Olatunji Ojo, "Child Slaves in Pre-colonial Nigeria, c.1725–1860," *Slavery & Abolition*, 33:3 (2012): 417–34.

[84] "Cuban Slaves in England," *Anti-Slavery Reporter and Aborigines' Friend*, 2:10 (1854): 234–9.

[85] Bolanle Awe and Omatayo Olutoye, "Women and Warfare in 19th Century Yorubaland: An Introduction," in Adeagbo Akinjogbin, ed., *War and Peace in Yorubaland, 1793–1893* (Ibadan: Heinemann Educational Books, 1998), 124.

[86] T. M. Ilesanmi, "The Yoruba Worldview on Women and Warfare," in Toyin Falola and Robin Law, eds., *Warfare and Diplomacy in Precolonial Nigeria* (Madison: African Studies Program, University of Wisconsin-Madison, 1992), 89.

other supporters" before "marching at the head of the army" against their attackers.[87] Evidence about women's involvement in warfare across the Yoruba-speaking states can also be derived from the accounts of some visitors to the region from the 1820s onwards. As Law has pointed out, after passing through Oyo-Ile in 1829 John Lander commented about the Aláàfin's wives who could be seen "armed with spears."[88]

Nevertheless, it was in neighboring Dahomey where women's role in warfare was taken to another level. There, at least from the eighteenth century, there had been female army corps, who had been armed with muskets and cutlasses. These female corps usually referred to as the Dahomean amazons or *mino*, a term that literally meant "our mothers," went to battle at least from the mid-nineteenth century, although differing opinions exist about whether their participation in organized warfare dates to the late eighteenth century. What seems certain is that after the *coup d'état* of 1818 that brought Ghezo to power, they were reorganized and their roles as regular troops were firmly established.[89]

Equally, children and teenagers were consistently employed in warfare during this period, frequently against their own wishes. In his article on children and slavery in pre-colonial Nigeria, Olatunji Ojo has discussed how enslaved children became, among other things, soldiers. In Ojo's opinion, across the interior of the Bights of Benin and Biafra, warfare had created "enough distrust to warrant military draft and child soldiering." He has also pointed out how in Oyo, "platoons of child soldiers called *jamaa* and *Ogo weere*", were deployed in conflicts of a military nature.[90]

The Fulani-led *jihād*, the wars in Nupe, Dahomey, and especially the persistent processes of war and enslavement that affected Oyo throughout these years led to the institutionalization of an endemic type of violence in all these territories. The demand for slaves to supply the markets was a crucial reason for the continual reproduction of conflict across the region. While war and raids constituted the main two ways of enslavement throughout the first half of the nineteenth century, they were not by any means the only ones. The most thorough study of the possible forms of falling into bondage produced at the time was carried out in Freetown by German linguist Sigismund Koelle in the late 1840s and early 1850s. Koelle interviewed at least 179 ex-slaves who had resettled in Sierra Leone after being liberated by the British authorities there. A second set of interviews was carried out, almost simultaneously, by the French Consul in Salvador de Bahia, Francis de Castelnau. Based on these two studies, and with the support of other sources, scholars have been able to look into the ways in which West Africans were enslaved

---

[87] Funso Afolayan, "Women and Warfare in Yorubaland during the Nineteenth Century," in Falola and Law, eds., *Warfare and Diplomacy*, 80.

[88] Robin Law, "The 'Amazons' of Dahomey," *Paideuma*, 39 (1993): 247.

[89] See e.g. Law, "The 'Amazons' of Dahomey," 245–60; Stanley B. Alpern, "On the Origin of the Amazons of Dahomey," *History in Africa*, 25 (1998): 9–25; Alpern, *Amazons of Black Sparta: The Women Warriors of Dahomey* (London: C. Hurst & Co., 1998); and Edna G. Bay, *Wives of the Leopard: Gender, Politics, and Culture in the Kingdom of Dahomey* (Charlottesville: University of Virginia Press, 1998), 198 onwards.

[90] Ojo, "Child Slaves in Pre-colonial Nigeria," 425–6.

and to draw some preliminary conclusions that point to a number of main reasons, including warfare, kidnapping, debt, and criminal punishment, among others.[91]

When in the early 1850s the ex-slave Wuene, or as he was now called William Cole of Freetown agreed to be interviewed by Koelle, he provided him with a glimpse of how some of the events discussed in this chapter had changed his life. When he was around 25 years old Wuene was forced to join the Bussa army that under the command of Gajere rushed to the support of Aláàfin Oluewu. Until that moment Wuene had had a regular and peaceful life in his hometown of Kaiama. Suddenly, however, he found himself a soldier in Gajere's army and a combatant at the battle of Ilorin, where he was taken prisoner and enslaved. After being sent to the coast Wuene found himself a slave on a vessel bound for the Americas that was seized by a ship of the British West African squadron. Ultimately, he was liberated by the Mixed Commission Court of Freetown, where he was still living several years after his ordeal took place.[92]

Among those interviewed by Koelle in Freetown there were many others who shed light on the many ways in which the wars that plagued the Central Sudan and the Yoruba-speaking states during those years affected men, women, and children. Many had been forced to join armies assembled to attack others in the search for slaves. Among these were Adamu, a Fulani from Kano who had been enslaved in 1845 during a war expedition against the Maladis, and Abali, a native of Borno who joined an expedition against one of the Hausa kingdoms where he was taken prisoner, and subsequently sent to Lagos. Some others among Koelle's informants had been enslaved by invading forces, while many others had been kidnapped to be sold as slaves in the ports of the Bights.[93]

That the wars that affected the Central Sudan and the Yoruba-speaking states from the early 1800s onwards produced the largest percentage of the slaves sent to Bahia and Cuba seems to be quite clear. Among those interviewed by Koelle, many of whom were natives of this region, 34 percent were prisoners of war, while another 30 percent were victims of kidnapping, usually carried out by small armies and raiding parties, also associated with the demands of the slave trade. Clapperton reported how the arrival of a Brazilian brig in Badagry had spurred the people of Ijanna to go on a slaving expedition against the neighboring town of Tabbo.[94] Slave raids and expeditions like this were widespread throughout the area as many of the surviving testimonies attest to.

Most of the Africans interviewed by French Consul Francis de Castelnau in Salvador in 1848 had been soldiers too. Mahammah, a Hausa known as Manuel in Bahia, had joined an army sent by the "Sultan of Kano" against the Zande people. Mahammah was part of the vanguard of the army, and confessed to have killed many

[91] See e.g. Philip Curtin and Jan Vansina, "Sources of the Nineteenth Century Atlantic Slave Trade," *Journal of African History*, 5:2 (1964): 185–208; P. E. H. Hair, "The Enslavement of Koelle's Informants," *Journal of African History*, 6:2 (1965): 193–203; Michael A. Gomez, *Black Crescent: The Experience and Legacy of African Muslims in the Americas* (Cambridge: Cambridge University Press, 2005), 117–18.
[92] Hair, "The Enslavement of Koelle's Informants," 197.
[93] Hair, "The Enslavement of Koelle's Informants," 195–9.
[94] Clapperton and Lander, *Journal of a Second Expedition*, 39.

enemies. He was finally made prisoner sometime afterward during another military expedition against Borgu, and taken down to Lagos via Ilorin and Ogbomoso.[95] Similar stories were told to Castelnau by Braz, another Hausa captured by the Oyo; Karo, a native of Borno seized by the Hausa; and notably by Boué or Bawa, a Hausa who admitted spending his entire life waging war against the "neighboring countries" before being himself apprehended and sold as a slave.[96]

As mentioned before, war and kidnapping were not, however, the only means of enslavement in the region at the time. The wars, the breakdown in family units, and the need for survival all combined to create a situation in which even relatives and friends would on occasion sell or entice their own into slavery. Some of those interviewed by Koelle confessed to have been sold into slavery by relatives or superiors. There were, for example, the cases of Fije and Dose, both from Mahi, north of Dahomey, who had been sold by their uncle and elder brother respectively as a result of domestic disputes, and also that of Aboyade from Ogbomoso, who had been sold by "a war-chief because he refused to give him his wife."[97]

Judicial processes and debt were also common reasons for the enslavement and sale of civilians.[98] Koelle had the opportunity to encounter a number of liberated Africans in Freetown who had been enslaved "on account of adultery"; among them there were men from Ijebu, Anfue, and Igala.[99] Following Clapperton's narrative Lovejoy has shown how criminal women in the Hausa-speaking territories seemed to have been frequently "sent to the coast for sale to the Americas."[100] Other examples were those of two men interviewed by Koelle, Oga from Gbeku and Tete from Dahomey, who had been sold due to debts they had contracted and which they were unable to repay.[101]

In the particular cases of northern Oyo, Sokoto, Borgu, Nupe, and Borno, males constituted the vast majority of those sent towards the coast. In a statistical study of the trade in the area in the first half of the nineteenth century based on a sample that included, among others the Africans interviewed by Castelnau and Koelle, Lovejoy has concluded that over 95 percent of those enslaved and sent towards the Bights in these years were men. Only three women and two girls (4.6 percent) from the Central Sudan also shared a similar fate.[102] The farther from the Atlantic coast, the likelier enslaved men were to do the journey surrounded by other men.[103] Among those enslaved in and sent to the coast from the southern Yoruba-speaking states and Dahomey, the male–female ratios were much more

[95] Francis de Castelnau, *Renseignements sur l'Afrique Centrale et sur une nation d'hommes à queue qui s'y trouverait* (Paris: Chez P. Bertrand, 1851), 10–25.

[96] Castelnau, *Renseignements*, 26–9 and 40.

[97] Hair, "The Enslavement of Koelle's Informants," 198.

[98] See Paul E. Lovejoy, "Civilian Casualties in the Context of the Trans-Atlantic Slave Trade," in John Laband, ed., *Daily Lives of Civilians in Wartime Africa: From Slavery Days to the Diamond Wars* (Westport, CT: Greenwood Press, 2007), 17–50.

[99] Hair, "The Enslavement of Koelle's Informants," 200.

[100] Lovejoy, "Background to Rebellion: The Origins of Muslim Slaves in Bahia," *Slavery & Abolition*, 15:2 (1994): 165.

[101] Hair, "The Enslavement of Koelle's Informants," 199.

[102] Lovejoy, "Background to Rebellion," 161–2.

[103] Lovejoy, "Background to Rebellion," 162.

balanced, women, while still in a minority, constituting between 38 and 42 percent of all those sent towards the ports.[104] The records of the Mixed Commission Court of Havana confirm the imbalance between males and females. Some of the vessels from the ports of the Bight of Benin for which sex percentages are available confirm a strong male preponderance, for example the ships *Mágico* (1826), 60.5 percent males; *Midas* (1829), 53.8 percent males; *Voladora* (1829), 70.3 percent males; *Indagadora* (1832), 91 percent males; *Negrito* (1832), 76.7 percent males; *Manuelita* (1833), 86.5 percent males; *Rosa* (1834), 60.3 percent males; *Julita* (1835), 70.9 percent males; *Tita* (1835), 65.6 percent males; and *Serra do Pilar* (1839), 55.6 percent males.[105] Additionally, when looking at the one group that can be accounted for as being from the north of Oyo (or farther north, i.e. Nupe), the Lucumí Tapa, the results are even clearer. Out of 82 Lucumí Tapa recorded by the Havana Mixed Commission Court between 1829 and 1835, 56 were male (68.3 percent). The consequences of the prevalence of males who were also often soldiers, were soon felt in both Bahia and Cuba, and will be discussed at length in the second part of this book.

CONCLUSIONS

From the late eighteenth century onwards the Bight of Benin and its interior were in a constant state of warfare that lasted many decades. Classic predatory states fought each other, more often than not for reasons intrinsically related to the control of the slave trade routes and markets.

That the slave trade was so intricately organized by the end of the eighteenth century from the Sahel to the Bights could help to explain why when the numbers of enslaved persons in the region increased after the beginning of the *jihād* and the wars in the Yoruba-speaking states the networks did not collapse but rather were ready and able to expand. Instead, Oyo was swiftly replaced as a slave exporter by Sokoto and Borno in the north, and by Dahomey and Ijebu Ode in the south.

Several large battles were fought by regular armies during this period. Some of them defined the boundaries of old states and constituted foundational elements in the creation of new ones. The battles fought in the north, beyond the thick forests, included both infantry and cavalry. In the south, however, infantry prevailed because hand-to-hand combat was practically the only way of fighting, and because horses there were more prone to falling victim to the animal trypanosomiasis caused by the tsetse fly.

Whereas large historically recorded battles were a common feature of the history of these peoples, small-scale raiding and brigandage, almost always associated with the enslavement of men, women, and children were likely the main source of slaves for the transatlantic slave trade. The bands of makeshift soldiers formed by Hausa-speaking ex-slaves based in Ilorin, the swarms of Oyo, Owu, and Egba refugees, and even the organized, but in the field rogue-like troops commanded

---

[104] Lovejoy, "Background to Rebellion," 163.   [105] <http://www.slavevoyages.org>.

by some of the flag bearers of the Shehu, enslaved many more across Oyo and the Central Sudan than major battles probably ever did.

In this respect, the predatory model delineated by Hubbell while examining the Sudanic states of the period, could be also applied to the countless number of individuals who lived for and profited from the supply of slaves for the region's markets. Those seized and sent towards the coast left behind a rapidly changing war-torn world. Although some of the actual dates of some of the events they lived through are still a matter of discussion, undoubtedly almost all of the slaves sent towards the coast were direct or indirect victims of small- and large-scale warfare. In more than one way, then, the identities of these men, women, and children were defined by more than their enslaved status. They were not only slaves, but also war prisoners and refugees, and it is as such that I intend to examine their actions in Bahia and Cuba in Chapters 4 and 5 of this book.

2

Between Home and the Sea
The West African Slave Trade to Bahia
and Cuba, 1790–1843

Whydah is now frequented only by the Brazilians and Spaniards who have
since 1819 carried on a great trade in Slaves.

Hugh Clapperton, 1825

In the last week of November 1825 Captain Hugh Clapperton landed in the slave
trading port of Badagry. After spending a short amount of time there Clapperton
and his entourage headed north, towards Oyo and Sokoto through the Egbado
trade corridor, the main slave trade road towards Oyo at the time.[1] The preference
for the Egbado among slave trading parties at the time had been a result of a series
of events that had occurred over the previous decades, which had led to the relocation of this main route towards the east time and again. As a matter of fact, when
Clapperton passed through it, the Egbado trade corridor was just a stage in a much
longer route; one that could often start in the sands of the Western and Central
Sudan and end up on remote plantations in the hinterland of northeastern Brazil
or western Cuba.[2]

In this chapter, I discuss the practice of the slave trade to Bahia and Cuba in the
first half of the nineteenth century, and offer a reassessment of the impact that processes and forms of enslavement and the transportation to the coast, and across the
Atlantic, had on the shaping of plantation societies on the other side of the ocean.
I also re-examine the figures of this trade with the purpose of making sense of
the numbers of the trade to Bahia and Cuba through statistical and demographic
methods. My ultimate goal is to engage with ongoing scholarly discussions around
the origins of the enslaved men, women, and children who were sent to Bahia and
Cuba from the ports of the Slave Coast. Who these men, women, and children
were and what sort of experience they were forced to endure, from the moment
of enslavement to their arrival in the New World, are questions that I intend to
address here to reveal how these origins—and all the cultural traits associated with

---

[1] Lockhart and Lovejoy, eds., *Hugh Clapperton into the Interior of Africa*, 93.
[2] The Egbado corridor was essentially part of a larger route that linked Sokoto with the Atlantic
ports; the one that Sultan Muhammad Bello referred to as a "line of trade with Christians between
Yarba (Yoruba) and Atagara." See Figure 2.1.

them—were, in fact, the common cohesive element that made the Bahian and Cuban cases so special and alike.

SLAVE TRADE FROM THE INTERIOR TO THE COAST

For many of those who were unfortunate enough to be taken away from their loved ones and sent towards the coast and across the ocean, the journey was neither easy nor quick. Slave trading routes in the area had existed for centuries and had overlapped with the routes followed by caravans, some of which had been in place for a much longer time. These routes had always been under the recurring threat of war and raids. Scholars of the Yoruba have discussed time and again how the main road to the Slave Coast was moved eastwards on a number of occasions throughout the eighteenth century.[3] The route went originally from its capital Oyo-Ile towards and around the Kumi swamps, and from there towards Ketu before reaching the ocean at Whydah. Morton-Williams, argued that this route was relocated by the Aláàfin of Oyo after Dahomey attacked and sacked Old Allada in 1724, to which Smith plausibly added that a break in the forest must have conveniently allowed the Oyo cavalry to accompany and protect the slave caravans that marched towards the coast, east of Whydah.[4]

Later in the century the route was moved eastward as a consequence of the constant threats coming from the kingdom of Dahomey. This new route, now under the control of Oyo, passed east of the Kumi swamps, and then through Ketu and the newly founded kingdom of Ifonyin or Anago towards the ports of Badagry and Porto Novo.[5] Thanks to this new route the kingdom of Ketu profited like no other from the slave trade throughout the eighteenth century, although it is fair to assert that its people were also occasionally enslaved and sent to the coast in the process.

Despite the changes affecting these routes, the two main ports where they ended, Whydah and Porto Novo, would still play a significant role in the transatlantic slave trade during the first half of the nineteenth century.[6] Whydah was probably the most important port of the Slave Coast, at least until the rise of Lagos in the nineteenth century; even then, under King Ghezo, his Chacha, or viceroy in Whydah, Francisco Felix de Souza and his slave trading partners, the human traffic there continued to prosper until the Brazilians finally abolished the slave trade in the middle

---

[3] See e.g. Smith, *Kingdoms of the Yoruba*; Morton-Williams, "The Oyo Yoruba," 25–45; Law, *The Oyo Empire*; Kola Folayan, "Trade Routes in Egbado in the Nineteenth Century," in I. A. Akinjogbin and Segun Osoba, eds., *Topics in Nigerian Economic and Social History* (Ile Ife: University of Ife Press, 1980), 83–95; and Lockhart and Lovejoy, eds., *Hugh Clapperton into the Interior of Africa*, 41–2.

[4] Morton-Williams, "The Oyo Yoruba," 29; and Smith, *Kingdoms of the Yoruba*, 45–6.

[5] Morton-Williams, "The Oyo Yoruba," 30–4; Smith, *Kingdoms of the Yoruba*, 45–6.

[6] Robin Law, *Ouidah: The Social History of a West African Slaving Port* (Athens, OH, and Oxford: Ohio University Press and James Currey, 2004); Catherine Coquery-Vidrovitch, *The History of African Cities South of the Sahara* (Princeton: Markus Wiener, 2005), 140–90; Paul E. Lovejoy, *Transformations in Slavery: A History of Slavery in Africa* (Cambridge: Cambridge University Press, 1983), 81–3, 100–2; John K. Thornton, *Warfare in Atlantic Africa, 1500–1800* (London: UCL Press, 1999), 78–9.

part of the century. In 1844 French Vice Admiral Charles Baudin reported on "the rich Spanish, Portuguese and Brazilian slave traders" who dominated a considerable part of the slave trade in the Bight of Benin from their Whydah headquarters.[7]

Porto Novo was situated on the north side of the lagoon, just under 50 miles east of Whydah. During the eighteenth century Porto Novo was a populous town which benefited almost as much as Whydah from the slave trade with the Europeans. This was particularly the case in the late part of the eighteenth century, when the route was moved east. During his visit to Porto Novo in the last decade of the eighteenth century Captain John Adams was keen to notice that the road to Oyo—where the slaves would come from—began just outside the city, "at the northwest extremity of the town."[8] Due to its proximity to Whydah, Porto Novo was recurrently subject to pressure from Dahomey. Not surprisingly, whenever the relations were tense, the slave trade there was affected, to the benefit of other neighboring ports, in particular Lagos.[9]

As the eighteenth century came to an end, the old route to Badagry via Egbado was retaken as a result of a series of occurrences that began with the renewed attempts of Dahomey to break Oyo's authority in the 1770s and culminated in the destruction of Badagry in 1784. As we have seen in the previous chapter, only a few years after these events took place, Oyo's Aláàfin Awole was forced to commit suicide, and the insubordination of the Are-Ona-Kakanfo Afonja in the north of Oyo brought about a long-lasting period of political instability that eventually led to the end of the empire. The new trading route—the Egbado trade corridor—would be under direct control of the Aláàfin of Oyo and would go southwards from Oyo, passing some important towns such as Saki, Ijanna, Ilaro, Ihumbo, and Ipokia before reaching the lagoon system at either Porto Novo or over time to the rebuilt and thriving port of Badagry.[10] This important port was located on the north side of this interior body of water, almost halfway between Porto Novo and Lagos.[11] When Clapperton and Lander visited Badagry in the mid-1820s the town was quite busy and the slave trade booming. A number of Portuguese, or more likely Brazilian slave traders were in residence and in full control of the slave trade there. Lander mentioned the existence of five factories in Badagry, where "upwards of one thousand slaves of both sexes, chained by the neck to each other" were waiting to be embarked.[12]

---

[7] Admiral Baudin to the Minister of Maritime and Colonial Affairs. Gorée, 12 November 1844. CAOM: FM-GEN 166/1341.

[8] John Adams, *Remarks on the Country Extending from Cape Palmas to the River Congo, including observations on the manners and customs of the inhabitants* (London: G. and W. B. Whittaker, 1823), 78.

[9] Pierre Verger, *Flux et reflux de la traite des Nègres entre le Golfe de Bénin et Bahia de Todos os Santos du XVIIe au XIXe siècle* (Paris: Mouton & Co. and École Pratique des Hautes Études, 1968), 271; Robin Law, "Trade and Politics behind the Slave Coast: The Lagoon Traffic and the Rise of Lagos, 1500–1800," *Journal of African History*, 24:3 (1983): 346.

[10] Morton-Williams, "The Oyo Yoruba," 37–41; Smith, *Kingdoms of the Yoruba*, 45–6; Caroline Sorensen-Gilmour, "Slave Trading along the Lagoons of South West Nigeria: The Case of Badagry," in Robin Law and Silke Strickrodt, eds., *Ports of the Slave Trade (Bights of Benin and Biafra)* (Stirling: Centre of Commonwealth Studies—University of Stirling, 1999), 84–95.

[11] "A Brief History of Badagry," c.1853. NA-UK: FO, 84/920.

[12] Richard Lander, *Records of Captain Clapperton's Last Expedition to Africa* (London: Henry Colburn and Richard Bentley, 1830), 286.

Finally, another route towards the coast that existed throughout the period passed through Ijebu Ode and the market town of Apomu, reaching the lagoon at Ikorodu or Ikosi on the lagoon, opposite of Lagos.[13] This route, sometimes referred to as the Remo Corridor, in its longer version passed through Ife, Ibadan—after its transformation into a major urban center in the late 1820s—and then went south towards the "western portion of Ijebu to the port of Ikorodu, whence across the lagoon to Lagos."[14] Lagos, also known as Onim and Eko, was undoubtedly the most important port in the area after the turn of the century. Originally a minor enclave under the authority of the powerful state of Benin and eclipsed by other ports like Whydah, Porto Novo, and Badagry, Lagos benefited from the several controls exercised on the trade at Whydah, and from the conflicts that affected the others. Lagos was situated on the south side of the lagoon, near its entrance. According to Robin Law, its "central position within the lagoon system, between the important kingdoms of Allada (and later, Dahomey) to the west and Ijebu and Benin to the east,"[15] was the main reason for its rise from the 1790s onwards. One thing that characterized Lagos traders was their policy of avoidance of the middlemen that were a common feature elsewhere along the Slave Coast.[16] Captain John Adams reported that these traders would "go in their canoes to Ardrah and Badagry, and to the towns situated in the NE. extremity of Cradoo lake" (i.e. Ijebu) where they would purchase the slaves that they would then supply to the Europeans.[17]

Although these routes served as channels for the bulk of the slave trade in the area, they were by no means the only ones. For generations the river Niger was also an important outlet. Ilorin (Affaga) and the ports of Rabba and Rakka seem to have been used for many years as points for assembling the caravans of slaves gathered in the area north of Oyo that were sent towards the coast.[18] Nupe merchants were probably the main traders in some of these places, or at least they were in the main port of Rabba. Based on Hugh Clapperton's notes and on a number of stories of enslavement that have survived it is possible to conclude that also Hausa-speakers, Bariba, and Oyo merchants were involved in sending slaves overland and possibly down the river towards the ocean.[19] In January 1824 Clapperton overheard a conversation between his servant and an envoy from Katagum concerning the port of Rakka and the slave trade in the river Niger. One of the things he heard was that Christian ships used to visit the

---

[13] Robert S. Smith, *The Lagos Consulate, 1851–1861* (Berkeley and Los Angeles: University of California Press, 1979); Lovejoy, *Transformations in Slavery*, 165, 177, and 257–8; Coquery-Vidrovitch, *The History of African Cities*, 252–4, 307–10, 328–9, and 373–4; Law, "Trade and Politics," 321–48.

[14] J. D. Y. Peel, *Religious Encounter and the Making of the Yoruba* (Bloomington: Indiana University Press, 2000), 39.

[15] Law, "Trade and Politics," 322.

[16] Adams, *Remarks*, 96. Law, "Trade and Politics," 322–3.   [17] Adams, *Remarks*, 96.

[18] Tambo, "The Sokoto Caliphate Slave Trade," 203–5; Hubbell, "A View of the Slave Trade from the Margin," 26–9; Anne O'Hear, "Ilorin as a Slaving and Slave Trade Emirate," in Paul E. Lovejoy, ed., *Slavery on the Frontiers of Islam* (Princeton: Markus Wiener, 2004), 56–7; Femi J. Kolapo, "The Southward Campaigns of Nupe in the Lower Niger Valley," in Lovejoy, ed., *Slavery on the Frontiers of Islam*, 69–86; and Law and Lovejoy, "Borgu in the Atlantic Slave Trade," 69–92.

[19] O'Hear, "Ilorin as a Slaving and Slave Trade Emirate," 56–7; Kolapo, "The Southward Campaigns," 69–86.

town to trade there; almost certainly one of the main "items" of trade, if not the principal, must have been slaves.[20]

Other important slave trade routes in the area were, much like the one across the river Niger was after the second decade of the century, strongly linked with the rising and establishment of the Sokoto Caliphate. When Clapperton visited Sokoto in the mid-1820s he was received by Sultan Muhammad Bello, whom he eventually persuaded to commit to the abolition of the slave trade. In his letter to the king of England Sultan Bello agreed to "prohibit the exportation of slaves by our merchants to Atagher, Dahomi and Ashantee."[21] Of these Atagher corresponds to Atagara or Idah, a town on the eastern banks of the Niger, referred to as a main point of trade with the Christians by Mohammed Bello's map (Figure 2.1).[22] The bare

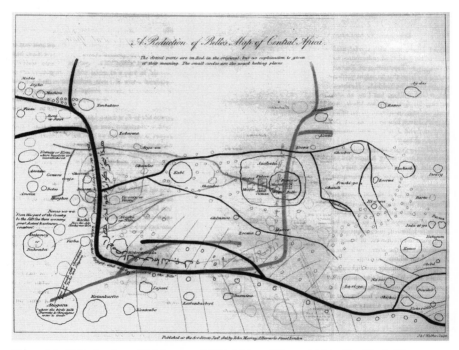

Figure 2.1 "A Reduction of [Mohammed] Bello's Map of Central Africa," by Hugh Clapperton. Courtesy of The Irvin Department of Rare Books and Special Collections, University of South Carolina Libraries. Originally published in Denham, *Narrative*, 1828.

---

[20] Dixon Denham et al., *Narrative of Travels and Discoveries in Northern and Central Africa in the Years 1822, 1823 and 1824*, ii: *From Murmur to Kano* (London: John Murray, 1828), 269.

[21] Muhammad Bello to King George IV. Sokoto, 18 April 1824. In Lockhart and Lovejoy, eds., *Hugh Clapperton into the Interior of Africa*, 58.

[22] See Bruce Lockhart and Lovejoy, eds., *Hugh Clapperton into the Interior of Africa*, 58. In Bello's map, printed in 1826, Atagara is described as the place "where the birds talk (Parrots) & Christians come to Trade." See Figure 2.1.

mention of the other two constitutes proof of the prosperous trade that, sponsored by Sokoto and Gwandu, was being conducted across Western and Central Sudan between cities such as Ilorin and Kano, through Borgu and Salaga and towards the kingdoms of Dahomey and Asante, both situated to the southwest and both places where the slave trade was thriving at the time.[23] Famously, Clapperton himself came across a group of merchants from Dahomey while he was visiting Borgu in 1826. Although they told him that they had been in Wawa for five months assisting the king of Yauri in his fight against the Fulani, these merchants were as a matter of fact slave traders who had been buying slaves in both Wawa and Yauri with the intention of taking them back to Dahomey.[24] Another significant example of this trade towards Dahomey and Asante is that of the previously mentioned Boué or Antonio, a Hausa interviewed by French Consul Francis de Castelnau in Bahia in the late 1840s, who after being enslaved was taken to the Gold Coast via Nupe and Kumasi.[25]

The slave trade from the interior of the Bight of Benin towards the coast was, then, far from a straightforward business, both in financial and geographical terms. Men, women, and children who were enslaved anywhere between Egbaland and Owu in the south and Borno, Gwandu, and Sokoto in the north could find themselves embarking on a lengthy and difficult journey that could take them through roads and rivers across vast parts of West Africa. In addition to the main routes there was a considerable number of what Toyin Falola has called "feeder routes" that criss-crossed the region in all directions.[26]

After being captured the destinies of these men, women, and children still depended on a number of factors and random decisions made by the most diverse people. For example, they could become domestic or plantation slaves somewhere in the Yoruba-speaking or Hausa-speaking territories;[27] they could be sent northwards towards the Ottoman Mediterranean World through the notoriously harsh Borno-Fezzan transaharan route—followed and documented by Clapperton in his first travel to the area—or through the apparently more secure Kano-Aïr-Ghadames

---

[23] Law, *Ouidah*, 28–9, 40–1, and 73–5; and Robin Law, "Central and Eastern Wangara: An Indigenous West African Perception of the Political and Economic Geography of the Slave Coast as Recorded by Joseph Dupuis in Kumasi, 1820," *History in Africa*, 22 (1995): 281–305; Coquery-Vidrovitch, *The History of African Cities*, 167–76; David Ross, "The Dahomean Middleman System, 1727–c.1818," *Journal of African History*, 28:3 (1987): 357–75.

[24] Lockhart and Lovejoy, eds., *Hugh Clapperton into the Interior of Africa*, 182–3; Robin Law, "Slave-Raiders and Middlemen, Monopolists and Free-Traders: The Supply of Slaves for the Atlantic Trade in Dahomey, c.1715–1850," *Journal of African History*, 30:1 (1989): 58.

[25] Francis de Castelnau, *Renseignements sur l'Afrique Centrale et sur une nation d'hommes à queue qui s'y trouverait* (Paris: Chez P. Bertrand, 1851), 40.

[26] Toyin Falola, "The Yoruba Caravan System of the Nineteenth Century," *International Journal of African Historical Studies*, 24:1 (1991): 125.

[27] Paul E. Lovejoy, "Plantations in the Economy of the Sokoto Caliphate," *Journal of African History*, 19:3 (1978): 341–68; and "Polanyi's 'Ports of Trade': Salaga and Kano in the Nineteenth Century," *Canadian Journal of African Studies/Revue canadienne des études africaines*, 16:2 (1982): 251, 268, and 272; Tambo, "The Sokoto Caliphate Slave Trade," 199–200; Stilwell, "Power, Honour and Shame," 396–7; and Ibrahim Hamza, "Slavery and Plantation Society at Dorayi in Kano Emirate," in Lovejoy, ed., *Slavery on the Frontiers of Islam*, 125–48.

route;[28] or, alternatively, they could be dispatched to the coast via the Gold Coast, Dahomey, Oyo, Benin, and as far as the ports of Lagos, Bonny, and Warri.

As noted in Chapter 1, there were several ways of falling into bondage in and around Oyo. Be it by military defeat, by war or slave raids, by debt, or by any other means of enslavement, men, women, and children were often traded at busy markets scattered throughout the territories and serving every existing trading route. In these markets their fate was frequently decided by who their buyers were. It does not seem to have been uncommon that once enslaved, a person could pass from one master to another within short periods of time. Certainly the narratives of Ali Eisami, Samuel Ajayi Crowther, and Joseph Wright indicate that this was often the case.[29]

As a direct consequence of the relentless advance of Sokoto and the escalating internal wars that engulfed Oyo by the 1820s slave markets were thriving with newly enslaved men, women, and children all across the region. During his first visit to Kano in 1824 Clapperton described the slave market there, commenting in detail about some of its features:

> The slave market is held in two long sheds, one for males, the other for females, where they are seated in rows, and carefully decked out for the exhibition; the owner, or one of his trusty slaves, sitting near them. Young or old, plump or withered, beautiful or ugly, are sold without distinction.[30]

The situation must have been quite similar in most of the major cities in the Bight of Benin. In his comparison of the markets of Salaga and Kano, Lovejoy stressed that "slaves were a major item of trade"[31] in both of them, and according to Anne O'Hear, after turning into an emirate, Ilorin had also become "a major slave-trading center" and by the middle of the nineteenth century "was reported to have the largest slave market in the region."[32] At least five of the Africans interviewed by Francis de Castelnau in Bahia in the 1840s had been enslaved in northern Oyo and taken to Ilorin on their way down to the bights.[33]

Slave markets also prospered within Oyo and some of its former territories. Among them those of Ijaye, Iseyin, and Igboho continued to trade well during this period. Iseyin in particular thrived after falling into the sphere of influence of

[28] Falola, "The Yoruba Caravan System of the Ninteenth Century," 113–14; A. Adu Boahen, "The Caravan Trade in the Nineteenth Century," *Journal of African History*, 3:2 (1962): 350–2; Ghislaine Lydon, *On Transaharan-Trails: Islamic Law, Trade Networks and Cross-Cultural Exchange in Nineteenth-Century West Africa* (Cambridge: Cambridge University Press, 2009), 122–5; and Michael La Rue, "The Frontiers of Enslavement: Bagirmi and the Trans-Saharan Slave Routes," in Lovejoy, ed., *Slavery on the Frontiers of Islam*, 31–54. For the Bornu–Fezzan route see: B. G. Martin, "Kanem, Bornu, and the Fazzan: Notes on the Political History of a Trade Route," *Journal of African History*, 10:1 (1969): 15–27; Montana, *The Abolition of Slavery in Ottoman Tunisia*.
[29] Philip D. Curtin, ed., *Africa Remembered: Narratives by West Africans from the Era of the Slave Trade* (Madison: University of Wisconsin Press, 1967).
[30] Denham et al., *Narrative of Travels and Discoveries*, ii: *From Murmur to Kano*, 10 February 1924, 287–8.
[31] Lovejoy, "Polanyi's Ports of Trade," 268.
[32] O'Hear, "Ilorin as a Slaving and Slave-Trading Emirate," 56.
[33] Castelnau, *Renseignements*. These were Mahammah or Manuel, Braz or Adam, Osman or Francisco, Grusa or Augusto, and Meidassara, all Hausa.

Ilorin from the second decade of the nineteenth century.[34] Not only was the town used as a base "for extensive raiding" in Ibarapa,[35] but presumably many of the slaves that were captured by Ilorin passed through Iseyin's market while en route to the Bights and, eventually, to the Americas.

With the ever increasing availability of slaves as a result of the jihadists' advances, the Owu wars, and the resurgence of Dahomey under King Ghezo, markets also prospered elsewhere. Olatunji Ojo has shown how after the attack and sacking of Emere, Ikereku, and Itoko by an Ife–Ijebu army reinforced by Oyo refugees in 1825, the prisoners made in these towns were taken to slave markets in Oko and other Ijebu towns, where they were sold and in some cases ransomed by their relatives.[36]

Other than Oko, Ijebu had important markets in the northern town of Oru[37] and to the south near the lagoon at Ikosi. More significantly its capital Ijebu Ode had at the time the largest slave market in the region. Thanks to its strategic position north of the Lagos lagoon, Ijebu managed to wade through the times of crisis in the Yoruba-speaking territories with a relative degree of success. Slave markets in Ijebu were flourishing during this period. As J. D. Y. Peel has argued, by the middle part of the nineteenth century "Ijebu Ode's great slave market, its control of the lagoon ports, its firm foothold in Ibadan. . . and the far-ranging activity of individual Ijebu as traders all made Ijebu the most formidable power in the south."[38]

For those who were sent to the coast, there was one last African leg of the journey before reaching the slave ships. Running parallel to the beaches of the Slave Coast there was a fluvial system often referred to as the lagoon. Most of the factories and ports renowned for sending hundreds of thousands of West Africans to the Americas as slaves were situated not by the ocean, but by this inland waterway, which also included various creeks and channels. All Grand and Little Popo, Whydah, Epe, Porto Novo, Badagry, and Lagos were situated by it. The lagoon was crossed west and east by expert canoemen who were in charge of taking the slaves from one place to another, depending on the shipping requirements existing at any moment; Robin Law has stated that the "lagoons operated in effect as feeders for the maritime trade."[39]

Because of the heavy surf and the sand banks existing alongside the Slave Coast, the role of the lagoon and its canoemen was crucial.[40] They were in charge of

---

[34] Lovejoy, *Identity in the Shadow of Slavery*, 119.   [35] Law, *The Oyo Empire*, 258.

[36] Olatunji Ojo, " '[I]n Search of their Relations, To Set at Liberty as Many as They Had the Means': Ransoming Captives in Nineteenth Century Yorubaland," *Nordic Journal of African Studies*, 19:1 (2010): 62. See also Sylviane A. Diouf, "The Last Resort: Redeeming Family and Friends," in Sylviane A. Diouf, ed., *Fighting the Slave Trade: West African Strategies* (Athens, OH, and Oxford: Ohio University Press and James Currey, 2003), 81–100.

[37] Margaret Thompson Drewal, *Yoruba Rituals: Performance, Play, Agency* (Bloomington: Indiana University Press, 1992), 138.

[38] Peel, *Religious Encounter*, 39.

[39] Robin Law, "Between the Sea and the Lagoon: The Interaction of Maritime and Inland Navigation on the Precolonial Slave Coast," *Cahiers d'études africaines*, 114:29/2 (1989): 222.

[40] The coast was affected by other hazards as well, including a very dangerous eastern current and the well-known sharks. See Markus Rediker, "History from Below the Water Line: Sharks and the Atlantic Slave Trade," *Atlantic Studies*, 5:2 (2008): 285–97.

delivering the slave and provision cargoes to the points of shipment, where other canoemen from the Gold Coast, who were specialists in dealing with the hazards associated with sea navigation, took on the cargoes and loaded them onto the European vessels anchored off the coast. While attempting to return to Europe after his journey to Oyo and Sokoto in the mid-1820s, Lander noticed these canoemen, who "passed repeatedly from Badagry to Cape Coast,"[41] a clear evidence of the intensity with which the trade was carried out at the time.[42] As Law has thoughtfully summarized this process, the "operation of European trade in this region was in fact critically dependent upon African navigational expertise."[43]

The journey from the regions north of Oyo, from Oyo, Igbomina, and Ekiti, from Ife and Owu, or from Ketu, Sabe, and Ijebu to the coast was always, to a larger or a minor extent a harrowing one for those who were enslaved, sold, and forced to march to the coast. Beyond the realm of statistics and the gravity of demographic numbers, the surviving narratives of those who were able to recount their stories of war, raids, and enslavement, tell us of a distressful passage towards the coast, often compounded by misery, hunger, and physical and psychological violence. For many, the journey ended even before arriving at the lagoon and the ocean, while for many others this was barely the beginning.[44] A long and disturbing transatlantic experience lay ahead: the Middle Passage. After that, for the vast majority of those who survived, the cities and plantations of Bahia and Cuba waited.

THE MIDDLE PASSAGE ABOARD SHIPS TO BAHIA AND CUBA: THE HUMAN EXPERIENCE

The transatlantic experience for those who were forced to cross the ocean in chains during the first half of the nineteenth century had a new twist. The triumph of the abolitionist movement in England in the first years of the century led to the Abolition Bill of 1807 and to the subsequent implementation of an international policy conducive to bringing other slave trading countries to join Great Britain in their efforts to suppress the trade. This policy was legitimized by bilateral treaties, by the establishment of Courts of Mixed Commissions, and by the always

[41] Richard Lander, "The Journal of Richard Lander from Kano to the Sea-Coast Partly by a More Eastern Route," in Clapperton and Lander, *Journal of a Second Expedition*, 326.

[42] It must be noticed that by the mid-nineteenth century the palm oil trade began a slow rise in the area. Palm oil would eventually become the main item of trade in the Bight of Benin once the slave trade entered its last period from 1851 onwards. See: Elisée Soumonni, "The Compatibility of the Slave and Palm Oil Trades in Dahomey, 1818–1858," in Robin Law, ed., *From Slave Trade to "Legitimate" Commerce: The Commercial Transition in Nineteenth Century West Africa* (Cambridge: Cambridge University Press, 1995), 78–92; and Martin Lynn, *Commerce and Economic Change in West Africa: The Palm Oil Trade in the Nineteenth Century* (Cambridge: Cambridge University Press, 2002).

[43] Law, "Between the Sea and the Lagoon," 209.

[44] It must be noted here that despite the lack of historical sources dealing with the march towards the coast, there seems to be enough evidence of resistance to enslavement during it. New human settlements appeared in the most remote parts of the lagoon system where those who had run away continued to live their lives after avoiding a life of slavery elsewhere. See Elisée Soumonni, "Lacustrine Villages in South Benin as Refuges from the Slave Trade," in Diouf, ed., *Fighting the Slave Trade*, 3–14.

efficient work of the British Royal Navy. The Middle Passage experience was thus profoundly affected by these new circumstances that made the operations of the slave traders more difficult and insecure. The effects were seen almost immediately, and were apparent from the moment of loading the human cargo to the end of the journey, irrespective of its fate. In particular from 1820 onwards the slave trade was conducted in a secretive manner in order to avoid contact with the ships of the West African, West Indies, and Brazil squadrons.

Once in the Bight of Benin slaves would be branded with the initials of one of those involved in their selling and purchase. It is still difficult to establish whether there was a regular system that could define who and where the initials burned onto the Africans' skins belonged to, because as Walter Hawthorne has recently argued "the branding of slaves is rarely mentioned in documents."[45] The records of the Courts of Mixed Commission in both Freetown and Havana recorded aspects of the newly arrived Africans, but not these marks, although on occasions they were described with words. The situation was different in Rio de Janeiro. There the commissioners took care of reproducing drawings of these branding marks on almost every single occasion. For example, in the case of the schooner *Emilia*, seized by the HMS *Morgiana* under the command of Captain William Finlayson in mid-February 1821 with a cargo of 397 Africans, mostly identified as Nagô, Nupe, and Hausa, the commissioners recorded Christian name, African "nation," branding mark, and where on the body the branding had been applied. All 352 surviving liberated Africans had the same mark (Figures 2.2 and 2.3), which almost certainly meant that they all belonged to the same person in the port of embarkation, Lagos.[46]

After being branded, the slaves would frequently be taken from one place to another inside the lagoon and creeks, that ran parallel to the coast while waiting to be sent to the ships (Figure 2.3). During this time they were kept in miserable conditions. German traveler C. H. Von Zütphen described what he saw while visiting the port of Lagos in 1831:

> The day before embarking these poor human beings can be seen near the river. They have been brought from the forest down the road to Onim. They are taken by the beach towards the barracoons in groups of 30, lined up and chained by their necks, guided by a freeman. From afar they resemble the march of a group of soldiers training, especially because each row stays always close to the next one. Before they are embarked, they are lined up again, all chained, and they look like a division of black demons. In the canoe they are released from their chains, but once they board the ship their feet are shackled again until they lose sight of the coast.[47]

[45] Walter Hawthorne, *From Africa to Brazil: Culture, Identity and an Atlantic Slave Trade* (Cambridge: Cambridge University Press, 2010), 121.

[46] Registro da Provizão do Ouvidor da Comarca do Rio de Janeiro sobre os Escravos Emancipados da Escuna Emilia. 10 July 1821. ANRJ: JC. 184/3. See also "Commissão Mixta no Rio de Janeiro, 1821." ANTT: DNE, 228. See also Walter Hawthorne, "Being now, as it were, one family: Shipmate bonding on the slave vessel Emilia, in Rio de Janeiro and throughout the Atlantic World," *Luso-Brazilian Review*, 45:1 (2008): 53–77.

[47] C. H. Von Zütphen, *Tagebuch einer Reise von Bahia nach Afrika* (Düsseldorf: Schreiner, 1835), 34.

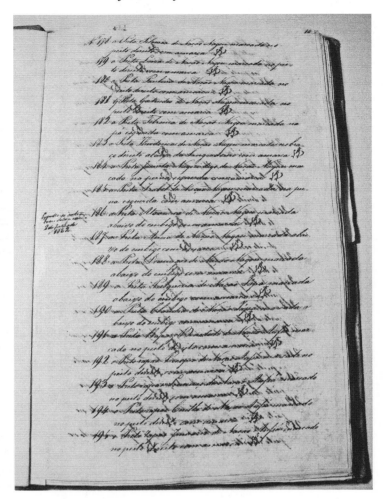

Figure 2.2 Register of the ship *Emilia*, 1821. ANRJ: JC.184/3. Courtesy of the Arquivo Nacional do Rio de Janeiro.

The actual shipping was in itself a daunting experience, especially for the many Africans who had never seen the ocean before and who had to endure the hazards of the notorious Slave Coast's surf. The procedure of loading them on to the ships would be carried out with urgency, usually within a few hours in order to diminish the chances of being spotted by the ships of the British West African Squadron. In his account Von Zütphen also commented how on 20 April 1831 a Spanish schooner had arrived in Lagos at around 8 a.m. with the intention of loading a cargo of slaves. By noon, he wrote, she was already en route to Havana with 429 Africans on board.[48] The ships of the West African Squadron loomed large constantly and the commanding officers

[48] Von Zütphen, *Tagebuch*, 33.

Figure 2.3 Branding mark given to the slaves of the ship *Emilia*, 1821. ANRJ: JC. 184/3. Courtesy of the Arquivo Nacional do Rio de Janeiro.

knew that any vessels found in the vicinity of Lagos, Badagry, Jakin, Porto Novo, Whydah, and Popo were likely to be waiting for the moment to load Africans in a hurry and then rush to Bahia or Cuba. The reports of the officers of the West African Squadron leave no doubt about the *modus operandi* of the slave traders in the Slave Coast. As a matter of fact, these officers had to adapt and refine their skills as the slavers became more and more cunning in their ways.[49]

An article that appeared in a Brazilian newspaper in December 1834 described the conditions in which the slave trade was being conducted since the abolition treaties had begun to be enforced:

> . . . the vessels being subject to search and to heavy penalties, the masters had recourse to every kind of artifice to elude it; at one time concealing the blacks under a load of wood where many were grievously bruised, at another immersing them in tanks of water, and at another putting them into cases where many expired from suffocation, and finally, at another time throwing them overboard to be devoured by fish, or in pipes, in order that, the danger being over, those who escaped with life might be turned to the best account.[50]

During her visit to Bahia in the early 1820s, Maria Graham had the opportunity to meet with William Finlayson, the captain of the HMS *Morgiana*, one of the British ships in charge of patrolling Brazilian waters and seizing slave vessels involved in the transatlantic slave trade. The descriptions she heard and annotated about the conditions in which the Africans had been frequently found by Captain Finlayson were dreadfully similar to the ones described above and confirmed the hardships to which the Africans bound for Bahia and Cuba were frequently exposed:

> Captain Finlaison [*sic*] tells me tales that make my blood run cold, of horrors committed in the French slave ships especially. Of young negresses, headed up in casks and thrown

[49] These deceiving ways were numerous. Slave ships frequently had more than one flag on board; they had fake logbooks and destinations (São Tomé and Príncipe being the favorite ones); and often they got away with a human cargo despite being subjected to inspections from the Royal Navy ships. British ships also developed new tricks to catch the slavers off guard. In his account Von Zütphen recounted how one of the brigs of the British West African Squadron was disguised to look like a Spanish slaver with the intention of seizing a Spanish schooner that was just about to load over 400 Africans. Von Zütphen, *Tagebuch*, 40.

[50] Extract [translated into English] from *O Justiceiro*, St Paulo, 25 December 1834. BPPO. Class A. Correspondence with the British Commissioners, at Sierra Leone, the Havana, Rio de Janeiro, and Surinam, relating to the slave trade. 1835.

overboard, when the ships are chased. Of others, stowed in boxes when a ship was searched, with a bare chance of surviving their confinement.[51]

The enslaved Africans were normally taken below deck where they would be crammed next to each other, spending the next weeks at sea in this way, often suffering from malnutrition and disease. Feeding the Africans taken on board was always a matter of utmost importance. That did not mean, however, that they were properly nourished. Countless reports exist about the mundane quality of the provisions given to the slaves during the Middle Passage. Among the most common were maize, yam, rice, beans, jerked beef, and sometimes spoiled undrinkable water. Mistakes at the time of calculating the amount of food and water that were needed in order to satisfactorily reach the other side of the Atlantic were not unheard of. The Mixed Commission judges and the commanding officers of the Royal Navy ships entrusted to seize slavers on the coasts of Africa, Brazil, and the Caribbean reported on numerous occasions about vessels loaded with starving and thirsty Africans on board. In addition to these shortages of food and water, there were several diseases that made the maladies of the Africans even worse.

Disease was a regular hazard that affected the slaves embarked all along the African continent's coast. Survival depended on the resistance of these men, women, and children to illnesses such as yellow fever, malaria, dysentery, and scurvy, among many others. Smallpox, even well into the nineteenth century, continued to be one of the illnesses with a higher degree of mortality.[52] In these cases, the expertise and talent of the slave trade surgeons could make all the difference between living and dying. Not surprisingly, the combination of all these ailments could lead to large human losses on board the ships. Examples of this kind abounded during this period. Contagious diseases became particularly lethal during this phase of the slave trade, since the slave traders often rushed to load their ships with Africans without checking their health and strength, in an attempt to avoid being captured by the vessels of the West African Squadron. Due to the inhumane conditions to which these men, women, and children were exposed after shipping, contagious diseases regularly spread like wildfire among them.

One case in question was that of the Brazilian schooner *Santo Jago*, captured by the HMS *Medina* in 1830 and taken to Sierra Leone where she was subjected to a thorough inspection by the Court of Mixed Commission surgeon upon arriving in Freetown. The situation of the 209 surviving Africans shipped at Whydah only a few days earlier, according to the surgeon, was desperate. He reported that "they were in a state of extreme debility from bad food and a tedious passage; that 1 was affected with the small-pox; and that about 30 were labouring under severe bowel

---

[51] Maria Graham, *Journal of a Voyage to Brazil and Residence there during Part of the Years 1821, 1822, 1823* (London: Longman, 1824), 151.

[52] From the 1830s slave traders began taking even more precautions with respect to the smallpox. In some cases they would provide the captains of ships bound for the Bights with vaccination kits and medicine chests and would instruct them to vaccinate the slaves bought against the smallpox as soon as possible. See e.g. José Francisco d'Azevedo Lisboa to Manoel José Delgado. Pernambuco, 20 February 1837. BPPO. Class A. Correspondence with the British Commissioners, at Sierra Leone, the Havana, Rio de Janeiro, and Surinam, relating to the slave trade. 1838–9.

complaints, and the dangerous accompanying evil of worms, and that 'craw-craw' prevailed."[53]

Other equally appalling cases were those of the Brazilian brig *Avizo*, seized by the HMS *Maidstone* after taking 467 slaves at Badagry in October 1824. Upon arriving in Sierra Leone, it was noted that 36 Africans had died in the passage, while a large number of those who had survived were "in a most wretched state of suffering from diarrhoea and dysentery."[54] In another case, the Portuguese ship *Legítimo Africano*, was reported to have lost at least 14 of the slaves shipped at Whydah; upon arrival in Sierra Leone the *Legítimo Africano* had several critical cases of dysentery and ophthalmia.[55] Similarly, the Portuguese brigantine *Deixa Falar* was seized by the HMS *Scout* off Lagos in November 1837. By the time of her arrival in Freetown the *Deixa Falar* had lost 24 Africans, most of them from dysentery, while at least 30 others were suffering from the same illness.[56]

The risks now posed by the Royal Navy vessels also led to more inhumane conditions on board, as the slavers found that they needed to maximize profits at any cost. Beyond the horrors associated with any transatlantic journey, the stories about excessive cruelties and mistreatments of the enslaved Africans in some of the ships bound to Bahia and Cuba in this period are truly horrific.

For example, while on her way back to Havana with 551 slaves loaded at Jakin (Godomey) the Spanish ship *Veloz Pasagera* was given chase by HMS *Primrose*. The captain José Antonio de la Vega determined to fight the British vessel and for that purpose he decided to use a number of the Africans he was carrying to Cuba as human shields. By the time the ship was taken, five of them "had been killed and one desperately wounded by the broadsides of the Primrose."[57]

On occasions, the slaves could be thrown overboard or abandoned altogether, as was the case of the Spanish brigantine *Orestes*. On this occasion the crew, after running aground on the Bahamas Green Banks in March 1826, abandoned ship and slaves to their fate and reached a cay where they were found by the British Navy. When Lieutenant Bennett boarded the ship after finding it in his way by sheer luck, he made mention of the wretched state in which they all were, lying among the corpses of their dead companions. He also recounted how some of them had

---

[53] Report of the Case of the Brazilian schooner "Santo Jago," Jozé Antonio de Souza Paladins, master. Sierra Leone, 10 October 1829. BPPO. Class A. Correspondence with the British Commissioners, at Sierra Leone, the Havana, Rio de Janeiro, and Surinam, relating to the slave trade. 1830. Craw-craw was the name given at the time to a skin disease called Onchocerciacis and caused by the larvae of the filarial worm.

[54] Report of the Case of the Brazilian brig "Avizo," Luiz Pacheco da Silva, master. Sierra Leone, [November 1824]. BPPO. Class A. Correspondence with the British Commissioners, at Sierra Leone, the Havana, Rio de Janeiro, and Surinam, relating to the slave trade. 1825–6.

[55] Report of the Case of the Portuguese schooner "Legítimo Africano," Jozé Manoel de Lima, master. Sierra Leone, 11 May 1835. BPPO. Class A. Correspondence with the British Commissioners, at Sierra Leone, the Havana, Rio de Janeiro, and Surinam, relating to the slave trade. 1835.

[56] Commissioners Macaulay and Lewis to Viscount Palmerston. Sierra Leone, 12 January 1838. BPPO. Class A. Correspondence with the British Commissioners, at Sierra Leone, the Havana, Rio de Janeiro, and Surinam, relating to the slave trade. 1838–9.

[57] Commissioners Findlay and Smith to the Earl of Aberdeen. Sierra Leone, 18 October 1830. Class A. Correspondence with the British Commissioners, at Sierra Leone, the Havana, Rio de Janeiro, and Surinam, relating to the slave trade. 1830. British Parliamentary Papers Online.

drowned in the surf trying to reach land, and how two others had been found dead of starvation and thirst in a nearby cay.[58]

Predictably, the harsh conditions associated with the Middle Passage often brought together the enslaved Africans who suffered it. Beyond old and new alliances and friendships, which strengthened and developed as means of survival, occasionally such bonding also led to overt resistance. While slave revolts were a common occurrence during the Middle Passage, ships bound to Bahia and Cuba from the Bight of Benin did not experience too many of them, or at least that is what the historical record tells us.[59] A case in question was that of the Brazilian yacht *Andonovi* in 1846. Although a massive revolt seems to have taken place on board this vessel, there is very little information about it, other than the fact that 80 of the 440 Africans shipped at Whydah were killed during the event by the crew.[60] If a considerably large uprising as the one on the *Andonovi* was barely recorded, we can only assume that many smaller events may have gone totally unnoticed by those in charge of the slave trade logbooks.

Even with a thorough examination of the *Slavevoyages* dataset and of the British Parliamentary Papers Online, information about uprisings at sea after the slave trade became illegal for most of the trading nations in 1820 is very limited. To be precise, only 14 cases are recorded on *Slavevoyages*. Of these, only two, the Brazilian brig *Veloz* in 1836 and the previously mentioned yacht *Andonovi*, were carrying slaves from the Bight of Benin.[61] When compared to the existing records for the previous century, when the slave trade was a legal affair, the difference is enormous. For the period 1700–1819, there are 422 confirmed cases recorded of slave ships where plots or uprisings were organized and carried out by the Africans on board.[62] It was precisely the very illegal character of the slave trade from the 1820s onward that contributed to keeping events like these in the shadows. Nevertheless, in spite of the absence of reliable statistics and descriptions of Atlantic plots and revolts, the fear of insurrections during the Middle Passage prevailed among the slave traders throughout the period.[63]

[58] Commissioners Kilbee and Macleay to George Canning. Havana, 23 March 1826. BPPO. Class A Correspondence with the British Commissioners at Sierra Leone, the Havannah, Rio de Janeiro and Surinam relating to the Slave Trade, 1826–7.
[59] Taylor, *If We Must Die*, 210–13.
[60] List of Vessels which have entered the Port of Bahia from Africa, during the quarter ending December 31, 1846. BPPO. Class B. Correspondence on the slave trade with foreign powers, parties to treaties, under which captured vessels are to be tried by mixed tribunals from January 1, 1847, to March 31, 1848, inclusive.
[61] <http://www.slavevoyages.org>. See entries for brig Veloz (Voyage No. 1836) and yacht Andonovi (Voyage No. 4563).
[62] <http://www.slavevoyages.org>. This vast amount of information has allowed some eighteenth-century scholars to evaluate the real impact of these slave movements upon the trade. See for example, Richard Rathbone, "Some Thoughts on Resistance to Enslavement in West Africa," *Slavery & Abolition*, 6:3 (1985): 11–22; Winston McGowan, "African Resistance to the Atlantic Slave Trade in West Africa," *Slavery & Abolition*, 11:1 (1990): 5–19; Joseph E. Inikori, "Measuring the Unmeasured Hazards of the Atlantic Slave Trade: Documents Relating to the British Trade," *Revue française d'histoire d'Outre-Mer*, 83:312 (1996): 53–92; and David Richardson, "Shipboard Revolts, African Authority, and the Atlantic Slave Trade," *William and Mary Quarterly*, 58:1 (2001): 69–92.
[63] In this passage of his book Turnbull commented: "From the intercepted correspondence of the slave dealers we have discovered how apprehensive they are of insurrections on ship-board, and of

Resistance in the Middle Passage could also take other forms. Slave ship surgeons habitually referred to cases of what they called melancholy or nostalgia. Defining the refusal to eat and therefore to live as an act of resistance could be considered as a contentious argument, especially because its connection with suicide may not be absolutely clear. There have been numerous descriptions of this "melancholy"—an emic term made popular in Europe since the seventeenth century—always associated with the sadness and despair felt by those who were forced to leave their homes as slaves. Even though it may have not been always a conscious act, the refusal to live, as I have argued elsewhere, must be considered as a possible form of resistance, since it was based on the belief of a physical return or escape to their African homes after dying, and on the clear fact that it represented a conscious rejection to live life as a slave and far away from home.[64] In Achille Mbembe's words, those who resorted to this act were able to "exercise control over mortality and to define life as the deployment and manifestation of [their] power."[65]

Again, from vessels leaving the Bight of Benin during this period, there are a few reported cases of this type of refusal to exist based on the belief of a physical return to Africa. One of them was that of the slaves taken by the HMS *Iphigenia* in April 1822 off Lagos. Of the 187 slaves captured on board the Portuguese polacca *Esperanza Felix*, 102 died within a few days, some of them of an unspecified illness, and the rest, "by far the greatest number" were victims of a "melancholy accident which befell" them.[66]

Though "melancholy" could have been the easiest way of refusing to live life as a slave and returning home, cases of jumping over board were not rare. According to a report written in 1834 by the British Commission judges in Freetown, suicide was the most frequent form of death among the Africans, surpassing even other illnesses:

> Suicide under such circumstances [i.e. melancholy], is an abundant case of the mortality on board of slave ships, and arises from the opinion entertained by these wretched beings, that after death they will revisit their own country. Almost every vessel that comes before the Court conveys melancholy proof of the prevalence of this idea.[67]

The changes that took place in the slave trade after 1820 had an undeniable impact upon the peoples of the Slave Coast and its interior, and upon the ways in which the trade was carried out. Whilst the actual experiences of those enslaved changed,

the struggles of the poor African for the recovery of their freedom." David Turnbull, *Travels in the West: Cuba; with Notices of Porto Rico and the Slave Trade* (London: Longman, 1840), 466.

[64] Manuel Barcia, *Seeds of Insurrection: Domination and Resistance on Western Cuban Plantations, 1808–1848* (Baton Rouge: Louisiana State University Press, 2008), 71–83.

[65] Achille Mbembe, "Necropolitics," *Public Culture*, 15:1 (2003): 11–12.

[66] Commissioners Gregory and Fitzgerald to the Marquis of Londonderry. Sierra Leone, 24 July 1822. BPPO. Class B. Correspondence with the British commissioners, at Sierra Leone, the Havannah, Rio de Janeiro, and Surinam, relating to the slave trade. 1822–3. It is probably worth noting here that this was the ship where Ajayi (Reverend Samuel Ajayi Crowther) found himself on his way to Bahia as slave.

[67] Commissioners Smith and Macaulay to Viscount Palmerston. Sierra Leone, 22 February 1834. BPPO. Class A. Correspondence with the British commissioners, at Sierra Leone, the Havana, Rio de Janeiro, and Surinam, relating to the slave trade. 1834.

so did the scale on which the trade was conducted and the demographic profiles of those enslaved and shipped away.

MIDDLE PASSAGE STATISTICS:
BAHIA AND CUBA

As we have seen, Africans leaving the Slave Coast from the early nineteenth century until the end of the transatlantic slave trade were taken mostly to two places: Bahia, in the northeastern part of Brazil and Cuba, and more specifically the western part of the island. Some other Atlantic places received smaller numbers of Africans exported from the Bight of Benin, notably Sierra Leone due to the many captured slave ships that were taken there from the late 1810s onwards, and also some of the British islands in the Caribbean, where a considerable number of liberated Africans were relocated after being freed by Mixed Commission and Vice-Admiralty Courts.

The volume of exports through the ports of the Slave Coast was always conditioned by both endogenous and exogenous factors. For example, internal warfare and changes of leadership in one or another state could bring about a temporary resurgence of the slave trade or have exactly the opposite effect. Events occurring elsewhere in the Atlantic World, notably the implementation of treaties between Great Britain and most of the slave trading nations from 1815 onwards, also had a direct effect on the volume of the trade and the manner in which it was conducted along the Atlantic shores of West Africa. A number of studies produced over the past decades have attempted to determine how many West Africans were exported to the Americas from the sixteenth to the nineteenth century. None has been so successful, and I would add useful, as the Transatlantic Slave Trade Database edited by David Eltis, David Richardson, Stephen Behrendt, and Herbert Klein and originally published by Cambridge University Press in 1999. This database, which is now available free of charge thanks to Emory University, has since been frequently updated, bringing scholars closer to the actual number of Africans who were forced to make their way across the Atlantic as slaves.[68]

The *Slavevoyages* database is then an essential tool for the understanding and interpretation of the figures of the trade from specific African regions and ports to the Americas. Whilst in some cases the records are quite complete and flawless, in other cases—due to the fragmentary characteristics of the data—additional work needs to be done to reach satisfactory approximates of the slave trade from and to these particular regions.

While it is correctly assumed that Brazil as a whole received more African slaves than any other region in the Americas—and this is especially the case for the first half of the nineteenth century—, Cuba was also a main destination for this trade. After 1820, men, women, and children leaving the Slave Coast were usually shipped towards Bahia and Cuba. That some of them ended up at other places such as Sierra Leone, St Helena, Rio de Janeiro, and the British West Indies was

---

[68] <http://www.slavevoyages.org>.

mostly a result of the vigilance and purpose shown by the British Navy in stopping the slave trade from the second decade of the century onwards.[69]

Between 1805 and 1845 the Bight of Benin alone exported no less than 209,667 slaves to the Americas.[70] Unquestionably most of those exported through these ports were the victims of the wars and raids that affected the area from the time of Afonja's insubordination in Ilorin and, probably more significantly, from the beginning of the Fulani-led *jihād* in 1804 and the Dahomean wars of expansion. As discussed before many victims of these same wars and raids were never sent to the ports of the Bight of Benin, but were instead taken west as far as the Gold Coast and southeastern ports like Warri and Bonny. Unfortunately, it is practically impossible to calculate the numbers of Yoruba and Hausa speakers, Nupe, Bariba, Borno, and some other neighboring groups taken down these routes based on the data we currently have, although it is undeniable that their numbers were not insignificant, since the combined human exports of these two regions (Gold Coast and Bight of Biafra) in the period were larger than those from the Bight of Benin (Tables 2.1–2.3).

Furthermore, the numbers of Africans exported from the Slave Coast between 1805 and 1845 were not always steady. As explained before, political, economic,

Table 2.1 Human exports from the Slave Coast, 1805–1845

	Total Exports, 1805–1845
Bight of Benin	209,667
Bight of Biafra	232,876
Gold Coast	31,265

Source: <http://www.slavevoyages.org>

Table 2.2 Bight of Benin human exports (five-year periods)

Years	Exported Africans
1805–10	51,678
1811–15	42,096
1816–20	17,801
1821–25	19,151
1826–30	20,852
1831–35	13,208
1836–40	23,147
1841–45	21,734
Total	209,667

Source: <http://www.slavevoyages.org>

[69] Christopher Lloyd, *The Navy and the Slave Trade: The Suppression of the African Slave Trade in the Nineteenth Century* (London: Cass, 1968).
[70] 159,963 out of the 209,667 slaves disembarked in the New World. This means that approximately 12 percent of the total slaves that arrived (i.e. 1,914,082) in the New World were embarked from the Bight of Benin. See <http://www.slavevoyages.org>.

Table 2.3 Slave exports from some of the principal ports of the Bight of Benin, 1805–1845

Years	Lagos	Whydah	Porto Novo	Grand Popo	Badagry
1805–10	7,483	2,808	1,654	484	1,866
1811–15	5,592	4,418	1,606	136	508
1816–20		760		433	
1821–25	5,497	4,934	843	558	1,862
1826–30	8,028	5,900		1,805	1,142
1831–35	4,719	5,671			
1836–40	14,327	5,684	490	1,004	
1841–45	11,861	2,588		1,687	354
Totals	57,507	32,763	4,593	6,107	5,732

Source: <http://www.slavevoyages.org>

and military changes could bring about changes in the numbers sent to the coast and eventually into the Atlantic slave trade. Since most of the slave trade in this period was conducted in an illegal manner the overall figures may be also misleading. The one thing that remains clear is that the exports of men, women, and children through the Bight of Benin can be traced on occasions to particular events.[71]

The possibilities of tracking down and identifying who these men, women, and children were and where they came from expand when we add specific ports of departure to the breaking down of the time into five-year periods. This way, and this again while assuming the figures may be inaccurately too low, the main trading ports continue to dominate the exports, especially Lagos and Whydah.

The dominance of Lagos as the main exporting port is obviously a result of a combination of the strengthening of Dahomey from 1818 onwards, of the wars that engulfed the southwest of the Yoruba states, and of the violence provoked by the Fulani-led *jihād* in the north. As explained before, Lagos's geographical position by the lagoon and its relative political calmness brought up an increase in the slave trade there that lasted until the middle years of the century.

Whydah, on the other hand, was able to hold on to a sizeable part of the market thanks to the strong control imposed over the trade by King Ghezo, to the efficiency, reputation, and contacts of his Chacha Francisco Felix de Souza and his slave trading partners, to the captives generated by Ghezo's own wars, and chiefly to the specialization of Dahomean merchants in the role of intermediaries in the trade, who, as seen before, went as far as Borgu and Nupe in search for slaves.

Impressive as it may seem, the overall figure of exports through the Bight of Benin to Bahia and Cuba is almost certainly inaccurately low. The reasons for these flaws lie in the very illegal character of the slave trade after 1820. The slave trade database compiled by Eltis et al., outstanding as it is, cannot always tell us the ports

---

[71] Henry B. Lovejoy is currently working on this issue by examining the Liberated African registries where the names and nations of the slaves were frequently annotated. His study may also throw new light into the chronology of warfare in the Yoruba-speaking states during the last years of Oyo. Lovejoy, "Old Oyo Influences."

where many slavers loaded their human cargoes in West Africa. In some cases, especially those of ships seized by the Royal Navy and taken as prizes, the details tend to be more accurate; in others, those that were never captured, important information such as port of departure and the numbers of slaves embarked and landed are difficult to be precise about. We know of more than 1,000 slave ships that arrived in Bahia and Cuba during these decades which left from unspecified places in West Africa and that at the very least landed the significant number of 15,069 in Bahia and the much larger figure of 304,197 in Cuba. These figures are a result of the calculations of British mixed commissioners and consuls, and the recalculations provided by the *Slavevoyages* database, and are not by any means conclusive.[72]

It is thanks to those commissioners and consuls that we have at least some approximate numbers. From 1820 onwards, whether from Rio de Janeiro, Salvador de Bahia, or Havana, they did their best to keep up with the illegal trade that was taking place right under their noses. They frequently reported human cargoes being landed along desolated shores and about ships arriving from Africa empty, or to use the commissioners' jargon in ballast, the clearest sign yet of their involvement in the transatlantic slave trade.[73]

Our understanding of how the illegal trade was carried out in these two regions is, however, affected by their own historical developments. Whilst Havana—a capital city—did have a Court of Mixed Commission from 1819 until well into the second half of the century, Salvador never did. The first court, an Anglo-Portuguese one, was established also in 1819 in the imperial capital Rio de Janeiro but it was dissolved in 1822 after Brazil gained its independence from Portugal. It was not until 1826 that a new court, an Anglo-Brazilian one, was created and, again, was located in Rio de Janeiro.[74] Thus, while Havana benefited from a number of British officers who reported on the every move of the slave traders there, Salvador de Bahia was covered only by British consuls, who, it must be said, were not always particularly keen on reporting slave trading activities.[75] Nonetheless, according to

---

[72] <http://www.slavevoyages.org>.

[73] Commissioners Kilbee and Jameson to the Marquis of Londonderry, Havana, 2 August 1822. Class B Correspondence with the British Commissioners at the Sierra Leone, the Havannah, Rio de Janeiro, and Surinam relating to the Slave Trade, 1822–1823. House of Commons Parliamentary Papers Online. The complaints of the British commissioners and consuls in Havana about illegal landings along Cuban coasts and about the ships arriving in ballast lasted until the early 1860s.

[74] For the Mixed Commission Courts of Rio de Janeiro see: Leslie Bethell, "The Mixed Commissions for the Suppression of the Transatlantic Slave Trade in the Nineteenth Century," *Journal of African History*, 7:1 (1966): 79–93; and "The Independence of Brazil and the Abolition of the Brazilian Slave Trade: Anglo-Brazilian Relations, 1822–1826," *Journal of Latin American Studies*, 1:2 (1969): 115–47; Jennifer L. Nelson, "The Mixed Commission and Emancipated Slaves in Nineteenth-Century Rio de Janeiro" (MA Diss. University of Leeds, 2011); See also ANRJ: JC, 184/3.

[75] Hamilton Hamilton to Vice-Consul John Whately. Rio de Janeiro, 24 October 1837. NA-UK: FO. 268/11. In this letter British Envoy Hamilton ordered the British Vice-Consul in Bahia, John Whately, to inform him, as exactly as possible, "what number of negroes has embarked in and what the number disembarked from each of the vessels engaged in the slave trade, whose arrival within your consular district from the Coast of Africa, you communicate to me; also the place of disembarkation together with any other circumstances connected with such speculations and with the trade in general which may appear to you important or interesting." The entire paragraph was originally underlined by Hamilton who was clearly not happy with finding himself "under the necessity of again calling" Whately's attention to this important matter.

Table 2.4 Approximate African imports in Bahia and Cuba, 1805–1845

	Slaves from the Bight of Benin		Slaves from unspecified ports		Total slaves (including unspecified ports)
	Number	%	Number	%	
Bahia	118,556	37.88	15,069	4.81	312,913
Cuba	22,928	5.14	304,197	68.23	445,795

Source: www.slavevoyages.org

their reports we know today that between 1805 and 1845 Salvador de Bahia was the final destination for a minimum of 118,556 Africans embarked in the Bight of Benin while, at the same time, the island of Cuba received at least 22,928 from the same region.[76]

If we keep in mind the much greater number of Africans that arrived in Cuba from unspecified African regions we could almost certainly assume that the number of Africans from the Slave Coast may have been much higher. Table 2.4 indicates that 5.14 percent of the total slaves that arrived in Cuba were embarked in the Bight of Benin. It is then reasonable to assume, based on this data, that 5.14 percent of the slaves that arrived in Cuba from unspecified ports were actually from the Bight of Benin. This suggests that approximately 15,635 slaves arrived in Cuba in addition to the 22,928 already registered. This approximation would imply that an estimated total of 38,563 Africans embarked in this region arrived in Cuba in this period. Yet, this figure still underestimates the actual number of slaves that arrived in Cuba from the Bight of Benin. Based on the fact that approximately 10 percent of the slaves that were exported from the whole of Africa during this historical period were shipped from the ports of the Bight of Benin, we could assume that 10 percent of the unspecified slaves that arrived in Cuba left from one of these ports. This would result in a much larger number than the one indicated by the calculations based on Cuban imports. We could then assert that between 1805 and 1845 approximately 30,419 Africans arrived in Cuba on top of the 22,928 already accounted for. This means that an estimated total of 53,347 slaves may have arrived in Cuba from the Bight of Benin alone during this period. Based on this analysis we can conclude that at least 11.96 percent of the slaves that arrived in Cuba during the 1805–45 period came from one of the ports of the Bight of Benin. This circumstance alone merits a reconsideration of any previous conclusions drawn about the ethnic composition of the Bahian and Cuban populations of African origin during this period. After all we have over 750,000 Africans of unknown origins whose cultural impact upon the slave societies of Bahia and Cuba is until today in the shadows.

---

[76] <http://www.slavevoyages.org>.

MIDDLE PASSAGE DEMOGRAPHICS: BAHIA AND CUBA

The issue of who was exported and to where, after 1805 from the Bight of Benin, is a puzzling one because whereas the historical records undisputedly tell us that Bahia and Cuba were the main destinations for those who left West Africa from these ports, the ethnic denominations used in these two New World places diverged from each other considerably. This, of course, has been until today a source of confusion with several scholars contributing with their takes on the different ways used by non-Africans to categorize their African slaves in the Americas.[77] Although the parallel slave trading histories of Bahia and Cuba during the period studied here are quite similar in many ways, there are a few issues that need clarification if we are to understand these common historical developments, particularly when we look at the slave uprisings that took place in both Bahia and Cuba throughout these years.

In Bahia, and this would seem to apply to the rest of Brazil as well, there was a combination of general and specific ethnic denominations used throughout the first half of the nineteenth century to refer to the slaves imported from Africa. While generic terms or *nações* such as Nagô, Hausa, Mina, and Jêje (Aja-Fon) were widely used as umbrella terms for vast numbers of Africans, more specific ones such as Tapa, Borno, Benguela, and Cabinda were also used on a day-to-day basis to identify other Africans from more explicit geographical regions or cultural origins. This circumstance has allowed historians to trace cultural traits from Africa to Brazil in a detailed fashion that until now has been unrivalled by scholars elsewhere in the American continent.[78]

In Cuba, on the other hand, illegally imported Africans were frequently identified by major diasporical ethnies or *naciones* with a very limited degree of specificity in reference as to where exactly they had come from. Among these *naciones* the main ones were Mandinga, Gangá, Mina, Arará (Aja- and Ewe-Fon), Lucumí, Carabalí, Congo, and Macua. This sort of classification was not always accurate, and as a result it has created major problems of interpretation for all those who have attempted to assess the geographical and cultural origins of the Africans that were taken to Cuba in the nineteenth century as slaves.[79]

Although the obstacles are undoubtedly challenging, there are certainly ways to achieve a better level of precision, even when the assessment has to be inevitably

---

[77] Gomez, *Exchanging our Country Marks*; and Hall, *Slavery and African Ethnicities in the Americas*.

[78] There are numerous studies addressing ethnicity in Brazil, including the foundational works of Raimundo Nina Rodrigues and Pierre Verger and the most recent articles and books written by João José Reis, Beatriz Gallotti Mamigonian, Maria Inês Côrtes de Oliveira, Nei Lopes, and Walter Hawthorne.

[79] See: Jesús Guanche, *Componentes étnicos de la nación cubana* (Havana: Fundación Fernando Ortiz, 1996); and also Barcia, *Seeds of Insurrection*, 13–24. For a discussion of the historical evolution of these studies see Oscar Grandío Moraguez, "The African Origins of the Slaves Arriving in Cuba, 1789–1865," in David Eltis and David Richardson, eds., *Extending the Frontiers: Essays on the New Transatlantic Slave Trade Database* (New Haven and London: Yale University Press, 2008), 176–201.

made on the basis of a limited number of primary sources. The best tool at our disposition is the registry from the Anglo-Spanish Mixed Commission Court that was established in Havana in 1819. There, the Commission judges were frequently careful enough to record the names of the seized Africans and on occasions they also recorded their ethnic and sub-ethnic denominations. In this way, Africans who would have been normally known and referred to in the Spanish historical record as Lucumí, were identified as, for example, Lucumí Elló (from Oyo); Lucumí Eba (from Egba); Lucumí Llabu (from Ijebu); and Lucumí Yesa (from Ijesa).[80] These records also allow us to identify men, women, and children that were not Lucumí, but who entered Cuba as such. Among them were Hausa speakers (Lucumí Jausá) and Nupe (Lucumí Tapa).[81] In other words, the Mixed Commission Court records also confirm that those Africans who entered Cuba frequently as Lucumí could come from anywhere in and around Oyo and could be, or not, Yoruba speakers.

The records of the Mixed Commission Courts established in Havana, Rio de Janeiro, and Freetown also offer fresh qualitative information that has until now been underestimated by scholars and that may certainly contribute to our understanding of the Nagô and Lucumí diasporas in Bahia and Cuba. A first aspect is that of kinship and fraternity links among these men, women, and children that had often existed in Africa and that were brought to Bahia and Cuba by the slaves. The Middle Passage may have been a terrible experience for all those who endured it, but precisely because of these difficult conditions, long-lasting friendships may have resulted from the day-to-day bonding aboard the ships and from the sharing of such a traumatic experience. As a matter of fact, in both destinations former shipmates coined terms to identify each other; in Bahia and other parts of Brazil the term *Malungo* prevailed, while in Cuba they used the term *Calabera* for the same purposes. As the years went by, in both destinations they also continued to interact with each other, creating solidarity networks that sometimes lasted all their lives. As Paul E. Lovejoy has correctly argued, in these slave vessels "shipmates formed strong allegiances, and the ethnic background of slaves further consolidated these ties."[82] That many slaves who left from the ports of the Bight of Benin knew each other before finding their way to the coast is a certainty. Many had been enslaved in wars in which their armies were involved and defeated and by raiding parties that attacked and destroyed their villages.

The Commission judges rarely, if ever, noticed these ties; although planters and authorities sometimes did after suppressing slave movements. However, what they did do was to carefully annotate any family unit links that existed among the Africans that they emancipated. Asking to establish existing kinship relations among the liberated Africans was a common procedure, so that those emancipated Africans who were related could be kept together after being assigned to their

---

[80] See the African Names Database at <http://www.slavevoyages.org/tast/resources/slaves.faces>.
[81] See the African Names Database at <http://www.slavevoyages.org/tast/resources/slaves.faces>.
[82] Lovejoy, "Background to Rebellion," 155.

guarantors. Any family relationships that were found to exist among them were duly annotated at the margin of the lists with the above idea in mind.[83]

What this noticeably shows is that strong connections existed among those men, women, and children who were enslaved and sent to Bahia and Cuba through the ports of the Slave Coast. That they undertook the Middle Passage together might have also been a massive boost to their chances of survival, since their mutual support may have proved decisive, and almost certainly may have been a reason behind uprisings. It is plausible to conclude that entire communities often found themselves still together across the Atlantic and on the other side of it, both in Bahia and Cuba. The emerging community of African-born slaves and former slaves, to which Paul E. Lovejoy referred while discussing the potential for revolt in Bahia, also made its way to Cuba.[84]

That these ships left from the Slave Coast to Bahia and Cuba, and that similar communities developed in both places, raises the inescapable question of why in Bahia Islam was one of the defining cultural traits among this population— together with the cult of the orishas or orixás—while in Cuba nothing of this sort happened. Even more so, the few existing indications to Islam among West African slaves in Cuba during these years are puzzling and by no means categorical. It is as if Islam, despite its overwhelming likelihood of arriving in Cuba, was conspicuously absent or forgotten in the island.

A few theories could help to clarify this absence, even if only partially. The formerly cited generalization of ethnic *naciones* could go a long way in proving what we know today, that not all those Africans listed as Lucumí were Yoruba speakers, and presumably, that not all of them revered the orishas. There is also a realistic chance that Spanish authorities, planters, and people in general deliberately chose to overlook the presence of Islam among their slaves; electing to civilize them instead, through their favorite means: Christianization. Thus, while Islam was clearly a social force in the first half of the nineteenth century in Bahia, historical evidence up to now tells us that it was missing in Cuba; yet, was it indeed so?

Islam almost certainly reached Cuba in the sixteenth century when Mandinga, Fula, Wolof, and Bambara slaves were brought to the island from Upper Guinea and Senegambia. In the nineteenth century waves of Muslim West African slaves continued to arrive at least from two main regions, the Upper Guinea Coast— mostly Mandingas—and the Bights of Benin and Biafra. The archive of the Court of Mixed Commission once again constitutes a relevant source to finally establish this Islamic presence among slaves from the Bight of Benin who disembarked in Cuba in the first half of the nineteenth century. Although these records must be regarded as a small sample of a larger commerce, the name registries covering the years between 1824 and 1835 offer a strong indication of this presence. As

---

[83] See e.g.: Vives to the Commissioners. Havana, 9 February 1826. NA-UK: FO 84/180; and Jáuregui, Kilbee and Quesada to Vives. Havana, 28 December 1824. In both cases the commission judges found a number of mothers and daughters, brothers and sisters, etc. Class A Correspondence with the British Commissioners at the Sierra Leone, the Havannah, Rio de Janeiro, and Surinam relating to the Slave Trade, 1824–1825. House of Commons Parliamentary Papers Online.

[84] Lovejoy, "Background to Rebellion," 155.

Table 2.5 reveals, dozens of names recorded in these registries are either accurately Muslim, or are otherwise of Hausa or Fulani origin, which would likely denote a direct connection with Islam, since by the 1820s most of the Hausa-speaking kingdoms of the savannah had been invaded by the Fulani-led *jihād* and its orthodox version of Islam.

Table 2.5 Likely Muslim, Hausa, and Fula names found in the registries of the Mixed Commission Court of Havana, 1824–1835

Name	≈	Likely (inferred from the sources)
Abdu		Muslim
Abdulage	Abdulaye	Muslim
Abu	Abubakar	Muslim
Adisa	Hadisa	Muslim
Ado	Adamu	Muslim
Aguale	Auwalu	Hausa
Aisa	Aisha	Muslim
Aisiatu		Hausa
Alado	Haladu	Hausa
Ali		Muslim
Alim		Muslim
Alimodu		Muslim
Aliu	Aliyu	Hausa
Allado	Haladu	Hausa
Alladu	Haladu	Hausa
Amadu		Muslim
Aquiles	Akil	Muslim
Aquilulu	Akil	Muslim
Aquiolu	Akil	Muslim
Argel		Hausa
Aruna		Muslim
Ayua	Ayyuba	Hausa
Baba		Hausa
Babanlo		Hausa
Buca	Buka	Hausa
Dada	Dauda	Muslim
Dogu	Dogo	Hausa
Fulala		Fulani
Fullavi		Fulani
Gambi	Gambo	Hausa
Gana	Gana	Hausa
Garuba	Garba	Hausa
Gauri		Hausa
Guari		Hausa
Jabi	Kabir	Muslim
Jabim	Jibirim	Muslim
Jaila	Jailani	Hausa
Lami	Laminu	Hausa
Mahoma		Muslim
Majama	Maijama	Hausa
Mauci	Musa	Muslim

(Continued)

(Continued)

Name	≈	Likely (inferred from the sources)
Momo	Mohammed	Muslim
Musu	Musa	Muslim
Sailu	Salihu	Muslim
Salu		Muslim
Seu	Sehu	Muslim
Suleye	*Suleyman*	Muslim

Source: <http://www.slavevoyages.org/tast/resources/slaves.faces>; John N. Paden, *Religion and Political Culture in Kano* (Berkeley and Los Angeles: University of California Press, 1973), 429–31; Sharifa M. Zawawi, *African Muslim Names: Images and Identities* (Trenton, NJ, and Asmara: Africa World Press, 1998), 111–17 and 124–35. I would also like to thank Olatunji Ojo for helping me identify some of the Muslim names in this list.

This inference is now supported by even stronger evidence.[85] The Havana Mixed Commission Court used to send Africans of the same ethnies as those who were aboard apprehended vessels upon their entrance in the port to investigate the number of *naciones* existing among the slaves. They did so with the sole purpose of "preparing the interpreters for each of the languages that would be found among them."[86] For example, in the case of the ship *Mágico* the Mixed Commission judges had to use interpreters for Lucumí Arará, Lucumí Jausá, Lucumí Popo, and Lucumí Elló. The very fact that the Mixed Commission had a Hausa-speaking interpreter at hand may go a long way to determining that Hausa-speaking slaves may have entered the island under the "Lucumí" label more often than had been supposed until now, and also with them their beliefs in Allah and Mohammed.[87]

Doubtlessly, Fula, Nupe, Bariba, and Borno slaves, many of whom may have been Muslims, also came into the island under the "Lucumí" denominator, mixing with other West African peoples without leaving too many traces. Whereas in Bahia, as stated earlier, there are numerous historical sources mentioning these groups and even their forms of enslavement, in Cuba they almost completely disappeared. Only a few dispersed, inconclusive allusions were left in the historical record. A Mandinga slave referred to as "Moro" or Moor could conceivably point to an Islamic, and feasibly Tuareg background, and Lucumí slaves who refused to drink alcohol could constitute another conceivable lead. Fredrika Bremmer's lines on "negro preachers and fortune-tellers,"[88] who were also Mandinga, and on a "negro of the Fellah tribe"[89] she encountered in the Havana countryside, are also indications of a Muslim tradition among African slaves in nineteenth-century Cuba. Another noteworthy allusion to the Islamic background of the Mandinga in Cuba was given by German traveler

[85] For a methodological approach to the identification of these names see G. Ugo Nwokeji and David Eltis, "The Roots of the African Diaspora: Methodological Considerations in the Analysis of Names in the Liberated African Registers of Sierra Leone and Havana," *History in Africa*, 29 (2002): 368–73.

[86] Report about the capture of the Spanish brig *Mágico*. Rafael Fernández, Secretary, and Rafael González. Havana, 5 February 1826. NA-UK: FO 313/42.

[87] Rafael Fernández, Secretary, and Rafael González. Havana, 5 February 1826. NA-UK: FO 313/42. The *Mágico* had taken its human cargo at Popo. The Mixed Commission was able to emancipate 87 Lucumí Elló, 67 Lucumí Arará, 14 Mina Popo, and 6 Lucumí Jausá.

[88] Fredrika Bremmer, *The Homes of the New World: Impressions of America* (New York: Harper and Brothers, 1856), 314.

[89] Bremmer, *The Homes of the New World*, 314.

C. Ritter, who in the early 1850s came across various West African men and women during his visit to a number of plantations in the outskirts of the capital, Havana. Ritter recounted the story of 75-year-old Bokary, who had spent the last 30 years in Cuba and who was a Mandinga. After saluting Ritter with a "Salama leco" (*sic*), Bokary told him that he had been the son of an Islamic scholar, and that in his country they prayed on top of mats made of hides and they usually shaved off their heads; all signs that corroborate Bokary's Muslim heritage.[90]

Moreover, and again thanks to the Mixed Commission Court judges, there is categorical evidence that there were many slave trade expeditions to Cuba in which West Africans from Nupe and Hausa origins were recorded as Lucumí. Among them were those of the schooner *Voladora* from Popo in 1829, the brig *Emilio Cesar* from New Calabar and the schooner *Santiago* from River Brass in 1830, the schooners *Joaquina* in 1833 and Maria in 1835 from Bonny, and the schooner *Tita* in 1835 from Whydah, all with Lucumí Tapa and some with Lucumí Jausá on board. Since, in that period, Lagos was normally considered as the "general market for the sale of slaves brought from Houssa,"[91] and since most of the slaves who arrived in Cuba from the Slave Coast had very likely been boarded there, we can safely assume that Hausa-speaking slaves—and very likely Nupe and Borno— arrived in Cuba on a regular basis during these decades.[92]

When assessing the potential impact of Islam and Islamic practice on Cuban cities and countryside, the rare remaining references that can be found in the historical record are for the most part unclear and by no means irrefutable. A few theories could help to explain this evident absence. The previously mentioned generalization of African *naciones* would suggest that not all those Africans registered as Lucumí necessarily worshipped the orishas.[93] It is also plausible that Spanish authorities, planters, and people in general, consciously decided to ignore the existence of Islam among their slaves, choosing to civilize them instead. This task, in the Cuban case might have been aided by the strength and penetration of the Catholic Church on the densely populated and relatively easy to control island of Cuba, especially when compared with the Bahian territorial expanses.

Specifically, among the Lucumí possible traces of Islamic beliefs can be found although, as Michael A. Gomez has warned, "there is little evidence that confirms a strong sense of Islamic identity among them."[94] This assessment may, of course, change depending on further discoveries. Some uniquely rich documents, such

---

[90] C. Ritter, "Mittheilungen über einige westafricanische Stämme in Cuba, gesamelt von Hesse," *Monatsberichte über die Verhandlungen der Gesellschaft für Erdkunde zu Berlin* (Berlin: Bei Simon Schropp und Comp., 1853), 12–16.

[91] Commissioners Gregory and Fitzgerald to the Marquis of Londonderry. Sierra Leone, 24 July 1822. Class B Correspondence with the British Commissioners at the Sierra Leone, the Havannah, Rio de Janeiro, and Surinam relating to the Slave Trade, 1822–1823. House of Commons Parliamentary Papers Online.

[92] The majority of Borno Africans interviewed by Francis de Castelnau in Bahia in the late 1840s had embarked in Lagos as well. It is likely, then, that Borno Africans made it to Cuba and were included under the Lucumí or, perhaps, Carabalí denominations.

[93] Lovejoy, "Old Oyo Influences," 70–106.   [94] Gomez, *Black Crescent*, 36.

as those produced in the aftermath of the Lucumí insurgency of 1833 in Banes, provide us with some hints of the presence of Muslim slaves among these Lucumí soldiers. After the armed movement was put down, colonial authorities in charge of investigating the events did something quite uncommon and wrote down the African names of the rebels alongside their new, Christian names. The resulting list reveals that some of them had ordinary Muslim names like Lalani (Lawani), Achumo (Asunmo or Ismail), and Alu (Aliyu), suggesting that at least in this movement, Muslim and non-Muslim Lucumí joined together against their new enemies.[95] A common ethnic background, and not religious beliefs seem to have played the most important role in this armed movement. Should other colonial prosecutors have recorded the African names of the Lucumí rebels they interrogated, we would probably have today many more pieces of evidence to back up this assessment. Unfortunately, in the vast majority of the cases only the Christian names of the Africans were recorded, depriving us of the necessary evidence to prove this Islamic heritage among the Lucumí conclusively.

As will be discussed in Chapters 4 and 5, by examining the African-led slave movements that unfolded in nineteenth-century Cuba, some faint clues appear to suggest that the Islamic element did not really vanish entirely, although it is beyond discussion that it never became the dynamic cohering element behind slave resistance that it was in Bahia during the same years. The "exiled, recreated and transformed Dar-el-Islam" that was present in Bahia may well have also existed in Cuba, although the historical sources up to now have failed to show whether it did, and if so, to what degree.[96]

CONCLUSIONS

As this chapter has revealed the number of West African peoples who were in direct contact with a series of historical events—e.g. the Fulani-led *jihād*, the Owu wars, the rise and expansion of Dahomey, the collapse of Oyo—was likely to be much higher that what we have so far believed. Accordingly, the contribution of the Nagô and the Lucumí, together with Hausa-speakers, the Aja- and Ewe-Fon, Borgu, Borno, Fulani, and other groups from these West African territories was tremendous in both Bahia and Cuba. During the first half of the nineteenth century they and their cultures became a powerful shaping force in both slave plantation societies.

Their own enslavement experiences, as shown here, explain to a large extent their behavior, and particularly their forms of resistance in the New World Societies to which they were taken. Put in other words, they, perhaps more than the Europeans themselves, made Bahia and Cuba alike.

---

[95] For a specific study on the origin of the names of the 1833 insurgents see: Lovejoy, "Old Oyo Influences," 104–17.

[96] José Cairus, "Instrumentum vocale, mallams e alufás: o paradoxo islâmico da erudição na diáspora africana no Atlântico," *Topoi*, 6 (2003): 129.

3

Between *Bozal* and *Ladino*
in Bahia and Cuba
The American Experience

Berimbau não é gaita. (A Berimbau is not a pipe.)

Afro-Brazilian proverb

On a dark night, probably in 1835 or 1836, a Brazilian slave ship landed its human cargo a few miles south of Salvador de Bahia, along the Barra Grande de Camamú. The slaves had been embarked a few weeks before somewhere in the Bight of Benin, and in order to avoid being seen by the cruisers of the Brazils Squadron they had been disembarked in haste and kept hidden in some nearby bushes in the vicinity of the village of Taipús, where their consignee, a certain Miguel Gahagem Champloni lived. The new Africans were kept in the bushes for some time until Champloni arranged for them to be sold. In due course the group was divided. Some of them were sold into slavery in the nearby villages of Maraú, Camamú, and Barra do Rio de Contas, while others were taken farther away to the regions of Santarém and Ilhéus. Many years after these events took place, in the late 1880s, some of these men and women, now in their 60s and 70s, came together before the Bahian authorities to reminisce about the time and conditions of their landing, the despair they had felt after confronting their new realities for first time, and the ways in which they were forced to get on with their lives in the state of Bahia in the aftermath of their arrival.[1]

This case illustrates some of the issues that I intend to discuss in this chapter. In both Bahia and Cuba, enslaved Africans had to deal with new tough destinations where they occupied the lowest echelons within two highly hierarchical slave societies. New as it was, nevertheless, this world was not entirely alien to them, as has been mentioned earlier. The natural world in both Bahia and Cuba resembled in many ways the homes they had left behind, while in the locations where they now had to live, whether urban or rural, they found ways to carry on with their lives, to practice their religions, to cook and eat their traditional food staples, to play their music, and to dance their dances in covert and overt ways. Here, slavery as an institution was quite different from the slavery they knew, but even in remote plantations these men, women, and children found solace in old friends

---

[1] For all the particulars of this case, see: Ricardo Tadeu Caíres Silva, "Memórias do tráfico ilegal de escravos nas ações de liberdade: Bahia, 1885–1888," *Afro-Ásia*, 35 (2007): 37–82.

and relatives—some of whom had made the Middle Passage alongside them—and in the reproduction of their cosmologies and cultures. The level of cosmopolitanism and ethnic variety in these two territories of the Americas was certainly new for most, but even the hectic city life in metropolitan centers like Havana and Salvador was not totally strange to some of them, especially to those who had come from Oyo, who by the early nineteenth century would have had the experience of living in a heavily urbanized African state.[2]

I argue that thanks to all these elements and many others that will be presented and discussed in this chapter, the former subjects of Oyo and their neighbors found themselves in an exceptional position to conspire and rise during the first half of the nineteenth century. This chapter, then, is crucial to understanding the historical significance and impact that the environment—both natural and social—had upon the numerous insurgencies that were simultaneously organized by West Africans in Bahia and Cuba during this period. I argue that these new environments provided more continuity than rupture, and allowed the Africans who were taken to these two regions of the Americas to reproduce their knowledge of the world in familiar environments that, on occasions, were conducive to conspiracy and rebellion.

INTERPRETING A NEW WORLD: THE ARRIVAL

The last days at sea during the Middle Passage were as dangerous for the slave traders—and the slaves—as the first days, when they were still close to the African coast and thus more prone to be seen by the vessels of the West African Squadron. On the other side of the Atlantic British cruisers lurked in the waters of the Caribbean Sea and along the vast coastline of Brazil, and often gave chase to the slavers as soon as their sails appeared on the horizon. Naturally, to the Africans on board that meant more discomfort and risk to their lives. Cases like that of the brigantine *Orestes*, mentioned in Chapter 2, or that of the Spanish ship *Guerrero* shipwrecked off the Florida Keys in 1827, illustrate these perils very well.[3]

Slave traders both in Bahia and Cuba devised ways to avoid the ships of the Royal Navy in order to disembark as many slaves as possible. For example, by the mid-1830s or perhaps much earlier, Cuba-based slave traders had posted pilots at Rocky Key, Crocodile, Isle of Pines, and French Key, in order to help the slave ships reach their desired destinations.[4] They also frequently provided slave ship masters with detailed instructions of where to land their cargoes and who to contact upon landing. A case in question is that of Jozé Moreira Sampaio, captain of the brigantine *Maria Theresa*, who was given instructions to disembark his "return cargo" of *bozal* slaves from Lagos in one of a number of locations where he was also expected to get in contact with agents designated by the owner of the ship and cargo. Among those people and places were: Juan de la Cabada in Matanzas,

---

[2] Coquery-Vidrovitch, *The History of African Cities*, 163–6, 181.

[3] Gail Swanson, "The Wrecking of the Laden Spanish Slave Ship Guerrero off the Florida Keys, in 1827," *The African Diaspora Archaeology Network Newsletter* (Sept. 2010). Online at: <http://www.diaspora.uiuc.edu/news0910/news0910.html#> (accessed on 3 January 2011).

[4] Turnbull, *Travels in the West*, 419.

Francisco Aguirre in Banes, Juan Manuel Martínez de Pinillos in Cabañas, and José Miró Pié in Majana and Guanímar.[5] The names of some of these agents, like those of Juan de la Cabada or José Miró Pié, were not unfamiliar to the British consuls and Mixed Commission judges in Havana. Their responsibilities went well beyond receiving the Africans, as will soon be discussed.

Bahia-based traders usually helped just as much. Every captain of a slave ship on its way back from Africa to Bahia knew in advance where his desired site of landing was, and who to contact upon arrival. Although, as explained before, Bahia never benefited from a Court of Mixed Commission that could provide detailed information of the illegal trade in human beings, the British Consuls in residence and some officers of the Brazils Squadron occasionally reported on the ways in which the slave trade to the city and its vicinity was carried out. In addition to the case of Champloni in the vicinity of Taipús, described in the opening paragraphs of this chapter, there were agents in many other parts of the Bahian coast in charge of receiving the new groups of Africans. For example, the depositions of some of the sailors of the Portuguese schooner *Providencia*, seized by a British cruiser in 1837 with a cargo of 198 slaves from Lagos, revealed details of the route that the ship master was to follow and the agents that he was supposed to contact upon his arrival in Rio Real, north of Bahia. According to Joaquím Martins Guimaraens, the master, he was expected to take his human cargo to Rio Real, where the Africans would be delivered to their main owner, Domingos José Rodrigues, who owned all but four of the slaves on board.[6] In another case, the British Consul in Bahia, John Parkinson, reported in 1833 that the Portuguese brig-schooner *Atrevido* had just entered Salvador in ballast. Parkinson described how before coming into port, the *Atrevido* had landed most of its cargo in a place "about a league distant from Torre, 18 leagues north of Bahia."[7] There, the vessel had been received by agents who had also sent some armed men on board to accompany it to Salvador, all of whom were still on board when Consul Parkinson visited it.[8]

Cases like the ones mentioned above constitute only a minor glimpse into the sophistication with which slave traders and slave ship captains went about business on a daily basis. Not only were they able to profit from the complicity and lack of interest of Brazilian and Cuban authorities in bringing the slave trade to an end, but they also used other less evident weapons in their favor.[9] Slave ship masters were more often than not experienced sailors who were also familiar with sea currents

[5] Report of the Case of the brigantine "Maria Theresa," Jozé Moreira Sampaio, Master, seized under Portuguese Colours. July 1837. BPPO. Class A. Correspondence with the British commissioners at Sierra Leone, the Havana, Rio de Janeiro, and Surinam, relating to the slave trade. From June 30th to December 31st, 1839.

[6] Commissioners Doherty and Lewis to Viscount Palmerston. Sierra Leone, 14 July 1837. BPPO. Class A. Correspondence with the British commissioners, at Sierra Leone, the Havana, Rio de Janeiro, and Surinam, relating to the slave trade. 1837.

[7] Deposition of John Parkinson Esq. HM Consul in Bahia. Bahia, 10 December 1833. BPPO. Class B. Correspondence with foreign powers, relating to the slave trade. 1834.

[8] Deposition of John Parkinson.

[9] José Luciano Franco, *Comercio clandestino de esclavos* (Havana: Ciencias Sociales, 1996); José Guadalupe Ortega, "Cuban Merchants, Slave Trade Knowledge, and the Atlantic World, 1790s–1820s," *Colonial Latin American Historical Review*, 15:3 (2006): 225–52; and Adrian J. Pearce, *British Trade with Spanish America, 1763–1808* (Liverpool: Liverpool University Press, 2007).

such as the Gulf Stream and with the winds that made the passage from West Africa to the Caribbean faster. Additionally, they also learned to take advantage of what the Bahian and Cuban geographical features could offer to accomplish their missions. The coastline of Bahia (see Map 3.1), from Rio Real in the north to the surroundings of Porto Seguro and Ajuda in the south had many convenient geographical

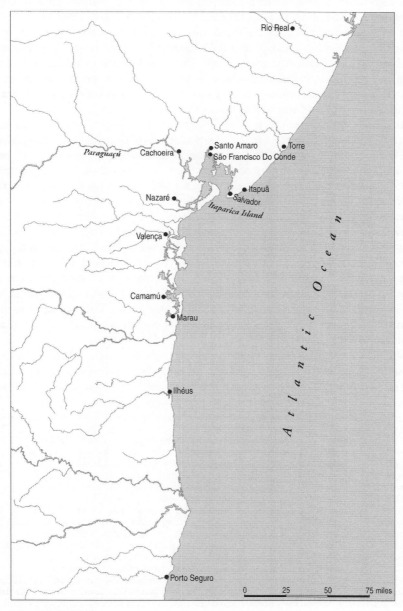

Map 3.1 Bahia

features for the smuggling of human beings from Africa, to the extent that by the late 1840s its blockade was considered to be "an impracticability."[10] Some areas along this coastline, like the section between Taipús and Valença, filled with small islands and natural waterways—including the delta of the Una river with more than 20 islands, and the archipelago of Tinharé—seemed to be tailor-made for this trade. Even the harbor of Bahia provided the slavers with similar sorts of advantages. The island of Itaparica offered slave ships the possibility of sneaking into the port without having to pass through the main entrance to the harbor. Itaparica, as well as the creek of Itapagipe and the region of Jaguaripe, were ideally placed to receive newly imported Africans.[11] British Consul Edward Porter documented one of these landings in August 1841. According to the news he was able to gather, the notorious slave ship *Picao* had disembarked 480 African slaves on the west side of the island of Itaparica, on the first day of that month.[12]

There are some other accounts of how slave ship masters benefited from the geographical characteristics of the Bahian coast to land their human cargoes safely. For example, in 1838 the American brig *Dido*, upon reaching the "sand hills, westwards of Bahia" noticed one of the Brazils Squadron vessels, the HMS *Sparrowhawk*, at anchor in the harbor. Upon sighting the ship, the slaver immediately hauled off and landed the 570 slaves that had been brought from Lagos that same evening "close to the point of Itapacau, at the village."[13] Next morning the *Dido* entered Bahia unmolested, all cleaned up and "under American colors."[14] In another similar case the Spanish brig-schooner *Musca* entered Bahia from Whydah with 228 slaves. According to the testimony of Ruffino Alexandre, one of the *Musca*'s sailors, after stopping at Torre to contact an agent who would arrange the delivery, the *Musca* spent four or five days cruising off Bahia until a *garoupeira* was sent out from the port to meet the slave ship at sea. The 228 Africans were then transshipped to the *garoupeira* and subsequently "safely landed at night in or about Bahia."[15]

The geographical vicinity of places like Itaparica and Jaguaripe to the City of Salvador also allowed traders and agents to bring their human cargoes to the slave market within hours. Some of the slaves disembarked by the previously mentioned

[10] Henry Matson, *Remarks on the Slave Trade and African Squadron* (London: James Ridgway, 1848), 92–3.
[11] The strait of Funil was frequently used by slave traders to get into Bahia's port without having to use the main entrance of the harbor. See Ubiratam Castro, "1846: um ano na rota Bahia-Lagos. Negócios, negociantes e outros parceiros," *Afro-Asia*, 21–2 (1998–9): 88
[12] Consul Edward Porter to Mr Ouseley. British Consulate, Bahia, 31 August 1841. BPPO. Class B. Correspondence with Spain, Portugal, Brazil, the Netherlands, Sweden, and the Argentine Confederation, relative to the slave trade. From January 1 to December 31 1841 inclusive.
[13] Commander Birch to Commodore Sulivan. Her Majesty's brig "Wizard," off Bahia, 12th November, 1838. BPPO. Class D. (Further series.) Correspondence with foreign powers, not parties to conventions giving right of search of vessels suspected of the slave trade. From February 2nd to May 3rd, 1839.
[14] Commander Birch to Commodore Sulivan.
[15] Deposition of Ruffino Alexandre, natural of Manila, and a sailor in the Spanish brig-schooner "Musca." Salvador, 10 April 1834. BPPO. Class B. Correspondence with foreign powers, relating to the slave trade. 1834. The *garoupeira* was a big fishing boat that took its name from the fish garoupa or grouper (*Polyprion americanus*) broadly fished in Brazilian waters at the time.

brig-schooner *Atrevido* in 1833 were sent in a *garoupeira* "which coasted along the Island of Itaparica to the Creek of Itapagipe" and landed the slaves in a sugar estate there.[16] Another group of around 40 slaves from the same ship was taken to Caes Dourado in Salvador, to "the house of Vicente de Paula Silva, into which they were admitted about 4 o'clock in the morning."[17] In most of these cases the slaves would be landed at night whenever possible and many of them would be found hours or days later in the main slave markets of the region.

In and around Cuba (see Map 3.2) slave trade captains profited from similar geographical features, to the point that British Commissioner Jameson noticed in the early 1820s that "no country in the world has coasts so well calculated for smuggling as the island of Cuba."[18] To reach the island of Cuba most of the slave ships would take advantage of the Gulf Stream. This strategy meant in reality that they would be forced to approach the island from the south, round Cape San Antonio and thence towards Havana cruising along the north coast. A second route involved abandoning the Gulf Stream and approaching Havana from the north passing between the northern coast of Hispaniola and Cuba and south of the Bahamas. Both routes counted a number of geographical elements that contributed to the success of many slave trading expeditions to Cuba, although they also had their disadvantages.

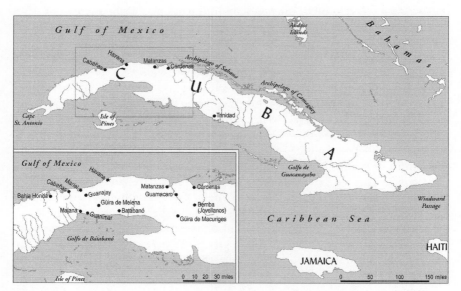

Map 3.2 Cuba

[16] Deposition of John Parkinson Esq. HM Consul in Bahia. Bahia, 10 December 1833. BPPO. Class B. Correspondence with foreign powers, relating to the slave trade. 1834.

[17] Deposition of John Parkinson.

[18] Robert Francis Jameson, *Letters from the Havana during the year 1820, containing an account of the present state of The Island of Cuba and observations on the Slave Trade* (London: John Miller, 1821), 31.

The southern route benefited in the first place from the Gulf Stream and favorable winds, but also from the Isle of Pines and the many small islands and cays that spread around it. For the slavers who chose this route the Isle of Pines was nothing short of a blessing. Even though a ship or two of the West Indies Squadron could lie in wait, the area to watch was so vast that they could barely cover but a small portion of it. The Isle of Pines added to this by offering an alternative route towards Cape San Antonio. Slavers could choose whether to proceed north or south of the Isle, making things even harder for the West Indies Squadron cruisers. In June 1832 the skipper of the HMS *Speedwell*, Lieutenant Warren, "had reason to suppose that a favourite track of slave vessels" was "to make the south side of the Isle of Pines" and so, he decided to return to the area and ambush future slavers in its surroundings.[19] He did not have to wait long, for as soon as he positioned himself south of the Isle, he encountered the Spanish schooner *Indagadora*, with more than 130 slaves from Lagos, which he seized and took to the Court of Mixed Commission in Havana.[20]

This route also benefited from a number of places in the south coast of Cuba that regularly served as emergency delivery sites. Particularly significant among them were the town of Trinidad in the south coast of the island, and the beaches of Guanímar and Majana, both conveniently situated south of Havana in the Gulf of Batabanó. Whenever a human cargo was disembarked in one of these places, the ship captain was expected to contact the local agents and to "dispatch a messenger to the owners in Havana, with the necessary information as to the number of slaves that have been landed, the classes of which they are composed, and other particulars" so that someone would be sent "to receive them."[21]

For those slave ships that decided to go round Cape San Antonio and attempted to land their human cargo in the north coast, there were a few landing locations where they could deliver the slaves they had brought from Africa. Before reaching Havana, they would come across three important natural harbors, namely Bahía Honda, Cabañas, and Mariel. Many of the Africans taken to Cuba during this period were disembarked there. West Indies Squadron cruisers, aware of this trend, often sailed off these harbors with the intention of seizing Cuba-bound slavers, and British officials in Havana repeatedly mentioned these three places in their correspondence, each time referring to incidences of slave landings.[22] Whenever possible, the slavers would seek refuge in one of these harbors and would land the Africans there; on other occasions they would have specific meeting places where the agents would wait for them, often in remote locations. The details of some of these landings were recollected by a group of liberated Africans who visited England on their way back to Lagos in the 1850s. One of them, Gabriel Crusati,

[19] Commissioner W. S. Macleay to Viscount Palmerston. Havana, 19 June 1832. BPPO. Class A. Correspondence with the British commissioners, at Sierra Leone, the Havana, Rio de Janeiro, and Surinam, relating to the slave trade. 1832.

[20] Abstract of the Evidence in the Case of the schooner "Indagadora." July 1832. BPPO. Class A. Correspondence with the British commissioners, at Sierra Leone, the Havana, Rio de Janeiro, and Surinam, relating to the slave trade. 1832.

[21] Turnbull, *Travels in the West*, 419–20.

[22] See correspondence of British Mixed Commissioners judges and British Consuls in Havana during the period in the British Parliamentary Papers Online.

remembered how they had been landed "in a wood, and thence taken to the bar-racoons" in Havana.[23] Another member of this group, Martina Seguí, narrated that she and the rest of the Africans who had come with her were "landed between two woods, at a retired place on the coast, and distributed as they were landed. They were expected."[24]

Approaching Havana from the north was not less dangerous. Here the slav-ers were at risk of coming across the always-threatening Haitian ships, while British cruisers were never far away, since the Bahamas was a British territory. Additionally, they did not have advantageous currents or winds to finish their journey. Nonetheless, continuous landings took place east of Havana during the period. Cárdenas, Camarioca, Matanzas, Puerto Escondido, and Canasí were mentioned by the British officials in Havana almost as much as they mentioned the landing spots west of the capital.

The illegal landing of African slaves, sometimes referred to by Cuban traders as *sacos de carbón* or *bultos*, and by Bahian traders as *paus de sangue* or *fardos*, was a constant occurrence during this period in both Cuba and Bahia.[25] For the Africans the end of the Middle Passage may have seemed a relief at first, but what awaited them was far from an easy ride. After disembarking, they were often forced to march for miles and miles to the main cities of Salvador and Havana where the slave markets functioned, or to plantations that on occasions could be even farther away.[26] Sometimes they could be found in the slave markets within hours of disem-barking.[27] The few and sparse testimonies about recently arrived Africans and slave markets that have survived have all one thing in common, namely their depiction of the horrors associated with the first days and weeks of the Africans in the New World.

According to testimonies and from the notary books of slave sales, the slave market in Salvador was located in the *Cidade Baixa* or Lower City, near the port. During her visit to Brazil in early 1820s British traveler Maria Graham was deeply overwhelmed by the slave markets that she found in the main cities that she vis-ited. About the slave market located in the Lower City of Salvador, she merely commented that this—the slave market—was a sight that she had "not yet learned to see without shame and indignation."[28] She did, however, use a quotation from another visitor who had earlier remarked about the place, "there are shops full of those poor wretches, who are exposed there stark naked and bought like cattle, over whom the buyers have the same power."[29]

---

[23] "Cuban Slaves in England," 236.   [24] "Cuban Slaves in England," 238.
[25] Both *bultos* and *fardos* can be translated as "bales." *Sacos de carbón* meant "bags of charcoal" in Spanish and *paus de sangue* "blood logwoods" in Portuguese.
[26] Michael Zeuske and Orlando García Martínez, "La Amistad de Cuba: Ramón Ferrer, contra-bando de esclavos, cautividad y modernidad atlántica," *Caribbean Studies*, 37:1 (2009): 104–8.
[27] David Turnbull referred to one of these cases when he mentioned that in late December 1838 the American frigate *Venus* had landed over 800 African *bozales* from Lagos near Havana and that the next day he had the opportunity of seeing the new Africans already for sale in the public barracoons. See Turnbull, *Travels in the West*, 456.
[28] Graham, *Journal of a Voyage to Brazil*, 137.   [29] Graham, *Journal of a Voyage to Brazil*, 137.

Maria Graham clearly did not find sufficient elements that would make this slave market different enough from the one she had recently visited in Pernambuco as to make a description of it. In the opinion of historian Mieko Nishida, Salvador never had "a commercially organized, large scale slave market," probably due to the "geographical features" of its port in which slaves were sold in many of the Lower City streets.[30]

In Recife, Maria Graham had confessed to being "sickened by the sight of the slave-market." [31] Her description was matched by an engraving in which some of the horrors for which the place was notorious were depicted (Figure 3.1). In this image it is possible to observe a toddler crawling away from the main group of new semi-naked Africans who were all sitting in the middle of a street, two of them were being beaten up by white men, while another was probably being taunted by another white man in uniform and by a dog. In the eyes of Miss Graham the place was:

> . . . thinly stocked, owing to the circumstances of the town; which cause most of the owners of new slaves to keep them closely shut up in the depôts. Yet about fifty young creatures, boys and girls, with all the appearance of disease and famine consequent upon scanty food and long confinement in unwholesome places, were sitting and lying about among the filthiest animals in the streets.[32]

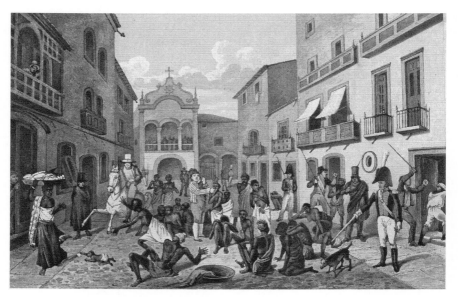

Figure 3.1 Slave Market in Pernambuco, 1820s, from Graham, *Journal of a Voyage to Brazil*, 107. Copyright of the University of Manchester.

---

[30] Mieko Nishida, *Slavery and Identity: Ethnicity, Gender and Race in Salvador, Brazil, 1808–1888* (Bloomington: Indiana University Press, 2003), 33. Nishida also mentions another slave market in the *Cidade Alta* or Upper City near the Black Church of Our Lady of the Rosary.

[31] Nishida, *Slavery and Identity*, 105.   [32] Nishida, *Slavery and Identity*, 105.

In Cuba, the situation would not differ much. One of the most shocking descriptions of a recently landed group of African *bozales* was given first hand by English traveler Henry Tudor, who visited Cuba at the end of 1831 and the beginning of 1832. In mid-January 1832, Tudor was taken on an excursion to Matanzas. There he had the opportunity to see a slave ship that had just entered the port with a cargo of approximately 250 Africans. His depiction of what he saw in the site where the slaves were being kept was the most distressing:

> I found them all huddled together in a large room, in which they were exposed to sale like a drove of pigs, in a state of complete nudity, with the exception of a bandage tied round their loins. They were disposed in lots of graduated ages, and were seated on the floor in groups of eight and ten, feeding out of a parcel of buckets, or rather devouring a miserable mess of the coarsest plantain, with a meagre sprinkling of bones and rice, exhibiting a colour as black as ink. It was, in truth, a species of pottage that I should have refused giving to my swine.[33]

Tudor also witnessed a slave auction that took place shortly before he left. He was genuinely shocked to see those he called "stony-hearted speculators on human flesh" bid for the Africans, even for those who were terminally ill.[34]

Another contemporary traveler, David Turnbull, during his first stay in Havana in the late 1830s visited the notorious slave barracoons of El Príncipe, where most of the slaves that were carried to Havana were sold to new owners.[35] Although Turnbull was somehow less critical of the conditions of existence of the Africans in the barracoons, he still called them "sad receptacles" and commented that in order to fetch higher prices "it was the policy of the importer to restore as soon as possible, among the survivors the strength that has been wasted and the health that has been lost during the horrors of the middle passage," and therefore visitors would not find "much immediate misery."[36] Turnbull also reflected on the age of those he saw, and criticized the increasing demands for younger victims among the slave traders.

The first days and weeks of the newly arrived Africans, although arguably constituting an improvement in the situation they had faced during the Middle Passage, were still full of anguish and despair. Hurried landings, often in the middle of the night, may have been a frightening experience to many. Still in chains and often sickly they were, at almost every opportunity, forced to march across the countryside for miles and miles until reaching the slave markets of Havana and Salvador or the rural estates where many would spend the rest of their lives. For those who survived these hardships a new world awaited; but they were soon to find out that this was a new world with many elements that they were able to recognize and relate to.

[33] Henry Tudor, *Narrative of a Tour in North America; comprising Mexico, the Mines of Real del Monte, the United States, and the British Colonies: with an Excursion to the Island of Cuba* (London: James Duncan, 1834), ii. 131.
[34] Tudor, *Narrative*, ii. 132.
[35] Most of the Africans who were interviewed in England in the 1850s declared they had been sold in these barracoons. See "Cuban Slaves in England," 234–9.
[36] Turnbull, *Travels in the West*, 60–1.

THE NATURAL WORLD

Although the experience of slavery in the New World is almost always presented as a dehumanizing one in which Africans were supposed to be stripped of their beliefs, cultures, and agency, some recent studies are beginning to challenge these views. Far from "socially dying" as implied by Orlando Patterson and other scholars,[37] these men, women, and children found ways of integrating themselves into social environments that kept much of the socialization and human interactions of the African places they came from. To the social element must be added another component of their lives that only recently has begun taking center stage in the discussions about what continued, what remained, and what disappeared from the various African cultures in the Americas, namely their understanding and knowledge of nature. By the time the Europeans had established a prosperous and profitable trade in human beings across the Atlantic, West Africans were still predominantly rural societies. This rural life, away from major urbanizations, allowed them to gather a large botanical knowledge, to domesticate animals, to master the melting and shaping of metals, and to rely on the planets and stars to determine the right timing for their festivities and harvests. On the other side of the Atlantic, all this knowledge was not wasted, but applied and indeed sometimes transformed and adapted to the new features of the world around them. That world was not an altogether different one, but rather one they found familiar in many ways.

From the moment they arrived in the regions of Bahia and Cuba these hundreds of thousands of men, women, and children were able to see with their own eyes a number of things that were well known to them. To begin with the Nagô, the Lucumí, and their neighbors, particularly those who had lived close to the Sahel and the Sahara and who had been associated with the caravan system, would have recognized many celestial bodies in their new skies. Because the homes of the Africans exported from the Bight of Benin were located at a latitude almost directly in between the latitudes of Cuba to the north, and Bahia to the south, the night sky would not have seemed that different to them.

At least for those who were sent to Cuba, the North Star or the Bilhady of the caravaners, who traded on the fringes of the Sahel, was visible all year round and could still be used as a point of orientation.[38] In Bahia, situated south of the Equator, the North Star was absent; nevertheless, other recognizable stars from both hemispheres were visible. Among them were the Pleiades, known by the Yoruba as *Kaza Maiyaya* (or the Hen with Chicken), and Altair (α-Aquila) also called by the Yoruba "the eagle star."[39] Other stars that were well known in West

---

[37] Orlando Patterson, *Slavery and Social Death: A Comparative Study* (Cambridge, MA: Harvard University Press, 1982). For some recent works that support Patterson's ideas of social alienation and death under slavery throughout history see: John Edwin Mason, *Social Death and Resurrection: Slavery and Emancipation in South Africa* (Charlottesville and London: University of Virginia Press, 2003); Smallwood, *Saltwater Slavery*; Margot Minardi, *Making Slavery History: Abolition and the Politics of Memory in Massachusetts* (Oxford and New York: Oxford University Press, 2010).

[38] Ghislaine Lydon has shown the significance of the North Star or Polaris to the caravaners across the Sahara. See Lydon, *On Transaharan Trails*, 29, 83, and 226.

[39] J. O. Urama, "Astronomy and Culture in Nigeria," in J. Holbrook et al. eds., *African Cultural Astronomy: Current Archaeoastronomy and Ethnoastronomy Research in Africa* (n.p.: Springer, 2008), 233.

Africa at the time—or so it seems from a nineteenth-century Hausa manuscript—and could be easily spotted in the tropical skies of Bahia and Cuba were Aldebaran or *Dabaran* for the Hausa (α-Taurus), Spica or *Simaku* (α-Virginis), and Antares or *Kalba* (α-Scorpio).[40]

References to planets were also common. Yoruba-speaking peoples in particular developed a number of proverbs in which the sun (*Oòrùn*), the moon (*Osù*), and planet Venus (*Àgùàlà*) appear regularly. Not surprisingly many of these proverbs are directly related to the countryside, and more importantly to crops and farming, while others reveal a traditional knowledge sprung from the regular observation of the sky:

> *Oòrùn ò kan àtàrí, owó ò dá* (The sun has not risen directly above the
>   head; working hands cannot cease their toil)
> *Fífé ni yiyìn osù; méjì-i rè kì í lé lójú òrun* (Adulation for the moon is a mark of
>   admiration for it; there are never two of them in the sky)
> *Àgùàlà mbá osù rìn, wón rò pé ajá-a rè ni* (The planet Venus follows the moon across
>   the sky, and people think it is the moon's dog)[41]

Although the cultural astronomy of West Africa remains poorly studied,[42] there are enough elements to reveal the practical uses of this knowledge on the daily lives of the Nagô, the Lucumí, and other neighboring peoples; a knowledge that almost certainly was transferred to the other side of the Atlantic and kept alive as the *bozal* Africans adapted to their new environments eventually becoming *ladinos*, or acculturated Africans. For example, one of the stars mentioned above, Altair (α-Aquila), was of utmost importance to Yoruba speakers and probably for the people of neighboring states like Nupe and Borgu, since its appearance in the morning skies signaled the advent of the harvest season.[43] According to J. O. Urama stars would determine the timing for a number of events, and would allow for the necessary synchronization of the beginning of the farming season (*Onwa Mvu*) with the coming of the rains, so that a good crop would be harvested.[44] Although very little is known about the ways in which this knowledge was transplanted to Bahia and Cuba, some references remain that point towards a continuation of the observance of a lunar calendar, as opposed to the Gregorian calendar adopted by the Christian West. A case in question, which will be discussed in Chapters 4 and 5, was that of Fermín Lucumí. A slave in the sugar estate La Sonora, he was apprehended by Cuban authorities upon the defeat of the slave movement he helped bring about and declared to them that he and his fellow Lucumí rebels had planned to rise "five moons earlier," clearly referring to four lunar months of 28 days each earlier.[45]

---

[40] Mervin Hiskett, "The Arab-Star Calendar and Planetary System in Hausa Verse," *Bulletin of the School of Oriental and African Studies*, 30–1 (1967): 158–76.

[41] Among the Yoruba, Venus was also referred to as the moon's dog (Ajá osù). For a complete list of these proverbs see: Oyekan Owomoyela, *Yoruba Proverbs* (Lincoln and London: University of Nebraska Press, 2005).

[42] Urama, "Astronomy and Culture in Nigeria," 237.

[43] Urama, "Astronomy and Culture in Nigeria," 233.

[44] Urama, "Astronomy and Culture in Nigeria," 237. See also Aimé Dafon Sègla, "De la cosmologie à la rationalisation de la vie sociale: ces mots idààcha qui parlent ou la mémoire d'un type de calendrier yoruba ancien," *Cahiers d'études africaines*, 46:1 (2006): 11–50.

[45] Deposition of Fermín Lucumí. Ingenio La Sonora. June, 1837. ANC: ME. 1178/B.

In Bahia, according to Dale Torston Graden, the *festa do inhame novo* (New Yam festival) was usually celebrated in November, coinciding with the harvest of the first roots of the season.[46] This festival, which was celebrated by Yoruba speakers, Igbo speakers, and other West African peoples in their homelands, attracted "an immense number of Africans" and was aimed at offering thanks to their deities and the dead "for the first fruits of the new harvest."[47]

The night sky was not, of course, the only thing that the new Africans from the Bight of Benin and its interior could and would relate to, since all three regions also shared tropical humid climates. West Africans recently transplanted to Bahia and Cuba were not exposed to drastic changes associated with relative seasonal humidity, precipitations, temperatures, or daily hours of sunlight. In Cuba hurricanes were a brand new experience, but even then strong winds were not totally unknown to them, since they were all familiar with the West African *harmattan*, a very different phenomenon but one that would often force them to seek refuge in a similar way as a tropical hurricane would.

Landscape settings, flora, and fauna were other features that would appear recognizable to the newly arrived Africans. The vast permanent and semi-permanent rain forests, mountains, swamps, and rivers that constituted their new surroundings were the sorts of sceneries that many of them had known throughout their lives.[48] This, of course, was the result of a common geological past. Both South America and Africa had been part of a supercontinent named West Gondwana that began to break up sometime between the early Jurassic and early Cretaceous periods (between 184 and 135 million years ago). Geological evidence indicates that South America and Africa took longer to separate than the rest of the West Gondwana, solidifying in this way "their shared evolutionary history."[49]

This common evolutionary history is also shared by Cuba. Together with the current territories of Florida and the Bahamas, the island of Cuba formed part of what Ron Redfern has called "a formidable piece of the Gondwana," also referred to as the Piedmont plate or the "top notch" region, in allusion to its geographical location with respect to the rest of the West Gondwana.[50] When compared with South America and West Africa, Cuba shares a significant number of indigenous, as opposed to imported at a later day, plant and animal families. Obviously, by the early nineteenth century, when the Nagô and the Lucumí became numerous in

---

[46] Dale Torston Graden, *From Slavery to Freedom in Brazil: Bahia, 1835–1900* (Albuquerque: University of New Mexico Press, 2006), 121.

[47] Graden, *From Slavery to Freedom in Brazil*, 121. See also Lillian Trager, *Yoruba Hometowns: Community, Identity, and Development in Nigeria* (London: Lynne Riener Publishers, 2001), 22.

[48] Carlos Galindo Leal and Ibsen de Gusmão Câmara, *The Atlantic Forest of South America: Biodiversity, Status, Threats, and Outlook* (Washington, DC: Island Press, 2003); Reinaldo Funes Monzote, *From Rainforest to Cane Field in Cuba: An Environmental History since 1492* (Chapel Hill: University of North Carolina Press, 2008).

[49] Robert A. Voeks, *Sacred Leaves of Candomblé: African Magic, Medicine, and Religion in Brazil* (Austin: University of Texas Press, 1997), 8.

[50] Ron Redfern, *The Evolution of Continents, Oceans, and Life* (Norman: University of Oklahoma Press, 2001), 159. See also Robert J. Pankhurst et al., *West Gondwana: Pre-Cenozoic Correlations across the South Atlantic Region* (London: The Geological Society, 2008), 49.

both Bahia and Cuba, many other species had crossed the Atlantic in all directions and were found in the most diverse places.

The first impressions must have been mixed. As Carney and Rosomoff have recently pointed out, newly arrived Africans would have still found many unknown plants and animals, but they would have also come across many other species that "would have been recognizable because they belong to plant genera found in both the Old and the New World."[51] Africans, in the words of Robert A. Voeks while referring to Bahia, "were viewing a mirror image of Mother Africa, a long-lost fraternal twin, one that had changed considerably since continental plate separation, but to the discerning eye was clearly of the same parental stock."[52]

These new landscapes were fundamental for the reproduction of West African cultures and beliefs on the other side of the ocean. Rainforests, as Voeks has argued in the case of Bahia and I argue for Cuba as well, provided an ideal environment "for animistic correspondence and substitution."[53] Both Bahia and Cuba featured "an array of physical features complementary to the ones to which they had previously attached cosmological significance."[54] Rivers, streams, and creeks, abundant in these two American lands, provided a habitat for Oshun, while Shango was never absent thanks to the frequent tropical thunderstorms that reminded the Nagô and the Lucumí of his existence and power. Those who practiced the religion of the orishas or orixás did not have major problems in finding some of the important African plants to honor their gods and ancestors, since many of them were readily available, while others were shrewdly replaced by new species from the same plant families they had used in tropical West Africa, giving way to what Carney and Rosomoff have aptly called a process of rediscovery.[55]

At a more material level these new landscapes provided Africans with a vast range of plants that could be used for medicinal or alimentation purposes. In the early nineteenth century important West African food staples such as rice, plantains, black eye-peas, millet, sorghum, and yams were all common to both territories. Guinea grass (*panicum maximum*) was ordinarily used for pasture in both Bahia and Cuba, and other plants, such as okra and the Guinea palm tree (*elaeis guineensis*) were easily available.[56] James Whetherell, during his visit to Bahia in the mid-nineteenth century, referred to the palm oil and the ways in which the Africans who lived there used it.[57] Similarly, Reverend Abiel Abbot commented on having seen several Guinea palm trees in Cuba, from which oil was being extracted. Abbot also observed that the palm tree oil was being produced to satisfy the needs of the Africans because

[51] Judith A. Carney and Richard Nicholas Rosomoff, *In the Shadow of Slavery: Africa's Botanical Legacy in the Atlantic World* (Berkeley and Los Angeles: University of California Press, 2009), 88–9. See also, Alwyn Gentry, "Diversity and Floristic Composition of Lowland Tropical Forest in Africa and South America," in Peter Goldblatt, ed., *Biological Relationships between Africa and South America* (New Haven: Yale University Press, 1993), 507–47.

[52] Voeks, *Sacred Leaves*, 7.   [53] Voeks, *Sacred Leaves*, 161.

[54] Voeks, *Sacred Leaves*, 161.   [55] Carney and Rosomoff, *In the Shadow of Slavery*, 102.

[56] Carney and Rosomoff, *In the Shadow of Slavery*, 166–70. See also Abiel Abbot, *Letters written in the Interior of Cuba between the Mountains of Arcana, to the East, and of Cusco, to the West, in the months of February, March, April and May, 1828* (Boston: Bowles and Dearborn, 1829), 57.

[57] James Whetherell, *Brazil: Stray Notes from Bahia: Being Extracts from Letters, &c., during a Residence of Fifteen Years* (Liverpool: Webb and Hunt, 1860), 114.

they would "prefer it to butter."[58] In Bahia, palm tree oil was called *dendê* and today still constitutes a main ingredient of Bahian cuisine.[59]

Animals, particularly wild animals, were in many ways different. The rich fauna of tropical West Africa differed from that of Bahia or Cuba in many ways. Lions, elephants, giraffes, and Hippopotamuses were not present in the Americas, although at least in the Brazilian rainforest the jaguar would have reminded Africans of its spotted and smaller close relative the leopard. In spite of this lack of large known mammals, other wild and domestic species indigenous to their new surroundings would have been familiar to most of them. Crocodiles, for example, could be found with little trouble in the rivers and streams of all three territories; and different types of snakes were well spread across these lands. Ants and termites were another component of the rural landscape that would have not escaped the eye of the new Africans.[60] Preventing the advance of ants and termites into inhabited areas was a very important piece of practical knowledge for West Africans. This ancestral knowledge inherited from their elders was also put into practice in the New World. In his notes of Bahia, taken during the 1840s and 1850s, James Whetherell referred at various opportunities to the threats posed by ants and termites to the humans who lived nearby.[61] Henry Tudor, during his visit to Cuba, also mentioned these ants that infested the soil and raised "mounds to an enormous height."[62] A fight between an African slave and the ants of one of these mounds was described by Abbot in one of his letters written in Cuba in the late 1820s. With great precision the South Carolinian minister highlighted the skills and bravery of this African man while dealing with the ants, who in his own words had "plunged into the very heart of their citadel" and who, "disregarding their bite, was transferring them with hand and shovel" to the fire he had started nearby. His abilities did not end up there though, as he sometimes also kindled "with husks a quick flame to destroy them in their cells."[63]

Among the many domesticated animals with which West Africans would renew direct contact in their new surroundings were horses, sheep, goats, dogs, guinea fowl, and African cattle that had arrived in the Americas well before the nineteenth century had begun.[64] All of them would be related to their day-to-day existence in their new homes. Of these, due to sacrificial reasons sheep and goats may have been particularly important for religious reasons for those Africans who were Muslims, while horses—widely spread and used in the north of the Yoruba-speaking states and throughout the Sahel—would eventually be used in the course of some of the insurrections that are discussed in Chapters 4 and 5.

---

[58] Abbot, *Letters*, 44–5.

[59] Caloca Fernandes, *Viagem gastronômica através do Brasil* (São Paulo: Senac, 2001), 103, 214, 233.

[60] See Ramón de la Sagra, *Historia física, política y natural de la Isla de Cuba* (Paris: Librería de Arthus Bertrand, 1840). See also the "Memórias zoológico-médicas relativas ao Brasil" sent in 1834 to the Museum of Rome, Italy, from Brazil. ASV: NAB, 6/23. Among the things mentioned in this memoir were alligators, boas, poultry, a large number of tropical plants, rocks, and minerals. Although the memoir is missing, the list of Brazilian flora and fauna specimens reveals the biological and geological richness to be found across Brazil at the time.

[61] Whetherell, *Brazil: Stray Notes from Bahia*, 40–1, 89, 108, 148.

[62] Tudor, *Narrative*, 130.   [63] Abbot, *Letters*, 12.

[64] Carney and Rosomoff, *In the Shadow of Slavery*, 158–63.

The existence of all these African food staples, including domestic animals and plants, combined with a familiar natural setting that did not represent a dramatic break from the world they had known, presented the recently arrived Africans with a number of elements that undoubtedly helped them to recreate their lost homes. Removed from one tropical region to another, these men, women, and children found inviting physical habitats that provided a balance against the social environments in which they were now forced to live slave lives. Furthermore, for those who decided to run away, the tropical forests and swamps offered welcoming hideouts where life would resume and communities could flourish away from the cities and plantations.

NEW SOCIETIES

Although the Bahian and Cuban societies where the Nagô, the Lucumí, and their neighbors were transplanted differed significantly, they were also alike in many ways. Both Bahia and Cuba featured slave societies heavily reliant on plantation systems that had benefited from the collapse of the sugar industry in Saint Domingue after the slave revolt of 1791 had begun. Throughout the first half of the nineteenth century both territories were dominated to a major or lesser extent by the wishes of political elites that were seriously committed to the continuation of the transatlantic slave trade, in spite of the bilateral treaties signed by their governments and Great Britain. Both places were also on the verges of a revolutionary world that was changing at a fast pace. In addition to the many African-led plots and insurrections that plagued them during this period, several movements of a different kind led by Creoles, peninsulars, and the free colored population also defined the course of history in both places. Bahia in particular, was the setting for a small-scale war of independence that lasted between 1822 and 1823. Cities, plantations, and smallholdings were all on the fringes of a transformative maelstrom that eventually led to the creation of the Empire of Brazil and to the consolidation of Spanish Colonial domination in Cuba, at a time when the rest of Spanish America attained independence.[65]

The solid relationship between merchants and planters on one side and the state on the other determined the course of history in these two territories of the Americas during the period. In Bahia their investment in sugar and slaves was nothing new, although the revolution in Saint Domingue was a catalyst for a rush

---

[65] See among others Hendrik Kraay, *Race, State and Armed Forces in Independence-Era Brazil: Bahia, 1790s–1840s* (Stanford, CA: Stanford University Press, 2004); Laird T. Bergad, *The Comparative Histories of Slavery in Brazil, Cuba, and the United States* (Cambridge: Cambridge University Press, 2007); Rafael de Bivar Marquese, "1808 e o impacto do Brasil na construção do escravismo cubano," *Revista USP*, 79 (2008): 118–31; Josef Opatrný, "Cuba en el contexto internacional," in Consuelo Naranjo Orovio, ed., *Historia de Cuba* (Madrid: CSIC-Doce Calles, 2009), 233–53; Sherry Johnson, "From Authority to Impotence: Arango's Adversaries and their Fall from Power during the Constitutional Period," in María Dolores González-Ripoll and Izaskun Álvarez Cuartero, eds., *Francisco Arango y la invención de la Cuba azucarera* (Salamanca: Ediciones Universidad de Salamanca, 2009), 193–213.

of new investments in what was considered by merchants and planters alike as an exceptional historical moment. The alliance in Bahia was so strong that even during the transition from captaincy to state, it remained unmoved. As would happen in Cuba, the revolution of the slaves in Saint Domingue caused concern and fear, leading to what Hendrik Kraay has aptly called a "shift to a binary racial system"[66] that augmented the oppression of slaves and free colored. [67]

For Bahian merchants and planters the army became a very necessary instrument to keep the peace and thus, to multiply their profits in a steady and confident manner. The opinions of some of them, like Luiz Paulino de Oliveira Pinto da França and Cipriano José Barata de Almeida, carried enough weight to influence politics at both the Bahian and Brazilian level.[68] Although Portuguese domination was eventually erased in the whole of Brazil, Bahia—to a large extent due to these merchants and planters—continued to be a focus for separatist ideas, and after 1822 only the existence of large numbers of African slaves in their cities and countryside stopped the Bahian elites from organizing more plots aimed at seceding from the imperial government of Rio de Janeiro.[69]

In Cuba things were not much different. In Havana a rising Creole planter elite led by Francisco de Arango y Parreño, Nicolás Calvo de la Puerta, and José de Ilincheta pushed its own agenda for the development of a plantation economy in the island from 1792 onwards, taking advantage of the disturbances in the neighboring French colony of Saint Domingue. In their attempt they were seconded by the mostly peninsular merchants that operated in the city, who saw a golden opportunity to get involved in the business of the transatlantic slave trade. Royal orders and decrees issued in Spain granted them trade privileges never seen before in Spanish America.[70] Before long, a prosperous sugar and coffee plantation economy took over the western part of the island and successfully supplanted Saint Domingue as the world leading producer and exporter of sugar. As in Bahia, too, the ever increasing number of Africans imported to work in the cities and plantations deterred them to push for a full independence.[71]

---

[66] Kraay, *Race, State and Armed Forces*, 23.

[67] For a new take on Haiti's impact on Brazil see: João José Reis and Flávio dos Santos Gomes, "Repercussions of the Haitian Revolution in Brazil, 1791–1850," in David Patrick Geggus and Norman Fiering, eds., *The World of the Haitian Revolution* (Bloomington: Indiana University Press, 2009), 284–314.

[68] Kraay, *Race, State and Armed Forces*, 109. See also Jeffrey D. Needell, *The Party of Order: The Conservatives, the State and Slavery in the Brazilian Monarchy, 1831–1871* (Stanford, CA: Stanford University Press, 2006), especially ch. 2 "The Threat of Revolution and the Reactionary Mobilization: 1831–1837."

[69] See e.g. Bethell, "The Abolition of the Brazilian Slave Trade," 71, 220, and 312; B. J. Barickman, *A Bahian Counterpoint: Sugar, Tobacco, Cassava and Slavery in the Recôncavo* (Stanford, CA: Stanford University Press, 1998), 104.

[70] See, among others, "Real Cédula reformando la libertad de comercio de negros otorgada a los virreinatos de Santa Fé y Buenos Aires, Capitanía de Caracas y Antillas Mayores." San Lorenzo, 24 November 1791, in Manuel Lucena Salmoral, *Regulación de la esclavitud negra en las colonias de América Española, 1503–1886* (Madrid: EDITUM, 2005), 256–9; and "Real Orden Reservada prorrogando el libre comercio de esclavos, ordenando respetar la cédula de 1789 para su tratamiento e importar esclavas para facilitar la procreación." AGI: IG, 2770.

[71] See, among others, Anthony P. Maingot, "Haiti and the Terrified Conciousness of the Caribbean," in Gert Oostindie, ed., *Ethnicity in the Caribbean: Essays in Honor of Harry Hoetink* (Amsterdam: Amsterdam

These two societies then, resembled each other in many different ways: powerful elites with serious interests in the continuation and growth of the slave trade and on the development of plantations; governments that acquiesced to most of their claims; armies of considerable size to keep their African population in check; and large, ever growing numbers of African-born slaves, many of whom had come from the Bight of Benin, and who now populated both their cities and countryside.

Buoyant economies dependent on sugar and slavery led to the expansion of plantations areas in the Recôncavo and the plains west and east of Havana. Their success transformed them into desirable destinations and investment opportunities for foreign businessmen from Europe and the rest of the Americas, ultimately changing both regions into cosmopolitan zones in an increasingly well-connected Atlantic World. American and European businessmen in particular migrated to Cuban and Bahian cities from the late 1810s onward. In Cuba, they took advantage of the new policies to foment white immigration, put in place by Intendant Alejandro Ramírez in 1818.[72] In Bahia, by the time the war of independence had begun, they were a group large and powerful enough to demand protection in the strongest possible terms from the American government through their Consul in Salvador, Woodbridge Odlin.[73]

Social tensions in this period were high, and the world that waited for the newly landed Africans was full of infighting between Creoles and peninsulars, independentists and loyalists, and in the Bahian case, republicans and monarchists. Even before the nineteenth century opened Salvador de Bahia was the stage for the *revolta dos Alfaiates* (Tailors' revolt) of 1798. This movement, in which free colored people were handsomely represented, sought among other things the creation of a federal republic in Bahia in which trade would not be restricted by royal dispositions and where slavery would be abolished.[74]

The French invasion of the Iberian Peninsula in 1808 had almost immediate consequences for both Bahia and Cuba. With the exile of the Portuguese royal court in Rio de Janeiro, Brazil soon became the center of the Portuguese Empire. Meanwhile, in Cuba a group of merchants and planters who called themselves liberals attempted to seize power in Havana by creating a *Junta de Gobierno* after the Spanish royal family were made prisoners by Napoleon Bonaparte that same year.[75] Although the

University Press, 2005), 65–7; Matt D. Childs, *The 1812 Aponte Rebellion*, 7–13, 30–2, 76, and 133; Ada Ferrer, "Speaking of Haiti: Slavery, Revolution, and Freedom in Cuban Slave Testimony," in Geggus and Fiering, eds., *The World of the Haitian Revolution*, 223–47.

[72] "Reglas para el domicilio de nuevos colonos y sus auxilios." 6 March 1818. ANC: AP, 298/2. For a reproduction of this document see Manuel Barcia, *The Great African Slave Revolt of 1825: Cuba and the Fight for Freedom in Matanzas* (Baton Rouge: Louisiana State University Press, 2012), appendix 2.

[73] Merchants and other American Citizens to Consul Woodbridge Odlin. Bahia, 13 September 1822. NA-US: MC-Bahian Consulate, R684.

[74] On the Tailors' movement of 1798, probably the most comprehensive study is István Jancsó, *Na Bahia contra o Império: história do ensaio da sedição de 1798* (São Paulo: Hucitec, 1976). Other important works on this event are: Luis Henrique Dias Tavares, *História da sedição intentada na Bahia em 1798* (São Paulo: Editora Pioneira, 1975) and Donald Ramos, "Social Revolution Frustrated: The Conspiracy of the Tailors in Bahia, l798," *Luso-Brazilian Review*, 13:1 (1976): 74–90.

[75] Francisco Ponte Domínguez, *La Junta de la Habana en 1808* (Havana: Guerrero, 1947); Johnson, "From Authority to Impotence," 193–213; and José Antonio Piqueras, *Sociedad civil y poder en Cuba: colonia y poscolonia* (Madrid: Siglo XXI, 2005), 71–3.

plan failed, there were clear signs of dissent among a previously pacific population that had until then given virtually no indication of having a rebel spirit.[76] A revolutionary movement uncovered in 1810, and the plot organized in 1811 and 1812 by the free colored people of Havana and other towns and villages known as the conspiracy or revolt of Aponte, rocked the formerly stable foundations of Cuban society and alerted the elites to the hard times that were to come.[77]

In the following years Cuba continued to experience social unrest. The new constitutional period ushered by the insurrection of the Spanish army that was about to sail for the New World from Cadiz to fight the South American rebels allowed the Cuban people a few liberties that had been missing until then. Freemasons took advantage of the new situation in Spain almost immediately and in connection with their Mexican partners soon began to conspire. The Soles y Rayos de Bolívar (Suns and Rays of Bolivar) plot, named after a freemasonic lodge and uncovered in 1823 was without a doubt the most serious menace to the Spanish Colonial domination in Cuba to date. The threats, however, were many and could arise from almost any sector of the Cuban society. In August 1824 army lieutenant Gaspar Rodríguez led a soldiers' rebellion in Matanzas, and not long after a new wider plot known as the Gran Legión del Águila Negra (Great Legion of the Black Eagle), with a leadership and contacts that spread across Central America and the Caribbean, required the full attention of the Spanish colonial authorities in the island.[78]

In Bahia the situation was much more complicated. To the already frequent African uprisings that had been affecting city and countryside since 1807, a new political and military conflict was added. While most of the other captaincies of Brazil embraced the new monarch Pedro I between 1821 and 1822, troops loyal to Portugal took the City of Salvador and triggered the most serious military conflict of the period, often referred to as the War of Independence of Bahia.[79] The war lasted for a year, until the Portuguese loyalists were finally defeated after a long blockade by land and sea that included a naval force under the command of the famous British Admiral Thomas Cochrane, who had been sent from Rio de Janeiro to help putting the insurrection down.[80] Even after the war concluded, tensions between Portuguese and Brazilian citizens continued to exist and were roused at various opportunities throughout the next two decades.

In the following years Bahia served as the stage for a series of uprisings of various kinds. In October 1824 the Levante dos Periquitos (Periquitos revolt) devastated Salvador. The authorities saw this military uprising as a "revolt of black soldiers

[76] José Antonio Piqueras, "La siempre fiel Isla de Cuba, o la lealtad interesada," *Historia Mexicana*, 58:1 (2008): 427–86.

[77] For the 1809–10 plot organized by Román de la Luz and Joaquín Infante see Luis Navarro García, *La independencia de Cuba* (Madrid: MAPFRE, 1992), 49–51. For the Aponte movement see Childs, *The 1812 Aponte Rebellion*.

[78] For the 1824 uprising of Gaspar Rodríguez see: "On Gaspar Rodríguez in Matanzas. The Conspiracy of 1824." AHN: ULT, 1603, 55. For the Águila Negra plot see Jacobo de la Pezuela, *Ensayo histórico de la isla de Cuba* (New York: Rafael, 1842), 557–64.

[79] See e.g. the essays published in Jurandir Malerba, ed., *A Independência brasileira: novas dimensões* (Rio de Janeiro: Editora FGV, 2006).

[80] Neill Macaulay, *Dom Pedro: The Struggle for Liberty in Brazil and Portugal, 1798–1834* (Durham, NC.: Duke University Press, 1986).

and ex-slaves."[81] As a direct consequence this insurrection offered a great opportunity to the local government to formally bring to an end the participation of free colored sections of the Bahian population in the military.[82] A few years later, in 1832, another insurgency broke out in the parishes of São Félix e Cachoeira. This movement, known as the Federação o revolta de Guanais (Federation or Revolt of Guanais) had an eminent autonomist and republican character and was successful for a brief period when the rebels managed to set up a provisional government. After the movement was suffocated by an army under the command of the Viscount of Pirajá, the main leader Bernardo Guanais Mineiro was captured and imprisoned in the Forte de São Marcelo, a circular fortress built in the seventeenth century in the waters of the harbor about 300 yards offshore from the Cidade Baixa of Salvador. Even then, a few months later in 1833, Guanais Mineiro succeeded in convincing the soldiers guarding the fort to rebel and from there bombarded the City of Salvador before being defeated once again.

The events of 1832 and 1833 constituted a threshold for two of the most significant insurrections in the history of Brazil. Firstly, in 1835, the revolt of the Malês, which will be discussed in Chapters 4 and 5, revived the fears of a racial war among the residents of Bahia. Then, in late 1837, a liberal and separatist uprising known as the *Sabinada*, named after its main leader Francisco Sabino Vieira, proclaimed the independence of the "República Bahiana" and brought the city and its countryside to a standstill that lasted for months. Although the Sabinada counted on free colored and slaves among their participants, its leaders were never comfortable with their involvement and demands. The movement, nevertheless, presented both Creole and African-born slaves with a new opportunity to challenge the status quo; an opportunity that they did not hesitate in taking.[83]

Meanwhile during the same period Cuba was affected by a deadly epidemic of cholera in 1833,[84] by new manifestations of social unrest activated by members of the free colored community, some of them former members of the Colored Militias[85] and some others foreigners, as in the case of Jorge Davidson in 1837[86],

---

[81] Hendrik Kraay, "Em outra coisa não falavam os pardos, cabras, e crioulos: o recrutamiento de escravos na Guerra da Independência na Bahia," *Revista Brasileira de história*, 22:43 (2002). Online at: <http://www.scielo.br/scielo.php> (accessed on 21 January 2011).

[82] Kraay, "Em outra coisa não falavam;" and Sérgio Armando Diniz Guerra Filho, "O povo e a guerra: participação das camadas populares nas lutas pela independência do Brasil na Bahia" (UFB Masters dissertation, 2004), 124–5.

[83] Hendrik Kraay, "'As terrifying as unexpected': The Bahian Sabinada, 1837–1838," *Hispanic American Historical Review*, 72:4 (1992): 501–25; and Juliana Serzedello Crespin Lopes, "Liberdade, liberdades: dilemas da escravidão na Sabinada (Bahia, 1837–1838)," *Sankofa: Revista de história da África e de estudos da diáspora Africana*, 6 (2010). Online at: <http://sites.google.com/site/revistasankofa/sankofa6/liberdade-liberdades> (accessed on 14 January 2011).

[84] Adrián López Denis, "Disease and Society in Colonial Cuba, 1790–1840" (Ph.D. diss. UCLA, 2007).

[85] Stephan Palmié, *Wizards and Scientists: Explorations in Afro-Cuban Modernity and Tradition* (Durham, NC: Duke University Press, 2002), 145–6; and Ivor Miller, *Voice of the Leopard: African Secret Societies and Cuba* (Jackson: University Press of Mississippi, 2009), 83–5.

[86] For the Davison case see Jane Landers, *Atlantic Creoles in the Age of Revolution* (Cambridge, MA: Harvard University Press, 2010), 215–18. For a discussion of other movements organized by the free colored population during the 1830s and early 1840s see Pedro Deschamps Chapeaux, *Los*

and by a new constitutional uprising in 1836 led by General Manuel Lorenzo, then Governor of Santiago de Cuba.[87] Among all these dangers, the presence of the British officials in Havana was perhaps the most daunting. By 1843 they had been repeatedly accused of interfering with Cuban affairs and one of them in particular, David Turnbull, had been forced out of the island in a couple of occasions as a result.[88]

When a massive conspiracy led by free colored men from Havana and Matanzas was uncovered late in 1843, the British, and Turnbull in particular, were immediately accused of being directly involved in the organization of the plot. This movement seems to have been an extended conspiracy that also included important numbers of Creole and African-born urban and rural slaves. To add to the Cuban authorities' fears, there were also indications that troops from Haiti could be ready to come and join the rebels once the insurrection had begun.[89] The repression that followed was in many ways similar to that implemented by the Bahian authorities in the aftermath of the revolt of the Malês in 1835. The free colored were singled out and dealt the harshest penalties; many of them were executed while others died in the dungeons of Havana and Matanzas during the months that followed the uncovering of the plot.[90]

Throughout these decades both Bahian and Cuban societies were plagued by discontent and fear. Peace was achieved, but the price paid was often high, especially for subaltern groups such as the free colored and the slaves. In the main cities and towns of both territories, recently arrived Africans had the opportunity to discover a new culture from which they took many traits and to which they contributed significantly. On the other hand, for those sent to plantations where slave life could remind them in many ways of their own past experiences, the process of settlement and acculturation would effectively last for much longer.

Urban or rural, domestic or field workers, their final destinations often determined the fate of the Africans taken to Bahia and Cuba. The conditions of existence in urban centers and plantations were more often than not harsh and full of deprivations. Nevertheless, those Africans who had the opportunity to interact within urban environments with other Africans, and Atlantic people in general, were more likely to learn a new language faster, to accumulate some wealth, and more importantly to have a greater degree of freedom.[91] In contrast, those who were sent to the

---

batallones de pardos y morenos (Havana: Instituto del Libro, 1976), 83–6; and Childs, *The 1812 Aponte Rebellion*, 175–9; María del Carmen Barcia, *Los ilustres apellidos*.

[87]   Christopher Schmidt-Nowara, *Empire and Anti-Slavery: Spain, Cuba, and Puerto Rico, 1833–1874* (Pittsburgh: University of Pittsburgh Press, 1999), 21–3. See also Manuel Lorenzo, *Manifiesto del General Don Manuel Lorenzo a la nación española* (Cádiz: Campe, 1837).

[88]   Paquette, *Sugar is Made with Blood*, 139–50; Manuel Barcia, "Entre Amenazas y Quejas: un acercamiento al papel jugado por los diplomáticos ingleses durante la Conspiración de la Escalera, 1844," *Colonial Latin American Historical Review*, 10:1 (2001): 1–26; David Murray, *Odious Commerce: Britain, Spain, and the Abolition of the Cuban Slave Trade* (Cambridge: Cambridge University Press, 2002), 138–62; and Karim Ghorbal, *Réformisme et esclavage à Cuba, 1835–1845* (Paris: Publibook, 2009), 160.

[89]   Paquette, *Sugar is Made with Blood*, 247–8; Barcia, *Seeds of Insurrection*, 27–9.

[90]   Bergad, *The Comparative Histories*, 212–13; Barcia, *Seeds of Insurrection*, 27–9.

[91]   See, among others, Stuart Schwartz, "The Manumission of Slaves in Colonial Brazil: Bahia, 1684–1745," *Hispanic American Historical Review*, 54 (1974): 603–35; Hebe Mattos, *Das cores do*

countryside, and particularly those who ended up living in sugar and coffee plantations, had very little chances of enjoying the same kind of freedom and interaction with their new social environment. Often forced to work under the whip of an overseer or a slave driver, and surrounded by fellow African slaves, they were able to retain and reproduce their cultures in a less contaminated manner within the relative isolation of the plantations. While urban life presented more opportunities for redemption through the use of legal channels and by exploiting the sympathy of good-hearted owners, plantation life offered very few chances for peaceful change. Interestingly enough, the partial freedom they enjoyed in cities and towns also played into their hands, and alongside less violent forms of resistance, these African men and women also convened and carried out fierce uprisings in both territories. As a result, both urban centers and plantations became adequate environments for the development of violent forms of resistance that were often West African in content and execution.[92]

Africans taken to these two American territories could benefit from a series of laws that, although devised to protect slave owners, also offered legal channels to the slaves, not only to gain freedom through manumission (including *coartación* or *coartação*, the right to buy their freedom by making an initial down payment that would set their price, and then paying the rest of the money over time) but also granted them the possibility of complaining about their masters and requesting to be sold to new ones.[93] Obviously urban slaves were able to take advantage of these laws because they had greater social mobility, they lived close to the tribunals where denunciations were presented, and because they knew Portuguese or Spanish and were able to learn about these laws and to understand how to use them to their own advantage.[94] For those Africans who found themselves surrounded by other Africans within plantation environments, the possibilities of complaining about the cruelties of their masters or to attain freedom through legal means were quite remote. The plantation world was to a large extent a diasporical African world where prisoners from many former enslaving wars in different African regions had found themselves with very limited rights and possibilities to improve their lives.

---

silêncio: os significados da liberdade no sudeste escravista: Brasil século XIX (Rio de Janeiro: Nova Fronteira, 1998); Gloria García, *La esclavitud desde la esclavitud: la visión de los siervos* (Havana: Ciencias Sociales, 2003), 36–44; Alejandro de la Fuente, "Slave Law and Claims-Making in Cuba: The Tannenbaum Debate Revisited," *Law and History Review*, 22:2 (2004): 339–69; Barcia, *Seeds of Insurrection*, 87–9.

[92] João José Reis and Eduardo Silva, *Negociação e conflito: a resistência negra no Brasil escravista* (São Paulo: Companhia das Letras, 1999), 62–78; Gwendolyn Midlo Hall, *Slavery and African Ethnicities in the Americas*, 46, 100, 123, 169–70; Barcia, *Seeds of Insurrection*, 105–25.

[93] See de la Fuente, "Slave Law and Claims-Making in Cuba," 339–69; On *coartación* in Cuba see Claudia Varella, "Esclavos a sueldo: la coartación cubana en el siglo XIX" (Ph.D. diss. Universidad Jaume I, 2010). On *coartação* in Brazil see: Eduardo França Paiva, "Coartações e alforrias nas Minas Gerais do século XVIII: as possibilidades de libertação escrava no principal centro colonial," *Revista de história*, 133 (1995): 49–57; and Vanessa Ramos, "A alforria comprada pelos 'escravos da religião' (Rio de Janeiro—1840–1871)," *História social*, 13 (2007): 121–37.

[94] Keila Grinberg, *Liberata. A lei da ambiguedade. As ações de liberdade da Corte de Apelação do Rio de Janeiro no século XIX* (Rio de Janeiro: Relume Dumará, 1994); and Barcia, *Seeds of Insurrection*, 87–9.

The world of the plantation slave was habitually filled with unpleasant commands and tasks. The work on sugar plantations in particular lasted often for as long as the sun was out and the actual tasks they were expected to do were all demanding and tiring. Nevertheless, the fact that Bahian and Cuban planters treated their slaves as machines did not mean that they were dehumanized. On the contrary, in spite of all the ruthless treatment and the endless working days, Africans still managed to reproduce their cultures and cosmologies, to interact with their new natural environments and to resist their slave condition.[95] They were repressed but by no means were they socially dead.

Not having the same opportunities to take advantage of the law that their urban counterparts enjoyed, resistance within plantations often took cultural forms. Religion, songs, dances, and drumming parties recreated 'Africa' and provided the slaves with necessary spaces to continue their traditions and beliefs. Although many could easily see acquiescence in these actions, they were really forms of resistance insofar as they undermined the social fabric of the slave systems where they had been forced to live. Bahian and Cuban authorities and planters were keen to erase the 'savage and uncivilized' Africa from the memories of their African slaves. By clinging on to their Nagô, Lucumí, Hausa, Jêje, or Arará diasporical identities, these men and women were effectively and, I would dare say, consciously contravening the wishes of their masters. Additionally, cultural forms of resistance should not be dismissed so straightforwardly, since it was during drumming parties and other social and religious gathering that many African insurrections started.[96]

Needless to say Africans also resorted to violent forms of resistance in both urban and rural settings, but it was in the countryside that suicide and runaway Africans more often opted to seek a better life away from the daily agony of the plantation life.[97] In the former case they did so with the conviction of ending their exile and going back in body and soul to their relatives and friends back in Africa. In the latter, they instead chose to recreate life as they knew it away from the white men, living in a closer interaction with nature and with the freedom

[95] Stuart Schwartz, *Sugar Plantations in the Formation of Bahian Society: Bahia, 1550–1835* (Cambridge: Cambridge University Press, 1985), 339–42, 484; Dain Edward Borges, *The Family in Bahia, Brazil, 1870–1945* (Stanford, CA: Stanford University Press, 1992), 32, 82–3; Barcia, *Seeds of Insurrection*, 73–5, 105–6, 118–19.

[96] This was the case in the 1825 African uprising in Guamacaro, Cuba, conceived and planned during Sunday festivities. It was also the case for the Urubu in 1826 in Bahia, where religious ceremonies at a Candomblé house owned by one Francisco de Tal seem to have served as a propitious environment for the organization of the Africans' resistance.

[97] This is not to say that urban slaves did not take their own lives or run away. Particularly in the case of Bahia, the African population of Salvador repeatedly escaped from their masters and formed *quilombos* in the outskirts of the city through the first four decades of the nineteenth century. See Stuart Schwartz, "Cantos e quilombos numa conspiração de escravos Haussás: Bahia, 1814," in João José Reis and Flávio dos Santos Gomes, eds., *Liberdade por um fio: história dos quilombos no Brasil* (São Paulo: Companhia das Letras, 1996): 381; and Flávio dos Santos Gomes, *A hidra e os pântanos: Mocambos, quilombos e comunidades de fugitivos no Brasil (séculos XVII–XIX)* (São Paulo: UNESP, 2005), 396–428.

of movement and expression that was denied to them on the plantations.[98] Plots and revolts were, nonetheless, the most extraordinary events associated with African populations not only in Bahia and Cuba, but also elsewhere in the New World. As will hopefully be demonstrated in Chapters 4 and 5, the series of armed movements that eroded colonial and imperial domination in Cuba and Bahia throughout the first half of the nineteenth century were in their majority, nothing but instances of a prolongation of West African warfare in the Americas.

CONCLUSIONS

As has been discussed in this chapter, the first days, weeks, and months for those West Africans taken to Bahia and Cuba were full of uncertainties. However, in spite of the intensity of their ongoing tragedies, many of them probably found hope in the most unsuspected of places. The world they encountered was in many ways akin to the one they had left behind. From plant families and animal species to climate and even the night skies, they found a myriad of familiar cosmological and cultural elements in their new homes. Furthermore, in urban centers as well as in rural estates they were able to link up with men and women who shared their own ethnic and cultural heritages, and who would ease out their introduction into the new harsh and oppressive social environments, and all this in spite of the noticeable differences existing between their homelands and their New World destinations.

Those things they found familiar and that reminded them of their homes in Africa have usually been understated elements of analysis for scholars attempting to explain the forms of resistance practiced by African slaves in the Americas. Familiarity with the surrounding environment, both natural and social, allowed them to carry out their emancipation plans according to the ancestral beliefs and knowledge of the world acquired on the other side of the Atlantic. Upon their arrival in Bahia and Cuba they found a world with more known than unknown elements, with more continuity than rupture, a convenient circumstance that permitted them to hang on to their West African identities and to continue to wage war in very analogous terms to the ways they had done so in their homelands. In the words of British Mixed Commission judge in Havana, Robert Jameson,

---

[98] On suicides see: João José Reis, *Death is a Festival: Funeral Rites and Rebellion in Nineteenth Century Brazil* (Chapel Hill: University of North Carolina Press, 2003), 145; Jackson Ferreira, "Por hojese acaba la lida: suicidio escravo na Bahia (1850–1888)," *Afro-Asia*, 31 (2004): 197–324; María Poumier Taquechel, "El suicidio esclavo en Cuba en los años 1840," *Anuario de estudios Americanos*, 43 (1986): 69–86; Louis A. Perez, *To Die in Cuba: Suicide and Society* (Chapel Hill: University of North Carolina Press, 2003), 25–64; Barcia, *Seeds of Insurrection*, 71–83. On runaway slaves see the essays featured in: Richard Price, ed., *Maroon Societies: Rebel Slave Communities in the Americas* (Baltimore and London: Johns Hopkins University Press, 1996); and Reis and Gomes, eds., *Liberdade por um fio*. For the Cuban case see also Gabino La Rosa Corzo, *Runaway Slave Settlements in Cuba: Resistance and Repression* (Chapel Hill: University of North Carolina Press, 2003).

"the African soil, from which they were torn, still cling[ed] to them."[99] As will be revealed and analyzed in Chapters 4 and 5 by establishing factual connections between the Bight of Benin and its interior with Bahia and Cuba, in the first half of the nineteenth century these two territories of the Americas became no less than physical extensions of the Dar-el-Harb, the West African realm of war, that these men, women and children had left behind.

---

[99] Robert Jameson, *Letters from the Havana, during the year 1820; containing an account of the present state of the island of Cuba, and observations on the slave trade* (London: John Miller, 1821), 20.

4

West African Warfare in Bahia and Cuba
Organization and Strategies

Awake, arise or be forever fall'n.

John Milton, *Paradise Lost*

On 15 June 1825 a group of slaves from the coffee plantation region of Guamacaro, southeast of Matanzas in Cuba, gathered together and proceeded to attack a number of neighboring rural estates, until they were finally repulsed and defeated around 12 hours later. Many of those who joined the movement perished in the various actions of that day, or later on, during the following days and months, as they were hunted down and killed. Some others were captured and interrogated by the colonial authorities who were eager to discover the motives that had led more than 200 of their own slaves to rebel against them.[1]

A curious aspect, found in the depositions given by those involved in this movement, was that irrespective of their ethnic background, practically none of them talked about a revolt, or a rebellion, or an insurrection, or anything of the sort. Instead, whenever they mentioned the events of that mid-June day, they referred to them as *the war*. For example, Pío, a slave in the La Hermita coffee plantation told the prosecutors about the three men who had promised him "weapons and gunpowder for the day of the war."[2] Similarly, José Luis, a slave in the El Solitario plantation confessed that a black man had come sometime before and had told them that "it was necessary to make war" against the whites, because they were punishing and killing all the blacks.[3] In the same vein, Tom Mandinga Soso declared that Lorenzo Lucumí and Federico Carabalí, the two ringleaders of the movement who were convinced that a long and protracted military campaign was about to begin, had come one night and encouraged him and his companions to "stop working in the fields, and to eat their chickens and other things that they might have, because with war everything was going to be lost."[4] Even a few years later in 1830, another African slave named Bozen Mandinga Moro referred to the events that had taken place five years earlier as the "war that took place against the blacks, many of whom were hanged."[5]

---

[1] Barcia, *The Great African Slave Revolt of 1825.*
[2] Deposition of Pío Carabalí. August 1825. ANC: CM. 1/5.
[3] Deposition of José Luis, slave of Gómez. August 1825. ANC: CM. 1/5.
[4] Deposition of Tom Mandinga Soso. August 1825. ANC: CM. 1/5.
[5] Deposition of Bozen Mandinga Moro. Limonar, July 1830. ANC: ME. 713/B.

References, like the ones cited above, given by Africans from different ethnies, help illustrate in unequivocal terms the different ways in which Africans on one side, and the rest of the inhabitants of these New World plantation societies on the other, saw the violent movements that historians have until today invariably considered as slave rebellions or revolts. For the authorities and planters of Bahia and Cuba there was little doubt that the Africans living in their cities and countryside plotted against them, and there were palpable proofs that they were avid to rebel, revolt, or engage in violent movements. It is clear that the ruling order and the planters and merchants feared such an uprising, as practically every time they referred to these actions they used the terms mentioned above, and from their point of view they were right. Whether free or slaves, these Africans were, after all, resisting the oppressive conditions that they had been forced to live in. In the eyes of authorities and planters of these two highly hierarchical plantation societies, the collective violent actions staged by their subordinate Africans were rebellions or revolts against the status quo and peace. However, for the Africans who led and participated in many of these events their actions seem to have meant only one thing: *war.*

How western concepts have been used to understand non-western societies has been a hot issue among historians, anthropologists, sociologists, and other scholars over the years. John K. Thornton, for example, while discussing the application of European models to the study of warfare in Africa, stressed how "military backwardness has been assumed as a parallel to economic backwardness" creating the false impression that Africans lived in primitive societies.[6] Curiously Thornton's conclusion could be applied not only to the contemporary scholars he was criticizing and but also to nineteenth-century Bahian and Cuban authorities and planters. The latter believed that the Africans they had imported to work on their cities and plantations were lawless savages living outside the Christian faith who were incapable of appreciating any civilized law or technological development, blinded by their own prejudices and preconceptions. Subsequently, in their opinion, their military actions—those revolts and insurrections they so often complained about—were heavily characterized by these backward traits and were never considered as actual organized military actions. This poor understanding of African warfare in the diaspora by contemporaries and by subsequent generations of historians is exceptionally problematic since it has conveniently overlooked the fact that African warfare was precisely the "ultimate source" of much of the population in these two slave societies.[7]

Told from the Africans' side, the story has a very different tone, as we will soon see. Yet, perhaps it is not so surprising that over a century after slavery was finally abolished in the Americas, the western concepts, terms, and models that were used during this historical period continue to be repeated over time without any serious questioning of their meanings and implications. While studying these African military movements historians—and I include myself among them—have until now continued to use the same western vocabulary and concepts used by authorities and planters while trying to understand the African side of the stories they are

---

[6] Thornton, *Warfare in Atlantic Africa*, 7.   [7] Thornton, *Warfare in Atlantic Africa*, 150.

meant to tell. Thus, a number of titles on slave conspiracies, revolts, and rebellions have been published—some of them nonetheless truly brilliant books—aiming at elucidating and explaining the African experience in Brazil and Cuba, from both above and below. Yet, in their vast majority they have failed to at least attempt to consistently recognize the movements they study as what they really were and what they meant to those who led them and participated in them. Moreover, this situation has not been exclusive to Brazil and Cuba, since many other titles focusing on other parts of the Americas have suffered from similar shortcomings.

As mentioned before, a main distinguishable characteristic common to all these military actions that shook the slave societies of Bahia and Cuba in the first half of the nineteenth century was, without any doubt, the fact that the protagonists consistently referred to their actions as *the war*. While discussing the understanding of African warfare by the Europeans many years ago, Robert S. Smith rightly highlighted an important issue that relates to the possibility of certain meanings getting lost in translation, in particular that of *war*. According to Smith, "in some languages a single word can imply a war, a battle, or just a skirmish,"[8] and this was particularly the case for some of the best-represented West African ethnies in the Bahian and Cuban cities and countryside. For example both Yoruba and Hausa speakers had well-defined words to refer to the distinctions of western concepts of *war* and *battle*. For the Yoruba speakers it was the term *ogun* while for the Hausa speakers it was the term *yaki*, although *fada* may have been occasionally used as well.

A brief look at the earlier written texts in Yoruba and Hausa languages from the mid-nineteenth century, offers an opportunity to assess the ways in which terms such as war and battle, as well as others, such as revolt and insurrection, were used at the time in West Africa. In his *Vocabulary of the Yoruba Language*, published in 1843, Samuel Ajayi Crowther used a number of words that could equate to war or battle in Yoruba.[9] Among them, the most important was *ogun*. Almost all other terms cited by Crowther included *ogun* in one way or another (e.g. *ija-ogun*) with the exception of *ija-pati*, which according to him described a pitched battle.[10] In the following years, Christian missionaries began an arduous work of translation of the various books of the Bible into the Yoruba language.[11] These translations, where passages of the Bible describing military actions are common, give us a unique window into the use and understanding of the terms that were used by Nagô and the Lucumí in Bahia and Cuba. Invariably, in each of the translated texts, the term *ogun* is used time and again when referring to actions of war, irrespective of whether they were large or small.[12] According to these translations,

[8] Robert S. Smith, *Warfare and Diplomacy in Pre-Colonial West Africa* (Madison: University of Wisconsin Press, 1976), 28.

[9] Samuel Crowther, *Vocabulary of the Yoruba Language* (London: Church Missionary Society, 1843), 13, 51, 139.

[10] Crowther, *Vocabulary of the Yoruba Language*.

[11] The most recent examination of these translation efforts is Sandra Nickel, "Spreading Which Word? Philological, Theological and Socio-political Considerations behind the 19th Century Bible Translation into Yoruba," *Leeds Working Papers for Linguistics and Phonetics*, 18 (2013): 54–84.

[12] See, among others, Exodus 32: 17 in Samuel Crowther, *The second book of Moses, commonly called Eksodus/translated into Yoruba for the use of the native Christians of that nation, by the Rev. Samuel*

however, Yoruba speakers also consistently used other terms to refer to instances of revolt or insurrection, notably *isote* and *sote*.[13] The fact that whenever they were asked about the origins or aims of the insurrections where they were the protagonists in Bahia or Cuba, they chose to respond using words like war or *ogun*, would then indicate a conscious choice on their part to refer to their own actions as actions of war.

In the case of the Hausa translations, one of the earliest available works is *Magana Hausa: Hausa Stories and Fables*, collected by James Frederick Schön, originally the work of Dorugu, a free slave who worked for explorers James Richardson and Heinrich Barth, and published for the first time in 1885. Hausa speakers in this period seemed to have interchangeably used the terms *yaki* and *fada* whenever they referred to actions of war, including battles. However, in one instance where a slave raid is carried out, none of these words is used, and instead the closest the author comes to equating war with raids, is a reference to the fact that he and the other captives were taken to a *sansani* or war camp after being captured. This repeated choice of *yaki* and *fada* to refer to actions of war, and the absence of any of these terms to refer to raids, and the use of the term *war* in Bahia, strongly suggest that Hausa speakers almost certainly considered the often-called revolts and insurrections that they organized on the other side of the Atlantic as military actions of war.

Therefore, the conscious choices of using the term *war* to define their own actions in Bahia and Cuba, strongly suggest that the Hausa, Nagô, Lucumí, and even other West African men and women interpreted their actions to be precisely that, actions of war. Moreover, other common aspirations mentioned time and again in the interrogatories of those who were captured after each of these movements took place seem to suggest that their actions were strongly connected to their main intention of waging war. For instance, they frequently denoted that among their objectives were to kill all the white men, to marry the white women, to take over the land, and to run away to the land of the blacks where they could all be free.[14]

Even keeping in consideration Smith's methodological question, references to West African warfare categorically remain the central element common to the vast majority of the African movements that took place in Bahia and Cuba between 1807 and 1844. The number of examples that support this statement are overwhelming, and even more so if we consider the obvious problems and deficiencies inherent in the existing primary sources for this period. In addition to the problems related to what may have gotten lost or misrepresented in translation, other issues that were present

Crowther, native missionary (London: British and Foreign Bible Society, 1854); and Numbers 31: 5, 31: 14, 31: 27, 31: 28, Deuteronomy 29: 7, Joshua 4: 13, and Judges 20: 18, 20: 20, all in Charles Gollmer Andrew and Samuel Crowther, *Bibeli Mimó eyi ni òro olorun ti Testamenti Lailai ati ti Titon: apa ekini ti Testamenti Lailai. Iwe ti Mose marun. Iwe ti Josua. Iwe ti awon Onidajo. Iwe ti Rutu* (London: A k fun awon egbe Bibeli ti a npè Britise at ti ilu omiran, 1867).

[13] See e.g. 2 Chronicles 21: 10, Ezra 4: 19, Nehemiah 9: 17, in Samuel Crowther, Adolphus Mann, D. O. Williams, and David Hinderer, *Iwe Mimo lati I. Samueli lo de Orin Solomoni* (London: A ko fun egbe Bibeli ti a npe ni Britise ati ti ilu miran, 1884). See also Crowther, *Vocabulary of the Yoruba Language*, 106, 214, 238.

[14] Examples of these testimonies are provided below, and in Chapter 5.

in almost every session of interrogation could lead to an even larger distortion of the reality than only those that the interrogated Africans were trying to describe.

While reading some of the testimonies about West African warfare, many of which will be reproduced below, I noticed a pattern that deserves a special mention: the habitual leading of the prisoners by those who interrogated them. Since the latter were bound to refer to the movements as insurrections, rebellions, revolts, etc., they frequently asked their questions using western terminology in Portuguese and Spanish, and in turn this often led the interrogated, and/or those who translated, to respond using the same terms. In those cases where it is obvious that the leading of the prisoners and witnesses did not take place, almost unanimously the interrogated Africans and/or their translators chose to use the term *war* to refer to the events in which they had been involved and which had led them to be questioned in first place.

Perhaps one of the clearest cases of African prisoners being coerced by the prosecutors is that of the interrogations carried out after the famous Malê movement was quashed in Bahia in January 1835. In this case the prosecutors seem to have used the word *insurreção* (insurrection) in almost every question they posed. Although the questions asked only rarely appear in the records—only the responses were consistently put on paper—, it is apparent from the written answers given from the first day that the interrogated Africans were being led to answer according to western terminology. As the days went by and the answers became longer and more intricate, references to *the war* suddenly started to appear in the depositions. For example, when given the opportunity to expand in her original response, Thereza, a Tappa (Nupe), told the authorities details such as that "the Saturday at night was the day of the war" and that when the Nagô came together they "talked about making war to the whites."[15] Other Africans such as Paulo, a Nagô, told the prosecutor that he had heard that his compatriot Lury had died "making war," while Agostinha, also a Nagô, declared that when she heard a noise coming from the street, Belchior told her that it was "the war of the Nagô" that she was hearing.[16] As happened in other movements in Bahia and Cuba, some Africans also used other terms that reflected their understanding of the world—as opposed to the more traditionally western terms used by the authorities—to refer to the military actions undertaken by them and their fellow Africans. Among these were the words *bulha* and *barulho* (noise, commotion), and at least once the word *banzé* (celebration, gathering). The fact that the imperial authorities recorded them reveals that even they were unable to forcefully translate the ideas and cultural expressions of the Africans they were interrogating into their own western terminology.

Something quite similar occurred in Cuba during the interrogations that followed the Lucumí armed movement of March 1843 which started on the grounds of the sugar plantation Alcancía, near the town of Bemba, southeast of Matanzas. In this case, the prosecutor also consistently led the witnesses provoking answers

---

[15] Deposition of Thereza, free woman of Tappa nation. "Devassa do levante de escravos ocurrido em Salvador em 1835," *Anais do Arquivo do Estado da Bahia*, 38 (1968): 34.
[16] Depositions of Paulo Nagô and Agostinha. "Devassa," *Anais*, 38 (1968): 35 and 100.

that replicated his own words, even though the vast majority of the prisoners had to testify using interpreters, who probably felt compelled to use the interrogator's own words as well. Nevertheless, when given their declarations some of the slaves referred to the events as the *bulla* (noise, commotion), a word that, as we have seen, was also used by the Nagô of Bahia. More to the point, at least one of the rebels, Marcos Lucumí declared that in his estate the Africans were "making war" and more intriguingly, in what seems to have been a reminiscence of his own African war-related past he also told the authorities that "since he had arrived in this land [Cuba] he had not yet seen anything like that," clearly implying that war actions similar to the one that he had just witnessed were not unfamiliar to him.[17]

In other cases, when the leading of prosecutors was not as blatant, African men and women were able to express themselves more freely, thus using their own words and expressions to describe events. Keeping in mind all the problems with existing sources, which are less rich in details for the Bahian case, it is still possible to find the word *war* used in the reports and court records that resulted from some of the most important African insurgencies of the period. In another specific case, after a large violent movement took place in Salvador de Bahia in April 1830, one of the Africans interrogated also referred to the events as the *bulha dos pretos* (noise caused by the blacks), and this in spite of the prosecutor using the word *revolução* (revolution) repeatedly in most of his questions.[18] Also after the first of these movements was uncovered in 1807 there were references to warfare. According to Howard Prince, the Hausa had conspired "to make war upon the whites."[19] More references to the act of war seem to have appeared in 1814 when two Hausa slaves told their master that they had overheard some of their fellow countrymen in the port talking among them of "a war against the whites."[20]

In the Cuban case, where the testimonies of the defeated Africans are more abundant, allusions and mentions to *the war* by them are more forthcoming. In addition to the examples from the 1825 movement in Guamacaro, provided at the beginning of this chapter, there were explicit references to the act of war in a handful of cases. In 1833, after more than 300 Africans, mostly Lucumí, attacked and ransacked a number of plantations and the town of Banes, west of Havana, some among those who were captured and interrogated also referred to the events as *the war*. Margarita Lucumí, for example, who was the partner of one of the ringleaders and military commanders of the African force, declared that her husband had told her that "they wanted to make war. . . against the whites, because they had enslaved them and were making them work, and because they punished them."[21] Gonzalo Mandinga, who was one of the non-Lucumí Africans to join this small army talked about the events in more than one occasion as "the war," while Atilano Lucumí, whose real name in West Africa was Bequé, referred to the beginning of the episode as "the moment when they went out to make war."[22]

[17] Deposition of Marcos Lucumí. April 1843. ANC: CM. 29/5.
[18] Deposition of Nicolau Nagô. April 1830. APEB: IE. 2845.
[19] Prince, "Slave Rebellion in Bahia," 89.   [20] Schwartz, "Cantos e quilombos," 381.
[21] Deposition of Margarita Lucumí. August 1833. ANC: ME. 540/B.
[22] Depositions of Gonzalo Mandinga and Atilano Lucumí (Bequé). August 1833. ANC: ME. 540/B.

Another case, in which the defeated Africans referred to their actions as *war* occurred in November 1843, after a large number of them, mostly Lucumí enslaved at the sugar plantations Ácana and Triunvirato, staged one of the largest slave military uprisings ever witnessed in colonial Cuba. Manuel, for example, explained how his companions at the Ácana plantation took with them "war drums," while Nicolás Gangá, also from the Ácana, declared that the objectives of the leaders were to "make war against the whites, be free and not to be exploited anymore."[23] Additionally, Damián Lucumí confessed to having been in charge of "playing the war drums."[24]

Documentary evidence suggests that what imperial and colonial authorities in Bahia and Cuba called insurrections, revolts, rebellions, uprisings, etc., to those who "rebelled" were more precisely, instances of armed struggle determined by previous knowledge and experiences of war, acquired and nurtured in West Africa. Naming them and considering them as such could give us fresh insights into the objectives and overall attitudes not only of those who defied enslavement, but also of hundreds of thousands of Africans who were transplanted to New World societies and who resisted oppression in other ways.

I am not proposing here the total abandonment of these traditional terms altogether, but rather to use them when looking at the manifestations of African warfare in these two slave societies mostly from the dominators' point of view. For instance, a number of books and articles published over the past decades specifically aim to explore the fundaments of the administration and functioning of these slave systems, including the control of their slave populations. They look, for example, into the Black Codes issued in various parts of the Americas and into the government and organization of slave economies.[25] For studies such as these, in which African customs and traditions—including their knowledge and understanding of warfare— are not at the center of the analysis, it makes sense to continue to regard and study these movements as slave revolts or slave rebellions.

However, when trying to assess the connotations and meanings attached to armed movements by those African men and women who participated in them, it makes sense to do so from a different perspective; and if at all possible, what could have been *their own* perspective. The military essence of these movements needs to be seriously taken into account every time we attempt to disentangle the meanings of their words and the reasons behind their actions. By using terms such as "slave revolt" or "slave insurrection" we continue to underestimate the vital military character of the vast majority of these movements. Perhaps it would make more sense to consider using more appropriate terms such as "slave military revolt" or "African military uprising," to mention but a couple of possibilities that would clarify at least in some measure the intrinsically martial character of each of these movements. From this point onwards, while referring

[23] Depositions of Manuel and Nicolás Gangá. November 1843. ANC: CM. 30/3.

[24] Deposition of Damián Lucumi. November 1843. ANC: CM. 30/3.

[25] See, among others, Manuel Moreno Fraginals, *El Ingenio: complejo económico social cubano del azúcar* (Havana: Ciencias Sociales, 1978), 3 vols.; Barickman, *A Bahian Counterpoint*; and Márcia Berbel, Rafael Marquese, and Tâmis Parron, *Escravidão e política: Brasil e Cuba, 1790–1850* (São Paulo: Hucitec/Fapesp, 2010).

to these events I will use terms such as the ones suggested above, or others more appropriate like armed movement, insurgency, military action, small army, and of course war, all of which, in my opinion, allow for a more critical assessment and understanding of what they meant to those who organized them and carried them into practice.

When examined this way, not surprisingly, the vast majority of armed struggle instances carried into practice by West Africans in Bahia and Cuba strongly resemble similar military actions that had taken place in their West African homelands. In many ways they—or at least an important number of them—were still fighting using similar weapons and following the same strategies they had observed, learned, and/or practiced before they had been enslaved. In various opportunities they took arms within days or weeks of being landed in the New World, and in some other cases they did so as soon as the chains came off their feet. To them, very likely, the white man was just a new enemy; there were clear signs that he was a powerful and resourceful foe, but all the same, there were no past experiences that pointed to the fact that he was invincible. As a matter of fact the vast majority of those Africans who were taken to Bahia and Cuba in the first half of the nineteenth century had never fought against the whites and equally, had not been enslaved by them. They had been defeated in war, or kidnapped and enslaved by other African men who then sold them to the whites, but that hardly pointed to any sort of military prowess held by the latter. If anything, they could have been considered as resourceful adversaries who were financially stronger since they had the means to buy Africans as slaves.

The fact, however, remains that white men had not defeated, in the battlefield, any of the West Africans they shipped towards these two plantation societies of the Americas. When combined with the fact that many of these Africans had been proud soldiers before being slaves—or while being slaves—this circumstance may have proven decisive when the time of confronting colonial and imperial authorities and the white population in general seemed propitious.[26] It was precisely because they were so familiar with war and with victory that they resorted to violent armed movements against those who had bought them but who had demonstrated to them no military skills in the battlefield so far.

Every so often these factors have been overlooked due to a number of diverse reasons. Many of the problems that had affected the study of pre-colonial West African warfare have also been evident in studies of these same men and women in the New World. Thornton has referred to this continual failure to see the obvious as a "historic blindness towards Africa."[27] When it comes to the history of African warfare in the Americas, this blindness translates as an implicit oversimplification and underrating of the vast majority of the insurgency movements led and

---

[26] As Ann O'Hear has rightly stated, most of those who were enslaved and sold in the region had been acquired "as a result of warfare and raids carried out by estates vying for importance as successors to the Oyo Empire, by non-Yoruba states, and by ambitious warriors." O'Hear, "The Enslavement of the Yoruba," 61. See also John Iliffe, *Honour in African History* (Cambridge: Cambridge University Press, 2005), 127.

[27] Thornton, *Warfare in Atlantic Africa*, 3.

protagonized by African men and women; something that has not happened with many of those organized by Creole slaves and freemen.[28]

In the same way that African wars associated with the transatlantic slave trade have sometimes been seen as "simply slave raids,"[29] African military actions in the Americas have frequently been considered simply as revolts lacking direction, organization, and clear objectives, when nothing could be farther from the truth. Consequently, the vast majority of the scholars who have studied slave societies in the New World have perpetuated the reasoning and explanations of these violent events offered by none other than the authorities who prosecuted the Africans, and by plantation owners, their employees, and the general non-slave population, which often lived in a permanent state of panic fearing the outbreak of a massive African insurgency.[30]

In my opinion this underestimation of African movements has generally occurred because African men and women fought their battles in ways that were not considered conventional at the time by European standards. More significantly, they have also been overlooked because in the minds of many scholars they failed to embody the so-called revolutionary ideas that had changed the political landscape in Europe and the Americas from the last decades of the eighteenth century onwards.[31] This underestimation may also be related to post-abolition backlash against Africans who refused to end slavery in Africa after the British had enforced the end of the human trade. This particular situation created an increasingly pessimistic and negative view of Africans as barbaric, which to a certain extent seems to have also infected the historiography that was to follow.

The truth, however, is that many of these movements were well planned, and their leaders had clear strategies and goals which were pursued once they rose in arms. As will be shown, they were more than simple attempts to overrun plantations or assassinate cruel overseers. In fact, in Bahia, as well as in Cuba such movements represented renewed efforts to achieve apparent and intentional goals, of which, logically, freedom, was the main one.

AFRICAN WARFARE IN BAHIA AND CUBA

In the late 1830s the white population of Salvador de Bahia was so tired of dealing with political unrest and the threat of African warfare that they fell into a very pessimistic psychological state. A Bahian newspaper moaned in January 1838:

> Ah, my God; will you permit such a terrible anathema upon the city of your Saint-, the capital of Salvador! Isn't your justice satisfied with so many knocks that you have

---

[28] See e.g. the treatment given to the Conspiracy of La Escalera in Cuba, and the movements led by Denmark Vesey and Nat Turner in the United States, to mention but a few examples. The exceptions are works by scholars such as Prince, Reis, and Lovejoy, among a few others.

[29] Thornton, *Warfare in Atlantic Africa*, 4.

[30] See e.g. Reis, *Rebelião Escrava no Brasil*, Part I; and Barcia, *The Great African Slave Revolt of 1825*, chs.1 and 2.

[31] Eugene Genovese, *From Rebellion to Revolution: Afro-American Slave Revolts in the Making of the Modern World* (Baton Rouge: Louisiana State University Press, 1979) and Paquette, *Sugar is Made with Blood*.

landed on us, with the roughness of the seasons, with the pest that has devastated our fields, with the problems that distress us, with the tears and desolation of so many scattered families; with so many lost possessions; with so many lives sacrificed and exposed?[32]

Barely a few years later, the white population in Cuba had reached a similar boiling point. Tired of dealing with internal and external threats of which African movements seemed to be the most dangerous and real, they even considered requesting, from the Captain-General, the immediate abolition of the slave trade to Cuba so that the increasing demographic imbalance shown in the censuses between the black and the white population could be addressed and resolved once and for all in their favor. Ninety-three Matanzas-based planters, led by Benigno Gener, begged Captain-General Leopoldo O'Donnell to reinforce security measures to protect them from their own slaves and to stop the slave trade to the island.[33] Not satisfied with this request, they also attempted to create an anonymous society with the intention of denouncing every new cargo of Africans that would arrive in Cuba.[34]

Although the slave trade continued for a few years after 1838 in Bahia and 1843 in Cuba, the truth is that control and surveillance measures increased in order to limit the probabilities of more violent actions led by Africans from taking place. By the time that both Bahian and Cuban inhabitants came to face their biggest fears in the form of large organized movements with the participation and leadership of West African freemen and slaves, they had already been subjected to frequent events of this kind which had prompted them to ask repeatedly for measures to safeguard their wealth and lives. These movements had started in earnest from the early years of the nineteenth century and by the 1830s and 1840s had peaked in both places, revealing to authorities and owners the hard-to-accept truth that both societies were more African than they would have liked them to be.

A particularly relevant incident occurred on the evening of 13 August 1833, when a large group of African-born men and women, mostly of Lucumí origin, took arms on the grounds of the Salvador coffee plantation, near the town of Banes, a few miles southwest of Havana. After causing considerable damage to the estate, they went on to the surrounding plantations and finally headed for Banes, causing more damage and killing almost every white person they found in their way.[35]

To the white residents and army officers that came across this West African contingent, the spectacle was both frightening and extraordinary. What they saw and heard that day was definitely something unknown to them. Not only did these African-born slaves behave and fight in what they considered to be eccentric ways, expertly using weapons as diverse as guns, machetes or cutlasses, spears, and horses, but they also marched to the terrifying rhythm of their Lucumí war drums

---

[32] "Santo Amaro," in *Pedro 2o, E Constituição*. Tuesday, 23 January 1838; No. 7, 1. ASV: NAB. B. 9, Fasc. 40. Bahia, 1838–40.

[33] Ghorbal, *Réformisme et esclavage à Cuba*, 670–2.

[34] José Luis Alfonso to Domingo del Monte. Cerro, 22 December 1843. In Domingo del Monte, *Centón epistolario* (Havana: Imagen Contemporánea, 2002), ii. 216.

[35] Uprising on the cafetal Salvador, owned by Francisco Santiago Aguirre. Banes, August 1833. ANC: ME, 540/B.

and songs. To this already mesmerizing and loud experience, the surviving witnesses added descriptions of African slaves protecting themselves with makeshift shields— a defense weapon in disuse for centuries by western armies—, and also carrying red umbrellas as war standards, an odd sight to western observers.

Umbrellas, shields, spears, war songs, war drums were all elements intrinsically associated with war in the regions of provenance of each of the African men and women who took arms that August night near Banes. Equally, the ways in which they planned their military operations, the objectives they pursued, and the reasons behind their actions were markedly different from what military men educated in the European and American wars of the period would have been used to experiencing or expect in the theater of war.[36] The use of bows, arrows, spears, and shields in warfare at that time was almost completely outdated across Europe since the arrival of firearms in the seventeenth century rendered most of them useless. Whenever found they normally had only an ornamental or ceremonial use. [37] Therefore, these African soldiers were definitely not the sort of foe that Bahian and Cuban military personnel would have had experience with before, either in Europe or in most of the Americas.

An examination of the macro and micro connections, transferences, and continuities existing between warfare in the interior of the Bight of Benin on the one hand, and Bahia and Cuba on the other will be discussed in the remaining pages of this book. In my opinion, it is of the utmost importance to start this examination by looking at the political background of these men and women, relying on the fact that many of these uprisings were undertaken and led by newly arrived Africans, who in some cases had barely spent days, even hours in their new places of destination. I will discuss who these African men and women were and what sort of military skills they had, with the intention of revealing even more direct connections and transfers to the warfare experiences they had previously acquired in their West African homelands. More importantly, I examine what elements may have weighed in favor of their decisions to go to war on the American side of the Atlantic, and how their plans were conceived and structured.

The vast majority of the instances of armed struggle planned and led by free and enslaved populations of African origin observed in Bahia and Cuba had an intrinsically West African character. From the organization and strategies devised by their leaders, to the actual ways in which battles were fought, it is practically impossible to find one of these events that did not have a significant number of elements belonging to contemporary West African warfare.

Descriptions of warfare in West Africa in the first half of the nineteenth century do not abound. More significantly, most of those who left impressions and accounts of how war was conducted in the period usually did not discuss in depth Oyo or other Yoruba-speaking states, focusing instead on Sokoto, Dahomey, Borno, and

---

[36] See, among others, Maurice Pearton, *Diplomacy, War, and Technology since 1830* (London: Burnett Books, 1982); and Geoffrey Jensen and Andrew Wiest, eds., *War in the Age of Technology: Myriad Faces of Modern Armed Conflict* (New York: New York University Press, 2001).

[37] W. Y. Carman, *A History of Firearms: From Earliest Times to 1914* (London: Taylor & Francis, 1955).

other nearby territories and estates.[38] Some of these accounts were produced by locals—notably the texts left by Uthman Dan Fodio, his son Mohammed Bello, and other *jihād* leaders—and others by European visitors like Mungo Park, Dixon Denham, Hugh Clapperton, and John and Richard Lander.[39]

In addition to written descriptions of warfare in the area, during this period, some of them also left a number of illustrations presenting soldiers belonging to various armies, and on occasion discussed how they compared to soldiers they had seen in other places they had visited before. Other sources that shed light on the ways warfare was undertaken in this region come from the bas-reliefs found in the palaces of Abomey, portraying scenes from the wars waged against the Yoruba-speaking peoples by the Dahomeans,[40] and from the traditional sculptures of warriors found across Oyo and other Yoruba-speaking states, many of which are preserved still today (Figures 4.1 and 4.2).[41]

Figure 4.1 The enemy flees: Abomey Palaces, Benin. Courtesy of Gaelle Beaujean-Baltzer.

[38] Notable exceptions are the memories of Samuel Ajayi Crowther, and the works of Koelle, Castelnau, and others.

[39] A. D. H. Bivar, "The Wathīqat Ahl Al-Sūdān: A Manifesto of the Fulani Jihād," *The Journal of African History*, 2:2 (1961): 235–43; Bello, *Infāq-ai-Maysūr* (London: Luzac and Co., 1957); Mungo Park, *Travels in the Interior of Africa* (Dublin: P. Hayes, 1825); Dixon Denham et al., *Narratives of Travels and Discoveries in Northern and Central Africa in the years 1822, 1823 and 1824* (London: John Murray, 1828), 2 vols.; Clapperton and Lander, *Journal of a Second Expedition*; Richard Lander, *Records of Captain Clapperton's Last Expedition to Africa* (London: Henry Colburn and Richard Bentley, 1830), 2 vols.; Richard Lander and John Lander, *Journal of an Expedition to Explore the Course and Termination of the Niger* (London: John Murray, 1833), 3 vols.

[40] Pierre Verger, "Note on the Bas-Reliefs in the Royal Palaces of Abomey," *Odu Journal of Yoruba and Related Studies*, 5 (1958): 3.

[41] Clapperton described them as "fetishes." See Clapperton and Lander, *Journal of a Second Expedition*, 380–5.

Figure 4.2 Battle scene: Abomey Palaces, Benin. Courtesy of Gaelle Beaujean-Baltzer.

In spite of the obvious potential effect that many of these sources may have for the understanding of episodes of African warfare in Bahia and Cuba, they rarely have been considered or used until today. When compared to the much richer descriptions of instances of West African warfare that occurred in Bahia and Cuba during the same period, these accounts can complement each other and enhance our knowledge of West African cultural elements associated with war and how and to what extent they were transferred from one continent to another.

The men and women who organized each of the many insurgencies that took place in Bahia and Cuba between 1807 and 1844 hailed from relatively close geographical areas in West Africa and were enslaved as part of the same processes of war and enslavement associated with the Fulani-led *jihād*, the Owu wars, the Dahomean attacks on the southwest of the Yoruba-speaking territories, and other contemporary occurrences. They were all quite acquainted with war. Some had been enslaved during military campaigns or surprise raids, and some of them were soldiers, even military leaders. Descriptions given by Africans who were enslaved and sent to the transatlantic slave trade, including those interviewed by French Consul in Bahia, Francis de Castelnau and by German missionary Sigismund Koelle in Sierra Leone, both around 1850, are a testament to such familiarity with warfare.[42]

The testimonies given by West African men and women in Bahia and Cuba occasionally offer clues related to this familiarity with war, and in some cases, go as far as mentioning their own war-related experiences back in their homelands.

[42] Castelnau, *Renseignements*; Segismund Koelle, *Polyglotta Africana, or a comparative vocabulary of nearly three hundred words and phrases, in more than one hundred distinct African languages* (London: Church Missionary House, 1854).

Such is the case of 39 Lucumí who were interviewed in the Havana barracoons in 1841 by Spanish lawyer Pedro María Fernández Villaverde, after the *Aquila,* the ship that they were taken in to Cuba, was captured by a British cruiser and brought before the Havana Mixed Commission Court. Fernández Villaverde benefited from the fact that two of the Africans, named Ensy and Ocotufachey, had learned some Spanish during the Atlantic crossing and were able to serve as interpreters. They told Fernández Villaverde that many among their companions had been "the victims of rapacity of other negroes of their own country, who carried them off by force in order to sell them," while others were "prisoners taken in the wars of the King of Oni with the King of Lusé," almost certainly referring to the wars between Ife and Ijesa that took place around the time.[43] With such declarations they left little margin for doubt that they were all victims of armed raids and warfare.

Another case, also recorded by the Mixed Commission Court of Havana in 1841, was that of Gavino Pinedo, a Lucumí who told how he had been enslaved around 1823 or 1824 "when travelling in the interior of his own country in quest of food, with several of his companions." Gavino recounted how "he fell into the hands of one of two parties, both of the Lucumí nation, who were fighting with each other for no other purpose than that of making prisoners and selling them to the white men engaged in the Slave Trade."[44]

Similar examples can be drawn from the testimonies of some of the Africans interviewed in Bahia by Francis de Castelnau in the late 1840s and mentioned before in this text. Among them were Mahammah, a Hausa, who confessed to have been part of military forces "under the orders of the sultan of Kano."[45] Mahammah, who was known in Bahia as Manuel, also described his specialized role within the sultan's army. He told Castelnau that he formed part of the army's vanguard and that he saw many people die and was also expected to examine their corpses.[46] Mahammah was eventually ambushed by a Borgu force, wounded in a leg by an arrow, captured, and sold as a slave in Ilorin, from where he was taken to Lagos and then to Bahia.[47]

Another Hausa, Boué or Bawa, who was known in Bahia as Antonio, boasted to the French Consul that "he had spent all his life making war against the neighboring countries," a statement he complemented by offering a detailed list of no less than twenty countries he claimed to have fought against.[48] Braz, also a Hausa known in Bahia as Adam, recounted that he had been participating in a military campaign against the country of Tiranca, when he was surprised in his sleep by the Oyo, seized, and taken to Ilorin, from where he was eventually sent to Lagos and Bahia.[49]

---

[43] Pedro María Fernández Villaverde to the Captain-General. Havana, 31 May 1841. BPPO: Class B. Correspondence with Spain, Portugal, Brazil, the Netherlands, Sweden, and the Argentine Confederation, relative to the slave trade. From January 1 to December 31 1841 inclusive. I would like to thank Professor Robin Law for his input on this issue.

[44] Gavino also related how he was taken to a factory by a navigable river called Ossa (likely the inland lagoon that runs parallel to the coast) and how after three months of waiting he was embarked and sent to Cuba in the Spanish ship *Dolores.* Deposition of Gavino Pinedo. Havana, 18 September 1841. BPPO. Class B. Correspondence with Spain, Portugal, Brazil, &c. &c. relative to the slave trade.

[45] Castelnau, *Renseignements*, 13. See also Chapter 2 for more details regarding the testimonies given by this group of Africans.

[46] Castelnau, *Renseignements*, 15.   [47] Castelnau, *Renseignements*, 21–3.

[48] Castelnau, *Renseignements*, 40.   [49] Castelnau, *Renseignements*, 26–7.

Direct references of a previous experience related to warfare in West Africa also surfaced during the days and weeks that followed insurgent movements in Bahia and Cuba. While being interrogated in 1844 in the aftermath of the discovery of the Conspiracy of La Escalera in Cuba, Marcelino Lucumí declared that his friend Manuel Lucumí was in charge of "playing the main drum, because in their homeland, he always carried the war drums."[50] Similarly, after the authorities in Bahia uncovered the Hausa conspiracy of May 1814, the slave João declared that among the arsenal that the plotters had gathered he had seen "weapons of his land," in another clear reference associated with a personal experience related to warfare in West Africa.[51]

Of course, anecdotes and accounts of war-related experiences were not limited to those who arrived from the interior of the Bight of Benin. On some occasions, Africans from other areas also talked of combat when compelled to by the authorities. In 1833 a small group of West African slaves at the Jimagua, Filomeno and Satre sugar estates spent the night dancing and singing "today is the last day, and tomorrow everything will end."[52] The Africans in question were all Gangá *bozales* from the Upper Guinea coast. According to Pío, one of the slaves, Vicente had told him that "he knew how to make war in his land, and that he wanted to join forces with other [slaves] to fight" against the whites.[53]

In both Bahia and Cuba merchants and planters knew that the men and women they were bringing from Africa to work on their plantations and cities were not unfamiliar with warfare and regular violence, and they made sure that the Portuguese, Brazilian, and Spanish authorities were aware of that fact. Nevertheless, they also trusted their own capabilities to keep the order and to repress them when necessary, as they did continuously throughout the first half of the nineteenth century in both territories.

As a matter of fact, middle and low ranking officers, slave hunters known as *capitães do mato* and *rancheadores*, and neighbors who were involved in repressing African movements, were often forced to refer to their organizational skills. Even though social structures were quite different from those in the African regions they originated from, West Africans in Bahia and Cuba carefully and systematically planned their attacks, and executed them with aplomb and with the skills they acquired from warfare experiences they had already engaged in before being transported.

ORGANIZATION AND STRATEGIES

Indeed, by the time they arrived in Bahia and Cuba virtually every man and woman from West Africa would have had some sort of understanding of how and why military campaigns were carried out. From the *hijra* of Uthman Dan Fodio to the

---

[50] Deposition of Marcelino Lucumí. Ingenio La Andrea. January 1844. ANC: CM, 37/1.
[51] Schwartz, "Cantos e quilombos," 386.
[52] Santiago Borrás to José María Gavilán. Ingenio Satre, 8 March 1833. ANC: GSC, 936/33046.
[53] José Cadaval to Captain-General Mariano Ricafort. Ingenio Bosmeniel, 25 February 1833. ANC: GSC, 936/33046.

well-planned annual or biannual wars that were common in these West African regions, the organization of military campaigns played a central role before they were launched.[54] In Bahia and Cuba, as noted by those who recorded instances of West African warfare throughout the first half of the nineteenth century, it also played a central role in a considerable number of movements.

João José Reis has noted how an "elaborate clandestine organization" appeared before the Hausa insurgency of May 1807, consisting of a well-prepared network that had a "captain in each parish of the city and a commander, known as the ambassador."[55] Reis also stressed how this political organization and the strategies of those involved in this movement were all part of "an experience lived in Africa."[56] Many other major movements registered in Bahia during the next decades featured complex levels of preparation. The 1809 insurgents, for example, came together in a *quilombo* located by the Prata River. Once they judged their force to be large enough, they fiercely attacked the town of Nazaré das Farinhas, "apparently in search of arms, ammunition, and food" that would allow them to strengthen their ranks with view to future actions.[57]

In February 1814 a synchronized Hausa-led force combined with runaway slaves coming from the *quilombos* and with slaves recruited from the places they attacked, proceeded to assault fishing marinas and the village of Itapuã.[58] The level of sophistication behind this movement was also noticed by Reis, when he stated that the 1814 rebels had been "carefully organized."[59] A few weeks later, another group of West Africans caused havoc in Iguape. Here, too, a well-conceived plan preceded the outbreak of hostilities. The Africans first met at the Ponta plantation, and from there decided on an attack against the town of Maragogipe.[60] Finally, when a new plot organized by the Hausa was denounced in May, the authorities immediately realized that they were faced with another complex plan. Here, as Stuart Schwartz has suggested, the Hausa had prepared a plan with "a tactic of deception" which included *quilombolas* and urban slaves from Salvador. They had linked with the runaway slaves from the Sangradouro forest, who had been given the task of getting things started by assaulting a gunpowder house in Matatú. The Hausa from the city would then wait for the authorities to send the army towards the maroons, in order to take the city.[61]

After the war of independence of Bahia came to an end in 1822, West Africans continued to surprise local residents and authorities with their organizational proficiency. Two well-prepared insurgencies broke out in Bahia in 1826. The first one took place in Cachoeira and, although little is known about it, it is not difficult to infer that a complex plot had preceded it, since at least its hierarchical

[54] Smith, *Warfare and Diplomacy*, 120–41; Richard Reid, *Warfare in African History* (Cambridge: Cambridge University Press, 2012), 107–47.
[55] Reis, *Rebelião escrava no Brasil*, 73.   [56] Reis, *Rebelião escrava no Brasil*, 73.
[57] Reis, *Rebelião escrava no Brasil*, 78–9.
[58] Reis, *Rebelião escrava no Brasil*, 82–4; Prince, "Slave Rebellion in Bahia," 104–7; Schwartz, "Cantos e quilombos," 380.
[59] Reis, *Slave Rebellion in Brazil*, 47.
[60] Reis, *Slave Rebellion in Brazil*, 49; Prince, "Slave Rebellion in Bahia," 106–7.
[61] Schwartz, "Cantos e quilombos," 385.

structure was clearly established by the existence of a king and a queen.[62] The second probably offered the most elaborated plan to date. A large number of Africans had concentrated in the Urubu *quilombo*, on the outskirts of Salvador. There, the insurgents had "expected many slaves to arrive from Salvador" with the intention to "invade the capital, kill the whites, and gain their freedom," showing a well-organized movement and awareness of the need for support from their urban-based fellow West Africans.[63]

Also another insurgent movement, which took place in downtown Salvador in 1830, revealed an intricate scheme. Aware of the fact that newly arrived Nagô slaves were being kept in a warehouse in Salvador, a group of approximately 20 West African men first proceeded to assault a number of hardware stores in the lower city with the aim of gathering swords, knives, and other weapons. Once this part of their plan was accomplished, they headed for the warehouse owned by Wenceslao Miguel de Almeida, where they killed a guard and then proceeded to liberate more than 100 fellow Nagôs, who did not hesitate in following them. The third step of the plan was then put into practice. Now well armed and with their ranks swollen, this Nagô contingent mounted an ambitious attack against the police station of Soledade, where they were eventually defeated and forced to retreat.

The strategy of the Nagô in 1830 showed a great understanding of what was needed to have a real chance of success, and followed a West African pattern and conception of how to make war. The Nagô first planned their moves, and then executed them in a logical, systematic, and progressive manner, taking advantage of the opportunities presented to them by unprotected hardware stores packed with weapons, and by the existence of likely reinforcements-in-wait in a nearby barely-protected warehouse.[64]

Taking advantage of newly arrived slaves was something plotters and military leaders saw as potential reinforcements that could determine the outcome of incoming battles in their favor. This was the case in 1833 in the coffee plantation Salvador, west of Havana, where the arrival of a large group of Lucumí *bozales* was seen by some of their compatriots already living there as the spark needed to put into practice their already arranged plan of action.[65] In a similar manner the Nagô force defeated after attacking a number of estates in the vicinity of Pirajá in March 1828, saw the need for enlisting recently arrived Africans (*escravos novos*) as a crucial part of their plan.[66]

In Cuba, as in Bahia, armed movements often followed a methodical process of planning. In the case of the Salvador estate in 1833, it is possible to add some others such as the case of 17 Lucumí *bozales* recently arrived at the Purísima Concepción estate, who taking advantage of the relative protection that speaking

[62] Reis, *Rebelião escrava no Brasil*, 100; Prince, *Slave Rebellion in Brazil*, 129–30.
[63] Reis, *Slave Rebellion in Brazil*, 57; Prince, *Slave Rebellion in Brazil*, 130–6.
[64] APEB: IE, 2845. "Criminal proceedings against Francisco, Nagô, and Nicolau, Nagô, slaves of Bernardo José Jorge." See also Prince, *Slave Rebellion in Brazil*, 147–51; and Reis, *Rebelião escrava no Brasil*, 115–21.
[65] Juan Iduarte, "Noticias sobre sublevaciones," 117–52.
[66] Prince, *Slave Rebellion in Brazil*, 140–1. APEB: IE, 2845.

in their own language offered, plotted to take arms and attempt an escape to the mountains, with the intention of freeing themselves from slavery.[67] Blas Lucumí, one of the Africans involved in the plot, confirmed the Africans' intentions when he declared through an interpreter and after swearing by "his own God," that their main objective was to flee to the mountains.[68]

The armed movement of March 1843 in the locality of Bemba also seems to have been carefully arranged. One of the Lucumí slaves involved, Fermín, recalled how they had intended an organized military offensive that would take them "from sugar estate to sugar estate" in order to swell their ranks with new recruits.[69] Something very similar was declared by Nicolás Gangá after the African movement of La Guanábana and La Cidra later that same year, was crushed by the authorities and the regular army. In the words of Nicolás, their objective "was to go from estate to estate, gathering the largest possible number of blacks to make war against the whites, to be free, and not to suffer any more."[70] For that, Nicolás explained, they "had different types of weapons, including many machetes, some long ones, pistols, spears, leather shields, and all the others they would get" on the places they intended to attack.[71]

Another clear case involving a well-planned attack occurred in 1837 on the sugar plantation La Sonora, located in Lagunillas. There 34 Lucumí slaves who had arrived on the estate less than six months earlier, violently and unexpectedly attacked the white employees who attempted to punish them. According to Fermín Lucumí, they had planned the offensive "approximately five moons before" (five months) when the plantation's overseer had punished one of them for first time.[72] Another African, Esteban Lucumí was even more specific when he stated that they "were just waiting for the next time that the overseer would get angry to fall all on him."[73] For such an attack they had crafted clubs and spears from nearby trees, which they had then hidden until the propitious time would come.[74]

Throughout these accounts, gathering, making, and hiding the weapons needed to carry out their plans were an important part of the organization of many of these movements, as in the cases of May 1814 in Bahia, and in the La Sonora estate in Lagunillas, in 1837, discussed above.[75] In the movement of May 1814, the Bahian Hausa manufactured a large number of *ferrões* (iron bars), which they then hid in the bush until they could prepare "metallic arrow heads" to turn each of them into a spear, one of the favorite weapons of infantry soldiers across West Africa.[76]

In other cases the Africans had to make do with finding weapons, as was the case during the insurgency of 1830 in Salvador, where the assault to the lower city hardware stores constituted a central part of the strategy of the Nagô, before

[67] Deposition of Victorino Rodríguez. Sibanacán, September 1832. ANC: ME, 570/S.
[68] Deposition of Blas Lucumí. Sibanacán, September 1832. ANC: ME, 570/S.
[69] Deposition of Fermín Lucumí. Bemba, April 1843. ANC: CM, 29/5-1.
[70] Deposition of Fermín Lucumí.   [71] Deposition of Fermín Lucumí.
[72] Deposition of Fermín Lucumí. Lagunillas, June 1837. ANC: ME, 1178/B.
[73] Deposition of Esteban Lucumí. Lagunillas, June 1837. ANC: ME, 1178/B
[74] Deposition of Esteban Lucumí.
[75] Schwartz, "Cantos e quilombos," ANC: ME, 1178/B.
[76] Schwartz, "Cantos e quilombos," 381.

moving on to free the recently arrived Africans who were being held in a nearby warehouse.[77] Also the attack on the town of Nazaré das Farinhas by the Hausa, in January 1809, seems to have been motivated by the need of arming their ranks before larger military operations could be undertaken.[78]

Something similar happened in Cuba on several occasions. The insurgents of 1825, in Guamacaro, raided one estate after another in search of weapons. This search was, to a certain extent, successful, since they managed to gather a few guns and sabers, which they subsequently used against the local neighbors and colonial troops sent from Matanzas to contain them.[79] In another case, the emancipated Africans from the brig *Negrito*, all Lucumí, who were at the time employed in the works of the Husillo aqueduct in Havana, attacked a house in the Jesús del Monte road where they found the machetes that they used later against the soldiers who eventually defeated them.[80]

Often, weapons were easily accessible, especially for those working in the cutting of sugar cane, for whom machetes were never too far out of reach. As a matter of fact, and as we will see in the following chapter, machetes, and often rocks, featured in almost every one of the rural movements examined here. But on some other occasions, when the required weapons were not easy to gather, improvising was paramount for the success of the movements. In either case, the procurement of appropriate weapons, whether African or not, was a *sine qua non* requisite in each of the dozens of movements organized and carried into practice by West African men and women in Bahia and Cuba during this period.

Meticulous organization and calculated strategies were then frequent among the armed movements that took place in these two territories of the Americas in the first half of the nineteenth century. African insurgencies were not always the result of spontaneous bouts of rage against masters and overseers with no sense of direction, as opposed to what was suggested by prosecutors, authorities, witnesses, and more problematic, by many historians who have continued to dismiss them for a variety of reasons. Yet, it is a matter of fact that the Africans were often able to calculate the pros and cons of their actions and to proceed accordingly due to the good organizational and strategic knowledge and military skills, which many of them had learned in their homelands.

They were conscious of the need to swell their ranks and subsequently worked incessantly to find the best ways of soliciting fellow Africans to their plans, logically opting for strategies involving military offensives that would take them from estate to estate, where the voluntary or forced enlistment of new soldiers was more likely to be achieved. For that they communicated in their own languages, using the few occasions they had to meet to discuss their ideas, and the best ways of carrying them into practice. They saw urban centers as propitious places to acquire

---

[77] APEB: IE, 2845. "Criminal proceedings against Francisco, Nagô, and Nicolau, Nagô, slaves of Bernardo José Jorge." See also Reis, *Rebelião escrava no Brasil*, 119.

[78] Reis, *Slave Rebellion in Brazil*, 43.

[79] Barcia, *The Great African Slave Revolt of 1825*, 104–6.

[80] Depositions of Miguel Lucumí and José Dávila Lucumí (through an interpreter). Havana, July 1835. ANC: CM, 11/1.

weapons and to solidify their military positions, as attacks on small towns, villages, and occasionally on larger cities were familiar to many of them. They were also aware of their need for weapons and thus devised their war plans accordingly, often putting together and concealing their arsenal until the time for action had arrived.

LEADERSHIP

The organization of each of these plots and their subsequent execution fell into the hands of men and women whose military background varied significantly. Historical evidence suggests that while some of them may have been innate military leaders in West Africa with a solid knowledge of what was required to lead troops in the battlefield, others were not as knowledgeable or capable.

As a matter of fact, the various degrees of expertise shown by these West African men and women could account to a certain extent for the ease with which some of them were defeated by colonial and, in the case of Bahia, imperial militias and armies. This particular disadvantage could possibly be applied to the fortunes of every African force to ever take on their European or American masters in the New World. Whereas the latter were able to rely on state-of-the-art weapons and on experienced army officers to lead the troops, Africans had to do with the human capital they were left with after the Middle Passage. As we will see, some of these leaders were often capable commanders, who had probably led troops of various sizes and types in the course of West African military campaigns. In other cases, however, they were probably makeshift leaders, who sometimes had some sort of previous experience related to war, but not necessarily as leaders.

As Smith and Smaldone have argued regarding Yoruba-speaking and Hausa-speaking territories respectively, irregular local armies of a reduced size were common across these territories.[81] Local leaders could raise these armies at short notice and would keep them "distinct on the battlefield."[82] Moreover, in his excellent study of warfare in Atlantic Africa, Thornton noticed that even in their own territories, these commanders were not always very adept, once again suggesting, even if indirectly, that on the other side of the Atlantic, where they were confronted by well-trained and equipped troops, this relative lack of proficiency may have been magnified.

The leaders of African military uprisings in Bahia and Cuba often received more attention than the rest of the participants in these movements. Authorities in both territories did their best to find out who they were, what their reasons to rise were, and what sort of ascendancy they had with the rest of their comrades. Whenever they managed to escape, they were relentlessly hunted down, sometimes for years. Unsurprisingly, maroon leaders, at least in Cuba, garnered a reputation of being invincible and impossible to capture, and on occasions became mythical figures among the slaves living in cities and the countryside. Witnesses in practically every

---

[81] Smith, *Warfare and Diplomacy*, 81, 86, 123; Smaldone, *Warfare in the Sokoto Caliphate*, 26–7.
[82] Thornton, *Warfare in Atlantic Africa*, 89.

one of the trials that followed these movements talked about them and described their best and worst qualities, sometimes referring to their organizational skills or to their military leadership while taking them to battle.

West African military commanders usually identified themselves with specific dresses or symbols, and by titles, which usually were described with western names. In West Africa as well as in Bahia and Cuba, specific dresses and clothing were generally believed to reflect roles within armed movements from the moment the planning had begun. In both Bahia and Cuba, West African insurgents frequently wore colorful dresses, sometimes prepared in advance or, alternatively, stolen during their military actions. One of the leaders among the insurgents of 1833 in Banes dressed in women's clothes;[83] while some of those who participated in the 1825 actions in Guamacaro stole and wore military jackets and feathered hats.[84]

In Bahia, some of the Muslim plotters in 1835 dressed in robes usually referred to as *abadá* garments, and in Cachoeira in 1826 a king and a queen, who wore a crown "decorated with ribbons" and "a cape of green duvetyn decorated with gilded hash marks" were reported to be the leaders of the armed movement.[85] Equally, among the plotters in the sugar estate La Andrea, uncovered at the beginning of 1844, there were captains, a king, and also a queen, who was supposed to wear a "white dress and a silk bandana for her head"; not a crown per se, but probably another connection to either Obatala or Islam.[86]

Some of the military symbols, or standards carried by the leaders of some of these armed movements point towards the existence of direct links to a royal or military authority in West Africa. Although it is well known that the titles of king, queen, and captain were often attached to many of the leaders of these movements, on occasions other clearer clues were apparent. In the particular case of the African military uprising of 1833 in Banes, west of Havana, two of the Lucumí leaders, Joaquín and Fierabrás, rode horses and carried open red umbrellas while leading their men to battle. While discussing this movement Henry B. Lovejoy has recently stated that "The prerogative of riding a horse with an umbrella was reserved for Yoruba kings; thus this umbrella on horseback was a potent symbol of sovereignty, especially in Oyo."[87] Additionally, Lovejoy has also pointed out that the fact that Fierabrás, who was known as Edu among the other Lucumí, was able to lead a battalion-size force into battle almost certainly suggests a previous military experience.[88]

This same movement provides us with another probable link to that West African soldierly past. One of the most mentioned names among those interrogated after the military uprising was crushed was that of Bale or Balé. He was said to command

---

[83] According to Henry Lovejoy, "The cross-dressing might relate to ilari (royal Oyo bodyguards initiated by Sango priests)." Lovejoy, "Old Oyo Influences," 197.

[84] Barcia, *The Great African Slave Revolt of 1825*, 119, 151.

[85] Reis, *Rebelião escrava no Brasil*, 206–11.

[86] Deposition of José Gangá. Ingenio La Andrea, January 1844. ANC: CM, 36/2. White clothes were also stolen and worn by the Lucumí during the military uprising of November 1843 in the districts of La Guanábana and La Cidra. Deposition of Joaquín Garcilaso de la Vega. Ingenio San Miguel, November 1843. ANC: CM, 30/3.

[87] Lovejoy, "Old Oyo Influences," 197.   [88] Lovejoy, "Old Oyo Influences," 197.

some of the rebels during the military actions of that day, and before he took his own life by shooting himself in the head, he was reported to have agreed to finish one of his comrades who had been wounded in battle. That the other Lucumí called him Bale, may have been a reference to his title rather than to his real name. Bale was the title given in Oyo and most of Yoruba states to village leaders who were frequently in charge of raising the previously mentioned small armies that would then join the Aláàfin in his military campaigns.[89] This Cuban Bale may well have been an Oyo commander leading his men into battle thousands of miles away from the battlegrounds that were familiar to them.

Another element that was frequently mentioned during the interrogations that followed these actions was the bravery of their leaders and the ways in which they led by example in the battlefield. John Iliffe has commented that "until the nineteenth century, honour in the several Yoruba kingdoms seems to have adhered closely to rank and civic virtue," and nothing denotes honor more than bravery and leadership.[90] Lucumís in Cuba, and Hausas and Nagôs in Bahia repeatedly asserted their leadership qualities during the period. Sometimes they shouted orders to their troops in their own languages, as it was the case during the military uprising in the sugar plantation San Juan de Dios de Macastá in 1834 in Cuba or during the defense of the Urubu *quilombo* in Bahia in 1826.[91]

There is little doubt that those who followed them were ready to take orders and die if necessary in the battleground. Time after time West African soldiers in Bahia and Cuba showed a deep commitment to their leaders, and often even explained their reasons to do so. In 1837 the Lucumís from the sugar estate La Sonora in Cuba were said to have obeyed whatever orders their leader, Esteban Lucumí, would give them. Esteban was reported to have called his fellow *bozales* to arms by stressing that white men could do nothing to them and that they should not be scared of them.[92] Something very similar happened a year before in the sugar estate San Pablo, where another Lucumí leader, José del Carmen, was immediately supported by all the *bozales* that had arrived with him to the estate from Africa merely a few months earlier.[93] One last episode involving not Lucumís, but Gangás, reveals the extent of these long-lasting West African loyalties. After being defeated by a militia that was sent from a nearby town to help putting their armed revolt down, Rafael Gangá, the only survivor of this movement in 1827, declared that the only reason he and his companions had had to rise against their master was their loyalty to their "captain from Africa," Tomás.[94]

Another aspect that will be discussed in detail in Chapter 5 which merits a mention in this section, is the fact that leaders were not always adult males. Just as could have happened in West Africa, there were cases in both Bahia and Cuba

[89] Smith, *Kingdoms of the Yoruba*, 109.
[90] Iliffe, *Honour in African History*, 67.
[91] Deposition of Manuel Blanco. Ingenio San Juan de Dios de Macastá, August 1834. ANC: ME, 451/E; Reis, *Rebelião escrava no Brasil*, 101.
[92] Deposition of Valentín Lucumí. Ingenio La Sonora, June 1837. ANC: ME, 1178/B.
[93] Depositions of Federico Lucumí and Nemesio Lucumí. Ingenio San Pablo, September 1836. ANC: ME, 1193/H.
[94] Deposition of Rafael Gangá. Catalina de Güines, September 1827. ANC: ME, 1069/B.

where Nagô and Lucumí women acted as military commanders.[95] Additionally, in at least one other instance, West African teenagers were reported to have led a Lucumí force across the streets of the Jesús del Monte neighborhood in Havana in 1835.[96]

The issue of leadership was central to most of the slave movements that took place in Bahia and Cuba during this period. The experience, bravery, and intelligence exhibited by some of these men and women while commanding their troops into battle became, on occasion, the stuff of legends. The fact that these men and women led by example and often lost their lives during armed confrontations only augmented their reputation among the other members of the West African communities in these two societies of the Americas.

CONCLUSIONS

Despite the inherent limitations of the sources used in this chapter, it is apparent that the transfer of West African practices and ethics associated with warfare made it across the Atlantic to the slave societies that flourished in the early nineteenth century in Bahia and Cuba. A comparison of the descriptions left by those who witnessed the organization and strategies of the military in West Africa and the depositions and correspondence left about the organization and planning of military operations in Bahia and Cuba, leaves little doubt that this well-nurtured knowledge about how to strike the enemy did not vanish during the Atlantic crossing.

When examined from an alternative viewpoint, these events also reveal that there is an African side to the story of slave resistance in the Americas; a story that has been told only partially. Virtually every African man and woman who participated in one of these movements had a previous experience related to warfare, either as victims, perpetrators or both. Not surprisingly they took this knowledge with them across the Atlantic, leading to what can only be described as a transplantation of African warfare in the Americas.

References to warfare, and more precisely to war, are commonly found in the depositions given by those African men and women who were interrogated following many of these movements. More importantly, their military actions resembled in many ways battles and skirmishes described by the first Europeans who visited their West African regions of origin; from organization and strategies to the crucial issue of leadership.

But these cultural transfers associated with warfare were hardly limited to organization, strategy, and leadership. As we will see, they were also apparent in the ways in which military operations were conducted and in their weaponry and war paraphernalia, and they were so from the moment of taking arms to the end of each of these instances of warfare in these two slave societies.

---

[95] Prosecutor's Report of Felipe Arango. Havana, 2 February 1844. ANC: CM, 30/3.
[96] Deposition of José Davila Lucumí. Havana, July 1835. ANC: ME, 11/1.

5

West African Warfare in Bahia and Cuba
Military Operations and Weaponry

War is deception; success in war is not great numbers or speed.

Abdullahi dan Fodio

On 23 March 1814 a large military uprising led by Hausa slaves shook the sugar plantation region of Iguape, at the heart of the Bahian Recôncavo valley. Right in the middle of the harvest season the slaves attacked their masters enacting a well-organized plan that had it been successful would have taken them first to the Ponta plantation and from there to the nearby town of Maragogipe. Major João Francisco Chobi, the local military chief, described the events in terrifying terms in a note sent to Antonio Augusto da Silva, the magistrate of Maragogipe. In his short missive, Chobi portrayed an Iguape landscape "in flames and under the attack of the negroes."[1]

As João José Reis has indicated, this military action was not the result of a naïve and spontaneous attempt at revenge, but a well-coordinated effort. However, in spite of the material damage caused by the slaves and the fear they provoked among the inhabitants of the region, very little else is known about it, and no reliable description of this Hausa military force was ever provided.[2] Something very similar could be argued for the Hausa-led insurrection that took place just a month before in the region of Itapuã, just outside Salvador de Bahia, and for other insurgencies for which we have even less information.[3]

The failure to deliver trustworthy descriptions of the operations of West African armed movements during this period was not limited to Bahia; Cuban authorities and planters often failed to offer meaningful accounts of these events as well. Predictably, even when they did, their interpretation of the ways in which West Africans organized themselves and fought their enemies were framed within their own military experiences and missed important cultural elements associated with the experience of warfare that these men and women had acquired in their homelands and displayed in Bahia and Cuba.

From the evidence it is clear that in most of those cases when the slaves took arms, they did so in accordance with the practices of their own places in West Africa and, as discussed in Chapter 4, they frequently described their actions as

---

[1] Reis, *Rebelião escrava no Brasil*, 86–7.
[2] Schwartz, *Sugar Plantations*, 483; Reis, *Rebelião escrava no Brasil*, 86–7.
[3] Prince, *Slave Rebellion in Bahia*, 104–5; Reis, *Rebelião escrava no Brasil*, 82–6.

military actions. On the few occasions that authorities and non-African inhabitants of Bahia and Cuba recalled their military clashes with West African fighters, they almost always described them as mobs, gangs, or hordes of uncivilized brutes, even though they had often obtained convincing proof that their movements had been meticulously planned and efficiently carried into practice.

In some exceptional instances, references to the use of horses, drums, songs, dances, and other particularities were mentioned by army officers and soldiers, plantation workers, and local inhabitants who witnessed West African armed forces in action. These descriptions, combined with those offered by the Africans themselves, give us a unique insight into how military operations were undertaken, into the tactics used by the insurgents from the moment they took arms to the time of their flight or surrender, into the composition of the troops, and into the weapons and war paraphernalia they employed.

MILITARY OPERATIONS AND TACTICS OF WAR

Perhaps no other group of Africans had a better opportunity to reproduce their knowledge of warfare in Bahia and Cuba than those who ran away from their masters and joined *quilombos, mocambos,* or *palenques.* In both territories they were known for coming out of their hideouts to carry out lightning raids on plantations and small towns and villages. Maroons, who it must be said were not always African-born, assaulted and robbed plantations and travelers, and occasionally confronted the slave hunters and armed forces sent by the authorities with the aim of bringing their freedom to an end. In some cases they even managed to fortify their hideouts in mountains, forests, and swamps with hidden deep trenches concealing sharp stakes and with other clever devices.[4] Maroons' actions were sometimes recounted by those sent to destroy them. In the aftermath of the defeat of the *quilombolas* of Urubu, in 1826, the attacks of the Africans against the imperial forces were described as a "furious charge,"[5] and in 1816 the Governor of Santiago de Cuba described local *cimarrones* as "hawks" who fell "with the speed of lightning" on the landholders living under his jurisdiction.[6]

In cities and plantations, conditions were much different. Organizational plans, like the ones presented in Chapter 4, required certain logistics that were often determined by an empirical knowledge of war learned and nurtured in West Africa. In these cases, as had happened in their homelands, West Africans benefited from the relative ease of assembling armies when people and weapons were readily available. It could be argued that tactics of war such as speed of movement, raiding

---

[4] Gabino La Rosa Corzo, *Armas y tácticas defensivas de los cimarrones en Cuba*, Reporte de investigación No. 2 (Havana: Academia de Ciencias de Cuba, 1989), 17–18; Barcia, *Seeds of Insurrection*, 64.

[5] Prosecutor's Report. [Piraja] 17 December 1826. APEB: IE, 2845. Inquest on the deaths of Manoel José Correia and others in the vicinity of Piraja. Reis has also referred to the "lightning raids and robberies perpetrated by residents of quilombos" during this period. Cf. Reis, *Slave Rebellion in Brazil*, 59.

[6] Barcia, *Seeds of Insurrection*, 55.

plantations, freeing other slaves and forcing them to join their troops, could have been the product of necessity, rather than that of imported cultural practices related to warfare. This type of simplistic approach, however, would overlook the personal experiences and ignore the historical context of those West African men and women, once again reinforcing Thornton's opinion about Africa's invisibility, both in Africa and in the African diaspora.[7]

As stated by Robert S. Smith, in West Africa small armies could be raised at short notice and without great expense precisely because of this ease of access to people and weaponry.[8] The fact that in Bahia and Cuba insurgent leaders, who occasionally had some experience as military commanders in their homelands, found themselves surrounded by men and women from those same regions, almost certainly constituted a catalyst for upheaval. Equally, the use of autochthonous languages that were not understood by their masters, their employees, and non-African neighbors also facilitated the undertaking of their military enterprises. That their plans usually involved moving from plantation to plantation with the aim of swelling their ranks suggests a deep awareness of the social situation of the regions to which they had been transplanted.

Additionally, some of the historical accounts of these armed movements indicate that West Africans were not necessarily intimidated or scared by their white masters, local militias, or even by regular troops. The best proof of their belief in their own martial capabilities is the fact that in spite of suffering a number of heavy defeats, they continued to rise in arms, time and again, in the hope of reclaiming their lost freedom. On some exceptional occasions some of their leaders were able to translate this belief into words. This was the case of Esteban Lucumí on the sugar plantation La Sonora in 1837, who was reported to have told his Lucumí followers "Companions, don't flee, don't; what can white men do to us? Let's go fight them."[9]

To the lack of fear of their oppressors and the existence of a pool of possible fighters to swell the ranks of any would-be military force, one final element could be added: a belief in the reincarnation of the soul. As we will see, the belief in an afterlife was common among West African men and women in Bahia and Cuba, regardless of their religion. Both Islam and the various West African religions transplanted to Bahia and Cuba offered the possibility of redemption, and in some cases, reincarnation, to their followers. Historians have repeatedly discussed the myth of the flying Africans over the years.[10] Suffice to say here that in many of the movements discussed in these pages, religious practices brought from West Africa seem to have had a meaningful cohesive function. This was the case in practically all Hausa-led armed insurgencies in Bahia between 1807 and 1816, as well as in the 1826 Urubu *quilombo* and the 1835 Malê insurrection in Salvador. Religion also seems to have played an important role in some of the movements

[7] Thornton, *Warfare in Atlantic Africa*, 1.   [8] Smith, *Warfare and Diplomacy*, 65.
[9] Deposition of Valentín Lucumí. Ingenio La Sonora, June 1837. ANC: ME, 1178/B.
[10] Gomez, *Exchanging our Country Marks*, 116–19; Adderley, *New Negroes from Africa*, 216–18; Barcia, *Seeds of Insurrection*, 71–83; Heather Russell, *Legba's Crossing: Narratology in the African Atlantic* (Athens, GA: University of Georgia Press, 2009), 116–17.

recorded in Cuba, notably in the 1833 uprising on the grounds of the Salvador coffee plantation, where several animal sacrifices were carried out as the revolt unfolded. Furthermore, the belief in an afterlife provided a way out for many of those who participated in the armed movements presented and discussed here.[11]

As was argued in Chapter 4, West African armed movements in Bahia and Cuba were often adequately prepared. This allowed many of them to go from the plotting stages to the actual military actions without being uncovered or betrayed. In these particular opportunities the leaders and their followers were able to display all their knowledge of how to make war in the new environments where they had been resettled. In the aftermath of some of these confrontations participants from both sides, as well as witnesses, recalled the events as they had seen them. The few existing descriptions of the unfolding of West African warfare in Bahia and Cuba constitute invaluable and informative accounts that reveal the extent to which the military actions undertaken by these men and women resembled contemporary narratives offered by those who described military actions in their West African regions of origin.

Participants and witnesses of the Salvador estate uprising near Banes, west of Havana, in 1833, gave one of the most detailed accounts of a West African force during the period. Their combined descriptions exposed in great detail elements such as rituals, the use of musical instruments and songs, the clothes they wore, leadership, weapons, and war paraphernalia. The 1833 force was mostly formed by Lucumí slaves; some had been living on the plantation grounds for some time, while others had just arrived from Africa weeks before. During the time that their military action lasted, they killed chickens and other animals presumably for ritualistic reasons. The leaders were reported to have been riding horses, wearing red umbrellas and colorful clothes—and at least one of them led his men while dressed in women's attire.[12] Their threats to kill those who refused to join them, their conscious separation of women and children from the ranks, their use of makeshift weapons and shields, and their constant use of the Lucumí language, were witnessed and reported again and again by slaves, masters, local residents, and authorities. While the 1833 military uprising was exceptionally well documented, to an extent that almost no other event of this type was, it was by no means unique. Many other armed movements were at least partially described and examined during these years in both Bahia and Cuba.

Not surprisingly the offensive tactics exhibited by West African insurgents were frequently at the center of witnesses' testimonies. Almost invariably, West African armed actions in Bahia and Cuba relied on fast-paced attacks that moved rapidly from one geographical setting to another—from estate to estate in the countryside, and from street to street in the cities—and which were all exceedingly violent and

---

[11] A number of studies on slave suicide in Bahia and Cuba have appeared over the past few years. See: Ferreira, "Por hoje se acaba a lida," 197–234; Ana Maria Galdini Raimundo Oda and Saulo Veiga Oliveira, "Registros de suicídios entre escravos em São Paulo e na Bahia (1847–1888): notas de pesquisa," Paper presented at the 3rd Encontro Escravidão e Liberdade no Brasil Meridional; Perez, *To Die in Cuba*; Barcia, *Seeds of Insurrection*, 71–83.

[12] Barcia, *Seeds of Insurrection*, 37; Lovejoy, "Old Oyo Influences," 196–7.

largely reminiscent of the ways in which similar actions had taken place in the various West African regions of origin of the participants. In Bahia there were various armed groups that followed these patterns unerringly. In some cases, as happened with the Hausa-led insurgency of February 1814 and the Nagô offensive of April 1828, they followed almost identical patterns and routes.[13] On these two occasions the insurgents attacked fishing marinas where they looked for reinforcements before heading for Itapuã. Both forces left several people killed in their wake, destroyed working instruments, and ransacked the area, before finally being defeated. The similarities between these two movements are so many, that this particular circumstance has led Reis to consider the events of 1828 a "re-enactment" of the actions of 1814.[14]

Other similar military offensives took place in March 1814 and September 1828, both in Iguape, and October 1829 in Cotegipe. All three featured violent attacks, torching of properties including buildings and cane fields, and the killing of any enemies who they found in their path.[15] Also the insurrectionary movements of 1830 and 1835 in Salvador de Bahia, although carried out against an urban background, revealed similar offensive tactics. In both cases the insurgents moved hastily across the city, with the intention of conducting their previously planned attacks on their military and civilian objectives.[16]

Military offensives carried out by West African men and women in Cuba also reflected an already existing knowledge of how to make war, which had been learned in their homelands and which differed significantly from the conventional ways of making war in Europe and the Americas at the time. Whenever opportunities arose, West African attacks were well concerted, ferocious, and fast. A case in question is that of the multiethnic uprising of 1825 in Guamacaro, southeast of Matanzas. There a force of just under 200 men attacked and ransacked plantation after plantation, killing men, women, and children until they were finally defeated near the crossroads of El Coliseo, 12 hours after the offensive had begun.[17] While doing so, they played their war drums, talked in their African languages, and dressed in military garments stolen from the estates they attacked. Equally, the armed movements of 1843 in Bemba (March) and La Guanábana and La Cidra (November) showed similar characteristics, going from estate to estate, killing, torching, and destroying everything they found in their path. In both cases the 1843 insurgents were reported to have carried out their actions amidst the sound of screams in Lucumí language and the beating of their Lucumí war drums.[18] Also, those who witnessed the Lucumí uprising of 1835 in Havana declared that the armed force had moved rapidly across the

---

[13] Reis, *Rebelião escrava no Brasil*, 82–3, 109–10.   [14] Reis, *Rebelião escrava no Brasil*, 109.
[15] Prince, *Slave Rebellion in Bahia*, 110–12, 141–5; Reis, *Rebelião escrava no Brasil*, 82–6, 110–15. For the movement of 1828 in Iguape see: APEB: JUI, 2270.
[16] Reis, *Rebelião escrava no Brasil*, 115–21; "Devassa," *Anais*, 38 (1968): 24, 62, 84.
[17] Barcia, *The Great African Slave Revolt of 1825*, esp. chs. 4 and 5.
[18] "Criminal enquiry following the uprising that took place in the jurisdiction of Cimarrones on the 27th of March." ANC: CM, 29/5/1–3; "Criminal proceedings against the authors and accomplices of the slave uprising that took place on the 5th of November by the slaves from the Triunvirato and Ácana estates." ANC: CM, 30/3.

outskirts of the city, before being confronted and defeated by the local authorities and militia.[19]

Another element common to many of these movements was the ways in which the leaders made use of threats to recruit more combatants. These threats, on occasion, led to the assassination of those who refused to comply.[20] For example, during the uprising of 1825 in Guamacaro, many slaves were forced to flee from the insurgents in order to save their lives, and at least one was taken prisoner and dragged for many miles after he refused to join the armed troop. Also in March 1843 the leaders of the Bemba uprising were reported to threaten with death all those blacks that would refuse to join them.[21]

In Bahia, West African insurgents often used similar intimidation methods in order to make sure their ranks would swell as much and as fast as possible. For example, both in February 1814 in Itapuã and two years later in February 1816 in Santo Amaro and São Francisco do Conde, Hausa-led forces threatened and killed those who refused to follow them.[22] In at least one other instance, in September 1828 in Iguape, a considerable force went on the offensive invading several plantations in the area. As the attack got under way they threatened and wounded any slave who refused to join their small army.[23]

It must be said that enforced recruitment did not always involve death threats. Some of these military leaders were also able to resort to alternative means to persuade those who were unwilling to follow them into battle to change their minds. For instance, in 1833 Fierabrás Lucumí, one of the main leaders of the uprising that began on the grounds of the Salvador coffee plantation, attempted to bribe Antonio Lucumí by "offering him a horse." After Antonio declined the offer, Fierabrás threatened to kill him should he continue to refuse to join the armed force.[24] Similarly, when the insurgents who rose on the Triunvirato sugar plantation in November 1843 invaded the neighboring Ácana estate, they gave those slaves who were in shackles the opportunity to choose between being released and joining the uprising, or to stay as they were should they decline to join it.[25]

Time and again these West African military forces were defeated and forced to flee by a combination of neighbors, loyal slaves, local militias, and regular troops. Only occasionally did they prevail and even then, their success was only momentary. Not surprisingly, and according to their previous martial experiences, they regularly resorted to confronting their foes in pitched battles that more often than not included hand-to-hand combat, just as they would have done in their homelands before. Here, once more, we do not have particularly rich descriptions for most of them. However, a few instances of hand-to-hand confrontations were recorded in both Bahia and Cuba. One such case is that of the 1830 insurgency that took

[19] Deposition of Bernardo Machado. Havana, July 1835. ANC: CM, 11/1.
[20] According to Johnson, in Oyo new recruits could be forced to join armies for fear of vengeance. Johnson, *The History of the Yorubas*, 195. I would like to thank Olatunji Ojo for pointing me to this reference.
[21] Deposition of Fermín Lucumí. Ingenio Alcancía, April 1843. ANC: CM, 29/5/1.
[22] Reis, *Slave Rebellion in Brazil*, 45, 50.   [23] Reis, *Rebelião escrava no Brasil*, 110–11.
[24] Deposition of Antonio (Pelu) Lucumí. Cafetal Salvador, August 1833. ANC: ME, 540/B.
[25] Deposition of Ynocencio Carabalí. Ingenio Ácana, November 1843. ANC: CM, 30/3.

place in downtown Salvador and that included a number of hand-to-hand clashes between the Nagô and the Bahian forces that fought and defeated them.[26] Similar instances were reported during the offensives of February 1814 in Itapuã, and April 1828 in Cachoeira, and during the Malê movement of 1835 in downtown Salvador.[27]

In Cuba, the level of detail of the descriptions of some of these hand-to-hand confrontations is much greater. Such was the case of the pitched battle that took place on September 1832 between 17 Lucumí *bozales* just arrived from Africa at the Purísima Concepción sugar estate and the plantation's white employees. The accounts of the encounter given by some of these white employees and other local neighbors reflect a truly non-western manner of facing the enemy, by attacking them without giving them an opportunity to strike back. According to Manuel Díaz, overseer of a nearby estate, when he came face to face with the Africans "he was not able to strike any of them, because they did not attack him frontally; instead they were always jumping, dancing and attacking him with their machetes, not being possible to face any of them directly, because every time he tried to, two or three would assault him from behind."[28] "Offbeat screams and contortions" were also referred to by Guillermo Monroy, overseer at the sugar plantation La Sonora in 1837, who was forced to fight a group of recently arrived Lucumí *bozales* who attacked him after he had attempted to punish some of them, and by the widow of a planter killed during the 1825 uprising in Guamacaro, who recalled how the Africans had been dancing, jumping, and celebrating while attacking a nearby estate.[29]

Those who witnessed the uprising that took place at the La Arratía estate in July 1842 gave an even more thorough account of the military actions undertaken by the West Africans they saw in battle. On this occasion the insurgents challenged the white employees of the estate and a troop of lancers shouting rallying cries in their own languages and wielding their machetes. According to one of the lancers who fought the African contingent, some of them "signaled to their heads, as a statement that they were ready to die."[30] On the battlefield, this group of Africans proved skillful soldiers. They were organized, fierce, and relentless when confronting a regular military force—something that even the plantation overseer struggled to understand—and showing expertise in facing firearms in the battlefield; when shot at, they all dodged the bullets by ducking to the ground, only to stand up again and resume their charge as soon as the barrage of fire had passed.[31]

[26] Prince, "Slave Rebellion in Bahia," 146–51; Reis, *Rebelião escrava no Brasil*, 115–21.

[27] Reis, *Rebelião escrava no Brasil*, 83–6; Magistrate José Cardozo da Silva to the President of the Province of Bahia. Cachoeira, 24 September 1828. APEB: JUI, 2270. "Devassa," *Anais*, 40 (1971), 54, 64.

[28] Deposition of Manuel Díaz, overseer of the ingenio Casa Barreto. Güira de Melena, September 1832. ANC: ME, 570/S.

[29] Deposition of Guillermo Monroy. Ingenio La Sonora, June 1837. ANC: ME, 1178/B. Deposition of Maria Luisa Saint-Gême Beauvais. Guamacaro, August 1825. ANC: CM, 1/5.

[30] Deposition of José Gorriti. Ingenio La Arratía, July 1842. ANC: CM, 28/1. In another incident involving Lucumí slaves a year earlier, they "brandished sticks and rocks while beating their buttocks and touching their genitals." Signaling to body parts while fighting their foes was something that Cuban authorities and slave owners found very unusual. Depositions of Valentín Toledo and Domingo Aldama. Havana, October 1841. ANC: GSC, 940/33154.

[31] Deposition of Fermín Ortega. Ingenio La Arratía, July 1842. ANC: CM, 28/1.

West African insurgents, of course, were also forced to fight many battles on the defensive. Taking strategic positions and choosing the terrain were important elements on these occasions. In Bahia, the *quilombolas* of Urubu fortified themselves in the bushes and, benefiting from their location, were able to fight a large armed force sent against them from Salvador in 1826. During the defense of their positions, the insurgents—most of whom were Nagôs—kept their lines and "fought back fiercely" killing three slave hunters and wounding three more, before being overpowered by a large regular army of more than 200 men.[32] The defense of *quilombos* in the outskirts of Salvador was nothing new, since regular troops and slave hunters had repeatedly assaulted them at least since April 1807 when the *quilombos* of Nossa Senhora dos Mares and Cabula came under attack by a force of more than 80 men sent from Salvador and commanded by Captain Severino da Silva Lessa.[33]

In Cuba, too, whenever possible, West Africans chose advantageous positions from which to battle against their foes. In 1830 a group of recently arrived *bozales* managed to repel a local militia for some time by hiding within the coffee bushes, from where they defended themselves throwing rocks at the militia men, injuring one and eventually forcing them to withdraw.[34] Ten years later, in a very similar instance at the coffee plantation Empresa, a large number of Lucumí slaves defied a local military force after taking the lives of their plantation's owner and overseer. When the colonial troops arrived to put down the insurrection, they were forced to retreat by the persistent attack that the slaves carried against them from their strategic position protected by the coffee bushes.[35]

In another incident which occurred on the grounds of the Banco sugar plantation near the town of Güines in June 1842, the descriptions of defensive tactics given were even more revealing. In this example the insurgent slaves, who were also recently arrived *bozales* from Africa, first moved towards the "entrance of the forest" where they "cleared a sizeable portion of woodland in the shape of a square [with the intention of using it] as a battle ground."[36] When they eventually were forced to withdraw to a more secure position, they chose a "narrow and difficult passage" to confront the colonial troops, rendering most of their weapons useless, and wounding the captain of the troop, Ignacio López Gavilán, who was ultimately forced to order his men to open fire, killing three and wounding one, while the others escaped even deeper into the woods.[37]

For those who did not lose their lives in battle, in an analogous way, as they would have done in West Africa, a quick withdrawal was the logical next step. Some ran away and joined *quilombos* and *palenques*, while others chose to kill themselves in the hope of being reborn in their homelands. In those cases where retreat maneuvers were described by the insurgents or those who hunted them, a lack of organization seems to have been the main common element. Even though

---

[32] Reis, *Slave Rebellion in Brazil*, 55–6.   [33] Reis, *Rebelião escrava no Brasil*, 69–71.

[34] Francisco Lechuga to Captain-General Vives. Wajay, 21 November 1830. ANC: GSC, 936/33032.

[35] Deposition of Captain Sixto Morejón. Cafetal Empresa, July 1840. ANC: GSC, 939/33131.

[36] Alejandro Pelosa to the Captain-General. Güines, 18 June 1840. ANC: GSC, 939/33130.

[37] Ignacio López Gavilán to Captain-General Prince of Anglona. San Nicolás, 15 June 1840. ANC: GSC, 939/33130.

defeated combatants "fled as best they could" in Bahia and Cuba, as they would have done in West Africa according to Thornton,[38] on occasion they attempted to reorganize themselves and counterattack. This was the case in September 1828. After the West African force that attacked several plantations in Iguape region was defeated by a local militia, those who survived regrouped in a nearby cane field with the intention, according to Reis, of mounting a counteroffensive. Unfortunately for them, their plans were frustrated when a large military force sent from Cachoeira arrived on the scene and forced them to escape into the forest.[39]

Failing to regroup and counterattack, insurgents had two alternative ways to get away from their pursuers. The first one was to find shelter in runaway slave communities, and to attempt to rebuild their lives away from plantations and cities. Both Bahia and Cuba offered propitious geographical locations for the establishment and defense of runaway slave settlements. The second available option was committing suicide. For many of these men and women taking their own lives equated to a physical return to their homelands, where they expected to be reborn among their kin. For that, whenever they had the time to do so, they gathered provisions for the journey and dressed in their best outfits. Nevertheless, for those who had been routed in the battlefield and who were on the run, provisioning for the journey seems to have been far from their main concern.[40]

On a number of occasions, beaten insurgents shared the journey back home together. Collective suicides were something that Bahian and Cuban authorities did not have to deal with until the nineteenth century. Even though for many years they had seen their African servants take their own lives due to what they called a "melancholic" state of mind, seeing entire groups of West Africans resorting to collective suicides took them by surprise as their own reports suggest.

In Bahia the first report of collective suicides was given in February 1814 after the armed uprising that affected the region of Itapuã. After the insurgents had been defeated a police report mentioned that many of the slaves had committed suicide "by drowning in the river or by hanging."[41] An even more unusual instance of collective suicide was described in December 1826 by the soldiers who attacked the Urubu *quilombo*, who recalled finding the bodies of five Africans who had "slit each other's throats."[42]

In Cuba, authorities were first forced to deal with a case of collective suicide after the first Lucumí uprising of the period, which took place at the coffee plantation Tentativa, and was suppressed in January 1827. According to army colonel Joaquín de Miranda y Madariaga up to 18 of the Africans who had risen in arms had been found hanging in the nearby forest.[43] Other similar acts of collective suicide followed the failed armed movements at the sugar plantations La Magdalena in 1835 and

[38] Thornton, *Warfare in Atlantic Africa*, 81.
[39] Jozé Paes Cardozo da Silva to the President of the Province of Bahia. Cachoeira, 24 September 1828. APEB: JUI, 2270. Cf. Reis, *Slave Rebellion in Brazil*, 110–12.
[40] Ferreira, "Por hoje se acaba a lida," 197–34; Perez, *To Die in Cuba*; Barcia, *Seeds of Insurrection*, 71–83.
[41] Reis, *Rebelião escrava no Brasil*, 82–3.   [42] Reis, *Rebelião escrava no Brasil*, 102.
[43] Joaquín de Miranda y Madariaga to Captain-General Francisco Dionisio Vives. Cafetal Reunión, 9 January 1827. ANC: RCJF, 150/7436.

Alcancía in 1843. In the former case, 14 Lucumí *bozales* who had arrived at the plantation only a few days earlier, rose in arms and fought the plantation's white employees until they were eventually defeated. In their reports, those who witnessed the insurrection and its aftermath reported that at least three of the Lucumí insurgents were found hanged, and another one had drowned in the river.[44] In the latter case, at least seven Africans were believed to have run away and hanged themselves after the uprising had concluded.[45]

As discussed so far, the ways in which West African military operations were conducted in Bahian and Cuban lands were occasionally reported, providing us with an exciting insight into how operations and tactics were transplanted from West Africa and adapted to the new American settings. To better understand these developments, a look into the composition of these armies is in order. Who was allowed to join and who was not? Were women and children simply witnesses of these movements? Were they willing participants instead, as they often had been in their West African homelands? Did ethnic background and geographical origin determine participation in each of them? These are some of the questions that will be explored and answered in the next section.

GENDER, ETHNICITY, AND THE COMPOSITION OF INSURGENT TROOPS

The membership of any given West African insurgency was determined by a number of factors that ranged from sex and age, to geographical and ethnic origins, not forgetting the significance of previously shared experiences. In Bahia as well as in Cuba women were from time to time involved in some of the most important West African armed actions of the period. For example, 22 women were reported to have joined insurgent forces during the uprising of May 1824 on the grounds of the Favorito coffee plantation in the locality of Puerta de la Güira.[46] West African women also participated in the uprisings of July 1835 in Havana and May 1843 on the Perseverancia coffee plantation.[47]

More to the point, as has been shown before, some of them were reported to have led and rallied West African soldiers in these two New World territories. For example, during the uprising that took place in the Cachoeira district in August 1826 one of the ringleaders seems to have been a woman, referred to as a "queen,"

---

[44] Proceedings against the rebel Lucumí slaves of the ingenio La Magdalena. Jurisdiction of Santa Ana, Matanzas, July 1835. ANC: ME, 232/Z. A similar case involving a force of 25 Lucumí bozales took place the following year on the grounds of the sugar estate San Pablo. See Proceedings against the slaves of the ingenio San Pablo, owned by Julián Zaldívar. Catalina de Güines, September 1837. ANC: ME, 1193/H.

[45] Deposition of Gil Lucumí. Ingenio Alcancía, April 1843. ANC: CM, 29/5/1.

[46] Antonio de Morejón Quixano to Captain-General Vives. Cafetal Favorito, 29 May 1824. ANC: AP, 28/8.

[47] Mutiny of the Slaves on the coffee plantation Perseverancia. Lagunillas, May 1843. ANC: GSC, 941/33203; Criminal proceedings against the negroes that on the afternoon of 12 July 1835 rose near the Chavez Bridge, committing various murders, injuries, robberies, and excesses. ANC: CM, 11/1.

who was eventually killed in combat by the troops sent to put down the movement.[48] Later that same year a Nagô woman called Zeferina acted as a leader for the many men and women who fought the soldiers sent against the Urubu *quilombo* in December. Zeferina was reported to have rallied the Urubu combatants, "keeping them on the line" with only a bow and some arrows.[49]

Two Lucumí women, Ferminia and Carlota, were the leaders of most likely the largest ever insurrection to take place in the Cuban countryside: the uprising of November 1843, which spread from the Triunvirato and Ácana plantations to the jurisdictions of La Guanábana and La Cidra. Both Ferminia and Carlota rallied the troops in different moments and became focal figures during the march that took this West African armed force from estate to estate. Ferminia Lucumí, in particular, was reported to have "a manly character. . . distinguishing herself among the most vicious men in the persecution and murdering of the whites."[50]

Cases such as these point to a military competence. As was discussed in Chapter 1, in Dahomey, and also in Yoruba-speaking states like Oyo and Ijesa, women were closely associated with war, and it was not rare for them to lead troops into battle. Zeferina, Carlota, and Ferminia may have been, to use Awe and Olutoye's words, "women of distinction or noble birth" in one of the Yoruba-speaking states before undergoing the transatlantic crossing.[51] Alternatively, and keeping in mind the level of confusion reigning at the time in order to determine the ethnies to which these women might have belonged, they could potentially be former Dahomean amazons or *mino*, who could have been mistakenly labeled as Nagô or Lucumí by Bahian and Cuban authorities or slave traders upon their arrival in Bahia and Cuba, almost certainly acquired before being sent to Bahia and Cuba.

On other occasions, as in the insurgent movement of 1833 in Banes, women and children were explicitly separated from the main troop following the orders given by Joaquín and Fierabrás, two of the leaders.[52] Children, or at least teenagers, almost certainly joined West African forces in both territories with frequency, and at least in one case, in July 1835 in Havana, some of them were among those who participated in the movement that began at the Puente de Chávez.[53] The armed force was said to be commanded by "a thirteen or fourteen years-old" African boy who "carried a machete and who was the meanest against the whites."[54]

The participation of West African women and children in actions of resistance, including military movements, in Bahia and Cuba is a topic that has not been

---

[48] Reis, *Rebelião escrava no Brasil*, 100.

[49] Imperial Police Guard, Military Division, Prosecutor's report. Bahia, 17 December 1826. APEB: IE, 2845. Cf. Reis, *Rebelião escrava no Brasil*, 102.

[50] Felipe Arango's Prosecutor Report, Havana, 2 February 1844. ANC: CM, 30/3. This uprising also included several other women who joined either by their own choice or after being forced to do so by the insurgents. Curiously, when a monument to these rebels was erected by the Cuban government in the 1970s, of three African human figures, two were men and one was a woman, even though historical evidence points to an armed forced led by two women and one man.

[51] Awe and Olutoye, "Women and Warfare in 19th Century Yorubaland," 124.

[52] Deposition of Matías (Eguyovi) Lucumí. Cafetal Salvador, August 1833. ANC: ME, 540/B.

[53] Criminal proceedings against the negroes that on the afternoon of 12 July 1835 rose near the Chavez Bridge, committing various murders, injuries, robberies, and excesses. ANC: CM, 11/1.

[54] Deposition of José de los Santos Sotomayor. Havana, July 1835. ANC: CM, 11/1.

properly studied so far. Other elements that led to the realization and cohesion of small West African armies on the American side of the Atlantic, however, have been perhaps better documented and studied. Take for example the issue of ethnicity. Debates about the role of ethnicity during slave and free men movements in Bahia and Cuba during the first half of the nineteenth century are not uncommon. Scholars such as Robert L. Paquette, Matt D. Childs, Michelle Reid-Vazquez, and more recently Aisha K. Finch have attempted to explore the role played by ethnic heritage during the conspiracies of Aponte and La Escalera in Cuba.[55] Even more to the point have been the discussions about the impact that large numbers of Hausa and Nagô Africans had upon slave and free men resistance in Bahia during the same period. From the groundbreaking work of Howard Prince and Stuart Schwartz, to the well-documented and masterfully written books and articles by João José Reis, ethnicity has become a major theme whenever West African-organized and -led movements have been studied, leading to constructive discussions that have increased our knowledge of the possible reasons that led these men and women to rise in arms.[56]

A particularly illuminating case is that of the diverging opinions expressed by Paul E. Lovejoy and João José Reis while discussing the actual reasons behind the Malê movement of 1835 in Bahia. This debate has centered on the role that Islam may or may have not played as a cohesive factor for the insurgents. While Lovejoy has argued that a *Nagoization* of the Muslim community in Bahia may imply that many of the movements that took place in Bahia between 1807 and 1835 "followed a pattern that suggests strong similarities with the *jihād* that was underway in the Central Sudan,"[57] Reis has pointed out that "the experience of Hausas and Nagôs suggests an ethnic rationale guiding their collective action." In other words, "one needed not be a follower of Allah to join in."[58]

While both approaches have merits of their own, and are by no means mutually exclusive, determining whether an ethnic rationale or a common belief in Allah had a central role in these movements is something worth examining and discussing. Although, for example, the documents produced as a result of some of the Hausa-led uprisings occurred before 1816 indicate that Islam may have been a crucial element in some of them, this is certainly not the case for the 1835 Malê insurrection which, incidentally, was continuously and consistently referred to by all those who testified after its suppression as the "war of the Nagôs" or the "uprising of the Nagôs."[59] The fact remains that at least some of the insurgencies that

[55] Paquette, *Sugar is Made with Blood*, 37–8; Childs, *The 1812 Aponte Rebellion*, 100–9; Michelle Reid-Vazquez, *The Year of the Lash: Free People of Color in Cuba and the Nineteenth-Century Atlantic World* (Athens, GA: University of Georgia Press, 2011), 58, 113; Aisha Finch, "Insurgency at the Crossroads: Cuban Slaves and the Conspiracy of La Escalera, 1841–1844" (Ph.D. diss. New York University, 2007), 293–5.

[56] Prince, "Slave Rebellion in Bahia," esp. ch. 1; Schwartz, *Sugar Plantations*, 480–1; Reis, *Rebelião escrava no Brasil*, 307–9; See also Nishida, *Slavery and Identity*; and Luis Nicolau Parés and Roger Sansi, eds., *Sorcery in the Black Atlantic* (Chicago: University of Chicago Press, 2011).

[57] Lovejoy, "Background to Rebellion," 170–1.

[58] João José Reis, "American Counterpoint: New Approaches to Slavery and Abolition in Brazil." Paper presented at the 12th Annual Gilder Lehman Center International Conference at Yale University, 29–30 October 2010, 18.

[59] "Devassa," *Anais*, 38 (1968): 72–3, 100, 129.

took place in Bahia were carried out by Hausas and Nagôs who mainly recruited men from their own ethnic backgrounds.

Evidence from Cuba also suggests that ethnic allegiances and alliances were more likely to be considered as indispensable by those organizing and leading these movements than any particular set of religious beliefs. The actions of West African insurgents, especially the Lucumí, often excluded West Africans identified under other ethnic denominators. One such case took place in 1842 in La Arratía sugar estate, where the Lucumí attacked the plantation's employees on their own, excluding Mina and Carabalí slaves, although letting two Arará slaves join them. Interestingly enough, and backing Henry B. Lovejoy's arguments about the unreliability of these ethnic denominators, some of these Arará slaves were not even sure to which group they actually belonged.[60] The testimony of Fidel Arará leaves no room for certainty. When asked about his origins, Fidel declared, "that he was Arará, although his companions were always saying that he was Lucumí."[61] In another opportunity, in an event that may have had a direct link to previous African rivalries, Arará slaves were expressly excluded from joining the insurgency that broke out at the La Sonora estate in Lagunillas in June 1837. In this case, the Arará slaves who were left out all declared that they did not speak the language of the Lucumí and that they did not mix with them, probably a direct reference to the conflicts that had seen the Yoruba-speaking states and Dahomey fight against each other from the early nineteenth century, when Adandozan and Ghezo began challenging the rule of Oyo.[62]

At times the combination of ethnic background and geographical origins could either bring insurgents together, or make insurrections unreachable to those who were considered untrustworthy outsiders. Multiethnic movements took place in both territories from early on in the century; for example, as early as in 1809, Bahian Hausas were keen to use Jêjes and Nagôs as allies in the movement they organized in January that year. Other Bahian insurgencies, including the 1835 Malê movement also included West Africans from different ethnies. In Cuba the situation was similar. The Guamacaro uprising of 1825, for instance, included men from a number of ethnic backgrounds, going so far as to accept a small number of Creole slaves among their ranks.[63] Equally, the force assembled at the Catalina coffee plantation in July 1828 counted among their ranks men belonging to the Macuá, Congo, Lucumí, and Carabalí ethnies.[64]

Opposed to these cases were others where Congo (Bantu) and Creole slaves were systematically left out. Congos, in particular, were considered unreliable by many West African men and women, and quite often were explicitly excluded from the plotting and undertaking of many of these movements. One of the most notable cases was that of the uprising of November 1843 in la Guanábana and La Cidra.

---

[60] Lovejoy, "Old Oyo Influences," 38–44.

[61] Deposition of Fidel Arará. Ingenio La Arratía, July 1842. ANC: CM, 28/1.

[62] Depositions of Simón Arará and Fermín Arará. Ingenio La Sonora, June 1837. ANC: ME, 1178/B. See also Law, *Ouidah*, 123–88.

[63] Barcia, *The Great African Slave Revolt of 1825*, 132.

[64] Proceedings against 18 runaway slaves from the cafetal Catalina. Guanajay, July 1828. ANC: GSC, 936/33025.

There, Congo slaves were not only segregated by the Lucumí who had organized and led the insurrection, but, probably as a reaction, they were reported to have done everything they could to protect and save the lives of their white masters and employees.[65]

Creoles were also frequently excluded from West African movements. Even in those cases where they were accepted, as in the 1825 uprising of Guamacaro, their presence regularly raised concerns among their West African comrades, who considered them "dumb or collaborators of the whites."[66] Creole slaves failed to feature in substantial numbers in almost every single movement organized by West African men and women throughout the first half of the nineteenth century in Bahia and Cuba. In fact, their absence was often noticeable. As Reis has correctly stated "Native-born blacks and *mestiços* did not take part in any of the more than twenty Bahian slave revolts prior to 1835."[67] Notably, they also failed to join the multiethnic Malê movement of 1835, which counted Nagôs, Jêjes, Hausas, Tapas, Bornos, and at least one Cabinda among its participants.[68] Thomas Skidmore has gone as far as claiming that Brazilian-born slaves were not enlisted because they were seen "as part of their enemy" by the West African insurgents.[69]

Relations between *bozal* and *ladino* (acculturated) Africans were even more challenging. Although more often than not *ladinos* of a West African origin were accepted by West African forces led by newly arrived men and women, on certain occasions they were not considered trustworthy enough, and thus were left out of conspiracies and insurrections. A number of instances point to an existing segregation between *bozales* and *ladinos*, irrespective of ethnic background, in both Bahia and Cuba.

In September 1828 a number of West African slaves rose in arms on the grounds of the Engenho Novo plantation in Bahia. According to Reis, on this occasion "even the Africans were divided: rebels comprised mainly recently arrived slaves."[70] Earlier that year, in another uprising which occurred in the vicinity of Cachoeira, it was reported that when the West African troops invaded the Herculano estate, only the *escravos novos* joined them, while all the *ladino* slaves refused to follow the insurgents.[71]

Bozal-only insurrections abounded in the Cuban case. Between 1832 and 1836, four significant armed movements exploded across the western Cuban countryside. All of them had as a common characteristic the fact that only *bozales* went into battle. These were the cases in the armed action that occurred in the Purísima Concepción estate in 1832, the Magdalena plantation in 1835, and the San Pablo sugar estate in 1836.[72] Even more to the point, during the August 1834 insurrection at the San

[65] Prosecutor's report of Felipe Arango. Havana, 2 February 1844. ANC: CM, 30/3.
[66] José Ildefonso Suárez to José Cadaval. Havana, 19 September 1825, ANC, CM, 1/5.
[67] Reis, *Slave Rebellion in Brazil*, 141.
[68] Reis, *Slave Rebellion in Brazil*, 141–6. At least in the case of Bahia, mulattos were occasionally the targets of West African forces. For example, during the Hausa-led uprising of February 1814 in Bahia, the insurgents urged "death for whites and mulattos" equally. Reis, *Slave Rebellion in Brazil*, 45.
[69] Thomas Skidmore, "Religion and Slave Rebellion in Bahia," *Current Anthropology*, 36:2 (1995): 390.
[70] Reis, *Slave Rebellion in Brazil*, 63.   [71] Reis, *Slave Rebellion in Brazil*, 62.
[72] For the uprising at the Purísima Concepción in September 1832 see ANC: ME, 570/S; for the insurrection at the Magdalena estate in June 1835 see ANC: ME, 232/Z; for the mutiny at the San Pablo plantation in September 1837 see ANC: ME, 1193/H.

Juan de Dios de Macastá sugar plantation, *ladino* slaves not only failed to join the insurgents, but fought against their recently arrived fellow slaves, taking the side of their masters.[73]

Inclusion or exclusion in each of the movements discussed in this book was determined by diverse factors that could come into play depending on the specific setting and circumstances. Although Creole slaves and Africans belonging to some particular ethnies were frequently excluded due to a lack of trust, which was probably a result of the lack of a common history, on certain opportunities they were permitted to join armed movements. Equally, although women and children were more often than not left out, at least in a few instances they became protagonists of some of these military actions, taking central stage once the insurgencies had begun to unfold. Obviously, the existence of previously acquired martial experiences was exceptionally relevant when plots were conceived and uprisings started. Ethnic affinity seems to have been of paramount importance throughout the period in both Bahia and Cuba. Even though interethnic military insurgencies were not uncommon, most of them still featured large numbers of West Africans from the same or close ethnic and geographical backgrounds, especially Nagô and Lucumí, and in the Bahian case, Hausa. This affinity was intrinsically related to the ways in which war was conducted in the West African regions they had come from, and probably even more importantly, to how weapons were obtained, distributed, and then used in the battlefield.

WEAPONRY

Irrespective of whether the weapons were manufactured, found, or taken from the places they assaulted, the fact that they were easy to acquire constituted an essential factor for these West African men and women in organizing their insurgencies. After all, they had come from places where weapons of war could be obtained relatively easily, sometimes at a very low cost, from local artificers, and at other times were even made at home.[74]

In both Bahia and Cuba, this was also the case. There, West African men and women armed themselves more often than not with weapons that were known to them from Africa, and in some cases that they even knew how to make with their own hands. Among them were some of offensive character such as blades, spears, bows and arrows, and also defensive ones like shields. As we will see, even rocks were used on occasion when other weapons could not be found. Additionally, they resorted to other war paraphernalia, including drums, amulets and charms, standards, and flags, all of which were considered as essential elements to guarantee the success of their martial enterprises.

Swords of various kinds were quite common in West Africa by the turn of the nineteenth century. Even though historians such as Jack Goody have suggested that swords were not particularly important as a weapon of war, material evidence

---

[73] Deposition of Tomás Mandinga. Ingenio San Juan de Dios de Macastá, August 1834. ANC: ME, 451/F.

[74] Smith, *Warfare and Diplomacy*, 65.

and some travelers' accounts seem to suggest otherwise.[75] As Smith has pointed out, in tropical West Africa "the large number of surviving swords, of both operational and ceremonial forms, attests to its having played a leading role in warfare over much of West Africa."[76] Some iconographic evidence points to this leading role. For example, the bas-reliefs found in King Ghezo's palace in Abomey depict various war scenes where swords are undoubtedly used as a main weapon for combat (Figures 4.1 and 4.2).[77] Smith has also noticed that all swords in the region, just like the machetes they would encounter in Bahian and Cuban plantations, "were designed for cutting or slashing," pointing to a martial use rather than to a ceremonial one.[78] More to the point, among these swords designed for cutting or slashing there were various types of cutlasses, including the common *idà*, the shorter version called *jomo*, and the heavier and longer *agedengbe*, widely used by the Owu soldiers against Ife and Ijebu during the Owu wars.[79] Cutlasses were commonly used among the Yoruba-speaking peoples for agricultural work, a situation that would also be common in Bahia and Cuba where the work on sugar plantations required their daily use.[80] According to Johnson, these weapons were often man-made locally across the Yoruba-speaking lands, where some of the most skilled blacksmiths in West Africa would manufacture them for both agricultural and military purposes. There, as would have subsequently happened in Bahia and Cuba, cutlasses or machetes were used in close quarters during military actions.

Of the different swords that were available to West African men and women in Bahia and Cuba, it was precisely the cutlass or machete that was the most common, at least in the countryside. Other agricultural working tools such as knives and sickles were also typical. West African soldiers reacquainted themselves with these blades on the other side of the Atlantic, as soon as they were taken to the many rural estates where their use was customary. Not surprisingly, cutlasses or machetes and other types of swords, like sabers, were habitual features among the weapons confiscated by Bahian authorities after instances of African warfare during the period. For example machetes and swords were used in battle by the *quilombolas* of Urubu in 1826,[81] while at least 12 swords with pommels stolen from a hardware shop were used by the Nagô insurgents of 1830 in Salvador.[82] Swords of various types were also displayed in the surprise offensive of 1826 in Pirajá, where at least an "old sword" was seized from the Africans.[83]

---

[75] Jack Goody, *Technology, Tradition and the State in Africa* (Cambridge: Cambridge University Press, 1971), 27, 34.

[76] Smith, *Warfare and Diplomacy*, 66.   [77] Verger, "Notes on the Bas Reliefs," 3–13.

[78] J. F. Ade Ajayi and Robert S. Smith, *Yoruba Warfare in the Nineteenth Century* (Cambridge: Cambridge University Press, 1971), 16.

[79] Crowther, *Vocabulary of the Yoruba Language*, 106; Johnson, *The History of the Yorubas*, 132; Ade Ajayi and Smith, *Yoruba Warfare in the Nineteenth Century*, 16.

[80] Samuel Johnson pointed out how until the nineteenth century agricultural work in the Yoruba-speaking territories was "carried on with simple and primitive instruments, viz. a hoe and a cutlass, and nothing more." Johnson, *The History of the Yorubas*, 117.

[81] Reis, *Slave Rebellion in Brazil*, 56.

[82] Cause against Francisco, Nagô, and Nicolau, Nagô, slaves of Bernardo José Jorge. APEB: IE, 2845.

[83] Inquest produced as a result of the deaths of Manoel José Correia and others, in the surroundings of Pirajá, 1826. APEB: IE, 2845.

Swords also featured prominently during the Nagô insurgency of 1835 in Salvador. They were described on a number of occasions by white, African, and African-descendant neighbors of the city. Inspector Leonardo dos Reis Vellozo recalled having seen "a group of negroes armed with swords" marauding the streets.[84] This testimony was backed by Henrique Nagô, who declared that the "negroes of his own nation" had "passed through the Pilar street armed with swords."[85] Other witnesses who mentioned the force of armed Nagôs marching through the city were Belchior, a Nagô,[86] and Domingos Marinho de Sá, a Creole tailor from Iguape.[87]

Due to the rural character of most of the African movements of the period in Cuba, swords, and especially cutlasses or machetes became the preferred weapon among African insurgents. References to machetes appear in almost every rural movement recorded between the mid-1820s and mid-1840s. Thanks to some travelers' accounts and recent archaeological excavations we also know that, together with the spear, they were the weapon of choice of maroons across the island.[88] Among the most remarkable instances of African warfare featuring machetes were those of the Purísima Concepción plantation in September 1832. Slaves there were reported to have used more than 20 during their attack, while displaying hand-to-hand combat tactics that left their white enemies confounded and perplexed.[89] Similarly, in June 1825, the insurgents used machetes and sabers during their offensive in Guamacaro.[90]

The sight of recently landed Africans wielding their machetes caused havoc in Havana in 1835, when some of the *emancipados* from the brig *Negrito* rose in arms and attacked a neighborhood of the city.[91] When another group of recently arrived Lucumí slaves confronted the white employees of the sugar plantation San Pablo in September 1836, they were reported to have armed themselves with machetes, which they then used against those who tried to contain them.[92] Working machetes were also used by the African insurgents at the La Arratía estate in 1842, and by the large African forces assembled in Bemba in March 1843, and La Guanábana and La Cidra in November 1843.

Alongside machetes and occasionally other types of swords, Africans also benefited from a number of working tools that were easily available to them, including knives, sickles, and hatchets. Knives were also common in West Africa. They were used for work and also in wars. Smith points out that among the Yoruba "iron throwing knives were important," and among the weapons depicted in one of the

---

[84] Deposition of Leonardo dos Reis Vellozo. Salvador, February 1835. "Devassa," *Anais*, 38 (1968): 21.

[85] Deposition of Henrique Nagô, slave of Vicente Ferreira de Mata. Salvador, January 1835. "Devassa," *Anais*, 38 (1968): 76.

[86] Deposition of Belchior, Nagô from Cobai, slave of Jozé Joaquim Xavier. Salvador, January 1835. "Devassa," *Anais*, 40 (1971): 19.

[87] Deposition of Domingos Marinho de Sá. Salvador, April 1835. "Devassa," *Anais*, 40 (1971): 64.

[88] La Rosa Corzo, *Armas y tácticas defensivas*, 12–13. See also Gabino La Rosa Corzo, "Arqueología del cimarronaje: útiles para la resistencia," *Boletín del Gabinete de Arqueología*, 6:6 (2007): 4–15.

[89] Deposition of Victoriano Rodríguez. Güira de Melena, September 1832. ANC: ME, 570/S.

[90] Barcia, *The Great African Slave Revolt of 1825*, 111–12, 117, 132, 150.

[91] Deposition of Bernardo Machado. Havana, July 1835. ANC: CM, 11/1.

[92] Deposition of Julián de Zaldívar. Catalina de Güines. September, 1836. ANC: ME, 1193/H.

illustrations left by Jean Barbot, one knife can be discerned to the bottom right of the image.[93] Another illustration (Figure 5.1) left by a visitor to West Africa in the 1850s shows two Mandingo men also armed with swords and knives.[94]

Not surprisingly, in both Bahia and Cuba knives frequently formed part of the arsenal of the African insurgents. The Bahian authorities found some of them, after the Hausa plot of 1807 was uncovered, and they featured among the diverse weapons used by the Urubu insurgents in 1826.[95] Knives equally constituted part of the arsenal of West African men and women in Cuba. In May 1824, for example, a group of African slaves from the coffee plantation Favorito in the locality of Puerta de la Güira, challenged the commands of their overseer and confronted him with machetes and at least 18 knives of various sizes and types.[96] Knives were also among the weapons first hidden in the bushes and then used by the Lucumí *bozales* of the sugar estate La Sonora in June 1837.[97]

Figure 5.1 Mandingo soldiers. Wagner, *Schilderung der Reisen*, 303.

[93] Jean Barbot, "A Description of the Costs of North and South Guinea," in John Green, ed., *A New General Collection of Voyages and Travels* (London: Thomas Astley, 1745), ii. 693. See also Smith, *Warfare and Diplomacy*, 76.

[94] Hermann Wagner, *Schilderung der Reisen und Entdeckungen des Dr Eduard Vogel in Central-Afrika: In der Grossen Wuste, in den Landem des Sudan* (Leipzig: Otto Spamer, 1860), 303.

[95] Reis, *Slave Rebellion in Brazil*, 43, 56.

[96] Antonio de Morejón Quixano to Captain-General Vives. Cafetal Favorito, 29 May 1824. ANC: AP, 28/8.

[97] Deposition of Guillermo Monroy. Lagunillas, June 1837. ANC: ME, 1178/B.

Although there are no references to the use of sickles in any of the instances of African struggle in Cuba, there were at least two cases in which they became part of the armory of their Bahian counterparts. Firstly, they were used in February 1814 by the Hausa force that attacked fishing marinas and the village of Itapuã.[98] Then they reappeared in 1826 among the weapons used by the *quilombolas* of Urubu.[99] In February 1814 the Hausa also made use of hatchets, a weapon they would have also known from Africa.[100]

Practical as machetes and knives were, for the vast majority of these West African men and women, given the choice they would have probably preferred spears and javelins when going to war. The spear was a "symbol of honour and office as well as a weapon of war" in many West African territories, including the Yoruba-speaking and Hausa-speaking states, Benin, and Dahomey, to mention but a few.[101] Spears and also javelins appear in almost every description and engraving left by those who visited West Africa in the late eighteenth century and throughout the nineteenth century. Thornton has noted how spears constituted offensive weapons broadly used from the Savannah to the Coast, and through Upper Guinea, the Gold Coast, and the Gap of Benin (see Figures 5.2 and 5.3).[102]

According to Smith, "West African spears consisted of wooden shafts to which an iron head was socketed or (less often) tanged."[103] If we are to trust the testimonies left by authorities and witnesses in both New World territories, this specific type of manufactured spear seems to have been common in Bahia and Cuba throughout the first half of the nineteenth century. The *ferrões* (iron bars) confiscated from the Hausa plotters in May 1814 in Bahia were supposed to be taken to the bush in order to fit them with "metallic arrow heads."[104] Equally, among the weapons taken from the insurgents in Pirajá in 1826 there was a wooden rod with an iron spike at the top, and what the authorities described as "various spears in preparation."[105]

A similar description was given by Spanish Captain Alejandro Pelosa, who was in charge of putting down an armed movement that began on the grounds of the Banco sugar estate in Güines in June 1842. In his letter, Pelosa described the spears carried by the Africans as "spikes made of wood from the heart" (of a tree, likely a cotton tree), which were then put into the fire to be hardened. After that, he commented, they were sharpened until their end was "as hard as an iron."[106] In this case the Africans had been forced to improvise, not having the needed iron heads they resorted to the closest they had, which was the hardening of the ending of the wooden spear with fire.

---

[98] Reis, *Slave Rebellion in Brazil*, 47.   [99] Reis, *Slave Rebellion in Brazil*, 56.
[100] Knives, sickles, and hatchets feature among the Central Sudanic weapons depicted by Denham and Clapperton in the mid-1820s. See also Smith, *Warfare and Diplomacy*, 71.
[101] Smith, *Warfare and Diplomacy*, 68.
[102] Thornton, *Warfare in Atlantic Africa*, 26, 44, 58, 80.
[103] Smith, *Warfare and Diplomacy*, 70.   [104] Schwartz, "Cantos e quilombos," 381.
[105] Prosecutor's report. 17 December 1826. APEB: IE, 2845.
[106] Alejandro Pelosa to Captain-General Jerónimo Valdés. Güines, 18 June 1842. ANC: GSC, 939/33130.

Figure 5.2 Bodyguard of the Sheik of Borno, 1820s. Denham, *Narrative of Travels and Discoveries*, 64.

Cuban archaeologist Gabino La Rosa has noticed how runaway slaves in Cuba generally used spear and spear-like weapons—likely javelins—as they were not particularly difficult to get or assemble from working tools such as the *herrones* (iron bars) used to open holes in the ground.[107] Spears were among the most common weapons featured in instances of African insurgencies in Cuba during the period. They were the main weapons among those wielded by a group of runaway slaves from the Catalina coffee plantation, near Guanajay, in 1828.[108] They also constituted part of the arsenal of another group of runaway slaves at the Flor de Cuba estate in Guamutas in 1843,[109] and were among the weapons used by another group of insurgents in the sugar estate Banco, near the town of Güines in June 1840 (see Figure 5.4).[110]

[107] La Rosa Corzo, *Armas y tácticas defensivas*, 12–13.
[108] Escape of 18 slaves from the cafetal Catalina. Guanajay, July 1828. ANC: GSC, 936/33025.
[109] Apolinar de la Gala to Captain-General Jerónimo Valdés. Cárdenas, 3 July 1843. ANC: GSC, 942/33231.
[110] Ignacio López Gavilán to the Prince of Anglona. San Nicolás, 15 June 1840. ANC: GSC, 939/33130.

Figure 5.3 Footsoldiers and cavalry of Borno, *c.*1860. Wagner, *Schilderung der Reisen*, 16.

Figure 5.4 Weapons used by Cuban maroons, nineteenth century. They include a knife, a machete, and a *herrón*. Courtesy of Professor Gabino La Rosa Corzo.

The use of spears was an intrinsically West African practice transferred by these men and women from their homelands to their destinations in Bahia and Cuba. Something very similar occurred with the use of bows and arrows, weapons that had been rendered obsolete from the early seventeenth century in Europe by the arrival of firearms.[111] Though in Europe they all but disappeared, in most of the Americas bows and arrows were still residually used by indigenous groups living away from the regions colonized by Europeans.

In West Africa, however, bows and arrows were still part of the armament of most of the armies. Relying on diverse primary sources, Joseph P. Smaldone has discussed the impact of archers during the Fulani *jihād*,[112] while Thornton has revealed how bows and arrows were consistently used throughout West African coastal areas until at least the nineteenth century.[113] Smith has argued that they constituted part of the infantry arsenal of West African armies, although in some areas, especially Oyo in the nineteenth century, cavalry forces sometimes used them as well.[114] According to John Lander, who visited Oyo in the mid-1820s, archery was widely practiced there at the time, and he notes that the bowmen were very skilled and capable of making extremely difficult shots.[115]

A number of drawings left by those who visited these areas during the period reveal the importance of the bow and arrow in West African warfare. Denham and Clapperton depicted a set, which also included a quiver, from the Western Sudan in the 1820s.[116] Denham also left us a drawing of a Munga bowman alongside a Kanem spearman, showing in detail their weaponry and apparel (Figure 5.5). Likewise, Francis Spilsbury, who visited Sierra Leone in the first decade of the nineteenth century, left us a sketch of a "warrior with poisoned arrows."[117]

In Bahia and Cuba the bow and arrow was a habitual weapon of West African insurgents, a circumstance that reveals another almost direct transfer of West African warfare practices across the Atlantic and to their American destinations. In May 1814 after uncovering a Hausa plot, the authorities in Bahia found more than "two hundred arrowheads, wood to make bows, and rod bundles to make arrows," indicating the existence of a process of collection of prime materials in order to manufacture what the slave João would call "weapons of his land."[118]

Bahian authorities had made a similar discovery a few years before, after uncovering the Hausa plot of 1807, when they found "four hundred arrows" and "a bundle of rods to be used as bows."[119] Bows and arrows were used against the Bahian army by the insurgents of February 1814, and by the African *quilombolas* of the Urubu in 1826.[120]

[111] Kenneth Chase, *Firearms: A Global History to 1700* (Cambridge: Cambridge University Press, 2003), 68–76.

[112] Smaldone, *Warfare in the Sokoto Caliphate*, 26–7.   [113] Thornton, *Warfare in Atlantic Africa*, 27, 44.

[114] Smith, *Warfare and Diplomacy*, 72; Robert S. Smith, "Yoruba Armament," *Journal of African History*, 8:1 (1967): 95.

[115] Smith, *Warfare and Diplomacy*, 72. Also the Baribas were reputed to be excellent archers and were credited with the victory at the battle of Gbodo. Bada, "The Frontier City of Ilorin," 163–4.

[116] Smith, *Warfare and Diplomacy*, 73.

[117] Francis B. Spilsbury, *Account of a voyage to the Western coast of Africa; performed by His Majesty's sloop Favourite, in the year 1805* (London: Richard Phillips, 1807), 39.

[118] Schwartz, "Cantos e quilombos," 386.   [119] Reis, *Slave Rebellion in Brazil*, 43.

[120] Reis, *Slave Rebellion in Brazil*, 47, 56–7.

Figure 5.5 Munga bowman and Kanem spearman, 1820s. Denham, *Narrative of Travels and Discoveries*, 166.

As in most cases, something analogous took place in Cuba, where West African men and women also made use of makeshift bows and arrows on a number of occasions. For example, when in 1827 a small group of Gangá Africans confronted their masters on their estate near the town of Catalina de Güines, they did so using firearms but also bows and arrows, which they had apparently made themselves sometime earlier.[121] As Cuban archaeologist Gabino La Rosa Corzo has suggested, having more time to manufacture specialized weapons such as bows and arrows allowed runaway slaves to often carry and use them in their raids. La Rosa has also noticed that there exist "many references to bows and arrows" being used by bands of maroons who "fabricated their weapons in correspondence with their experiences and technical knowledge."[122]

 Much easier to manufacture and often very effective weapons were clubs made of wood. Clubs formed part of the weaponry of soldiers throughout tropical West

---

[121] Deposition of Rafael Gangá. Catalina de Güines, September 1827. ANC: ME, 1069/B.
[122] La Rosa Corzo, *Armas y tácticas defensivas*, 13.

Africa. These clubs could be used for hand-to-hand combat, but could also be used as missiles, as was the case in both the Gap of Benin and Upper Guinea, according to Thornton.[123] Clubs were "probably the oldest, and certainly the simplest" weapon in West Africa, and well into the nineteenth century still constituted part of the "secondary armament" of the armies across this vast region.[124] In the Yoruba-speaking states, according to Smith, they were a basic weapon, better known as *kondo*, "a stick selected from the forest, having its branches trimmed, and one end cut from the thick intersection of branches with the main stem to form the club head."[125] Clubs could be easily manufactured by cutting branches from nearby trees and shaping them in any desired form, something that seems to have been the rule in West Africa and that certainly continued to happen at least in Cuba.

Clubs made of nearby woods were used by the large group of Lucumí insurgents that took arms on the grounds of the coffee plantation San Juan de Dios de Macastá in the summer of 1834;[126] and they were also used by another group of Africans in July 1842 at the sugar estate La Arratía, near Matanzas.[127] The armed force that rose on the grounds of the sugar estate Salvador in August 1833 took advantage of the nearby trees to arm themselves with clubs before they left for the neighboring plantations in the zone of Banes.[128]

Although cutting off and shaping tree branches was a very easy way of creating an arsenal, it was practically impossible to find more elementary and easy-to-find weapons than rocks. Subsequently, in a few cases West Africans were reported to have used them to attack and defend themselves, at least in the case of Cuba. For example, in November 1830 a group of West Africans at a coffee plantation near the town of Wajay, south of Havana, attacked their master and then proceeded to successfully repel a force under the command of the Captain of the Jurisdiction, with a "great number of rocks."[129] Ten years later, another group of Lucumí insurgents attacked and killed their master and overseer, and then confronted the local militia again using rocks.[130] Other African movements, mostly Lucumí, also resorted to the use of rocks as an offensive weapon. These were the cases of the insurgencies started at the sugar estates Salvador in 1833, San Juan de Dios de Macastá in 1834, La Sonora and San Pablo, both in 1837, and La Arratía in 1842.

One last type of weapon often featured among those used by West African men and women in Bahia and Cuba during the period: firearms. Guns of various types and sizes were not unknown to many of those who arrived as slaves on the shores of these two territories during the first half of the nineteenth century. Smith maintains that by the late seventeenth century the use of firearms extended throughout the Gold and the Slave Coasts reaching as far as Borno and the Hausa-speaking

---

[123] Thornton, *Warfare in Atlantic Africa*, 80; Smith, *Warfare and Diplomacy*, 76.

[124] Smith, *Warfare and Diplomacy*, 76.

[125] Smith, "Yoruba Armament," 98–9.

[126] Deposition of Manuel Díaz, overseer. Bauta, 3 August 1834. ANC: ME, 451/F.

[127] Deposition of Vicente Echeverría. Ingenio La Arratía, 22 July 1842. ANC: CM, 28/1.

[128] Deposition of Luis de Zepeda. Cafetal Salvador, August 1833. ANC: ME, 540/B.

[129] Francisco Lechuga to Captain-General Vives. Wajay, 21 November 1830. ANC: GSC, 936/33032.

[130] Sixto Morejón to the Captain-General. Ceiba del Agua, 2 July 1840. ANC: GSC, 939/33131.

states, although he also noticed that their potential value was not always appreciated.[131] Based on the analysis of scholars such as Smith, Thornton, and Richard Reid one would expect that only a fraction of those West African men and women who arrived in Bahia and Cuba during the first half of the nineteenth century had any knowledge of how to use them. However, this fraction should not be straightforwardly dismissed, since Dahomey, Benin, and Ijebu Ode, among others, were all using firearms in their military campaigns, often against Yoruba-speaking states, by the second decade of the nineteenth century.[132] As a matter of fact, the fall of Owu has been traditionally attributed to the use of firearms by the Ijebu army that rushed to support the Ife against the Owu.[133] Other Yoruba-speaking soldiers would have faced these weapons while fighting against Dahomey, and possibly among themselves during the many wars that plagued the Yoruba-speaking states throughout the nineteenth century.[134]

Among the previously mentioned weapons confiscated in May 1807 by the Bahian authorities were pistols and a shotgun.[135] Equally, one of those involved in the Hausa plot of May 1814 in Salvador confirmed to have seen "firearms hidden in a sugar box."[136] Also in 1826 Bahian authorities recounted how a large number of men and women at the *quilombo* of Urubu had small- and large-bore shotguns among their weapons.[137] Firearms were not uncommon among West African insurgents in Cuba either. They were used by the armed multiethnic force that rampaged through the lands of Guamacaro in 1825, although to no avail, since none of their victims was killed or wounded by them, a circumstance that reveals their probable lack of familiarity with these weapons.[138] Among the arms used by the Lucumí force that attacked numerous estates in the areas of La Guanábana and La Cidra in November 1843 were, according to the slave Nicolás Gangá, a number of pistols.[139] This testimony was confirmed by at least one other African, Manuel Gangá, who declared to have seen Narciso Lucumí carrying "one of the pistols they had taken from the [estate's] carpenter."[140]

An even more revealing episode took place in 1833 among the insurgents of the coffee plantation Salvador. Here, the Africans—mostly Lucumí—were forced to improvise when they found themselves with firearms but without ammunition. The solution found by some of the leaders was to load the guns with crushed glass, with some degree of success, at least according to Ayaí and Oyo, who observed the incident.[141]

---

[131] Smith, *Warfare and Diplomacy*, 80–3.

[132] According to Law, during the eighteenth century both Dahomey and Asante "rested their military power principally upon firearms." Robin Law, "Horses, Firearms and Political Power in Pre-colonial West Africa," *Past and Present*, 72 (1976): 122.

[133] Johnson, *The History of the Yorubas*, 132, 206; Ajayi and Smith, *Yoruba Warfare in the Nineteenth Century*, 17–20.

[134] For a more detailed study of how firearms spread across West Africa from the sixteenth century onwards see Raymond A. Kea, "Firearms and Warfare on the Gold and Slave Coasts from the Sixteenth to the Nineteenth Centuries," *Journal of African History*, 12:2 (1971): 185–213.

[135] Reis, *Slave Rebellion in Brazil*, 43.   [136] Schwartz, "Cantos e quilombos," 386.

[137] Reis, *Slave Rebellion in Brazil*, 56.   [138] Barcia, *The Great African Slave Revolt of 1825*, 132.

[139] Deposition of Nicolás Gangá. Ingenio Ácana, 20 November 1843. ANC: CM, 30/3.

[140] Deposition of Manuel Gangá. Ingenio Ácana, 12 November 1843. ANC: CM, 30/3.

[141] Depositions of Ayaí (Pascual Lucumí) and Oyo (Hermenegildo Lucumí). Cafetal Salvador, August 1833. ANC: ME, 540/B. Pistols were also used by some of the insurgents in 1833.

Alongside offensive weapons, West African soldiers frequently protected themselves with various types of armory. Shields in particular seem to have been used across the region and from the coast to the Sahel. Shields were commonly used across Fulani and Hausa-speaking states throughout the first half of the century.[142] According to Smith they were also part of the military accouterments of both infantry and cavalry soldiers in the various Yoruba kingdoms. Shields were almost always made of wood, basketwork, and ox and elephant hides.[143]

Predictably, the knowledge of how to make shields also made their way across the Atlantic with these men and women. Although there are no references to shields being used in Bahia, at least a handful were recorded in Cuba. The 1833 Lucumí insurgents from the coffee plantation Salvador manufactured shields out of abandoned sugar wagons. According to Gonzalo Mandinga, they found the "two sugar wagons and stripped them of their leather covers to make armor-plates to defend themselves."[144]

Also the armed West African force that took the Alcancía sugar estate in Bemba in 1843 and then proceeded to attack the neighboring plantations was reported to count shields among their accouterments.[145] Later that year, another Lucumí force attacked the zones of La Guanábana and La Cidra, not far from Matanzas. Witnesses once again reported the use of shields made of hides. Manuel Gangá, a slave in the Ácana plantation, declared that "almost all the Lucumí blacks used leathers as shields."[146] Nicolás Gangá, who stated that they had carried many weapons with them including "leathers to defend themselves," supported Manuel's testimony.[147]

All the weapons previously presented and discussed formed part of the arsenal of soldiers across West Africa, and not surprisingly the historical record confirms that they also continued to be used in both Bahia and Cuba. As in West Africa, however, these weapons were rarely used alone. A vast quantity of war-related accessories constituted essential components of the soldiers' accouterments. Armies hardly ever proceeded without making sure that they were found among their ranks. Once again, these elements appear to have made the Atlantic crossing with these West African men and women, to appear again—and despite the obvious deficiencies of the primary sources that recorded them—in Bahia and Cuba.

WAR PARAPHERNALIA

In the first half of the nineteenth century, West African soldiers would carry with them a number of objects other than weapons into battle. Smith has rightly argued, this "less utilitarian impedimenta" was of great importance for the morale of the troops.[148]

---

[142] Thornton, *Warfare in Atlantic Africa*, 25, 80.
[143] Smith, *Warfare and Diplomacy*, 79; Thornton, *Warfare in Atlantic Africa*, 80.
[144] Deposition of Gonzalo Mandinga. Banes, August 1833. ANC: ME, 540/B.
[145] Barcia, *Seeds of Insurrection*, 40.
[146] Deposition of Manuel Gangá. Ingenio Ácana, November 1843. ANC: CM, 30/3.
[147] Deposition of Nicolás Gangá. Ingenio Ácana, November 1843. ANC: CM, 30/3.
[148] Smith, *Warfare and Diplomacy*, 79.

Among these were the almost indispensable war drums with their expert drummers, who encouraged the soldiers to advance into enemy territory, and also served to convey messages between different sections of the armies. Trumpets, and the singing of appropriate war themes, accompanied by the sound of drums, were also frequent. An assortment of charms and amulets endowed with magical powers that could convince the soldiers of their invisibility or protect them from being wounded or killed by the weapons of their foes were also of the utmost importance.[149] These charms could be Islamic or not. According to Smith "Koranic verses, were in demand" indistinctly among both pagan and Muslim soldiers. These amulets were often stitched to their clothes or worn around their necks. For cavalry soldiers it was also common to affix them to their horses' necks.[150]

Flags and standards, including umbrellas or parasols, were also part of the paraphernalia taken to battle across West Africa. Among the *jihād* forces commanded by Dan Fodio and his generals, flags were "the ensign of Muslim leadership and the insignia of command rank."[151] During this period, flags were also carried to battle by the Fulani, Dahomean, and Ashanti armies, among others.[152] In some cases they were accompanied by standards of a different kind. Yoruba-speaking armies, for example, would take a "staff covered with charms and amulets" to war. In Smith's words, this standard constituted "a symbol of their strength and also had a mysterious power of its own."[153] Oyo and Dahomean armies would also take umbrellas to war, a circumstance described by European visitors and also by some drawings of the period (Figure 5.6).[154]

Finally, West African armies also relied on religious and cultural elements that had an impact on their understanding of how to wage and win a war. For example, symbols of leadership were very important among them. In the Gold Coast the black stool of the Ashanti was one of those items. Crowns, hats, decorated armories and helmets, jewelry, the privilege of riding a horse, and the use of specific colors could all denote leadership, honor and power, not only in this region but all across West and West Central Africa.[155]

Many of these ancestral beliefs and customs could be found during outbreaks of war in both Bahia and Cuba during the same period. Musicians often formed part of the West African armed movements that occurred in these two territories of the Americas. Among the war-related paraphernalia of the Hausa plotters of 1807 there was at least one drum that was presumably destined to be taken to war once this had begun.[156] Reis has pointed out, in the *quilombos* which he aptly calls "free territories" in the outskirts of Salvador, "war drums boomed in worldly celebrations, in homage to African deities, and to call warriors to battle."[157]

---

[149] Smith, *Warfare and Diplomacy*, 33, 79–80. [150] Smith, *Warfare and Diplomacy*, 33.

[151] Smaldone, *Warfare in the Sokoto Caliphate*, 25–6; J. Alfred Skertchly, *Dahomey as it is: Being a Narrative of Eight Months' Residence in that Country* (Whitefish: Kessinger Publishing, 2004), 259, 291–2; and Thomas Birch Freeman, *Journals of Various Visits to the Kingdoms of Ashanti, Aku, and Dahomi, in Western Africa* (Cambridge: Cambridge University Press, 2010), 256.

[152] Smaldone, *Warfare in the Sokoto Caliphate*, 25–6.

[153] Smith, *Warfare and Diplomacy*, 79. [154] See Chapter 1.

[155] Smith, *Warfare and Diplomacy*, 64–98; Iliffe, *Honour in African History*, 31–53, and 67–99.

[156] Reis, *Slave Rebellion in Brazil*, 43. [157] Reis, *Slave Rebellion in Brazil*, 41.

Armed Women, with the King at their head, going to War.

Figure 5.6 Military Parade: Dahomey, 1790s. Dalzel, *The History of Dahomey*, 136. Copyright of the University of Manchester.

When in 1826 the *quilombo* of Urubu was finally taken by Imperial troops, among the many items they found in three huts were drums, and also shells, rattles, and other objects.[158] Equally, in 1835 during the Nagô armed insurgency in Salvador, drums seem to have been beaten during the military offensive that shook authorities and neighbors across the city.[159]

In Cuba, war drums featured heavily in many of the armed movements carried out by West African men and women during this period. In 1825, for example, the insurgents in Guamacaro beat their war drums while moving from plantation to plantation until they were finally defeated.[160] War drums were also played by Lucumí *bozales* and accompanied by songs of war during the armed movement of 1833 in Banes, west of Havana. According to the overseer of the estate, Diego Barreiro, the slaves began with their meeting song, the "Ho-Bé," which was then followed by their song of war, the "Oní-Oré," to which a chorus of Lucumí slaves then replied with "O-Fé."[161]

---

[158] Reis, *Slave Rebellion in Brazil*, 57.   [159] Reis, *Slave Rebellion in Brazil*, 200.
[160] Barcia, *The Great African Slave Revolt of 1825*, 119, 151.
[161] Barcia, *Seeds of Insurrection*, 37. For a possible explanation of these terms see Lovejoy, "Old Oyo Influences," 198.

The Lucumí war drums accompanied by songs were also heard uninterruptedly during the military offensive of March 1843 in Bemba. Various witnesses, both free and slaves, referred to them in their depositions, mentioning the war songs they sang while marching into battle.[162] Later that year Lucumí war drums reemerged during another armed movement, this time in the localities of La Guanábana and La Cidra, closer to Matanzas. Here the West African insurgents were reported to carry two war drums with them during their attack.[163]

In another apparent cultural transfer from West Africa, charms and amulets also appear with frequency in instances of African warfare in both Bahia and Cuba. The Count of Ponte mentioned the "phoney amulets" and the "fanatical prayers and blessings" that were in display among the runaway slaves living on the outskirts of the city of Salvador in 1807.[164] In the Nagô insurgency of 1835 where Islamic beliefs played an important role, amulets consisting of "pieces of paper containing passages from the Koran and powerful prayers," were confiscated from those involved (see Figure 5.7).[165] One of those charms was described by the Bahian authorities as a little bundle or leather pouch containing a piece of paper with Arabic characters written on it and "several pieces of insignificant things such as cotton wrapped in a little powder [*sic*], others with tiny scraps of garbage, and little sacks with some seashells inside."[166] Other charms were found during the search conducted in the house of Belchior and Gaspar da Silva Cunha, among them there was one in a piece of paper claiming to "protect the body against any weapon."[167]

The use of charms and amulets was also recorded on occasions in Cuba. Italian physician, José Leopoldo Yarini wrote, in the late 1830s, that his slaves "carried necklaces, the so called brugerías [*sic*], amulets they believe [make them] infallible."[168] Among the many things these charms could be made of were pieces of glass, birds' feathers of different colors, snails, dogs' fangs, cocks' spurs, and dried weeds, among other items.[169] Africans from the Upper Guinea coast, especially the Mandinga, were reputed to be respected sorcerers and at least one of them, Campuzano Mandinga, was accused of selling charms during 1843 and 1844 in Matanzas to many of those involved in the La Escalera conspiracy. Following Smith's conclusions and given that Campuzano had almost certainly come to Cuba from an Islamic region of West Africa and was probably a Muslim himself, one could safely assume that his charms were probably Islamic, as they were highly

---

[162] Depositions of José Cano and Germán, a slave at the ingenio Peñalver. Alcancía estate. April 1843. ANC: CM, 29/5/1.

[163] Depositions of Manuel Gangá and Camila Criolla. Ingenio Ácana, November 1843. ANC: CM, 30/3.

[164] Count de Ponte to Viscount Anadia. Salvador, 7 April 1807, in *Anais da Biblioteca Nacional de Rio de Janeiro*, 37 (1918): 450–1. Translation by Reis, *Slave Rebellion in Brazil*, 42.

[165] Reis, *Slave Rebellion in Brazil*, 99.   [166] Reis, *Slave Rebellion in Brazil*, 99.

[167] Translation of the papers found in the house of the blacks Belchior and Gaspar da Silva Cunha. Salvador, 7 February 1835. *Anais do Arquivo do Estado da Bahia*, 38 (1968): 130–1. The authorities found other amulets in the same house, containing instructions and protection prayers for those who would participate in the planned military action that came to be known years later as the revolta dos Malês.

[168] Barcia, *Seeds of Insurrection*, 123–4.   [169] Barcia, *Seeds of Insurrection*, 124.

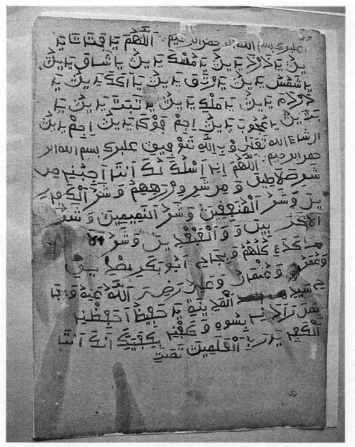

Figure 5.7 Arabic text confiscated in the aftermath of the Malê movement, 1835. APEB: IE, 2845. Courtesy of the Arquivo Público do Estado de Bahia.

sought after by both Muslim and non-Muslims at the time.[170] Similarly, Agustín Mina, an African also involved in the plot, was accused by a number of witnesses of carrying around his neck an amulet that would protect him from bullets and sabers. Among the things inside the small bag were "many bones, snakes' heads, frogs, chameleons and red ocher powders."[171] Material evidence collected in the past decades supports the information offered by the written historical record. Cuban archaeologists Lisette Roura and Jorge Garcell have recently discovered some religious items possessed and carried by runaway slaves, similar to those described by the slave hunters of the period.[172] Among these items they found a

---

[170] Barcia, *Seeds of Insurrection*, 45.   [171] Barcia, *Seeds of Insurrection*, 45.
[172] Gabino La Rosa Corzo, "Rescate de Olórum: (estudio de arqueología afroamericana)," *América negra*, 12 (1996): 48–9; Barcia, *Seeds of Insurrection*, 64–5.

Figure 5.8 Orisha Elegba figure made out of wood. Courtesy of Lisette Roura and Jorge Garcell.

wood carved orisha Elegba with a red and black crown in the Cheche hills near Tapaste, south of Havana (Figure 5.8).[173]

Standards, flags, and other magical items were also essential elements in many plots and military actions in both Bahia and Cuba during the period. Among the items taken from the African force defeated in Cachoeira in August 1826 there was a red flag, the color of the ancestral King of Oyo and orixá Shango.[174] Also in 1826, among the things found in the *quilombo* of Urubu were a number of items, most of them painted red, including statues of cows.[175]

In Cuba there were also references to objects of this sort. At least once, in 1844, flags were prepared and ready to be taken into battle by the Africans from the sugar estate La Andrea, with a Lucumí slave named Marcelino being the appointed flag bearer.[176] More notably, in 1833 the Lucumí insurgents in Banes carried open red

[173] This is not the only icon found by archaeologists in Cuba over the past decades. For another example see Gabino La Rosa Corzo, "Aproximaciones antropológicas a las bandas cimarronas de las ciénagas de Cuba," *Boletín del Gabinete de Arqueología*, 7:7 (2008): 4–15. Even more striking are the sculptures and wall paintings of Oduduwa, Olorun, and Obatala found in 1938 by a Shell-Mex oil prospector in the purposely called Cave of the Idols, in the jurisdiction of Ceiba del Agua. These manifestations of Lucumí art reflect the continuation of the cult of the orishas in the diaspora by runaway men and women. See La Rosa Corzo, "Rescate de Olórum," 38–56.

[174] Reis, *Slave Rebellion in Brazil*, 55.   [175] Reis, *Slave Rebellion in Brazil*, 57.

[176] Deposition of Gabriel Criollo. Ingenio La Andrea, January 1844. ANC: CM, 37/1.

umbrellas into the battlefield. According to some of the slaves who participated and witnessed the event, they were displayed as war standards and carried by each of the commanders as symbols of leadership.[177]

The colors chosen by the insurgents to dress in and to decorate their war paraphernalia was another area where the correspondences between warfare in West Africa and Bahia and Cuba could be observed. The color red featured prominently among the objects taken by the authorities from the insurgents in Cachoeira and Urubu in 1826 in Bahia. The red flags and animal figures discussed before, and the red hats with feathers, strongly suggest links to Shango. Green, the color associated with Ogun, the orixá of iron and war, was the color of the duvetyn cape of the presumable leader, referred to as "the King of the Blacks" in the movement of August 1826 in Cachoeira.[178] Bahian authorities also noticed the white garments called *abadá* worn by the participants in the 1835 movement, which reflected not just an association to Islam but that were also a "symbol of social superiority."[179]

The use of clothing in specific, meaningful colors was not unknown in Cuba either. The red umbrellas carried by the Lucumí of the Salvador sugar estate in 1833 are but one among many cases. For example, in 1825 the Africans who attacked a number of plantations in the zone of Guamacaro stole and wore military uniforms and hats, some of which were green, the color of Ogun, the orisha of war. Many among the insurgents were reported to wear hats with feathers, a symbol of status in many of their regions of origin in West Africa.[180] Among the many instances of African warfare in Cuba, the Lucumí insurgents of November 1843 in La Guanábana and La Cidra, were reported to have stolen a number of pieces of clothing, all white, from the plantations they attacked. In this case the connection may well have been to either Islam—although there are no other elements that suggest this was the case—or the orisha Obatala, Olorun's representative on earth.[181] In other cases, however, the Africans stripped off their clothes—bar women carrying children on their backs—and faced the authorities naked.[182]

CONCLUSIONS

Historical evidence suggests that the military operations and tactics displayed by the men and women who took arms in Bahia and Cuba during the period studied here were in every significant way a continuation of war practices learned and practiced first in West Africa. As shown by contemporaries and scholars, hand-to-hand

[177] Depositions of Diego Barreiro, Guillermo, and Gonzalo Mandinga. Cafetal Salvador, August 1833. ANC: ME, 540/B.
[178] Reis, *Slave Rebellion in Brazil*, 55.
[179] Reis, *Slave Rebellion in Brazil*, 55, 57, 103. Similar tunics were described by the Bahian authorities in 1807.
[180] See e.g. Ruben G. Mendoza, "West African Empires: Dates 400–1591 C.E.," in John Powell, ed., *Weapons and Warfare* (Pasadena: Salem Press, 2001), 293.
[181] Deposition of Joaquín Garcilaso de la Vega. Ingenio San Miguel, November 1843. ANC: CM, 30/3.
[182] Apolinar de la Gala to Captain-General Valdés. Cafetal Perseverancia, 18 September 1842. ANC: GSC, 941/33194.

combat, the use of familiar weapons, and the use of symbols that denoted leadership, among other factors discussed in this chapter, were characteristics common to most of these movements.

Additionally, and often forgotten, the belief in their chances of beating their enemies in spite of their apparent inferiority might have played a crucial role when plotting and carrying into practice their plans. Having the odds against them did not necessarily mean a guaranteed failure. The effectiveness of small irregular armies across Yorubaland and Hausaland is well documented. Even the mighty Fulani-led *jihād* of the early nineteenth century started as a movement of resistance against the authority of the Sarki of Gobir that was almost crushed before it could develop into a more organized army. Only a providential victory at Tabkin Kwotto in 1804 transformed the defensive attitude of the followers of Dan Fodio into an offensive that went on to conquer most of the Hausa states, Nupe, and parts of other neighboring states, including Oyo. Tabkin Kwotto and many other battles that took place in the interior of the Bight of Benin in the following years constituted poignant proof that numerical or armament inferiority could be overturned with clever strategies and through the achievement of early military victories.[183] Many of the irregular troops that fought in each of the battles discussed throughout this book in Bahia and Cuba did so, to a certain extent, by exemplifying classic tactics of guerrilla warfare related to slave raids, as they had done before in their West African regions of origin.

Furthermore, gender and ethnic inclusion were determined by the qualities and background of the leaders of each movement. Perhaps surprisingly, women such as Zeferina, Ferminia, and Carlota were able to impose themselves and to lead armed troops. However, war was an almost exclusively adult male affair that was put into practice by West African men who were not intimidated by the white men, who had never defeated them, and who were able to devise sophisticated plans and to gather the necessary arsenal to carry out their projects. Insurgents formed alliances with those they trusted, which in practice meant excluding Creole and most of the Bantu slaves, and sometimes even acculturated West Africans.

If it is true that traditional armaments and war paraphernalia may have indeed been left behind in Africa, new weapons—often reproductions probably made by men who had been arms manufacturers in West Africa—were crafted or adapted from raw materials, or stolen from their white oppressors. The sight of West African soldiers marching into battle protected by shields made of hides and wielding blades in the air, often accompanied by drums and standards, was almost as common in Bahia and Cuba as it was in the Bight of Benin and its hinterland during the first half of the nineteenth century. The links between West Africa on one side and Bahia and Cuba on the other revealed by the historical sources are compelling, and although even now they are not yet fully explored, they provide an insight into how the Nagô, the Lucumí, the Hausa, and their comrades in arms, organized themselves and fought their new enemies according to the knowledge of warfare they had acquired in West Africa.

---

[183] Smaldone, *Warfare in the Sokoto Caliphate*, 27.

Conclusion
Soldier Slaves in the
Atlantic World

When, in 1844, a recently arrived Lucumí *bozal* renamed Manuel was brought before the colonial authorities during the enquiries that followed the uncovering of the Conspiracy of La Escalera in Cuba, something quite unusual happened. Aware of his lack of understanding of Spanish, the Military Commission public prosecutor in charge of his examination first called an interpreter to help with the interrogation. Upon realizing that Manuel had not yet been baptized, the prosecutor unexpectedly requested to know the name of the "God of his nation."[1] After the African replied that the name of the god he believed in was Olorun, the public prosecutor demanded that he swear by Olorun that he would only answer with the truth to the questions he was about to be asked. By accepting Olorun, the god of the Lucumí, as a legally binding deity, colonial authorities implicitly acknowledged the legitimacy of Manuel's West African beliefs and traditions, and the cultural differences existing between Spanish and West African cultures. In other words, this Spanish military prosecutor recognized something that many others before and after him, even today, have failed to acknowledge: the inexorable impact that African history and culture had on the many instances of West African armed struggle that took place in Bahia and Cuba in the first half of the nineteenth century.

The case of Manuel was not unique. In the course of similar criminal interrogations, other Africans were often asked to swear by their own gods. Yet rarely did the authorities go as far as soliciting their deities' names and writing them down in legal documents. To a large extent, Manuel Lucumí and his God Olorun, represented for the briefest of moments in time, the social, political, and religious conflicts created by the transplantation of West African men, women, and children to the slave plantations of Bahia and Cuba in the early nineteenth century. Manuel, like many fellow newly arrived Africans, had a life experience that involved war and enslavement in their homelands, and a Middle Passage trauma that was not likely to be forgotten or easily overcome. Like many others, Manuel was stripped of his name and sent to work under the sun in a remote Cuban plantation. Not surprisingly, he found himself involved in the aftermath of one of the many West African armed movements conceived and put into practice in Bahia and Cuba during this period. Like many, Manuel was probably a prisoner of war who had found himself toiling for the white man in a foreign land. Thus he found himself a victim of the repression that followed one of the best-known conspiracies in the history of the Americas.

---

[1] Interrogation of Manuel Lucumí. Ingenio La Andrea, January 1844. ANC: CM, 37/1.

The Lucumí and the Nagô, like the Hausa, the Arará, the Carabalí, and many of their West African neighbors, had been exposed to centuries of endemic warfare. Those who were taken to Bahia and Cuba in the late eighteenth century and early nineteenth century had inadvertently become important actors and witnesses of a transformative historical age that led to the creation of new states and to the destruction of others. Cities like the important capital of Oyo, Oyo-Ile, had been plundered and eventually abandoned by the late 1830s, while others such as Sokoto in the north and Abeokuta and Ibadan in the south thrived in the midst of these wars.

These men, women, and children had seen it all. In their near totality, they had been separated from their loved ones, usually forever, before being sent towards the Atlantic slave ports en route to Bahia and Cuba. Many had seen relatives and friends killed by regular armies or by random bands of armed men, like the one described by Samuel Ajayi Crowther. Others had been affected by disease and malnutrition from the onset. For those who made it alive across the Atlantic, a new life of enforced labor waited. Not surprisingly, they would soon find themselves at the center of the two largest and most violent cycles of armed movements to take place in the almost 400 years of slavery in the Americas. Not surprising either, is that these two cycles took place almost simultaneously, and at least from the 1820s onwards were consistently blamed, with much reason, on the Nagô and the Lucumí.

As a result of warfare-related knowledge acquired by these men and women in their West African homes, their understanding of war was directly transferred to their new homes, where they adapted it and reproduced it, keeping it as close to its original essence as they were able and allowed. The Nagô and the Lucumí soon attained a reputation of being violent people with no fear of the white man. In Bahia, during the aftermath of the 1835 Malê movement, French consul A. J. Baptiste Marcescheau referred to them as "intelligent, strong, and courageous."[2] This opinion was shared by the British consul in Havana, Joseph T. Crawford, who almost replicated Marcescheau's words when he commented that the Lucumí in Cuba were "famed for being the most hardy of the Africans, warlike in their own country."[3]

João José Reis has concluded that after the 1835 events had taken place, "The proud and predominant Nagôs were the favorite object of criticism"[4] not only among the white population, but also among their fellow slaves and Africans. For example, José da Costa, a Jêje who was interrogated a few weeks after the Malê movement was defeated, in an obvious reference to the long-existing rivalries between Dahomeans and Oyos, declared that "he was from a nation that was wholly inimical to the blacks who disturbed the city's peace."[5] Likewise, Domingos Borges, a Hausa, declared that a Nagô had stabbed him when he refused to join the first uprising of the Nagô—in reference to the 1830 armed insurgency in Salvador. Domingos also added that he hated the Nagô and had no dealings with them.[6]

[2] Marcescheau to French Minister of Foreign Affairs, Salvador, 29 January 1835. Cited by Reis, *Slave Rebellion in Brazil*, 147.
[3] Joseph T. Crawford to the Earl of Aberdeen. Havana, 18 April 1843. NA-UK: FO, 72/634.
[4] Reis, *Slave Rebellion in Brazil*, 157.   [5] Reis, *Slave Rebellion in Brazil*, 157–8.
[6] Reis, *Slave Rebellion in Brazil*, 158

In Cuba, the Lucumí created a comparable reputation among their fellow slaves. In 1844, Perico Criollo, a slave at the La Andrea sugar estate, declared that the Lucumí "had said that they did not want to be slaves anymore, and that they would fight until achieving freedom or that they would die trying."[7] Perico also mentioned what other African slaves he knew were saying about the Lucumí. Marcelino Gangá, for example, had told him that "they were always thinking about rising up, only to end up killed."[8] According to José Cano, a neighbor in the jurisdiction of Bemba, Francisco Mandinga, had commented, "these Lucumí rascals are going to finish their masters and everything else."[9]

As a matter of fact, the protagonism of the Nagô and the Lucumí in slave resistance was so noticeable that many of the movements recorded by the authorities in both territories and discussed here were simply referred to by means of phrases such as the "uprising of the Nagô," the "Lucumí conspiracy," etc., in a clear sign that they were often perceived to act on their own by almost everybody else. It must be stated that in Bahia between 1807 and 1816, something very similar happened to the Hausa. This perception was nothing but a direct reflection of the West African warfare past that has been repeatedly mentioned and discussed in this book. From the very basic issues of recruitment and the provision of weapons, to the more complex ones of tactic and strategy, and the leading of troops into battle, the resemblances between descriptions provided by travelers and witnesses in West Africa, Bahia, and Cuba are uncanny. That on occasion they were able to surmount ethnic differences inherited from West Africa should not come as a surprise either since, as John K. Thornton has stated, "virtually all slaves exported from a port would be from the cultural zone that was already united by commerce in other goods."[10]

For decades now historians have argued over the socio-economic and socio-political aspects that drove African slaves to take arms against their oppressors throughout the New World, and especially in the Portuguese and Spanish Americas. With some prominent exceptions that include the works of Monica Schuler, John K. Thornton, Raymond A. Kea, and Walter Rucker, they have repetitively revealed how many slave movements were motivated by political and ideological reasons related to the diasporical experiences of these men and women, yet, all too often overlooking that their personal and group journeys began in Africa.[11] These points

---

[7] Deposition of Perico Criollo. La Andrea, February 1844. ANC: CM, 37/1.

[8] Deposition of Perico Criollo.

[9] Deposition of José Cano. Bemba, April 1843. ANC: CM, 29/5/1.

[10] Thornton, *Africa and the Africans*, 194.

[11] Most of these works focus on African slave movements that took place in the eighteenth century. See, for example, Monica Schuler, "Akan Slave Rebellions in the British Caribbean," *Savacou*, 1:1 (1970): 8–31; John K. Thornton, "African Dimensions of the Stono Rebellion," *American Historical Review*, 96:4 (1991): 1101–13; "'I am the Subject of the King of Congo': African Ideology in the Haitian Revolution," *Journal of World History*, 4:2 (1993): 181–214; "African Soldiers in the Haitian Revolution," *Journal of Caribbean History*, 25:1 (1993): 58–80; Raymond A. Kea, "'When I Die, I Shall Return to my Own Land': An 'Amina' Slave Rebellion in the Danish West Indies, 1733–1734," in John Hunwick and Nancy Lawler, eds., *The Cloth of Many Colored Silks: Papers on History and Society Ghanian and Islamic in Honor of Ivor Wilks* (Evanston, IL: Northwestern University Press, 1997), 159–94; and Walter Rucker, *The River Flows On: Black Resistance, Culture, and Identity Formation in Early America* (Baton Rouge: Louisiana State University Press, 2006).

of view, although valid on occasion, have too easily ignored, dismissed, or under-estimated the role that West African memories, ideas, ideologies, and war-related ethics and technologies, brought with the enslaved across the Atlantic, had upon the violent events which took place in Brazil and the Spanish Caribbean.

As this book has hopefully revealed, historical events and processes that took place in West Africa had a profound effect on the lives and destinies of those who were enslaved and sold to slave traders along the West African coast, and then taken to Bahia and Cuba. It has been argued here that the understanding of the world that these enslaved men, women, and children had acquired from an early age in their West African homes had a more intense and direct impact upon their decision to fight their new enemies than any gossip or story they could have heard about emancipation-related events occurring in the Americas. This is especially the case if we consider that their new homes were not particularly different from the ones where they had been born and raised. In both Bahia and Cuba, these men, women, and children found solace among their own compatriots, and were able to worship their gods, to fabricate or acquire weapons, and more importantly, to find support for their military enterprises.

Certainly the very fact that Dan Fodio's *jihād*, the Oyo wars, and the expansion of Dahomey in the first decades of the century all produced large numbers of slaves for the transatlantic trade constitutes, in itself, uncontested proof of the direct impact they had upon the military uprisings which they carried into practice in Bahia and Cuba. A number of references given by West African men and women in both territories alluding to these specific West African conflicts and how they had played a central role in their pre-Middle Passage lives, corroborate this fact.

The Lucumí and the Hausa, like the Gangá, the Mandinga, the Carabalí, the Arará, and the Jêje all possessed war-related knowledge and proficiencies that included hand-to-hand combat, pitched battles, forays into enemy territory in search for slaves, brigandage, and victories and defeats, none of which had ever included the white man. Since Europeans and later on Americans, Brazilians, and Cubans bought their slaves in the slave ports situated on the coast of the various regions involved in this human traffic from the Senegambia to the south of Benguela, they lacked any sort of reputation as able soldiers among those Africans who were sent to Bahia and Cuba during the period studied here. In other words, they were not the invincible and formidable foes that traditional historiography—without ever questioning such an odd belief—assumed they were.

Indeed West Africans in Bahia and Cuba had ideological and political beliefs, but they were not necessarily derived from ideas formed and developed in Europe or the Americas during the Age of Revolution. Contrary to what some historians would suggest, the fact that they heavily relied on their own West African traditions, knowledge, and beliefs instead of adopting foreign ones, does not make them less revolutionary or their struggle less relevant. That they frequently refused the help or support of the free colored population which was more in contact with the burgeoning ideas associated with the French and Haitian Revolutions and British Abolitionism, does not make them less politically motivated actors either.

The quintessentially West African forces described in Bahia and Cuba in similar terms by witnesses from Europe, Africa, and the Americas were just that, West African. Although their actions may have been modified to a certain extent by their experiences of enslavement and transplantation to another continent, they still behaved and fought according to the knowledge they had acquired in their homelands. Put in other words, they had their own reasons to go to war, not least because they were prisoners who had been turned into slaves, and more often than not they did so not due to new ideologies or tales of revolutions occurring elsewhere, but because they were driven by the knowledge and ideas that they had accumulated through their own lives in West Africa. Consequently, they organized themselves and fought as they would have done in their homelands.

The French and Haitian Revolutions were not the only meaningful historical events to take place in the Atlantic World during this time, and the ideas that emanated from these events were not the only ones to challenge and change previous social and political structures and beliefs. It is time that the history of West Africa, and all African regions affected by the slave trade, were seriously and consistently taken into account while writing the history of the African diasporas in the Atlantic World. By looking at West African warfare and its protagonists from a comparative viewpoint, this study has endeavored to do just that.

APPENDIX 1

Chronology of Slave Movements in Bahia, 1807–1835

Date	Place	Leadership	Participants	Notes
1807—May	Salvador and the Recôncavo	Hausas	7 African (6 Hausas and 1 Mandinga) slaves & free men	Conspiracy
1809—Jan.	Nazaré das Farinhas	Hausa slaves	More than 300 Hausa slaves (Jêjes & Nagôs also participated)	Revolt
1814—Feb.	Recôncavo	Hausa slaves	More than 250 rebels; mostly Hausas (some Nagôs also participated)	Conspiracy & revolt
1814—Mar.	Iguape	Hausas	Hausa slaves & free men	Revolt
1816—Jan. 1816—Feb.	Santo Amaro & São Francisco do Conde		Large number of African born slaves	Revolt
1822—May	Itaparica island		280 slaves	Revolt
1822—Sept.	São Marcos		African slaves & free men	Revolt (against whites & mestiços)
1822—Dec.	Mata Oscura & Saboeiro		Nearly 200 slaves	Revolt (slaves attacked the army)
1824	Engenho *Santana*, Ilhéus		Creole slaves	Revolt (formed quilombo until 1828)
1826—Aug.	Cachoeira	African born slaves	African born slaves	Revolt
1826—Dec.	Pirajá; *Urubú Quilombo*	Nagôs	Less than 50 slaves; most of them Nagôs	Revolt
1827—Mar.	Cachoeira		African slaves from different plantations	Revolt
1827—Apr.	São Francisco do Conde		Slaves from 10 plantations	Revolt

(*Continued*)

(Continued)

Date	Place	Leadership	Participants	Notes
1827—Sept.	Abrantes			Revolt
1828—Mar.	Itapuá	African-born slaves (probably Nagôs)	Large number of African-born slaves	Revolt
1828—Apr.	Cachoeira			Two revolts on 17 & 21 April
1828—Sept.	Iguape	African-born slaves	Nearly 40 African-born slaves	Revolt (slaves rebels killed some mulattos)
1828—Nov.	Santo Amaro	African-born slaves	African-born slaves	Revolt
1829—Oct.	Cotegipe		Slaves	Revolt
1829—Oct.				Revolt
1830—April	Salvador	Urban slaves	More than 100 slaves; mostly Nagôs	Revolt; included also a large number of *escravos novos*
1835—Jan.	Salvador	Mostly Nagôs; also Hausas, Tapas, etc.	A large number of urban and rural slaves and free men	Conspiracy & revolt

Chronology of Slave Movements in Cuba, 1798–1844

Date	Place	Leadership	Participants	Notes
1798—July	Trinidad (district of Barlovento)	A foreign slave from Curaçao & another slave (possibly a Creole)	Urban, rural slaves & free men	Conspiracy (plot to take control over the city)
1798—Aug.	Puerto Príncipe		23 slaves	Revolt
1798—Oct.	Ingenio Nueva Holanda, Güines			Revolt; used machetes & spears
1799—Feb.	Ingenio of Ponce de León		36 *bozal* Africans recently arrived	Revolt; used machetes & handmade spears
1802—June	Ingenio San Juan Bautista. Managua			Revolt
1802—June	Cafetal of Juan de Santa María. San Antonio Abad			Slaves refused to work & played their drums daily
1806—April	Güines y Güara. Havana	A Creole & a slave came from Saint Domingue		Conspiracy (planned to take the main fortress of Havana & consequently also the city)
1812	Bayamo			Revolt
1812	Puerto Príncipe			Revolt
1812	Peñas Altas. Havana			Revolt
1812	Conspiración de Aponte	José Antonio Aponte & other free men from Havana		Conspiracy
1814	Puerto Príncipe			
1817	Cafetal La Esperanza. Havana		Five slaves, probably African born	Revolt (all five rebels executed)
1822	Cayajabos. Pinar del Rio			

(*Continued*)

(Continued)

Date	Place	Leadership	Participants	Notes
1822	Ingenios in El Mariel. Havana			
1824—May	Cafetal Favorito. Puerta de la Güira		Mostly African-born slaves. At least 22 women participated	
1824	Guanímar. Eastern Cuba			
1825—June	Guamacaro & Coliseo. Matanzas	Lorenzo Lucumí, Federico Carabalí, & Pablo Gangá	Multiethnic movement. More than 200 slaves, most of them African born	Conspiracy & revolt (several people killed, both whites & slaves)
1825—June	Río Blanco del Norte. Havana		10 to 15 slaves	Revolt (overseer wounded)
1826—Sept.	Pinar del Rio	Luis Lucumí & Estevan Mina	Two slaves	Revolt against the overseer
1826	Puerto Príncipe			
1827	Ingenio Industria; Cafetal Esperanza			
1827—Jan.	Cafetal Tentativa		57 slaves (most of them African born)	Revolt. Overseer and manager killed. Other casualties from both sides; (at least 18 slaves committed suicide)
1827—Sept.	Catalina de Güines	Rafael Gangá (probably all the rebels were gangás)	6 slaves	Revolt. Master & overseer assassinated; (slaves used bows & arrows)
1827—Oct.	Cafetal Carmen. Güira de Melena	Simón Mina, Celedonia Mandinga, & Ventura Congo.	Most of the plantation slaves participated	Revolt (rebels tried to murder overseer)
1830—July	Cafetal Arcadia; Ingenio Laguna de Palos. Guamacaro. Matanzas	Federico Mandinga & Antonio Gangá	Gangá, Mina, Mandinga, Carabalí, Lucumí, Congo, & Creole slaves	
1830—Nov.	Cafetal of Cabañas. Wajay			Revolt (overseer held for hours & a soldier injured)

(Continued)

Date	Place	Leadership	Participants	Notes
1830	Cafetal Nuestra Sra. de la Asunción			
1831	Cafetal Nueva Empresa			
1832—Sept.	Ingenio Purísima Concepción. Güira de Melena	Lucumí slaves	17 recently landed Lucumí slaves	Revolt (one white & two slaves killed)
1833—Feb. –Mar.	Ingenios Jimagua, Filomeno, & Satre. San Nicolás			Possible conspiracy
1833	Ingenio Encarnación. Campo Florido			
1833—Aug.	Cafetal Salvador. Banes, Guanajay	3 Lucumí slaves	330 African-born slaves (most of them Lucumís)	Revolt (recently landed slaves involved)
1834	Ingenio San Juan de Macastá. Bauta	Antonio Lucumí	African-born slaves (most of them Lucumís)	Strike & revolt
1834	Ingenio Stma. Trinidad. Güines			
1835—July	Puente de Chávez. Havana	Lucumí *bozal* emancipados	Lucumís emancipated from Brig Negrito	Revolt (some young men, possibly children, participated and led the others)
1835—Aug.	Ingenio Carolina & Cafetal Burato. Macuriges		130 slaves (most of them African born)	
1835—Aug.	Ingenio Intrépido		30 slaves (most of them African born)	
1835—July	Ingenio Magdalena. Santa Ana		14 Lucumí slaves	Revolt & suicides
1836	El Cerro, Havana		Lucumí slaves	Revolt
1837—June	Ingenio La Sonora. Lagunillas		34 Lucumí slaves (both *ladinos* & *bozales*)	Revolt (possible previous plot against the overseer)
1837—Sept.	Ingenio San Pablo. Catalina		25 Lucumí slaves (18 of them recently arrived *bozals*)	Revolt against the overseer (two suicides)
1837—Dec.	Cafetal Santa Ana de Biajacas. Ceiba Mocha		Mostly African-born slaves	Revolt (maroon slaves involved)

(*Continued*)

(Continued)

Date	Place	Leadership	Participants	Notes
1838	Cafetal Clarita. Batabanó		African-born slaves	
1838	Ingenio San Gabriel de Corredera. Rio Blanco del Norte	Congo slave		Revolt (white labourer injured)
1838—Apr.	Trinidad	Creoles	Creoles and African-born slaves and free men	Conspiracy (39 went to trial & 3 were executed)
1839—May	Ingenio La Conchita. Macuriges		9 Lucumí slaves (all *bozales*)	Revolt
1840—June	Cafetal Armonía			
1840—June	Ingenio Banco. Güines		10 Lucumí slaves	Revolt (3 slaves executed)
1840—July	Ingenio La Esperanza			Revolt (overseer and one slave killed)
1840—July	Cafetal Empresa. Ceiba del Agua	Tranquilino Lucumí	25 to 30 African-born slaves, most of them Lucumís	Revolt (master & overseer killed)
1840—Aug.	Ingenio Catalina & Cafetal Concepción. Guanajay	2 Carabalí slaves	Mainly Carabalí slaves	Conspiracy
1840—Aug.	Guamutas. Havana	Marcial Gangá, José Dimas Lucumí, Dionisio Lucumí and Eugenio Lucumí		Alleged plot
1841—Oct.	Palace of Domingo Aldama. Havana	Tomás Lucumí	19 Lucumí *bozales* recently arrived	Revolt (6 slaves killed & 7 wounded)
1842—Mar.	Ingenio Loreto, Managua		All the slaves of the ingenio (40 slaves)	Revolt
1842—May	Cafetal Jesús Nazareno. Bejucal			Strike (change of overseer was the reason)
1842—July	Ingenio La Arratía. Matanzas		26 Lucumís, 11 Ararás, 4 Minas, and 1 Congo	Revolt (attacked an army company; 2 soldiers & 7 slaves injured)
1842—Sept.	Cafetal Perseverancia. Lagunillas		African-born slaves	Attempt of revolt

(Continued)

Date	Place	Leadership	Participants	Notes
1843—Mar.	Ingenio Alcancía, Bemba	Lucumí slaves	Mostly Lucumí slaves	Collective suicides (around 400 slaves lost their lives)
1843—May	Ingenios *Santa Rosa* and *Majagua*. Sabanilla	African-born slaves	African-born slaves	Revolt
1843—June	Ingenios Ácana & Concepción			
1843—June	Ingenio Flor de Cuba, Guamacaro			More than 300 slaves ran away
1843—July	Ingenio La Arratía	Lucumí slaves	More than 40 slaves	Revolt
1843—Nov.	Ingenios Triunvirato & Ácana	Lucumí leaders, including 2 women	More than 300 slaves, most of them Lucumís	Revolt
1843—Dec.	La Escalera	Plácido, Miguel Flores, Luis Guigaut, etc.	Thousands of free colored & slaves (both urban and rural)	Conspiracy(ies)
1844—Apr.	Cafetal Recompensa. Bejucal			Rumour of conspiracy

Glossary

abadá robe used by Muslim Africans in Bahia

Aláàfin Monarch of Oyo

Are-Ona-Kakanfo Supreme military commander of Oyo

Bale Village heads in Oyo and across other areas of Yorubaland

Basorun Leader of the Oyo Mesi council and commander of the troops based in Metropolitan Oyo

bozal name given in Cuba and other parts of the Americas to Africans who had arrived recently and who were not yet acculturated

cabildos de nación associations formed by Africans in Cuba and other parts of the Americas; they were often formed alongside ethnic lines

cafetal coffee plantation

calavera (or calabera) name given in Cuba to Africans who had been shipmates in the Middle Passage

Candomblé Afro-Brazilian religion with elements from various African religions, but with a predominant Yoruba element

capitão de mato name given to slave hunters in Brazil

coartação name given in Brazil to a special type of manumission by which slaves could buy their freedom by monetary installments

coartación as above, but for Spanish American territories

Dar-el-Harb the realm of war

Dar-el-Islam the realm of Islam

dendê name given to palm oil in Bahia

engenho sugar plantation (Portuguese)

garoupeira small boat used in the Brazilian Atlantic to fish garoupa (grouper)

ingenio sugar plantation (Spanish)

irmandades Brazilian institution similar to the *cabildos de nación* in Spanish America.

jihād Islamic Holy War

ladino acculturated African

malungo name given in Brazil to Africans who had been shipmates in the Middle Passage

mocambo one of the names given to runaway slave settlements in Brazil

naciones name given to the various African ethnic groups in the Americas

naçoes as above, but in Brazil

palenque name given to runaway slave settlements throughout Spanish America

quilombo one of the names given to runaway slave settlements in Brazil

rancheador name given to slave hunters in Spanish America

Santería Also known as the Rule of Ocha. Afro-Cuban religion with Yoruba supremacy

Bibliography

ARCHIVAL SOURCES

Archivo General de Indias, Seville (AGI)
Indiferente General (IG)
Archivo Histórico Nacional, Madrid (AHN)
Ultramar (ULT)
Arquivo Público do Estado da Bahia, Salvador (APEB)
Insurreções de Escravos (IE)
Juizes (JUI)
Archivo Nacional de Cuba, Havana (ANC)
Asuntos Políticos (AP)
Comisión Militar (CM)
Gobierno Superior Civil (GSC)
Miscelánea de Expedientes (ME)
Real Consulado y Junta de Fomento (RCJF)
Arquivo Nacional do Rio de Janeiro (ANRJ)
Junta do Comércio (JC)
Arquivo Nacional de Torre da Tombo, Lisbon (ANTT)
Documentos dos Negócios Estrangeiros (DNE)
Archivio Segreto Vaticano, Vatican City (ASV)
Nunziatura Apostólica in Brasile (NAB)
British Parliamentary Papers Online (BPPO)
Centre des Archives D'Outremer, Aix-en-Provence (CAOM)
Fondos Ministerieles–Généralités (FM-GEN)
Département des Manuscrits Arabes et Ajami, Niamey, Niger (DMAA)
Collection Niamey (CN)
National Archives, London (NA-UK)
Foreign Office (FO)
HM Treasury (T)
National Archives, Washington, DC (NA-US)
Miscellaneous Correspondence (MC-Bahian Consulate)
Newspapers *Friends Intelligencer* (Philadelphia, PA)
O Justiceiro (São Paulo)
Pedro 2o, E Constitução (Bahia)
The Anti-Slavery Reporter and Aborigines' Friend (London)

PRINTED PRIMARY SOURCES

Abbot, Abiel. *Letters written in the Interior of Cuba between the Mountains of Arcana, to the East, and of Cusco, to the West, in the months of February, March, April and May, 1828.* Boston: Bowles and Dearborn, 1829.

Adams, John. *Remarks on the Country Extending from Cape Palmas to the River Congo, including observations on the manners and customs of the inhabitants.* London: G. and W. B. Whittaker, 1823.

Barbot, Jean. "A Description of the Costs of North and South Guinea," in John Green, ed., *A New General Collection of Voyages and Travels.* London: Thomas Astley, 1745. 2 vols.

Bello, Muhammed. *Infaq Al-Maisur. 1812,* in C. E. J. Whitting, ed., *Infaku'l Maisuri.* London: Luzac & Company, 1957.

Birch Freeman, Thomas. *Journals of Various Visits to the Kingdoms of Ashanti, Aku, and Dahomi, in Western Africa.* Cambridge: Cambridge University Press, 2010.

Bivar, A. D. H. "The Wathīqat Ahl Al-Sūdān: A Manifesto of the Fulani Jihād," *The Journal of African History,* 2:2 (1961): 235–43.

Bremmer, Fredrika. *The Homes of the New World; Impressions of America.* New York: Harper and Brothers, 1856.

Castelnau, Francis de. *Renseignements sur l'Afrique Centrale et sur une nation d'hommes à queue qui s'y trouverait.* Paris: Chez P. Bertrand, 1851.

Clapperton, Hugh, and Richard Lander. *Journal of a Second Expedition into the Interior of Africa from the Bight of Benin to Soccatoo.* London: John Murray, 1829.

Crowther, Samuel. *Vocabulary of the Yoruba Language.* London: Church Missionary Society, 1843.

Crowther, Samuel. *The second book of Moses, commonly called Eksodus/translated into Yoruba for the use of the native Christians of that nation, by the Rev. Samuel Crowther, native missionary.* London: British and Foreign Bible Society, 1854.

Crowther, Samuel, Adolphus Mann, D. O. Williams, and David Hinderer, *Iwe Mimo lati I. Samueli lo de Orin Solomoni.* London: A ko fun egbe Bibeli ti a npe ni Britise ati ti ilu miran, 1884.

"Cuban Slaves in England," *The Anti-Slavery Reporter and Aborigines' Friend,* 2:10 (1854): 234–9.

Dalzel, Archibald. *The History of Dahomy, an Island Kingdom of Africa; Compiled from Authentic Memoirs; with an Introduction and Notes.* London: T. Spilsbury and Son, 1793.

Dan Fodio, Uthman. *Tanbihu'l Ikhwan.* Translated in H. R. Palmer, "An Early Fulani Conception of Islam (Continued)," *Journal of the Royal African Society,* 14:53 (1914): 407–14.

Dan Fodio, Uthman. *Kitāb al-farq.* Translated in M. Hiskett, "Kitāb al-farq: A Work on the Habe Kingdoms Attributed to Uthman Dan Fodio," *Bulletin of the School of Oriental and African Studies,* 23:3 (1960): 567–69.

Denham, Dixon, et al. *Narratives of Travels and Discoveries in Northern and Central Africa in the years 1822, 1823 and 1824.* London: John Murray, 1828. 2 vols.

"Devassa do levante de escravos ocurrido em Salvador em 1835," *Anais do Arquivo do Estado da Bahia,* 38 (1968).

"Devassa do levante de escravos ocurrido em Salvador em 1835," *Anais do Arquivo do Estado da Bahia,* 40 (1971).

Gollmer, Charles Andrew, and Samuel Crowther, *Bibeli Mimó eyi ni òro olorun ti Testamenti Lailai ati ti Titon: apa ekini ti Testamenti Lailai. Iwe ti Mose marun. Iwe ti Josua. Iwe ti awon Onidajo. Iwe ti Rutu.* London: A k fun awon egbe Bibeli ti a npè Britise at ti ilu omiran, 1867.

Graham, Maria. *Journal of a Voyage to Brazil and Residence there during Part of the Years 1821, 1822, 1823.* London: Longman, 1824.

Jameson, Robert. *Letters from the Havana, during the year 1820; containing an account of the present state of the island of Cuba, and observations on the slave trade.* London: John Miller, 1821.

Koelle, Segismund. *Polyglotta Africana, or a comparative vocabulary of nearly three hundred words and phrases, in more than one hundred distinct African languages.* London: Church Missionary House, 1854.

Lander, Richard. *Records of Captain Clapperton's Last Expedition to Africa.* London: Henry Colburn and Richard Bentley, 1830.

Lander, Richard, and John Lander. *Journal of an Expedition to Explore the Course and Termination of the Niger.* London: John Murray, 1833. 3 vols.

Lorenzo, Manuel. *Manifiesto del General Don Manuel Lorenzo a la nación española.* Cádiz: Campe, 1837.

Matson, Henry. *Remarks on the Slave Trade and African Squadron.* London: James Ridgway, 1848.

Mockler-Ferryman, Augustus. *Up the Niger.* London: G. Phillip & Son, 1892.

Monte, Domingo del. *Centón epistolario.* Havana: Imagen Contemporánea, 2002. 4 vols.

Park, Mungo. *Travels in the Interior of Africa.* Dublin: P. Hayes, 1825.

Pezuela, Jacobo de la. *Ensayo histórico de la isla de Cuba.* New York: Rafael, 1842.

Ritter, C. "Mittheilungen über einige westafricanische Stämme in Cuba, gesamelt von Hesse," *Monatsberichte über die Verhandlungen der Gesellschaft für Erdkunde zu Berlin.* Berlin: Bei Simon Schropp und Comp., 1853, 12–16.

Sagra, Ramón de la. *Historia física, política y natural de la Isla de Cuba.* Paris: Librería de Arthus Bertrand, 1840.

Sandoval, Alonso de. *Treatise on Slavery: Selections from De Instauranda Aethiopum Salute.* Indianapolis and Cambridge: Hackett, 2008.

Schön, James Frederick, and Samuel Crowther. *Journals of the Rev. James Frederick Schön and Mr. Samuel Crowther who, with the Sanction of Her Majesty's Government accompanied the Expedition up the Niger, in 1841.* London: Hatchard and Son, 1842.

Skertchly, J. Alfred. *Dahomey as it is: Being a Narrative of Eight Months' Residence in that Country.* Whitefish: Kessinger Publishing, 2004.

Spilsbury, Francis B. *Account of a voyage to the Western coast of Africa; performed by His Majesty's sloop Favourite, in the year 1805.* London: Richard Phillips, 1807.

Tudor, Henry. *Narrative of a Tour in North America; comprising Mexico, the Mines of Real del Monte, the United States, and the British Colonies: with an Excursion to the Island of Cuba.* London: James Duncan, 1834. 2 Vols.

Turnbull, David. *Travels in the West: Cuba; with Notices of Porto Rico and the Slave Trade.* London: Longman, 1840.

Von Zütphen, C. H. *Tagebuch einer Reise von Bahia nach Afrika.* Düsseldorf: Schreiner, 1835.

Wagner, Hermann. *Schilderung der Reisen und Entdeckungen des Dr Eduard Vogel in Central-Afrika: In der Grossen Wuste, in den Landem des Sudan.* Leipzig: Otto Spamer, 1860.

Whetherell, James. *Brazil Stray Notes from Bahia: Being Extracts from Letters, &c., during a Residence of Fifteen Years.* Liverpool: Webb and Hunt, 1860.

PRINTED SECONDARY SOURCES

Adderley, Rosanne M. *New Negroes from Africa: Free African Immigrants in the Nineteenth-Century Caribbean.* Bloomington: Indiana University Press, 2007.

Adekunle, Julius O. *Politics and Society in Nigeria's Middle Belt: Borgu and the Emergence of a Political Identity.* Trenton, NJ, and Asmara: Africa World Press, 2004.

Adeyinka, Augustus A. "King Gezo of Dahomey, 1818–1858: A Reassessment of a West African Monarch in the Nineteenth Century," *African Studies Review,* 17:3 (1974): 541–8.

Afolayan, Funso. "Women and Warfare in Yorubaland during the Nineteenth Century," in Falola and Law, eds., *Warfare and Diplomacy in Precolonial Nigeria: Essays in Honor of Robert Smith,* 87–92.

Aguirre Beltrán, G. "Tribal Origins of Slaves in Mexico," *Journal of Negro History,* 31 (1946): 269–352.

Ajayi, J. F. Ade. "Samuel Ajayi Crowther of Oyo," in Curtin, ed., *Africa Remembered: Narratives by West Africans from the Era of the Slave Trade,* 289–316.

Ajayi, J. F. Ade, and Robert S. Smith. *Yoruba Warfare in the Nineteenth Century.* Cambridge: Cambridge University Press, 1971.

Akinjogbin, Adeagbo, ed. *War and Peace in Yorubaland, 1793–1893.* Ibadan: Heinemann Educational Books, 1998.

Akinjogbin, I. A., and Segun Osoba. *Topics in Nigerian Economic and Social History.* Ile Ife: University of Ife Press, 1980.

Alpern, Stanley B. "On the Origin of the Amazons of Dahomey," *History in Africa,* 25 (1998): 9–25.

Alpern, Stanley B. *Amazons of Black Sparta: The Women Warriors of Dahomey.* London: C. Hurst & Co., 1998.

Araujo, Ana Lucia. "Dahomey, Portugal and Bahia: King Adandozan and the Atlantic Slave Trade," *Slavery & Abolition,* 33:1 (2012): 1–19.

Atanda, J. A. "The Fall of the Old Oyo Empire: A Re-consideration of its Cause," *Journal of the Historical Society of Nigeria,* 5:4 (1971): 477–90.

Awe, Bolanle, and Omotayo Olutoye. "Women and Warfare in 19th Century Yorubaland: An Introduction," in Akinjogbin, ed., *War and Peace in Yorubaland,* 121–30.

Bada, Chief Samuel Ojo. "The Frontier City of Ilorin," in Toyin Falola, ed., *Yoruba Gurus: Indigenous Production of Knowledge in Africa.* Trenton, NJ, and Asmara: Africa World Press, 2000, 157–72.

Barcia, Manuel. "Entre amenazas y quejas: un acercamiento al papel jugado por los diplomáticos ingleses durante la Conspiración de la Escalera, 1844," *Colonial Latin American Historical Review,* 10:1 (2001): 1–26.

Barcia, Manuel. "Revolts amongst Enslaved Africans in Nineteenth-Century Cuba: A New Look to an Old Problem," *Journal of Caribbean History,* 39:2 (2005): 173–200.

Barcia, Manuel. *Seeds of Insurrection: Domination and Resistance on Western Cuban Plantations, 1808–1848.* Baton Rouge: Louisiana State University Press, 2008.

Barcia, Manuel. "A Not-so-Common Wind: Slave Revolts in the Age of Revolutions in Cuba and Brazil," *Review: The Journal of the Fernand Braudel Center,* 31:2 (2008): 169–94.

Barcia, Manuel. *The Great African Slave Revolt of 1825: Cuba and the Fight for Freedom in Matanzas.* Baton Rouge: Louisiana State University Press, 2012.

Barcia, María del Carmen. *Los ilustres apellidos: negros en la Habana colonial.* Havana: Bologna, 2009.

Barickman, J. *A Bahian Counterpoint: Sugar, Tobacco, Cassava and Slavery in the Recôncavo.* Stanford, CA: Stanford University Press, 1998.

Bay, Edna G. *Wives of the Leopard: Gender, Politics, and Culture in the Kingdom of Dahomey.* Charlottesville: University of Virginia Press, 1998.

Berbel, Márcia, Rafael Marquese, and Tâmis Parron. *Escravidão e política: Brasil e Cuba, 1790–1850.* São Paulo: Hucitec/Fapesp, 2010.

Bergad, Laird T. *The Comparative Histories of Slavery in Brazil, Cuba, and the United States.* Cambridge: Cambridge University Press, 2007.

Bethell, Leslie. "The Mixed Commissions for the Suppression of the Transatlantic Slave Trade in the Nineteenth Century," *Journal of African History,* 7:1 (1966): 79–93.

Bethell, Leslie. "The Independence of Brazil and the Abolition of the Brazilian Slave Trade: Anglo-Brazilian Relations, 1822–1826," *Journal of Latin American Studies*, 1:2 (1969): 115–47.

Bivar, A. D. H. "The Wathiqat ahl Al-Sudan: A Manifesto of the Fulani Jihad," *Journal of African History*, 2:2 (1961): 235–43.

Boahen, A. Adu. "The Caravan Trade in the Nineteenth Century," *Journal of African History*, 3:2 (1962): 349–59.

Borges, Dain Edward. *The Family in Bahia, Brazil, 1870–1945*. Stanford, CA: Stanford University Press, 1992.

Bowser, Frederick P. *The African Slave in Colonial Peru, 1524–1650*. Stanford, CA: Stanford University Press, 1974.

Bruce Lockhart, Jamie, and Paul E. Lovejoy, eds. *Hugh Clapperton into the Interior of Africa: Records of the Second Expedition, 1825–1827*. Leiden: Brill, 2005.

Cairus, José. "Instrumentum vocale, mallams e alufás: o paradoxo islâmico da erudição na diáspora africana no Atlântico," *Topoi*, 6 (2003): 128–64.

Candido, Mariana. *An African Slaving Port and the Atlantic World: Benguela and its Hinterland*. Cambridge: Cambridge University Press, 2013.

Capone, Stefania. *Searching for Africa in Brazil: Power and Tradition in Candomblé*. Durham, NC: Duke University Press, 2010.

Carman, W. Y. *A History of Firearms: From Earliest Times to 1914*. London: Taylor & Francis, 1955.

Carney, Judith A., and Richard Nicholas Rosomoff. *In the Shadow of Slavery: Africa's Botanical Legacy in the Atlantic World*. Berkeley and Los Angeles: University of California Press, 2009.

Castro, Ubiratam. "1846: Um ano na rota Bahia-Lagos: negócios, negociantes e outros parceiros," *Afro-Asia*, 21–2 (1998–9): 83–110.

Chambers, Douglas. "Ethnicity in the Diaspora: The Slave-Trade and the Creation of African 'Nations' in the Americas," *Slavery & Abolition*, 22:3 (2001): 25–39.

Chase, Kenneth. *Firearms: A Global History to 1700*. Cambridge: Cambridge University Press, 2003.

Childs, Matt D. *The 1812 Aponte Rebellion and the Struggle against Atlantic Slavery*. Chapel Hill: University of North Carolina Press, 2006.

Coquery-Vidrovitch, Catherine. *The History of African Cities South of the Sahara*. Princeton: Markus Wiener, 2005.

Curtin, Philip D., and Jan Vansina. "Sources of the Nineteenth Century Atlantic Slave Trade," *Journal of African History*, 5:2 (1964): 185–208.

Curtin, Philip D., ed. *Africa Remembered: Narratives by West Africans from the Era of the Slave Trade*. Madison: University of Wisconsin Press, 1967.

Deschamps Chapeaux, Pedro. *Los batallones de pardos y morenos*. Havana: Instituto del Libro, 1976.

Diouf, Sylviane A. "The Last Resort: Redeeming Family and Friends," in Diouf, ed. *Fighting the Slave Trade*, 81–100.

Diouf, Sylviane A., ed. *Fighting the Slave Trade: West African Strategies*. Athens, OH, and Oxford: Ohio University Press and James Currey, 2003.

Dupigny, E. G. M. "Nupe Province," in Anthony Hamilton Millard Kirk-Greene, ed., *Gazetteers of the Northern Provinces of Nigeria: The Central Kingdoms: Kontagora, Nassarawa, Nupe, Ilorin*. London: Frank Cass, 1972, iii. 8–10.

Eltis, David. "Welfare Trends among the Yoruba in the Early Nineteenth Century: The Anthropometric Evidence," *Journal of Economic History*, 50:3 (1990): 521–40.

Eltis, David. "The Diaspora of Yoruba Speakers, 1650–1865: Dimensions and Implications," in Falola and Childs, eds., *The Yoruba Diaspora*, 17–39.

Eltis, David, and David Richardson, eds. *Extending the Frontiers: Essays on the New Transatlantic Slave Trade Database*. New Haven and London: Yale University Press, 2008.

Falola, Toyin. "A Research Agenda on the Yoruba in the Nineteenth Century," *History in Africa*, 15 (1988): 211–27.

Falola, Toyin. "The Yoruba Caravan System of the Nineteenth Century," *International Journal of African Historical Studies*, 24:1 (1991): 111–32.

Falola, Toyin, ed. *Yoruba Gurus: Indigenous Production of Knowledge in Africa*. Trenton, NJ, and Asmara: Africa World Press, 2000.

Falola, Toyin, and Matt D. Childs, eds. *The Yoruba Diaspora in the Atlantic World*. Indianapolis: Indiana University Press, 2004.

Falola, Toyin, and Matthew Heaton. *A History of Nigeria*. Cambridge: Cambridge University Press, 2008.

Falola, Toyin, and Robin Law, eds. *Warfare and Diplomacy in Precolonial Nigeria: Essays in Honor of Robert Smith*. Madison: African Studies Program. University of Wisconsin-Madison, 1992.

Fernandes, Caloca. *Viagem gastronômica através do Brasil*. São Paulo: Senac, 2001.

Ferreira, Jackson. "Por hojese acaba la lida: suicidio escravo na Bahia (1850–1888)," *Afro-Asia*, 31 (2004): 197–234.

Ferreira, Roquinaldo. *Cross-Cultural Exchange in the Atlantic World: Angola and Brazil during the Era of the Slave Trade*. Cambridge: Cambridge University Press, 2012.

Ferrer, Ada. "Speaking of Haiti: Slavery, Revolution, and Freedom in Cuban Slave Testimony," in Geggus and Fiering, eds., *The World of the Haitian Revolution*, 223–47.

Finch, Aisha. "Insurgency at the Crossroads: Cuban Slaves and the Conspiracy of La Escalera, 1841–1844," Ph.D. diss. New York University, 2007.

Flint, John E., ed. *The Cambridge History of Africa*. Cambridge: Cambridge University Press, 1975. Vol. v.

Folayan, Kola. "Trade Routes in Egbado in the Nineteenth Century," in Akinjogbin and Osoba, *Topics in Nigerian Economic and Social History*, 83–95.

Franco, José Luciano. *La Conspiración de Aponte*. Havana: Archivo Nacional, 1963.

Franco, José Luciano. *Comercio clandestino de esclavos*. Havana: Ciencias Sociales, 1996.

Fuente, Alejandro de la. "Slave Law and Claims-Making in Cuba: The Tannenbaum Debate Revisited," *Law and History Review*, 22:2 (2004): 339–69.

Fuglestad, Finn. "A Reconsideration of Hausa History before the Jihad," *Journal of African History*, 19:3 (1978): 319–39.

Funes Monzote, Reinaldo. *From Rainforest to Cane Field in Cuba: An Environmental History since 1492*. Chapel Hill: University of North Carolina Press, 2008.

Gailey, Harry A. *Lugard and the Abeokuta Uprising: The Demise of Egba Independence*. London: Frank Cass, 1982.

Galdini, Ana Maria, Raimundo Oda, and Saulo Veiga Oliveira. "Registros de suicídios entre escravos em São Paulo e na Bahia (1847–1888): notas de pesquisa," Paper presented at the 3rd Encontro Escravidão e Liberdade no Brasil Meridional. Florianopolis, May 2007.

García, Gloria. *Conspiraciones y revueltas: la actividad política de los negros en Cuba, 1790–1845*. Santiago de Cuba: Oriente, 2003.

García, Gloria. *La esclavitud desde la esclavitud: la visión de los siervos*. Havana: Ciencias Sociales, 2003.

Geggus, David P. "Sex, Ratio, Age and Ethnicity in the Atlantic Slave Trade: Data from French Shipping and Plantation Records," *Journal of African History*, 30 (1989): 23–44.

Geggus, David P., and Norman Fiering, eds. *The World of the Haitian Revolution.* Bloomington: Indiana University Press, 2009.

Genovese, Eugene. *From Rebellion to Revolution: Afro-American Slave Revolts in the Making of the Modern World.* Baton Rouge: Louisiana State University Press, 1979.

Gentry, Alwyn. "Diversity and Floristic Composition of Lowland Tropical Forest in Africa and South America," in Peter Goldblatt, ed., *Biological Relationships between Africa and South America.* New Haven: Yale University Press, 1993.

Ghorbal, Karim. *Réformisme et esclavage à Cuba, 1835–1845.* Paris: Publibook, 2009.

Goldblatt, Peter, ed. *Biological Relationships between Africa and South America.* New Haven: Yale University Press, 1993.

Gomes, Flávio dos Santos. *A hidra e os pântanos: mocambos, quilombos e comunidades de fugitivos no Brasil (Séculos XVII–XIX).* São Paulo: UNESP, 2005.

Gomez, Michael A. *Exchanging our Country Marks: The Transformation of African Identities in the Colonial and Antebellum South.* Chapel Hill: University of North Carolina Press, 1998.

Gomez, Michael A. *Black Crescent: The Experience and Legacy of African Muslims in the Americas.* Cambridge: Cambridge University Press, 2005.

González-Ripoll, María Dolores, and Izaskun Álvarez Cuartero, eds. *Francisco Arango y la invención de la Cuba azucarera.* Salamanca: Ediciones Universidad de Salamanca, 2009.

Goody, Jack. *Technology, Tradition and the State in Africa.* Cambridge: Cambridge University Press, 1971.

Gorgondière, Louise de la, Kenneth King, and Sarah Vaughan, eds. *Ethnicity in Africa: Roots, Meanings and Interpretations.* Edinburgh: Centre of African Studies, 1996.

Graden, Dale Torston. *From Slavery to Freedom in Brazil: Bahia, 1835–1900.* Albuquerque: University of New Mexico Press, 2006.

Graden, Dale Torston. "Interpreters, Translators, and the Spoken Word in the Nineteenth-Century Transatlantic Slave Trade to Brazil and Cuba," *Ethnohistory,* 58:3 (2011): 393–419.

Grandío Moraguez, Oscar. "The African Origins of the Slaves Arriving in Cuba, 1789–1865," in David Eltis and David Richardson, eds., *Extending the Frontiers: Essays on the New Transatlantic Slave Trade Database.* New Haven and London: Yale University Press, 2008, 176–201.

Grinberg, Keila. *Liberata. A lei da ambiguedade. As ações de liberdade da Corte de Apelação do Rio de Janeiro no século XIX.* Rio de Janeiro: Relume Dumara, 1994.

Guanche, Jesús. *Componentes étnicos de la nación cubana.* Havana: Fundación Fernando Ortiz, 1996.

Guerra Filho, Sérgio Armando Diniz. "O povo e a guerra: participação das camadas populares nas lutas pela independência do Brasil na Bahia." UFB MA diss., 2004.

Hair, P. E. H. "The Enslavement of Koelle's Informants," *Journal of African History,* 6:2 (1965): 193–203.

Hall, Gwendolyn Midlo. *African Slaves in Colonial Louisiana.* Baton Rouge: Louisiana State University Press, 1992.

Hall, Gwendolyn Midlo. *Slavery and African Ethnicities in the Americas: Restoring the Links.* Chapel Hill: University of North Carolina Press, 2007.

Hamza, Ibrahim. "Slavery and Plantation Society at Dorayi in Kano Emirate," in Lovejoy, ed., *Slavery on the Frontiers of Islam,* 125–48.

Hawthorne, Walter. "Being now, as it were, One Family: Shipmate Bonding on the Slave Vessel Emilia, in Rio de Janeiro and throughout the Atlantic World," *Luso-Brazilian Review,* 45:1 (2008): 53–77.

Hawthorne, Walter. *From Africa to Brazil: Culture, Identity and an Atlantic Slave Trade.* Cambridge: Cambridge University Press, 2010.

Higman, Barry W. *Slave Populations of the British Caribbean, 1807–1834.* Baltimore and London: Johns Hopkins University Press, 1984.

Hiskett, Mervyn. "The Arab-Star Calendar and Planetary System in Hausa Verse," *Bulletin of the School of Oriental and African Studies,* 30–1 (1967): 158–76.

Hiskett, Mervyn. "The Nineteenth-Century Jihads in West Africa," in John E. Flint, ed., *The Cambridge History of Africa.* Cambridge: Cambridge University Press, 1976, V. 125–69.

Howard, Rosalyn. "Yoruba in the British Caribbean: A Comparative Perspective on Trinidad and the Bahamas," in Falola and Childs, eds., *The Yoruba Diaspora,* 157–76.

Hubbell, Andrew. "A View of the Slave Trade from the Margin: Souroudougou in the Late Nineteenth-Century Slave Trade of the Niger Bend," *Journal of African History,* 42:1 (2001): 25–47.

Hunwick, John, and Nancy Lawler, eds. *The Cloth of Many Colored Silks: Papers on History and Society Ghanian and Islamic in Honor of Ivor Wilks.* Evanston, IL: Northwestern University Press, 1997.

Iduarte, Juan. "Noticias sobre sublevaciones y conspiraciones de esclavos. Cafetal Salvador, 1833," *Revista de la Biblioteca Nacional José Martí,* 73:24, 1–2, 3ra época (1982): 117–52.

Ilesanmi, T. M. "The Yoruba Worldview on Women and Warfare," in Falola and Law, eds., *Warfare and Diplomacy in Precolonial Nigeria,* 87–92.

Iliffe, John. *Honour in African History.* Cambridge: Cambridge University Press, 2005.

Inikori, Joseph E. "Measuring the Unmeasured Hazards of the Atlantic Slave Trade: Documents Relating to the British Trade," *Revue française d'histoire d'Outre-Mer,* 83:312 (1996): 53–92.

Jancsó, István. *Na Bahia contra o Império: história do ensaio da sedição de 1798.* São Paulo: Hucitec, 1976.

Jensen, Geoffrey, and Andrew Wiest, eds. *War in the Age of Technology: Myriad Faces of Modern Armed Conflict.* New York: New York University Press, 2001.

Johnson, Samuel. *The History of the Yorubas: From the Earliest Times to the Beginning of the British Protectorate.* Cambridge: Cambridge University Press, 2010.

Johnson, Sherry. "From Authority to Impotence: Arango's Adversaries and their Fall from Power during the Constitutional Period," in María Dolores González-Ripoll and Izaskun Álvarez Cuartero, eds., *Francisco Arango y la invención de la Cuba azucarera.* Salamanca: Ediciones Universidad de Salamanca, 2009, 193–213.

Kea, Raymond A. "Firearms and Warfare on the Gold and Slave Coasts from the Sixteenth to the Nineteenth Centuries," *Journal of African History,* 12:2 (1971): 185–213.

Kea, Raymond A. "'When I Die, I Shall Return to my Own Land': An 'Amina' Slave Rebellion in the Danish West Indies, 1733–1734," in Hunwick and Lawler, eds., *The Cloth of Many Colored Silks,* 159–94.

Kirk-Greene, Anthony Hamilton Millard, ed. *Gazetteers of the Northern Provinces of Nigeria: The Central Kingdoms: Kontagora, Nassarawa, Nupe, Ilorin.* London: Frank Cass, 1972.

Kolapo, Femi J. "The Southward Campaigns of Nupe in the Lower Niger Valley," in Lovejoy, ed., *Slavery on the Frontiers,* 69–86.

Kraay, Hendrik. "'As terrifying as unexpected': The Bahian Sabinada, 1837–1838," *Hispanic American Historical Review,* 72:4 (1992): 501–25.

Kraay, Hendrik. *Race, State and Armed Forces in Independence-Era Brazil: Bahia, 1790s-1840s.* Stanford, CA: Stanford University Press, 2004.

Kraay, Hendrik. "Em outra coisa não falavam os pardos, cabras, e crioulos: o recrutamiento de escravos na Guerra da Independência na Bahia," *Revista Brasileira de história*, 22:43 (2002). Online at: <http://www.scielo.br/scielo.php> (accessed on 21 January 2011).

Laband, John, ed. *Daily Lives of Civilians in Wartime Africa: From Slavery Days to the Diamond Wars*. Westport, CT: Greenwood Press, 2007.

Laitin, David D. *Hegemony and Culture: Politics and Change among the Yoruba*. Chicago: University of Chicago Press, 1986.

Landers, Jane. *Atlantic Creoles in the Age of Revolution*. Cambridge, MA: Harvard University Press, 2010.

La Rosa Corzo, Gabino. *Armas y tácticas defensivas de los cimarrones en Cuba*. Reporte de investigación No. 2. Havana: Academia de Ciencias de Cuba, 1989.

La Rosa Corzo, Gabino. "Rescate de Olórum (estudio de arqueología afroamericana)," *América Negra*, 12 (1996): 39–57.

La Rosa Corzo, Gabino. *Runaway Slave Settlements in Cuba: Resistance and Repression*. Chapel Hill: University of North Carolina Press, 2003.

La Rosa Corzo, Gabino. "Aproximaciones antropológicas a las bandas cimarronas de las ciénagas de Cuba," *Boletín del Gabinete de Arqueología*, 7:7 (2008): 4–15.

La Rue, Michael. "The Frontiers of Enslavement: Bagirmi and the Trans-Saharan Slave Routes," in Lovejoy, ed., *Slavery on the Frontiers of Islam*, 31–54.

Law, Robin. "The Chronology of the Yoruba Wars of the Early Nineteenth Century: A Reconsideration," *Journal of the Historical Society of Nigeria*, 5:2 (1970), 211–23.

Law, Robin. "The Constitutional Troubles of Oyo in the Eighteenth Century," *Journal of African History*, 12:1 (1971), 25–44.

Law, Robin. "The Owu War in Yoruba History," *Journal of the Historical Society of Nigeria*, 2:1 (1973): 141–7.

Law, Robin. "A West African Cavalry State: The Kingdom of Oyo," *Journal of African History*, 16:1 (1975): 1–15.

Law, Robin. "Horses, Firearms and Political Power in Pre-colonial West Africa," *Past and Present*, 72 (1976): 112–32.

Law, Robin. "Ethnicity and the Slave Trade: 'Lucumi' and 'Nago' as Ethnonyms in West Africa," *History in Africa*, 24 (1997), 205–19.

Law, Robin. "Making Sense of a Traditional Narrative: Political Disintegration in the Kingdom of Oyo," *Cahiers d'études africaines*, 22:87/88 (1982), 387–401.

Law, Robin. "Trade and Politics behind the Slave Coast: The Lagoon Traffic and the Rise of Lagos, 1500–1800," *Journal of African History*, 24:3 (1983): 321–48.

Law, Robin. "Slave-Raiders and Middlemen, Monopolists and Free-Traders: The Supply of Slaves for the Atlantic Trade in Dahomey, c.1715–1850," *Journal of African History*, 30:1 (1989): 45–68.

Law, Robin, "Between the Sea and the Lagoon: The Interaction of Maritime and Inland Navigation on the Precolonial Slave Coast," *Cahiers d'études africaines*, 114: 29/2 (1989): 209–37.

Law, Robin. *The Oyo Empire, c.1600–c.1836*. Oxford: Oxford University Press, 1991.

Law, Robin. "The 'Amazons' of Dahomey," *Paideuma*, 39 (1993): 245–60.

Law, Robin. "Central and Eastern Wangara: An Indigenous West African Perception of the Political and Economic Geography of the Slave Coast as Recorded by Joseph Dupuis in Kumasi, 1820," *History in Africa*, 22 (1995): 281–305.

Law, Robin, ed. *From Slave Trade to "Legitimate" Commerce: The Commercial Transition in Nineteenth Century West Africa*. Cambridge: Cambridge University Press, 1995.

Law, Robin. "Local Amateur Scholarship in the Construction of the Yoruba Ethnicity, 1880–1914," in Louise de la Gorgondière, Kenneth King, and Sarah Vaughan, eds., *Ethnicity in Africa: Roots, Meanings and Interpretations*. Edinburgh: Centre of African Studies, 1996, 55–90.

Law, Robin, ed. *Contemporary Source Material for the History of the Old Oyo Empire, 1627–1824*. Toronto: Harriet Tubman Resource Centre on the African Diaspora, 2002.

Law, Robin. *Ouidah: The Social History of a West African Slaving Port*. Athens, OH, and Oxford: Ohio University Press and James Currey, 2004.

Law, Robin. "Ethnicities of Enslaved Africans in the Diaspora: On the Meanings of 'Mina' (Again)," *History in Africa*, 32 (2005): 247–67.

Law, Robin, and Paul E. Lovejoy. "Borgu in the Atlantic Slave Trade," *African Economic History*, 27 (1999), 69–92.

Law, Robin, and Silke Strickrodt, eds. *Ports of the Slave Trade (Bights of Benin and Biafra)*. Stirling: Centre of Commonwealth Studies-University of Stirling, 1999.

Leal, Carlos Galindo, and Ibsen de Gusmão Câmara. *The Atlantic Forest of South America: Biodiversity, Status, Threats, and Outlook*. Washington, DC: Island Press, 2003.

Levtzion, Nehemiah. *Muslims and Chiefs in West Africa: A Study of Islam in the Middle Volta Basin in the Pro-Colonial Period*. Oxford: Oxford University Press, 1968.

Lloyd, Christopher. *The Navy and the Slave Trade: The Suppression of the African Slave Trade in the Nineteenth Century*. London: Cass, 1968.

Lohse, Russell. "Africans in a Colony of Creoles: The Yoruba in Colonial Costa Rica," in Falola and Childs, eds., *The Yoruba Diaspora*, 130–56.

Lopes, Juliana Serzedello Crespin. "Liberdade, liberdades: dilemas da escravidão na Sabinada (Bahia, 1837–1838)," *Sankofa: Revista de história da Africa e de estudos da diáspora Africana*, 6 (2010). Online at: <http://sites.google.com/site/revistasankofa/sankofa6/liberdade-liberdades> (accessed on 14 January 2011).

Lopes, Nei. *Enciclopédia Brasilera da diáspora Africana*. São Paulo: Selo Negro, 2004.

López Denis, Adrián. "Disease and Society in Colonial Cuba, 1790–1840." Ph.D. diss. UCLA, 2007.

López Valdés, Rafael L. "Notas para el estudio etnohistórico de los esclavos Lucumí de Cuba," in Menéndez, ed., *Estudios afro-cubanos*, ii. 311–479.

Lovejoy, Henry B. "Old Oyo Influences on the Transformation of Lucumí Identity in Colonial Cuba." Ph.D. diss. UCLA, 2012.

Lovejoy, Paul E. "Plantations in the Economy of the Sokoto Caliphate," *Journal of African History*, 19:3 (1978): 341–68.

Lovejoy, Paul E. "Polanyi's 'Ports of Trade': Salaga and Kano in the Nineteenth Century," *Canadian Journal of African Studies/Revue Canadienne des études Africaines*, 16:2 (1982): 245–77.

Lovejoy, Paul E. *Transformations in Slavery: A History of Slavery in Africa*. Cambridge: Cambridge University Press, 1983.

Lovejoy, Paul E. "Background to Rebellion: The Origins of Muslim Slaves in Bahia," *Slavery & Abolition*, 15:2 (1994): 151–80.

Lovejoy, Paul E. "The African Diaspora: Revisionist Interpretations of Ethnicity, Culture and Religion under Slavery," *Studies in the World History of Slavery, Abolition and Emancipation*, 2:1 (1997). Online at: <http://ejournalofpoliticalscience.org/diaspora.html> (accessed on 12 March 2012).

Lovejoy, Paul E. "Jihad e escravidão: as origens dos escravos muçulmanos da Bahia," *Topoi: revista de história*, 1:1 (2000): 11–44.

Lovejoy, Paul E. ed. *Slavery on the Frontiers of Islam*. Princeton: Markus Wiener, 2004.

Lovejoy, Paul E. "The Urban Background of Enslaved Muslims in the Americas," *Slavery & Abolition*, 26:3 (2005): 349–76.

Lovejoy, Paul E. "The Yoruba Factor in the Trans-Atlantic Slave Trade," in Falola and Childs, eds., *The Yoruba Diaspora*, 40–55.

Lovejoy, Paul E. *Slavery, Commerce and Production in the Sokoto Caliphate of West Africa*. Trenton, NJ, and Asmara: Africa World Press, 2005.

Lovejoy, Paul E. "Civilian Casualties in the Context of the Trans-Atlantic Slave Trade," in Laband, ed., *Daily Lives of Civilians in Wartime Africa*, 17–50.

Lovejoy, Paul E., ed. *Identity in the Shadow of Slavery*. London: Continuum, 2009.

Lovejoy, Paul E. "Identifying Enslaved Africans in the African Diaspora," in Lovejoy, ed., *Identity in the Shadow of Slavery*, 1–29.

Lucena Salmoral, Manuel. *Regulación de la esclavitud negra en las colonias de América Española, 1503–1886*. Madrid: EDITUM, 2005.

Lydon, Ghislaine. *On Transaharan-Trails: Islamic Law, Trade Networks and Cross-Cultural Exchange in Nineteenth-Century West Africa*. Cambridge: Cambridge University Press, 2009.

Lynn, Martin. *Commerce and Economic Change in West Africa: The Palm Oil Trade in the Nineteenth Century*. Cambridge: Cambridge University Press, 2002.

Mabogunje, A. L., and J. Omer-Cooper. *Owu in Yoruba History*. Ibadan: Ibadan University Press, 1971.

Macaulay, Neill. *Dom Pedro: the Struggle for Liberty in Brazil and Portugal, 1798–1834*. Durham, NC: Duke University Press, 1986.

McGowan, Winston. "African Resistance to the Atlantic Slave Trade in West Africa," *Slavery & Abolition*, 11:1 (1990): 5–19.

Maingot, Anthony P. "Haiti and the Terrified Consciousness of the Caribbean," in Oostindie, ed., *Ethnicity in the Caribbean*, 53–80.

Malerba, Jurandir, ed. *A Independência brasileira: novas dimensões*. Rio de Janeiro: Editora FGV, 2006.

Marquese, Rafael de Bivar. "1808 e o impacto do Brasil na construção do escravismo cubano," *Revista USP*, 79 (2008): 118–31.

Martin, B. G. "Kanem, Bornu, and the Fazzan: Notes on the Political History of a Trade Route," *Journal of African History*, 10:1 (1969): 15–27.

Martínez García, Daniel. "La sublevación de la Alcancía: su rehabilitación histórica en el proceso conspirativo que concluye en La Escalera (1844)," *Rábida*, 19 (2000): 41–8.

Mason, John Edwin. *Social Death and Resurrection: Slavery and Emancipation in South Africa*. Charlottesville and London: University of Virginia Press, 2003.

Mason, Michael. "The Antecedents of Nineteenth-Century Islamic Government in Nupe," *International Journal of African Historical Studies*, 10:1 (1977): 63–76.

Mattos, Hebe. *Das cores do silêncio: os significados da liberdade no sudeste escravista: Brasil século XIX*. Rio de Janeiro: Nova Fronteira, 1998.

Mbembe, Achille. "Necropolitics," *Public Culture*, 15:1 (2003): 11–40.

Mendoza, Ruben G. "West African Empires: Dates 400–1591 C.E.," in John Powell, ed., *Weapons and Warfare*. Pasadena, CA: Salem Press, 2001.

Menéndez, Lázara, ed. *Estudios afro-cubanos: selección de lecturas*. Havana: Universidad de la Habana, 1990.

Miller, Ivor. *Voice of the Leopard: African Secret Societies and Cuba*. Jackson: University Press of Mississippi, 2009.

Minardi, Margot. *Making Slavery History: Abolition and the Politics of Memory in Massachusetts*. Oxford and New York: Oxford University Press, 2010.

Mirzai, Behnaz A., Ismael M. Montana, and Paul E. Lovejoy, eds. *Slavery, Islam and Diaspora*. Trenton, NJ, and Asmara: Africa World Press, 2009.

Montana, Ismael M. *The Abolition of Slavery in Ottoman Tunisia*. Gainesville: University Press of Florida, 2013.

Moreno Fraginals, Manuel. *El ingenio: complejo económico social cubano del azúcar.* Havana: Ciencias Sociales, 1978. 3 vols.

Morton-Williams, Peter. "The Oyo Yoruba and the Atlantic Trade, 1670–1830," *Journal of the Historical Society of Nigeria*, 3:1 (1964): 25–45.

Murray, David. *Odious Commerce: Britain, Spain, and the Abolition of the Cuban Slave Trade*. Cambridge: Cambridge University Press, 2002.

Nadel, Siegfried Frederick. *A Black Byzantium: The Kingdom of Nupe in Nigeria*. Oxford: Oxford University Press, 1951.

Naranjo Orovio, Consuelo, ed. *Historia de Cuba*. Madrid: CSIC-Doce Calles, 2009.

Navarro García, Luis. *La independencia de Cuba*. Madrid: MAPFRE, 1992.

Needell, Jeffrey D. *The Party of Order: The Conservatives, the State and Slavery in the Brazilian Monarchy, 1831–1871*. Stanford, CA: Stanford University Press, 2006.

Nelson, Jennifer L. "The Mixed Commission and Emancipated Slaves in Nineteenth-Century Rio de Janeiro," MA diss. University of Leeds, 2011.

Nickel, Sandra. "Spreading Which Word? Philological, Theological and Socio-political Considerations behind the 19th Century Bible Translation into Yoruba," *Leeds Working Papers for Linguistics and Phonetics*, 18 (2013): 54–84.

Nicolau Parés, Luis, and Roger Sansi, eds. *Sorcery in the Black Atlantic*. Chicago: University of Chicago Press, 2011.

Nishida, Mieko. *Slavery and Identity: Ethnicity, Gender and Race in Salvador, Brazil, 1808–1888*. Bloomington: Indiana University Press, 2003.

Northrup, David. "Igbo and Myth Igbo: Culture and Ethnicity in the Atlantic World, 1600–1850," *Slavery & Abolition*, 21:3 (2000): 1–20.

Nwabara, Samuel N. "The Fulani Conquest and Rule of the Hausa Kingdom of Northern Nigeria (1804–1900)," *Journal de la Société des Africanistes*, 33:2 (1963): 231–42.

Nwokeji, G. Ugo, and David Eltis, "The Roots of the African Diaspora: Methodological Considerations in the Analysis of Names in the Liberated African Registers of Sierra Leone and Havana," *History in Africa*, 29 (2002): 368–73.

O'Hear, Ann. *Power Relations: Ilorin Slaves and their Successors*. Rochester, NY: Rochester University Press, 1997.

O'Hear, Ann. "Ilorin as a Slaving and Slave Trade Emirate," in Paul E. Lovejoy, ed., *Slavery on the Frontiers of Islam*. Princeton: Markus Wiener, 2004, 55–68.

O'Hear, Ann. "The Enslavement of the Yoruba," in Falola and Childs, eds., *The Yoruba Diaspora*, 56–75.

Ojo, Olatunji. "Islam, Ethnicity and Slave Agitation: Hausa 'Mamlucks' in Nineteenth-Century Yorubaland," in Mirzai, Montana, and Lovejoy, eds., *Slavery, Islam and Diaspora*, 103–24.

Ojo, Olatunji. "'[I]n Search of their Relations, To Set at Liberty as Many as They Had the Means': Ransoming Captives in Nineteenth Century Yorubaland," *Nordic Journal of African Studies*, 19:1 (2010): 58–76.

Ojo, Olatunji. "Child Slaves in Pre-colonial Nigeria, c.1725–1860," *Slavery & Abolition*, 33:3 (2012): 417–34.

Oliveira, Maria Inês Cortês de. "Retrouver une identité: jeux sociaux des Africains de Bahia (vers. 1750–vers. 1890)". Ph.D. diss. Université de Paris-Sorbonne, 1992.

Oostindie, Gert, ed. *Ethnicity in the Caribbean: Essays in Honor of Harry Hoetink*. Amsterdam: Amsterdam University Press, 2005.

Opatrný, Josef. "Cuba en el contexto internacional," in Naranjo Orovio, ed., *Historia de Cuba*, 233–53.

Ortega, José Guadalupe. "Cuban Merchants, Slave Trade Knowledge, and the Atlantic World, 1790s–1820s," *Colonial Latin American Historical Review*, 15:3 (2006): 225–52.

Ortiz, Fernando. *Los negros esclavos*. Havana: Ciencias Sociales, 1987.

Owomoyela, Oyekan. *Yoruba Proverbs*. Lincoln and London: University of Nebraska Press, 2005.

Oyewumi, Oyeronke. "Making History, Creating Gender: Some Methodological and Interpretive Questions in the Writing of Oyo Oral Traditions," *History in Africa*, 25 (1998), 263–305.

Paden, John N. *Religion and Political Culture in Kano*. Berkeley and Los Angeles: University of California Press, 1973.

Paiva, Eduardo França. "Coartações e alforrias nas Minas Gerais do século XVIII: as possibilidades de libertação escrava no principal centro colonial," *Revista de história*, 133 (1995): 49–57.

Palmié, Stephan. *Wizards and Scientists: Explorations in Afro-Cuban Modernity and Tradition*. Durham, NC: Duke University Press, 2002.

Pankhurst Robert J., et al. *West Gondwana: Pre-Cenozoic Correlations across the South Atlantic Region*. London: The Geological Society, 2008.

Paquette, Robert L. *Sugar is Made with Blood: The Conspiracy of La Escalera and the Conflict between Empires over Slavery in Cuba*. Middleton, CT: Wesleyan University Press, 1987.

Patterson, Orlando. *Slavery and Social Death: A Comparative Study*. Cambridge, MA: Harvard University Press, 1982.

Pavy, David. "The Provenience of Colombia Negroes," *Journal of Negro History*, 52 (1967): 35–58.

Pearce, Adrian J. *British Trade with Spanish America, 1763–1808*. Liverpool: Liverpool University Press, 2007.

Pearton, Maurice. *Diplomacy, War, and Technology since 1830*. London: Burnett Books, 1982.

Peel, J. D. Y. *Religious Encounter and the Making of the Yoruba*. Bloomington: Indiana University Press, 2000.

Perez, Louis A. *To Die in Cuba: Suicide and Society*. Chapel Hill: University of North Carolina Press, 2003.

Person, Yves. "Chronologie du royaume gun de Hogbonu (Porto Novo)," *Cahiers d'études africaines*, 15:58 (1975): 217–38.

Piqueras, José Antonio. *Sociedad civil y poder en Cuba: colonia y poscolonia*. Madrid: Siglo XXI, 2005.

Piqueras, José Antonio. "La siempre fiel Isla de Cuba, o la lealtad interesada," *Historia Mexicana*, 58:1 (2008): 427–86.

Ponte Domínguez, Francisco. *La Junta de la Habana en 1808*. Havana: Guerrero, 1947.

Poumier Taquechel, María. "El suicidio esclavo en Cuba en los años 1840," *Anuario de estudios Americanos*, 43 (1986): 69–86.

Powell, John, ed. *Weapons and Warfare*. Pasadena, CA: Salem Press, 2001.

Price, Richard, ed. *Maroon Societies: Rebel Slave Communities in the Americas*. Baltimore and London: Johns Hopkins University Press, 1996.

Prince, Howard M. "Slave Rebellion in Bahia, 1807–1835". Ph.D. diss. Columbia University, 1972.

Ramos, Donald. "Social Revolution Frustrated: The Conspiracy of the Tailors in Bahia, 1798," *Luso-Brazilian Review*, 13:1 (1976): 74–90.

Ramos, Vanessa. "A alforria comprada pelos 'escravos da religião' (Rio de Janeiro – 1840–1871)," *História social*, 13 (2007): 121–37.

Rathbone, Richard. "Some Thoughts on Resistance to Enslavement in West Africa," *Slavery & Abolition*, 6:3 (1985): 11–22.

Redfern, Ron. *The Evolution of Continents, Oceans, and Life*. Norman: University of Oklahoma Press, 2001.

Rediker, Markus. "History from Below the Water Line: Sharks and the Atlantic Slave Trade," *Atlantic Studies*, 5:2 (2008): 285–97.

Reginaldo, Lucilene. "Irmandades e devoções de africanos e crioulos na Bahia setentista: histórias e experiências atlânticas," *Stockholm Review of Latin American Studies*, 4 (2009): 25–35.

Reid, Richard. *Warfare in African History*. Cambridge: Cambridge University Press, 2012.

Reid-Vazquez, Michelle. *The Year of the Lash: Free People of Color in Cuba and the Nineteenth-Century Atlantic World*. Athens, GA: University of Georgia Press, 2011.

Reis, João José. *Slave Rebellion in Brazil: The Muslim Uprising of 1835 in Bahia*. Baltimore: Johns Hopkins University Press, 1995.

Reis, João José. *Death is a Festival: Funeral Rites and Rebellion in Nineteenth Century Brazil*. Chapel Hill: University of North Carolina Press, 2003.

Reis, João José. *Rebelião escrava no Brasil: a história do levante dos Malês em 1835*. São Paulo: Companhia das Letras, 2003.

Reis, João José, and Eduardo Silva. *Negociação e conflito: a resistência negra no Brasil escravista*. São Paulo: Companhia das Letras, 1999.

Reis, João José, and Beatriz Gallotti Mamigonian. "Nagô and Mina: The Yoruba Diaspora in Brazil," in Falola and Childs, eds., *The Yoruba Diaspora*, 77–110.

Reis, João José, and Flávio dos Santos Gomes. "Repercussions of the Haitian Revolution in Brazil, 1791–1850," in Geggus and Fiering, eds., *The World of the Haitian Revolution*, 284–314.

Richardson, David. "Shipboard Revolts, African Authority, and the Atlantic Slave Trade," *William and Mary Quarterly*, 58:1 (2001): 69–92.

Roberts, Kevin. "The Influential Yoruba Past in Haiti," in Falola and Childs, eds., *The Yoruba Diaspora*, 177–83.

Rodrigues, Raimundo Nina. *Os africanos no Brasil*. São Paulo: Editora Nacional, 1932.

Ross, David. "The Dahomean Middleman System, 1727–c.1818," *Journal of African History*, 28:3 (1987): 357–75.

Rucker, Walter. *The River Flows On: Black Resistance, Culture, and Identity Formation in Early America*. Baton Rouge: Louisiana State University Press, 2006.

Russell, Heather. *Legba's Crossing: Narratology in the African Atlantic*. Athens, GA: University of Georgia Press, 2009.

Schmidt-Nowara, Christopher. *Empire and Anti-Slavery: Spain, Cuba, and Puerto Rico, 1833–1874*. Pittsburgh: University of Pittsburgh Press, 1999.

Schuler, Monica. "Akan Slave Rebellions in the British Caribbean," *Savacou*, 1:1 (1970): 8–31.

Schwartz, Stuart. "The Manumission of Slaves in Colonial Brazil: Bahia, 1684–1745," *Hispanic American Historical Review*, 54 (1974): 603–35.

Schwartz, Stuart. *Sugar Plantations in the Formation of Bahian Society: Bahia, 1550–1835*. Cambridge: Cambridge University Press, 1985.

Schwartz, Stuart. "Cantos e quilombos numa conspiração de escravos Haussás: Bahia, 1814," in Reis and Gomes, eds., *Liberdade por um fio*, 373–406.

Sègla, Aimé Dafon. "De la cosmologie à la rationalisation de la vie sociale: ces mots idàà-cha qui parlent ou la mémoire d'un type de calendrier yoruba ancien," *Cahiers d'études africaines*, 46:1 (2006): 11–50.

Silva, Ricardo Tadeu Caíres. "Memórias do tráfico illegal de escravos nas ações de liberdade: Bahia, 1885–1888," *Afro-Asia*, 35 (2007): 37–82

Simpson, Alaba. *Oral Tradition and Slave Trade in Nigeria, Ghana and Benin.* Paris: UNESCO, 2004.

Skidmore, Thomas. "Religion and Slave Rebellion in Bahia," *Current Anthropology*, 36:2 (1995): 389–90.

Smaldone, Joseph P. *Warfare in the Sokoto Caliphate: Historical and Sociological Perspectives.* Cambridge: Cambridge University Press, 1977.

Smallwood, Stephanie. *Saltwater Slavery: A Middle Passage from Africa to American Diaspora.* Cambridge, MA: Harvard University Press, 2007.

Smith, Robert S. "Yoruba Armament," *Journal of African History*, 8:1 (1967): 87–106.

Smith, Robert S. *Kingdoms of the Yoruba.* London: Methuen & Co., 1969.

Smith, Robert S. "Event and Portent: The Fall of Old Oyo, a Problem in Historical Explanation," *Africa: Journal of the International African Institute*, 41:3 (1971): 186–99.

Smith, Robert S. *Warfare and Diplomacy in Pre-Colonial West Africa.* Madison: University of Wisconsin Press, 1976.

Smith, Robert S. *The Lagos Consulate, 1851–1861.* Berkeley and Los Angeles: University of California Press, 1979.

Sorensen-Gilmour, Caroline. "Slave Trading along the Lagoons of South West Nigeria: The Case of Badagry," in Law and Strickrodt, eds., *Ports of the Slave Trade*, 84–95.

Soumonni, Elisée. "The Compatibility of the Slave and Palm Oil Trades in Dahomey, 1818–1858," in Law, ed., *From Slave Trade to "Legitimate" Commerce*, 78–92.

Soumonni, Elisée. *Dahomey y el mundo Atlántico.* Amsterdam and Rio de Janeiro: SEPHIS, 2001.

Soumonni, Elisée. "Lacustrine Villages in South Benin as Refuges from the Slave Trade," in Diouf, ed., *Fighting the Slave Trade*, 3–14.

Stilwell, Sean. "Power, Honour and Shame: The Ideology of Royal Slavery in the Sokoto Caliphate," *Africa: Journal of the International African Institute*, 70:3 (2000): 394–421.

Swanson, Gail. "The Wrecking of the Laden Spanish Slave Ship Guerrero off the Florida Keys, in 1827," *The African Diaspora Archaeology Network Newsletter* (Sept. 2010). Online at: <http://www.diaspora.uiuc.edu/news0910/news0910.html#2.> (accessed on 3 January 2011).

Sweet, James H. *Recreating Africa: Culture, Kingship and Religion in the African-Portuguese World, 1441–1770.* Chapel Hill: University of North Carolina Press, 2003.

Tambo, David C. "The Sokoto Caliphate Slave Trade in the Nineteenth Century," *International Journal of African Historical Studies*, 9:2 (1976): 187–217.

Tavares, Luis Henrique Dias. *História da sedição intentada na Bahia em 1798.* São Paulo: Editora Pioneira, 1975.

Taylor, Eric Robert. *If We Must Die: Shipboard Insurrections in the Era of the Atlantic Slave Trade.* Baton Rouge: Louisiana State University Press, 2006.

Thompson Drewal, Margaret. *Yoruba Rituals: Performance, Play, Agency.* Bloomington: Indiana University Press, 1992.

Thornton, John K. "African Dimensions of the Stono Rebellion," *American Historical Review*, 96:4 (1991): 1101–13.

Thornton, John K. "'I am the Subject of the King of Congo': African Ideology in the Haitian Revolution," *Journal of World History*, 4:2 (1993): 181–214.

Thornton, John K. "African Soldiers in the Haitian Revolution," *Journal of Caribbean History*, 25:1 (1993): 58–80.

Thornton, John K. *Africa and the Africans in the Making of the Atlantic World, 1400–1800*. Cambridge: Cambridge University Press, 1998.

Thornton, John K. *Warfare in Atlantic Africa, 1500–1800*. London: UCL Press, 1999.

Trager, Lillian. *Yoruba Hometowns: Community, Identity, and Development in Nigeria*. London: Lynne Riener Publishers, 2001.

Urama, J. O. "Astronomy and Culture in Nigeria," in J. Holbrook et al. eds., *African Cultural Astronomy: Current Archaeoastronomy and Ethnoastronomy Research in Africa*. n.p.: Springer, 2008, 231–8.

Van Norman Jr., William C. *Shade-Grown Slavery: The Lives of Slaves on Coffee Plantations in Cuba*. Nashville: Vanderbilt University Press, 2013.

Varella, Claudia. "Esclavos a sueldo: la coartación cubana en el siglo XIX". Ph.D. diss. Universidad Jaume I, 2010.

Verger, Pierre. "Note on the Bas-Reliefs in the Royal Palaces of Abomey," *Odu Journal of Yoruba and Related Studies*, 5 (1958): 3–12.

Verger, Pierre. *Flux et reflux de la traite des Nègres entre le Golfe de Bénin et Bahia de Todos os Santos du XVIIe au XIXe siècle*. Paris: Mouton & Co. and École Pratique des Hautes Études, 1968.

Verger, Pierre. *Trade Relations between the Bight of Benin and Bahia from the 17th to the 19th Century*. Ibadan: Ibadan University Press, 1976.

Voeks, Robert A. *Sacred Leaves of Candomblé: African Magic, Medicine, and Religion in Brazil*. Austin: University of Texas Press, 1997.

Warner-Lewis, Maureen. "Ethnic and Religious Plurality among Yoruba Immigrants in the Nineteenth Century," in Lovejoy, ed., *Identity in the Shadow of Slavery*, 113–28.

Zawawi, Sharifa M. *African Muslim Names: Images and Identities*. Trenton, NJ, and Asmara: Africa World Press, 1998.

Zeuske, Michael, and Orlando García Martínez. "La Amistad de Cuba: Ramón Ferrer, contrabando de esclavos, cautividad y modernidad atlántica," *Caribbean Studies*, 37:1 (2009): 104–8.

Index

Printed and bound by CPI Group (UK) Ltd, Croydon, CR0 4YY